Evidence and Proof in Scotland

To my Scottish family – Aileen, Jamie and Helen

Evidence and Proof in Scotland

Context and Critique

Donald Nicolson

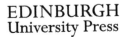

EDINBURGH
University Press

Edinburgh University Press is one of the leading university presses in the UK. We publish academic books and journals in our selected subject areas across the humanities and social sciences, combining cutting-edge scholarship with high editorial and production values to produce academic works of lasting importance. For more information visit our website: www.edinburghuniversitypress.com

Edinburgh University Press Ltd
The Tun – Holyrood Road
12 (2f) Jackson's Entry
Edinburgh EH8 8PJ

Typeset in 11/13pt Monotype Baskerville by
Manila Typesetting Company,
and printed and bound in Great Britain

A CIP record for this book is available from the British Library

ISBN 978 1 4744 1199 8 (hardback)
ISBN 978 1 4744 1200 1 (paperback)
ISBN 978 1 4744 1201 8 (webready PDF)
ISBN 978 1 4744 1202 5 (epub)

Published with the support of the University of Edinburgh Scholarly Publishing Initiatives Fund.

Contents

Expanded Table of Contents

Table of Cases

Table of Legislation

Preface

This book has had a long and convoluted history. It developed out of an innovative evidence course John Blackie and I taught at the University of Strathclyde which looked not just at the law of evidence but also far more broadly at how evidence is dealt with in the Scottish legal system and the various contextual factors which affect the process of proof. The idea was to write a textbook with two parts: the first on the processes and contexts of proof; and the second an analysis of the law of evidence in terms of these processes and contexts. However, John took early retirement and after a while I realised that the book would take much longer than originally anticipated due to the vast and constantly emerging literature, not to mention the need periodically to feed the voracious REF minotaur. It also seemed desirable for the first book in Scotland – if not the English-speaking world – aimed at covering both the law and practice of evidence to provide a level of detail and sophistication which is impossible in a traditional textbook. Consequently, I decided to divide the book into two separate volumes corresponding to the two parts of the originally planned textbook. Whether the second volume will ever appear remains to be seen, given that I have now moved to a new challenge as Director of the University of Essex Law Clinic.

In any event, the current book should still play an important role as a supplement to existing books on Scots evidence, since some of the topics are relevant to particular evidence rules. For example, the description of police and lawyer practices in Chapters Four and Six is directly relevant to the law on confessions. Similarly, the discussion of scientific expertise in Chapter Five has important implications for the law on expert evidence, as does the discussion of fact finder's ability to evaluate witness testimony in Chapter Six.

Arguably, however, this book is a necessary and not just a useful supplement to existing evidence books in Scotland, since the latter concentrate almost entirely on the law of evidence. As argued in Chapter One, the law has only a very marginal impact on the way evidence is handled and facts proved in the legal system, and hence this book fills a significant gap in the literature. This does not mean that it completely ignores the legal regulation of evidence and proof. Instead, discussion is limited to ensuring a comprehensive picture of the factors affecting evidence and proof or to covering issues such as the regulation of identification evidence, which are rarely covered by others.

Finally, this book is not intended merely as a necessary, let alone useful, supplement to existing discussions of evidence and proof in Scotland, but also – to borrow Jacques Derrida's memorable phrase – a 'dangerous supplement'. Accordingly, it provides a critical interrogation of the supposed aims and methods of evidence and proof in Scotland to explore both whether these aims are achieved and methods followed in actual practice, and whether they are worth pursuing in the first place.

In the years it has taken me to produce this dangerous supplement, I have accumulated many debts. The most obvious one is to John Blackie, who helped start the project and on occasion acted as a grossly overqualified research assistant to remedy gaps in my knowledge of Scots law and procedure. He supplemented an embarrassingly long list of student research assistants who helped tame the dense jungle of literature from myriad disciplines: Emma Boffey, Alex Brock, James Campbell, Helen Donnelly, Roisin Donnelly, Elise Lang, Fergus Lawrie, Craig Leslie, Stacey Martin, Kathryn Millar, Christina Rae, Caley Rattray, Ben Shepperd and Clara Smeaton. Also incredibly helpful have been a number of academic colleagues both in Scotland and beyond who have provided guidance on points of detail. These include Pamela Ferguson, Charles Hennessy, John Jackson, Fiona Leverick, Tom Mullen and my own live-in Scottish legal polymath Aileen McHarg, who also provided her usual acute comments on the final draft of the book. Finally, and most importantly, I must thank her and my children, Jamie and Helen, for their love, support and forbearance over the long years it has taken to produce this Forth Bridge of a book.

Isle of Mull
April Fool's Day 2018

CHAPTER ONE

Introduction: Facts in Law

1 Taking Facts Seriously[1]

1.1 Introduction

This book is about how facts are dealt with in the Scottish legal system. Such facts can be of two kinds. 'Adjudicative facts' are those relevant to decision-making by courts and other legal officials deciding disputes or other specific issues like eligibility for state benefits, whereas 'legislative facts' involve propositions about relevant aspects of the world, society, people and so on, adopted by administrative and legislative bodies when regulating areas of social activity.[2] Given that the process of determining legislative facts is not regulated nor subjected to study, and that this book is designed to supplement those on evidence law which regulates the use of adjudicative facts, legislative facts will be excluded from discussion.[3]

Nevertheless, even with this more limited focus, facts play an incredibly important role in law. While occasionally law might function merely as a means of signalling valued social norms, usually it applies to actual people, objects, historical events, and past or future states of affairs.[4]

---

[1] Title of Chapter 2 of W. Twining, *Rethinking Evidence: Exploratory Essays* (2nd edn, 2006). See also ibid., Chapter 14; J. Frank, 'Why Not a Clinical Lawyer School' (1933) 81 *University of Pennsylvania Law Review* 907; J. Frank, *Law and the Modern Mind* (1949) and *Courts on Trial: Myth and Reality in American Trials* (1949, reprinted 1973), preface; D. Nicolson, 'Facing Facts: The Teaching of Fact Construction in University Law Schools' (1997) *International Journal of Evidence and Proof* 132; P. W. Murphy, 'Teaching Evidence, Proof and Facts: Providing a Background in Factual Analysis and Case Evaluation' (2001) 51 *Journal of Legal Education* 568; P. Roberts, 'Rethinking the Law of Evidence: A Twenty-First Century Agenda for Teaching and Research' (2002) 55 *Current Legal Problems* 297.

[2] See K. C. Davis, 'An Approach to Problems of Evidence in the Administrative Process' (1942) 55 *Harvard Law Review* 364, 402ff.

[3] Though, admittedly, they cannot be clearly distinguished from adjudicative facts: M. Rustad and T. Koenig, 'The Supreme Court and Junk Social Science: Selective Distortion in Amicus Briefs' (1993) 72 *North Caroline Law Review* 91, 117.

[4] But cf. D. M. Walker, *The Scottish Legal System* (8th edn, 2001), 103, 110–11. See also H. L. Ho, *A Philosophy of Evidence Law: Justice in the Search for Truth* (2008), 6, referring also to 'processes' such as continual stalking or gradual poisoning, as well as states of affairs and events.

As Jerome Frank – one of the intellectual inspirations for this book – put it, laws are usually expressed in the form of 'a conditional statement referring to facts. Such rules seem to say in effect, "if such and such a fact" exists, then this or that legal consequence should follow.'[5] Facts are thus central to law's operation and the activities of legal actors and therefore should, as Frank argued, be a central part of legal education and legal scholarship. Yet eight decades after he first made this case, both focus predominantly on the law – its content, how it is applied to the facts and, less commonly, its justice and effectiveness.

Admittedly students do encounter law's factual dimension indirectly, most obviously through decided cases. Snails in ginger beer bottles, edentulous grannies, 'coos' which turn on taps, and bingo-loving pensioners[6] help law come alive and live in the memory. Students may learn that the facts of cases are important in influencing their outcome, perhaps even that 'everything depends on the facts'. Facts also play a more concrete role in the distinguishing of cases and reasoning by analogy. Furthermore, students will encounter facts – albeit of a notoriously artificial nature – in numerous tutorial and examination problems.

However, both case reports and problem questions tend to convey the impression that facts exist pre-given, ready for the application of the only skills worth teaching – those involved in interpreting and applying law. Some problem questions may leave the facts open-ended so that students can explore how legal solutions differ according to what facts are found to exist, but this only provides practice in applying the law to the facts, not exposure to how facts are determined. Many, if not most, legal academics now acknowledge that the legal rules are neither static nor always clearly defined, but have to be interpreted and applied by judges and other legal actors, who in doing so may make new law. In short, rather than just being applied, law is made or, to adopt postmodernist terminology, 'constructed'. By contrast, legal education and scholarship tend to treat facts as concrete entities which arrive neatly pre-packaged in appeal courts. Facts may affect the way appeal courts construct the law, but the impression given is that they are not themselves constructed and hence little attention is paid to the way that they are handled.

One aim of this book is to correct the erroneous impressions that legal education and legal scholarship convey about the role of facts in law, and hence about how law operates and about the skills that lawyers require.

---

[5]   Frank, *Courts on Trial*, above n. 1, 14.

[6]   See, respectively, *Donoghue* v. *Stevenson* 1932 SC (HL) 31, 1932 SLT 317; *McColl* v. *Strathclyde Regional Council* 1983 SLT 616; *Cameron* v. *Hamilton's Auction Marts Ltd* 1955 SLT 74; *Robertson* v. *Anderson* 2003 SLT 235.

However, its main aim is to take facts seriously by exploring the processes involved in, and the factors affecting, how facts are used as evidence to prove that certain events occurred, or states of affairs existed, for legal purposes. Unlike other books on evidence in Scotland, and indeed elsewhere, this book is not primarily about *the law* regulating evidence and processes of proof, largely – as we shall see – by rules excluding certain facts from consideration by courts of law. Instead it supplements these textbooks by exploring how a vast range of legal actors – not just lawyers and courts – go about handling facts both within and outwith the courts when the law of evidence is either not relevant or simply provides a very general framework for the handling of facts.

This chapter sets out to show why it is important to take facts seriously by looking first at the centrality of facts to the legal process and legal practice and then at why the law has only a sporadic and decreasingly significant impact on the process of proof. It then sets out an alternative approach to understanding evidence and proof in terms of the various contexts in which facts are handled in law.

1.2 The Centrality of Facts in Law

A starting point for understanding the importance of facts is to recognise that, as we shall see throughout this book, 'reality' is unbounded, multi-faceted, confusing and subject to varying interpretations. The facts relevant to legal issues have therefore always to be selected, interpreted and communicated.[7] This process is not like leaving a video to record a simple event like a plant growing, nor even filming a documentary, but far more like filming and editing a fictional story.[8] Just as no documentary, nor indeed fictional account,[9] attempts to narrate everything about an incident and its protagonists, or can present what it records without consciously or subconsciously interpreting the significance of events, so legal actors have to edit and interpret the slice of life relevant to their legal purpose. Moreover, those seeking to persuade some decision-maker or other audience will do more than just edit 'reality'. Instead, they will deliberately seek to ensure that the

---

7   See, for example, W. W. Cook, '"Facts" and "Statements of Fact"' (1936) 4 *University of Chicago Law Review* 233.
8   See A. Dershowitz, *A Reversal of Fortune: Inside the von Bulow Case* (Penguin, 1991), xxi, cited in M. Fox and C. Bell, *Learning Legal Skills* (3rd edn, 1999), 129; Chapter 6, section 2.
9   Even James Joyce could not narrate every single second of Lionel Bloom's day in the hundreds of pages of *Ulysses*.

'raw' or 'brute'[10] facts which make up the social world are transformed into a favourable version of *the* facts of a case which form the object of the application of law. In other words, rather than existing in pre-packaged, concrete form, the facts relevant to law are constructed.[11]

A second erroneous impression left unchallenged by legal education's failure to engage with the process of fact construction is the idea that facts and law are discrete entities. Separating law and facts is important for a number of legal and procedural reasons.[12] Of most relevance to the process of proof, they delineate a division of labour between judge and jury: the latter determines the facts and decides how they fit the legal rules identified by the judge, who will also decide on sentence.[13] In addition, rights of appeal are largely confined to decisions of law and not fact.[14] Finally, litigants need only prove the existence of facts, as courts are presumed to know the law.

The traditional view is that law and fact can be easily distinguished in conceptual terms.[15] In practice, however, matters are complicated by 'fact-value complexes' such as negligence, dishonesty, provocation and murder which involve 'mixed questions of fact and law'[16] in the sense that whether one person can be said, for instance, to have murdered another does not just depend on the factual question of what they did, but also the legal question of what constitutes murder. Even so, in most circumstances the problem is resolved by the courts simply declaring (often for political reasons such as the desire not to leave politically controversial issues to lay adjudicators and especially juries)[17] that for legal purposes a particular question (and hence its answer) is either a factual or a legal one. But even if there remain difficulties in categorising issues as ones of fact or law, conceptually law and facts seem to be different

---

[10] J. R. Searle, *The Construction of Social Reality* (1995), 1–2, though confining the term to facts which exist independently of what one believes rather than facts which exist only because we believe them to exist, such as marriage, money, governments, etc. – what he calls 'institutional facts'.

[11] For examples of this process, see this chapter at nn. 21 and 26 and accompanying text; Chapter 2, section 4.2; Chapter 4 passim and Chapter 7 passim. See also the references cited in R. Cotterrell, *The Sociology of Law: An Introduction* (2nd edn, 1992), 222–5, 342; B. Jackson, *Law, Fact and Narrative Coherence* (1988), 101–6 and *Making Sense in Law: Linguistic, Psychological & Semiotic Perspectives* (1995), esp. Chapters 1 and 3.

[12] See Walker, above n. 4, 104ff.

[13] However, on the rare occasion when juries decide civil cases, they determine the amount of damages.

[14] See section 2.3 for details.

[15] See, for example, J. Jackson, 'Questions of Fact and Questions of Law', in W. Twining (ed.), *Facts in Law* (1983); A. A. S. Zuckerman, 'Law, Fact or Justice?' (1986) 66 *Buffalo University Law Review* 487; H. L. Ho, *A Philosophy of Evidence Law: Justice in the Search for Truth* (2008), 2ff.

[16] J. Stone, *Social Dimensions of Law and Justice* (1966), 737.

[17] See C. Boyle and M. MacCrimmon, 'To Serve the Cause of Justice: Disciplining Fact Determination' (2001) 20 *Windsor Yearbook of Access to Justice* 55, 62–9.

entities: law tells us how to behave or how certain facts situations will be treated; facts are the raw material of life to which these norms apply.[18] Put another way, law exists to perform a normative function; facts just exist. Of course, the process of describing 'raw' facts can be and often is normative. The words, tone and body language used, and what aspects of the facts one decides to concentrate on, can carry important normative messages.[19] However, this normative function is usually an implicit and inevitable by-product of finding or describing the facts, whereas in the case of law its primary purpose is to regulate society through setting and enforcing norms.

Nevertheless, even if there is clear conceptual distinction between law and fact, in terms of how the legal process actually operates, it is misleading to treat law and fact as discrete entities. In practice, the processes of fact and law construction do not take place in hermetically sealed environments, with facts first being discovered against the background of clear law, and then the law being applied, interpreted and sometimes modified against the background of clear facts. When lawyers investigate, analyse and argue about facts, the law may be unclear; and when they investigate, analyse and argue about law, the facts may be unclear.

In addition, the processes of law and fact construction are intertwined. Thus, when adjudicators have jurisdiction to determine both issues of fact and law, the decision is, as Frank – himself a judge – states, 'frequently an undifferentiated composite which precedes any analysis or breakdown into facts and rules'.[20] But even when the two jurisdictions are separate, it is clear that facts affect findings of law and vice versa.[21] In other words, the two categories 'leak' into each other.

Thus judges notoriously distinguish precedents on their facts and frequently manipulate logic and legal rules in order to reach the decision which they think is warranted by a case's merits. This is aptly illustrated by the cases of *R* v. *Thornton No. 1* and *R* v. *Ahluwalia*.[22] Both provided compelling grounds for changes in the law of provocation to take into account the experience of

---

[18] If persuasive, this seems to answer the point made, by P. Tillers, 'The Values of Evidence in Law' (1988) 39 *Northern Ireland Quarterly* 176 and R. J. Allen and M. S. Pardo, 'Facts in Law and Facts of Law' (2003) 7 *International Journal of Evidence and Proof* 153, that there is no difference between law and fact in the sense that law is as much a fact as what are traditionally called facts.

[19] See further Chapter 2, section 3.2.2.2; Chapter 7, section 4.2.

[20] *Law and the Modern Mind*, above n. 1, ix; *Courts*, above n. 1, Chapter 12.

[21] See, for example, A. E. Taslitz, 'Patriarchal Stories: Cultural Rape Narratives in The Courtroom' (1996) 5 *Southern California Review of Law and Women's Studies* 387, 418–22.

[22] [1992] 1 All ER 306 and [1992] 4 All ER 889, discussed by D. Nicolson, 'Telling Tales: Gender Discrimination, Gender Construction and Battered Women Who Kill' (1995) *Feminist Legal Studies* 185; C. Bell and M. Fox, 'Telling Stories of Women Who Kill' (1995) 5 *Social and Legal Studies* 471.

battered women. But although Sara Thornton's actions better fitted the existing law, in that she had stabbed her husband seconds after his last provocative conduct, and although Kiranjit Ahluwalia had premeditated her husband's death, it was in *Ahluwalia* that the judges made the law more amenable to battered women who kill. The judgments strongly suggest that the courts' perceptions of the facts, and in particular the women's character, was crucial to their decisions. Sara Thornton challenged the pattern of demure femininity which women have been traditionally required to display by having many sexual relationships, and a broken marriage, working while her husband was unemployed, drinking in pubs and acting, in a witness' view, 'aggressively'. By contrast, Kiranjit Ahluwalia appeared to be meek, obedient and submissive, terminating her legal studies and entering an arranged marriage in order to please her parents, and doing everything to save her marriage for the sake of her children and loyalty to her husband, despite his brutality and adultery. Arguably, then, it was the judges' judgment of the two women in terms of their perceived conformity with social norms of appropriate female behaviour that determined the level of judicial sympathy accorded them and the judicial willingness to reform the law. We thus see that even in appellate decisions where the facts of cases are meant to be concretised by lower court findings, the inherent fluidity and uncertainty of facts means that the way they are presented and interpreted may influence the development of the law.

However, the opposite is also true: decisions as to the facts are influenced by the law. As already noted, reality is unbounded. It has no beginning or end. The most important determinant of the 'slice of reality' on which a court case will focus is the law. Facts can only be presented in legal trials if they are relevant to the substantive law issues raised by the case. For example, the law says that a defendant's motive is irrelevant to criminal liability and therefore courts must ignore the fact that an accused broke into an abandoned house because she was homeless.

Moreover, law does not just exclude facts; it also influences the way that they are interpreted and hence the ultimate findings of fact. In other words, law and fact cannot be separated because law and the discourses with which it is associated are part of the process by which facts are defined.[23] As also already noted, reality is often ambiguous, contradictory and confusing. A prime example is the area of sexuality. People often give off signals at odds with those they think they are communicating and may even be unsure themselves as to what they want and what they perceive others to want. There are also a great many variations between being attracted to

---

[23] Cotterrell, above n. 11, 222.

someone and wanting to have sexual intercourse with them. However, for years the law required proof of force and defined rape from the perspective of men, in the sense that, to be convicted, the accused must have known that the complainant was not consenting.[24] This reinforces social myths about what constitutes 'real' rape, which in turn encourage juries to dismiss rape allegations unless they involve strangers using extreme force.[25] The law thus forces the facts into black and white – either the woman freely gave her consent and no crime occurred, or she was the victim of vicious force and a rape was committed; either the woman is promiscuous or the defendant is a violent rapist – and then encourages juries to see the facts as involving the former.[26] This leaves little legal space for women who consent to some form of sexual activity less than intercourse, but do not want to engage in intercourse itself.

1.3 The Centrality of Facts in Legal Practice

We thus see that, just as facts affect how law is constructed, so law influences the construction of the facts of cases. One implication of this interrelationship is that where the law is unclear or unfavourable or where, as often occurs, it only provides a general idea as to the case's outcome, the interpretation of the law and the disposition of the case may be crucially affected by what facts are found and how they are perceived. In order to bring about law reform or favourable dispositions, lawyers should therefore devote much time and effort seeking to establish favourable facts, deny unfavourable facts, and present facts in ways which engage the court's sympathies. As a leading US advocate famously stated: 'In an appellate court, the statement of the facts is not merely a part of the argument, it is more often than not the argument itself.'[27]

Admittedly the lower courts have limited scope for changing the law and appeal courts limited scope for interfering with findings of fact. But even though it is essential to have one's view of the facts accepted at trial and even though arguments about law theoretically only have potential to bring about legal changes on appeal, lawyers need to have the possibility of appellate proceedings in mind at the outset of a case just in case they do not win at first instance. For this reason and also because legal decision-makers tend,

---

[24] P. R. Ferguson and C. McDiarmid, *Scots Criminal Law* (2nd edn, 2014), 323ff.

[25] The classic work is S. Estrich, *Real Rape* (1987); for a recent study of the continuing effects of rape myths, see L. Ellison and V. E. Munro, 'Of "Normal Sex" and "Real Rape": Exploring the Use of Socio-Sexual Scripts in (Mock)Jury Deliberation' (2009) 18 *Social and Legal Studies* 291.

[26] See, for example, T. Jefferson, 'The Tyson Rape Trial: The Law, Feminism and Emotional "Truth"' (1997) 6 *Social and Legal Studies* 281.

[27] J. W. Davis, 'The Argument of an Appeal' (1940) 26 *American Bar Association Journal* 895, 896.

as we have seen, to consider law and facts simultaneously, lawyers frequently consider how to construct facts and law simultaneously. Consequently it seems obvious that even if the focus of legal study should be on law and its creation, it should also include attention to the handling of facts.

The need to do so becomes even more obvious when one considers that most lawyers spend most of their time dealing with facts rather than law.[28] Practising lawyers spend very little time interpreting and arguing about law – according to one survey only an hour a week on average[29] and in another study as little as fifteen minutes.[30] Instead, most of their time is spent on matters of procedure, facilitating client affairs (through, for example, establishing trusts, drafting wills and contracts, and incorporating companies) and, crucially, dealing with the facts. Take, for example, a delictual claim. Here the main issue is rarely the intricacies of the law, but usually ascertaining what happened, predicting the court's findings of fact – a far more difficult task than predicting their findings of law – and, where relevant, presenting the facts in a way to achieve the desired result. Even when lawyers help clients facilitate their future affairs, they are likely to spend more time ascertaining details about the client's life than dealing with the law.

Consequently it is prima facie arguable that legal education should concentrate far more on the factual, as compared to the legal, dimension of law and legal practice. On closer examination, however, this is neither practical nor necessary since students cannot learn the facts relevant to future cases in the way that they can attempt to know the law. Nor is it possible to introduce students to all disciplines which throw light on how the world works in the same way that it is possible (but rarely attempted) to introduce them to all disciplines that illuminate how law works. Nevertheless, just as one of the main aims of a legal education is not simply to learn the law, but how to handle law and legal arguments through learning to think like a lawyer, so it is possible to learn how to handle facts and factual arguments. Arguably this takes longer in the case of learning how to handle legal materials, but this does not mean that factual skills should be ignored almost entirely.

---

[28] Recognised even by Blackstone: '[E]xperience will abundantly show, that above a hundred of our lawsuits arise from disputed facts, for one where the law is doubted of': *Commentaries on the Laws of England* (1765–9) 330, quoted by J. H. Langbein, *The Origins of Adversary Criminal Trial* (2003), 1.

[29] C. M. Campbell, 'Lawyers and their Public', in D. N. McCormick (ed.), *Lawyers in their Social Setting* (1976), 209.

[30] D. Kidd, *The Information Needs of Scottish Solicitors* (unpublished PhD, Edinburgh, 1979), cited in W. Twining, *Blackstone's Tower: The English Law School* (1994), 118. See also L. Loevinger, 'Facts, Evidence and Legal Proof' (1958) 9 *Western Reserve Law Review* 154.

At the same time, this book does not seek to fill all the gaps left by legal education's silence on law's factual dimension. William Twining, the main intellectual inspiration for this book, argues that it requires more than one or two courses to introduce students to all aspects of legal fact handling.[31] Equally a book with this subject-matter would be unduly long. However, this book need not cover all factual skills, given that many practical skills which involve handling facts like interviewing, negotiating and drafting are dealt with in law clinics and the vocational stages of legal education. Consequently, in line with the current, admittedly artificial, divide between the academic and vocational stages of legal education, this book concentrates on the intellectual processes involved in establishing facts relevant to law and providing an overview of the various factors which influence this process. It does not seek to train prospective lawyers in how to deal with facts nor introduce them to every factor which may affect fact handling. Rather, it seeks to illuminate the various processes of, and factors affecting, fact handling in order to provide a more accurate understanding of law and alert students to the special skills and research relevant to fact handling, thus enabling them to investigate further when necessary once in practice. Contrary to Paul Roberts,[32] who argues that evidence teachers should not relieve their colleagues of responsibility for teaching fact skills, the apparently Sisyphean nature[33] of the campaign to persuade law academics to take facts seriously suggests that it seems better for converts to attempt as much as is possible where they can. Moreover, given that one can never satisfactorily cover all possible issues in the detail desired and hence one always needs to make the most effective use of the limited time available, in my experience it *is* possible to introduce students to all aspects of fact handling (barring vocational skills like interviewing), including the governing law, in a standard evidence class.

1.4 What is Evidence and Proof?
As we shall see in more detail in Chapter Seven, fact handling involves at least four different tasks:

- fact investigation – discovering facts in the first place;
- fact analysis – evaluating the extent to which these facts are likely to lead to the conclusions required;

---

[31] Twining, above n. 1, 21 and 'Taking Facts Seriously Again', in P. Roberts and M. Redmayne (eds), *Innovations in Evidence and Proof: Integrating Theory, Research and Teaching* (2007), 74.
[32] Above n. 1, 305.
[33] Twining, ibid., 17.

- fact presentation (or advocacy) – presenting the facts in a way which persuades an adjudicator to reach the required conclusion;
- fact adjudication – determining what "*the* facts" are in a case.

However, as this book seeks not just to help prepare students for practice, but also to increase general understanding of the factual dimension of the legal process, it is important to note that facts are not only handled by law-yers and courts, and that most fact handling occurs outwith formal legal proceedings. As already noted, lawyers need to establish the facts in order to facilitate their clients' affairs through contracts, wills, etc. Even more significantly, people's legal rights are subject to decisions by administra-tive officials far more frequently than by courts. Every year thousands of decisions are made about the allocation of housing, social welfare benefits, immigration and so on, whereas numerous officials like the police, health and safety inspectors and trading standards officers have power to inter-vene in people's lives.

In all these cases, legal actors may engage in fact investigation, anal-ysis and adjudication in order to arrive at a determination of '*the* facts' relevant to the particular issue. These facts can be called 'legal facts' to distinguish them from the mass of 'brute facts' which make up life's rich tapestry and from which the legal facts are derived. As we have seen, by no means do all 'brute facts' pertaining to legally relevant incidents or situations become part of the legal facts. Nor, indeed, are all legal facts necessary for the application of law. From the brute facts, the fact finder must decide what 'actually happened' and on that basis decide what legal consequences apply. To take a simple example, a court might decide that on a particular day the accused committed various acts and that the deceased for whose murder she was charged died, but only if the prosecu-tion has proved that the accused caused the deceased's death intentionally and without any legal defence can she be found guilty of the crime of murder. The conditions of the intentional causing of death without a legal defence are variously described as the facts in issue, the ultimate, material, operative or dispositive facts.[34] When raw facts tend to establish the facts in issue, they are called evidentiary facts or simply *evidence*. Evidence, in turn, has been usefully defined by Jeremy Bentham as 'any matter of fact, the effect, the tendency or design of which, when presented to the mind, is to produce a persuasion concerning the existence of some other matter

---

[34]   For example, Murphy, above n. 1, 578; Zuckerman, above n. 15; A. L. Corbin, 'Legal Analysis and Terminology' (1919) 29 *Yale Law Journal* 163, 164. See further Chapter 7, section 2.4.1.

of fact; a persuasion either affirmative or disaffirmative of its existence.'[35] Traditionally[36] evidence is divided into:

- testimony – which can be either by 'observational' witnesses who observe events or other relevant legal facts or expert witnesses asked to investigate or give an opinion;
- documents – contracts, wills, receipts, registration certificates, ransom notes, etc.;
- real evidence – objects (and arguably also witness demeanour and appearance)[37] which fact finders can observe for themselves, such as weapons and defective goods which were involved in the events in question, or items that can throw light on such events, such as photographs, CCTV and sensor images, and a variety of pictorial representations of the world, such as charts, maps and diagrams.

Sometimes, judicial knowledge (namely facts known to the court without the need for proof in terms of the doctrine of judicial notice[38]) is regarded as a fourth category,[39] whereas Terence Anderson, David Schum and William Twining[40] add the category of 'accepted facts', which are taken-for-granted facts which do not require proof, like tables of chemical compounds, tide tables, or the fact that heroin is a drug. An even wider approach sees evidence as simply anything which the fact finder legitimately considers in reaching a decision, including, for instance, the demeanour of witnesses while not giving evidence, arguments by lawyers, in loco inspections (where the court visits the locality relevant to particular legal issues), and demonstrations, such as by computer re-enactments.[41]

---

[35] *Rationale of Judicial Evidence* (1827), quoted in W. Twining, *Theories of Evidence: Bentham and Wigmore* (1985), 29. For similar definitions, see, for example, Murphy, above n. 1, 570: L. R. Patterson, 'Evidence: A Functional Meaning' (1965) 18 *Vanderbilt Law Review* 875, 887.

[36] But see, for example, R. E. Conway and B. McCann, *The Civil Advocacy Skills Book* (2015), 14, who distinguish 'demonstrative evidence' like photographs from real evidence and the rather different approach discussed in Chapter 7, section 3.

[37] G. D. Nokes, 'Real Evidence' (1949) 65 *Law Quarterly Review* 57.

[38] See F. Raitt, *Evidence – Principles, Policy and Practice* (2nd edn, with E. Keane, 2013), Chapter 14.

[39] But see T. Anderson, D. Schum and W. Twining, *Analysis of Evidence* (2nd edn, 2005), 91 n. 22, arguing that judicially noticed and admitted facts are not evidential sources because, like irrebuttable presumptions of facts, they are 'inferences that triers of fact are instructed to accept as proven'.

[40] Ibid., 76.

[41] See S. W. Howe, 'Untangled Competing Conceptions of "Evidence"' (1997) 30 *Loyola of Los Angeles Law Review* 1199.

Moreover, as we shall in more detail in Chapter Seven,[42] all types of evidence can take the form of *direct* evidence, which establishes the facts in issue directly, such as CCTV footage of an assault, or *circumstantial* evidence, in which some inference additional to that relating to the direct evidence's authenticity has to me made, such as if one infers guilt from the fact that a suspect ran from the scene of an alleged crime. Sometimes, cases turn solely on the credibility and reliability of witnesses, or – albeit more rarely – on the impact of documents or real evidence, but most commonly on a mixture of both.[43]

The process by which evidence is converted into a final determination of the facts of a case and the question of whether the facts in issue have (or have not) been established is known as *proof*,[44] though in Scotland a trial involving disputed facts is also called 'a proof' and generally 'proof' can refer not to the process of establishing legal facts but to evidence which is sufficient to establish the facts in issue.[45] In this book, unless otherwise indicated, 'proof' will be used to refer to the process of establishing legal facts by courts and other bodies with adjudicative power. By contrast, 'fact finding'[46] will be used to refer more widely to all processes of determining the facts relevant to a legal issue, not only in court, but also by legal actors in other settings, such as lawyers managing their client's affairs or administrative officials making decisions. Finally, 'fact handling' refers more widely to both formal fact adjudication and informal fact finding as well as the investigation, analysis and presentation of facts.

2 Taking Evidence Seriously

2.1 Evidence Law
In covering all aspects of fact handling in the Scottish legal process, this book differs markedly from other evidence books in Scotland (and indeed elsewhere). Whether entitled 'Evidence' or more accurately

---

[42] Section 3.4.

[43] See, for example, W. Young, N. Cameron, and Y. Tinsley, *Juries In Criminal Trials, Part Two: A Summary of Research Findings* (1999), 27, who observed forty-eight New Zealand criminal trials. See further, Chapter 5, section 1 and 7.3.2; Chapter 6, section 1.

[44] See H. Lai Ho, 'The Process of Proof: Nature, Purposes and Values' (1998) *Singapore Journal of Legal Studies* 215, 217ff for this and other conceptions of the notion of proof.

[45] Loevinger, above n. 29, 160–1; Patterson, above n. 34, 881; A. B. Wilkinson, *The Scottish Law of Evidence* (1986), 9.

[46] But cf. J. A. Jolowicz, 'Fact-Finding: A Comparative Perspective', in D. L. Carey Miller and P. R. Beaumont (eds), *The Option of Litigating in* Europe (1993), 135, who confines the term to adjudication.

'The Law of Evidence', existing Scottish books on evidence and proof have almost entirely concentrated on the relevant law and primarily on its application in the courts.[47] A quick glance at these books reveals that, as in all Anglo-American jurisdictions,[48] evidence law comprises an incoherent set of highly technical and conceptually difficult rules, principles and standards largely governing the proof of facts in court, though also having an impact on certain aspects of extra-curial legal process, such as the way police officers obtain confessions and conduct searches of premises.

These rules govern a number of issues: who must prove what in court (the burden of proof); how much evidence is needed for proof (the standards of proof and the requirement of corroboration); when proof is not required (for example, because of judicial notice or a presumption of proof); who is and is not allowed to give evidence (competency) and who can and cannot be forced to give evidence (compellability); and the manner of proof (for example, rules prohibiting leading questions). But mostly evidence law comprises a miscellany of admissibility rules that exclude evidence from being led in court because it is thought unreliable and/or misleading (such as hearsay evidence or previous convictions), was obtained unfairly (confession) or because its admission would be contrary to public policy (for example, in breaching official secrecy or client confidentiality). As in all Anglo-American jurisdictions, Scots evidence law is primarily 'devoted to the determination of what is not admissible evidence'.[49] And thus, given that these books are almost entirely devoted to the law, they ignore what *is* evidence and create the impression that studying evidence law is sufficient for understanding the topic of evidence and proof.[50] This impression is highly misleading, as we shall now see.

---

[47] See D. P. Auchie, *Evidence* (4th edn, 2014), 1, describing the subject of evidence as 'really about what happens (or should happen) in a court room'. See also J. Chalmers, *Evidence* (2006), 1. Two recent books extend the focus slightly. F. P. Davidson, *Evidence* (2007) provides a chapter on the law's history and procedural context (ch. 1), and a brief discussion of probability theories (18–21). Raitt, above n. 37, includes a short chapter on the adversarial system, and the importance of facts, and fact construction, but as she admits (at 3), the vast bulk of her book is devoted to 'the treadmill of teaching the rules'. The situation is somewhat better south of the border, though usually only in the form of introductory chapters and only with regard to some of the relevant issues (see, for example, C. Allen, C. W. Taylor and J. Nairns, *Practical Guide to Evidence* (5th edn, 2016) Chapters 1–3 passim; I. Dennis, *The Law of Evidence* (6th edn, 2017) Chapter 4, but see the more extensive discussion by P. Roberts and A. Zuckerman, *Criminal Evidence* (2nd edn, 2010), passim.

[48] See, for example, Twining, above n. 1, Chapter 6; Murphy, above n. 1, 569.

[49] R. Bagshaw, *Cross and Wilkins: An Outline of the Law of Evidence* (7th edn, 1996), 2.

[50] See Twining, above n. 1, Chapters 5–6, upon which the following draws heavily.

2.2 The Reach of Evidence Law

Textbooks[51] sometimes state that evidence law comprises three important concepts: relevance (what facts tend to prove the legal facts), admissibility (what evidence may be considered in deciding these facts) and weight (the extent to which particular evidence goes towards proving legal facts). However, what evidence is relevant and how influential it is has never been – and generally could never be – legally regulated, given that it is a matter of logic, common sense and the persuasive abilities of those presenting facts.[52] Consequently discussion of relevance is largely confined to defining and explaining the concept and rare judicial dicta on whether proffered evidence is sufficiently relevant to the issues in question.[53] Similarly, as regards weight, while the law does specify, albeit in very schematic form, how much evidence is required to constitute proof and requires essential facts in criminal cases to be corroborated, this involves the somewhat different issue of evidential sufficiency, which in general involves the question of whether there is enough evidence to satisfy the burden of proof and whether in the case of corroboration the essential elements of liability are supported by at least two independent items of evidence. By contrast, law rarely if ever directs fact finders on how much weight to attach to particular items of evidence or the evidence as a whole, and whether it satisfies the relevant burden of proof.[54] Such decisions are also matters of 'ordinary practical reasoning and commonsense knowledge' rather than law.[55]

However, even when we turn from the very minimal regulation of relevance and sufficiency to the far more extensive rules of admissibility, they pale into insignificance alongside the so-called principle of 'free proof'.[56] While not an explicit legal principle, in effect it allows anyone to use virtually any information to prove their case as long as it is relevant to the legal issues. By comparison to this principle, evidence law is extremely marginal. Even if always faithfully applied, it provides only disparate and sporadic exceptions to the principle of free proof. Moreover, there are a number of factors which make these exceptions even less significant than is suggested by Evidence books.

---

[51] For example, Allen, Taylor and Nairns, above n. 46, 7ff; C. Tapper, *Cross and Tapper on Evidence* (12th edn, 2010), 64ff, but cf. the wider approach in Raitt, above n. 37, Chapter 2.

[52] J. B. Thayer, *A Preliminary Treatise on Evidence at Common Law* (1898), 314: 'The law has no mandamus on the logical faculty', quoted by Twining, above n. 1, 203.

[53] See, for example, Davidson, above n. 46, 29–37; cf. also C. Boyle, 'A Principled Approach to Relevance: the Cheshire Cat in Canada', in Roberts and Redmayne, above n. 30.

[54] Moreover, the legal rulings that do exist are confined to specifying what inferences may be led from particular evidence and only very rarely those that may not: see Stair, *Laws of Scotland: Stair Memorial Encyclopaedia* (1990), vol. 10, 458–61.

[55] Twining, above n. 1, 210.

[56] Ibid., 208ff. See also W. Twining, 'Freedom of Proof and the Reform of Criminal Evidence' (1997) 31 *Israel Law Review* 439.

2.3 The Applicability of Evidence Law

Influenced by the black-letter tradition, the 'Upper-Court Myth',[57] or suffering from 'appellate-court-itis',[58] these Evidence books present evidence law as operating in the way portrayed in statutes and appeal court decisions. However, aside from ruling on evidence law's peripheral exceptions to the principle of free proof, appeal courts very rarely deal with factual issues[59] and never rehear the evidence.[60] Procedurally, appeal courts are generally[61] required to treat the facts as found by the trial courts, given that evidence is often a matter of assessing witness reliability and honesty, and this requires observation of their demeanour, tone of voice, body language, etc. Consequently, disputes of fact and the process of proof are almost entirely confined to the lower courts, as well as other adjudicative fora such as administrative tribunals.

More importantly, only a fraction of legal disputes is resolved in this way. Most criminal charges result in guilty pleas,[62] whereas most civil cases are settled[63] or resolved through various forms of alternative dispute resolution (henceforth, ADR), such as mediation, arbitration or by an Ombudsman. In deciding whether or not to plead guilty, settle, accept the outcome of ADR or drop the dispute altogether, parties and their advisors

---

[57] Frank, *Law and the Modern Mind*, above n. 1, xii; *Courts on Trial*, above n. 1, Chapter 15.

[58] Twining, above n. 1, 169.

[59] Appeals are only possible on matters of law from some civil courts (C. Hennessy, *Civil Procedure and Practice* (4th edn, 2014), ch. 20), whereas prosecutors can only appeal on points of law and then in solemn cases only in relation to sentence or other forms of disposition: R. W. Renton and H. H. Brown, *Criminal Procedure According to the law of Scotland* (6th edn, 1996 by G. H. Gordon, assisted by J. Chalmers), Chapter 28.

[60] In case of appeals to a sheriff principal, however, further evidence may be allowed: I. D. MacPhail, *Sheriff Court Practice* (3rd edn, 2006), 660–1.

[61] Appeal courts can only interfere with factual decisions in civil cases when it can be said with certainty that they are unsound or that trial courts had insufficient evidence to support their decision, in criminal cases if new and significant evidence has come to light, and, in the case of jury decisions, when no reasonable jury properly directed could have returned the verdict: Davidson, above n. 47, Chapter 16.

[62] For example, 90 per cent of all cases in 2016/17, though far less of High Court cases (45 per cent) and somewhat more of summary cases (94 per cent): Crown Office and Fiscal Service, *Statistics on Last 5 Years: 2012–2017*. Available at http://www.copfs.gov.uk/images/Documents/Statistics/Statistics%20-%20COPFS%20Performance%20201617/Statistics%20on%20Case%20Processing%20Last%205%20Years%202012-17.pdf (last accessed 14 March 2018).

[63] Unlike with regard to criminal cases, statistics are not officially kept, but see Hennessy, above n. 58, 248 and D. R. Parratt, "'Something Old, Something New, Something Borrowed . . .": Civil Dispute Resolution in Scotland – a Continuing Story', in C. H. van Rhee (ed.), *Judicial Case Management and Efficiency in Civil Litigation* (2008), 171, both suggesting a figure of around 95 per cent.

will base their decisions partly on their view of the facts. Indeed, with all legal disputes and other legally relevant situations that may be litigated and adjudicated, there are a number of stages and processes involved that need not be consecutive or clear-cut,[64] but precede the very remote possibility of formal adjudication. At each stage, facts will be investigated and evaluated.

The process starts with the recognition of an issue that might give rise to a legal claim. For example, someone thinks that they have been defamed or sees a figure climbing through a broken window in a neighbour's house. The final stage in the first case might be a determination by the highest appeal court that what was said was not legally defamatory, and in the second case a decision as to parole of the convicted and imprisoned burglar. In between these start and end points, there are various stages in which fact handling is central.

For instance, the possible burglary witness needs to decide whether to call the police. On closer analysis, the 'burglar' may turn out to be the occupant who has locked herself out. More formally, if called, the police have to decide whether there is enough evidence to arrest and charge, and the prosecutor fiscal as to whether there is sufficient evidence to prosecute. Similarly the defamation victim may decide on reflection that the words spoken were not particularly insulting or that pursuing a claim involves too much effort, anxiety and expense. If they do decide to proceed, their lawyer may advise against suing because of evidential or other obstacles to success.

Either before or after these strategic decisions are made, the relevant legal actor – the police officer, procurator fiscal, lawyer or even the defamation victim herself – will look for further information and test the credibility and strength of existing evidence. Then, at some stage during or after such fact investigation is finished, they will start to prepare their case. This includes thinking about the logical relevance of the facts to the law, what inferences can be drawn from available evidence, whether they will be sufficient to succeed in court, and how to present the evidence – in what order, with what emotional slant, what witnesses to call, etc. Then, when in court or other adjudicative fora such as a parole board, the evidence must be presented to the adjudicator in the form of witnesses, real evidence and documents, in terms of arguments and/or stories, and, where relevant, through examining and cross-examining witnesses.

---

[64] W. L. F. Felstiner, R. L. Abel and A. Sarat, 'The Emergence and Transformation of Disputes: Naming, Blaming, Claiming . . .' (1980–1) 15 *Law and Society Review* 631.

However, while in all these stages facts are being investigated, evaluated and/or presented, the impact of evidence law, even as occasional exceptions to the principle of free proof, does not apply equally in all types of proceedings. The further one gets from the formal process of proof as exemplified by a criminal trial involving a jury, the less strict the procedures and exclusionary rules are. Even in civil trials, the range of evidence law is far less extensive than in criminal trials, and now non-existent in lower-value claims in the sheriff court (non-injury claims under £5,000) governed by the new Simple Procedure rules.[65]

But it is only when one considers all the many legal actors involved in fact finding that the full extent of the marginality of evidence rules becomes clear. Thus evidential rules do not govern negotiation or various forms of ADR.[66] Admittedly lawyers engaged in such proceedings may consider the possibility that, if the dispute were to end up in court, they will be subject to evidence rules which will either strengthen or weaken their position, and evidence law can therefore be said to cast a long shadow over legal disputes handled outside court.[67]

The same, however, does not apply to fact finding by state officials, whose decisions are largely unaffected by evidence law even though they might be as – if not more – important than those of the courts.[68] Admittedly the law may set standards of belief to justify particular acts, such as requiring police officers to have reasonable grounds for suspecting the commission of a crime before detaining a suspect.[69] Furthermore, the principles of natural justice frequently require procedural safeguards affecting fact finding. However, state officials may rely on evidence which would be inadmissible in court and some, such as immigration officers, may even rely on information which is secret to them and never disclosable to the applicant.[70]

---

[65] See Chapter 3, section 4.2.

[66] Unless parties so stipulate or where an arbiter is unable to perform his or her function without reference to the rules: F. P. Davidson, *Arbitration* (2000), 230–1.

[67] Cf. R. Mnookin and L. Kornhauser, 'Bargaining in the Shadow of Law' (1979) 88 *Yale Law Journal* 950.

[68] For example, mistaken decisions by administrative officials may have life-and-death consequences, such as those in relation to asylum applications (as presumably occurred in *M* v. *Home Office* [1994] 1 AC 377; see also the various cases culminating in *AA (Zimbabwe)* v. *SSHD* [2007] EWCA Civ 149), whereas court proceedings might be extremely routine and/or of a comparatively low level of seriousness, such as debt recovery and minor traffic offences.

[69] See Gordon and Gane, above n. 59, para. 6.08.

[70] Cf. B. Gorlick, 'Common Burdens and Standards: Legal Elements in Assessing Claims to Refugee Status' (2003) *International Journal of Refugee Law* 357, 362–3; and further Chapter 3, section 4.2.

Falling somewhere between the comparatively highly regulated decisions of courts, at one extreme, and the totally unregulated decisions of lawyers acting for clients and most ADR participants and minimally regulated administrative officials at the other extreme, is an incredibly wide variety of public bodies, such as inquiries, commissions[71] and administrative tribunals, as well as domestic tribunals dealing with matters like professional discipline. Compared to the courts, these bodies are relatively, but not completely, free of evidence rules, though the precise position varies from one body to the next.[72] More recently, the radical reduction of myriad UK-wide tribunals[73] has led to much greater standardisation of the approach taken to evidence rules, with one set of procedures for all the New Upper Tribunal which is repeated for almost all first Chambers.[74] There has been a similar consolidation of tribunals in Scotland,[75] but this has not yet led to a standardisation of the approach to evidence law.

More generally, sometimes a general revision of evidence rules will provide explicitly for its application to a particular body or type of body.[76] More frequently, the legislation governing a particular body may specify the application of some evidence rules[77] or expressly permit evidence to be admitted notwithstanding its inadmissibility in the courts.[78] In some cases, secondary legislation specifies the position regarding evidence rules in a code.[79] Legislation also frequently expressly gives the body a discretion

---

[71] Most are investigatory bodies and therefore do not apply evidence rules: see, for example, P. Duff, 'Criminal Cases Review Commissions and "Deference" to the Courts: The Evaluation of Evidence and Evidentiary Rules' (2001) *Criminal Law Review* 341.

[72] See, for example, Tapper, above n. 51, 21–8; and for a useful discussion of the various issues, albeit focused on Australia, see E. Campbell, 'Principles of Evidence and Administrative Tribunals', in E. Campbell and L. Waller, *Well and Truly Tried* (1982).

[73] In terms of the Tribunals, Courts and Enforcement Act 2007. For the details, see, for example, M. Elliot and J. N. E. Varuhas, *Administrative Law: Texts and Materials* (5th edn, 2017), 738ff.

[74] Though interestingly the Tribunal Procedure (First-tier Tribunal) (Immigration and Asylum Chamber) Rules 2014 (SI No. 2604 (L. 31)) does not include the usual discretion to exclude evidence on the grounds of unfairness.

[75] In terms of the Tribunals (Scotland) Act 2014.

[76] See s. 9 of the Civil Evidence (Scotland) Act 1988, applying civil rules of hearsay to arbiters, inquiries and tribunals.

[77] See, for example, sch. 2, pt 3, para. 12(4) to the Mental Health (Care and Treatment) (Scotland) Act 2003; sch. 1, para. 4(ii) to the National Health Service (Tribunal) Scotland Regulations SSI 2004/38; s. 22 of the Inquiries Act 2005.

[78] See, for example, s. 15 2(a) of the Tribunal Procedure (Upper Tribunal) Rules 2008 (SI 2008 No. 2698 (L. 15)), which is repeated in all the regulations for first-tier tribunals. This does not preclude the application of such rules if the tribunal so decides, though this may amount to a reviewable error of law: *Coral Squash Clubs Ltd* v. *Matthews* [1979] ICR 607.

[79] See, for example, General Medical Council Preliminary Proceedings Committee and Professional Conduct Committee (Procedure) Rules Order of Council SI 1988/2255.

to decide on the application of evidence law and how to deal with evidence more generally (for example, by requiring it to be given on oath or allowing cross-examination), either on a case-by-case basis or through rules.[80] Where there is no statutory guidance on the matter or matters are left to the body's discretion, the courts may require the tribunal to handle evidence fairly in terms of the principles of natural justice. As a general proposition, natural justice does not require application of evidence rules,[81] but the closer the proceedings approximate criminal proceedings, the more likely it is that the criminal standard of proof and evidence rules must be applied.[82] Such rules have also been argued to be more applicable where the proceedings are more adversarial than inquisitorial in nature.[83] Moreover, the general tendency towards legalism in tribunals[84] has meant that evidence is treated in ways which mirror the courts, and that when normally inadmissible evidence is admitted, notice be given of its intended use.[85]

We thus see that the applicability of evidence rules depends very much on the type of fact finder concerned. It also depends on what stage in the legal proceedings is involved. A particular item of information can be treated very differently in different stages of the proceedings.[86] For instance, previous convictions are generally inadmissible in criminal trials.[87] Yet the fact that particular people have previous convictions for crimes which fit what the police call their MO (modus operandi – that is, their mode of operating) might alert their suspicion, leading to an arrest

---

[80] See, for example, r. 19 of the Town and Country Planning (Inquiries Procedure) (Scotland) Rules SI 1997/796; sch. 2, pt 3, para. 10 to the Mental Health (Care and Treatment) (Scotland) Act 2003; ss 17 and 41 of the Inquiries Act 2005.

[81] *R* v. *Deputy Industrial Injuries Commissioner, ex parte Moore* [1965] 1 QB 456, 488; *Walker* v. *Amalgamated Union of Engineers and Foundry Workers and Another* 1969 SLT 150; *Mahon* v. *Air New Zealand* [1984] AC 808, 821.

[82] See, for example, *R* v. *Commission for Racial Equality: Ex parte Hillingdon London Borough Council* [1980] 1 WLR 1580; *Lanford* v. *General Medical Council* [1990] 1 AC 13, 19.

[83] Tapper, above n. 51, 26; J. G. Logie and P. Q. Watchman, 'Social Security Appeal Tribunals: An Excursus on Evidential Issues' (1989) 8 *Civil Justice Quarterly* 109, 113, 125.

[84] See, for example, H. Genn, 'Tribunals and Informal Justice' (1993) 56 MLR 393, which summarises the more detailed discussion in H. Genn and Y. Genn, *The Effectiveness of Representation at Tribunals: Report to the Lord Chancellor* (1989).

[85] Logie and Watchman, above n. 82, 128. This formalisation of the process may also have negative effects such as providing the potential for lawyers to exploit legal technicalities: R. Hunter, 'Evidentiary Harassment: The Use of the Rules of Evidence in an Informal Tribunal', in L. Ellison and M. Childs (eds), *Feminist Perspectives on Evidence* (2000).

[86] See Twining, above n. 1, 212–13.

[87] See Raitt, above n. 38, Chapter 12.

and perhaps the suspect's harsh treatment.[88] If a confession ensues, the police know that it might be excluded. However, just because the confession is excluded does not mean that it is not evidence and might not contribute to proof. Confessions might confirm police officers' suspicions, hence justifying them going to the effort of trying to find independent evidence of guilt. Moreover, the confession and previous convictions, even if excluded from proof of guilt, might again become important at the sentencing stage. Thus a court is likely to decide to impose a higher sentence because of previous convictions and because the accused put the prosecution to proof despite having previously confessed to something which the court found to be true.

2.4 The Application of Evidence Law

We thus see that most fact handling in law and even the formal process of proof is untouched by evidence law. But even where applicable, the law is not always applied in the way required by appellate decisions and legislation, if at all. In civil cases, the parties may waive the application of all or some evidence rules. More problematically, fact finders – especially those without legal training – may misunderstand and hence misapply the rules. Even more worryingly, fact adjudicators may simply ignore the rules, for instance where they regard the case as too trivial to require formal rules.[89] Indeed, it is sometimes said that it takes a 'brave lawyer who raises technical points on the law of evidence' before Justices of the Peace or magistrates.[90] In theory, misunderstandings and disregard of the law can be rectified on appeal, but those who are unrepresented are unlikely to be aware of this possibility, whereas even those who are aware may not have the money or emotional energy to appeal. Thus only a small percentage of decisions are appealed[91] and, even then, there is no guarantee of success.[92]

---

[88] See, for example, M. McConville, A. Sanders and R. Leng, *The Case for the Prosecution* (1999), esp. 23–4.

[89] See D. McBarnet, *Conviction* (1981), Chapter 7 and further Chapter 4, section 3.2.

[90] Twining, above n. 1, 212, citing P. Carlen, *Magistrates' Justice* (1976), presumably at 103.

[91] Given the way that statistics are recorded, it is impossible to gain an idea of the rate in civil cases (see Scottish Government, Civil Justice Statistics in Scotland 2015–16, available at <http://www.gov.scot/Resource/0051/00515767.pdf> (last accessed 14 March 2018)) or an exact figure in criminal cases, but in 2008/9, the last year the Scottish Government collected criminal appeal statistics, it reported that the 'total of 2,191 concluded appeals in 2008–09 was equivalent to 2% of the total number of persons with a charge proved in criminal proceedings in 2007–08': http://www.gov.scot/Publications/2009/10/28140800/5 (last accessed 14 March 2018).

[92] Of all criminal appeals in 2008/9 which were not abandoned or sifted out at an earlier stage, just over half were successful, but 80 per cent of these were against sentence, not conviction: Scottish Government, ibid.

2.5 The Reform of Evidence Law

However, even if evidence law was to be given full effect, the extent to which it interferes with the principle of free proof is on the wane. This is because evidence rules, especially those excluding evidence, are gradually being whittled away. Many, such as those excluding hearsay evidence, requiring corroboration and regulating documentary evidence have been abolished in civil cases.[93] Moreover, even when retained, much evidence law has been transformed from rules providing categorical directions about how to treat evidence into standards of evaluation that require adjudicators to weigh up competing considerations and exercise judgment as to admissibility. As a result, some evidence which in the past would have been excluded might now be admitted and therefore more evidence is likely to be admitted overall than when strict exclusionary rules applied.

Some evidence scholars regard the reduction in the scope and application of evidence law in a positive light.[94] Thus, as long ago as the nineteenth century, Bentham argued that the only justifiable evidence rules were those designed to reduce cost, vexation and delay.[95] More recently, perhaps the most eminent UK evidence law scholar, Rupert Cross, stated: 'I am working for the day when my subject is abolished.'[96]

What is revealing about Cross' view is not just his opinion that most evidence law is unnecessary, but also the suggestion that in the absence of laws regulating evidence and proof, there is nothing worth examining. As this book will show, this view is well wide of the mark. It ignores the fact that, even if there was no law, we still need to know how legal actors go about proving and determining facts: for instance, what techniques do they use; what factors help or hinder them; how does proof differ in the various stages of the legal process; what assumptions underlie the way in which legal actors go about obtaining and using evidence?

On these and many more questions concerning the process of establishing facts both in and outwith court, there exists an extensive range of information emanating from a wide variety of disciplines. For instance, the philosopher Bentham started the study of the principles of proof, which was taken over by the legal academic John Henry Wigmore, who analysed the various logical processes involved in proving and disproving

---

[93] By the Civil Evidence Scotland Act 1988.

[94] See Twining's discussion of Bentham, Thayer and Cohen, above n. 35, 448ff, but cf. A. Stein, *Foundations of Evidence Law* (2005).

[95] This involved not only a rejection of exclusionary rules but also those regarding weight, credibility, and burdens and standards of proof. See further, Twining, above n. 35, Chapter 2 passim.

[96] Witnessed by Twining, above n. 1, 1.

facts. More recently, the dominant role of logic in proof has been questioned by psychologists who report that fact finders evaluate evidence in terms of competing stories and other non-logical factors. Psychologists have also extensively researched the reliability of witness testimony and the ability of fact finders to evaluate evidence accurately, while forensic science and the sciences in general are becoming increasingly important with developments such as DNA testing. Also relevant is socio-legal work on the impact of court procedures, lawyers' ethics, and even court architecture and the language of trial proceedings, on the processes of legal proof. Finally, recent years have seen the development of a debate about the validity of using mathematical probability theories in matters of proof, given that they are almost always about the likelihood rather than certainty of alleged facts.

Opening such a 'Pandora's box'[97] of non-legal disciplines might raise the objection that legal scholars, never mind students, cannot be expected to acquire the necessary expertise in these disciplines to make use of them. However, as this book hopes to show, with the exception of probability theories and some scientific issues, the insights of relevant disciplines are relatively easy to grasp, particularly if, as Roberts suggests, one takes their lessons on trust.[98] Moreover, as Twining persuasively argues, even if opening up the study of evidence to other disciplines may involve difficulties, one cannot simply pretend that such disciplines are irrelevant; instead one must deal with them as best one can.[99]

3 Treating Evidence Contextually[100]

Clearly, then, the topic of evidence is much wider than the few rules which regulate the process of proof in courts, usually by excluding apparently relevant and useful evidence. It involves, in addition to the rules, the techniques and processes by which facts are investigated, analysed, presented and determined. However, such techniques and processes do not take place in a vacuum, but are influenced by various contextual factors such as intellectual assumptions about fact handling, institutional factors like the type of procedures in place, the values of the legal system, power relations between the parties involved, court architecture, and the language used in dealing with facts both inside and outwith court, as well as human

[97] Ibid., 26–8.
[98] See Roberts, above n. 1, 338.
[99] Twining, above n. 1, 27–8.
[100] Cf. ibid., 167, Chapter 5.

capabilities in dealing with facts. Accordingly, the rest of this book will be organised around five major contexts to fact finding that between them encompass the various processes and techniques of proof. The term 'context' is thus used broadly to include both factors external to legal actors like legal procedures and factors internal to them such as theoretical assumptions about fact finding and psychological thought processes.

In organising this book around the wide range of extra-legal contexts to evidence and proof, this book is thus very different to most other books about evidence and proof, not just in Scotland but more generally, where the focus is either almost exclusively on the law of evidence or on isolated contexts to evidence and proof. Whereas some evidence scholars like Twining[101] acknowledge the importance of understanding evidence in its various contexts, and others like Paul Roberts and Adrian Zuckerman integrate various contextual information into their main focus on the law, this is the first book to treat the various contexts of evidence and proof as the central focus of attention in order to provide a far more accurate picture of how evidence is treated and proof constituted in the Scottish legal process and indeed many other jurisdictions.

Chapter Two starts by looking at the *theoretical* context of the process of proof in Scotland, namely the ideas, assumptions and values that underlie the process of dealing with evidence. This provides a means to understand and evaluate the other contexts (as well as evidence law itself). Chapter Three then looks at the particular *procedural* factors which influence the way facts are dealt with in the Scottish legal system and in particular give rise to particular assumptions about the best way of achieving the theoretical goals and values adopted in relation to evidence and proof. This leads onto the empirical question of whether these aims and values are actually achieved and upheld. This takes us first, in Chapter Four, into what will be called the *sociological* context of fact finding in that it draws upon socio-legal work on the actual workings of the legal system in relation to fact handling. Secondly, Chapter Five looks at the *scientific* context of fact finding as represented by the reliance on experts from a wide spectrum of disciplines ranging from the physical and natural sciences through the forensic to the social sciences. While some of these social scientists can assist in the evaluation of testimony by witnesses, they and other experts are primarily useful in helping to understand the importance of documents and real evidence, and how the world works more generally. Consequently, an understanding of witness testimony is left to Chapter Six which, together

---

[101] See above n. 1, passim but especially Chapters 5 and 7; W. Twining, 'Evidence and Legal Theory' (1984) 47 *Modern Law Review* 261.

with Chapter Seven, explores the *psychological* context of fact finding. Thus Chapter Six discusses psychological studies of people's ability to perceive and report on observed facts, whereas Chapter Seven explores the psychological processes and techniques involved in investigating, analysing, presenting and determining facts in general.

Before moving on to discuss these contexts, it is important to note two important points about the focus of discussion. The first is that the nature of the relevant socio-legal research means that much of the discussion of the various contexts of fact handling concentrates on litigation, particularly on court proceedings and even more so on that in criminal cases. This somewhat undermines the argument that questions of evidence and proof should not be confined to the activities of the courts, let alone the appeal courts, but should extend to what happens in lawyers' offices, in negotiation, in administrative tribunals, etc. On the other hand, although the enforced focus on litigation[102] only provides a partial picture of the procedural and sociological contexts of fact finding, the theoretical assumptions, thought processes and psychological issues relating to the investigation, analysis, presentation and evaluation of facts remain largely the same whatever the particular legal activity. For instance, the reasoning processes used in investigating and analysing facts (as opposed to background assumptions about the world) do not differ noticeably between police officers and lawyers. Similarly witnesses in court do not have worse or better memories than those in administrative tribunals.

The other problem flowing from the state of literature on fact handling in law is that, some notable but by now rather outdated exceptions apart,[103] most studies involve England and Wales, the USA and other Anglo-American jurisdictions, where the relevant psychological and socio-legal work is better established. However, this Anglo-American bias is far less problematic than the court- and criminal justice-centred nature of much of the literature. This is because, despite the different civilian tradition of Scots law as regards substantive law, there are no great procedural, and certainly no philosophical, differences between the Scottish processes of proof and fact handling and those in other Anglo-American jurisdictions. Most importantly, all fit within the Anglo-American approach to legal procedure, have the same concepts of proof, very similar

---

[102] But cf. Twining, above n. 1, 193, where the focus on litigation is voluntary, though he interprets litigation rather broadly. See also at 251–2.

[103] For example, McBarnet, above n. 89; S. R. Moody and J. Tombs, *Prosecution in the Public Interest* (1982); Z. K. Bankowski, N. R. Hutton and J. J. McManus, *Lay Justice?* (1987).

rules regulating evidence and the same theoretical assumptions about how one goes about dealing with facts and proving things. Moreover, whatever one might think of the psychological and emotional differences between Anglo-Saxons and Scots, it would be very surprising if there were substantial differences as to their psychology as witnesses and fact finders, while scientific expertise is obviously universally applicable.[104]

4 Conclusion

It should be now be clear that this book will adopt a *Realist*[105] approach to evidence and proof,[106] in the sense of starting from the premise that the law involves more than just legal rules found in books and that the actual operation of the law may be very different to the way it is portrayed on paper. More specifically, in line with Frank's insight that the uncertainty of predicting legal outcomes because the uncertainty of predicting decisions about the facts vastly outweighs the uncertainty involved in predicting decisions about the law,[107] it is designed to go beyond the formal law regulating evidence and proof to explore the vast field of activity involving the actual investigation, evaluation and presentation of evidence itself. In addition, I will seek to ascertain how facts are handled in a wide variety of legal settings, ranging from trials courts to administrative bodies and officials to lawyers in their offices. This book is also therefore *contextual*[108] in seeking to understand fact handling in terms of the contexts in which it operates and *multi-disciplinary* in seeking to use whatever areas of knowledge help understand the processes of fact handling. As will become apparent when looking at these contexts, especially the theoretical and sociological, I will also adopt a *critical* approach in seeing law, and by extension its fact-finding processes, as involving forms of social, economic and political power and therefore not necessarily being beneficial to all in society or neutral between its various members. Finally, as the next chapter on the theoretical context seeks to justify, I will also adopt a *sceptical* approach to the assertion that it is possible to make objective claims about knowledge, truth, morality and justice.

---

[104]   As recognised in *Holland* v. *HM Advocate*, 2005 SLT 563, para. 49.

[105]   For an introduction, see, for example, M. D. A. Freeman, *Lloyd's Introduction to Jurisprudence* (9th edn, 2014), Chapter 9.

[106]   Though not to epistemology: see Chapter 2.

[107]   What he called 'fact-' as opposed to 'legal scepticism': see Frank, *Law and the Modern Mind*, above n. 1, viii–xiii.

[108]   Twining, above n. 1, 167 and 177, and see further, W. Twining, *Law in Context: Enlarging a Discipline* (1997), esp. 43–5.

CHAPTER TWO

The Theoretical Context:
Truth, Reason and Justice

1 Introduction

As we saw in the last chapter, the theoretical context of evidence and proof involves the central theoretical ideas, beliefs, assumptions and values relating to fact handling in law. And, as we shall see in the next chapter, some of these flow from the specific procedural context which governs fact finding in Scotland, and hence may change as this context itself changes. In this chapter, however, we will discuss those 'first-order' ideas, beliefs, assumptions and values which are likely to endure irrespective of – and provide the broad parameters for – the particular procedural, sociological and legal contexts in which facts are handled. The most important of these relate to:

- *The aims of fact finding* in trials and other legal arenas such as pre-trial proceedings, immigration decisions, etc. – is it truth, a peaceful resolution to disputes, social regulation, etc?
- *The thought process involved in fact handling* – how do we persuade and come to be persuaded that particular facts do or do not exist, or that a particular case is or is not proven?

There are at least two reasons why it is important to examine the theoretical context of evidence and proof. First, and most obviously, nothing in life takes place in a theoretical vacuum. All action, whether of a personal or institutional nature, occurs against a background of explicitly or implicitly held ideas and values.[1] When legal actors handle facts, they do so in terms of conscious beliefs or unacknowledged assumptions about the

---

[1] Cf. F. Northrop, *The Complexity of Legal and Ethical Experience* (1959), 6: 'the only difference between a person without a philosophy and someone with a philosophy is that the latter knows what his philosophy is'.

possibility of obtaining accurate facts, the best way to do so, and the aims of legal processes. Understanding their theoretical assumptions may thus lead to a better understanding of their actions, and even improve their own self-knowledge.

Secondly, and perhaps more importantly, understanding current ideas and assumptions about the aims and methods of fact handling in law allows us to critically evaluate them. This critique can take one of two forms. Most chapters in this book will involve an 'immanent critique' in taking orthodox beliefs and assumptions about fact handling at face value and examining whether they are actually upheld in practice. This chapter, however, will critique such orthodox beliefs and assumptions on their own terms. In doing so it will draw upon a wide variety of writers working in diverse areas such as sociology, anthropology, psychology, history and even the physical sciences, as well as law itself, but primarily on philosophers known as epistemologists. Thus, for centuries epistemologists have debated some of the central concerns of evidence theory, such as whether true knowledge is possible, and if so, how it is best obtained.[2] Many of these ideas have percolated into the background assumptions of legal actors. But even if they have not, we may draw upon them in seeking to improve our understanding of evidence and proof, and perhaps also in suggesting alternatives to its current aims and methods. First, however, it is necessary to have an idea of the existing ideas and assumptions about these aims and methods.

2 Existing Approaches to Evidence and Proof

2.1 The Hard-nosed Practitioner and Atheoretical Academic

By far the most pervasive approach to fact handling is far from theoretical. Rather than being based on abstract reflection, it involves a set of working and largely subconscious assumptions on the part of various legal actors who are only indirectly influenced by existing evidence theory. For instance, lay participants in the legal system are likely to owe their ideas to various aspects of popular culture, such as films, TV and novels,[3] whereas

---

[2] Cf. J. Bentham, *An Introductory View of the Field of Evidence*, VI, *Works*, 5: 'The field of evidence is no other than the field of knowledge', cited in W. Twining, *Rethinking Evidence: Exploratory Essays* (2nd edn, 2006), 135. See also M. S. Pardo, 'Juridical Proof, Evidence, and Pragmatic Meaning: Towards Evidentiary Holism' (2000) 95 *Northwestern University Law Review* 399, 424; P. Roberts 'Rethinking the Law of Evidence: A Twenty-First Century Agenda for Teaching and Research' (2002) 55 *Current Legal Problems* 297, 324–48.

[3] S. S. Diamond, 'What Jurors Think', in R. E. Litan (ed.), *Verdict: Assessing the Civil Jury System* (1993), 299–300.

legal practitioners absorb lessons from their practical training and their work environment.

There is little relevant research on the assumptions (as opposed to the actual behaviour)[4] of the vast variety of lay participants. Nevertheless, it is clear from their own writing and studies of their behaviour that – as we shall see in Chapter Four – William Twining is correct to characterise lawyers as 'hard-nosed practitioners'. Such practitioners, he notes, subscribe to views such as 'I am not concerned with justice or truth, my aim is to win cases' or '[t]he adversary trial is a game'.[5] Once elevated to the bench, judges might make lofty claims about the aims of legal fact finding,[6] but most lawyers' primary goal is to win cases, rather than to search for such a fickle mistress as truth or anything as elevated as justice. This attitude is explicitly fostered by practitioner handbooks and by professional legal ethics.[7] It also owes something to atheoretical evidence academics who write most evidence textbooks, which are almost totally silent on theory and hence fail to challenge the hard-nosed practitioner stance.[8] As this stance is not an explicit position within evidence theory, it is impossible to gauge whether the hard-nosed practitioner (and indeed the atheoretical evidence scholar) knowingly challenges, unwittingly departs from or regards their more pragmatic, unreflective approach as compatible with orthodox views on the aims and methods of legal fact handling.[9] Thus, although incredibly important in relation to the actual practice of fact handling, this chapter does not discuss the hard-nosed stance. Instead, it is confined to orthodox evidence theory, arguing inter alia that it is, at least partly, responsible for the hard-nosed practitioner's apparent cynicism and the atheoretical academic's complacency towards the aims and assumptions of evidence and proof.

---

[4]   See Chapter 4 section 4; Chapter 5 section 7; Chapter 6 section 3; and Chapter 7 section 5.

[5]   Twining, above n. 2, 105.

[6]   For example, 'there seems to me to be no reason why there should be anything more sacred than the ascertainment of truth and the doing of justice': *Lennie* v. *Lennie* 1948 SLT 382, 385; '[The trial judge's] object, above all, is to find out the truth, and to do justice according to the law': *Jones* v. *National Coal Board* [1957] 2 QB 55, 63. See also Chapter 3, n. 58; H. L. Ho, *A Philosophy of Evidence Law: Justice in the Search for Truth* (2008), 52.

[7]   See Chapter 4, section 2.3.

[8]   See Chapter 1, n. 46 regarding Scottish evidence textbooks, and Roberts, above n. 2 and Twining, above n. 2, Chapter 3 regarding English evidence textbooks.

[9]   For example, as we shall see in Chapter 3, lawyers doing all they can to win rather than search for truth is argued to enhance the prospect of finding truth.

2.2 The Rationalist Tradition

Following Twining, it is now common to refer to orthodox evidence theory as the 'Rationalist Tradition'.[10] Having surveyed Anglo-American[11] scholarship from the late eighteenth century until the early 1980s, Twining concluded that it shares 'very similar assumptions, either explicitly or implicitly, about the nature and ends of adjudication, about knowledge or belief about past events and about what is involved in reasoning about disputed questions of fact in forensic contexts'.[12] Boiled down to its essentials, these assumptions involve a holy trinity of truth, reason and justice, interrelated as follows: the primary aim of fact finding is truth; the means to that truth is through reason; justice is achieved by applying law to true facts.

More specifically, as its name suggests, the core of the Rationalist Tradition is the belief that proof of facts can and should involve human reasoning in relation to the presented evidence.[13] It thus involves a rejection of earlier, medieval forms of proof which involved some sort of test, such as trial by combat or ordeal, which was believed to allow an omniscient god to reveal where the truth lay. Instead, the Rationalist Tradition regards legal disputes as resolvable by ordinary citizens deciding on the basis of testimony, documents and real evidence presented to them.

This change in the method of legal proof reflected a major change in Western thought from the pre-modernist approach of seeing knowledge as flowing deductively from some authority, such as the church, the Bible or early scholastic writers, to the new modernist belief in the power of humans to know and shape the world. The modernist approach developed from around the seventeenth century with the advent of the Enlightenment or Age of Reason (or Man). Inspired by the great scientific discoveries of Copernicus, Galileo, Kepler and Newton, reliance on religious beliefs was replaced with knowledge based on scientific observation and reason. Also influential was Protestantism, with its emphasis on individual conscience

---

10 Most fully described by Twining, above n. 2, Chapter 3. For similar analyses, see M. Ariens, 'Progress Is Our Only Product: Legal Reform and the Codification of Evidence' (1992) *Law and Social Enquiry* 213; S. W. Howe, 'Untangled Competing Conceptions of "Evidence"' (1997) 30 *Loyola of Los Angeles Law Review* 1199; B. J. Shapiro, '"To a Moral Certainty": Theories of Knowledge and Anglo American Juries 1600-1850' (1986) 38 *Hastings Law Journal* 153.

11 Though noting (above n. 2, 85) that the Rationalist Tradition might fit Continental fact-finding processes better than Anglo-American processes: an issue explored in Chapter 3, section 3 passim.

12 Ibid., n. 2, 77.

13 In addition to the references in n. 10, the following draws on L. J. Cohen, 'Freedom of Proof', in W. Twining (ed.), *Facts in Law* (1983); J. D. Jackson, 'Theories of Truth Finding in Criminal Procedure: An Evolutionary Approach' (1988) 10 *Cardozo Law Review* 475.

and direct access to God. Accordingly, in terms of the 'principle of universal cognitive competence',[14] it came to be believed that everyone was capable of understanding the world through reason.

Reason was conceptualised in two main ways. 'Pure reason' such as that involved in mathematics involves logical deduction from abstract principles, themselves derived logically a priori from self-evident propositions, without reference to human experience or observation. Because this method is more appropriate to disciplines like mathematics and perhaps also because of its Continental rather than British roots, Anglo-American evidence writers have been primarily[15] influenced by a different conceptualisation of reason, which is derived from philosophers like Bacon, Locke, Hume and Mill. This has been variously called British or English Empiricism, scientific rationality or the classical scientific method, since it is modelled on the experimental methods used by scientists. In terms of this latter approach, knowledge is based on a mixture of information derived from observation using human senses and the drawing of inferences from this basic data using general principles such as cause and effect, which are themselves based on our experience of how the world works. In other words, instead of deducing conclusions from a priori principles, knowledge is seen as built 'bottom up' through induction[16] from the observation of natural phenomena and other raw data, such as when Newton deduced the existence of gravity from observing a falling apple. Such an approach is usually called empirical or experiential foundationalism because it sees knowledge as based on the secure foundations of what we perceive with our senses.

Another important difference with the pre-Enlightenment period, where knowledge was thought to be based on the 'truth' of God or nature, was that Enlightenment philosophers like Locke accepted that once one moves from disciplines like mathematics to those concerned with past events, absolute certainty is impossible. At best, one can obtain conclusions based upon an assessment of probabilities that no reasonable person could doubt, and hence Rationalist Tradition adherents accept that truth of the world is a matter of probabilities rather than certainties.

On the other hand, most Enlightenment thinkers assumed that a real world exists independent of human observation. This 'realist' ontology or

---

[14] Cohen, ibid.

[15] But cf. below at nn 25–7 regarding the influence of Scottish 'common sense' philosophy.

[16] As understood in the sense discussed at n. 80 below, rather than at nn 133–5 and in Chapter 7, section 3.

metaphysics[17] was combined with what is sometimes called a cognitivist epistemology and theory of language which holds that the world is capable of being discovered and accurately represented in words. Furthermore, in terms of the correspondence theory of truth, true knowledge is regarded as that which corresponds with reality.

While a realist ontology, cognitivist epistemology and correspondence theory of truth are more or less explicit rationalist positions in relation to factual inquiries, it is difficult to know whether – as seems likely[18] – Rationalists adopt a similar position in relation to questions about justice. This is because all that is required by the very narrow notion of what Twining calls 'expletive justice' (more usually termed 'formal justice')[19] is the logical application of substantive law and adherence to principles of procedural justice, such as the right to a hearing, equality of arms, and various protections for criminal suspects.

In ignoring the possibility that the substantive law applied might be immoral or unjust, the Rationalist Tradition seems to have been influenced[20] by the nineteenth-century jurisprudential theory of legal positivism,[21] itself partly influenced by the Enlightenment. Thus the latter's privileging of science as the optimum means of truth led to the positivistic belief that observation and drawing inferences from observation can be conducted in a neutral, value-free fashion, and indeed represents the only valid form of knowledge. On the ground that they cannot be objectively observed and analysed, positivism excludes as irrelevant all judgments of value, and all political, moral or other policy questions.

This approach was adopted in other disciplines like law and philosophy, with science becoming the paradigm to be emulated. Thus in the nineteenth century legal positivists like Jeremy Bentham and John Austin insisted on a strict separation between determining law's validity and evaluating its justice and morality. Admittedly, contemporary positivists do not deny that one can criticise law on moral and political grounds (and indeed frequently do so), but in practice, generations of lawyers exposed to a positivist legal education have been unconcerned about justice and morality. In other words, legal positivism tends to lead to legal formalism

---

[17] Ontology or metaphysics involves the philosophical study of existence.

[18] Cf. Twining, above n. 2, 48 and the discussion at section 3.3.2 below.

[19] For an overview of legal formalim, see for example S. Bottomley and S. Bronitt, *Law in Context* (4th edn, 2012), Chapter 2.

[20] Rarely acknowledged, and only then in passing: see for example Twining, above n. 2, 77; J. Winter, 'The Truth Will Out? The Role of Judicial Advocacy and Gender in Verdict Construction' (2002) 11 *Social and Legal Studies* 343, 343.

[21] See, for example, R. Cotterrell, *The Politics of Jurisprudence* (2nd edn, 2003), Chapters 3 and 4.

in which the only concern of practitioners is to apply law in ways which suit their clients, and that of judges is to apply law logically to the facts. Similarly, the only concern of academics and students is to describe and understand law, with any evaluation confined to the question of law's logical coherence.

While positivism and formalism can be logically combined with any view of society, in practice they usually operate in tandem with liberalism, which accepts that modern Western societies and the majority of their laws are generally just. As is well known, liberalism celebrates the freedom of individuals to pursue their own goals.[22] However, because unconstrained individual freedom may lead to anarchy and oppression of some by others, it regards neutral laws as necessary to ensure a level playing field and maximum freedom for all. These rules provide individuals with rights against the state and other individuals, while a principle of legality ensures that these rights are only infringed after due process of law and on legal grounds. Of particular importance to legal fact finding are various procedural rights designed to protect litigants and particularly criminal accused against unfair treatment and unfair trials.

Based on this survey, we can summarise the core assumptions of orthodox Anglo-American scholarship, as follows:

- There exists an objective reality independent of human knowledge;
- Truth is knowledge which corresponds to this objective reality;
- Although present knowledge about past events is typically based upon incomplete evidence and hence a matter of probabilities, the best way to discover truth is through 'rational' means;
- The best rational method of discovering truth is through induction, more specifically using common knowledge about how the world works to draw logical inferences from evidence observed by the fact finder;
- Although there are a number of other values to be protected in fact finding, such as national security, the rights of suspects, etc., the 'rectitude' (in other words, correctness) of decisions has a high priority;
- The aim of adjectival law (that is, evidence and procedural law) is to ensure correct decisions;
- Justice is achieved through the application of substantive law to correct facts;
- Just substantive law ensures the equal protection of everyone's legal rights and freedoms.

---

[22] See, for example, Bottomley and Bronitt, above n. 19, Chapter 1.

Since Twining offered his 'tentative hypothesis'[23] about the shared assumptions of Anglo-American evidence scholars, it has become received wisdom.[24] Moreover, there is little to suggest a unique Scottish approach, notwithstanding some differences in philosophical influences.[25] Thus the uniqueness of the Scottish evidence scholar James Glassford[26] is limited[27] to arguing that fact finders evaluate evidence holistically rather than atomistically in terms of the individual impact of separate items of evidence, as Rationalists assume.[28] Moreover, his views seem to have been entirely ignored by Scots evidence scholars.[29]

Of Anglo-American evidence scholars who do address theory, Twining notes that underlying their 'truly remarkable homogeneity' over the conceptions of truth, reason and justice there nevertheless exist 'strains and disagreements'.[30] One debate centres on how to reconcile conflicts between competing aims and values. For instance, some like Bentham regard truth as virtually the only value of fact finding, whereas others regard factors like the need to protect civil liberties as overriding.[31] Indeed, in his most recent description of the Rationalist Tradition, Twining lists protection of the public interest as its fourth pillar.[32] While he seems to confine it to civil liberties and the state's interests, it could also be said to include the notion of expediency, which is usually taken to involve the avoidance of the three

---

[23] Above n. 2, 78.

[24] See, for example, P. Tillers, 'The Values of Evidence in Law' (1988) 39 *Northern Ireland Law Quarterly* 176; D. M. Risinger, 'Unsafe Verdicts: The Need for Reformed Standards for the Trial and Review of Factual Innocence Claims' (2005) 41 *Houston Law Review* 1281, 1286–7.

[25] For example, 'common sense' philosophy holds, contrary to English empiricism, that the world is revealed to people's consciousness without mediation by human judgment. However, although adopted by at least one Scottish writer (Glassford – see below), and one other evidence writer (Shapiro, above n. 10, 176), it does not seriously challenge orthodox evidence theory.

[26] *An Essay on the Principles of Evidence and their Application to Subjects of Judicial Enquiry* (1820), discussed by M. A. Hareira, 'An Early Holistic Conception of Judicial Fact-Finding' (1986) *Juridical Review* 79.

[27] See Glassford, ibid., 1, 119, 185, 216, accepting that the 'Discovery of Truth is the primary and fundamental objective' in fact finding, and, while difficult, is possible.

[28] See further, Chapter 7 passim.

[29] G. Tait, *A Treatise on the Law of Evidence in Scotland* (3rd edn, 1834), xviii, acknowledges Glassford's 'enlarged and interesting views on the general sources and principles of evidence' but then proceeds to a black-letter analysis of evidence law. F. Raitt, *Evidence – Principles, Policy and Practice* (2nd edn, with E. Keane, 2013), at 2 places 'truth' in inverted commas, suggesting scepticism towards the existence of objective truth, but also states (at 6) that '[f]acts are *rarely* pure, neatly defined or objective" (emphasis added). The contradictory and en passant nature of these indicia do not suggest a developed theoretical position.

[30] Above n. 2, 77.

[31] See Chapter 3, section 3.1.

[32] W. Twining, 'Taking Facts Seriously – Again', in P. Roberts and M. Redmayne (eds), *Innovations in Evidence and Proof: Integrating Theory, Research and Teaching* (2007), 75.

evils of undue cost, delay and vexation identified by Bentham.[33] Thus resources to pursue truth and justice have to compete with other public goals,[34] whereas lengthy fact-finding proceedings prevent participants getting on with their lives, and prolong associated vexations, such as anxiety, embarrassment, the glare of publicity, the indignity of cross-examination, etc. and most notably being imprisoned on remand. Accordingly, timeliness is sometimes regarded as required by procedural fairness in terms of Article 6 of the European Convention on Human Rights.[35] At the same time, it is also linked to accuracy, given that memory fades with time, as do the chances of all witnesses being available. Moreover, delay and cost raise issues involving justice as equality, in that they have differential impact on the parties and this in turn may affect the likelihood of ascertaining true facts.

Twining also distinguishes between different strands of rationalism.[36] Thus he contrasts *complacent* rationalists, who simply assume that the goals of truth, reason and justice are met in practice, with *aspirational* rationalists, who see them as ideals to be strived for, though not necessarily achieved. Moreover, in relation to this latter group, he distinguishes between *optimistic* rationalists, who assume these aspirations are achievable, from *pessimistic* rationalists, who do not. At the same time, Twining notes that it is important not to see the Rationalist Tradition as setting unachievably high ideals.[37] For instance, the standard of rationality to be achieved is 'modest' or 'soft', in that it is not assumed that everyone in society is capable of competent, objective and impartial reasoning about facts. Nevertheless, despite these differences as to the achievability of its goals, rationalists are extremely complacent about their theoretical validity, recording '[h]ardly a whisper of doubt about the possibility of knowledge, about the validity of induction, or about human capacity to reason'.[38]

---

[33] See W. Twining, *Theories of Evidence: Bentham and Wigmore* (1985), Chapter 2 passim and on expediency in general: R. W. Fox, 'Expediency and Truth-Finding in the Modern Law of Evidence', in E. Campbell and L. Waller (eds), *Well and Truly Tried* (1982).

[34] See, for example, A. A. S. Zuckerman, 'Reform in the Shadow of Lawyers' Interests', in A. A. S. Zuckerman and R. Cranston (eds), *Reform of Civil Procedure: Essays on 'Access to Justice'* (1995), 73–4 and 'Quality and Economy in Civil Procedure – the Case for Commuting Correct Judgment for Timely Judgments' (1994) 14 *Oxford Journal of Legal Studies* 353.

[35] R. S. Summers, 'Evaluating and Improving Legal Processes – A Plea for "Process Values"' (1974) 60 *Cornell Law Review* 1, 10–11; A. A. S. Zuckerman, *Zuckerman on Civil Procedure: Principles of Practice* (2nd edn, 2006), Chapter 2.

[36] See, for example, Twining, above n. 2, 83–4.

[37] Ibid., 104.

[38] Twining, above n. 2, 80. See also at 104.

2.3 The New Evidence Scholarship[39]

By contrast, from the 1980s certain Rationalist assumptions began to be questioned by what has come to be known as the 'New Evidence Scholarship'.[40] This designation was directed originally and sometimes exclusively[41] at evidence scholars, primarily in the US, who began to debate the plausibility of using competing probabilities theories in legal fact finding.[42] However, not only did this fierce debate become increasingly arcane, it is also firmly rooted within the epistemological assumptions of the Rationalist Tradition.[43]

Other New Evidence Scholars have engaged with a much wider range of issues, such as procedure, fact finder reasoning and the impact of science and technology, while drawing on various disciplines relevant to evidence and proof, such as sociology, psychology and semiotics (the study of signs and signification). Much of this literature only challenges complacent rationalism in questioning the extent to which rationalists' aspirations are met in practice, rather than their theoretical plausibility.[44] Indeed, much of it is arguably motivated by the 'pursuit of scientific rationality'.[45] On the other hand, contrary to Twining,[46] not all socio-legal scholars critical of the legal process accept the Rational Tradition's conceptions of truth, reason and justice.[47] More fundamentally, some of the empirical research, especially on human witnessing and reasoning capabilities, implicitly challenges the Rationalist Tradition by suggesting that some of its aspirations are unachievable even if current methods of proof are reformed.[48] This has led some New Evidence Scholars to echo Glassford's questioning of the Rationalist conception of reason as involving the 'atomistic' evaluation

---

[39] For an overview, see J. D. Jackson, 'Analysing the New Evidence Scholarship: Toward a New Conception of the Law of Evidence' (1996) 16 *Oxford Journal of Legal Studies* 309 and 'Modern Trends in Evidence Scholarship: Is All Rosy in the Garden?' (2003) 21 *Quinnipiac Law Review* 893.

[40] Following R. Lempert, 'The New Evidence Scholarship: Analyzing the Process of Proof', in P. Tillers and E. D. Green (eds), *Probability and Inference in the Law of Evidence* (1988).

[41] Cf. R. C. Park, 'Evidence Scholarship, Old and New' (1990–1) 75 *Minnesota Law Review* 849, 854ff.

[42] See, for example, the symposia published in 1986 in the *Boston University Law Review* and in 1991 in the *Cardozo Law Review*; the discussion in Chapter 7, section 3.8.2.

[43] J. Jackson, 'Analysing the New Evidence Scholarship', above n. 39. 314–16 and 'Modern Trends in Evidence Scholarship', ibid., 895.

[44] Twining, above n. 2, Chapter 4; J. Jackson, above n. 13, 513–14; and 'Modern Trends in Evidence Scholarship', above n. 39, 896–7.

[45] P. Haldar, 'The Return of the Evidencer's Eye: Rhetoric and the Visual Technologies of Proof' (1999) *Griffith Law Review* 86, 87 and see further J. Jackson, 'Modern Trends in Evidence Scholarship', above n. 39.

[46] Above n. 2, 80 and Chapter 4.

[47] See, for example, D. McBarnet, *Conviction: Law, The State and the Construction of Justice* (1981) 11, 12 and 16, impliedly rejecting the correspondence theory of truth by claiming that 'truth' and 'reality' are 'subjective and relative', though admittedly she is not consistent in her language.

[48] See Chapters 6 and 7.

of evidence in terms of the logical relationship between individual facts[49] rather than holistically in terms of competing theories and/or stories. However, notwithstanding the apparent link between holistic reasoning and a conception of truth which sees true statements as those which most coherently explain the data rather than correspond to reality, most evidence scholars have left untouched the Rationalist Tradition's concepts of truth as well as justice.[50] Thus, whereas some New Evidence Scholars reconceptualise reason, truth remains an objective truth and justice, expletive justice: the transport has been modernised but the destination remains the same.

By contrast, an even smaller group of scholars interested in issues relating to evidence and epistemology, influenced variously by semiotics, postmodernism, critical theory, pragmatism and feminism, have challenged the Rationalist Tradition's conceptions of truth and justice as well as its valorisation of rationality.[51] More specifically, they have questioned whether objective reality can be captured by human knowledge, whether there are

[49] See Chapter 7.
[50] For example, while Twining expressly positions himself as a relatively detached excavator, rather than evangelical supporter, of the Rationalist Tradition (for example, above n. 2, 82 and 'Hot Air in the Redwoods: A Sequel to Wind in the Willows' (1988) 86 *Michigan Law Review* 1523, 1528), and criticises its complacency about truth, ultimately he only questions its conception of reason and even then rather hesitantly (see Chapter 7, section 6). See also Roberts above n. 2; Ho, above n. 6 and 'The Process of Proof: Nature, Purposes and Values' [1998] *Singapore Journal of Legal Studies* 215; J. Jackson, 'Analysing the New Evidence Scholarship', above n. 319–20 and 'Modern Trends in Evidence Scholarship', ibid., 39, 896–7 (but cf. above n. 13, 519 where he comes very close to recognising that holistic reasoning challenges the correspondence theory of truth); M. Redmayne, 'Rationality, Naturalism, and Evidence Law' 2003 *Michigan State Law Review* 849; A. Stein, *Foundations of Evidence Law* (2005), esp. 36, 39; D. M. Paciocco, 'Evidence About Guilt: Balancing the Rights of the Individual and Society in Matters of Truth and Proof' (2001) 80 *Canadian Bar Review* 433; D. Grano, 'Ascertaining the Truth' (1992) 77 *Cornell Law Review* 1061; and, slightly more ambivalently, M. Damaška, 'Truth in Adjudication' (1997–8) 49 *Hastings Law Journal* 289; W. P. Marshall, 'In Defence of the Search for Truth as a First Amendment Justification' (1995) 30 *Georgia Law Review* 1; R. Allen, 'Truth and its Rivals' (1997) 49 *Hastings Law Journal* 309.
[51] See, for example, Z. Bankowski, 'The Value of Truth: Fact Scepticism Revisited' (1981) *Legal Studies* 257; K. W. Graham, 'There Will Always be an England: The Instrumental Ideology of Evidence' (1987) 85 *Michigan Law Review* 1204; L. Harmon, 'Etchings on Glass: Reflections on the Science of Proof' (1999) 40 *South Texas Law Review* 483; B. S. Jackson, *Law, Fact and Narrative Coherence* (1991); K. L. Scheppele, 'Foreword: Telling Stories' (1989) 87 *Michigan Law Review* 2073 and 'Just the Facts, Ma'am: Sexualised Violence, Evidentiary Habits, and the Revision of Truth' (1992) 37 *New York Law School Law Review* 123; D. Nicolson, 'Truth, Reason and Justice: Epistemology and Politics in Evidence Discourse' (1994) 57 *Modern Law Review* 726; 'Feminist Perspectives on Evidence Theory: Gender, Epistemology and Ethics', in L. Ellison and M. Childs (eds) *Feminist Perspectives on Evidence* (2000) and 'Taking Epistemology Seriously: "Truth, Reason and Justice" Revisited' (2012) 17 *International Journal of Evidence and Proof* 1; J. Fiske, 'Admissible Postmodernity: Some Remarks on Rodney King, O. J. Simpson, and Contemporary Culture' (1995) 30 *University of South Florida Law Review* 917; M. L. Seigel, 'A Pragmatic Critique of Modern Evidence Scholarship' (1993) 88 *Northwestern University Law Review* 995.

other forms of truth at play in fact finding other than 'rectitude of decision', and whether there is more to justice than 'correctly' applying law to facts.

However, battle has not been directly joined between critical evidence scholars and modified rationalists. When not ignoring the sceptical challenge altogether, the latter have tended to deny its intellectual pedigree by arguing that philosophical sceptics are 'rare birds',[52] their arguments are 'naïve' and unsubstantiated by 'sophisticated theoretical arguments',[53] and that scepticism is a self-defeating position for those seeking to contribute to debates over evidence and proof.[54] However, apart from citing their favourite philosophers, rationalists have done little to explore whether orthodox approaches to truth, reason and justice can be justified on their own terms or at least in modified form.

The rest of this chapter seeks to fill this gap by subjecting the rationalists' theoretical assumptions to the critical evaluation, first of philosophical sceptics and then of critical legal theory. It will concentrate on the core beliefs of orthodox evidence theorists and the views of their favourite philosophers, leaving debates over whether truth should be the overriding aim of legal fact finding until Chapter Four. It will also concentrate on theoretical issues which are specific to fact handling in law and thus side-step debates over the value of liberalism and the existence of objective moral and political values,[55] not least because the objective existence and knowability of the factual domain of evidence (people, things and events) seems more plausible than that of moral and political values and is in fact far less philosophically controversial.

3 Truth, Reason and Knowledge: Philosophical Explorations[56]

3.1 Introduction
3.1.1 The Protagonists: Realism v. Scepticism
In exploring these issues, we will compare the main epistemological approaches of realism and scepticism. Each involves a number of different positions. Thus *ontological* or *metaphysical realism* involves the idea that there

---

[52] Twining, above n. 2, 110. See also Chapter 4 passim, though acknowledging at 142 that he has yet to respond to recent critics.

[53] Roberts above n. 2, 325.

[54] Dealt with in detail in section 3.3.2 below.

[55] But, see respectively, for example, D. Nicolson, 'Critical Approaches', in S. Halliday (ed.), *An Introduction to the Study of Law* (2012), D. Nicolson and J. Webb, *Professional Legal Ethics: Critical Interrogations* (1999), 201–3, and Nicolson and Webb, ibid., 43–6.

[56] This section is based on the more detailed discussion in Nicolson, 'Taking Epistemology Seriously' above n. 51.

exists a factual (and indeed moral) reality out there independent of human knowledge and understanding. *Semantic, linguistic* or *representational realism* holds that the meaning of 'assertoric'[57] statements is affected by and may reflect the world as it exists. The term *realist epistemology* can be used to describe the 'cognitivist' position that knowledge is capable of being presented in true statements which correspond with reality. Finally, while it is more tendentious to describe the view of rationality associated with British Empiricism as a form of realism, it is not entirely inappropriate given that it is based on the drawing of inductive inferences from perceptions of the real world.

It is important to note that these different realist positions do not comprise a job lot. One can, for instance, adopt metaphysical realism and a correspondence theory of truth, but reject the realist view of rationality. Similarly, one can adopt all or some aspects of realism in one sphere of human activity, such as the natural sciences, but reject all or some aspects in other spheres, such as the human sciences or morality.

The same applies to scepticism.[58] Scepticism is as old as philosophy itself, traceable as far back as 539 BC,[59] and varying in intensity. Thus a mild form, which can be called *anti-dogmatic scepticism*,[60] merely questions the possibility of infallible and certain knowledge, pointing to the unlikelihood of human knowledge ever being complete or free from errors, preconceptions or biases. However, philosophers usually have in mind a more thorough-going scepticism (*cognitive scepticism*), which questions the very possibility of obtaining knowledge or at least obtaining it through the evidence of one's senses. Closely related to cognitive scepticism is the more recent *semantic scepticism*, which questions whether assertoric statements can directly reflect an external world out there. Finally, *ontological scepticism* goes even further to deny the existence of the world itself. Thus those variously called idealists, phenomenalists or solipsists maintain that the world exists only in the ideas and minds of individuals.[61]

Recently, these traditional forms of scepticism have been given a more radical edge by the loose collection of writers described as postmodernist or poststructuralist. Their scepticism extends beyond philosophy to all disciplines

---

[57] That is, those that assert some fact rather than express some feeling (for example, 'yuck') or perform a 'speech act' (for example, 'I do' in a marriage ceremony).

[58] The term scepticism is preferred to anti-realism because the latter is usually confined to semantic scepticism and usually has negative overtones, suggesting that one is unrealistic, whereas, as argued below (section 3.3.2), scepticism can be regarded in positive terms.

[59] A. Musgrave, *Common Sense, Science and Scepticism: A Historical Introduction to the Theory of Knowledge* (1993), 10.

[60] Cf. M. Williams, *Unnatural Doubts: Epistemological Realism and the Basis of Scepticism* (1996), 251.

[61] See Musgrave, above n. 59, Chapter 7.

and arguably represents more than just a theoretical position but a radically new way of looking at the world.[62] This new stance was sparked largely by the failure of many aspects of the Enlightenment project. For instance, not only has science struggled to discover the truth about the world and how to make it a better place, but it has led to many contemporary problems such as large-scale environmental destruction, and made possible some of the most horrific episodes in human history, such as the Holocaust and Hiroshima.

Modernism's failures have led postmodernists to assert that truth, reason and justice involve relative rather than absolute standards. Building on philosophers such as Friedrich Nietzsche, Martin Heidegger and Ludwig Wittgenstein, and influenced by various critical theories, such as feminism and Marxism, and disciplines like literature, psychoanalysis and the sociology of knowledge, writers such as Jean-François Lyotard, Jacques Derrida, Michel Foucault and Richard Rorty have launched a thorough-going critique of modernist philosophy. For postmodernists, knowledge is seen as partial in both senses of the word: in other words, as incomplete and as affected by subjective perspectives and values. Indeed, postmodernists see knowledge and truth, as well as reason, not just as impossible dreams, but also as imbued with and legitimating existing relations of power. Similarly, language is seen as a value-laden means of constructing truth, rather than a means simply of describing it. Even individuals themselves are regarded as being constructed by language and other discourses rather than as autonomous epistemological subjects whose minds represent a mirror onto which reality is reflected in ways unaffected by their social context.[63] Moreover, rather than science and philosophy being held up as the foundation for all knowledge, postmodernists even reject the continuing value of epistemology and metaphysics, with their search for universal foundations for knowledge and adjudicating truth claims. Finally, 'grand (or meta-) narratives' which attempt to construct large-scale 'totalising' theories of complex and wide-ranging phenomena are rejected in favour of provisional, small-scale theories that pay attention to a plurality of different voices, stories and experiences.

3.1.2 Battle Joined

As some modified rationalists now realise,[64] it is no longer possible to claim – if indeed it ever was – that philosophical sceptics are 'rare birds'.[65]

---

[62] See, for example, D. Harvey, *The Condition of Postmodernity* (1989); J. Flax, *Thinking Fragments: Psychoanalysis, Feminism, and Postmodernism in the Contemporary West* (1990), Chapter 1; S. Best and D. Kellner, *Postmodern Theory: Critical Interrogations* (1991).

[63] See R. Rorty, *Philosophy and the Mirror of Nature* (1979).

[64] For example, Damaška above n. 50; Allen, above n. 50, 310–11.

[65] Twining, above n. 2, 110.

The issue is now whether realism or scepticism provides a more plausible approach to evidence theory. Given that few contemporary sceptics, let alone evidence scholars,[66] deny that there is an objective world independent of human knowers, there seems little point in debating the esoteric and ultimately irresoluble issue of whether there *actually is* an 'out there' out there.[67] The real issue is thus whether *knowledge* of such an objective reality is possible; in other words, the debate is epistemological, not ontological.

Orthodox epistemologists usually define knowledge as 'justified true belief'. Truth is required in order to distinguish belief from knowledge, whereas the justification requirement is designed to ensure that lucky guesswork cannot count as knowledge. We will start with the justification requirement since it is regarded by traditional epistemologists as more fundamental.[68] In fact, evaluating traditional theories of justification simultaneously involves evaluating the Rationalist Tradition's approach to rationality. This is because theories of justification and rationality overlap in that rational beliefs are regarded as those that are adequately justified (albeit not necessarily true).[69] Accordingly, we will first explore the various traditional theories of rational belief and realist responses to traditional scepticism before turning to the arguments of contemporary sceptics. However, given that the justification criterion for knowledge only overlaps with what is called theoretical or epistemic rationality (namely, that which governs what is rational to *believe*), it is necessary to engage in a more general critique of rationality. This encompasses both theoretical rationality and practical rationality, which governs what is rational to *do*.

3.2 Justification and Reason

3.2.1 Realist Theories

3.2.1.1 EMPIRICIST FOUNDATIONALISM

As already noted, the Rationalist Tradition's favoured form of reason, and hence epistemic justification, is that of empiricist foundationalism, which, as we have seen,[70] treats justified knowledge as that which is built upon a mixture of the evidence of one's senses and logical inferences. Over the centuries,

---

[66] But cf. Graham, above n. 51, 1225, who flirts with ontological scepticism.

[67] See, for example, Rorty, above n. 63, 276, *Contingency, Irony and Solidarity* (1989), 4–5 and *Objectivism, Relativism and the Truth: Philosophical Papers – Volume One* (1991), 83.

[68] R. Fumerton, 'Theories of Justification', in P. K. Moser (ed.), *The Oxford Handbook of Epistemology* (2002), 204.

[69] See, for example, R. Audi, 'Theoretical Rationality', in R. Mele and P. Rawling (eds), *The Oxford Handbook of Rationality* (2004), 17.

[70] Section 2.2.

sceptics have raised numerous problems with this approach.[71] However, even if these problems can be overcome, empiricist foundationalism drastically reduces the range of possible justifiable knowledge. This is because most of the knowledge which we quite reasonably or at least inevitably rely on is gained, not by our own perceptions, but indirectly from others – parents, teachers, books, films, television, etc. – much of which they in turn obtained from others, who also obtained it from others, and so on.

But even within the confines of directly observed evidence, sceptics have long noted the fallibility of our senses. Not only do they frequently deceive us, but they can never provide us with knowledge of the external world; only with knowledge of what we perceive – of how things appear, not how they are. Moreover, as we shall see in much more detail in Chapter Six,[72] different people may perceive the same things differently, and even the same person can perceive things differently if the conditions of observation are altered. Our perceptions might even be the result of dreaming, hallucinations or, as René Descartes famously hypothesised,[73] an evil demon deceiving us into thinking that we perceive the real world rather than one of his making. Furthermore, there seems to be no non-circular way of justifying beliefs based on sensory perceptions. This is because we can only attempt to distinguish what is real from mere appearance according to prior beliefs. Yet, if these beliefs are based on prior experiences, they are subject to the same problems.

More generally, as again we will see in Chapter Six,[74] perceptions are not simply delivered by our senses; we have to interpret them.[75] This is done in terms of pre-existing concepts used to categorise information ('this is pain', 'that looks red', etc.), and these in turn involve a comparison with past experiences, thus undermining the foundationalist nature of the experiential 'givens'. Moreover, we do not know such experience words like 'pain', 'red', etc. simply through direct acquaintance. Experience is usually[76] filtered through the medium of language, which, as we shall see later,[77] is composed of categories which themselves are not derived directly from experience.

---

[71] See, for example, Musgrave above n. 59, Chapters 3–8 passim; Williams, above n. 60; Fumerton above n. 68, 210–20; J. Dancy, *Introduction to Contemporary Epistemology* (1985), Chapter 1; S. Haack, *Evidence and Inquiry: Towards Reconstruction in Epistemology* (1993), Chapter 2.
[72] Section 2.2.
[73] See the references at n. 81 below.
[74] Section 6.3.
[75] See, for example, Fumerton above n. 68, 216ff.
[76] But cf. A. I. Goldman, *Knowledge in a Social World* (1999), 18–19.
[77] Sections 3.2.2.2 and 3.3.2.

Nevertheless, even if our senses could provide unmediated knowledge of the world, David Hume famously argued that we cannot use it to make infallible inferences about things we do not experience.[78] This is because we can never be certain that future events or unobserved past events will repeat the pattern of past experiences. For instance, just because bread nourished me from Monday to Saturday does not mean that it will nourish me on Sunday, let alone always nourish me or everyone else.[79] There is always an inevitable evidential gap between our beliefs about future events and other unobserved facts, and our evidence for them. Consequently, what Hume called 'experimental inference' (but is now called 'inductive generalisation')[80] can never generate certain conclusions about unobserved or future facts. Consequently, Hume concluded that, while inevitable, our everyday way of understanding the world through inductive inferences from past experiences is in fact irrational. If true, this could be devastating to the Rationalist Tradition's claim to rationality.

One[81] solution is to resile from 'strong' or 'radical'[82] forms of empiricist foundationalism and accept that absolutely secure foundations for knowledge are impossible. This approach argues that anti-dogmatic cognitive sceptics only establish that particular items of knowledge are fallible; not that secure knowledge is never possible.[83] For instance, while our senses sometimes deceive us, they do not always do so. Similarly, while it is theoretically possible that our perceptions are caused by an evil demon,[84] we need only exclude realistic and not highly unlikely scenarios in order to claim justified knowledge. In other words, epistemological standards must be realistic and reflect the world in which we live, rather than a 'highly

---

[78]   See Musgrave, above n. 59, Chapters 8 and 9; J. Greco, 'Virtues of Epistemology', in Moser, above n. 68, 304–5.

[79]   Example taken from Musgrave, ibid., 151–4.

[80]   J. Jackson, above n. 13, 496.

[81]   Cf. also the attempt is to seek foundational knowledge in 'pure reason' as exemplified by Descartes, who relied on self-evidence as the source of reason and justified knowledge (see, for example, Williams, above n. 60, passim; Musgrave, above n. 59, Chapter 11), and Kant, who relied on logical necessity (Musgrave, ibid., Chapter 12; Dancy, above n. 71, 92–5, Chapter 14; A. Casullo, 'A Priori Knowledge', in Moser, above n. 68). However, for the reasons summarised in Nicolson, 'Taking Epistemology Seriously', above n. 51, 13–14, both attempts ultimately fail and hence few if any philosophers now regard pure reason as capable of providing an adequate alternative to empiricist foundationalism.

[82]   Terms taken, respectively, from Haack, above n. 71, Chapter 1; N Lemos, 'Epistemology and Ethics', in Moser, above n. 68, 492–3 and Williams, above n. 60, 120.

[83]   Williams, ibid., n. 2, 135–6; N. Rescher, *Rationality* (1988), esp. 99ff and Chapter 10 – a position adopted by many contemporary orthodox evidence scholars: for example, Twining, above n. 2, 109; Stein, above n. 50, 58–9; Ho, above n. 6, 55.

[84]   Or the contemporary equivalents of a machine called Braino or a mad scientist controlling a brain in a vat: Musgrave, above n. 59.

rarefied, theoretical context'.[85] Consequently, we can accept that knowledge claims can never be certain, exact and free from doubt, or that we can ever possess all the relevant facts to rule out all possible errors or new explanations for our beliefs. But this does not mean we have to accept that knowledge claims can never be justified. According to Nicholas Rescher, '[i]f we have done all that reasonably can be asked of us, the best that can reasonably be done, then there can be no need for *further* assurance . . . A wholly justified claim to certainty and knowledge is compatible with a nagging element of theoretical doubt.'[86]

This suggests that Hume wrongly concluded that we cannot rationally rely on past experience to make inferences about future or unobserved facts. Accordingly, we can put the 'rational' back into the Rationalist Tradition, especially as it accepts that legal proof does not require absolute certainty but only probable certainty. However, while good pragmatic reasons exist for eschewing a standard so high that it is rarely met, two problems remain.[87] The first is that once we abandon absolutely certain basic beliefs as the source of our derived beliefs, it is difficult to know how far down the line to stop – virtually certain, reasonably certain, fairly certain or merely more likely than not?[88] And even if we can fix on a standard, applying it to the facts involves much discretion and hence further scope for watering down standards for justified knowledge. Both problems arise in legal fact finding where the justification standard in civil cases is as low as merely a balance of probabilities.

3.2.1.2 ALTERNATIVES TO FOUNDATIONALISM

Another solution to the problems with classic foundationalism lies in developing alternative theories of justification. The oldest and best known of these is coherentism, which treats justification holistically by seeking particular beliefs as warranted if they cohere with other relevant beliefs in the sense of being compatible and mutually supportive.[89] Thus, instead of justification being built up atomistically from basic beliefs to derived beliefs

---

[85] Williams, above n. 60, 185. See also, for example, Haack, above n. 71, 88–9 and Chapter 10 passim.
[86] Above n. 83, 40–1.
[87] Cf. also Rescher, ibid., 79–80, who denies that probabilities provide a sufficiently robust method of deriving justified beliefs.
[88] Cf. H. Kornblith, 'In Defence of a Naturalized Epistemology', in John Greco and Ernest Sosa (eds), *The Blackwell Guide to Epistemology* (1999), 160.
[89] The following draws on Dancy, above n. 71, Chapters 8 and 9; Moser, above n. 68 passim, esp. 87–90, 226–30, 241, 288, 356–8, 500–1; Williams, above n. 60, 228–33 passim, Chapter 7ff; Audi, above n. 69, 27–9; Haack, above n. 71, 17–33 passim, 52–7, 60–1; L. Bonjour, 'The Dialectic of Foundationalism and Coherentism', in Greco and Sosa ibid.

in the form of an inverted pyramid, it is analogised to a raft in which no belief is more fundamental than any other, but each forms part of a web of mutually supporting beliefs. However, consistency alone does not justify beliefs; the belief set must also be comprehensive, otherwise justification can too easily be ensured by simply omitting inconsistent beliefs.

This approach has many advantages. One is that it fits actual practice better than foundationalism in that we naturally rely on a mutually supportive mixture of prior beliefs, empirical observations and other forms of acquiring knowledge, which we recognise merely as provisional and subject to revision in the light of conflicting evidence. Moreover, our beliefs can derive, not just from perception (and 'pure reason', as in the case of mathematics), but also from the reports of others. Thus, instead of seeing individuals as struggling to construct their own beliefs, we can recognise the crucial social dimension to epistemology.[90] Finally, as we shall see,[91] coherentism accords with contemporary scepticism, which argues that we have no access to anything beyond language and existing beliefs and hence that we can never expect more than coherence as a justification for knowledge.

On the other hand, coherentism is criticised as both too strong and too weak a standard of justification. It is too strong in suggesting that even one small inconsistent belief can 'destroy the possibility of there being *any* epistemic justification for believing *any* proposition'.[92] It also suggests that we must be aware of an enormous number of beliefs which must cohere before we can justify even simple acts of knowing. For instance, to say that a siren is sounding we need to be aware of numerous enabling conditions (both practical, such as being able to hear, and conceptual, most notably that we possess the concept of a siren) and to exclude countless alternatives for the sound.[93] And if it is unrealistic to expect one to be aware of these myriad enabling conditions in relation to single facts, it is even more unrealistic in relation to all of one's knowledge.

But coherentism is also too weak in suggesting that coherence and comprehensiveness are sufficient to justify beliefs. Descartes' evil demon scenario shows that a set of beliefs can be perfectly coherent yet have no basis in reality. In addition, coherentism is said to treat beliefs acquired by wishful thinking equally to those involving the painstaking evaluation of evidence. Without some explanation of how consistency of belief somehow

---

[90] See further at sections 3.2.2 and 3.3 below.
[91] Section 3.2.2 below.
[92] Fumerton, above n. 68, 227.
[93] Example taken from Audi, above n. 69, 28.

delivers truth, the adoption of a coherence theory of justification seems to be incompatible with realism's correspondence theory of truth.

Faced with these problems, many[94] contemporary epistemologists have abandoned theories like foundationalism and coherentism that require epistemological subjects to be aware of the factors thought to justify their knowledge. Compared to such 'internalist' approaches, so-called 'externalists' look for guarantees of truth that need not be known by the subject.[95] While there are various versions of externalism, the most influential is reliabilism,[96] which simply requires reliably produced beliefs that are said to be justified because they are probably true. Reliabilism is argued to involve a common-sense response to cognitive scepticism in that, as long as our normal sources of knowledge (for instance, perception, introspection, logical intuitions and reason) are reliable, it matters not that we can never know whether they are reliable. Equally it avoids foundationalism's problems of circularity and coherentism's undue demands on the abilities of epistemological subjects, while also allowing justification to vary in degree according to the level of reliability of the belief-producing method.

However, a number of problems with reliabilism and externalism generally have limited their appeal. One is that there is no universally acceptable reliability measure. Secondly, there is a danger that setting it too high makes knowledge impossible and setting it too low provides ammunition for sceptics. More generally, pointing to examples such as clairvoyants who through unknown processes are able to produce reliable beliefs, traditional epistemologists argue that externalist accounts of justification are counterintuitive and that, even if there is an epistemological role for reliabilism and other versions of externalism, some form of internalist justification is required.

Others argue that '[w]e cannot be simply "reliable": we can only be reliable about certain things *under certain conditions*'.[97] This has led to a contextualist approach to justification,[98] which argues that it is impossible to

---

94 Others have sought to combine coherentism and foundationalism in a way that resolves the problems of each. See, for example, Haack's 'foundherentism', which analogises justification to a crossword puzzle with experiential evidence representing the clues and background information the existing entries (Haack, above n. 71) but like other similar mixed approaches, it has failed to garner much support (Nicolson, 'Taking Epistemology Seriously', above n. 51, 17–18).

95 On the two approaches, see Bonjour, above n. 89; E. Sosa, 'Skepticism and the Internal/External Divide', in Greco and Sosa, above n. 88.

96 See Fumerton, above n. 68, 220–3; Dancy, above n. 71, 31–2; Haack, above n. 71, Chapter 7; Greco, above n. 78; Bonjour ibid.

97 Williams, above n. 60, 329 (emphasis in original).

98 See Williams, ibid., passim; K. DeRose, 'Contextualism: An Explanation and Defense', in Greco and Sosa, above n. 88.

have a consistent system of knowledge across all contexts and therefore that justification can only be legitimately demanded within localised areas of knowledge such as disciplines like philosophy or law, or particular activities such as scientific experimentation or medical diagnosis. However, while contextualism provides additional reasons for being sceptical about the possibility of universally infallible knowledge, it is questionable whether it constitutes an independent approach to justification, rather than simply a qualification to reliabilism or other externalist theories, or more radically a denial of the possibility of objective standards of justification.

3.2.2 Contemporary Scepticism
3.2.2.1 INTRODUCTION
This last position is the one expressly adopted by contemporary sceptics who, unlike traditional epistemologists, tend to treat justification and truth together. Moreover, they are far less concerned with analysing either concept or debating the merits of traditional theories of justification and truth. Instead, they attack the idea that knowledge can be objectively true and justified for all people at all times and in all places, and argue that claims to knowledge, reason and truth are relative to place and time, and implicated in existing power relations. Nevertheless, despite this more holistic approach, it is possible to distinguish contemporary sceptics' views on the plausibility of realist conceptions of justification from their views on truth.

3.2.2.2 KNOWLEDGE, PERSPECTIVE AND POWER[99]
Starting with justification, a central criticism of traditional epistemology is that its highly selective view of how humans learn about the world ignores issues of power, overestimates its ability to understand and improve the processes of knowledge acquisition, and radically underestimates the impact of perspective on knowledge and the degree of uncertainty inherent in knowledge claims.[100]

---

[99] See, in general, J. Jackson, 'Theories of Truth', above n. 13 and 'Analysing the New Evidence Scholarship', above n. 39; Fiske, above n. 51; Scheppele, above n. 51 (both references); Williams, above n. 60; Flax, above n. 62; Rorty, above nn. 63, 67 (both references) and *Consequences of Pragmatism* (1982); J. Bruner, 'The Narrative Construction of Reality' (1991) 8 *Critical Inquiry* 1; L. Alcoff and E. Potter (eds), *Feminist Epistemologies* (1993); K. Lennon and M. Whitford (eds), *Knowing the Difference: Feminist Perspectives in Epistemology* (1994); L. Code, *What Can She Know? Feminist Theory and the Construction of Knowledge* (1999).

[100] See L. M. Antony, 'Embodiment and Epistemology', in Moser, above n. 68; Alcoff and Potter, ibid., esp. Chapters 2, 6 and 7; Code, ibid.

One reason is that traditional epistemology treats knowledge of the objects of scientific research or inanimate medium-sized objects like chairs as paradigmatic, rather than more complex phenomena like people or events. Moreover, knowledge is narrowly conceptualised as propositional knowledge of the kind: 'S [a person] knows that P [some fact that can be formulated as a proposition (that is, statement of fact)]', rather than practical knowledge (for example, 'knowing how to ride a bicycle, etc.') or knowledge of people (for example, 'knowing Janet'). In fact, knowledge of others is not only the earliest form of knowledge humans develop, but also one that is as – if not more – important than propositional knowledge. As already noted,[101] we do not obtain most of our knowledge of the world from personal observation and/or reason, but from the personal reports of others, books, films and television, etc.

This is particularly true in law because legal fact finders frequently lack personal access to the facts, but usually have to rely on witness testimony.[102] Here what is as, if not more, important than reason or other sources of knowledge emphasised by traditional epistemology is the more or less instinctive and emotional, and hence far more complex and uncertain, decision as to whether to trust someone. According to Lorraine Code: knowing others 'admits of degree in ways that knowing the book is red does not' and 'is an ongoing, communicative, interpretative process'.[103] This, and the fact that acquaintance with others might alter both parties' perspective, contrasts markedly with the stable and permanent knowledge associated with physical objects in which neither subject nor object is affected by the process of knowledge acquisition. It also contrasts with the traditional epistemologist's image of individuals using a laboratory microscope or sitting in their studies contemplating whether they are being manipulated by an evil demon. Indeed, knowledge production is a highly social activity in which questions of credibility and trust in others, and communal practices of acknowledgment, correction and critique, are as essential as perception and reason.

But even propositional knowledge is far less stable, certain and objective than the most anti-dogmatic realist would acknowledge. While personal perspective *might* not affect knowledge of physical objects, Chapter Six will show that it is ineradicable in relation to knowledge of events, which is far more relevant to legal fact finding. As the proto-postmodernist Friedrich Nietzsche asserted: '[t]here is *only* a perspectival seeing, *only* a perspectival knowing'.[104]

---

[101] Section 3.2.1.1.
[102] On the importance of expert and lay testimony, see Chapter 5, section 1 and Chapter 6, section 1.
[103] Code, above n. 99, 37–8.
[104] *On the Genealogy of Morals and Ecce Homo* (1969), 119.

For instance, different people may disagree as to whether some form of physical contact is mere touching, a slap or an aggressive hit. As Chapter Six explores in more detail later, phenomena are not simply absorbed by blank minds like images captured by photographic material.[105] The mind makes sense of any incoming information in terms of pre-existing categories, which are formed in response to individual experiences, as well as received information from others, and hence depend crucially on each person's background. For instance, men subjected to childhood violence and women in general might be more likely to interpret physical contact as violence than other men. In other words, epistemological subjects are not neutral observers, substitutable one for another, but embodied individuals with specific histories who are located in specific communities with particular ideas and values which inevitably affect how they interpret new experiences as well as which parts of reality they notice. As Rorty argues: to 'notice a sort of "thing" is to notice under a description, not just to respond discriminatively to it'.[106]

According to contemporary sceptics, there is no escaping the categories and concepts by which we view the world. Knowledge is therefore constructed by language and other means of communicating ideas (for example, art, architecture and even clothes) – collectively described as 'discourse' – which in turn are constructed by their cultural setting. And, when it comes to interpreting events, we rely heavily on narratives: commonly occurring stories with self-contained narrative structure and in-built significance and interpretations of matters like causation, motive and responsibility.[107] Echoing coherentism, contemporary sceptics argue that the plausibility of narratives is evaluated in terms not of their correspondence to some independently existing reality, but their internal coherence and consistency with existing stories about the world.

If persuasive, this means that evaluating facts can never be based on 'the whole truth and nothing but the truth'. Value judgments and background assumptions, not to mention prejudice and biases, will inevitably affect the choice of what is noticed and how it is evaluated. Knowledge is, therefore, never point-of-viewless. It only appears so when we are exposed to the same phenomenon under the same conditions and share the same

---

[105] See section 2.2; also B. Barnes and D. Bloor, 'Relativism, Rationalism and the Sociology of Knowledge', in M. Hollis and S. Lukes (eds), *Rationality and Realism* (1982), 37ff.

[106] Rorty, above n. 63, 183; see also 'Foucault and Epistemology', in D. C. Hoy (ed.), *Foucault: A Critical Reader* (1986), 48.

[107] See Chapter 7, esp. section 5.

conceptual framework[108] – or, in postmodernist terminology,[109] participate in the same language games.

If values and all factors which cause different people to have different perspectives on the world affect belief and if different individuals and social groups both have different values and perspectives and differing abilities to have their views heard, disseminated and imposed on others, then what counts as knowledge in any society will reflect, and in turn legitimate and reinforce, existing power relations. As critical theorists put it, the perspectives and values of the powerful in society are privileged, and their power and privileges are maintained, by elevating their views from mere belief into knowledge.

Moreover, the process whereby this occurs is enhanced by the very idea of objective standards of justification and knowledge reflecting truth, and by the possibility of producing a single, authoritative representation of the 'real world',[110] stripped of all traces of human biography, culture and social background. Accordingly, by seeking absolute and objective foundations to knowledge, traditional epistemology is argued to constitute an exercise in the legitimation of the status quo.[111] By purporting to be able to discover the universal grounds that distinguish opinion from knowledge, belief from truth and fact from value, and to provide the universalistic and objective foundations of knowledge and truth claims, realist epistemology appears to cleanse knowledge, fact and truth of perspective, politics and power.

Even more radically, following Nietzsche,[112] it is argued that the will to knowledge is indissociable from the will to power. According to Foucault, 'there is no power relation without the correlative constitution of a field of knowledge, nor any knowledge that does not presuppose and constitute at the same time power relations'.[113] Thus, rather than emancipation and unadulterated progress, the Enlightenment ideals of knowledge

---

[108] Scheppele, 'Foreword', above n. 51, 2090.

[109] Popularised by J. F. Lyotard, *The Postmodern Condition: A Report on Knowledge* (1979), discussed by Best and Kellner, above n. 62, Chapter 5, Flax, above n. 62, 202ff, but see Wittgenstein's original more technical meaning at n. 163, below.

[110] Code, above n. 99, 258.

[111] This has been a theme particularly of Rorty: see, for example, above n. 63, esp. Introduction and Part III; *Objectivism, Relativism and the Truth*, above n. 67, esp. 21–2, 35 and 'Foucault and Epistemology', above n. 106, 44. See also Flax, above n. 62, 30–4, 190–4.

[112] For example, *The Will to Power* (1968), esp. Book III.

[113] See *Power/Knowledge: Selected Interviews and Other Writings*, 1972–1977 (1980); *Discipline and Punish* (1979) and *The History of Sexuality, Volume One* (1984), discussed by G. Turkel, 'Michel Foucault: Law, Power and Knowledge' (1990) 17 *Journal of Law and Society* 170. See further, Best and Kellner, above n. 62, Chapter 2.

and truth have ensured increasing control and repression. Foucault argues that we live in a 'disciplinary' society in two senses. First, power is exercised most effectively through subtle processes, involving 'devious and supple mechanisms of power',[114] which maintain social *discipline* through persuading individuals to uphold social and legal norms specifying appropriate behaviour. Secondly, normalisation occurs through the knowledge and techniques of various *disciplines*, such as pedagogy, medicine, psychiatry and demography, which since the Enlightenment have sought to 'qualify, measure, appraise and hierarchize'[115] all aspects of human life, thus subjecting individuals to increasing surveillance and control.

3.2.2.3 REASON AND EXCLUSION

Given that such categorisation, classification and other forms of ordering and subjecting of humans to scientific knowledge are often associated with Enlightenment ideals of rationality, Foucault is equally critical of the way that these ideals have been used to control society – though he does not reject the ideal of rationality per se.[116] Similarly, while it can be argued that to see the 'disenchantment of the world' through an 'iron cage' of bureaucratic rationalism,[117] the single-minded focus of economic man on cost-benefit calculations, and the technocratic logic of Hitler's final solution[118] are distortions rather than logical extensions of Enlightenment rationality, many see pristine Enlightenment rationality as itself problematic.

We have already seen that centuries of debate have not delivered consensus on epistemic rationality. Also problematic is practical rationality, which covers the question of whether behaviour is rational. Together these two forms of rationality are combined into what is sometimes called the 'Standard Picture'.[119] This Standard Picture sees both rational beliefs and behaviour as controlled by the intellect and specifically by rules of logic and probabilities, and various others principles like consistency, uniformity, coherence, simplicity and efficiency.[120] In subsequent chapters, we will see

---

[114] *The History of Sexuality, Volume One* (1984), 86.

[115] Ibid., 144.

[116] See Best and Kellner, above n. 62, 37–8, 52–3. For similar approaches, see at nn. 140–1 below.

[117] M. Weber, *The Protestant Ethic and the Spirit of Capitalism* (1958).

[118] Cf., for example, D. Harvey, *The Condition of Postmodernity* (1989), esp. 12–15, Chapter 8.

[119] E. Stein, *Without Good Reason* (1996); R. Samuels and S. Stich, 'Rationality and Psychology', in Mele and Rawling, above n. 69, 285; A. I. Goldman, 'The Sciences and Epistemology', in Moser, above n. 68, 148.

[120] Stein, ibid.; R. J. Allen, 'Factual Ambiguity and a Theory of Evidence' (1994) 88 *Northwestern University Law Review* 604, 628, quoting Rescher, above n. 86, 16–18; G. Harman, 'Practical Aspects of Theoretical Reasoning', in Mele and Rawling, above n. 69, 48ff. See also Rorty, *Objectivism, Relativism and the Truth*, above n. 67, 25, 28, 35ff.

that in fact people use a much wider variety of reasoning methods – not only narrative and other forms of holistic reasoning,[121] but also what is called heuristic reasoning (rough-and-ready rules of thumb which are generally reliable but may lead to mistakes and biases),[122] abductive reasoning and the closely related lateral thinking (the creative search for explanations and solutions for situations).[123] In addition, rational thinking is inextricably tied up with, and not necessarily more likely than, emotion, intuition and empathy to deliver the truth.[124] Sigmund Freud exploded the idea of the conscious mind able to escape the murkier depths of the unconscious.[125] Instead of reason being unproblematically associated with truth, it may suppress the desire for truth. As Blaise Pascal famously put it, '[t]he heart has its reasons that reason knows nothing about'.[126]

Whether this makes humans irrational, and whether or not narrative, heuristic and abductive reasoning are regarded as forms of rationality capable of leading to justified beliefs, can be said to be a matter of definition.[127] If so, this suggests that the meaning of 'reason' and 'rationality' may vary according to time and place. Even the rules of logic have been argued to be no more than descriptions of the inferences we habitually accept.[128] Moreover, critical theorists argue that 'reason' and 'rationality' are politically loaded. The designation 'rational' usually connotes more than behaviour which is controlled by logic or the intellect more generally, but involves a value judgment as to its soundness.[129] Rather than being neutral, such judgments are likely to reflect social power differences, with the closer to dominant values and ideas the outcome the more likely they are to be deemed rational. For example, it has long been suggested that women, black people and the 'lower' classes are ruled less by logic and the mind than by emotion and the heart. Accordingly, when they challenge those in power their views can be dismissed as irrational and overly emotional. Being associated with emotion, intuition and passion, women in

---

[121] Chapter 7, section 5.2.

[122] Chapter 5, sections 6.2 and 7.3.2; Chapter 7, section 5.1.

[123] See Chapter 7, sections 2.1 and 2.2.

[124] See, for example, Code, above n. 99, 47; Williams, above n. 60, esp. 71–2; Jackson, above n. 13; P. Greenspan, 'Practical Reasoning and Emotion', in Mele and Rawling, above n. 69; K. Jones, 'Gender and Rationality', in Mele and Rawling, ibid., 304.

[125] Flax, above n. 62, 59–63.

[126] *Pensées* (1660), cited by M. R. Damaška, *Evidence Law Adrift* (1997), 42.

[127] See Goldman, above n. 76, 153; and see Chapter 7 section 5.3 below.

[128] Rorty, above n. 63, 321; Barnes and Bloor, above n. 105, 45–6.

[129] See Greenspan, above n. 124, 210.

particular have been disqualified as capable knowers.[130] Moreover, the Age of Reason justified women's relegation to the domestic sphere and occupations requiring their 'natural' female traits of nurturing, leaving politics, economics, law and other arenas of public power to be debated in the language and experiences of men – defined as rationality.

Thus the centuries-old Platonic distinction between reason and emotion, which solidified into the positivistic desire to expel values from knowledge, has acted to reinforce existing power relations in society. So has the positivistic belief that knowledge obtained through reason and empirical observation using sense-perception can be objective, neutral and value-free, and that rational knowers can escape the influences of their social context to produce value-neutral knowledge. This neutral and objective stance is, however, only available to those who reflect the experiences, perspectives and norms of those with power in society, whose views in turn are protected from challenge by the Enlightenment myth of a rational epistemological subject capable of achieving the 'view from nowhere'.[131]

A similar legitimising effect is achieved by the Standard Picture's privileging of formal logic.[132] Formal logic is likely to be emphasised by those who are content with the premises involved in a reasoning process.[133] It encourages attention to be focused solely on the logical application of those premises rather than their content. This applies particularly to the Rationalist Tradition's favoured form of logic: inductive reasoning, or at least to how it is conceived by some evidence theorists.[134] Deductive logic or syllogistic reasoning involves a major premise (a generalisation about the world), a minor premise (a fact) and a conclusion. For example, if one applies the major premise infamously articulated by one English judge that 'women, in particular, and small boys are liable to be untruthful and invent stories'[135] to a female witness as the minor premise, the conclusion follows that she is prone to lie. Inductive logic, on the other hand, is said to involve only two stages: the minor premise (this is a woman) and the

---

[130] See in the context of law, N. Naffine, *Law and the Sexes: Explorations in Feminist Jurisprudence* (1990), Chapters 1 and 2.

[131] T. Nagel, *The View from Nowhere* (1986). See further, section 3.2.1.

[132] See also at section 3.3.2 regarding the use of logic to delegitimise critique, and B. Hernstein-Smith, 'Unloading the Self-Refutation Charge' (1993) 2 *Common Knowledge* 81 regarding such strategies in general.

[133] Graham, above n. 51, 1219–20; K. T. Bartlett, 'Feminist Legal Methods' (1990) 103 *Harvard Law Review* 829.

[134] See Chapter 7, section 1.

[135] Quoted, for example, by A. McColgan, 'Common Law and the Relevance of Sexual History Evidence' (1996) 16 *Oxford Journal of Legal Studies* 275, 277 and echoed by at least one police officer in advice to colleagues: A. Firth, 'Interrogation' (1975) 28 *Police Review* 1507.

conclusion (she is likely to be lying). However, by not expressly articulating the major premise, it appears to be axiomatic and unproblematic, which may in turn encourage its unconscious acceptance by others.

Given these problems with the Standard Picture, critical theorists – and to some extent modified rationalists[136] – have argued for rationality to be reconceptualised as including holistic, narrative and dialectic forms of thinking and decision-making,[137] as well as practical judgment and common sense,[138] and intuition.[139] Some also go beyond the decision-making processes of individual actors to see rationality as involving a commitment to the free, tolerant, non-dogmatic and respectful exchange of views in what Jurgen Habermas describes as "ideal speech situations".[140] According to Rorty, rationality so conceived can be regarded not as a method, but as a moral virtue or mark of civilisation denoting our willingness to use persuasion rather than force.[141]

3.2.2.4 THE REALIST RESPONSE

While evidence theory realists have largely ignored the political (as opposed to psychological) critique of rationality, some realist epistemologists have responded to the sceptical attack on traditional accounts of knowledge and justification by relying on a distinction between the process of knowledge acquisition (often called 'discovery') and that of its justification. Thus, while acknowledging the perspective-laden, highly social and context-dependent nature of discovery, they argue that these problems can be cured by the subsequent application of universal standards of justification.[142]

---

[136] See section 2.3, above.

[137] Twining, above n. 50, esp. 1544; Jackson, above n. 13. See also J. C. Rideout, 'Storytelling, Narrative Rationality, and Legal Persuasion' (2008) 14 *Legal Writing: Journal of the. Legal Writing Institute* 53.

[138] R. A. Posner, 'The Jurisprudence of Skepticism' (1988) 86 *Michigan Law Review* 827; W. Twining, 'Civilians Don't Try: A Comment on Mirjan Damaška's "Rational and Irrational Proof" Revisited' (1997) 5 *Cardozo Journal of International and Comparative Law* 69, 76.

[139] See, for example, Harmon, above n. 51, 505.

[140] See, for example, J. Habermas, *Theory of Communicative Action* (1981), discussed by Best and Kellner, above n. 62, 237ff; J. Jackson, 'Two Methods of Proof in Criminal Procedure' (1988) 51 *Michigan Law Review* 549, 563–4.

[141] Rorty, *Objectivism, Relativism and the Truth*, above n. 67, esp. 36–7, 62. See also Code, above n. 99, esp. at 169.

[142] Damaška, above n. 50, 292–3; W. S. G. Gey, 'Why Rubbish Matters: The Conservative Underpinnings of Social Constructionist Theory' (1999) 83 *Minnesota Law Review* 1707, 1720–1; Goldman, above n. 119; M. S. Moore, 'The Interpretative Turn in Modern Theory: A Turn for the Worse?' (1989) 41 *Stanford Law Review* 871, 909–11; R. K. Sherwin, 'The Narrative Construction of Legal Reality' (1993) 18 *Vermont Law Review* 681, 700ff; J. R. Searle, *The Construction of Social Reality* (1995), 151ff; S. Haack, *Manifesto of Passionate Moderate* (1998), passim but esp. 94, 105, 130–1, 142ff.

However, sceptics question whether even this latter, more reflective, process can completely erase the trace of individual perspective, language and human categories on knowledge acquisition,[143] not least because of the difficulty of spotting and eradicating factors which influence our thinking. Furthermore, discovery and justification cannot be neatly separated.[144] We may shape our processes of knowledge acquisition according to what we think are accepted models of justification (foundationalism, coherence, reliabilism, etc.), whereas these justification models are likely to reflect the processes by which traditional epistemologists think knowledge is acquired. More fundamentally, the process of justification only consciously commences once knowledge is acquired, and if perspective excludes certain enquiries from being undertaken or certain types of information from being noticed, there is little for justification to cure.

Even more fundamentally, it is difficult to see how we can escape existing categories, concepts and theories to distinguish justified from non-justified beliefs. Doing so requires both universal standards of justification *and* the ability to measure their success according to objective standards. In the next section we will evaluate whether realist concepts of truth can play the latter role. But as regards objective, universalistic standards of justification, it can be asked why, if they existed, centuries of debate have failed to produce consensus on their content, and why existing theories look suspiciously like the epistemic habits of Western, middle-class men and mimic the cool, rational and detached investigative methods of scientists. In fact, numerous studies have been summarised as finding 'East Asians to be more *holistic*, attending to the entire field and assigning causality to it, making relatively little use of categories and formal logic, and relying on "dialectical" reasoning, whereas Westerners are more *analytic*, paying attention primarily to the object and the categories to which it belongs and using rules, including formal logic, to understand its behaviour.'[145] This suggests that individual beliefs are transformed into knowledge, not by some objective process of ratification, but by being regarded as legitimate within particular epistemic communities. As Rorty asserts, belief 'goes all the way down',[146] in that 'nothing counts as justification unless by

---

[143] S. Harding, 'Rethinking Standpoint Epistemology: What is "Strong Objectivity"?', in Alcoff and Potter, above n. 99, 56, 70.

[144] Bankowski, above n. 51, 261–2.

[145] R. E. Nisbett et al., 'Culture and Systems of Thought: Holistic Versus Analytical Cognition' (2001) 18 *Psychological Review* 291.

[146] Rorty, *Contingency, Irony and Solidarity*, above n. 67, xiii; see also C. Norris, 'Law, Deconstruction and the Resistance to Theory' (1988) 15 *Journal of Law and Society* 166, 172.

reference to what we already accept, and there is no way to get outside our beliefs and our language so as to find some test other than coherence'.[147]

Thus contemporary sceptics believe that justification is merely a matter of community acceptance or at best the most coherent account of existing beliefs. However, realists could still rescue their notion of universally and objectively correct justification processes by showing that particular forms of justification in fact can deliver truth in relation to knowledge claims.[148] But this in turn assumes such a thing as objective and universalistic truth, which is the issue to which we now turn.

3.3 Truth

3.3.1 The Correspondence Theory and its Critics

Compared to justification, epistemologists pay relatively little attention to the concept of truth, perhaps because it seems obvious that, as Aristotle asserted, truth involves 'to say of what it is, that it is, or of what it is not, that it is not'.[149] Certainly most people[150] understand truth as involving a correspondence between a true proposition (statement, sentence, thought, etc.) and reality, the facts, the world out there, etc.[151] For example, 'the cat is on the mat' is true if the cat really is on the mat.

This correspondence conception of truth is inextricably linked with a theory of meaning (or semantics).[152] 'True' does not refer to the world or reality; the world or reality is not true, it is just the world or real. 'True' refers to a statement's status as accurately reflecting how things really are. The correspondence theory thus adopts a referential, representational or cognitivist theory of meaning in which language is assumed to be capable of accurately representing the world, and which analogises language as a picture of the facts, and the mind as a mirror on which the world is reflected.

Sceptics see profound problems with this view of truth and language. One is that it can only apply to descriptive rather than evaluative statements and struggles to cope with negative statements like 'the cat is not on

---

[147] Rorty, above n. 63, 178.
[148] See, for example, Haack, above n. 71, 196, 199. This strategy is particularly associated with reliabilism: see, for example, Goldman, above n. 76, Chapter 1.
[149] *Metaphysics* (1908): 1011b26-9, quoted in Haack, above n. 142, 21.
[150] See Musgrave, above n. 59, 248.
[151] For overviews, see Musgrave, ibid., Chapter 14; Searle, above n. 142, Chapter 9; Goldman, above n. 76, Chapter 2, esp. 59–66.
[152] Cf. Dancy, above n. 71, 85; E. Lepore and B. C. Smith (eds), *The Oxford Handbook of Philosophy of Language* (2006), esp. Chapters 9, 11, 25 and 36.

the mat'[153] or those which are vague like 'the man is handsome'.[154] More fundamentally, the correspondence theory treats two different things – language and the world – as the same.[155] Admittedly, the rules or conventions of language can deliver analytical truths – those statements Kant described as true by virtue of semantic definition, such as 'all bachelors are single'. However, the correspondence theory leaves mysterious how the world makes a meaningful contribution to language and hence delivers all other types of truths – those which Immanuel Kant described as synthetic truths whose truth depends on facts beyond the meaning of words.

To work, the correspondence theory requires 'truth-makers' – worldly entities which correspond to and hence make factual statements synthetically rather than analytically true. The most obvious candidate seems to be facts (or states of affairs), but facts come embedded with – and hence are constructed by – language. They do not exist pre-packaged, but have to be isolated and described. For instance, events like an assault have no natural start or end point, no natural boundaries determining what contemporaneous factors are included or excluded (motive, facial expressions, etc.). Nor is there a natural word to describe an act like putting one's hands on another's neck: was it caressing, touching, pressing, throttling, strangling?[156] Even the favoured facts of traditional epistemology – physical objects like rocks or 'mid-sized' objects like chairs – are creations of language: when, for instance, does a pebble become a stone, a stone a rock, a rock a boulder? As already noted,[157] we never encounter reality except under a description. Consequently, if John Searle is correct that institutional facts are those which depend for their existence on human institutions[158] and analytical truths are propositions which are true by definition, it would seem there are no such things as Searle's 'brute', non-institutional, facts or synthetic truths: all facts are institutional and all truths analytical.

Facts can thus be seen not as naturally occurring but as hybrid entities composed of 'physical stimuli and our antecedent response to such

[153] Rorty, *Objectivism, Relativism and the Truth*, above n. 67, 80.
[154] Cf. G. Segal, 'Truth and Meaning', in Lepore and Smith, above n. 152, 190.
[155] See, for example, Rorty, above n. 63, esp. Chapter 6; *Contingency, Irony and Solidarity*, above n. 67 Chapter 1; *Objectivism, Relativism and the Truth*, above n. 67, 78ff, 120ff and 151ff; and *Consequences of Pragmatism*, above n. 99, esp. Introduction and Chapters 1 and 9; D. Paterson, *Truth and Law* (1996), Chapters 1 and 3 passim. See also B. S. Jackson, 'Truth or Proof?: The Criminal Verdict' (1998) 11 *International Journal for the Semiotics of Law* 227, 252ff.
[156] Example taken from Scheppele, 'Foreword', above n. 51. For descriptions of fact construction in law, see Chapter 1, section 1.2, Chapter 4 passim, and Chapter 7, section 4.
[157] At n. 106.
[158] Searle, above n. 142, esp. 1–2, 27.

stimuli'[159] which are mediated via language, concepts and categories. Thus, as illustrated by the many Orcadian words for rain[160] and, even more strikingly, the fact that the Karam of New Guinea categorise bats as birds but cassowaries as sui generis,[161] different cultures categorise reality differently. In other words, the world does not represent itself. It has to be represented through some means of communication such as language, and all such means are human constructs. Moreover, given that language and other forms of discourse are social constructions and that society is hardly a value-free environment, descriptions of the world may involve moral and political value judgments – by no means always, but more than most people recognise. For example, while the sexism of using 'men' and other male terms to include women or as an allegedly gender-neutral designation for positions of authority or valued occupations is perhaps now widely recognised, it is still likely to influence children as they learn language, whereas the sexism of words like 'seminal' is far less obvious, as is the tendency for men to be named before their female partners.[162]

We see then that the world does not decide between different truth-claims, for instance whether the cat is – or is not – on the mat. Rather, it is our common view of the world as expressed through our accepted language conventions that decides, for instance, that what we call a 'cat' is what we call 'sitting' on what we call a 'mat'. We learn and understand the meaning of words by seeing how other people use them or, as Wittgenstein put it, by learning the rules of particular language games.[163] Meaning is not a matter of matching sentences with the facts which make them true, but a matter of assertability – what we are allowed to say by other language-users in our community. No matter how close we think descriptions come to representing reality, language and others forms of communication always intercede, making the description valid only in terms of its coherence with language or other means of communication as a whole, or in terms of conventional understandings of such communication. Moreover, a concept of truth cannot specify when knowledge claims are true in terms of something outside language because no one can adopt what is variously called the 'view from nowhere',[164] 'God's Eye point of

---

[159] Rorty, *Objectivism, Relativism and the Truth*, above n. 67, 83.

[160] Musgrave above n. 59, 265.

[161] Barnes and Bloor, above n. 105, 38.

[162] P. Hegarty et al., 'When Gentlemen are First and Ladies are Last: Effects of Gender Stereotypes on the Order of Romantic Partners' Names' (2011) 50 *British Journal of Social Psychology* 21.

[163] *Philosophical Investigations* (2001).

[164] Nagel, above n. 131.

view'[165] or 'Archimedean point'[166] and manage to step outside both language and the world, as well as their own biases, motives, interests, values and preconceptions, to inform the rest of us when we have finally arrived at the truth.[167]

3.3.2 The Realist Rejoinder

Instead of attempting to answer these points directly, many realists and certainly all those within orthodox evidence theory have treated attacks on scepticism as the first (and only) line of defence of realism.

Thus, it is commonly argued that truth-scepticism is self-refuting in the sense that one cannot deny truth (or indeed the possibility of obtaining knowledge) without relying on the concept of truth (or knowledge)[168] – along the lines that 'if scepticism is right, it is wrong; and if it is wrong, therefore it is wrong'.[169] Sceptics could respond that the realist argument is itself illogical in being question-begging because it assumes that what they explicitly and wittingly deny (the existence of objective truth) is the same as what they implicitly and unwittingly affirm (the existence of objective truth).[170] In fact, when sceptics deny objective truth they would not assert this as an objective truth – merely a warranted belief. But realists can then respond that if the denial of truth is not objectively true it remains logically possible that it *may* be wrong; in which case, objective truth *might* exist.

At this point, rather than pursuing whether such a marginal and highly esoteric 'flaw' can stem the tide of contemporary scepticism and whether the whole edifice of objective truth can be supported by the mere logical possibility of its existence, sceptics might be tempted to respond with a 'whatever' and get on with the task of exploring the value-laden nature of knowledge acquisition and justification. But before doing so, they need to deal with the more searching and pertinent realist argument that truth-scepticism is politically and ethically dangerous in undermining, if not totally negating, the ability and indeed the desire to search for truth

---

[165] H. Putnam, *Reason, Truth, and History* (1981), Chapter 3.

[166] See, for example, Rorty *Objectivism, Relativism and the Truth*, above n. 67, 155; H. Nelson, 'Epistemological Communities', in Alcoff and Potter, above n. 99, 129.

[167] Rorty, above n. 63, 281–2; see also his *Consequences of Pragmatism*, above n. 99.

[168] For example, Stein, above n. 50, 59; Twining, above n. 50; Williams, above n. 60, 270; Goldman, above n. 76, 35, 40; Gey, above n. 142, 1720–1; Moore, above n. 142, 897, 912–14; P. K. Moser, 'Introduction', in Moser, above n. 68, 11–12; C. Sunstein, 'On Finding Facts', in J. Chandler, A. I. Davidson and H. D. Harootunian (eds), *Questions of Evidence: Proof, Practice and Persuasion across the Disciplines* (1994), 197.

[169] Allen, above n. 50, 314 (though not endorsing this position).

[170] Cf. Hernstein-Smith, above n. 132, 84.

and to challenge injustice and the impact of bias on truth-claims.[171] Thus it is argued that truth-sceptics cannot legitimately evaluate knowledge claims and related action as valid or invalid; in other words, that 'truth' can only act as an ideal or goal to be strived for and as a means of evaluating knowledge and resisting biased and oppressive knowledge claims if understood in objective terms; as 'Truth'.[172]

However, it is difficult to see why a recognition that perspective, language and other forms of discourse always intercede between knowledge claims and "Truth" means that 'truth', understood as the most persuasive, comprehensive and coherent account of facts, cannot be an ideal for sceptics. Realists have, after all, recognised, not only that absolute certainty is unattainable, but also that what is really being sought are 'theories [which are] better or worse supported by the evidence'[173] or the 'best reasons'.[174] In other words, abandoning the notion of 'Truth' does not necessarily mean 'sawing off the branch of the tree of knowledge on which evidence is perched'[175] or abandoning 'truth' as an ideal or aspiration.[176] We can thus understand truth not in correspondence terms but as involving: (1) the best possible description or explanation we can muster of all relevant information – what can be called 'truth as aspiration';[177] and (2) a commitment to being as assiduous and as honest as we can be in our inquiries and communications – what can be called 'truth as integrity'.[178]

Nor does the denial of objective truth entail, as realists seem to assume, a form of relativism which accords all views equal value.[179] Admittedly,

---

[171] See generally Haack, above n. 20, 195–201 and n. 90, Chapters 7 and 8; Goldman, above n. 76, Chapter 1; Coleman and Leiter, above n. 78, 276; Gey, above n. 142; and in an evidence context, Roberts, above n. 2, 325–6; Twining, above n. 2, 124, 134–5, 155–6 n. 152 and, above, n. 50; Ho, above n. 6, 55–6; Marshall, above n. 50, 24; J. Jackson, 'Analysing the New Evidence Scholarship', above n. 39; Allen, above n. 50, 319; Stein, above n. 50, 57; Sunstein, above n. 169; D. J. Galligan, 'More Scepticism about Scepticism' (1988) 8 *Oxford Journal of Legal Studies* 249, 250.

[172] Cf. Twining, above n. 50.

[173] Haack, above n. 103, 131.

[174] Stein, above n. 50, 56–60.

[175] Roberts, above n. 2, 325–6.

[176] Cf. M. Henket, 'Taking Facts Seriously', in A. Wagner, W. Werner and D. Cao (eds), *Interpretation, Law and the Construction of Meaning: Collected Papers on Legal Interpretation in Theory, Adjudication and Political Practice* (2007), esp. 118.

[177] Cf. Rorty, above n. 63, 385.

[178] This idea, but not the exact phrase, derives from B. Jackson, above n. 51, 172–3.

[179] For this and other counterarguments, see, for example, E. Laclau and C. Mouffe, 'Post-Marxism Without Apologies' (1987) 166 *New Left Review* 79, 85, 101–2; A. C. Hutchinson, 'Inessentially Speaking (Is There Politics After Postmodernism?)' (1991) 89 *Michigan Law Review* 1549; A. Hepburn, 'On the Alleged Incompatibility between Relativism and Feminist Psychology' (2000) 10 *Feminism and Psychology* 91.

it does entail that there are no objectively 'valid or invalid' arguments. But that does not mean that there are no 'strong' or 'weak' arguments.[180] Although sceptics cannot claim to rely on Truth (or Reason or Justice similarly conceived in objective terms), they can argue that their views are more coherent both in terms of internal logic and compatibility with existing beliefs, better grounded, more accurate or at least more convincing (or rational or morally superior) than competing views.[181] Such arguments can be persuasive because, in relation to issues of fact, they can draw upon a world of sufficiently common experiences and because, in relation to issues of morality and justice, they can draw upon a language and system of values understandable within prevailing discourse.[182] Thus, while not seeing concepts like truth, justice and due process as having some foundation beyond social discourse, they are equally available to sceptics in criticising social practices. Indeed, to worry that there is nothing outside existing discourse to provide the foundations with which to criticise social practices suggests little faith in our society's existing values and its openness to new values.[183]

Realists, however, have one more throw of the dice. Thus, even accepting that the denial of objective truth does not logically preclude sceptics from criticising beliefs or action which are poorly supported by evidence, they argue that in practice a belief in objective truth is likely to be more effective in highlighting and combating biased and abusive knowledge claims.

In response, sceptics note that throughout history dominant groups have legitimated various forms of oppression through recourse to the language of 'Truth', 'Reality', 'Normality', 'Human Nature', etc.[184] Moreover, their views are defended by portraying relativism and scepticism as leading to a moral abyss. While it is tempting for those confronting these views to take a contrary absolutist position, according to sceptics, this refuge is dangerous in that challenging one 'Truth' with another 'Truth' carries with it the danger that one allegedly biased and oppressive claim to truth might simply be replaced by another less obviously biased and oppressive truth-claim. Moreover, it maintains the idea that there are absolute truths and that it is simply a question of who has access to them. Given the intersection between truth and power in society, this creates the potential for disputes

---

[180] Quotations from Twining, above n. 50, 1544.
[181] Cf. B. Jackson, above n. 51, 172–3, 193–4; S. Harding, 'Feminism, Science and Anti-Enlightenment Critiques', in L. Nicholson (ed.), *Feminism/Postmodernism* (1990), 100.
[182] Cf. C. Mouffe, 'Radical Democracy: Modern or Postmodern?', in A. Ross (ed.), *Universal Abandon: The Politics of Postmodernism* (1988), 37–8.
[183] Cf. Hutchinson, above n. 179, 1572.
[184] Best and Kellner, above n. 62, 231.

over competing versions of these absolute truths to be resolved by truth following power, thus reducing the chances of successful challenges to dominant views.[185]

Indeed, it can be argued that as long as sceptics avoid the slide into nihilism or an 'anything goes' relativism that allows dominant groups to exploit their greater power to influence the formation of views, scepticism offers a more effective bulwark against oppression, immorality and injustice, in that realism arguably encourages ethical and political complacency.[186] Thus it is a short step from believing in objective notions of truth, reason and justice to accepting that particular claims to truth, reason or justice are that absolute version. Rather than condemning one to silence, the denial of objective truth should compel one to constant reflection, evaluation and critique. Constant awareness that claims to truth can never be more than just claims discourages complacency and constantly invites the questions: under what conditions has this claim been made, by whom and whose interests is it likely to serve? It is perhaps revealing that such questions have only been vaguely and half-heartedly raised in relation to the Rationalist Tradition by modified rationalists.[187] While there is not necessarily a link between a realist epistemology and the failure to question the politics of the Rationalist Tradition, it is arguable that a theory which denies the existence of objective truth and which focuses on the social construction of truth is more likely to keep alive a critical approach to all truth-claims.[188]

3.3.3 Conclusion

However, given the counterargument that realism prevents complacency by encouraging the 'humbling recognition' that one's beliefs can always be wrong,[189] we are clearly very much in the realm of conjecture. Moreover, because it is impossible to establish which of the two predictions of complacency towards truth-claims are more accurate, it seems that we must return to the philosophical arguments about whether realism can withstand the sceptical attack on objective notions of truth. In this regard, it should now be clear that the sceptical rather than the realist approach will be adopted in this book. This does not mean going as far as Rorty, who called for epistemology to be abandoned in favour of political and ethical questions, and

---

[185] Fiske, above n. 51, 924–5.
[186] Bankowski, above n. 51, 260; Flax, above n. 62, 141–2.
[187] See Chapter 7, section 6.
[188] Cf. Bankowski, above n. 51.
[189] Gey, above n. 142, 1711, also at 1713. See also Marshall, above n. 50, 29.

a commitment to continuing 'the conversation of mankind'.[190] While this chapter has sought to establish that epistemology should never be pursued without due attention to issues of morality, politics and power, nevertheless there remains important epistemological work to be done. But rather than seeing this largely in terms of a search for the one true theory of justification or a plausible alternative to truth as correspondence, the focus of this book will be on how knowledge is actually acquired and how its acquisition may be improved.[191] Moreover, the various theories of justification can be used to evaluate knowledge claims, and the notions of 'truth as aspiration' and 'truth as integrity' can act as ideals to be pursued.

Finally, while the aim of this section to evaluate the epistemological assumptions of orthodox evidence has necessitated a focus on the claims of traditional and realist epistemology, it can be argued that closer attention needs to be paid to alternative epistemological positions. For instance, feminists argue that, given that perspective and personal interest is an inevitable epistemic fact of life, an awareness and recognition of their impact is more likely to achieve accurate information than attempts to replicate the allegedly detached and neutral stance of scientists.[192] Standpoint epistemology goes further to argue that the oppressed in society have a better understanding of the world than their oppressors, as they must understand the former's perspective as well as their own, but not vice versa,[193] and they will at the very least understand the details of their own lives better than others.[194] Similarly, while recognising that more voices may cause clarity and accuracy to be lost in a babble of noise, it makes sense to listen to postmodernist calls for a plurality of views and localised rather than universalistic knowledge claims.[195] Given that knowledge is always produced from the partial perspective of individual knowers, maximising the number of relevant perspectives drawn upon is likely to improve the knowledge obtained.

---

[190] Rorty, above n. 69, 264, quoting but not referencing Michael Oakshott. See also ibid., 209ff, 373–8, and *Contingency, Irony and Solidarity*, above n. 76, 68.

[191] See L. Code. 'Taking Subjectivity Into Account' and L. H. Nelson, 'Epistemological Communities', in Alcoff and Potter, above n. 99.

[192] S. Harding, 'Rethinking Standpoint Epistemology: What is "Strong Objectivity"?', in Alcoff and Potter, ibid.; C. Menkel-Meadow, 'The Trouble with the Adversary System in a Post-Modern, Multi-Cultural World' (1996) *Journal of the Institute for the Study of Legal Ethics* 801.

[193] See, for example, Harding, ibid.; D. Haraway, 'Situated Knowledges: The Science Question in Feminism and the Privilege of Partial Perspective' (1988) 14 *Feminist Studies* 575.

[194] Though not necessarily understand the structural causes of their oppression: see, for example, Haack, above n. 142, 126; M. Kelman, 'Reasonable Evidence of Reasonableness', in Chandler, Davidson and Harootunian, above n. 168, 179–82.

[195] See, for example, Menkel-Meadow, above n. 193; Scheppele, 'Foreword', above n. 51, 2097.

This has clear implications for the design of fact-finding procedures and hence will be picked up on in the next chapters. First, however, we need to complete the theoretical critique of orthodox theory by drawing upon jurisprudential theory in relation to its conception of justice.

4 Justice and Jurisprudence: The Politics of Evidence Theory

4.1 Jurisprudential Challenges to Orthodox Evidence Theory

As regards jurisprudence, as we have seen,[196] orthodox evidence theory has been influenced, first by legal positivism and its uglier offspring legal formalism in its attitudes to the relevance of justice to law and, secondly, by liberalism as regards its conceptualisation of justice. In the twentieth century, all three jurisprudential approaches and in particular their amalgamation into what Critical Legal Studies interchangeably calls liberal legalism, or legal liberalism,[197] has come under attack.[198]

Thus in the first half of the twentieth century Frank and his American Realist colleagues exploded the myth that law operates syllogistically and that legal decisions are unaffected by considerations of social policy and morality. Later, motivated by the apparent link between the positivist outlook of German lawyers and their failure to challenge the legality of Nazi rule, natural lawyers criticised legal positivism for failing to pay due regard to the moral basis of law and for discouraging German lawyers from standing up to legal injustice. Finally, various critical legal theories such as Marxism, feminism, Critical Legal Studies and latterly postmodernism joined with natural law to criticise legal positivism for its silence on issues of justice and morality, and with individual liberals who accepted that, even in democratic and generally just societies with reasonably just legal systems, the conflation of law with morality ignores the possibility that individual laws can be unjust. However, critical legal theory goes further than natural law to deny that law can ever be a neutral tool in society or at least in fundamentally unjust Western societies where law legalises and legitimises unequal power relations based on class, gender, race, sexuality, etc. According to these theories, law's neutrality and the universality of liberal freedoms are mere mirages. The rules are written and administered by

---

[196] Section 2.2.

[197] See, for example, A. Hunt, 'The Theory of Critical Legal Studies' (1986) 6 *Oxford Journal of Legal. Studies* 1.

[198] For overviews, see, for example, Cotterrell, above n. 21; Nicolson, 'Critical Approaches', above n. 55.

the powerful (or at least in terms of ideologies which support them) and hence tend to promote their interests at the expense of others. Moreover, the types of freedoms protected are those which favour the powerful. For example, freedom to exploit property is protected whereas freedom from starvation or unhealthy living and working conditions is downplayed. Likewise, freedom of sexual expression is protected, but not women's freedom from sexual violence. Admittedly, the law does now incorporate the interests of the powerless; otherwise it would not act as a legitimatory ideology. Nevertheless, despite these gains for the less powerful in society, ultimately whether one benefits from the liberal order depends to a large extent on one's place in the social hierarchy. Yet, at the same time, whereas law is complicit in ensuring social injustice, legal liberalism creates the impression that law *is* justice.

4.2 Orthodox Evidence Theory and Legal Closure

It is not difficult to see that these criticisms apply to the hard-nosed practitioner who expressly rejects the relevance of issues of truth and justice to legal practice. However, they can also be levelled at orthodox evidence theory for portraying legal fact finding as hermetically sealed from issues of justice, morality and politics, and therefore as helping to legitimate moral and political values contained in law and dominant societal ideology.[199]

As we have seen, apart from elements of procedural justice, orthodox evidence theory sees the aim of legal fact finding as making correct decisions on the relevant facts of cases. In other words, truth is conflated with what can be called 'factual truth'. However, legal fact finders do not just determine factual truth; every decision is in itself a truth in creating a reality[200] for the parties: acquittal/punishment; exculpation/damages. More importantly, decisions and trials may communicate truths of a more overtly moral and political nature. For example, the frequent acquittal of rape accused, especially those known to the complainer, may confirm ideas that women routinely make false allegations, 'ask for it' by dressing inappropriately and that 'real rape' involves a violent attack by a stranger. [201]

---

[199] See R. P. Burns, 'The Distinctiveness of Trial Narrative', in A. Duff et al. (eds), *The Trial on Trial: Volume 1 – Truth and Due Process* (2004). Cf. Jackson, 'Modern Trends in Evidence Scholarship', above n. 39, 904, who neatly illustrates the difference between the modified Rationalists and critical evidence theorists by regarding the law's attempt 'to provide closure to the issues under examination' not as politically problematic, but as compromising truth.
[200] Or what Ho, above n. 6, 20 calls an institutional fact.
[201] See Chapter 1 at n. 24.

The cases of Sara Thornton and Kiranjit Ahluwalia provide a more detailed illustration of this and other aspects of the politics of fact finding.[202] As we saw in Chapter One, both women were convicted of murder despite years of violence and abuse, but on appeal their murder convictions were reduced to manslaughter on the grounds of diminished responsibility, although Sara Thornton needed two appeals in order to achieve this.[203] On one level, the cases communicate truths of a banal nature. Sara Thornton's trial and first appeal[204] tell us that she was a murderer, whereas Kiranjit Ahluwalia's appeal[205] tells us that she killed while suffering from diminished responsibility. However, these decisions cannot be separated from legal definitions of murder, provocation and diminished responsibility, gender stereotypes and social perceptions of violence by and against women. Criminal law, for instance, tells us that it is excusable to kill in a fit of temper immediately after being provoked (especially if a man catches his wife in adultery), but not if one finally snaps through a mixture of anger, fear and frustration at years of domestic violence; in other words, that male patterns of violence are excusable, but female patterns are not. Kiranjit Ahluwalia's case also suggests that women who passively accept years of extreme violence and adultery for the sake of their marriages and children will be sympathetically treated. By contrast, Sara Thornton's trial and first appeal teaches that women who have a number of relationships and failed marriages, work, drink and are seen as aggressive will not. In other words, both judgments did more than just rule on factual truth; they laid down truths of a moral and political nature.[206]

However, by concentrating on factual truth, orthodox evidence theory erects a protective barrier around the morality and politics contained within law. This closure is reinforced by beliefs as to the best procedural method of finding factual truth and related conceptions of the lawyer's role. Thus many rationalists seem to accept the assumption behind the current adversarial system of justice that truth is best discovered by strong arguments on both sides of a dispute being presented to impartial judges.[207] Under this

---

[202] The following analysis draws on D. Nicolson, 'Telling Tales: Gender Discrimination, Gender Construction and Battered Women Who Kill' (1995) 3 *Feminist Legal Studies* 185.

[203] *R* v. *Thornton (No 2)* [1996] 2 All ER 1023.

[204] *R* v. *Thornton* [1992] 1 All ER 306.

[205] *R* v. *Ahluwalia* [1992] 4 All ER 889.

[206] At most, modified rationalists like Twining are ambivalent about the dangerous sexual stereotypes purveyed as truth by the legal system, being unsure whether they are 'objectionable because they are inaccurate or because this is an offensive way of speaking irrespective of the accuracy of the stereotypes for some other reason': T. Anderson and W. Twining, *Analysis of Evidence* (1991), 378.

[207] See Chapter 4, section 2.2.

adversarial system of fact finding, lawyers are expected to act like latter-day knightly champions of their clients. More specifically, they are *neutral* partisans in being excused or even prohibited (as in the case of advocates) from being concerned with the morality or politics of client ends or the means necessary to achieve those ends. As long as lawyers refrain from pursuing illegal ends or using tactics prohibited by law or professional rules, they are regarded as performing an inherently moral function by ensuring the proper working of the adversarial system and hence the discovery of factual truth.[208] Consequently, it is no surprise that, despite the formal constraints on prosecutors,[209] the barrister prosecuting Sara Thornton sought to portray her as a woman of loose morals notwithstanding the irrelevance of her sexual morality to guilt and his personal opinion that she did not deserve a murder conviction.[210] This limitation on the lawyer's role to ascertaining truth through a process of competitive argumentation further reinforces the conflation of truth with factual truth and the closure around law's values.

This process is strengthened even further by the Rational Tradition's conceptualisation of reason. As already noted,[211] the emphasis on formal logic rather than other forms of rationality focuses attention on the logical application rather than content of the premises involved in reasoning processes, whereas inductive logic enables their concealment, thus suggesting that they are axiomatic and unproblematic. In any event, however, reason is largely an instrumentalist concept. It does not tell us what we should reason from or what we should reason to, but only how to get there.[212] In terms of orthodox evidence theory, reason links facts with factual truth, and factual truth with substantive law. Apart from elements of procedural justice, this logical application of substantive law to correct facts is what is meant by justice.

As a result, legal fact finding is portrayed as involving a closely controlled system in which truth, reason and justice all fall under law's shadow. Thus the starting point – the facts – are to a large extent selected by substantive law. As noted in Chapter One, evidence is admissible in court if relevant to the governing substantive law. The principle of relevance thus filters out facts which might challenge the politics, morality and justice of existing law. Conversely, facts may be admitted as relevant to substantive legal norms of a politically or morally dubious nature. Moreover, since this principle is regarded as merely an empty conduit pipe for the application of whatever

---

[208] See Nicolson and Webb, above n. 55, Chapters 6 and 7.

[209] Ibid., Chapter 8.

[210] J. Nadel, *Sara Thornton: The Story of a Woman Who Killed* (1993), Chapters 7 and 8 passim, and 152.

[211] At n. 132, above.

[212] H. Wigmore, 'The Problem of Proof' (1913) 8 *Illinois Law Review* 77; H. A. Simon, *Reason in Human Affairs* (1983) 7–11.

can be presented as reason,[213] the exclusion of evidence which might challenge the politics contained in substantive law can be represented not as a political decision but as simply the neutral application of logic to substantive legal rules. Thus, to return to criminal law's treatment of battered women who kill, feminists have argued that it is largely based upon male-oriented standards of behaviour and morality.[214] Given that many men react immediately to insults and violence in a fit of anger, the provocation defence requires a 'sudden impulse of resentment'.[215] Consequently, facts which establish a time lag or 'cooling off' period between domestic violence and killing are admitted as relevant, whereas the woman's subjection to years of physical and mental abuse by male partners has often been excluded as irrelevant. Of course, substantive law is constantly being developed, but such developments tend to be kept within narrow confines by legal methodology and dominant social ideas.

The concept of legal relevance is similarly far from an iron cage. Given that the evidence presented in court is rarely confined strictly to the core events or state of affairs in question (the alleged killing, the position of the fence between disputing neighbours, etc.), but includes background information explaining these events, states of affairs or situation (premeditation, provocation, the buying of the property, etc.), the way is opened to the widespread admission of arguably irrelevant information. Why, for instance, was it relevant that Sara Thornton had 'several relationships with young men which did not work out' and met her husband 'in a public house',[216] or that on the afternoon before killing her husband Kiranjit Ahluwalia had 'visited her mother-in-law' and 'returned home with her younger son, who was unwell'?[217] These facts clearly go beyond the legal requirements of provocation and diminished responsibility. Nevertheless, in a sense the law made them necessary. Theoretically, those accused of homicide are placed in one of the following categories: fully blameworthy (murder), morally justified (self-defence), partly excused (provocation), fully or partly medically excused (insanity or diminished responsibility) or not guilty. However, the male orientation of self-defence and provocation law meant that the only categories realistically available to the women were those of murder or diminished responsibility. In choosing between them, the judges drew

---

[213] C. Tapper, 'Evanescent Evidence' (1993) 1 *International Journal of Law and Information Technology* 35, 51–2.

[214] See, for example, A. McColgan, 'A Feminist's Perspective on General Defences', in L. Bibbings and D. Nicolson (eds), *Feminist Perspectives on Criminal Law* (2000).

[215] (Baron) D. Hume, *Commentaries on the Law of Scotland Respecting Crimes*, Vol. 1 (4th edn, 1844), 239.

[216] Above n. 204, 309.

[217] Above n. 205, 892.

on prevailing discourses about 'appropriate femininity', in terms of which women are expected to be submissive, passive and demure, but also pathologically subject to biological control, and about female criminality, in terms of which female violence is seen as resulting from either maladjusted femininity or excessive pathology.[218] It was in relation to these discourses that the arguably irrelevant information was used to construct Sara Thornton as a cold-hearted killer and Kiranjit Ahluwalia as a helpless victim of circumstances beyond her control, and hence as justifiably attracting the labels of murder and diminished responsibility respectively.

As noted in Chapter One,[219] substantive law's influence over the facts of cases is not limited to their selection, but extends to their construction. In *Thornton* and *Ahluwalia* it was held that, despite considerable domestic violence and provocative acts by their husbands shortly before being killed, neither woman was provoked. This conclusion was not simply one of 'historical fact'.[220] Instead, it flowed from the law's definition of provocation as a sudden loss of self-control immediately following provocation. Indeed, the law's constructive impact extends beyond 'fact-value complexes'[221] like provocation, intention and murder to all facts. If anti-realists are right that facts are constructed by the various political, moral and other discourses which are part of the language we use, then law's definitions and terminology will also crucially influence the minutia of cases – in other words, all facts of cases, not just *the* facts (what in Chapter One[222] were called the legal facts). For instance, it is plausible that the law's description of any time gap between provocation and murder as a 'cooling off', rather than a 'boiling over', period may have influenced witnesses and adjudicators to conclude that there was a significant time gap between domestic violence and killing.

According to orthodox evidence theory, however, the case outcomes are just if substantive law was logically applied to 'correct' facts. The response by critical legal theorists to this formalistic concept of 'expletive' justice is obvious: the value of achieving factual truth (even if that were possible) is significantly reduced if the actual decision is morally or politically unacceptable. For example, it may have been 'true' that there was a time gap between Deepak Ahluwalia's provocative acts and his killing, yet it hardly follows that it was just to reject Kiranjit's provocation defence.

---

[218] See Nicolson, above n. 202.
[219] Section 1.2.
[220] Cf. Twining, above n. 50, 1545.
[221] J. Stone, *Social Dimensions of Law and Society* (1966), 737.
[222] See section 1.4.

4.3 Conclusion: Fact Positivism, Formalism and Realism

What the above discussion reveals is a striking similarity between the Rationalist Tradition and legal positivism. Both focus attention on logic, whether of rules or of proof, and away from the inherently political and partial nature of law and facts. While their most reflective adherents address political and moral issues, both seem to have discouraged generations of legal academics, practitioners and judges from doing so. Thus, just as legal positivism seems to lead many to adopt legal formalism, so it can be argued that the Rationalists' failure to address issues of justice, morality and politics leads to the stance of hard-nosed practitioners and atheoretical academics. In other words, there is a close resemblance between legal positivism and the Rationalist Tradition on the one hand, and legal formalism and hard-nosed practitioners and atheoretical academics on the other. This, along with the clearly positive connotations associated with the term 'Rationalist Tradition' (who wants to be seen as irrational?) and the apparent grudging respect for the 'hard-nosed practitioner' (what is wrong with doing the best for one's clients?), suggests that the terms 'fact positivism' and 'fact formalism' seem to be more appropriate descriptors of the evidential equivalents of legal positivism and legal formalism.[223]

Similarly, it also seems appropriate to rename the modified rationalists of the New Evidence Scholarship as fact realists. This reflects not only their epistemological stance, but also their similarities with the American Legal Realists. Thus the fact realists' questioning of the role of formal logic in fact handling echoes the American Realists' critique of formalist accounts of legal adjudication, whereas their failure to question the justice of substantive law and its social context mirrors the American Realists' acceptance of the broadly just nature of American society. Similarly, just as some legal realists are ambivalent about the limited role that logic plays in adjudication, so are some fact realists ambivalent about the 'dangerous' role of narrative in subverting legal principles.[224] The implication is that, if only it were possible, it would be preferable to confine fact finding to facts logically relevant to substantive law.[225]

---

[223] See Nicolson, above n. 51 (all references); I. Anderson, 'Gender, Psychology and Law: Studies in Feminism, Epistemology and Science' (2002) 12 *Feminism and Psychology* 379, 384; P. Haldar, 'Book Review' (2003) 11 *Feminist Legal Studies* 109, 109.

[224] See the discussion in Chapter 7, section 6.

[225] Cf. also, above n. 33, 149 where Twining paraphrases Wigmore's belief that to 'harp continually on the fallibility of common sense and relativity of knowledge would be . . . inimical to . . . public confidence in the legal system'.

Critical theorists, by contrast, would question whether law's failure to achieve impregnable closure around its underlying values is necessarily to be deplored. Instead, stories and a concept of relevance expanded to include background and other information necessary to make sense of the crucial events or state of affairs may provide a space for challenging the political and moral values currently embedded in law. The issue for critical theorists is not that stories are dangerous – as Foucault said, 'everything is dangerous'.[226] The issue is whether those likely to challenge the status quo have access to the legal process and, if they do, whether they are in fact able to provide a sufficiently radical challenge to the law's political and moral values. Thus, as we saw, even though the judges did not keep their discussion of the facts strictly relevant to legal rules in *Thornton* and *Ahluwalia*, they managed to remain within its broad parameters and apply a different, but equally mainstream, set of norms, namely those designating appropriate gender behaviour. No doubt other legal actors are likely to be more radical in moving beyond the narrow confines of legal fact finding, but whether they are likely to be effective will be explored in the chapters that follow.

However, the point is not so much that law creates an impregnable closure around the values contained within law and its supporting social ideologies, but that fact positivism portrays fact finding as a value-free exercise and that fact realism, where it does acknowledge the leakage of political and moral values into fact finding, seems to regard this as regrettable and presumably to be resisted. Accordingly, while willing to debate the politics and justice of adjectival laws, they leave untouched questions of the politics and justice of substantive law and its social context, and hence do little to challenge the seemingly inevitable slide into fact formalism of the majority of those actually engaged in fact handling.

5 Taking Stock

If so, this neatly supports the view expressed in the Introduction to this chapter that looking at theoretical assumptions about evidence and proof is important for understanding why legal actors behave in the way that they do. However, as also argued, it is equally important to evaluate these assumptions to see if they are persuasive on their own terms. And here

---

[226] 'Afterword', in H. Dreyfus and P. Rabinow, *Michel Foucault: Beyond Structuralism and Hermeneutics* (2nd edn, 1983), 232.

we summarise the conclusions that can be drawn from our evaluation of orthodox evidence theory as follows:

- While there might be an objective reality which exists independently of human knowledge, it can only be through the mediation of language and other forms of discourse which are socially constructed; and hence
- There is no such thing as 'true' knowledge corresponding with this objective reality; at best, truth involves warranted assertability;
- Knowledge can only be regarded as justified in terms of existing community standards;
- Given that the requirements of knowledge are a matter of theoretical definition rather than ontological essence, knowledge (understood as true justified belief) *is* possible so long as one does not expect objective or universalistic truth and justification;
- While inductive logic is useful in fact finding, it does not represent the only rational method;
- While rectitude of decisions has a high priority in fact finding, along with procedural justice and other public-interest values, consideration needs also to be taken of substantive justice, morality and politics.

In addition, one could also draw from this chapter the following lessons:

- It is not just '*the* facts' of cases which are constructed out of the raw material of 'brute facts', but each 'brute fact' itself;
- Issues of power and perspective are inextricably mixed up with fact construction, evidence and proof and no ex post facto process of justification is likely to be able to remedy this;
- For this reason and also because, as many contemporary epistemologists argue, knowledge is best gained by drawing on multiple perspectives, legal fact finding needs to be open to those traditionally excluded from power and to expand the range of information beyond that regarded as relevant to existing legal values.

These lessons will be applied where relevant in evaluating the law and practice of fact handling in the chapters that follow. However, equally important in evaluating legal fact handling is to supplement the immanent critique of orthodox evidence theory's assumptions about truth, reason and justice with an external critique. Consequently, the rest of the book will explore whether these assumptions are met in practice and, if not, whether the law and practice can be reformed to ensure that they are, or whether all or some of the alleged aims and methods of legal fact handling need to be abandoned and replaced with more realistic or useful versions. This takes us first to the procedural context of evidence and proof.

CHAPTER THREE

The Procedural Context: Truth, Justice and Institutional Design

1 Introduction

All fact finding, except perhaps in very informal settings involving small groups of people well known to each other, follows some procedure demarcating at the very least[1] how claims are to be made, decided and by whom. Otherwise the process will tend to suffer from a number of flaws. For instance, unless there are means to bring issues to a close and avoid unnecessary repetition of arguments, fact finding might be unduly time-consuming. Unless there are rules as to who speaks when and for how long, proceedings may be chaotic and potentially fractious, as well as unfair in favouring those who are more powerful or simply more assertive.

Inevitably, attempts to resolve such problems through designing procedures will involve assumptions about what procedures work best and how they fit with the more general aims of fact finding. As Mirjan Damaška, the doyen of the comparative study of evidence and procedure, states, 'few ideas and attitudes about fact finding are completely untouched by changes in their procedural environment and entirely immune to contamination by procedural ecology'.[2] Indeed, it is often difficult to distinguish between matters of evidence and procedure.[3] Hence it is vital at the outset

---

[1] Cf. further R. S. Summers, 'Evaluating and Improving Legal Processes – A Plea for "Process Values"' (1974) 60 *Cornell Law Review* 1, 8.

[2] M. R. Damaška, *Evidence Law Adrift* (1997), 76. See also M. Cappelletti and B. G. Garth, 'Introduction – Policies, Trends and Ideas in Civil Procedure', in M. Cappelletti (ed.), *XVI International Encyclopedia of Comparative Law* (1987). See also C. Hennessy, *Civil Procedure* (4th edn, 2014), 2–4.

[3] W. Twining, *Rethinking Evidence: Exploratory Essays* (2nd edn, 2006), 218. Consequently, some argue that it is better to deal with evidence law and procedure together in their different criminal and civil contexts (for example, P. Roberts and A. Zuckerman, *Criminal Evidence* (2nd edn, 2010), esp. 6–8, but cf. contra Twining, above n. 3, 218ff; J. Jackson, 'Taking Comparative Evidence Seriously', in P. Roberts and M. Redmayne (eds), *Innovations in Evidence and Proof: Integrating Theory, Research and Teaching* (2007), 293, 296.

to have an understanding of the impact of the procedural context on legal fact handling. However, the procedural context of fact finding is important, not just because it affects fact-handling practice, but also because it contains certain 'second-order' assumptions about how best to achieve orthodox evidence theory's 'first-order assumptions' about the aims of fact finding. Both sets of assumptions thus need to be evaluated when considering whether the practice of fact finding upholds orthodox evidence theory about evidence and proof.

While, in terms of detail, this chapter will concentrate on the Scottish legal system, it will also draw more widely on discussion of other legal systems. One reason for this comparative approach is that the form and values of Scottish legal procedure are generally[4] regarded as being shared, albeit to greater and lesser extents, with all Anglo-American[5] legal systems.[6] Consequently, discussion of these other systems can enhance our understanding of Scottish legal procedure. However, given that there is great variation between Anglo-American jurisdictions, we will describe their predominant features in terms of what the sociologist Max Weber calls an 'ideal type':[7] a heuristic device not meant to reflect reality in vivid detail, but in exaggerated form in order to aid explanation and comparison.[8] As we shall see, what we shall call the classical Anglo-American procedural model has never been fully implemented in Scotland or elsewhere. Nor has it ever applied equally across all proceedings. Instead, it differs according to the type of proceedings involved (criminal, civil, administrative, etc.), the level of court or other legal forum, the stage which proceedings have reached and the level of formality involved in fact finding.

---

[4] But see S. Goldstein, 'The Odd Couple: Common Law Procedure and Civilian Substantive Law' (2003) 78 *Tulane Law Review* 291, 292; P. Michalik, 'Justice in Crisis: England and Wales', in A. A. S. Zuckerman and R. Cranston (eds), *Reform of Civil Procedure: Essays on 'Access to Justice'* (1995), 127 n. 4.

[5] That is, those which have voluntarily followed English procedure or more commonly had it imposed following colonisation.

[6] C. Gane, 'Classifying Scottish Criminal Procedure', in P. Duff and N. Hutton (eds), *Criminal Justice in Scotland* (1999), esp. 57, 59; *The Laws of Scotland: Stair Memorial Encyclopaedia Civil Procedure Reissue* (1999), paras 4–14; D. Edward, 'Fact-Finding: A British Perspective', in D. L. Carey Miller and P. R. Beaumont (eds), *The Option of Litigating in Europe* (1993), esp. 46.

[7] See, for example, A. Hunt, *The Sociological Movement in Law* (1978), Chapter 5.

[8] See, for example, M. R. Damaška, *Faces of Justice and State Authority: A Comparative Approach to the Legal Process* (1986), 4–6; J. Jackson, 'The Effect of Human Rights on Criminal Evidentiary Processes: Towards Convergence, Divergence or Realignment?' (2005) 68 *Modern Law Review* 737, 740–5; M. Langer, 'From Legal Transplants to Legal Translations: The Globalization of Plea Bargaining and the Americanization Thesis in Criminal Procedure' (2004) 45 *Harvard International Law Journal* 1, 7–9.

Moreover, recent years have seen moves away from the classical model even in proceedings where it has been most fully implemented.

A second reason for a comparative approach is because it enhances the understanding of one's own system[9] and will be particularly useful in the next chapter in evaluating whether the Scottish procedural context is best suited to achieving the goals of legal fact finding. Consequently, in common with most discussions of Anglo-American procedure, we will contrast it with its polar opposite ideal-type, namely procedure in Civilian legal systems or more specifically those in Continental Europe, which shall accordingly be called the classical Continental model.

First, however, a confession and avoidance. In Chapter One it was noted that legal proceedings leading to a contested trial are rare and that most legal fact finding takes place outwith the court system in lawyers' offices, police stations, social welfare benefit offices, parole hearings, administrative tribunals, etc., which vary in their formality from a total lack of regulation to something resembling formal legal proceedings. Given the plethora of such proceedings, describing each individually would require a book of its own. Consequently, we will concentrate first on the formal fact-finding system before noting how it has been modified to varying degrees in other proceedings. Admittedly, starting with and devoting so much attention to formal proceedings risks over-exaggerating both their prevalence and practical significance. However, apart from the dearth of discussions of what can be loosely called 'informal fact-handling' occurring outside the court system, there are at least three[10] possible mitigating excuses for starting with formal proceedings in this chapter.

The first is that many of their features cast a long shadow over informal legal proceedings.[11] Thus if pre-trial negotiations or various forms of alternative dispute resolution fail, or an administrative decision is faulty, the parties may end up in court. Secondly, judges and evidence scholars have largely formulated the aims of fact finding only with trials or at most formal proceedings leading to trials in mind. Finally, the formal system – particularly

---

[9]   See, for example, Damaška, above n. 2, esp. 4, 7–8.

[10] Another is that evidence law was developed in the context of and applies mainly to formal, especially trial, proceedings.

[11] See, for example, R. H. Mnookin and L. Kornhauser, 'Bargaining in the Shadow of the Law: The Case of Divorce' (1979) 88 *Yale Law Journal* 950; C. Menkel-Meadow, 'The Trouble with the Adversary System in a Post-Modern, Multi-Cultural World' (1996) 1 *Journal of the Institute for the Study of Legal Ethics* 49, 63; A. Duff et al., *The Trial on Trial: Volume 3 – Towards a Normative Theory of the Criminal Trial* (2007), 7–8, 13.

as regards serious criminal cases[12] – is extremely important in inculcating a certain mindset among regular participants, most notably legal practitioners and judges, from whom others like clients and court officials will take their cue. As the next chapter reveals,[13] this mindset is often one of competitive adversariality and spreads from formal legal proceedings to all aspects of legal fact finding. It is thus another reason why the procedural context is so crucial to understanding the processes of evidence and proof.

2 Scottish Legal Procedure: Adversarial or Merely Anglo-American?

It is usually thought[14] that the most important feature distinguishing Anglo-American from Continental legal systems is the former's adversarial[15] character. Here, Damaška's description is commonly cited.

> The adversarial mode of proceeding takes its shape from a contest or a dispute: it unfolds as an engagement of two adversaries before a relatively passive decision maker whose principal duty is to reach a verdict. The nonadversarial mode is structured as an official inquiry. Under the first system, the two adversaries take charge of most of the procedural action; under the second, officials perform most of the activities.[16]

---

[12] P. Roberts, 'Faces of Justice Adrift? Damáska's Comparative Method and the Future of Common Law Evidence', in J. Jackson, M. Langer and P. Tillers (eds), *Crime, Procedure and Evidence in a Comparative and International Context: Essays in Honour of Procedure Professor Mirjan Damáska* (2008), 319. Cf. also D. Nicolson and J. Webb, *Professional Legal Ethics: Critical Interrogations* (1999), Chapter 7 as regards legal ethics.

[13] Section 2. See also at n. 282, below (Menkel-Meadow re: ADR).

[14] At least by Anglo-American commentators. Continental counterparts rarely use this comparison because the greater differences between Continental procedural systems make it more difficult to speak of a uniform approach: J. F. Nijboer, 'Common Law Tradition in Evidence Scholarship Observed from a Continental Perspective' (1993) 41 *American Journal of Comparative Law* 299, 334.

[15] Some prefer the term 'accusatorial' (for example, Nijboer, ibid., 314; A. S. Goldstein, 'Reflections on Two Models: Inquisitorial Themes in American Criminal Procedure' (1973) 26 *Stanford Law Review* 1009, 1016–18), but cf. M. Damaška, 'Evidentiary Barriers to Conviction and Two Models of Criminal Procedure' (1973) 121 *University of Pennsylvania Law Review* 506. 555–9; J. Jackson and S. Doran, *Judge Without Jury: Diplock Trials in the Adversary System* (1995), Chapter 3, noting other uses within both Continental and Anglo-American systems.

[16] Above n. 2, 3. See also Damaška, ibid., 'Presentation of Evidence and Factfinding Precision' (1975) 123 *University of Pennsylvania Law Review* 1083, esp. 1088–9 and 'The Uncertain Fate of Evidentiary Transplants: Anglo-American and Continental Experiments' (1997) 45 *American Journal of Comparative Law* 839. The following discussion also draws on J. Jackson and Doran, ibid., Chapter 2; Langer, above n. 8; G. Van Kessel, 'Adversary Excesses in the American Criminal Trial' (1991) 67 *Notre Dame Law Review* 403; J. McEwan, *Evidence and the Adversarial Process* (2nd edn, 1998). Chapter 1; S. Doran, J. D. Jackson and M. Seigel, 'Rethinking Adversariness in Nonjury Criminal Trials' (1995) 23 *American Journal of Comparative Law* 1, 13–25.

While Damaška's use of the term 'nonadversarial' reflects a desire to avoid the misleading and pejorative association of Continental procedure with the Holy Inquisition, this chapter will follow more common usage and refer to Continental procedure as 'inquisitorial' even though many Continental lawyers describe their legal systems as 'mixed' in involving both adversarial and inquisitorial elements.[17]

In fact, it is universally recognised that one cannot speak of any jurisdiction, let alone jurisdictional family, as being purely adversarial or inquisitorial. Instead, each jurisdiction falls somewhere on a continuum between the two ideal types[18] and in fact may differ dramatically from others within their procedural family. Thus it is generally accepted that the US system has more adversarial elements than the British systems, whereas Continental systems range even more widely from the more inquisitorial French, Spanish, Dutch and Belgian to those like the Italian or Scandinavian[19] which may more legitimately be described as 'mixed', containing adversarial and inquisitorial elements in more or less equal parts. Describing Anglo-American jurisdictions as adversarial and Continental jurisdictions as inquisitorial is only true to the extent that the former have more adversarial elements than the latter, which, in turn, especially in criminal proceedings, contain more inquisitorial features than the classical Anglo-American model.[20] Similarly, although the Scottish system is by no means solely adversarial, it is generally[21] regarded as far more adversarial than inquisitorial.[22] In other words, 'adversarial' and 'inquisitorial' are useful terms to describe procedural arrangements, but operate more appropriately as adjectives or adverbs (as in 'Scots procedure is more adversarial than inquisitorial' or 'Scottish lawyers act adversarially') than as nouns (as in 'the Scottish adversarial system').

Moreover, the terms are best used as descriptions, not of entire legal systems, let alone jurisdictional families, but of particular elements in particular legal systems depending, most importantly, on whether they are criminal or civil, trial or pre-trial, and formal or informal. To complicate matters further, procedural arrangements are not static. Apparently,

---

[17] Cf. Damaška, above n. 15, 558.
[18] Cf. M. R. Damaška, 'Epistemology and Legal Regulation of Proof' (2003) 2 *Law, Probability and Risk* 117, 120.
[19] See McEwan, above n. 16, 9; Nijboer, above n. 14, esp. at 303.
[20] Nijboer, ibid., 304.
[21] But see at n. 4 above.
[22] See, for example, Hennessy, above n. 2, 1–2; F. Raitt, *Evidence: Principles, Policy and Practice* (2nd edn, 2013), Chapter 1; F. P. Davidson, *Evidence* (2007), 14; A. V. Sheehan and D. J. Dickson, *Criminal Procedure* (2nd edn, 2003), 57–8.

indigenous Scottish proceedings were adversarial in nature,[23] but for centuries criminal proceedings incorporated inquisitorial elements. Thus until the late nineteenth century justices of the peace decided on whether to commit suspects for trial based on declarations taken from them, and judges investigated the facts and examined witnesses.[24] While the move to a purer adversarial model was possibly tied up with general reception of English law,[25] even in England the modern-day adversarial trial is traced to the period after 1830 when lawyers, who hitherto had been prohibited from defending felony accused, began to take over the examination of witnesses from judges and juries, and judges began to adopt a more passive role[26] – an approach which then spread to civil cases.[27] However, the classical adversarial model was relatively short-lived. As we shall see,[28] recent procedural developments require greater judicial activism with a consequent dilution of party autonomy. Furthermore, there are signs that Anglo-American and Continental systems are converging and may be far closer than commonly portrayed if one looks behind the formal position at actual practice.[29]

The final and most crucial reason why the terms 'adversarial' and 'inquisitorial' are misleading descriptors of Anglo-American and Continental jurisdictions respectively is that each contains prominent features which have no necessary connection to the core notions of contest and inquest, respectively.[30] Thus, in his highly influential book,

---

[23] V. V. Palmer (ed.), *Mixed Jurisdictions Worldwide: The Third Legal Family* (2001), 64, 224–5, 249. But see the unsupported claim by S. R. Moody and J. Tombs, *Prosecution in the Public Interest* (1982), 10 that the adversary system was imported from England.

[24] Gane, above n. 6, esp. 61–2.

[25] Cf. D. R. Parratt, "'Something Old, Something New, Something Borrowed . . .'" Civil Dispute Resolution in Scotland – a Continuing Story', in C. H. van Rhee (ed.), *Judicial Case Management and Efficiency in Civil Litigation* (2008), on the influence of English civil procedure.

[26] J. H. Langbein, *The Origins of Adversary Criminal Trial* (2003). See also A. Duff et al., above n. 11, Chapter 2; J. Hunter, 'Battling a Good Story: Cross-examining the Failure of the Law of Evidence', in Roberts and Redmayne, above n. 3, 266–8.

[27] But cf. Davidson, above n. 22, 8–9, questioning whether the earlier appearance of counsel in civil cases might have influenced criminal procedure rather than vice versa and noting that counsel represented accused in Scottish criminal cases from the seventh century.

[28] Section 4.2, below.

[29] R. S. Frase, 'Comparative Criminal Justice as a Guide to American Law Reform: How Do the French Do It, How Can We Find Out and Why Should We Care?' (1990) 78 *California Law Review* 539 and references contained therein. See further section 5.2.

[30] See, for example, Damaška, above n. 1, 3, 69, 74, though many conflate the terms adversarial and inquisitorial more widely with other aspects of the classical Anglo-American and Continental models: for example, Goldstein, above n. 15, 1018; P. Devlin, *The Judge* (1979), Chapter 3; P. Alldridge, 'Scientific Expertise and Comparative Criminal Procedure' (1999) 3 *The International Journal of Evidence and Proof* 141, 143–7; L. Ellison, *The Adversarial Process and the Vulnerable Witness* (2001), passim.

Faces of Justice and State Authority,[31] Damaška categorises procedural systems in terms of two ideal-type axes, which together explain the fundamental features of each classical model. One axis overlaps with the adversarial/ inquisitorial distinction, but instead of looking at the external form of legal proceedings Damaška focuses on their aims. He relates these to two types of state authority:[32] activist states, which impose a perception of the good life on society and see legal proceedings as aimed at regulating society rather than resolving disputes; and reactive states, which merely provide the legal framework for citizens to pursue their own vision of the good life and see legal proceedings as designed merely to resolve disputes. Damaška then argues that active states design legal proceedings as inquests aimed at policy implementation, whereas reactive states see proceedings as contests.

While the distinction between policy implementation and conflict resolu-tion does not completely overlap with that between proceedings as inquests or contests, respectively,[33] it remains very insightful. It explains, for instance, the rarity of allowing guilty pleas in Continental systems[34] and their ini-tial ambivalence towards what in Anglo-American jurisdictions is loosely[35] called plea bargaining, whereby an accused agrees to plead guilty in return for a lesser charge, lower sentence or some other incentive from the prosecu-tion, such as the exclusion of certain features of the offence charged to save the accused embarrassment.[36] Thus, where legal proceedings are designed to provide public condemnation of criminal behaviour, their outcome should not depend on the parties' decision to waive formal proceedings. Similarly,

---

[31] Above n. 8: evaluated by, for example, Roberts, above n. 12; Twining, above n. 3, 195–6; A. Stein, 'A Political Analysis of Procedural Law' (1988) 51 *Modern Law Review* 659; I. Markovits, 'Playing the Opposites Game: On Mirjan Damaška's "The Faces of Justice and State Authority"' (1989) 41 *Stanford Law Review* 1313.

[32] See Damaška, ibid., esp. Chapters 3 to 5.

[33] Almost all legal proceedings, even those involving policy-implementing schemes like state welfare benefits, frequently involve the resolution of disputes (Twining, above n. 3, 196; H. Kötz, 'Civil Litigation and the Public Interest' (1982) 1 *Civil Justice Quarterly* 237), whereas, as we shall explore in more detail in Chapter 4, section 3, and as Damaška, above n. 8, 12, implicitly recognises, dispute resolution serves the policy goal of reducing social conflict.

[34] See, for example, Goldstein, above n. 15, 1019, 1022, but also J. McEwan, 'From Adversarialism to Managerialism: Criminal Justice in Transition' (2011) 31 *Legal Studies* 519, 525 regarding the increasing acceptance of guilty pleas because of stretched resources.

[35] Technically the term is confined to bargaining over charges already instituted: A. Duff et al., above n. 11, 171, but for the sake of convenience we will use it to cover all forms of bargaining.

[36] See, for example, A. Duff et al., ibid., 171–80; Goldstein, above n. 15, 1022–3; M. McConville, 'Plea Bargaining', in M. McConville and G. Wilson (eds), *The Handbook of the Criminal Justice Process* (2002); F. Leverick, 'Tensions and Balances, Costs and Rewards; The Sentence Discount in Scotland' (2004) 8 *Edinburgh Law Review* 360 and 'Plea and Confession Bargaining in Scotland' (2006) 10 *Electronic Journal of Comparative Law*, available at http://www.ejcl.org (last accessed 14 March 2018).

the dominance of policy issues in administrative decision-making might explain the inquisitorial nature of such procedures in Anglo-American jurisdictions.[37]

And while the distinction between active and reactive states no longer maps onto procedural differences between Anglo-American and Continental systems,[38] Damaška's emphasis on the impact of political culture on procedural design is important in helping to explain why different legal systems developed, and continue to retain, inquisitorial or adversarial proceedings.[39] Indeed, along with related differences in legal culture, political attitudes also explain many of the features covered by Damaška's other categorising axis, which relates to the structure of judicial authority.[40] Thus, motivated by a desire for certainty in decision-making flowing from both Civilian legal culture and the needs of policy implementation, 'hierarchical' forms of authority involve a professional and hierarchically organised corps of officials who make decisions according to technical standards. Conversely, motivated by a greater legal tolerance for tempering strict legal logic with equitable considerations and the same distrust of powerful centralised governments that underlies the preference for a reactive state, 'co-ordinate' forms of authority involve non-professional decision-makers who hold power for short periods, are organised into a single level of authority and make decisions by applying community standards.[41]

As we shall see in more detail,[42] different approaches to judicial authority led to significant features of each classical model. For instance, the importance of superior control and review in hierarchical systems means that all proceedings are recorded in a comprehensive and integrated 'dossier' and decisions are fully reasoned. The Civilian preference for logic over emotion means that trials involving potentially unruly live witnesses are de-emphasised in favour of basing decisions on the dossier's contents. By contrast, because of the difficulties and expense of bringing together relatively large groups of amateur decision-makers, systems with co-ordinate judicial authority opt for hearing all evidence in one continuous trial.

---

[37] See section 4.3.1 below.

[38] Thus the UK is in this regard far more similar to Continental countries than the US and some other former British colonies.

[39] In addition to the references in n. 16, see, for example, N. Jörg, S. Field and C. Brants, 'Are Inquisitorial and Adversarial Systems Converging?', in P. Fennel et al. (eds), *Criminal Justice in Europe: A Comparative Study* (1995), 54; O. G. Chase, 'American "Exceptionalism" and Comparative Procedure' (2002) 50 *American Journal on Comparative Law* 277.

[40] Above n. 8, Chapters 1 and 2.

[41] Cf. Edward, above n. 6, referring to 'lay' as opposed to 'judicial' fact-finding systems.

[42] Section 3.2.

Moreover, superior review of decisions is minimal, not least because juries do not provide reasons for their decisions.

At the same time, it should be noted that the impact of differing approaches to the state and judicial authority have a varied impact. Thus celebrated features of Anglo-American procedural systems, such as the primacy of oral evidence, the concentrated 'day in court' and the role of the jury and other forms of lay justice, are sometimes incorporated into inquisitorial proceedings, whereas Anglo-American procedural systems sometimes adopt paradigmatic features of Continental proceedings such as a series of separate hearings and, most notably, adjudication by professional judges.

As regards the Scottish position, from at least the establishment of the Court of Session in 1532, civil proceedings were partly based on the Romano-canonical procedure then prevailing on the Continent.[43] Thus the facts were not determined by judges following oral evidence, but on the basis of documents prepared by different judges who had heard witnesses in earlier proceedings. It was only in the nineteenth century that this was replaced by the climactic 'day in court' trial at which all evidence was presented orally, civil juries were reintroduced and rights of appeal were severely curtailed. Criminal proceedings had always retained juries for serious crimes, but resembled Continental proceedings until the early twentieth century as regards the pre-trial judicial examination of accused.[44] Today, while the fit is far from exact,[45] especially after the total abolition of pre-trial judicial examination, and the increasing pressures to introduce more episodic fact finding and written evidence,[46] as well as to reduce jury trials, Scottish legal procedure resembles the co-ordinate authority model far more closely than the hierarchical model.[47]

Given its significant impact on many aspects of Scottish legal procedure, the co-ordinate judicial authority model thus deserves to be treated along with adversariality as a dominant feature of its procedural system. Although analytically distinct, we shall see that the adversarial and co-ordinate judicial authority models combine comfortably in a procedural system.[48] Moreover, together they go a long way to explaining another important

[43] *The Stair Encyclopaedia*, loc. cit. n. 6; Parratt, above n. 25; Edwards, above n. 41, 50–4.
[44] Gane, above n. 6, 61–2.
[45] See Moody and Tombs, above n. 23, Chapter 3, regarding the organisation of procurator fiscals.
[46] See section 4.2 below.
[47] See, for example, Gane, above n. 6, 65–9 regarding criminal proceedings; *The Stair Encyclopaedia*, loc. cit. n. 6, regarding civil proceeding, but again cf. contra Goldstein, loc. cit. n. 15.
[48] As do the inquisitorial and co-ordinate judicial authority aspects of Continental systems: Damaška, above n. 8, 13–14, Chapter 6.

difference between Anglo-American and Continental systems, namely the former's greater subjection of evidence and proof to complicated and technical legal rules. At the same time, however, not all these rules derive from the adversarial nature of legal proceedings or the co-ordinate nature of judicial authority. In addition to miscellaneous aspects of public policy which apply similarly in both procedural families, many rules, particularly in criminal cases, are designed to ensure a fair trial and protection of the rights and dignity of the parties and, more recently, also witnesses. However, given that Continental proceedings contain similar protections, issues of procedural justice will be treated as a separate feature of the procedural context.

3 The Classic Anglo-American Procedural Model[49]

3.1 The Adversarial Nature of Proceedings

3.1.1 Introduction

Judges sometimes flatter themselves by thinking that their function is the ascertainment of truth. This is so only in a very limited sense. Our system of administering justice in civil affairs proceeds on the footing that each side, working at arm's length, selects its own evidence . . . It is on the basis of two carefully selected versions that the judge is finally called upon to adjudicate . . . He is at the mercy of contending sides whose whole object is not to discover truth but to get his judgment . . .

A litigation is in essence a trial of skill between opposing parties, conducted according to recognised rules, and the prize is the judge's decision. We have rejected inquisitorial methods and prefer to regard the judges as entirely independent. Like referees at boxing contests, they see that the rules are kept and count the points.

Lord Justice-Clerk Thomson[50]

This statement, like Lord Denning's better-known equivalent,[51] vividly illustrates the essential adversarial nature of Anglo-American legal proceedings,

---

[49] For an overview, see Twining, above n. 3, 197–8, relying on J. Jacob, 'Fundamental Features of English Civil Justice', in W. E. Butler (ed.), *Justice and Comparative Law: Anglo-Soviet Perspectives on Criminal Law. Procedure, Evidence and Sentencing Policy* (1987); see also J. Jacob, *The Fabric of English Civil Justice* (1987), Chapter 1.

[50] *Thompson* v. *Glasgow Corporation* [1961] SLT 237. See also his similar comments in *Islip Pedigree Breeding Centre* v. *Abercromby* [1959] SLT 161, 165, but see Lord Justice Auld in *R* v. *Gleeson* [2004] 1 Cr App R 29, [2003] EWCA 3357 [para. 36] denying that criminal trials at least are games giving criminal accused a sporting chance.

[51] *Jones* v. *National Coal Board* [1957] 2 QB 55, 64.

its links with medieval trial by combat[52] and its frequent characterisation as a sporting contest,[53] a fight[54] or even war.[55] In this vein, one can plausibly analogise adversarial litigation to a football match, with the court being the referee, the courtroom the pitch, the principle of relevancy the perimeter lines and rules like offside equivalent to those of admissibility.[56] By contrast, the inquisitorial method resembles a scientific investigation in which investigators develop a hypothesis, test it by experiments in the laboratory of pre-trial proceedings and then seek confirmation of the results through peer review at the trial and any subsequent appeal.[57]

This is not to say, as Lord Justice-Clerk Thomson seems to,[58] that Anglo-American fact finding is unconcerned with truth. After all, classical Greek philosophy used the adversarial method of 'Socratic dialogue', medieval scholars sought knowledge through public 'disputations' and debates, and some modern disciplines are turning to adversarial methods.[59] As we shall see,[60] not only are many non-adversarial features of Anglo-American fact finding thought to promote truth finding, but it is even argued that adversarial methods perform better than inquisitorial methods at doing so. Requiring competing parties to persuade a neutral arbiter is said to ensure the discovery of more information and prevent fact finders from jumping to conclusions before encountering all the evidence. This indicates that the preference for adversarial fact finding is compatible with, at least

---

[52] For example, Davidson, above n. 22, 1ff.

[53] For example, R. Pound, 'The Causes of Popular Dissatisfaction with the Administration of Justice' (1964) 10 *Crime & Delinquency* 355; P. Stein, 'Legal Thought in Eighteenth Century Scotland' (1957) *Juridical Review* 1, 15–17.

[54] For example, Devlin, above n. 30, 58; J. Frank, *Courts on Trial: Myth and Reality in American Trials* (1949, reprinted 1973), 26, Chapters 2 and 6.

[55] For example, Devlin, ibid., 54, 56ff; C. Finlayson, 'Proving Your Case – Evidence and Procedure in Action' (1991–2) 13 *Cardozo Law Review* 257, 258.

[56] But cf. W. T. Pizzi, *Trials without Truth* (2000) Chapter 1, arguing that this makes proceeding more like highly regulated and stop-start American football matches; F. Pollock and F. W. Maitland, *The History of English Law Volume II* (1898), 671, using a cricket metaphor given that umpires only make decisions at the players' instigation.

[57] Pollock and Maitland, ibid.; J. D. Jackson, 'Theories of Truth Finding in Criminal Procedure: An Evolutionary Approach' (1988) 10 *Cardozo Law Review* 475, esp. 496–8.

[58] But cf. his dictum in *Lennie* v. *Lennie* 1948 SLT 382, 385 cited in Chapter 2 at n. 6, and see also *Duke of Argyll* v. *Duchess of Argyll and Another* 1962 SLT 333, 338 where the court denied that litigation is just a game rather than a search for truth.

[59] Menkel-Meadow, above n. 11, 54–5; R. Elliott et al., 'An Adjudicated Hermeneutic Single-Case Efficacy Design Study of Experiential Therapy for Panic/Phobia' (2009) *19 Psychotherapy Research* 543.

[60] Chapter 4, section 2.

optimistic, rationalism,[61] and that its adoption may be rooted not just in political attitudes to the state but also in an epistemological position based on a division of labour between relevant legal actors.

3.1.2 The Passive Adjudicator[62]

In this division of labour, the roles allotted to the adjudicator and parties represent opposite sides of a coin: if the former plays an active role, the latter play a more passive role, and vice versa. Thus under the classical Continental inquisitorial model,[63] exemplified by criminal rather than civil proceedings,[64] the state's direct interest in the outcome means that the judiciary actively engages in all aspects of fact finding. Once proceedings have started, judges control – though do not necessarily personally conduct – the search for information, decide which witnesses to question, question witnesses before trial, control proceedings at trial and decide on the outcome; though to ensure a degree of judicial objectivity and to prevent weak cases going to trial, different tasks may be allocated to different judges. Moreover, even in criminal cases, judges are meant to seek the truth rather than build a case against the accused.

In Anglo-American proceedings, by contrast, adjudicators are expected to adopt a passive role and remain aloof from the dust of the arena.[65] This is especially true of judges and sheriffs in jury trials, lest they impinge on the jury's autonomy by signalling their views. Certainly adjudicators have no power to investigate, choose the witnesses they want to hear[66] or call for information not presented to them. Apart possibly from cases involving

---

[61] Twining, above n. 3, 86; D. M. Risinger, 'Unsafe Verdicts: The Need for Reformed Standards for the Trial and Review of Factual Innocence Claims' (2004) 41 *Houston Law Review* 1281, 1288–9; J. Jackson, above n. 57, 502–3, arguing that both procedural models represent alternatives within empiricist rationality; but see J. Hodgson 'Conceptions of the Trial in Inquisitorial and Adversarial Procedure', in A. Duff et al. (eds), *The Trial on Trial: Volume 2 – Judgement and Calling into Account* (2006), 225; E. Grande, 'Dances of Criminal Justice: Thoughts on Systemic Differences and the Search for the Truth', in J. Jackson, Langer and Tillers, above n. 12, esp. 147, arguing that Anglo-American systems work with a more relativist notion of 'interpretive truth' based on the parties' opposing views.

[62] See generally, S. Doran and J. Jackson (eds), *The Judicial Role in Criminal Proceedings* (2000).

[63] The following description draws on the references in n. 16, as well as J. A. Jolowicz, 'Fact-Finding: A Comparative Perspective', in Miller and Beaumont, above n. 6; R. S. Thompson, 'Decision, Disciplined Inferences and the Adversary Process' (1991) 13 *Cardozo Law Review* 725, 746–9.

[64] Since the French Revolution, Continental systems have allowed civil litigants greater mastery over proceedings and have limited the judge's active role: see Damaška, above n. 2, 106–7, 120 and 'The Uncertain Fate of Evidentiary Transplants', above n. 16, 841–4.

[65] See *Yuill* v. *Yuill* [1945] P 15, 20.

[66] US judges are authorised to call witnesses and appoint experts, but rarely do so: Goldstein, above n. 15, 1022; van Kessel, above n. 16, 429.

unrepresented accused or litigants faced with a represented opponent, adjudicators may not intervene to help the parties present their cases through questioning witnesses.[67] Instead questions should be limited to clarifying points either for themselves or where applicable for the jury.[68] While jurors may ask witnesses questions, they are not told of this and often discouraged from doing so,[69] such as by the Scottish requirement that questions have to be submitted in writing for judicial approval.[70] Consequently, such questioning is rare.[71] More positively, adjudicators must declare a winner, while judges must ensure also fair play through upholding procedural, evidential and ethical rules so that no one gains an unfair advantage. This secondary role, especially in relation to the exclusion of inadmissible evidence and issues insufficiently supported by the evidence and, where relevant, instructing the jury, means that Anglo-American judges are more than a *mere* umpire. Nevertheless, their role is far removed from that of the Continental judge.

3.1.3 Party Autonomy

The latter's activist role means that party control over fact investigation and proof in the classical Continental model is correspondingly limited, particularly in criminal cases. Apart from bringing disputes to state notice, parties are more 'the object of the inquiry rather than the subject of the action'.[72] Witnesses are regarded as evidentiary sources of the bench rather than the parties[73] and only questioned by the latter after they have first related their evidence in a relaxed, informal way, and had it judicially tested, albeit in a more relaxed manner than adversarial cross-examination,[74] in order to clarify points or evince additional

---

[67] Otherwise, they risk an appeal on the grounds of bias (*Tallis* v. *HMA* (1982) SCCR 91), though only if this prejudices one party (*Livingstone* v. *HMA* (1974) SCCR (sup); but see now *CG* v. *UK* 2002 34 EHRR 31 indicating that judicial interruptions *may* render a trial unfair under Article 6 of the European Convention on Human Rights).

[68] Sheehan and Dickson, above n. 22, 200.

[69] But cf. experiments with juror questioning in some US states: for example, B. Schafer and O. K. Wiegand, 'It's Good to Talk – Speaking Rights and the Jury', in A. Duff et al., above n. 61, 120–1 and see further Chapter 4 at n. 263.

[70] *Renton & Brown's Criminal Procedure According to the Laws of Scotland* (6th edn, 1996, by G. H. Gordon assisted by J. Chalmers and C. H. W. Gane), para. 18.52.

[71] For example, in one study only 18 per cent of the 44 per cent of English Crown Court jurors interviewed who wanted to ask questions did so: M. Zander and P. Henderson, *Crown Court Study* (Royal Justice Commission Research Study No. 19, 1993).

[72] Doran, Jackson and Seigel, above n. 16, 16.

[73] Though they are in practice more readily associated with civil litigants: Damaška, 'The Uncertain Fate of Evidentiary Transplants', above n. 16, 843.

[74] But cf. McEwan, above n. 16; B. McKillop, 'Anatomy of a French Murder Case' (1997) 45 *American Journal of Comparative Law* 527 regarding the Netherlands and France respectively.

information. Parties or their lawyers may suggest further avenues for investigation, but the bulk of information gathering and testing is performed by the judge, with the parties' lawyers largely confined to protecting their clients' right to a fair trial. Lawyer cross-examination is rare and, compared even to that of Continental judges, restrained. Equally, factual and legal arguments are far less partisan and rhetorical than is characteristic of adversarial advocacy.

Under the Anglo-American model, by contrast, fact investigation and presentation is left almost entirely to the parties. They only seek and present information they regard as favourable. They set the issues through the pleadings and can agree the existence or non-existence of facts. Although judges can insist on such issues being argued where the factual basis is uncertain, according to Damaška such arguments are likely to be 'artificial, contrived, lifeless and anaemic'.[75] Indeed, remarkably from the Continental perspective,[76] whole cases can be removed from adjudication via plea bargaining. Similarly, it is the parties' responsibility to trigger procedural and evidential mechanisms and to challenge the admissibility of unfavourable evidence or undermine its persuasiveness through cross-examination and contrary evidence. In general, parties are stuck with the consequences of failing to make such challenges and in Scotland, except for the failure to object to inadmissible evidence in solemn criminal cases, omissions cannot be rectified on appeal.[77] Moreover, when parties call witnesses favourable to them, such witnesses are regarded as their 'property' rather than a resource at the court's disposal – even in the case of experts.[78]

In the past, 'trial by ambush' was regarded as part of the adversarial nature of proceedings.[79] Pleadings had to disclose intended arguments, but not their supporting evidence. More recently, it has been recognised that 'truth is most likely to emerge when each side seeks to take the other by reason rather than by surprise'[80] and that this is unlikely in competitive fact-finding systems where there is a serious 'inequality of arms' regarding

---

[75] Above n. 1, 104.

[76] See at n. 34 above, regarding the rarity of allowing guilty pleas. Recently, schemes allow accused to avoid court proceedings for less serious offences by paying fixed penalties or even negotiated sums (Jörg, Field and Brant, above n. 39, 48), whereas practices similar or even equivalent to Anglo-American plea bargaining are developing (Langer, above n. 8; T. Weigend, 'The Decay of the Inquisitorial System: Plea Bargaining Invades German Criminal Procedure', in J. Jackson, Langer and Tillers, above n. 12).

[77] See Raitt, above n. 22, 281–2, 283–4, 292–3.

[78] Raitt, ibid., 59. See further Chapter 5 section 7.2 and also section 8 as regards the Continental practice of judicially appointing experts.

[79] Though according to McEwan, above n. 16, 20, this is rare and not very effective.

[80] Justice Traynor, quoted in Doran, J. Jackson and Seigel, above n. 16, 15.

access to crucial information. Consequently, parties have for some time been required to disclose some, but not all,[81] forms of information in their possession prior to trial. Thus, in general,[82] what in Scotland[83] is called 'recovery' in civil procedure and 'disclosure' in criminal procedure, requires parties to list and allow inspection of documents in their possession and provide the contact details of witnesses where they intend to rely on such documents and witnesses in court.[84]

3.1.4 Fragmented Testimony Style, and Rules of Presentation and Proof

The centrality of party autonomy and 'witness ownership' has important implications for how proof is regulated in Anglo-American procedural systems. Because fact finding is structured as a contest, rules about the burden and standard of proof are required to determine who must do what to win. Thus, generally, unlike on the Continent where state fact finders simply form a subjective belief about what happened, the burden of proof is on the person bringing proceedings, and adjudicators must be satisfied on a balance of probabilities in civil cases and can only convict criminal accused if satisfied beyond reasonable doubt.[85] In this way, adversarial fact finding avoids philosophical problems regarding whether truth is possible by redefining it into 'more manageable proportions'[86] from 'truth' to 'proof'.[87] In Scottish (but not other Anglo-American)[88] jury trials, the bar is lowered even further by allowing verdicts based on a bare majority, though criminal juries can compromise by using the unique 'not-proven' verdict, which allows them to acquit where they are not convinced of innocence but recognise that the charges have not been proved beyond reasonable doubt.[89]

---

[81] Full disclosure is said to undermine the incentives on parties to adequately investigate the facts: Damaška, above n. 2, 133.

[82] But see the special position of prosecution and criminal accused, discussed at n. 214 below.

[83] And 'discovery' in many other Anglo-American jurisdictions.

[84] See Hennessy, above n. 2, 213–17; P. Duff, 'Disclosure in Scottish Criminal Procedure: Another Step in an Inquisitorial Direction?' (2007) 11 *The International Journal of Evidence and Proof* 153.

[85] Or as Lord Devlin put it, whereas Continental adjudicators ask 'what is the truth of the matter?', their Anglo-American counterparts ask 'are the shoulders of the party upon whom is laid the burden of proof . . . strong enough to carry and discharge it?': above n. 30, 54.

[86] D. McBarnet, *Conviction: Law, the State and the Construction of Justice* (1983), 12; see also B. S. Jackson, 'Truth or Proof?: The Criminal Verdict' (1998) 11 *International Journal for the Semiotics of Law* 227.

[87] B. Jackson, ibid.

[88] Where unanimity cannot be reached, a maximum of two dissenters is permitted in England and Wales, and three in the US.

[89] See G. Maher, 'The Verdict of the Jury', in M. Findlay and P. Duff (eds), *The Jury Under Attack* (1988).

As regards the presentation of evidence, by contrast to flexible Continental proceedings, Anglo-American trials are strictly structured around the two competing cases.[90] Unlike in most other Anglo-American jurisdictions, in Scotland the parties do not make opening statements setting out what they intend to prove except in rarely held civil jury trials,[91] thus ensuring that neither party benefits from the psychological impact of having the first word.[92] Instead, the prosecution or pursuer simply calls their first witness and, in order to elicit all – and only – the evidence necessary to establish their case, subjects them to what is called examination-in-chief. However, witnesses do not testify in the familiar way of providing chronological accounts of events, largely uninterrupted and in episodes long enough to constitute independent narrative assertions. Instead of this 'narrative' testimony style characteristic of Continental proceedings, Anglo-American testimony is 'fragmented'.[93] Described by Jeremy Bentham as 'the very glory of English procedure',[94] witnesses provide short answers to very specific questions which puncture the flow of testimony[95] to ensure control of the information elicited. Examination-in-chief does not usually involve the extreme form of limiting testimony to simple yes or no answers, but allows witnesses to give brief narrative accounts. These are, however, carefully controlled to ensure that only favourable information emerges. On the other hand, examination-in-chief

---

[90] The following description of the Scottish position draws on Raitt, above n. 22, Chapters 16 and 17; Sheehan and Dickinson, above n. 22, Chapter 6; Hennessy, above n. 2, Chapter 18; Davidson, above n. 22, Chapter 7.

[91] Jury trials are confined to the Court of Session and even then are extremely rare, usually involving personal injury claims: see, for example, A. Hajducki, *Civil Jury Trials* (2nd edn, 2006).

[92] S. M. Kassin, 'The American Jury: Handicapped in the Pursuit of Justice' (1990) 51 *Ohio State Law Journal* 687, 698 n. 43; M. R. Leippe, 'The Case for Expert Testimony about Eyewitness Memory' (1995) 1 *Psychology, Public Policy and Law* 909, 931, but see S. M. Wood et al., 'The Influence of Jurors' Perceptions of Attorneys and Their Performance on Verdict' (2011) 23 *Jury Expert* 23, where the opening statements had either no or a negative effect on verdicts.

[93] See W. M. O'Barr, *Linguistic Evidence: Language, Power and Strategy in the Courtroom* (1982), esp. 76–83; B. Danet, 'Language in the Legal Process' (1980) 14 *Law and Society Review* 445; B. S. Jackson, 'Narrative Models in Legal Proof' (1988) 1 *International Journal of the Semiotics of Law* 225, 228–9.

[94] Cited in J. D. Jackson, 'Law's Truth, Lay Truth and Lawyers' Truth: The Representation of Evidence in Adversary Trials' (1992) 3 *Law and Critique* 29; see also M. Stone, *Proof of Fact in Criminal Trials* (1984), 273.

[95] Witnesses may also be interrupted by objections to the admissibility of the answers given, sometimes necessitating a pause in proceedings to allow legal debate (with adverse effects on the quality of evidence according to jurors in one study: W. Young, N. Cameron, and Y. Tinsley, *Juries In Criminal Trials, Part Two: A Summary of Research Findings* (1999), 23–4), though the staccato of rapid-fire unsubstantiated lawyer objections is not seen in Scottish trials, if indeed outwith US film and television dramas.

cannot involve leading questions, which put the answer into the witness' mouth or suggest the expected answer.[96] Whether obvious, such as 'Was the approaching car driving fast?', or more subtle, such as 'What did the accused do after killing the victim?', as we shall see,[97] psychological research shows how effective leading questions are in influencing witness testimony.

Once witnesses have given their evidence, the other side has a right to cross-examine them,[98] and in doing so will attempt through cross-examination to shake testimony by finding gaps and inconsistencies and seek to contradict even seemingly unimpugnable evidence. In doing so, they may ask leading questions and, albeit under limited circumstances, tender witnesses' out of court statements which contradict their testimony, notwithstanding the normal ban on hearsay evidence in criminal cases.[99] More generally, cross-examiners will seek to impugn witnesses' credibility by, for example, suggesting that there are lying, have bad memories or could not possibly have seen or heard the events accurately. However, there are limits on such tactics; for example, general attacks on witnesses' character are prohibited and cross-examiners cannot lead evidence to rebut witness denials of attacks on their credibility.[100]

Although cross-examination is usually associated with undermining opposition witnesses, it is also used to obtain favourable information. But, whether used negatively or positively, cross-examination involves the fragmented testimony style at its most extreme. Cross-examiners attempt to confine witnesses merely to contradicting themselves or agreeing with the cross-examiner, who generally can go far further in using aggressive tactics than those engaged in examination-in-chief. One exception applies when a witness called by one party turns out to be more favourable to the opponent. Such 'hostile' witnesses may be subject to the full range of cross-examination techniques. There are no specific rules in Scotland as to when this is justified;[101] instead the party calling the witness is left to make the tactical decision as to when to switch from examination to cross-examination. Nor is it clear how hostile witnesses fit the adversarial nature of proceedings: they

---

[96] Though, to speed up proceedings, this does not apply to matters of uncontroversial details such as witness names and addresses.

[97] Chapter 6, section 2.4.3.

[98] In Scotland, unlike in some Anglo-American jurisdictions, any unchallenged witness testimony is not treated as conclusively established.

[99] See Raitt, above n. 22, 281–2.

[100] Raitt, above n. 22, 12.

[101] Cf., for example, Roberts and Zuckerman, above n. 3, 338–40 regarding the English position.

clearly no longer 'belong' to the side calling them but do they now 'belong' to the opponent, thus preventing cross-examination by the latter?[102]

Finally, the party who calls a witness is given the opportunity to re-examine her in order to clear up any doubts or ambiguities or repair any damage caused by cross-examination. However, witnesses can only be questioned on matters not raised in examination-in-chief or cross-examination with leave of the court, whereas witnesses who have finished testifying can only be recalled if their new testimony could not have reasonably been anticipated when first examined.

In criminal cases, after all prosecution witnesses have been examined, the accused can submit that there is no case to answer because their evidence falls short of a prima face case. But if the court does not dismiss the case, the accused, like the defender in civil cases after completions of the pursuers' evidence, will then call her witnesses and the process of examination-in-chief, cross-examination and re-examination will be repeated for each. Once complete, the parties will deliver closing arguments (or 'speeches' in jury trials) designed to draw together the testimony into a meaningful and persuasive whole, with the defence having the last word. In jury trials, the judge will then deliver the charge to the jury, instructing it on the law, as well as summarising, though not giving a personal view of, the facts.[103] Finally, the adjudicator delivers its decision either immediately or after reserving judgment.

3.2 Co-ordinate Judicial Authority and its Implications

3.2.1 Introduction: The Continental Hierarchical Model[104]

Those exposed to fictional courtroom dramas in the English-speaking world will immediately recognise this description of the Anglo-American trial. By contrast, the classical Continental procedural model will be unrecognisable, because of the absence of a climactic trial in which all the evidence is led and a decision finally made. Indeed, many regard this as the 'grand discriminant'[105] between the two classical models. Continental cases are built up incrementally through a series of fact-finding episodes at which various state

---

[102] M. Newark, 'The Hostile Witness and the Adversarial System' [1986] *Criminal Law Review* 441.
[103] Cf. Renton and Brown, above n. 70, para. 18-79.0.4.
[104] For an overview, see Damaška, n. 1, Chapter 3 and loc. cit., n. 40 esp. 58–73.
[105] B. Kaplan, 'An American Lawyer in the Queen's Courts: Impressions of English Civil Procedure' (1971) 69 *Michigan Law Review* 821, 841. See also Jolowicz, above n. 63, 134 (relating this in turn to the existence of the jury in Anglo-American systems), but cf. contra J. H. Langbein, 'The German Advantage in Civil Procedure' (1985) 52 *University of Chicago Law Review* 823, 862–3; J. C. Reitz, 'Why We Probably Cannot Adopt the German Advantage in Civil Procedure' (1989) 75 *Iowa Law Review* 987, 1008.

officials investigate, and gradually move to a decision on, the facts. A dossier is kept containing a written record of all procedural steps taken during the investigation, the results of questioning the parties and other witnesses, and all relevant documents. The trial is usually relatively brief, involving more of the formal public confirmation of the results of the dossier than a full-blooded hearing of the issues.[106] Decisions are not based solely on judges' personal observation of oral testimony,[107] but on the whole dossier, which only includes a summary, rather than a verbatim record, of oral testimony before examining judges. Moreover, given the Continental focus on accurate decision-making rather than on simply deciding a contest, on appeal decisions are subject to a re-hearing on the merits and hence are supported by detailed written reasons. This lack of finality in fact finding also means that new evidence can be easily considered when it arises. Consequently, whereas the classical Anglo-American model sharply distinguishes between pre- and post-trial proceedings and the trial itself, Continental lawyers speak simply of 'proceedings', with what Anglo-Americans call the trial being merely one of the stages. As we have seen,[108] Damaška argues that this procedural model flows naturally from the existence of a highly bureaucratised professional judiciary organised according to distinct functions (investigation, decision to proceed, adjudication, and hierarchical review) and in a hierarchical pyramid, and which makes decisions according to the logical application of technical decisional standards.

3.2.2 Concentrated Fact Finding: the 'Day in Court' and Finality

By contrast, many central features of classical Anglo-American procedure flow from both the jury's historical role as the primary fact finder in the UK – albeit one later augmented by a relatively large corps of 'gentlemen' Justices of the Peace (henceforth JPs) in Scotland[109] and a smaller group of second-career judges (that is, those promoted from the bar) – and from the failure to establish state institutions to investigate and pursue cases. Thus a small and largely amateur judiciary is unable to play an active role in gathering facts. Moreover, having cases decided by fifteen jurors as in Scottish criminal cases or even twelve in civil cases makes concentrated

---

[106] See, for example, McKillop, above n. 74, 565, noting the 5 per cent average acquittal rate in France for the period 1988–92.

[107] But as is apparent from A. A. S. Zuckerman, 'Justice in Crisis: Corporate Dimensions of Civil Procedure', in A. A. S. Zuckerman (ed.), *Civil Justice in Crisis: Comparative Perspectives of Civil Justice* (1999), passim, the extent of orality varies dramatically in Continental civil cases, though seems to be uniformly decreasing.

[108] Loc. cit. n. 40.

[109] The Scottish equivalent of magistrates.

fact finding in a trial, while not logically necessary,[110] virtually inevitable. It would be incredibly impractical, if not impossible, to repeatedly convene juries or unpaid JPs for each investigative stage of episodic fact finding.

Consequently, the classical Anglo-American model developed around the climactic trial at which all evidence is presented. Moreover, limited judicial resources and hierarchical levels militate against complete re-hearings and confine appeals to errors of law and procedure, egregious factual errors and the emergence of new evidence considered likely to have affected the original decision.[111] Indeed, appeal courts ask not what they but rather what a reasonable trial court would have decided and frequently refer decisions back rather than reaching a decision themselves. Decision finality[112] also flows from the fact that, even if regarded as desirable,[113] it is unrealistic to expect a diverse group of lay people to provide reasons for their decision in a form which supports review. In fact, unless an appeal is launched, the lower civil courts need only provide brief reasons[114] and the lower Scottish criminal courts none at all.[115]

A number of important implications flow from the concentrated nature of fact finding. One is that adjudicators usually approach cases cold. Although judges and sheriffs *may* read the pleadings prior to trial, most adjudicators and certainly juries first encounter the evidence when the first witness begins to testify. Unlike the original 'self-informing' jury,[116] adjudicators are expected to decide purely on evidence presented at trial and not on relevant personal knowledge obtained outside the court room. Indeed, the law goes to great lengths to protect juries from outside influence.[117] A second consequence is that, compared to Continental proceedings, trials are often dramatic spectacles, subject to surprises and unexpected turns of events – the last-minute discovery of missing documents, witnesses who crumple under cross-examination, turn 'hostile' or go missing, etc. Evidence may also go missing in the sense that witnesses may partly or totally forget facts they encountered months and sometimes years before – though they are allowed to 'refresh memory' by looking at notes made con-

---

[110] Jury trials could follow episodic fact finding by professional judges, but this would vastly expand the required commitment of the lay public.

[111] For details, see Chapter 1, section 2.3.

[112] See generally, J. D. Jackson, 'Managing Uncertainty and Finality: The Function of the Criminal Trial in Legal Inquiry', in A. Duff et al. (eds), *The Trial on Trial: Volume 1 – Truth and Due Process* (2004).

[113] But see section 3.2.4 regarding the perceived values of jury autonomy.

[114] Hennessy, above n. 2, 156–7, 173.

[115] See Sheehan and Dickson, above n. 22, 234.

[116] See section 3.2.4 below.

[117] See, for example, Sheehan and Dickson, above n. 22, 192–3.

temporaneously with the events in question.[118] Such missing evidence or other surprise events can prove determinative given that remedial action must occur before the trial ends. Thirdly, and perhaps most importantly, the limited timescale in which to pursue new evidential leads and re-question witnesses when new evidence emerges or to compare a witness' court testimony against earlier recorded statements means that other 'powerful engines'[119] have had to be devised for evaluating evidence.

3.2.3 Orality, Immediacy and Publicity[120]
These engines centre on the important principle of orality, which generally requires that all evidence must be given orally in person. Even when parties want to tender documents or items of real evidence, they must be 'spoken to' by a witness who can explain their origin and significance. Moreover, in terms of the hearsay rule, orally delivered evidence must involve what is personally observed by the witness rather than reported by someone else.[121] As Bentham put it, witnesses are 'the eyes and ears of justice'.[122]

There are many reasons for this faith in oral testimony. One is the general preference for speech over writing in Western philosophy[123] and the Platonic belief that truth will emerge from continued discussion, question and answer, dialogue and interrogation.[124] These ideas combine with the British empiricist version of Enlightenment thinking which, as we saw in Chapter Two,[125] treats evidence of the senses as the central means of knowledge acquisition.[126] However, it is not so much that live testimony is regarded as more accurate than other forms of evidence, but that it can be subject to greater safeguards.

---

[118] As long as such documents are made available to the opposition and do not substitute for oral evidence: Raitt, above n. 22, 275–6.

[119] Damaška, above n. 8, 61.

[120] See generally, A. Duff et al., above n. 11, passim; Ellison, above n. 30, esp. Chapter 2 (expanding on 'The Protection of Vulnerable Witnesses in Court: an Anglo-Dutch Comparison' (1999) 3 International Journal of Evidence and Proof 29); T. Honoré, 'The Primacy of Oral Evidence?', in C. Tapper (ed.), Crime, Proof and Punishment: Essays in Honour of Sir Rupert Cross (1981), esp. 186–9.

[121] For the details, see, for example, Raitt, above n. 22, Chapter 11.

[122] Cited by P. Halder, 'The Return of the Evidencer's Eye – Rhetoric and the Visual Technologies of Proof' (1999) 8 Griffith Law Review 86, 91.

[123] Ibid., 90.

[124] J. Jackson, above n. 94, 35.

[125] Sections 2.2 and 3.2.1.

[126] Cf. Schafer and Wiegand, above n. 69; A. Duff et al., 125, 132, arguing that British Empiricism also influenced the development of the adversarial system, though if Langbein (above n. 26) is correct and the immediate catalyst was a judicial willingness in English felony cases to allow defence lawyers a more active role, at best it can only have provided background intellectual support.

One is the oath or affirmation to tell the truth. However, unless one regards the solemnity of swearing or affirming to tell the truth in court, along with the formality and official nature of court proceedings, as encouraging honesty, what is most crucial in discouraging dishonesty is the fear of perjury charges;[127] in which case, sworn written evidence can be regarded as equally safe. A prima facie more plausible reason for the faith in oral evidence is the opportunity it gives adjudicators to observe witnesses' demeanour: facial expressions, body language and voice intonation.[128] These are assumed to provide valuable clues as to whether someone is lying or not and, on the assumption that confidence is correlated to accuracy, the certainty of their assertions. However, as we shall see in Chapter Six,[129] psychological research raises serious doubts about these assumptions.

Consequently, it would seem that the most plausible justification for the principle of orality is that it ensures that witnesses can be subjected to cross-examination before the adjudicator. As John Henry Wigmore famously opined, cross-examination is 'the greatest legal engine ever invented for the discovery of truth'.[130] By enabling questioners to expose lying, mistaken or otherwise unreliable witness through uncovering inconsistencies, illogicalities and inaccuracies in evidence, cross-examination is the primary method used to test the veracity and accuracy of evidence. Moreover, cross-examination may work as much by deterring unreliable witnesses from giving false testimony or even taking the stand through fear of being exposed.[131]

In fact, the value of cross-examination can be said to extend beyond its instrumental 'truth-certifying' role. By allowing those who face allegations an opportunity to test their veracity, cross-examination upholds principles of natural justice and makes participants more likely to accept adverse outcomes as legitimate.[132] Related to the right to examine is the belief that truth finding is enhanced by dialectical immediacy and the eyeball-to-eyeball confrontation between accuser and accused. Not only

[127] Cf. D. Kurzon, 'Telling the Truth: The Oath as a Test of Witness Competency' (1989) II *International Journal for the Semiotics of Law* 49.
[128] See, for example, *Kilpatrick* v. *Dunlop* (1911, unreported), cited in *Murray* v. *Fraser* 1916 SC 623, 624.
[129] Section 3.3.
[130] *A Treatise on the Anglo-American System of Evidence in Trials at Common Law*, Vol. 5, (1974), para. 1367, quoted, for example, by Hunter, above n. 26, 262.
[131] R. A. Posner, 'An Economic Approach to the Law of Evidence' (1999) 51 *Stanford Law Review* 1477, 1490.
[132] See, for example, Thompson, above n. 63, 749; G. Richardson and H. Genn, 'Tribunals in Transition: Resolution or Adjudication' [2007] *Public Law* 116, 131, and see further section 4.3.2.2.

is the idea of such confrontation closely associated with adversarial fact finding, but it is also thought that witnesses who might otherwise be able to get away with lying will crumple when faced with the gaze or questions of those who know the truth.[133]

Finally, it is thought that the values of orality and immediacy are enhanced by holding proceedings in open court, where they are subject to public scrutiny and report by the media. According to Wigmore, this renders witnesses less inclined to falsify,[134] whereas Bentham went further to argue that without publicity all other guarantees of truth finding are insufficient. 'Publicity', he wrote, 'is the soul of justice. It is the keenest spur to exertion and the surest of all guards against improbity.'[135] However, publicity is only fully applicable to the trial, where orality and the concentrated day-in-court make it easier for the public to attend and comprehend proceedings. It is far less applicable to formal pre-trial proceedings. For instance, it is impossible to accommodate all who might want to observe discussions in judges' chambers. And it is not applicable at all when parties speak to prospective witnesses or to opponents. Consequently, the problems of inequality and injustice which we will see arising in plea bargaining and negotiation of civil claims[136] remain hidden from public view.

3.2.4 Lay Adjudication

As already noted,[137] the British suspicion of centralised state control led to entrusting adjudication to ordinary citizens. Thus, from 1609, Scottish JPs were intended to have administrative and policy as well as adjudicative powers in minor criminal cases. The jury has a much longer history.[138] Notwithstanding Lord Devlin's characterisation of it as 'a particularly English institution',[139] the Normans also imported it into Scotland. Norman juries were initially composed of lay members of the community who were expected to base decisions on their own knowledge of events and the parties. However, with the breakdown of small communities and law's growing complexity, the jury was gradually reduced to its present size, lost its self-informing nature and became judicially controlled. The

---

[133] See, for example, *Coy* v. *Iowa* 487 US 1012, 1019 (1988).

[134] Above n. 130. Vol. 6, 435.

[135] Quoted by A. A. S. Zuckerman, *Zuckerman on Civil Procedure: Principles of Practice* (2nd edn, 2006), 88–9; and see in general Zuckerman, ibid., 88–93; A. Duff et al., above n. 11, Chapter 9.

[136] See Chapter 4, section 2.4.2.

[137] Text following n. 40, above.

[138] See I. D. Willock, *The Origins of the Jury in Scotland* (1966). For a briefer description, see Davidson, above n. 22, 4–5, and in relation to England, P. Devlin, *Trial by Jury* (1956), Chapter 1.

[139] Ibid., 121.

civil jury even fell into desuetude, having to be revived in 1815, but even today it is only used in the higher courts and then only rarely. Jury trials are more common in criminal cases, but even then only in relation to serious offences. Moreover, for reasons relating primarily to cost,[140] the proportion of jury trials in Scotland has been even further reduced by enlargement of the jurisdiction of summary courts, and there has never been a right to a jury trial. Thus juries are responsible for only a very small fraction of formal fact finding, whereas the role of Scottish JPs has never been that extensive.[141] Nevertheless, historically, lay adjudication and particularly the institution of the jury has had an impact on fact finding out of all proportion to its current-day practical significance.

We have already seen that lay adjudication encouraged the continuous nature of – and finality attached to – the Anglo-American trial.[142] The perceived need to prevent lay people from being misled by unreliable and unduly prejudicial evidence played a crucial role in prompting admissibility rules of an 'intrinsic' exclusionary nature which are intended to make accurate evaluation of the facts more likely by excluding evidence thought to be unreliable, misleading or otherwise prejudicial – as opposed to the rather less common rules of 'extrinsic' exclusionary nature which exclude evidence for reasons other than truth finding.[143] Whether juries are indeed more susceptible to paying undue regard to unreliable, misleading or prejudicial evidence is a moot point. Moreover, if the lack of legal training is indeed so important,[144] then the rules could also be said to be necessary to protect, not just JPs, but also those involved in alternative dispute resolution and administrative decisions who lack legal training, but as we saw in Chapter One[145] are largely unencumbered by evidence rules.

The jury also gave rise to the complex specialisation of functions between judge and jury whereby judges rule on the law (and criminal sentence) and juries on the facts (and occasionally the level of civil damages). The

---

[140] Other factors in England and Wales involve fears of jury 'nobbling' and jurors' ability to deal with complex cases such as those involving fraud, and pressures from the police and other sections of the law-and-order lobby who regard juries as soft on criminals and the protection of national security – see, for example, A. Duff et al., above n. 11, 1–2, 51–2.

[141] Gane, above n. 6, 67.

[142] Section 3.2.2. Whereas the ubiquity of 'bench trials' means that episodic fact finding is now more feasible, the retention of the limited right to appeal decisions on the facts still makes sense because judges sitting alone have the exclusive opportunity to observe oral testimony.

[143] See, for example, Damaška, above n. 2, 13–14 and n. 15, 514–23.

[144] Cf. C. R. Callen, 'Cognitive Strategies and Models of Fact Finding', in Jackson, Langer and Tillers, above n. 12, 176, with Damaška, above n. 2, 31–2 and 'Propensity Evidence in Continental Legal Systems' (1994) 70 *Chicago-Kent Law Review* 55, 65–6.

[145] Section 2.3.

distinction is not, however, completely clear-cut. Thus judges have the power to withhold facts from juries by ruling evidence inadmissible,[146] withdraw particular issues from consideration on the grounds of insufficient supporting evidence, and may even decide that there is no case to answer at all. Similarly, although the charge to the jury is intended largely to clarify the law, the entitlement to comment on the plausibility and credibility of witnesses[147] creates the potential for a fair amount of subconscious or even conscious influence over jury decisions.[148]

However, the jury's significance extends well beyond its historical impact. Thus, while not everyone goes as far as Hale, who regarded jury trials as 'the best method of searching and sifting out the truth',[149] many – including Scottish lay justices themselves[150] – regard lay adjudicators as in some ways superior fact finders to professional judges.[151] Thus, sharing the social background, life experiences, values and assumptions of witnesses and the parties, lay adjudicators – albeit jurors more than JPs who come from a narrower range of social backgrounds[152] – are thought likely to more accurately assess the credibility of witness testimony and understand events. Juries have the added advantage of being able to draw upon the combined life experiences – and, when it comes to the final decision, the memory – of up to fifteen fact finders, who will not be case hardened and hence more willing to treat each case on its unique facts. On the other hand, even those who espouse the truth-finding advantages of lay adjudication concede that legal education and experience make professional adjudicators better at drawing inferences from accepted testimony,

---

[146] For the details, see Davidson, above n. 22, 392–8. Where there is no jury the judge may either decide on admissibility immediately or allow the evidence in 'under reservation'.

[147] But cf. Renton and Brown, above n. 70, para. 18-79.0.4, noting that such comments must be accurate and balanced so that judges do not encroach on the jury's role as master of the facts.

[148] For evidence that this potential is realised, see Chapter 4, section 4.2.2.

[149] Quoted by B. J. Shapiro, *Beyond Reasonable Doubt and Probable Cause: Historical Perspectives on the Anglo-American Law of Evidence* (1991), 11–12.

[150] See Z. Bankowski, N. R. Hutton and J. J. McManus, *Lay Justice?* (1987), Chapter 6 – a view not shared by the lawyers appearing before them: ibid., Chapter 8.

[151] See, for example, Risinger, above n. 61, 1308–9; Posner, above n. 131 1493; Damaška, above n. 15, 538–9; Devlin, above n. 138, 140–1. Empirical research suggests that juries do a good job in this regard: see, for example, M. Redmayne, 'Theorising Jury Reform', in A. Duff et al., above n. 61, 102; M. Galanter, 'The Regulatory Function of the Jury', in R. E. Litan (ed.), *Verdict – Assessing the Civil Justice System* (1993), 70; though cf. contra J. Baldwin and M. McConville, *Jury Trials* (1979).

[152] Bankowski, Hutton and McManus, above n. 150, Chapter 3 reports that they tend to come from lower middle and upper working class backgrounds.

evaluating complex evidence and avoiding the distorting impact of emotion and prejudice.[153]

Indeed, most supporters of lay adjudication see its value as lying beyond superior fact finding.[154] Historically, the 'right' to be judged by one's own peers was regarded as a safeguard against state tyranny and corruption – 'the lamp that shows that freedom lives'.[155] But leaving aside the fact that Scottish accused have never had such a right, since the prosecution decides whether solemn or summary proceedings are appropriate,[156] it is doubtful whether random selection, coupled with 'self-deselection' by those able to avoid jury service, ensures judgment by one's peers. Moreover, some question whether 'overprotection' by sympathetic juries is desirable, let alone necessary, in a state subject to the rule of law.[157]

A more promising justification is that lay adjudication democratises the legal process and ensures individualised and substantive justice. By bringing an element of common sense, equity, flexibility, popular and community justice, and a human face to the austerity and harshness which may emanate from the strict application of law, juries and JPs are said to inject 'lay acid' into adjudication.[158] Like professional adjudicators, they are implicitly delegated the power to rely on extra-legal norms in applying legal standards of reasonableness, fairness, honesty, etc. But, in addition, because they do not provide reasons for their decisions and are largely immune from appeal,[159] jurors can apply their own notions of justice and ignore the clear dictates of the law. Such 'jury nullification'[160] may directly prompt law reform or at least cause legislators to consider the likely jury response to proposed laws. This power to act as a 'little Parliament'[161] is not formally extended to JPs, but their freedom from having to give reasons for decisions unless there is an appeal[162] means that in practice they have much greater scope than professional judges to favour their own conception of substantive

---

[153] For evidence of this, see Chapter 7, section 5 passim.

[154] In addition to the above, see, for example, Findlay and P. Duff, above n. 89.

[155] Devlin, above n. 138, 164.

[156] English and Welsh accused are entitled to opt for a jury trial in cases 'triable either way', whereas Magna Carta (which does not apply in Scotland) refers to a right to be judged by one's peers.

[157] See, for example, Redmayne, above n. 150, 106; P. Darbyshire, 'The Lamp That Shows That Freedom Lives – Is It Worth The Candle?' (1991) *Criminal Law Review* 740, 750–1.

[158] Bankowski, Hutton and McManus, above n. 150, 181; Z. Bankowski, 'The Jury and Reality', in Findlay and P. Duff, above n. 89, 20.

[159] See section 3.2.2. above.

[160] But see R. D. Friedman, 'Generalized Inferences, Individual Merits, and Jury Discretion' (1986) 66 *Buffalo University Law Review* 509, 510, who argues that this power exists not as a matter of principle but due to the impracticality of eliminating it.

[161] Devlin, above n. 138, 162.

[162] See section 3.2.2 above.

justice over factual truth and expletive justice. Of course, whether or not one regards this power to keep 'the law from ossifying into a rigid ballet of bloodless categories'[163] as outweighing the benefits of legal certainty depends on whether one prioritises substantive justice over Rule of Law values. Similarly, whether entrusting such power to an unelected, unaccountable and not necessarily representative group of citizens is regarded as enhancing or detracting from democratic constitutionalism depends on how much faith one has in Parliamentary democracy.[164]

Nevertheless, it is clear that lay adjudication provides a recognised exception to orthodox evidence theory's emphasis on factual truth and expletive justice. Less explicitly recognised is the challenge to the politics of fact positivism represented by the weakened commitment of lay adjudicators to scientific rationality, which helps close off any politics, morals or conception of justice other than those already contained in law.[165] Lacking practice in legal reasoning with its emphasis on formal logic, lay adjudicators seem more likely than judges to escape the straitjacket of scientific rationality. The assumption that jurors in particular are significantly influenced by emotion, passion and prejudice,[166] as well as the knowledge that they can make decisions against the grain of law, is likely to encourage those appearing before them to increase the emotive content of their rhetoric, which in turn increases the chances of jurors departing from scientific rationality and expletive justice.

3.3 The Legal Regulation of Evidence

Certainly, as we have already seen,[167] assumptions about the inferior cognitive abilities of jurors underlie the much greater regulation of fact finding in Anglo-American systems as compared to that on the Continent.[168] Accordingly, the desire to protect jurors from potentially unreliable, misleading and prejudicial evidence was a significant source of many exclusionary evidential rules in Anglo-American systems. Continental systems also have 'extrinsic exclusionary rules' protecting public-interest immunity and even more types of evidentiary privileges, whereas Continental fact finders might as a matter of discretion give little or no weight to evidence thought to be unreliable, misleading or otherwise prejudicial. However,

---

[163] R. P. Burns, "The Distinctiveness of Trial Narrative", in A. Duff et al., above n. 112, 160.
[164] Cf Darbyshire, above n. 157, 750.
[165] Chapter 2, section 4.2.
[166] An assumption which motivates much of the criticism of the institution of the jury cited in n. 157 above.
[167] Section 3.4.2.
[168] The following draws upon Damaška, above n. 2, esp. Chapter 1.

there is no Continental analogue to the variety of Anglo-American 'intrinsic exclusionary rules', most notably those which require all evidence to have been personally observed by witnesses giving oral evidence rather than hearsay reports of others, preventing fact finders from relying on a person's character and propensity for committing certain types of acts rather than evidence of actually having committed the alleged act and (with the exception of experts) to involve merely an observation of the facts and not an opinion on what they might mean.[169]

Apart from exclusionary rules, there are other significant differences in the legal regulation of proof between the Anglo-American and Continental procedural models. While Continental appeal court rulings on the adequacy of evidential support for factual findings may influence future decision-makers, they are non-binding and hence cannot be said to constitute rules.[170] By contrast, Anglo-American systems not only have exclusionary rules, but also rules regulating how decision-makers should evaluate and determine the facts, such as those on the burdens and standards of proof, those regulating what need not be proved (presumptions, judicial notice, etc.), sufficiency of evidence (most notably in Scotland, the corroboration requirement), as well as 'partial admissibility' rules which state that certain information can be considered for limited purposes only. In addition, judges can direct jurors to ignore inadmissible evidence to which they were accidentally exposed or to treat with caution other evidence regarded as misleading, unreliable or otherwise prejudicial. Arguably this is more likely to affect how evidence is treated than Continental judges making a mental note to disregard or downplay evidence thought to be misleading, unreliable or prejudicial, or even issuing warnings to lay assessors on mixed panels.[171] Consequently, in the absence of a developed body of binding rules regulating the presentation and evaluation of evidence, most regulation of fact finding on the Continent comprises detailed procedural rules governing the process of evidence-gathering. By comparison, at least until recently, Anglo-American evidence law has paid far less attention to directly regulating pre-trial fact handling, though the exclusion of improperly obtained confessions and other improperly obtained evidence indirectly regulates fact

---

[169] That is, the hearsay, character and opinion evidence rules: see Raitt, above n. 22, Chapters 11, 12 and 3 respectively; and see also ibid., Chapter 9 on confessions which, to the extent that they are excluded for being given in circumstances suggesting a lack of voluntariness, rather than simple unfairness, can also be regarded as involving an intrinsic exclusionary rule.

[170] See also Nijboer, above n. 14, 302, 314ff.

[171] See also M. Damaška, 'Free Proof and its Detractors' (1995) 43 *American Journal of Comparative Law* 343, 350–2.

investigators by cautioning them to act legally lest improperly obtained evidence be ruled inadmissible.[172]

The two classical models differ in terms, not just of the number and focus of their rules, but also their nature. Thus, compared to Continental systems, Anglo-American law is marked by its complexity and lack of coherent structure: its 'maze of disconnected rules, embroidered by exceptions and followed by exceptions to exceptions', in Damaška's apt description.[173] Moreover, the rules are incredibly technical in nature, having little connection to ordinary methods of factual inquiry, and very difficult for an untrained mind to comprehend. A final notable distinction is that the centrality of party autonomy in the Anglo-American model means that, unlike in the Continental model, the parties are in control of many evidence rules and hence, as we saw in Chapter One,[174] can decide to waive their application.

3.4 Procedural Justice in the Anglo-American Classical Model
3.4.1 Overview: Scope, Application and Rationale
Given that Continental fact finding is conducted as a direct search for truth rather than a contest, there is no need for the sort of rules of the game designed to ensure fair play between competitors. Thus, to the extent that Continental systems have rules of procedural justice, they exist more for reasons of intrinsic fairness rather than to ensure that outcomes are the product of factual truth rather than competitive advantage.[175] In fact, however, not least because of different approaches to the role of the state, 'intrinsic' civil liberties were initially slower to develop on the Continent than in Anglo-American systems. However, this process has now accelerated under the influence of the European Convention on Human Rights (hereafter ECHR), which is arguably causing the approach to procedural justice in both systems to 'converge'.[176] This is also likely to flow from the European Union Charter of Fundamental Rights, the content of which overlaps with the ECHR as regards procedural justice. However, given that its status is now highly precarious following the vote to leave the European Union, discussion will be confined to the common law and the ECHR. Moreover, given that this book is meant to supplement Evidence

---

[172] See, for example, A. Duff et al., 'Introduction: Towards a Normative Theory of the Criminal Trial', in A. Duff et al., above n. 111, 11–12.

[173] Above n. 2, 10.

[174] Section 2.4.

[175] See, for example, J. D. Jackson and S. J. Summers, *The Internationalisation of Criminal Evidence: Beyond the Common Law and Civil Law Tradition* (2012), Chapter 3.

[176] See at nn. 222–5 below.

Law textbooks and these rarely – especially in Scotland – provide an overview of the law upholding procedural justice, this section will confine itself merely to providing a broad overview of the position in Scotland, which in turn reflects the general procedural values found in Anglo-American legal systems and which, as we saw in the previous chapter,[177] have become an increasingly important goal of the fact-finding process.

This overview will reveal a complex picture of the legal basis, scope and underlying rationale of procedural justice values. To simplify matters, we will concentrate on aspects of procedural justice (sometimes, especially in the US, called due process) most directly related to issues of evidence and proof.[178] These involve the right to a fair trial and what shall be called the right to fair treatment, which applies to all aspects of conduct impinging on fact finding other than the trial or hearing itself and encompasses a broad range of civil liberties, such as the rights to bodily integrity, privacy and to freedom from arbitrary arrest and illegal searches. The distinction between fair trials and fair treatment is not, however, clear-cut. Certain rights to a fair trial have implications for pre-trial behaviour (for instance, the right to effective trial participation requires prior notice of accusations), whereas unfair treatment outside court (such as improperly obtained confessions) may lead to evidence being excluded at trial.

Matters are further complicated by the fact that, while many of the legal requirements for fair trials and fair treatment are found in the common law and domestic legislation, this law is now significantly overlaid and considerably strengthened by the ECHR.[179] Although not directly incorporated into Scots law, Acts of the Scottish Parliament that conflict with the ECHR are invalid, whereas the Convention must be taken into account by the courts in developing the common law, and interpreting and applying UK and Scots legislation, and by executive authorities in exercising discretionary powers. Similarly, while not technically binding, decisions of the European Court of Human Rights (henceforth ECtHR)

---

[177] Section 2.2.

[178] In addition, it includes inter alia rights of access to court, the right not to participate in or at least invoke a legal process (voluntariness), the requirement that decisions be based upon prospectively promulgated, clear rules rather than arbitrary discretion which bind adjudicators as well as the parties (procedural legality) and procedural rationality, discussed below at n. 208: see Summers, above n. 1, 20ff; J. L. Mashaw, 'Administrative Due Process: the Quest for a Dignity Theory' (1981) 61 *Buffalo University Law Review* 885, 899ff; M. Boyles, 'Principles for Legal Procedure' (1986) 5 *Law and Philosophy* 33, 53ff.

[179] See, for example, R. Reed and J. Murdoch, *A Guide to Human Rights Law in Scotland* (2nd edn, 2011), above n. 8, esp. Chapter 1 on the Convention's legal status, and for a useful overview of relevant provisions, A. Ashworth and M. Redmayne, *The Criminal Process* (4th edn, 2010), 29–38.

are effectively binding in all UK cases involving Convention rights, though the ECtHR does allow domestic law a 'margin of appreciation' in applying Conventional rights to local conditions. Moreover, in deciding on the compatibility of domestic procedures the ECtHR looks at their overall fairness rather than acting on isolated technical breaches.[180] These rights, especially those to a fair trial contained in Article 6,[181] overlap substantially but not entirely with domestic law and echo its much greater procedural protection of criminal suspects and accused than participants in other proceedings. Thus, in addition to certain basic aspects of the right to a fair trial provided by Article 6(1), Articles 6(2) and 6(3) provide for specific rights for criminal accused, although some of these have been held to apply impliedly to civil litigants as well. Furthermore, not only do many aspects of fair treatment involving the protection of civil liberties, such as the rights against arbitrary arrest and illegal searches, arise more frequently in criminal cases, but many procedural protections, such as the duty to tell suspects of their rights on arrest, are simply not applicable to civil litigants.

Nevertheless, whether confined to criminal suspects and accused or extending more widely, many regard both fair trial and fair treatment protections as necessary to ensure respect for values regarded as intrinsic to our common humanity. In terms of the Western human rights tradition traceable back to Immanuel Kant, which requires people to be treated equally and as subjects in their own right rather than means to others' ends, everyone is considered to be entitled to be treated with minimal invasions of their freedom, dignity and self-respect, and to participate in decisions likely to harm their welfare.[182]

There are, as already noted, additional instrumental reasons for upholding procedural justice in adversarial fact finding. Most obviously, the requirement of an impartial adjudicator, and of effective and equal rights to put one's case, serve the goal of truth finding. The same is said of other aspects of a fair trial, such as the absence of delay[183] and arguably also publicity,[184] as well as certain aspects of fair treatment, such as the prohibition

---

[180] See Reed and Murdoch, ibid., respectively at Chapter 3, esp. 285–91 and Chapter 5, esp. 520–1.

[181] Not least because UK lawyers played a key role in its drafting: J. Jackson, above n. 8, 748–9.

[182] See, for example, Summers, above n. 178: Mashaw, above n. 178; T. M. Massaro, 'The Dignity Value of Face to Face Confrontations' (1988) 40 *University of Florida Law Review* 863; and, for a more critical approach, D. Galligan, *Due Process and Fair Procedures* (1996), esp. 75ff; P. Roberts, 'Theorising Procedural Tradition: Subjects, Objects and Values in Criminal Adjudication', in Duff et al., above n. 61.

[183] See Chapter 2, section 2.2.

[184] Section 3.2.3 above.

on obtaining confessions through violence or deceit. A less obvious instrumental effect of procedural fairness, discussed in more detail in the next chapter,[185] is that it promotes the peaceful resolution of disputes by dissuading aggrieved individuals from resorting to self-help. Thus unsuccessful litigants are said to be more likely to accept outcomes if they had a chance to influence the decision of an impartial adjudicator, whereas if the public sees justice being done and fair methods of fact investigation and adjudication being followed, confidence in the administration of justice will be enhanced. Also discussed in the next chapter[186] is another more recent additional rationale for procedural fairness in relation to criminal proceedings to the effect that, if the state is to legitimately call to account alleged criminals, it must itself uphold, and be seen to uphold, standards of legality and fairness at all stages of proceedings. Indeed, given that civil cases also communicate normative behavioural standards, this 'principle of integrity' arguably also requires civilised procedural standards in civil proceedings.

There are, however, specific protections for criminal suspects and accused. Some, like the presumption of innocence, largely[187] operate at trial. Others, like the right to silence and the limitation on the prosecution's adversarial stance, may also have an impact on conduct outside trial. Some commentators maintain that these protections are intrinsically required as a mark of society's respect for individual dignity[188] or the principle of integrity.[189] However, the standard rationale points to the imbalance in resources between state and accused, and the serious consequences of unjust convictions.[190]

Thus prosecution authorities have substantial investigative advantages over suspects in the form of the police and other investigative agencies, the ability to appeal to the public for information, usually greater financial resources and the ability to obtain damaging admissions through arrest and interrogation. By contrast, defence lawyers frequently cannot rely on their clients' assistance because they are either incapable or incarcerated. In court, the state has the advantage of greater credibility. Judges and

---

[185] Section 3.

[186] Ibid.

[187] But cf. Robert and Zuckerman, above n. 3, 223 n. 12, arguing that the presumption of innocence also reinforces specific protections of criminal suspects and accused outside the court room.

[188] See, for example, Roberts and Zuckerman, ibid., 240ff; D. Luban, 'Are Criminal Defenders Different?' (1993) 91 *Michigan Law Review* 1729.

[189] See, for example, Roberts and Zuckerman, above n. 3, 22, 188–91; A. Duff et al., above n. 11; R. A. Duff, *Trials and Punishments* (1986), esp. Chapter 4; I. H. Dennis, 'Reconstructing the Law of Criminal Evidence' (1989) *Current Legal Problems* 21.

[190] In addition to the specific references in the rest of the section, see, for example, Roberts and Zuckerman, ibid., 15, 58ff; D. Luban, *Lawyers and Justice: An Ethical Study* (1988), 58ff.

juries tend to believe police witnesses and disbelieve accused, commonly assuming that accused would not be in the dock without good reason. Whereas prosecuting criminals seems legitimate and in accordance with democratic government, attempts to evade criminal liability are likely to be viewed with greater suspicion. As we shall see in the next chapter, sociologists observe that the whole nature of legal proceedings and court atmosphere operate to make criminal convictions more likely than not, frequently persuading accused to plea bargain even when innocent. To this can be added the danger – dramatically highlighted by notable miscarriages of justice[191] – of overzealous police convinced by guilt or motivated by less worthy goals trampling underfoot civil liberties and manipulating evidence to secure convictions at all cost. But even in routine cases involving 'harassed over-worked bureaucrats'[192] wanting merely to dispose of cases quickly, imbalances in power between state and defendant may result in punishment being imposed on the innocent or excessively on the guilty. Not only may they innocently lose their property or liberty, but they also potentially face public condemnation, loss of reputation and social discrimination for having criminal records. In fact, even if acquitted, the prosecution process involves intense anxiety and possibly also financial expense, lost employment and disrupted family lives.

In this light, the plethora of legal protections for criminal suspects and accused are generally regarded as aimed not simply at protecting human dignity or the integrity of proceedings, but at 'overprotecting'[193] suspects and accused by placing significant obstacles in the way of convictions so as to equalise power imbalances between state and citizen. On the assumption that no rules could effectively protect the innocent from conviction while simultaneously allowing conviction of every guilty person, it is famously declaimed that 'it is better to let ten guilty men go free than to convict one innocent'.[194] This 'principled asymmetry'[195] is sometimes also augmented by the argument that protecting the freedom of criminal defendants indirectly protects the freedom of all. As Barbara Babcock

---

[191] See, for example, C. Walker and K. Starmer (eds), *Miscarriages of Justice: A Review of Justice in Error* (1999).
[192] Luban, above n. 189, 1730ff, refuting W. H. Simon, 'The Ethics of Criminal Defense' (1993) 91 *Michigan Law Review* 1703, 1707ff.
[193] Luban, above n. 188, 60–3.
[194] Blackstone, *Commentaries* (1765–9) 4.27, followed in *Hobson* 1 Lew CC 26, but cf. Roberts and Zuckerman, above n. 3, 19–20, noting other ratios ranging from 5:1 to 1000:1; M. Risinger, 'Innocents Convicted: An Empirically Justified Factual Wrongful Conviction Rate' (2007) 97 *The Journal of Criminal Law and Criminology* 761, 791, arguing that there is no magic in the numbers; they simply symbolise a normative commitment.
[195] Roberts and Zuckerman, above n. 3, 19.

colourfully puts it, 'the criminally accused are the representatives of us all. When their rights are eroded, the camel's nose is under and the tent may collapse on anyone.'[196]

3.4.2 The Right to a Fair Trial[197]

This overview suggests that we can categorise procedural justice as it affects legal fact finding in terms of three broad categories of rights: to a fair trial; to fair treatment generally; and to fair treatment and protection as a criminal suspect or accused.

As regards the right to a fair trial, this comprises five more specific rights which apply in both criminal and civil cases, though more extensively in the former:

(1) *The right to an impartial and independent tribunal*

In terms of the *nemo iudex in sua causa* principle of natural justice, those who adjudicate disputes or other legal proceedings must not only be free from bias and a personal interest in the case, but also free from the appearance of partiality. Article 6(1) goes further and requires an independent tribunal, which has been interpreted to require independence from the parties as well as from the other organs of government.

(2) *The right to a fair hearing*

In terms of this right, everyone must be given both an *effective* and an *equal* opportunity to participate in the decision-making process. More specifically, the *audi alteram partem* principle of natural justice requires that those facing decisions seriously affecting their interests must be given a hearing before the decision is made. Moreover, to make this right effective, a number of subsidiary rights are provided by the common law, and expressly and impliedly by Article 6. One is the right to prior and timely notice of the case to be met so as to enable adequate preparation time. Criminal accused must also be afforded adequate facilities to prepare, and the charges must be sufficiently detailed and intelligible. Arguably, however, such notice as well as the proceedings themselves should also be intelligible to participants, particularly the parties. Article 6 also expressly provides criminal accused with the right to defend themselves in person or through legal assistance of their own choosing and to free legal representation if required. Whereas the right to state-funded counsel only

---

[196] 'Defending the Guilty' (1983) 32 *Cleveland State Law Review* 175, 177.

[197] The following is based on Zuckerman, above n. 135, Chapter 2; Jackson, above n. 8, 48ff; Reed and Murdoch, above n. 178, Chapter 5.

extends exceptionally to civil litigants when party resources are grossly disparate, they seem to have the same rights as criminal accused to represent themselves or be represented. Certainly, they are entitled to examine (or have examined) witnesses and to obtain the attendance and examination of witness under the same conditions as witnesses against them. Furthermore, the implicit reference to equality in Article 6(1) has given rise to a more general notion of 'equality of arms' regarding the rights of parties to present their case, learn of the opponent's case and respond to it. On the other hand, while the right to confrontation is often regarded as associated with the right to a fair trial in enhancing the dignity of those accused of wrongdoing,[198] this does not extend to a right to face-to-face confrontation nor even a right to cross-examine witnesses, as opposed to challenging evidence more generally.

(3) *The right to a public hearing*

We have already seen that publicity is regarded as an important means of upholding truth-finding guarantees,[199] and guaranteeing other aspects of the right to a fair trial. As Lord Hewart LCJ famously put it, 'justice should not only be done but should manifestly and undoubtedly be seen to be done'.[200] This is recognised by Article 6(1), which specifically requires both a public hearing and a publicly pronounced judgment, though it also allows for limitations on press and public attendance to protect juveniles, privacy, the interests of justice and national security. More recently, as we have seen,[201] many see the public nature of criminal trials in even wider terms, as necessary to play the important role of legitimising the verdict to the accused and collectively reaffirming applicable legal norms.[202]

(4) *The right to a timely and final hearing*

We have also already seen that, in the well-known phrase, 'justice delayed is justice denied', in that delay may impact on the accuracy of outcome, as well as exacerbating all the anxieties and other material consequences of having important decisions hanging over one's head.[203] Consequently,

---

[198] See, for example, Ellison, above n. 30, 71–2; T. Massaro, above n. 182; S. J. Clark, '"Who Do You Think You Are?" The Criminal Trial and Community Character', in A. Duff et al., above n. 61, 91–4.

[199] Section 3.2.3 above.

[200] *R* v. *Sussex Justices, ex p McCarthy* [1924] 1 KB 256, 259.

[201] At n. 188 above.

[202] See Chapter 4, section 3.1.

[203] Chapter 2, section 2.2.

Article 6 requires cases to be heard within a reasonable time. The converse of this principle of timeliness is that of finality. However, while finality is, as we have seen,[204] prioritised in Anglo-American systems, this is generally more a matter of expediency than fairness. One clear exception is the double jeopardy rule preventing someone being charged with the same offence arising out of the same set of facts, but even so it has been limited recently.[205]

(5) *The right to a reasoned decision*
Finally, although not expressly provided for by the ECHR and certainly not by the common law,[206] a right to be given reasons for decisions against one has been implied into Article 6, subject to exceptions such as in the case of juries. This requirement not only makes rights of appeal meaningful (though these in themselves are not required by the Convention), but can also be said to concentrate the tribunal's mind. Indeed, the ECtHR has stated that in principle the right to a reasoned judgment requires courts to examine and address the evidence and arguments presented by the parties.[207] To this extent, it can be said that procedural justice includes a principle of 'procedural rationality' which requires evidence and arguments to be carefully and calmly ascertained, canvassed and weighed, and decisions supported with reasons.[208]

3.4.3 General Fair Treatment Rights
Although legal protections governing the process of information-gathering and pre-trial procedures apply equally in criminal and civil cases, they are far more likely to arise and be strictly applied in the former. Whether or not they lead to the exclusion of unfairly obtained information in addition to criminal and/or delictual liability and remedies for breach of the ECHR[209] will depend on the seriousness and type of consequent harm to the affected individual and the extent to which reliability of information is affected. Given that these issues are discussed in detail in books on evidence law, delict and human rights, here we need simply note the most important forms of unfair treatment, namely:

---

[204] Section 3.2.2.
[205] See the Double Jeopardy (Scotland) Act 2011.
[206] See at nn. 114 and 115, above.
[207] *Quadrelli* v. *Italy* (11 January 2000); *Hiro Bolani* v. *Spain* (1994) A 303-B.
[208] Cf. Summers, above n. 178, 26–7.
[209] For the details, see Reed and Murdoch, above n. 179, Chapters 4, 6 and 8.

- the use or threat of torture and other violations of physical integrity (as contrary to criminal law and Article 3 of the ECHR);
- coercive interrogation techniques such as abusive and oppressive questioning (as contrary to Article 3's prohibition on inhuman or degrading treatment);
- the extraction of harmful admissions through deception (not criminally or delictually actionable, but likely to affect admissibility);
- illegal arrest and illegal and intrusive bodily searches and seizures (delictually actionable and contrary to Articles 5 and 8);
- invasions of privacy through unauthorised surveillance techniques (delictually actionable contrary to Article 8);
- unauthorised searches and seizures of property (delictually actionable and contrary to Article 8 and possibly also Article 1 of Protocol 1 of the ECHR).

3.4.4 Specific Fair Treatment Protection for Criminal Suspects and Accused

The fact that any involvement with the police or other state investigatory agencies involves at least some degree of coercion and restriction on freedom, and hence invasion of the citizen's human rights, has led to a number of legal protections being developed which may result in the exclusion of any evidence emerging in the course of unfair treatment even if such evidence appears totally reliable. Such protections are myriad, complex and highly detailed. They emanate from case law, domestic legislation and the ECHR, are either explicit or more uncertain in flowing from rulings on inadmissible evidence, and involve a variety of different types of protection, a wide range of state activities and special provisions for certain types of offences such as terrorism and serious fraud.[210] Once again, given their extensive treatment elsewhere, it is necessary again only to note the more important examples of the protection of suspects and accused in order to gain an idea of the procedural values they embody. These are:

- conditions, including the content and sufficiency of supporting evidence, justifying surveillance, stop and search (of persons), the search of premises, taking of samples, and arrest, detention and charge;
- requirements for suspects to be informed why they are being searched, arrested or detained and of their procedural rights, including their right to silence, to inform someone of their detention and to a legal advisor;

---

[210] For the details, see Renton and Brown, above n. 70, Chapter 7.

- regulation of the taking of samples, the holding of identification parades and the conditions under which questioning is conducted, relating for instance to adequate breaks, refreshments, heating and ventilation, and the tape-recording of interviews;
- regulation of the maximum periods of arrest and detention, and for the granting or refusal of bail to those charged and awaiting trial.

In addition to their unique fair trial and fair treatment rights, criminal suspects and accused are accorded three other significant forms of 'over-protection' in order to prevent unjust convictions, and arguably also to uphold their dignity and the integrity of criminal proceedings. The first is the presumption that criminal accused are innocent until proved guilty,[211] which is now incorporated into Article 6(3) of the ECHR. This is given specific expression in the common law's placing of the burden of proof on the prosecution and by the courts seeking to limit as far as possible legislation purporting to impose burdens of proof on accused. Thus, unless the burden is legislatively reversed, the state has to do all the running in evidence-gathering and persuasion of the court, allowing the accused, at least in theory, to sit back and simply deny that the burden of proof has been satisfied. Moreover, the heightened 'beyond reasonable doubt' standard of proof means that much more is needed by way of evidence to establish a criminal as opposed to a civil case, whereas uniquely in Scotland – at least currently[212] – convictions require corroborated evidence.

Related to the presumption of innocence are the right to silence and the privilege against self-incrimination,[213] which, while not exactly equivalent conceptually, have similar practical effects. To some extent, their protection overlaps with the independent prohibition on the state using force, threats of force or other oppressive or unfair means to gain confessions, and the common law freedom of suspects to refuse to respond to requests for information from anyone other than the police in relation to certain personal details. However, in addition, the privilege against self-incrimination exempts criminal accused from the normal rules compelling all those thought to possess relevant information to testify in court, whereas the right to silence protects them from the normal probative effect of remaining silent when accused with wrongdoing by prohibiting fact finders from drawing the obvious inference that their silence either in or

---

[211] For a useful analysis, see Roberts and Zuckerman, above n. 3, Chapter 6.
[212] Abolition was recommended by *The Carloway Review – Report and Recommendations* (2011), but has yet to be implemented.
[213] See Roberts and Zuckerman, above n. 3, Chapter 9 for a useful discussion.

outwith court stems from consciousness of guilt and an absence of any exculpatory reasons.

In order to weigh further the scales against convictions, certain limitations and unique obligations are placed on the prosecution, creating a relation of asymmetry vis-à-vis the accused. Thus professional ethics norms give greater leeway to defence lawyers in acting as an accused's champion, while also expecting prosecution lawyers to act as 'ministers of justice' with a duty to truth rather than winning cases.[214] Moreover, the prosecution is subject to more onerous requirements of disclosure relating to documents and witnesses than the defence.[215] Perhaps reflecting the fact that so many miscarriages of justice involve the suppression of inculpatory evidence,[216] the prosecution is expected to disclose to the court and, in solemn cases prior to trial, to the defence (even without a request) any information in their possession which would tend to exculpate the accused or is likely to be of material assistance in the preparation or presentation of their defence, such as a witness' previous convictions.[217] Indeed, the authorities must provide criminal accused with timeous access to their police case files or other information which might assist in the preparation of their defence.[218] Finally, there a number of other structural asymmetries in the position of prosecution and accused, such as the very limited right of the prosecution to appeal against an acquittal.[219]

4 Modifications to the Classical Anglo-American Procedural Model

4.1 Two Classical Models?

Having described the classical Anglo-American procedural model and compared it with its Continental alter ego, we need to ascertain to what extent it currently holds sway in Scotland. First, however, it might be useful to highlight explicitly what might by now be apparent, namely that the classical model is far more prevalent in civil as opposed to criminal proceedings. Thus the specific procedural protections afforded to suspects and

---

[214] See, for example, Moody and Tombs, above n. 23, 28–9; J. Fionda, *Public Prosecutors and Discretion: A Comparative Study* (1995), 66.

[215] Though for both more so in solemn as compared with summary procedures: Sheehan and Dickson, above n. 22, 115, 123–7, 155–6, 165–6 respectively.

[216] Roberts and Zuckerman, above n. 3, 55.

[217] Renton and Brown, above n. 70, para. 13-12.3.

[218] See, for example, *Haase* v. *Germany*, Application No. 7412/76, 11 DR 108; *Dowsett* v. *United Kingdom*, Application No. 39482/98, (2004) 38 EHRR 41.

[219] Only in summary cases and only on a point of law.

accused give the adversarial nature of criminal proceedings a very different shape. In civil cases, as long as formal equality between the parties is maintained, the outcome is accepted even though the resultant 'truth' that emerges may owe much to disparities in power and resources. In criminal cases, by contrast, the law places obstacles in the way of convictions in a rough-and-ready attempt to equalise the inherent disparity in power and resources between state and accused. Moreover, while fact accuracy remains important, the law is more concerned about ensuring that the innocent go free rather than that the guilty are punished. While civil cases constitute contests between disputants, if criminal proceedings resemble a contest at all, they are more in the nature of a handicap horse race than a football match. In fact, however, they are better described as a 'state-sponsored examination of an accused's alleged criminal wrongdoing'.[220]

At the same time, criminal proceedings remain adversarial to the extent that the adjudicator remains passive, and fact investigation and presentation remain largely in the hands of prosecution and defence. Nevertheless, so fundamental is the asymmetrical nature of the criminal 'contest' that it makes sense to speak of two Anglo-American models – one criminal and the other civil – though both are largely adversarial and both involve a co-ordinate model of judicial authority.

4.2 Recent Developments

We have already seen that there are a number of significant departures from the two classical Anglo-American models which, when combined with parallel developments on the Continent, reveal a narrowing of differences between the families of legal systems, especially as regards the already relatively similar civil proceedings.[221] While there remain – and for the foreseeable future are likely to remain – significant differences in the structure of fact finding in the two criminal models, many aspects of the two classical criminal models are being altered to take on features of their alter ego.[222] Nevertheless, it remains to be seen whether the two models will converge towards each other or whether, as some predict, there

---

[220] Roberts and Zuckerman, above n. 3, 9.
[221] See Damaška, above n. 2, Chapter 5, 150; K. D. Kerameus, 'A Civilian Lawyer Looks at Common Law Procedure' (1986) 47 *Louisiana Law Review* 493.
[222] See, for example, Langer, above n. 8, 27–8; Jörg, Field and Brant, above n. 39; C. M. Bradley, 'The Convergence of the Continental and the Common Law Model of Criminal Procedure' (1996) 7 *Criminal Law Forum* 471. For examples, see C. Bradley, *Criminal Procedures: A Worldwide Study* (2nd edn, 2007), esp. xxiff, where he argues that the movement has been much more from the Anglo-American to the Continental classical model than vice versa.

will emerge a new 'third way' influenced by ECtHR case law,[223] a common drive for 'economy and expedition',[224] and developing international procedural norms.[225]

In the meantime, there are clearly important developments in both classic Anglo-American models. One is the already noted decline in the use of the jury, though rumours of its death in the 1980s now seem to have been greatly exaggerated as regards criminal cases. In civil cases, by contrast, its virtual abandonment[226] has contributed to the substantial reduction of exclusionary rules given that many were motivated by the perceived need to protect juries from unreliable and misleading evidence, whereas any remaining exceptions, such as those excluding improperly obtained evidence and character evidence, are rarely applied. However, although many categorical rules have been transformed into discretionary powers to decide on admissibility and other forms of evidential regulation, most traditional regulation of criminal evidence remains.

The predominance of 'bench trials' has another consequence. Thus research shows that judges who are solely responsible for factual accuracy and freed from worrying about influencing the jury, may be tempted to intervene more actively in the trial and pursue their own lines of inquiry.[227] Proceedings remain adversarial, but are transformed from a no-holds-barred forensic battle between the parties into a calmer, though still intense, contest that includes direct engagement with the judge. This illustrates that, although analytically distinct, in practice the contest and co-ordinate authority dimensions of Anglo-American procedure are intimately entwined so that like a cloth made up of cross-cutting contest and co-ordinate authority threads, a pull on one thread (adjudication by lay jurors) pulls out of line a connected thread (the passive adjudicator).

In addition to the gradual decline of the jury, there are three much more recent developments of significance for the classical Anglo-American model. One which is confined to criminal proceedings has been the rise – or, perhaps more accurately, recent resurgence – of what Peter Duff[228] calls penal populism, in terms of which politicians and the general population have

---

[223] See, for example, Jackson, above n. 8; Jörg, Field and Brants. above n. 39; and for a summary of the impact of the ECHR on Scottish civil procedure: Hennessy, above n. 2, Chapter 22.

[224] McEwan, above n. 34, esp. at 519.

[225] J. Jackson and Summers, above n. 175.

[226] See at n. 91 above.

[227] Cited in Doran, J. Jackson and Seigel, above n. 16, 39–40. See in more detail, J. Jackson and Doran, above n. 15.

[228] 'Scottish Criminal Law Adrift?', in P. Duff and P. Ferguson (eds), *Current Developments in Scottish Criminal Evidence Law* (2017), 227–34.

supported specific measures that disrupt the balance between protecting civil liberties and the public interest in being protected from crime, but without necessarily conflicting with ECHR jurisprudence. Most notable has been the abolition of the double jeopardy rule, but also relevant is the suggested abolition of the corroboration requirement.[229]

Another development is confined to civil cases in Scotland, though more widely used in England and Wales.[230] Whether characterised as part of a populist trend or as a legitimate response to threats to national security, the relatively recent rise of secret trials strikes directly at the heart of many cherished Anglo-American procedural values. Initially confined to immigration cases, then extended to cases involving suspected terrorists, they now extend to all types of civil litigation in the UK when disclosure of sensitive material might be 'damaging to the interests of national security'.[231] Not only does this negate the benefits of publicity, but the appointment of special advocates to represent those excluded from closed hearings also negates both the right to a representative of one's choice and to participating in decisions affecting one's interests.[232]

Finally, a far more widespread and significant development has altered many features of classical Anglo-American procedure in both criminal and civil cases and brought it closer to the Continental model than it has been in centuries.[233] Motivated by a 'managerialist ideology'[234] that emphasises efficiency, from the 1960s US judges began to take responsibility for directing the course of civil litigation through a series of pre-trial conferences designed to reduce costs and delay through setting and enforcing timetables, and by encouraging early settlements.[235] This practice then spread throughout the Anglo-American world, though, despite

---

[229] By *The Carloway Review – Report and Recommendations* (2011), but not yet acted upon.

[230] See J. Jackson, 'The Role of Special Advocates: Advocacy, Due Process and the Adversarial Tradition' (2016) 20 *International Journal of Evidence and Proof* 343.

[231] S. 6 of the Justice and Security Act 2013.

[232] Cf., however, *Secretary of State for the Home Department* v. *AF* [2010] 2 AC 269, where it was held that affected persons had to be given sufficient information about the allegations against them to enable them to give effective instructions to mount a defence.

[233] C. H. van Rhee, 'The Development of Civil Procedural Law in Twentieth Century Europe: From Party Autonomy to Judicial Case Management and Efficiency', in van Rhee, above n. 25, 11.

[234] P. Duff, 'Changing Concepts of the Scottish Criminal Trial: The Duty to Agree Uncontroversial Evidence', in A. Duff et al., above n. 112, esp. 29; see more generally, McEwan, above n. 34; P. Duff, above n. 228, 234–41.

[235] See, for example, essays by Zuckerman, Marcuse and Michalik in Zuckerman, above n. 4. Case management has a much longer history in Europe dating from the late nineteenth century: see van Rhee, above n. 25, passim.

recommendations for its more widespread use,[236] currently remains relatively limited in Scotland.[237]

Thus, in Court of Session personal injury litigation, 'case flow management' involves setting timescales for various procedural steps to be taken, with the court having power to call parties to account for failure to comply. More significantly, parties are obliged to meet a few weeks before trial to discuss settlement, the quantification of the claim and to try to reach agreement on the facts in order to narrow down the issues for proof and reduce the number of witnesses at proof. In all commercial actions, judges have extensive case management powers designed to encourage them to take innovative approaches to case management and control of evidence. For instance, they can order production of documents and witness details, and witness statements and/or affidavits to be lodged in connection with any of the issues, and can fix evidential hearings on distinct parts of the case. The rules of ordinary actions in the Court of Session and the sheriff court do not provide such explicit powers, although there are provisions which, if used imaginatively, would allow judges to manage cases and influence the nature and extent of any climactic hearing. Proposed reforms are intended to increase these case management powers,[238] but so far this has been confined to the Simple Procedure rules,[239] which apply to lower-value claims in the sheriff court (non-injury claims under £5,000) and replace existing Small Claims procedure. Sheriffs are required to be interventionist, with a priority to do whatever needs to be done to resolve the dispute, including actively encouraging settlement and directing the parties as to what is expected from them. In particular, any trial can be conducted by sheriffs in whatever way they consider appropriate, parties need not be put on oath and there are no rules of evidence.

Case management is more widespread in criminal cases, applying in both summary and solemn proceedings, though it is more narrowly confined, largely to ensuring that a trial is still necessary and that the parties are prepared, with the aim of reducing the number of cancelled, adjourned and overly lengthy trials.[240] However, the recently introduced obligation to

---

[236] See, for example, Parratt, above n. 25, and *The Development and Use of Written Pleadings in Scots Civil Procedure*, (2006), Chapter 5.

[237] For the details, see Hennessy, n. 2, Chapters 6, 8 and 11.

[238] *Report of the Scottish Civil Courts Review* (The Gill Review), available at http://www.scotcourts. gov.uk/docs/default-source/civil-courts-reform/report-of-the-scottish-civil-courts-review-vol-1-chapt-1---9.pdf?sfvrsn=4 (last accessed 14 March 2018), Chapter 5.

[239] Act of Sederunt (Sheriff Court Rules Amendment) (Miscellaneous) 2017. For a discussion, see C. Hennessy, 'Sheriff Court', in the *Scottish Lawyer's Factbook* Section (2017).

[240] P. Duff, above n. 228, 236–46. Renton and Brown, above n. 3, Chapters 17 and 20.

ensure that parties agree and reduce to writing uncontroversial evidence is thought likely to require 'rigorous' questioning of the parties, which in turn leads to a 'silent move'[241] from traditional judicial passivity and, along with the pre-trial lodging of documents, the principle of orality and the concentrated trial. If, as occurs in civil cases,[242] the same judge presides at trial, case management will also undermine the claim that Anglo-American proceedings prevent the rush to judgment before all evidence is presented.[243] Moreover, the benefits of publicity will be undermined where proceedings involve written witness statements.[244] Finally, whereas party autonomy is arguably not overly compromised by the increased judicial activism required by case management,[245] it is seriously affected by the judicial power in solemn proceedings to override one party's insistence on leading allegedly uncontroversial evidence orally at trial. Indeed, in general, the duty to agree uncontroversial evidence can be said to weaken the privilege against self-incrimination, especially if, as evidence discussed in the next chapter suggests,[246] some defence lawyers display insufficient zeal in representing their clients.

Nevertheless, despite its problematic impact on the classical procedural models, case management is here to stay and likely to grow – as, in criminal cases, is the increased use of plea bargaining and the diversion of cases from prosecution through, for example, fixed penalty offences and the consequent undermining of the fact-finding function of legal proceedings.[247] A potential development equally disruptive of the classical procedural model is the suggested use of pre-recorded witness statements.[248] However, while also motivated by managerialist considerations and problematic in terms of the ability to cross-examine witnesses, such statements are likely to at least reduce the negative impact of delay on witness memory and availability.

[241] Scottish Law Commission, *Responses to 1993 Review of Criminal Evidence and Criminal Procedure (and) Programming of Business in the Sheriffs Courts* (1993), para. 8. See also R. L. Marcus, 'Déjà Vu All Over Again? An American Reaction to the Woolf Report', in Zuckerman and Cranston, above n. 4, 236.
[242] Hennessy, above n. 2, 89, 148.
[243] Marcus, above n. 241, 239–40. See J. Resnik, 'Managerial Judges' (1982) 96 *Harvard Law Review* 374, for the classic critique of case management.
[244] Zuckerman, above n. 135, 94; C. Hehn, 'The Woolf Report: Against the Public Interest', in Zuckerman and Cranston, above n. 4, 150–1.
[245] Gane, above n. 6, 65; Parratt, above n. 25, 181; but cf. N. Morrison, *The Cullen Report* (1996), *Scots Law Times* 93, 96–7.
[246] Section 2.4.2.
[247] As regards the Scottish position, see P. Duff, above n. 228, 235–6.
[248] See P. Duff, ibid., 244–6.

Other pressures on the classical Anglo-American models stem from arguably more laudable objectives. One possible influence is the ECtHR's 'holistic' approach to evidence admissibility.[249] Instead of looking at each item of allegedly inadmissible evidence separately, it considers whether apart from the evidence wrongly admitted there is sufficient evidence to justify the decision. As domestic courts have to apply this test when evidence is objected to rather than retrospectively, it is likely to require them to take a 'more proactive and dominant role'.[250]

A final source of increased judicial activism derives from the commendable desire to improve the treatment of witnesses and reverse the marginalisation of victims in the criminal justice system, which traditionally has regarded them simply as passive sources of information rather than interested participants. Thus, instead of 'stealing'[251] disputes from victims, some jurisdictions have created various forms of 'restorative justice' alternatives to standard criminal proceedings that aim to reconcile victims and offenders, through mediation and undoing the harm caused, and to reintegrate offenders into society. Some have also introduced programmes providing for victims to be supported in court, informed of the progress of proceedings and the reasons for decisions not to proceed further, given the opportunity to meet with perpetrators and even to contribute to discretionary decisions.[252] Although Scotland lags behind other Anglo-American jurisdictions in this regard, it has introduced measures designed to protect children and adult witnesses whose evidence is at serious risk of being affected by reason of 'mental disorder' or 'fear and distress in connection with giving evidence at the trial'.[253] Not only do these provisions enhance judicial activism through their discretionary nature, but the pre-trial video-recording of evidence and the use of written out-of-court statements conflict with the 'day in court' idea, whereas reliance on written statements conflicts with the principle of orality, and the use of pre-trial video-recording, live television links and physical screens in

---

[249] J. Jackson, above n. 8, 755–6; A. Ashworth, 'The Human Rights Act 1998: Part 2: Article 6 and the Fairness of Trials' (1999) *Criminal Law Review* 261, 272.

[250] J. Jackson, ibid., 756.

[251] N. Christie, 'Conflicts as Property' (1997) 17 *British Journal of Criminology* 1.

[252] M. Hildebrandt, 'Trial and "Fair Trial": From Peer to Subject to Citizen', in A. Duff et al., above n. 61; J. Shapland, 'Victims and the Criminal Process: A Public Service Ethos for Criminal Justice', in Doran and J. Jackson, above n. 78; L. Ellison, 'Witness Preparation and the Prosecution of Rape' (2007) 27 *Legal Studies* 171. For general evaluations of restorative justice, see, for example, A. Duff et al., above n. 11, 290ff; D. O'Mahoney and J. Doak, *Reimagining Restorative Justice: Agency and Accountability in the Criminal Justice Process* (2017).

[253] S. 271(1) of the Vulnerable Witnesses (Scotland) Act 2004 and see generally, Raitt, above n. 22, 35–45.

court removes the face-to-face confrontation aspect of the principle of immediacy. On the other hand, given that, in line with ECHR principles, Scots law retains the accused's right to cross-examine and the courts can limit protective measures in the interest of a fair trial or justice more generally, these measures do not seem to detract from fact-finding accuracy or procedural fairness in any meaningful way.[254]

We thus see considerable modification of the classical civil and criminal procedural models of fact finding. Moreover, it is not easy to predict future directions. Whereas many developments enhance the adjudicator's role and diminish that of the parties, and some do so in order to enhance the civil liberties of suspects and accused or victims and other witnesses, those associated with managerialism are antithetical to civil liberties and enhance the power of managers and not necessarily adjudicators, while retaining the basic contest nature of proceedings.[255] Very different modifications to the classical models are also possible as other new developments take hold.[256] For example, the increasing use of scientific and other forms of evidence too technical for non-expert adjudicators to understand creates pressure for the increased use of written reports, as already occurs extensively in England and Wales,[257] and, as we shall see in Chapter Five, delegation of the resolution of certain issues to specialist tribunals. Of equal potential significance is the ever-increasing tendency of social phenomena such as ecological disasters to have wide-ranging impacts giving rise to collective lawsuits and potential conflicts between litigants, which then require judicial supervision. Finally, the classical bipartisan model of litigation is also challenged by the temptation of fact finders to rely on evidence which emanates not from the parties, but from specialist state agencies who have investigated relevant complex factual scenarios such as anti-competitive market behaviour.

4.3 Alternatives to the Classic Models

4.3.1 The Informal Fact-finding Landscape

However, not only is the likelihood of these possible changes to the classical procedural models very uncertain, but they are dwarfed in importance

---

[254] Certainly, the ECtHR has accepted that protection of (especially vulnerable) witnesses is in principle compatible with Article 6: J. Jackson, above n. 8, 760–1; Ellison, above n. 30, Chapter 4.

[255] See McEwan, above n. 34.

[256] See Damaška, above n. 1, 139–40, ch. 6; J. Jackson, above n. 129, 144–5; T. Weigend, "Why Have a Trial When You Can Have a Bargain?" in A. Duff et al., above n. 61, 210–11.

[257] Whereas s.30 of the Criminal Justice Act 1988 merely allows written reports to be adduced instead of oral evidence, r.35.5 (i) of the Civil Practice Rules requires written reports unless otherwise authorised. In Scotland, the principle of orality still holds sway.

by the fact that most fact finding takes place in a procedural context which has never reflected these models. As emphasised in Chapter One,[258] most legal decisions are taken by administrative officials deciding on whether to grant state benefits like immigration status, welfare assistance or planning permission, or to impose fiscal or other burdens on citizens. Such decisions may be purely 'adjudicative' in involving only an application of law to determined facts, or 'polycentric'[259] in also involving consideration of policy factors, such as whether a business takeover is in the public interest, and the prediction of future events, such as whether bail applicants will abscond.[260] In some cases, such as in planning, those charged with policy decisions may conduct an inquiry to inform their decision, which may involve a public hearing.[261] Judicial inquiries play a rather different role. Although the investigation of sudden unnatural deaths by Procurators Fiscal[262] will seek to establish the facts of some matter of public importance, and might also aim at conveying lessons learnt from such events and holding state bodies to account, in formal terms they have no concrete outcome.

Other fora which were intended to provide for more informal fact finding are the myriad tribunals established to prevent the formal courts being swamped, make legal proceedings more accessible to citizens in terms of cost, comprehensibility and ease of use, and enable adjudication by specialists.[263] Accordingly, certain private disputes such as those involving employment and some, but not all, appeals from primary decision-making by administrative agencies have been allocated to tribunals (and their functional equivalents).[264] For similar reasons, as already noted in relation to the new Simple Procedure Rules, private disputes involving relatively small amounts of money are dealt with in the lower courts by procedures designed, like those in tribunals, to be far less formal than standard legal

---

[258] See esp. section 2.3.

[259] Cf. L. L. Fuller, 'The Forms and Limits of Adjudication' (1978) 92 *Harvard Law Review* 353, 395ff.

[260] Similar decisions may be involved in what the Americans call public interest litigation involving complex issues of public policy and attempts to adjust future behaviour rather than compensate for past wrongs (see, for example, A. Chayes, 'The Role of the Judge in Public Law Litigation' (1976) 89 *Harvard Law Review* 1281) but such litigation is less common in the UK.

[261] On all forms of inquiry, see C. Harlow and R. Rawlings, *Law and Administration* (4th edn, 2009), Chapter 13.

[262] See, for example, Sheehan and Dickson, above n. 22, 54.

[263] See, for example, R. Sainsbury and H. Genn, 'Accces to Justice: Lessons from Tribunals', in Zuckerman and Cranston, above n. 4; Harlow and Rawlings, ibid., Chapter 11.

[264] Thus, while not designated as such and hence not joining the sixty or so tribunals under the jurisdiction of the Tribunals Council, bodies such as the Crofters Commission act like tribunals: cf. Sainsbury and Genn, ibid., 413. See also Chapter 1 at nn. 73 and 75 regarding the amalgamation of both UK-wide and Scottish tribunals.

procedure.[265] Similar in terms of procedure, but historically and functionally distinct, are certain bodies like the Children's Panel which deal with the care and protection of children as well as child offending,[266] the Parole Board, which deals with issues relating to the early release of prisoners,[267] and more recently the Scottish Criminal Cases Review Commission, which decides whether convictions should be re-opened because of alleged miscarriages of justice.[268]

To add to the complexity of procedural variation are various forms of what is commonly called Alternative Dispute Resolution (henceforth, ADR),[269] though, because most disputants settle disputes outwith litigation,[270] it is now sometimes termed Appropriate or Primary Dispute Resolution.[271] In fact, however, settlement is usually achieved by inter-party negotiation without any third-party intervention. Consequently, it is not normally regarded as a form of ADR, but as the combined and continuous process of 'litigoation' – defined as 'the strategic pursuit of a settlement through mobilising the court process'[272] – with the latter held in reserve if negotiation fails.

Nevertheless, negotiation underlies all consensual forms of ADR where resolutions are only binding once agreed and shares many of its alleged benefits. Thus, compared to litigation, especially of an adversarial nature, ADR involves reduced costs, greater speed, and the avoidance of uncertainty as to adjudicative outcome. Accordingly, the judicial encouragement of settlement is already well established in Employment Tribunals,[273] has been extended from Small Claims proceedings to all Simple Procedure

---

[265] See at n. 239 above and cf. Hennessy, above n. 2, Chapter 12; D. Kelbie, *Small Claims Procedure in the Sheriff Court* (1994), esp. 70–1, 90–1 for the erstwhile small claims procedure.

[266] See K. M. Norrie, *Children's Hearings in Scotland* (3rd edn, 2013).

[267] See J. Jackson, 'Evidence and Proof in Parole Hearings: Meeting a Triangulation of Interests' (2007) *Criminal Law Review* 417.

[268] See, for example, Sheehan and Dickson, above n. 22, 355–6.

[269] Restorative justice schemes have been excluded because technically criminal proceedings do not involve disputing parties and no fact finding is involved given that guilt has first to be acknowledged or judicially determined. Moreover, restorative justice schemes are rare in Scotland but, where established, resemble those used in mediation and hence fit model 4 below: R. E. Mackay, 'Alternative Dispute Resolution and Scottish Criminal Justice', in S. R. Moody and R. E. Mackay, *Green's Guide to Alternative Dispute Resolution in Scotland* (1995).

[270] For estimates of numbers, see Chapter 1, at nn. 62 and 63.

[271] The following discussion draws on Moody and Mackay, above n. 269; K. Mackie et al., *The ADR Practice Guide. Commercial Dispute Resolution* (3rd edn, 2007), Chapters 1–3; K. Mackie (ed.), *A Handbook of Dispute Resolution: ADR in Action* (1991), esp. Chapter 1 and Part I; H. Brown and A. Marriott, *ADR Principles and Practices* (3rd edn, 2012), esp. Chapters 1–7, 16.

[272] M. Galanter, 'Worlds of Deals: Using Negotiation to Teach About Legal Process' (1984) 34 *Journal of Legal Education* 268, 268. For empirical supporting evidence, see, for example, H. Genn, *Hard Bargaining: Out of Court Settlement* (1987).

[273] See, for example, G. Pitt, *Employment Law* (9th edn, 2014), 5–8.

claims[274] and has been recommended by the Gill Review for extension to all Scottish courts.[275] In addition, the consensual and co-operative nature of ADR means that parties have more control over outcomes, and that procedures are far more likely to foster interpersonal respect and civility than adversarial litigation. This, and the fact that outcomes are not limited to all-or-nothing decisions based upon applying technical legal rules to facts nor are remedies confined to damages and interdicts, means that ADR is more likely to accommodate both parties' interests and be accepted by them, thus promoting reconciliation and more amicable future relationships. Finally, various types of ADR may be suitable to deal with disputes such as those between neighbours which rarely reach court.

On the other hand, ADR sceptics[276] argue that the absence of formal legal protection works to the detriment of parties with weaker bargaining power, especially those in close personal relationships, who may be coerced into agreeing settlements because of power imbalances. ADR is also said to rob courts of the opportunity to develop the law, especially in ways which challenge an unjust status quo. Consequently it is important to see litigation as one of a range of 'appropriate dispute resolution' mechanisms alongside those which fall under the ADR rubric, even though legal policy-makers are increasingly seeking ways to encourage the use of ADR,[277] and even to annexe ADR to court procedures.[278]

Also increasing is the variety of ADR mechanisms and the ways in which they are being combined.[279] The form which most resembles court proceedings is arbitration. Like all forms of ADR, parties can choose any procedure they wish, but usually they present their cases adversarially in private before a neutral arbiter who makes a binding decision (subject to limited rights of appeal). Similar in nature is a form of fast-track arbitration known as 'contractual adjudication', which is largely confined to construction disputes and which gives parties the option to reject the decision. Also adjudicative in form, but not function, are various types of 'evaluative ADR', popular in the

---

[274] See at n. 239 above.

[275] Above n. 238, Chapter 5. However, the Courts Reform (Scotland) Act 2014 only empowers rather than requires the different courts to adopt procedures to encourage settlement.

[276] Most notably, O. Fiss, 'Against Settlement' (1984) 93 *Yale Law Journal* 1073. For a useful summary of the respective merits and demerits of formal versus informal proceedings, see T. F. Marshall, 'Neighbour Disputes: Community Mediation Schemes as an Alternative to Litigation', in Mackie, above n. 271.

[277] Mackie et al., above n. 271, Chapters 4–6; Brown and Marriott, above n. 271, Chapter 3.

[278] Cf. Brown and Marriott, ibid., Chapter 5; and for a critique, S. Roberts, 'Alternative Dispute Resolution and Civil Justice: An Unresolved Relationship' (1993) 56 *Modern Law Review* 452.

[279] For example, 'med-arb' involves mediation switching to arbitration to resolve unsettled issues, and 'arb-med' involves the results of initial arbitration being kept secret unless mediation fails.

US though beginning to be used in the UK, which model court proceedings in order to provide disputing parties with an idea of whether and how they should settle cases. For example, 'mini-trials' or 'executive tribunals' involve lawyers arguing each party's case before the parties themselves sitting with a neutral adviser as the tribunal. Other forms of evaluative ADR involve an investigation and opinion by a neutral expert. Then again, a common form of dealing with complaints is for the state, regulatory bodies or even industries themselves to establish schemes whereby Ombudsmen or other independent bodies or officers investigate and rule on complaints which bind the parties or at least the subject of the complaint.[280]

However, the most used form of ADR is mediation – sometimes, but decreasingly, called conciliation – which involves a neutral third party attempting to facilitate the reaching of consensus ('facilitative' mediation) and also making suggestions as to how consensus might be reached or even how the issues should be resolved ('evaluative' or 'directive' mediation). Although both the governing procedure and final outcome are wholly dependent on agreement, controversially some jurisdictions require parties to certain types of disputes to attempt mediation. Moreover, because the emphasis is on reconciling the parties rather than simply ending the dispute, discussion can range beyond alleged past wrongs to future relationships and arrangements. Consequently, as long as both parties agree on how to move forward, there is no need to determine, even by agreement, the exact nature of the facts giving rise to the dispute. Indeed, it is arguable that rigorously probing for factual accuracy may distract attention away from and hence impede the consensual and peaceful resolution of disputes, whereas the '[p]ublic exposure of true facts can in some situations revive a dispute that was losing steam'.[281] Nevertheless, given that their views of the facts may still play an important role in affecting the parties' willingness to settle their dispute, with serious disagreements as to past events or future situations likely to prevent a resolution,[282] it seems appropriate to include 'co-operative' as well as 'adjudicative' forms of ADR in a discussion of the procedural context of evidence and proof.

4.3.2 Informal Fact-finding Procedural Models
The above sketch of informal fact finding reveals a plethora of different proceedings, with almost as many procedural structures as there are types of

---

[280] See, for example, Harlow and Rawlings, above n. 261, 480–3.
[281] Damaška, above n. 18, 123.
[282] For evidence of the central role facts may play in negotiations, see S. Wheeler, *Reservation of Title Clauses: Impact and Implications* (1991), esp. 36, 198.

informal fact finding. Indeed, even within each type, proceedings will differ markedly between, for instance, different tribunals, Ombudsmen schemes and types of ADR, and – given the freedom of presiding officers and ADR parties to vary procedure as deemed appropriate – even within each individual dispute or other form of fact finding. Nevertheless, despite this almost limitless variation, the various forms of informal fact finding can be placed on a continuum ranging between four ideal-type procedural models, though it has to be noted that some procedures straddle two categories rather than fitting neatly into one or other.[283] Moreover, proceedings in some fora may follow one model in theory but another in practice. For instance, there is a tendency for many adjudicative fora to be far more formal and adversarial than envisaged by their enabling legislation.[284] Given also that many types of informal proceedings can be conducted in the manner regarded as most suited to the dispute, much may also depend on the approach of presiding adjudicators and in particular whether they adopt an enabling approach which, while not fully inquisitorial, goes beyond adversarial neutrality in seeking to compensate for the disadvantages faced by an unrepresented party. Finally, other proceedings like those before parole boards show signs of migrating from one model to another because of factors like the impact of the ECHR.[285]

(1) *The Modified Anglo-American Model*

A fair amount of informal fact finding adopts the classical Anglo-American civil procedure model in terms of party control, judicial passivity and a single hearing based on oral testimony, examination and cross-examination, as well as in some cases an element of lay adjudication.[286] Examples include the usual practice in arbitration, except that in order to expedite proceedings and ensure confidentiality it is conducted in private and

---

[283] For example, inquiries and adjudication straddle the second and third models, given that the former involve an inquest rather than a contest, but also may be held in public and involve a right to cross-examine witnesses and other adversarial procedures, whereas 'adjudication' involves a decision by a neutral party based purely on paper representations by the disputing parties and thus reflects the adversarial but not oral nature of Anglo-American proceedings.

[284] See, for example, Kelbie, above n. 265, 69–70; Gill Review, above n. 238, para. 126; J. G. Logie and P. Q. Watchman, 'Social Security Appeal Tribunals: An Excursus on Evidential Issues' (1989) 8 *Civil Justice Quarterly* 109, esp. 126; H. Genn, 'Tribunals and Informal Justice' (1993) 56 *Modern Law Review* 393, 422; and esp. H. Genn and Y. Genn, *The Effectiveness of Representation at Tribunals. Report to the Lord Chancellor* (1989). A similar 'judicialisation' of ADR has also been detected, at least in the US (cf. Mackie et al., above n. 271, 8 regarding arbitration): C. Menkel-Meadow, 'Pursuing Settlement in an Adversary Culture – A Tale of Innovation Co-opted or "The Law of ADR"' (1991) 19 *Florida State University Law Review* 1.

[285] See J. Jackson, above n. 267 regarding a move from model 3 to 2 discussed below.

[286] See Brown and Marriott, above n. 271, 53–4.

without evidence rules.[287] At least where both parties are represented, proceedings in tribunals like Employment Tribunals and those hearing immigration appeals also resemble the classical Anglo-American model, except as regards the application of evidential rules, and the fact that in some cases proceedings may be postponed for the hearing of further evidence.

(2) *The Modified Continental Model*

Where, however, one party is not represented, these tribunals and courts hearing Simple Procedure claims, along with other tribunals such as those hearing appeals involving social security benefits (at least in practice)[288] and proceedings in 'mini-trials', are meant to be much more similar to Continental civil procedure in involving 'quasi-inquisitorial process within the stylised rules of an adversary game'.[289] Thus they mix orality, adherence to procedural justice requirements and party control with minimal adherence to evidence rules and a fair degree of judicial activism in questioning witnesses and developing independent lines of inquiry. Adjudicators may also adopt a more episodic approach to fact finding and actively seek to ensure that parties engage in settlement negotiations. On the other hand, except where necessary, for instance, to protect children, proceedings are in public, usually oral,[290] and usually involve cross-examination by the parties as well as questions from the adjudicator.

(3) *The Pure Continental Model*

Much more like the archetypically inquisitorial criminal proceedings of Continental Europe are the procedures followed by Ombudsmen, the Children's Panel, the Scottish Criminal Cases Review Commission, forms of evaluative ADR, individual state officials and administrative bodies making adjudicative and discretionary decisions, and some tribunals such as those hearing social security appeals. Here decisions are usually made in private,[291] the rules of natural justice apply in attenuated form and evidence rules not at all. Fact finding follows the form of an investigation, usually by the same person or body which makes the final decision[292] and

---

[287] For details of the applicability of evidence rules in all forms of informal fact finding, see Chapter 1, section 2.2.

[288] See Genn and Genn, above n. 284, 158ff – in theory they are meant to be more inquisitorial.

[289] I. Ramsay, 'Small Claims Courts in Canada: A Socio-Legal Appraisal', in C. J. Whelan (ed.), *Small Claims Courts: A Comparative Study* (1990), 33.

[290] But see on tribunals: Richardson and Genn, above n. 132.

[291] Though the press may attend Children's Hearings.

[292] Again, Children's Hearings are an exception, making them more like most Continental criminal proceedings where different judges investigate and adjudicate.

often only on the basis of written submissions. Even when there is a hearing, the investigator also questions those with relevant information, though they might also hear oral submissions from interested parties. Finally, in the case of administrative decision-making, there is substantial hierarchical control in the form of a *de novo* appeal to a tribunal and perhaps also an interim internal review.

(4) *The Consensual Dispute Resolution Model*

Fitting into neither of the classical Anglo-American or Continental models are the sui generis procedures used in co-operative forms of ADR. For example, while parties can agree any form of procedure most likely to ensure resolution of their dispute, mediation typically involves alternating between, first, private meetings between mediator and each party, and then mediated meetings involving both parties. Such meetings can be confined to one occasion or broken up into a number of sessions, and may be preceded by submission of at times extensive documentation. Sometimes legal representatives are excluded and sometimes meetings can be confined to representatives. No rules of procedural justice, let alone of evidence, formally apply, though arbiter bias and the failure to give each party an equal opportunity to present their case is likely to prevent a settlement emerging, whereas making ADR mandatory and binding may breach Article 6 by removing the possibility of parties going to the courts for a formal determination subject to the principles of procedural justice.[293]

5 Conclusion

This overview of the procedural context has taken us from the paradigmatic but statistically rare form of formal fact finding in courts to the far more common but less formal fact finding in court-substitutes and even less formal fact finding by inquiries and administrative agencies, and finally to ADR and administrative processes where outcomes are not solely dependent on the application of law to determined facts. We have also seen that the classical Anglo-American procedural model is generally retained in civil proceedings, albeit with an ever-increasing diminution of evidential rules and party autonomy, largely caused, respectively, by the demise of lay adjudication and the advent of the judge's more active role under case management. By contrast, the classical model has long been significantly

---

[293] See Mackie et al., above n. 271, Chapter 10.

altered in criminal cases to compensate for the power imbalances between state and accused and the harsh consequences of unjustified criminal convictions, and accordingly to provide suspects, accused and more recently victims and witnesses with additional procedural rights both pre-trial and at trial. However, when we move from proceedings in and leading up to the formal courts, fact finding ranges along a continuum from those resembling the classical civil model relatively closely, on the one hand, to those that are sui generis in involving the resolution of legal issues through co-operation between the parties rather than adjudication, where fact finding does not play a central role.

But whatever the centrality of fact finding to the particular type of legal proceedings, it can be seen that different procedural models give rise to different methods of seeking truth, most notably those utilised by the Anglo-American and Continental classical models. It thus becomes necessary to compare these different methodologies to ascertain which is more effective in actual practice. However, we have also seen that factual truth and expletive justice no longer appear to be regarded by everyone and in all legal fora as the only, let alone the overriding, objective of legal fact finding even in formal legal proceedings. Instead, the fact positivist view of evidence and proof has to be qualified by the recognition not only of occasional pragmatic considerations, but also far-reaching requirements of procedural justice, which especially in criminal cases can obstruct the search for truth. Indeed, we have seen that some legal scholars regard procedural justice as serving goals other than truth, such as the dignity of participants in the legal process, the need to provide a civilised forum for dispute resolution or the communication of society's normative behavioural standards. Such views clearly flow from a liberal view of law and the legal process and hence to this extent are compatible with orthodox evidence scholarship. But, as we have still to explore, while fact realists have recognised this rather large modification to fact positivism,[294] to the extent that it has addressed the issue, there is little consensus in orthodox evidence theory on how to reconcile these liberal values with the Holy Trinity of 'Truth, Reason and Justice'.

By contrast, orthodox evidence scholarship has made virtually no attempt to get to grips with adjudicative, never mind polycentric, decisions taken by administrative agencies, tribunals or inquiries, or with fact finding in ADR, but has focused largely on court decisions.[295] Admittedly, it was probably never intended to deal with anything other than adjudicative

---

[294] See Chapter 2, section 2.3.
[295] See, for example, Twining, above n. 3, Chapter 3 passim.

decisions in the formal courts. Nevertheless, the fact that so much fact handling occurs in pre-trial proceedings and various forms of informal fact finding raises the possibility that orthodox theory may be contradicted by much of the actual practice of fact finding. Indeed, it is also possible that actual practice in the courts itself contradicts assumptions about obtaining factual truth, ensuring procedural justice and achieving expletive justice. We thus turn to studies of the actual operation of legal fact finding to see what light they can shed on the viability of orthodox assumptions about the aims and procedural methods of evidence and proof.

CHAPTER FOUR

The Sociological Context: Truth, Justice and Institutional Practices

1 Introduction: Sociology and Three Views of Fact Finding

We begin the task of testing orthodox theoretical assumptions about fact handling by looking at what can be loosely called the 'sociological context' of evidence and proof. At one level, the term denotes no more than the discussion draws on studies which use sociological techniques[1] to study fact-handling processes. However, the term 'sociological' also distinguishes this chapter from Chapters Six and Seven, which examine the psychological context of evidence and proof. This context involves factors which are inherent and internal to the minds of legal actors, such as their ability to accurately perceive and remember events, to reason logically, etc. In this chapter we will look at the actual behaviour of lawyers, judges and other legal officials as influenced by the social milieu or institutional practices of legal fact finding. Admittedly, it is rather artificial to distinguish between the sociological and psychological contexts, in that external sociological factors are only relevant if they affect people's behaviour and hence the two contexts are closely related. Similarly, conduct by legal actors will be influenced by their assumptions about how people's minds work. If, for instance, advocates did not expect fact finders to be influenced by appeals to emotion or prejudice, they would be less likely to couch their arguments in these terms. However, the distinction being drawn here is between psychological factors which are inevitably present irrespective of the external context in which people find themselves and sociological factors which are context-dependent and could be altered.

---

[1] While as we shall see in Chapter 6, section 1, these techniques include laboratory and 'field' (for example, in police stations, lawyer's offices, etc.) experiments, this chapter relies on the observation of actual fact-finding activity or interviews with actual participants.

As our discussion of the procedural context of fact handling suggests, there is unlikely to be one uniform sociological context to evidence and proof. Instead, there are myriad different processes – formal and informal, legal and administrative, criminal and civil, trial and pre-trial, to name but the most important distinctions – each with unique sociological characteristics. Unfortunately, however, while there are some empirical studies on how administrative officials and tribunals make decisions and on pre-trial proceedings in civil cases, as noted in Chapter One,[2] a disproportionate amount of information about the sociological context of fact finding involves criminal cases, where the institutional setting is very different to that of civil and administrative fact finding. There are two other reasons to be cautious about the generalisability of the findings discussed. The first is that there are very few studies undertaken in Scotland,[3] yet its relevant institutional settings might differ to those in the Anglo-American jurisdictions where the studies discussed occurred – though, where possible, findings from England and Wales are cited given that it is most similar in terms of state institutions and ideological orientations. More problematic is the fact that much of the research relied upon is relatively old, and at least some of it might have been overtaken by recent developments highlighted in the previous chapter, particularly those relating to procedural justice. Nevertheless, while there might be subtle changes to the overall impression provided by the studies we discuss, it should become clear that they provide sufficiently compelling grounds for questioning many of the assumptions about evidence and proof found in orthodox theory.

As we saw in the previous chapter,[4] one assumption is that the Anglo-American method of fact finding, and in particular its adversarial nature, is an effective – if not *the* most effective – means of finding truth. Accordingly, complacent fact positivists assume that legal fact finding can achieve the goal of factual truth and thereby expletive justice. An alternative view held among those who share fact positivism's liberal view of law's social role does not deny the value of factual truth and expletive justice, but sees upholding procedural justice as deserving equal respect. This is because it helps ensure that legal processes provide a civilised means of dispute resolution, thus discouraging disputes from being resolved by self-help and preventing society descending into anarchy. In addition, it is said

[2]   Section 3.
[3]   But cf. D. McBarnet, *Conviction: Law, the State and the Construction of Justice* (1981); Z. Bankowski, N. R. Hutton and J. J. McManus, *Lay Justice?* (1987); G. Chambers and A. Millar, *Prosecuting Sexual Assault* (1986); S. R. Moody and J. Tombs, *Prosecution in the Public Interest* (1982).
[4]   Section 2.1.

to communicate valued social norms, thus legitimising legal proceedings. Finally, procedural justice can be regarded as necessary simply in order to uphold the intrinsic value of human dignity.

However, a third view of legal fact handling which emerges from many sociological studies echoes contemporary critical theory in seeing the legal process in terms of power, control and the imposition of the views of the powerful in society over the less powerful. More specifically, in relation to criminal justice, it is argued that fact-handling processes tend to reflect what Herbert Packer[5] has famously described as a crime-control model in which both law and practice prioritise the suppression of crime through high rates of detection and conviction, and seek to achieve this with maximum efficiency and speed, and minimal cost, preferably outwith the courts, with procedural protections limited to those necessary to retain confidence in the system. This critical view is likely to seem overblown to modified rationalists who adhere to the liberal view of fact finding, and will certainly do so for fact positivists. By contrast, both these groups are likely to argue that the law's increased emphasis on procedural justice reflects Packer's competing due process model in which law's principled asymmetry, and its consequent overprotection of criminal suspects and accused, acts as a hurdle in the way of unjust convictions, as well as respecting law's moral integrity in criminal justice.

The question then arises as to which, if any, of these three views of the legal process and its approach to evidence and proof is most accurate. In answering this question we will start with an evaluation of the complacent fact positivist argument about the effectiveness of Anglo-American methods of fact finding.

2 Complacent Fact Positivism: Legal Fact Finding as Truth Finding

2.1 Beyond Fact Positivism: Informal Fact Finding

In evaluating the fact positivist argument about the effectiveness of Anglo-American methods of fact finding, it needs firstly to be recognised that, even if empirically supported, it would apply only to a fraction of fact finding. This is because, as the previous chapter shows, the classical Anglo-American procedural model is only fully applicable to formal fact finding

---

5   *The Limits of the Criminal Sanction* (1968), usefully evaluated by A. Sanders, R. Young and M. Burton, *Criminal Justice* (4th edn, 2010), 21ff.

in the courts,[6] and even then decreasingly so.[7] In informal fact finding, the search for factual truth is frequently downplayed often for legitimate reasons, such as in the case of polycentric administrative decisions,[8] where policy decisions are as important as, and merge inextricably with, assessing the facts, or where ascertaining factual truth plays second fiddle to settling disputes in negotiation and co-operative forms of ADR.[9] Given that it is impossible for the purpose of analysis and evaluation to isolate decisions about the existence of facts from other aspects of these types of legal proceedings, we will omit them from discussion and focus exclusively on fact-finding processes which, at least in theory, resemble those found in formal legal proceedings.

Thus, in principle, theoretical assumptions about the centrality of truth to evidence and proof should apply to adjudicative administrative decisions, given that fact finders are required simply to determine the facts and apply legal standards in much the same way as the courts.[10] Indeed, the normative standards for administrative decision-making are very similar to those postulated by orthodox evidence theory. Thus, echoing fact positivism, Roy Sainsbury asserts that the concept of administrative justice prioritises factual accuracy and the correct application of relevant legal rules to the facts, with fairness, in the sense of prompt, impartial, participatory and accountable decisions, being a secondary albeit very important consideration.[11]

In reality, however, sociological research on a wide range of administrative decision-making suggests that many officials readily allow the search for factual truth to bow to less elevated considerations.[12] In addition to inadequate training, a more understandable, albeit regrettable, reason for officials inadequately investigating and cursorily evaluating the facts is the pressures they almost invariably face in coping with heavy caseloads caused by

---

[6]   Section 3.1.

[7]   Section 4.

[8]   See Chapter 3, section 4.3.1.

[9]   See H. L. Ross, *Settled Out of Court: The Social Process of Insurance Claims Adjustments* (1970), esp. Chapter 3; G. Davis, *Partisans and Mediators: The Resolution of Divorce Disputes* (1988), Chapters 5 and 10; S. E. Merry, *Getting Justice and Getting Even: Legal Consciousness among Working Class Americans* (1990), esp. 118.

[10] Cf. W. Twining, 'Rationality and Scepticism in Judicial Proof: Some Signposts' (1989) II *International Journal for the Semiotics of Law* 69, 79.

[11] 'Administrative Justice: Discretion and Procedure in Social Security Decision-Making', in K. Hawkins (ed.), *The Uses of Discretion* (1992), 302–6.

[12] In addition to the specific studies cited below, see M. Lipsky, *Street-Level Bureaucracy: Dilemmas of the Individual in Public Services* (1980); D. J. Galligan (ed.), *A Reader on Administrative Law* (1996), esp. 35–8, 247–405; Hawkins (ed.), ibid., passim, but esp. K. Hawkins, 'The Use of Legal Discretion: Perspectives from Law and Social Science'.

insufficient resources[13] – a factor likely to have intensified since the imposition of economic 'austerity' measures in recent years.[14] Even when not expressly prioritising speed, officials often cope by focusing on the surface appearance of cases which, using common sense and experience, they place into what they see as commonly occurring categories. Those categories themselves, as well as assessments of applicants' credibility, may well flow from moralistic evaluations of them as worthy or unworthy, deserving or undeserving, etc. Such 'shallow' decision-making means that those whose situations do not neatly fit the favoured categories may well be wrongly denied state benefits, especially as their almost invariable lack of representation means that they frequently lack the knowledge to submit necessary information and arguments themselves.[15] A study of the application of homelessness legislation also suggests that officials vary the depth of investigation of eligibility according to policy considerations, such as the amount of available housing stock.[16] In other words, expediency and other policy factors are not occasional side-constraints on truth finding and expletive justice, but an ever-present competing and often overriding goal of administrative fact finding.

Breach of these ideals is particularly egregious in the case of asylum decisions, since these may have life-and-death consequences for those who had to flee violence.[17] Numerous studies report that officials consistently make basic errors regarding applicants' names and the details of their claim, and rely on background information which is sometimes absurdly inaccurate and frequently out of date.[18] Here a number of factors suggest

---

[13]   Expressly admitted by just over one-quarter of officials adjudicating income support claims in the study by J. Baldwin, N. Wikeley and R. Young, *Judging Social Security: The Adjudication of Claims for Benefits in Britain* (1992), 39. See also, more recently, The National Audit Office, *Getting It Right, Putting It Right: Improving Decision-Making and Appeals in Social Security Benefits*, HC 1142, Session 2002/2003; Report of the President of the Appeals Service, 2004/2005, available at http://www.appeals-service.gov.uk/Publications/publications.htm (accessed on 15 March 2018). Work and Pensions Committee, First Special Report of Session 2009–10, *Decision Making and Appeals in the Benefits System*, HC 313.

[14]   R. Thompson and J. Tomlinson, 'Mapping Current Issues In Administrative Justice: Austerity And The 'More Bureaucratic Rationality' Approach' (2017) 39 *Journal of Social Welfare and Family Law* 380.

[15]   See H. Genn and Y. Genn, *The Effectiveness of Representation at Tribunals: Report to the Lord Chancellor* (1989), esp. Chapter 5.

[16]   I. Loveland, *Housing Homeless People: Administrative Law and the Administrative Process* (1993), esp. Chapters 7 and 9.

[17]   See Chapter 1, n. 68.

[18]   See, for example, Asylum Aid, *Still No Reason at All: Home Office Decisions on Asylum Claims* (May 1999), available at http://www.asylumaid.org.uk/wp-content/uploads/2013/02/Still_No_Reason_At_All.pdf (accessed on 15 March 2018); Amnesty International UK, *Get it Right: How Home Office Decision Making Fails Refugees* (February 2004), available at https://www.amnesty.org.uk/files/get_it_right_0.pdf (accessed on 15 March 2018); D. Stevens, *UK Asylum Law and Policy: Historical and Contemporary Perspectives* (2004), 307–10; G. Clayton et al., *Textbook on Immigration and Asylum Law* (5th edn, 2012), 414–15.

that poor decision-making undoubtedly results from overwork and inadequate or no training. More worryingly, it also stems from internal policy decisions and a 'culture of disbelief that runs from top to bottom',[19] in which officials seem to see their job as allowing entry to as few asylum seekers as possible – an impression confirmed by the 'offensive and inhuman' tone[20] in which applications are dealt with, and evidence of racism within relevant departments.[21] Thus, for example, investigating alleged repression is notably lacking in relation to countries with which the UK has commercial and diplomatic ties, whereas the reasoning behind decisions is frequently highly tenuous if not illegal. Rather than genuinely investigating the substance of claims, many officials interviewing and assessing applicants seem more intent on catching them out through minor discrepancies in their accounts and then, without exploring the underlying reasons, using such discrepancies as evidence of a lack of credibility.[22] Similarly, where officials find applicants' accounts or supporting medical evidence implausible, they often fail to provide an opportunity to provide substantiating information, relying instead on their own assumptions about conditions in the applicant's country.

Admittedly, errors in initial decision-making can be cured by the fact that most administrative decisions are liable to a *de novo* appeal and sometimes also internal review. However, the value of these mechanisms is somewhat limited, especially for those without access to legal representation.[23] For example, internal reviewers of asylum refusals,[24] as well as certain categories of social security claimants,[25] tend simply to replicate the inadequacies of the initial decision-making process. Rather more hopeful are figures released by the now-abolished Administrative Justice and Tribunals Council that show that in 2010 appeals were successful in 41 per cent of social security and child support cases, 37 per cent of immigration and asylum, 31 per cent of education admission and 43 per cent of criminal

[19] Asylum Aid, ibid., 65. See also JUSTICE/ILPA/ARC, *Providing Protection: Towards Fair and Effective Asylum Procedures* (1997), 38ff.
[20] Asylum Aid, ibid., 59ff.
[21] Ibid., 59–60.
[22] An approach which is also applied in other areas of immigration, notwithstanding judicial disapproval: see Clayton et al., above n. 18, 210, 309, 387–8.
[23] See Genn and Genn, above n. 15; R. Berthoud and A. Bryson, 'Social Security Appeals: What do the Claimants Want?' (1997) 4 *Journal of Social Security Law* 17.
[24] Asylum Aid, above n. 18, 73.
[25] For example, those claiming unemployment and contribution benefits rather than income support: Baldwin, Wikely and Young, above n. 13, Chapter 3.

injury compensation cases.[26] Then again, in the case of social security appeals, it has been estimated that roughly 20 per cent of appellants lose despite having arguable cases, and in roughly another third there was sufficient latitude to go the other way.[27] In addition, there remain many types of decisions from which there are no appeals, and more recently appeal rights have been drastically reduced in the case of immigration decisions. By contrast, the introduction of mandatory internal reconsideration of benefit decisions led to a dramatic increase in the rate of appeals, but not necessarily an improvement in decision-making.[28] But even if appellants appealed more often and more successfully, it is argued that the appeal system legitimises the social security regime by coating it 'with a veneer of procedural fairness which may serve to deflect attention from the severe and rigid nature of many of the benefit rules which lie beneath it'[29] – a criticism which can be levelled at many other areas of administrative decision-making, such as immigration and housing.

To the extent that these somewhat dated studies are still applicable to as well as representative of the many other areas of administrative fact finding that have never been researched, they provide little support for thinking that the optimistic assumptions about the accuracy of fact finding held by some fact positivists applies as much to informal fact finding as it does to formal fact finding. But this raises the question of how accurate those assumptions are in the far more limited sphere of formal fact finding.

2.2 Formal Fact Finding: Orthodox Assumptions

As we saw in Chapter Three,[30] there are many reasons given by complacent fact positivists for regarding the Anglo-American procedural model as an effective – if not *the* most effective – means of finding factual truth. One is the rules of evidence. However, leaving aside their effectiveness, which is a question beyond the scope of this book, we saw in Chapter One[31] that they are of very limited application. Also regarded as important are the principles of orality, publicity and the dialectic confrontation between

---

[26] Stevens, above n. 18, 308–9 (but cf. also 298–9 where the Home Office's own figure of 30 per cent is cited and JUSTICE/ILPA/ARC, above n. 18, 15, which estimated that only 5 per cent of this 20 per cent were on substantive grounds); Baldwin, Wikely and Young, above n. 13, 99.

[27] Ibid., 99.

[28] T. Mullen, 'Access to Justice in Administrative Law and Administrative Justice', in E. Palme et al. (eds), *Access to Justice: Beyond the Policies and Politics of Austerity* (2016), 90–9.

[29] Baldwin, Wikely and Young, above n. 13, 22, referring to T. Prosser, 'Poverty, Ideology and Legality: Supplementary Benefit Appeal Tribunals and their Predecessors' (1977) 4 *British Journal of Law and Society* 39.

[30] Section 3, passim.

[31] Section 2.

accuser and accused, which are said to discourage people from lying and
to allow the accurate evaluation of truthfulness through observation of
demeanour, body language and tone of voice.[32]

However, as we shall see in Chapter Six, the ability of fact finders accurately to assess the reliability of oral testimony from demeanour, body
language and tone of voice is grossly overrated.[33] As regards the principles
of immediacy and publicity, there is simply no empirical evidence supporting their truth-enhancing qualities.[34] Indeed, contrary to traditional
assumptions, common sense suggests that witnesses are likely to be less
rather than more honest when they give evidence about someone present
in court.[35] Moreover, what evidence does exist establishes that testifying
publicly, especially as regards intimate or otherwise embarrassing matters,
and in the close presence of a criminal accused, causes witnesses to experience stress and anxiety.[36] This in turn reduces their ability to accurately
recall and convincingly relate information, increases their susceptibility to
suggestion by cross-examiners intent on manipulating their evidence, and
may lead fact finders to misinterpret signs of stress and anxiety as indicating lies or a lack of confidence. Indeed, it is these problems that led to
he special measures protecting witnesses seen as particularly vulnerable,
namely rape complainers, children and those with learning disabilities,
which were referred to in the previous chapter.[37] Arguably, vulnerability
to the stress and anxiety of dialectic confrontation and publicity is not
confined to these groups and hence the principles of immediacy and publicity undermine as much as enhance truth finding, and may in fact deter
witnesses from coming forward to testify.[38]

A contrasting problem with publicity is that, if opening up proceedings
to the light of the public and media gaze does in fact deter violations of
evidence and proof values,[39] the vast majority of legal fact handling takes
place in private. This is particularly problematic for criminal suspects,
given that, as we shall see, their fate is often sealed long before trial and
there is rarely much that can be done at trial to compensate for prior

[32] See Chapter 3, section 3.2.3.
[33] See section 2.
[34] L. Ellison, *The Adversarial Process and the Vulnerable Witness* (2001), 45.
[35] T. M. Massaro, 'The Dignity Value of Face to Face Confrontations' (1988) 40 *University of Florida Law Review* 863, 901.
[36] Ellison, above n. 34, Chapter 2.
[37] Section 4.2, at n. 253.
[38] A. Duff et al., *The Trial on Trial: Volume 3 – Towards a Normative Theory of the Criminal Trial* (2007), 264–5.
[39] Cf. Duff et al., ibid., 260, 267, arguing that show trials in the Soviet Union and elsewhere were in fact legitimated rather than challenged by their highly public nature.

treatment which is unfair or obstructive of the truth, even if trials were held in the full glare of publicity. In fact, however, the public and the media only attend a small fraction of trials.[40]

Consequently, the main argument for the accuracy of Anglo-American fact finding lies with its adversarial nature: the idea that 'truth is best discovered by powerful statements on both sides of the question'.[41] Unfortunately, however, the general claim[42] about the superiority of adversarial over alternative – in effect, inquisitorial – methods cannot be empirically verified. Not only is it impossible to establish the comparative factual accuracy of particular systems since, as the previous chapter made clear, none exists in pure form, but it is impossible to verify the accuracy of any adjudicative decision since no one can ever definitively ascertain the 'true' facts of cases. As David Luban memorably noted: 'A trial is not a quiz show with the right answer waiting in a sealed envelope.'[43] Consequently, the arguments for the Anglo-American system's truth-finding superiority rest primarily on intuitive 'armchair psychology'[44] arguments backed up by some laboratory experiments.

Thus, the Fuller[45] or bias[46] thesis is based on the 'natural human tendency' to be too quick to convert preliminary hypotheses about cases into fixed conclusions in that 'all that confirms the diagnosis makes a strong imprint on the mind, while all that runs counter to it is received with diverted attention'.[47] An adversarial presentation of evidence remedies this by holding the case 'in suspension between two opposing interpretations', leaving 'time to explore all of its peculiarities and nuances'. In addition, the incentive thesis argues that those seeking to win cases have greater incentives than neutral investigators to investigate cases thoroughly, especially where the facts initially found are

---

[40]   McBarnet, above n. 3, 144; Duff et al., ibid., 266.

[41]   *Ex parte Lloyd* (1822) Montagu's Reports 70 n. 72, cited with approval in *Jones* v. *National Coal Board* [1957] 2 QB 55, 63.

[42]   Assessed by, for example, M. Damaška, 'Presentation of Evidence and Fact-finding Precision' [1975] 123 University of Pennsylvania Law Review 1083; D. Luban, *Lawyers and Justice: An Ethical Study* (1988), 68–74; D. Nicolson and J. Webb, *Professional Legal Ethics: Critical Interrogations* (1999), 183–8; C. R. Callen, 'Cognitive Strategies and Models of Fact-Finding', in J. Jackson, M. Langer and P. Tillers (eds), *Crime, Procedure and Evidence in a Comparative and International Context: Essays in Honour of Procedure Professor Mirjan Damáska* (2008), 169–74.

[43]   Luban, ibid., 68.

[44]   Ibid., 69.

[45]   Named after its main proponent: see L. L. Fuller and J. D. Randall, 'Professional Responsibility: Report of the Joint Conference' (1958) 44 *ABA Journal* 1159, 1160; L. L. Fuller, 'The Adversary System', in H. J. Berman (ed.), *Talks on American Law* (revised edn, 1971).

[46]   J. H. Langbein, *Comparative Criminal Procedure: Germany* (1977), 150–1.

[47]   Quotations from Fuller and Randall, above n. 45, 1160.

unfavourable.[48] Consequently, adjudicators are likely to be presented with more facts under adversarial as compared to inquisitorial proceedings.

Both hypotheses have been confirmed by experiments simulating evidence gathering and presentation in the two systems.[49] However, not only has their methodology been criticised,[50] but it is doubtful whether laboratory experiments involving reading statements of facts to students effectively replicates the special atmosphere, undercurrents and dynamics of trials, not to mention the dramatic personal confrontations of adversarial trials, and the use of rhetoric and various tactical devices used to persuade fact finders. Nor does 'buying' facts from experimenters resemble frequently harassed lawyers deciding whether to fully investigate cases or to fall back on their court room skills.

But even at the level of conjecture and intuition, both hypotheses come up against counter-arguments. Regarding the first, William Simon has noted that, even if the adversarial system does prevent a rush to judgment, it has not been established that allowing lawyers to attempt to distort or obfuscate the facts 'increases the likelihood that the balance will ultimately be struck in favor of the correct interpretation . . . Prejudices, after all, are often very accurate, and in a world of shared values and common experiences, one expects "familiar patterns" to have a certain reliability.'[51] In answer to the second argument, it can be replied that, while partisans may investigate more facts, they will only present those that support their case. Moreover, in addition to deliberate attempts at ensuring witness bias, it seems likely that some witnesses will subconsciously alter their evidence in subtle ways to benefit those calling them.[52] In Damáska's arresting image, the overall effect is that, 'as in a car driving at night, two narrow beams . . . illuminate the world presented to the adjudicator'.[53] More generally, according to Carrie Menkel-Meadow, 'polarized debate distorts the truth, leaves out important information, simplifies complexity, and

---

[48] See, for example, P. Devlin, The Judge (1979), 61: 'Two prejudiced searchers starting from opposite ends of the field will between them be less likely to miss anything than the impartial searcher starting in the middle.'

[49] J. Thibaut and L. Walker, Procedural Justice: A Psychological Analysis (1975); the studies cited in S. M. Kassin, *The American Jury Handicapped in the Pursuit of Justice* (1990), 697 n. 41. See also M. Freedman, *Understanding Lawyers' Ethics* (1990), 30–1, citing anecdotal evidence from lawyers who have practised in both systems; research on the confirmation bias in Chapter 5, sections 5.3 and 6.2.

[50] Damaška, above n. 42, 1095–1100; P. Brett, 'Legal Decisionmaking and Bias: A Critique of an "Experiment"' (1973) 45 *University of Colorado Law Review* 1.

[51] W. H. Simon, 'The Ideology of Advocacy: Procedural Justice and Professional Ethics' [1978] *Wisconsin Law Review* 29, 76, quoting Fuller and Randall, loc. cit. n. 45.

[52] See experiments by B. H. Sheppard and N. Vidmar, 'Adversary Pretrial Procedures and Testimonial Evidence: Effects of Lawyer's Role and Machiavellianism' (1980) 39 *Journal of Personality and Social Psychology* 320.

[53] *Evidence Law Adrift* (1997), 92.

obfuscates rather than clarifies'.[54] However, the main argument against Anglo-American fact finding is encapsulated by Jerome Frank's rhetorical assertion that encouraging adversarial parties to do everything they can to win rather than find the truth is rather like encouraging nurses to throw pepper in the eyes of surgeons.[55] In other words, the adversarial system's effectiveness is undermined by the adversarial ethos it generates.

2.3 The Adversarial Ethos

As regards such adversariality, the role of lawyers – for litigants lucky enough to have one – is particularly problematic. As we saw in Chapter Two,[56] subject to certain minimal legal and professional conduct constraints, lawyers are expected to do their utmost for their clients irrespective of the morality of their client's objectives or behaviour. Indeed, adversarial proceedings are said to require this stance of neutral partisanship because, without lawyers, clients may not be capable of adequately investigating the facts and putting their cases as forcefully as possible.

However, for many it is this adversarial ethos itself which undermines the adversarial system's effectiveness at finding the truth. As we saw in Chapter Two,[57] lawyers are educated and socialised into being hard-nosed practitioners who see legal proceedings as civilised battles or sporting contests in which winning is everything and, while outright lying is regarded as unsporting, truth and justice are seen as irrelevant.[58] As a result, based on admittedly now rather old anecdotal evidence[59] and empirical research,[60] it is claimed

---

[54] 'The Trouble with the Adversary System in a Postmodern, Multicultural World' (1996) 1 *Journal of the Institute for the Study of Legal Ethics* 49, 50.

[55] *Courts on Trial: Myth and Reality in American Trials* (1949, reprinted 1973), 85.

[56] Section 4.2.

[57] Section 2.1.

[58] Nicolson and Webb, above n. 42, Chapter 6; L. Ellison, 'Rape and the Adversarial Culture of the Courtroom', in M. Childs and L. Ellison (eds), *Feminist Perspectives on Evidence* (2000), 45.

[59] See, for example, Frank, above n. 55, Chapter 6; R. Eggleston, 'What is Wrong with the Adversary System?' (1975) 49 *Australian Law Journal* 428; M. Frankel, *Partisan Justice* (1980) Part I (expanding 'The Search for Truth' (1975) 123 *University of Pennsylvania Law Review* 1031). Although the observations were made in relation to other Anglo-American jurisdictions, it is doubtful whether the situation differs much in Scotland.

[60] In addition to the references below, see G. Davis, S. Cretney and J. Collins, *Simple Quarrels* (1994), 98–9, Chapter 6, and 259; H. Genn, *Hard Bargaining: Out of Court Settlement in Personal Injury Actions* (1987), Chapters 7 and 8. For other surveys of the evidence, see Luban, above n. 42, Chapters 1 and 2; D. L. Rhode, 'Ethical Perspectives on Legal Practice' (1985) 37 *Stanford Law Review* 589, 595–604 and 'Institutionalizing Ethics' (1994) 44 *Case Western Reserve Law Review* 665, 667–73; J. McEwan, *Evidence and the Adversarial Process: The Modern Law* (2nd edn, 1998), Chapter 1; and for evidence of similar approaches of non-legal professions involved in legal disputes, see S. Wheeler, *Reservation of Title Clauses: Impact and Implications* (1991).

that lawyers are prepared to make 'the true look false and the false look true'[61] and to 'bend, fold, and spindle, if not mutilate, the facts', in a way which 'either cheats her way to justice or cheats justice'.[62] Thus Anglo-American lawyers are said to engage in numerous tactics – both before and during trial – which undermine the adversarial system's ability to ensure accurate fact finding.

Such pre-trial tactics include outlining the law before hearing clients' stories and subtly – or not so subtly – coaching clients and witnesses[63] so as to get useful rather than necessarily true stories – though research suggests that such tactics are not always necessary in that witnesses may subconsciously change their stories to suit adversarial lawyers interviewing them.[64] Other notorious tactics involving 'shopping' around for favourable expert evidence, and even pressurising experts to adapt or amend their opinions,[65] providing incomplete or evasive responses to disclosure applications, and overlooking or even conniving in the non-disclosure of material evidence. More fundamentally, lawyers may try to prevent cases from getting to court by sapping the energy and resources of opponents,[66] such as by making frivolous counter-claims, spurious procedural manoeuvres, misleading negotiation strategies, excessive requests for recovery, or burying opponents under a mound of irrelevant documents when they seek recovery. And even when unsuccessful, as already noted,[67] delay affects witnesses' memory and potential availability.

On the other hand, to the extent that Scottish lawyers display similar adversariality, the increasing role of case management in both criminal and civil proceedings[68] might lead to a general watering down of adversariality. Evidence of this has emerged in the US[69] and England

[61] M. L. Schwarz, 'On Making the True Look False and the False Look True' (1988) 41 *Southwestern Law Journal* 1135.

[62] Luban, above n. 42, 13–15.

[63] See, for example, M. McConville et al., *Standing Accused: The Organisation and Practices of Criminal Defence Lawyers in Britain* (1994), 97ff, 156–8, 251–2, but cf. P. Rock, *The Social World of the English Crown Court* (1993), Chapter 4 passim, regarding lawyers who were wary of coaching.

[64] Sheppard and Vidmar, above n. 52.

[65] See further Chapter 5, section 7.2.

[66] For example, in the notorious 'McLibel' case (*McDonald's Corporation* v. *Steel & Morris* [1997] EWHC QB 366), McDonald's lawyers ensured that unrepresented and indigent defendants had to undergo the longest case in English legal history, ultimately resulting in the ECtHR finding that they had been denied a fair trial (*Steel & Morris* v. *United Kingdom* [2005] EMLR 15).

[67] Chapter 2, section 7.

[68] See Chapter 3, section 2.2.

[69] See, for example, R. L. Marcus, 'Déjà Vu All Over Again? An American Reaction to the Woolf Report', in A. A. S. Zuckerman and R. Cranston (eds), *Reform of Civil Procedure: Essays on 'Access to Justice'* (1995), 232–4.

and Wales,[70] though south of the border there has been more wide-ranging case management, control of discovery and even court-appointed experts,[71] and even then the impact has not lived up to expectations.[72]

As regards lawyer behaviour in court, lawyers will obviously seek to create the most favourable evidence possible. Witness answers can be commented on or paraphrased to subtly alter their meaning. More regularly, strict editorial control is exercised over testimony through asking precise, closed questions which limit the possible range of answers or leading questions that suggest the required answer. In addition, witnesses may be prevented from adding information that was not requested.[73] As one American judge sarcastically commented: 'Lawyers' texts on cross-examination teach the classic wisdom of successful veterans concerning the disaster of asking one question too many on cross; that blundering next question may give the entrapped witness a chance to *explain*, heaven forfend, to tell how it really was . . .'[74]

Other tactics are more negative in trying to negate unfavourable facts, most notoriously through cross-examination.[75] Supposedly, as we have seen,[76] the greatest truth-generating engine ever invented, cross-examination, can just as easily be used to the opposite effect. As we shall see in more detail in Chapter Six,[77] leading and other forms of suggestive questioning can alter testimony. Truthful witnesses can be confused, or made to contradict themselves by questions on irrelevant issues or unimportant and unmemorable minute details merely in order to discredit them, and by complex vocabulary and syntax such as questions containing

---

[70] Summarised in M. Zander, 'Zander on Woolf' (2009) 159 *New Law Journal* 367, but cf. E. Samuel, *Commercial Procedure in Glasgow Sheriff Court* (Scottish Executive Social Research, 2005); R. Clancy, 'The New Commercial Cause Rules: Part 1' (1997) *Scots Law Times* 6, 45, 46, noting improvement in terms of speed and reduced cost.

[71] For an overview, see, for example, A. A. S. Zuckerman, *Zuckerman on Civil Procedure: Principles of Practice* (2nd edn, 2006), Chapter 1.

[72] Not least because the greater emphasis on pre-trial paperwork is expensive, thus further enhancing the advantages of wealthy litigants: McEwan, above n. 60, 278; see also S. Issacharoff, 'Too Much Lawyering, Too Little Law', in Zuckerman and Cranston, above n. 69, 251ff.

[73] See, for example, P. Goodrich, *Languages of the Law: From Logics of Memory to Nomadic Masks* (1990), 197–201; R. Du Cann, *The Art of the Advocate* (1993), Chapters 5–8; K. Evans, *The Golden Rules of Advocacy* (1993), 73ff; S. Lubet, *Modern Trial Advocacy: Analysis and Practice* (4th edn, 2009), Chapter 5, esp. 101ff.

[74] Frankel, *Partisan Justice*, above n. 59, 16.

[75] See, for example, Rock, above n. 63, 29–30; Rock, 'Witness and Space in a Crown Court' (1991) *British Journal of Criminology* 266, 267–9; Ellison, above n. 34, Chapter 5 (expanding on 'The Protection of Vulnerable Witnesses in Court: An Anglo-Dutch comparison' (1999) 3 *International Journal of Evidence and Proof* 29) and above n. 58.

[76] See Chapter 3, section 3.2.3.

[77] Chapter 6, sections 2.3.4 and 2.4.3.

multiple propositions, embedded clauses and double or even triple negatives. Lawyers may ask the same question repeatedly, fire off questions in
rapid succession and juxtapose unrelated topics. All of this can be done
politely and courteously, but some use aggressive or sarcastic language,
tone of voice and physical gestures in order to intimidate. Witnesses may
be challenged with allegations of mendacity, impropriety and malice, and
asked about sensitive and intimate information merely to cause embarrassment. Cross-examination thus tends to be a stressful and difficult
ordeal even for practised expert witnesses, but it is particularly so for rape
complainers, children and other vulnerable witnesses.[78] As we will see,
this may diminish their ability to recall and communicate information
accurately and fact finders' ability to evaluate witness accuracy and honesty.[79] Moreover, it may discourage victims from coming forward.[80]

Finally, lawyer tactics extend to a variety of other rhetorical, and sometimes just plain 'dirty',[81] tricks. These include attempting to distract attention from unfavourable testimony, such as the American prosecution lawyer
who broke wind repeatedly during defence counsel's speech,[82] pretending
to possess a determinative document in order to intimidate a witness into
providing favourable evidence, making spurious objections to disrupt the
flow of evidence and suggest that it is suspect in some way, and bringing
into court a client's children or wife to help garner the court's sympathy.
Furthermore, advocates may appear to put not just their technical skills,
but their reputation and even soul into arguing their cases.[83] They can

---

[78] For example, rape complainants are made to feel as if they were on trial (if not subjected to a
     form of legal rape) by being accused of acting provocatively and wearing sexually suggestive
     clothing, and asked irrelevant questions about drug use, drinking and abortions. See Ellison,
     above nn. 58 and 76, the classic studies of Z. Adler, *Rape on Trial* (1987) and J. Temkin, *Rape and
     the Legal Process* (1987), and the shorter Scottish study of G. Chambers and A. Millar, 'Proving
     Sexual Assault: Prosecuting the Offender or Prosecuting the Victim?', in P. Carlen and
     A. Worrall (eds), *Gender, Crime and Justice* (1987). Legal reforms discussed in Chapter 3, section 4.2 pro-
     tecting sexual offence complainers (and other vulnerable witnesses) from being cross-examined
     face-to-face and on their previous sexual history, but leave untouched other adversarial tac-
     tics: Ellison, above n. 34, esp. 131, which apparently continue: M. Burman, 'Evidencing Sexual
     Assault: Women in the Witness Box' (2009) 56 *Probation Journal* 1.
[79] Chapter 6, sections 2.4.3 and 3.
[80] J. Hunter, 'Battling a Good Story: Cross-examining the Failure of the Law of Evidence', in
     P. Roberts and M. Redmayne (eds), *Innovations in Evidence and Proof: Integrating Theory, Research and
     Teaching* (2007), 286.
[81] D. Luban, 'Are Criminal Defenders Different?' (1993) 91 *Michigan Law Review* 1729, 1761.
[82] For this and other examples, see Du Cann, above n. 73, 5; D. Napley, *The Technique of Persuasion*
     (4th edn, 1991), 134–5; D. Pannick, *Advocates* (1992), 27–8.
[83] See, for example, Pannick, ibid., 153–4.

express indignation at suggestions of client wrongdoing, pull the heart-strings of juries and make self-righteous appeals to the very notions of truth and justice they seem intent on bending to their purpose.

Viewed in this light, Frank's analogisation of the adversarial presentation of evidence to throwing pepper in a surgeon's eyes does not seem too overblown. As another American judge said, it may be that 'litigators' devices . . . have utility in testing dishonest witnesses, ferreting out falsehoods, and thus exposing the truth. But . . . these devices are, like other potent weapons, equally lethal for heroes and villains.'[84] On the other hand, like all weapons, they may blow up in the face of those wielding them by causing a backlash on the part of fact finders who regard advocates as overdoing their adversarial role.[85] Nevertheless, their use of truth-obstructing tactics is likely to lead to a vicious circle. While all lawyers might recognise that they should refrain from truth-obstruction, they will know that this benefits less scrupulous colleagues, and consequently the use of such tactics is likely to escalate incrementally.

2.4 Adversarial Checks and Balances?
2.4.1 The Neutral Arbiter
Supporters of the adversarial system have two responses to these problems. The first points to the role of judges or other adjudicators as neutral umpires who can ensure that adversariality does not go so far as to undermine truth finding. However, this response is beset with problems.

One is that trial judges are limited by the laxity of procedural and ethical rules, and the difficulty of reconciling the tension between maintaining fairness and their passive role. Given the spectre of reversal on appeal and their own socialisation into an adversarial mindset, they are likely to restrain only the very worst excesses.[86] While they may occasionally be more interventionist, this seems to stem from factors like impatience and the less adversarial nature of some proceedings such as those involving family disputes,[87] but not necessarily from the more legitimate goal of helping

[84] Frankel, 'The Search for Truth', above n. 60, 1039.
[85] See, for example, M. Selvin and L. Picus, *The Debate over Jury Performance: Observations from a Recent Asbestos Case* (1987), 28–31.
[86] Ellison, above n. 34, 110, 133–4, above n. 58, 48, Hunter, above n. 80, 281, 287, and for evidence, Rock, above n. 63, 87–8. See also A. A. S. Zuckerman, 'Reform in the Shadow of the Lawyers' Interests' and M. Zanders, 'Why Lord Woolf's Proposed Reform of Civil Procedure should be rejected', in Zuckerman and Cranston, above n. 69, respectively at 77 and 87–8 on judicial culture more generally.
[87] Davis, Cretney and Collins, above n. 60, Chapter 10.

unrepresented litigants struggling with legal and procedural complexities and an adversarial opposing lawyer.[88]

Secondly, there is considerable evidence[89] to suggest that, particularly in the lower criminal courts, judicial neutrality is not always maintained. Adjudicators tend to believe state witnesses and particularly the police, and disbelieve accused, especially as judges and JPs become case-hardened over time. Consequently, they frequently interrupt the testimony of defence witnesses or the effective cross-examination of prosecution witnesses, such as by reacting indignantly to suggestions of police lies[90] – though probably less so after revelations of the police's role in notorious miscarriages of justice.[91] Nor are judges likely to act more even-handedly because of a potential appeal. As we have seen,[92] even if inclined,[93] appeal courts have very limited scope to reverse findings of fact, whereas the process may be time-consuming, costly and stressful, and thus appeals are rare and success even rarer.

Finally, and most crucially, most disputes do not reach court. As we have also seen,[94] the vast majority of criminal cases are resolved by plea bargaining and voluntary guilty pleas, whereas an even higher percentage of civil cases are settled by negotiation or, as is increasingly common, by mediation or other forms of ADR. Here the court will have very little or no role at all in ensuring that outcomes are likely to accurately reflect factual truth or even the values of procedural justice.

---

[88] See E. Samuel, *In the Shadow of the Small Claims Court: The Impact of Small Claims Procedure on Personal Injury Claimants and Litigation* (1998), 76–7 and the older US study of W. M. O'Barr and J. M. Conley, 'Litigant Satisfaction Versus Legal Adequacy in Small Claims Narratives' (1985) 19 *Law & Society Review* 661.

[89] See, for example, McEwan, above n. 60, 12–23; McConville et al., above n. 63, Chapter 9; Bankowski, Hutton and McManus, above n. 3, passim; S. Doran, 'The Necessarily Expanding Role of the Criminal Law Judge', in S. Doran and J. Jackson (eds), *The Judicial Role in Criminal Proceedings* (2000), 13, but cf. W. Young, N Cameron and Y. Tinsley, *Juries in Criminal Trials, Part Two: A Summary of Research Findings* (1999), 35, who found that jurors in their study rarely held such views of the judges presiding over their cases.

[90] See, for example, McBarnet, above n. 3, 56, Chapter 7 passim; P. Darbyshire, 'For the Lord Chancellor – Some Causes for Concern About Magistrates' (1997) *Criminal Law Review* 861, 862, 869.

[91] See, for example, C. Walker and K. Starmer (eds), *Miscarriages of Justice: A Review of Justice in Error* (1999).

[92] Chapter 1, section 2.4.

[93] See, for example, *R* v. *Hircock and Others* [1970] 1 QB 67, where a jury decision was upheld despite the judge during the defence making gestures of impatience, sighing and loudly uttering 'Oh God' several times and then laying his head down and making groaning noises. See generally on appeal court deference to trial courts: R. Nobles and D. Schiff, 'The Right to Appeal and Workable Systems of Justice' (2002) 65 *Modern Law Review* 676.

[94] Chapter 1, section 2.3.

2.4.2 Battle of the Equals

The other response to criticisms of adversarial truth finding is that, while both parties may seek to obstruct the truth, their excesses cancel each other out. If one tries to pull the wool over the tribunal's eyes, their opponent will provide the other side of the story. Here, however, attention to the realities of the 'litigoation'[95] landscape suggest that this argument suffers from the same myopia that underlies classical laissez-faire economic theory with which it is ideologically linked.[96] Just as it seems a pious hope that, as Adam Smith conjectured, an 'invisible hand' will ensure that the pursuit of individual self-interest improves everyone's living standards, so it seems naive to expect truth to emerge from two adversaries doing their utmost to obstruct it.

Sociological studies of civil disputes[97] reveal that the assumption of a level playing field with two protagonists equally able to safeguard their interests is as misplaced as the equivalent assumptions made by classical economic theory. Most obviously,[98] huge wealth differences combine with a free market in lawyer services only partially – and decreasingly – ameliorated by legal aid to ensure that access to competent and zealous lawyers is far from evenly distributed.[99] Money also buys more thorough fact investigation, advantageous access to expert witnesses and a greater ability to engage in truth-obstructing tactics like delay and recovery abuses, whereas those desperate for a financial settlement may be unable to invest in their cases or wait for drawn-out litigation to conclude. Reinforcing these differences are the advantages enjoyed by 'repeat players' like big companies and state agencies who are regularly involved in litigation and benefit from superior knowledge of the legal process, ready access to legal specialists and crucial information, economies of scale, low start-up costs, the opportunity to develop informal relations with institutional incumbents, and an ability to play for higher stakes and to make gains over the long run.[100] By comparison, if 'one-shotters' (those involved in litigation for the first time or only very rarely) are not deterred from commencing legal proceedings in the first place, financial and other obstacles (most notably in Scotland, geographical location) mean that many

---

[95] See Chapter 3 at n. 272.

[96] Cf. Frank, above n. 55, 92–5; Frankel, *Partisan Justice*, above n. 60, 10–11.

[97] See Ross, above n. 9; Davis, Cretney and Collins, above n. 60; Genn, above n. 60; Wheeler, above n. 60; D. R. Harris et al., *Compensation and Support for Illness and Injury* (1984); S. Ingleby, *Solicitors and Divorce* (1992), Chapter. 6.

[98] But cf. also the impact of gender, for example, in family law disputes: for example, Davis, above n. 9, Chapter 6.

[99] H. Genn and A. Paterson, *Paths to Justice: What People in Scotland Do and Think about Going to Law* (2001).

[100] M. Galanter, 'Why the "Haves" Come Out Ahead: Speculations on the Limits of Legal Change' (1974) 9 *Law & Society Review* 95.

will lack the necessary protection against powerful opponents. Thus research shows that initial advice and representation significantly affect the outcome of cases in court and tribunals,[101] and unrepresented litigants face distinct disadvantages in formal fact-finding fora due to their lack of knowledge of proper procedures and how to orientate their stories to the governing law.[102]

But, as important as representation is, it does not guarantee a level playing field. Despite being repeat players, lawyers who represent one-shotters and other less powerful members of society in civil law disputes tend themselves to come from the less powerful sectors of the profession, have less specialised knowledge and operate with tighter profit margins than their opponents' lawyers.[103] Consequently they tend to limit their investigation of the facts and force them into pre-determined categories involving standardised remedies by controlling client interviews.[104] Moreover, rather than zealously pursuing their clients' interests, many lawyers seem more intent on maintaining co-operative relationships with colleagues and court officials or looking after their own economic interests, such as by ensuring economies of scale through the speedy through-put of cases or by not frightening away more lucrative prospective clients.[105] Admittedly, at least when both sides are equally co-operative, this less adversarial stance may in fact benefit both parties. Unfortunately, however, studies show that the watering down of lawyer zeal is not always confined to a desire to co-operate in the client's interest. Indeed, lawyers are willing to (ab)use all their powers of persuasion and aura of authority, and even mislead clients into agreeing to outcomes which they and the academics researching their activities regard as unfavourable.

Given the structural inequalities between state and the accused and the serious consequences of wrongful convictions, it is even more worrying

---

[101] Genn and Genn, above n. 15, though noting at 213–14, 243–4 that experienced lay representatives may be as, if not more, effective than lawyers; Wheeler, above n. 60, 185–7.

[102] O'Barr and Conley, above n. 88, 684–90.

[103] Galanter, above n.100, 114–17.

[104] In addition to the British sources cited above at n. 97, see C. J. Hosticka, 'We Don't Care About What Happened, We Only Care About What is Going to Happen: Lawyer-Client Negotiations of Reality' (1978–9) 26 *Social Problems* 599; J. B. Atleson, 'The Legal Community and the Transformation of Disputes: The Settlement of Injunction Actions' (1989) 23 *Law & Society Review* 41, esp. 60–1, 69–70; G. Bellow, 'Turning Solutions into Problems: The Legal Aid Experience' (1977) 34 *NLADA Briefcase* 106; A. Sarat and W. L. F. Felstiner, 'Law Strategy in the Divorce Lawyer's Office' (1986) 20 *Law & Society Review* 93, 109–13; S. Macaulay, 'Lawyers and Consumer Protection Laws' (1979) 14 *Law & Society Review* 115; G. Neustadter, 'When Lawyer and Client Meet: Observations of Interviewing and Counseling Behavior in the Consumer Bankruptcy Law Office' (1986) 35 *Buffalo Law Review* 177, 195ff, 239–41.

[105] In addition to studies already cited in nn. 97 and 104, see Davis, above n. 9, esp. Chapter 9 (though he notes that there was no evidence that the lack of adversarial zeal led to clients losing out); P. Rock, *Making People Pay* (1973), 185–6.

that countless studies reveal that this stance is equally displayed by criminal defence lawyers.[106] In fact, this research reveals that inequalities between state and accused go beyond the inevitable consequences of the state's more powerful role and resources, and that the various safeguards designed to redress them frequently fail to materialise.[107]

Thus, not surprisingly, given the model of criminal procedure, the police adopt an adversarial attitude which further exacerbates defence disadvantages and directly undermines the chances of truth emerging. Officers do not seek the truth with open minds, but from the outset construct cases against suspects based on early hunches and confident beliefs that they have 'got their man (or far less frequently, woman)'[108] – beliefs which can be based on stereotypes about typical criminals and crimes, and affected by mistaken interpretations of the behaviour of those from minority social groups.[109] Thus they gather evidence not *about*, but *against*, suspects and, once incriminating evidence passes a threshold, tend not to look for other explanations and certainly not for exculpatory evidence. Admittedly the process of converting early case theories into confident conclusions through psychological processes such as 'premature closure' (reaching a conclusion before investigation), 'confirmation bias' (only seeking information relevant to that conclusion) and 'ironing out and selective synthesis' (ignoring and glossing over 'inconvenient contradictory detail, unwanted uncertainty, gaps, vagueness, ambiguity and anomaly') is common to most fact investigators. Nevertheless, police officers seem to work with very strong initial prejudices and 'working rules'[110] as to who or what patterns of behaviour

---

[106] See Chapter 3, section 3.3.2.1.

[107] In addition to specific studies referred to below, the following description draws on McBarnet, above n. 3; McConville et al., above n. 64; Sanders, Young and Burton, above n. 5, esp. Chapters 2–5, 8–10; P. Carlen, Magistrates' Justice (1976); A. E. Bottoms and J. D. McClean, Defendants in the Criminal Process (1976); J. Baldwin and M. McConville, Negotiated Justice: Pressures on Defendants to Plead Guilty (1977); A. Sanders, 'Constructing the Case for the Prosecution' (1987) 14 Journal of Law and Society 229; M. McConville, A. Sanders and R. Leng, The Case for the Prosecution: Police Suspects and the Construction of Criminality (1993).

[108] E. Shepherd and R. Milne, 'Full and Faithful: Ensuring Quality Practice and Integrity of Outcome in Witness Interviews', in A. Heaton-Armstrong, E Shepherd and D. Wolchover (eds), Analysing Witness Testimony: A Guide for Legal Practitioners and Other Professionals (1999), esp. 126–67. See further Chapter 5 section 6.2 and Chapter 6 passim); K. Abimola, 'Questions and Answers: The Logic of Preliminary Fact Investigation' (2002) 29 Journal of Law and Society 533, for a detailed example of such processes at work.

[109] M. B. Powell and T. Bartholomew, 'Interviewing and Assessing Clients from Different Cultural Backgrounds: Guidelines for All Forensic Professionals', in D. Carson and R. Bull (eds), Handbook of Psychology in Legal Contexts (2003), 637–8.

[110] B. Schafer, J. Keppens and Q. Shen, 'Thinking With and Outside the Box: Developing Computer Support for Evidence', in P. Roberts and M. Redmayne (eds), Innovations in Evidence and Proof: Integrating Theory, Research and Teaching (2007), 144.

are worth investigating, which have consequences that are more serious than with many other forms of fact investigation. Moreover, they display what has been called an 'investigator bias', which makes them more suspicious of the truth of what they are told.[111] More problematically, stop and search, arrest and detention are often not motivated by the strength of incriminating evidence, but by extraneous reasons such as asserting police authority on the street, obtaining witness statements, whereas decisions to charge may be designed to save face over unjustified arrests.[112]

Following arrest, police officers exercise control and authority over suspects in order to soften them up to serve the imperative of confessions and guilty pleas. Thus custodial conditions (already likely to ensure vulnerability) can be exploited by, for instance, controlling access to food, toilets, toilet paper, sanitary towels and even lawyers, notwithstanding ECHR rights, and imposing strip or intimate searches. Then, in interrogating suspects, the police may use a mixture of threats (for example, to pursue family members), aggressive questioning, humiliation, abuse and insults, inducements (for example, of early release or reduced charges), and feigned empathy or concerned but misleading advice.[113] Far more sophisticated, but legally unchallengeable, are various questioning techniques designed to subtly shape the answers of both suspects and witnesses to the questioner's purpose, such as the use of closed, leading and imperfect syllogistic questions (which force the suspect to accept dubious statements because they follow logically). Moreover, in the case of witness interviews, which unlike those of suspects need not be recorded, the police will attempt to turn ambiguity into certainty by choosing the wording of formal witness statements. Finally, not only do the police rarely seek out exculpatory material (or indeed corroborative material even when corroboration is required)[114] but when it is raised, may seek to suppress it and even cause exculpatory physical evidence to 'disappear'.

Theoretically, weak cases should be weeded out at later procedural stages, such as the decision to charge or to go to trial, or at trial itself. However, leaving aside the infringement of civil liberties and stress caused by such late action, empirical studies paint a pessimistic picture of the

---

[111] See D. Bradford and J. Goodman-Delahunty, 'Detecting Deception in Police Investigations: Implications for False Confessions' (2008) 15 *Psychiatry, Psychology and Law* 105, 108–9.

[112] See, for example, Sanders, Young and Burton, above n. 5, Chapters 2–4.

[113] See Chapter 6, sections 2.4.3 and 2.5.2 as regards the effectiveness of such techniques.

[114] Cf. C. J. Ayling, 'Corroborating Confessions: An Empirical Analysis of Legal Safeguards against False Confessions' (1984) 1984 *Wisconsin Law Review* 1121, 1193.

system's ability to identify weak cases.[115] They suggest that weak and strong cases are not simply matters of the objective weight and cogency of the evidence, but are products of police[116] and prosecution activity. According to research south of the border, around 50 per cent of suspects are not charged, yet such decisions seem to stem as much from factors such as workload and ideas of 'true' criminality as from evidential insufficiency.[117] Indeed, there is often little difference between cases dropped and those that, because of the factors discussed in this section, lead almost inevitably to a conviction, usually after a guilty plea. Thus, as far as the outcome and hence factual accuracy of cases is concerned, the die is often cast at an early stage of proceedings, out of sight and reach of those responsible for ensuring factual accuracy in what is in effect a trial before the trial, albeit one in secret.

For example, decisions not to charge or to drop charges are rarely if ever reviewed, whereas the files for cases selected for prosecution which arrive before superior police officers and prosecution lawyers are already heavily constructed in favour of prosecution, with ambiguities removed by amending and omitting problematic material, and facts forced into stereotypical situations regarded as unproblematically criminal. Moreover, police officers and prosecution lawyers making decisions to charge and prosecute are often reluctant to question the views of those investigating cases, lack adequate time and resources to conduct independent evaluations, especially of 'trivial' cases, and are themselves subject to a conflicting adversarial requirement of obtaining convictions. Consequently Susan Moody and Jacqueline Tombs found, albeit more than three decades ago, that only 8 per cent of cases are dropped by Scottish prosecutors and in only 6 per cent of cases did they request additional evidence, despite recognising the selective nature of police files.[118]

Admittedly, many of those who are actually or technically innocent are acquitted. However, as we have already noted,[119] adjudicators, especially in the lower courts, tend to operate with a presumption of guilt. Far more importantly, even if adjudicators are willing and able to act as robust and neutral evaluators of the accuracy of the prosecution's case, the prevalence of plea bargaining means that in most cases they are unable to do so.

---

[115] For a good overview, see A. Sanders, 'Prosecution Services', in M. McConville and G. Wilson (eds), *The Handbook of the Criminal Justice System* (2002).

[116] Especially in relation to public order offences when the only evidence required might be an officer's subjective view that the accused was abusive, causing alarm or distress, etc.

[117] McConville, Sanders and Leng, above n. 107, Chapter 6.

[118] *Prosecution in the Public Interest* (1982), 9, 47, 57.

[119] Section 2.4.1, above.

No doubt many 'cop a plea' because they recognise their guilt and likely conviction. The knowledge that guilty pleas frequently attract lower sentences[120] and the desire to get 'things over with' in order to avoid extended anxiety and disruption of their lives may make such decisions sensible, especially when lesser charges or some other incentive for pleading guilty are offered. On the other hand, some decisions may only be sensible because the dice are already so loaded against an accused because of police control of pre-trial proceedings and pro-prosecution adjudicative biases.

Even more problematic is the fact that suspects may face undue pressure, subterfuge and even deception and betrayal of confidence by their lawyers. As one prominent study concludes: 'Not only are the overwhelming majority of defendants convicted, and convicted by their own plea, but conviction is achieved in the office of their own adviser through a process whose methodologies most closely resemble those of the police themselves.'[121] While undue pressure is arguably, and deception certainly, unethical, given the evidence against clients (often from their own mouths) and the sociological realities of trials, advice to plead guilty may obviously be sensible. However, sociological research consistently finds that such advice often reflects the lawyer's rather than their client's interests,[122] and that innocent clients are sometimes pressurised into reluctantly pleading guilty[123] not least because it is rational for the prosecution to offer the innocent the most favourable plea-bargaining deals![124] Some of the reasons for lawyers using adversarial zeal *against* rather than *for* their clients duplicate those motivating civil law practitioners, namely the economic advantages of settling cases and the desire to maintain good relationships with police officers, prosecution lawyers and court officials with whom they daily interact, even to the extent of volunteering confidential information about the case in the absence of any duty to do so.[125] However,

---

[120] F. Leverick, 'The Rise and Fall of the Sentence Discount' (2013) *Scots Law Times News* 259.

[121] McConville et al., above n. 63, 160.

[122] In addition to studies cited above, see, for example, J. Baldwin, *Pre-Trial Justice: A Study of Case Settlement in Magistrates' Courts* (1985).

[123] The most persuasive demonstration of this is Baldwin and McConville, above n. 108, Chapter 4, but see also Bottoms and McClean, above n. 107, 219–26 (estimating the figure to be about 18 per cent); McConville, Sanders and Leng, above n. 117, 169–70; M. Zander, 'The "Innocent" (?) Who Plead Guilty' (1993) 143 *New Law Journal* 85 (but see M. McConville and L. Bridges, 'Pleading Guilty Whilst Maintaining Innocence' (1993) 143 *New Law Journal* 160 criticising Zander's methodology).

[124] C. M. Bradley, 'The Convergence of the Continental and the Common Law Model of Criminal Procedure' (1996) 7 *Criminal Law Forum* 471, 474.

[125] See, for example, Baldwin, above n. 122, 19, Chapters 2 and 3; McConville et al., above n. 63, 36.

in addition, some defence lawyers seem to assume that their clients are, if not guilty of the exact crime charged, then at least of doing something similar, and may even share police and prosecution 'crime-control' views[126] about the need to convict and punish criminals with minimum state expenditure. Consequently their constructions of the facts may be 'precisely tailored to legitimate and support', rather than rival, those of the police.[127]

However, whatever the precise causes of what Abraham Blumberg famously described as a confidence game in which lawyers act as 'double agents' serving the needs of 'assembly line justice' rather than their clients,[128] far too few live up to their image as fearless and zealous champions of criminal suspects. Indeed, most guilty pleas and the pressure to accept them are made almost inevitable by the singular lack of effort put into criminal defence work. Thus defence lawyers – or often their staff, who might be inexperienced or recruited from the police – may do little or nothing to protect clients from police pressure in interrogation, concentrating instead on persuading them to be co-operative and waive their right to silence. Instead of independently investigating the facts of cases, such as by fully interviewing clients, following evidential leads and searching for independent witnesses, lawyers and their staff tend to rely on police documents, ignore or are sceptical about the client's version of events, guide client answers into pre-determined stereotypical assumptions about the facts, and ignore possible defences and the opportunity to challenge police malpractice. Indeed, they may even delegate fact investigation to clients themselves, which is problematic enough for those on bail but almost impossible if on remand. Moreover, they spend less time preparing for trial – a practice not helped by solicitors who deliver case files to counsel at the last minute, and by counsel who return briefs at the last moment and are reluctant to speak to clients and witnesses. Finally, much court-room advocacy is perfunctory, often designed simply to show clients that the lawyer is doing their job,[129] with many lawyers worried more about their own credibility with the court than defending clients' interest, even to the extent of sometimes effectively selling them out.

This does not necessarily mean that clients are better off unrepresented. Certainly, tactics used to discourage suspects from gaining legal

---

[126] See at n. 5, above.

[127] McConville et al., above n. 63, 149.

[128] 'The Practise of Law as Confidence Game: Organizational Co-Optation of a Profession' (1967) 1 *Law & Society Review* 15.

[129] See the quotation at n. 217 below.

advice[130] suggest that the police do not think so, though in fact many criminal suspects themselves waive their right to representation because of misplaced optimism, fatalistic pessimism or an understandable distrust of lawyers. But evidence does suggest that suspects without lawyers are less resistant to police attempts to get them to break their right to silence, adapt their answers to fit police constructions of the facts and confess to crimes that they may not have committed or for which they could possibly avoid being convicted.[131]

Unrepresented accused are similarly disadvantaged in court.[132] It is much more difficult to tell a long story without the assistance of someone to converse with, especially in formal settings and where faced by an opponent poised to seize on any small mistakes, exaggerations or omissions. Moreover, unrepresented witnesses lack knowledge of court procedure, such as when to cross-examine and when to mount their defence, resulting in them being frequently silenced for speaking out of turn. This is likely to intimidate them so that when their turn to speak does arrive they are cowed into silence. But when they do try to cross-examine, the effect will be blunted because they will be unaware of its usual form and technique. Conversely, and paradoxically, criminal accused who show some knowledge of court procedures and law or display advocacy skills are treated with suspicion by adjudicators, who may assume that their knowledge comes from previous contact with the criminal justice system or regard them as cheeky upstarts. What is praiseworthy conduct in lawyers may thus be silenced or subjected to negative comment if performed by unrepresented accused.

These features of criminal cases hardly seem calculated to enhance truth finding in a system premised on the vigorous representation of opposing positions before a neutral adjudicator. Occasionally constraints on the prosecution, protections for an accused and lawyers committed to zealous defence of their client's interest may more or less cancel out state advantages. Equally, lacklustre performance by defence lawyers may be matched by lacklustre prosecution lawyers and poor police preparation. Usually, however, the state is faced either by accused who are unrepresented and out of their depth or represented by compliant lawyers equally as keen as the state to routinely channel accused towards a plea of guilty irrespective of possible defences. In such circumstances, factual accuracy

---

[130] See, for example, E. Cape, 'Advising and Assisting Defenders before Trial', in McConville and Wilson, above n. 115.

[131] See G. Gudjonsson, *The Psychology of Interrogations and Confessions: A Handbook* (2003), 71, 139 and 150, comparing this with the overall low rate of reliance on the right to silence by suspects: see ibid. at 49 and 148.

[132] See esp. McBarnet, above n. 3, 124–8; Carlen, above n. 107, Chapters 3 and 4.

never comes to be adversarially tested and as a consequence thousands of accused will be convicted each year on charges which are insufficiently supported by the evidence or to which there are legal defences. In fact, because most accused plead guilty at least to some charges, there is less incentive for police to get the facts right before they arrest and charge, leading to mass arrests in 'sweeps' or based merely on matching the crime with the modus operandi of local criminals.[133] This not only leads to unjustifiable human rights violations, but also, given the difficulty of derailing unjustified cases once started, increases the possibility of unjustified convictions. Admittedly, the even lower level of checks on decisions not to arrest, charge or prosecute where there *is* sufficient evidence to convict mean that the overall truth-deficit in the criminal process cuts both ways. But, for the reasons repeatedly stressed,[134] fundamental criminal justice values entail that this is far less of a problem.

We thus see that, depending on the exact configuration of the competing parties and access to resources, the adversarial system may be undermined as much by lawyers and other parties exercising insufficient zeal as by those displaying excessive zeal. This is exacerbated by the way in which the presence or absence of such zeal coincides with inequalities in other resources, often leading to cases being settled out of court without judicial oversight. In other words, the assumptions behind the truth-finding qualities of adversarial fact finding only works, if at all, when both parties are equally matched or there is a neutral adjudicator present, willing and able to rectify the impact of power imbalances. Such conditions are, however, far more the exception than the rule.

2.5 The Anglo-American Procedural Model: Replacement or Reform?

The failings of the Anglo-American procedural model and particularly its adversarial structure have led to much debate within and outwith fact positivism. Ranged against those who consider the classical Anglo-American model as the best means of truth finding are 'adversary sceptics'[135] who call for its replacement by the classical Continental model, not least because its similarity to scientific fact finding better reflects the Rationalist Tradition. More specifically, in addition to avoiding many of the problems

---

[133] See, for example, McConville, Sanders and Leng, above n. 107, Chapter 2, esp. 23–4; M. McConville, 'Plea Bargaining', in McConville and Wilson, above n. 116, 367.

[134] See esp. Chapter 3, section 3.3.2.

[135] D. M. Risinger, 'Unsafe Verdicts: The Need for Reformed Standards for the Trial and Review of Factual Innocence Claim' (2005) 41 *Houston Law Review* 1281, 1288.

of adversarial fact finding, we can recall from Chapter Three a number of features of the Continental model that can be claimed with varying degrees of plausibility to make it better at truth finding, and – as managerialist reforms assume – cheaper and more efficient:[136]

- the fact that witnesses are judicially examined soon after the events in question rather than months, if not years, later reduces problems with memory decay and contamination,[137] while also reducing the chances of witnesses being unavailable;
- witnesses give evidence in a natural and arguably more reliable manner;
- the episodic nature of fact finding and its lack of finality mean that proceedings can easily be reconvened and conclusions altered if new facts emerge;
- greater judicial control is exercised over out-of-court settlements and plea bargains;
- the use of trained professional adjudicators;
- judgments are based on logical inferences from a written record and reached in circumstances conducive to calm reflection;
- all evidence can be considered and any dangers of unreliable evidence assessed on their merits rather than by applying blanket policies of exclusion.

However, just as it is impossible to establish that the classical Anglo-American model is any better than its Continental counterpart, neither can it be established that it is any worse. While the two main arguments in favour of adversarial fact finding can be met with counterarguments, even Frank, one of the most vociferous critics of the adversarial system, admits that it contains 'a core of good sense'.[138] And whatever the problems with cross-examination, some sociological studies indicate its worth in ferreting out the truth.[139] Conversely, perceived problems with Continental fact finding have led to the introduction of adversarial and other Anglo-American features in some Continental jurisdictions, though mainly in

---

[136] As argued for by, for example, B Kaplan, 'Civil Procedure – Reflections on the Comparison of Systems' (1959) 9 *Buffalo Law Review* 409; J. H. Langbein, 'The German Advantage in Civil Procedure' (1985) 52 *University of Chicago Law Review* 823.

[137] See Chapter 6, section 2.3.

[138] Above n. 55, 80.

[139] See, for example, Davis, Cretney and Collins, above n. 60, 246ff, but see Chapter 5, section 7.4 and Chapter 6, section 4.2 regarding its more limited role in relation to scientific and witness testimony.

order to ensure greater protections for criminal accused.[140] There is thus no overwhelming case for totally re-modelling fact finding on the classical Continental procedural model, not least because doing so would involve enormous costs in terms of effort, expense, confusion, anxiety, disorientation, and inadvertent miscarriages of justice due to unfamiliarity with a new system.[141] In addition, the classical Continental model is argued to be incompatible with Anglo-American distrust of officialdom and the beliefs that things are best done by individual effort and in competition with others.[142]

Consequently the solution might be to follow aspirational rationalists, as well as those taking a more critical approach, and seek to remove those aspects of the Anglo-American system which obstruct truth finding, most notably its excessively adversarial character. Alternatively, many[143] suggest borrowing specific aspects of Continental practice, such as the:

- extension of the current limited duties of disclosure of all known facts and documents;
- use of neutral state agencies to investigate and even present facts and question witnesses;
- abandonment of the climactic and final nature of trials to allow full investigation whenever new facts emerge;
- allowing judges and juries a more active role in questioning witnesses in order to improve their understanding of cases;
- replacement of juries with 'mixed panels' of professional judges and lay assessors.

More specifically in the criminal justice sphere, some suggest abolishing or at least radically curtailing plea bargaining and its greater judicial supervision to ensure that plea bargains are factually supported, fair and

---

[140] See the references in nn. 175 and 223 in Chapter 3.

[141] See, for example, Luban, above n. 42, 92–103; S. R. Gross, 'The American Advantage: The Value of Inefficient Litigation' (1987) 85 *Michigan Law Review* 734, 751–2.

[142] Freedman, above n. 49, 38–9; R. J. Kutak, 'The Adversary System and the Practice of Law', in D. Luban (ed.), *The Good Lawyer: Lawyer's Roles and Lawyer's Ethics* (1983), 173.

[143] See, for example, Eggleston, above n. 59; McEwan, above n. 60, Chapter 8; Hunter, above n. 80; Langbein, above n. 136; M. Jacob, *Civil Litigation: Practice and Procedure in a Shifting Culture* (2001), passim, but esp. 18, 115, 264; T. Weigend, 'Why have a Trial when you can have a Bargain?', in A. Duff et al. (eds), *The Trial on Trial: Volume 2 – Judgement and Calling into Account* (2006); B. Schafer and O. K. Wiegand, 'It's Good to Talk – Speaking Rights and the Jury', in A. Duff et al., ibid.; T. Hornle, 'Democratic Accountability and Lay Participation in Criminal Trials', in A. Duff et al., ibid.

in the public interest.[144] A detailed discussion of the merits of these suggested reforms – and indeed a whole raft of other reforms to police and prosecution practices – is beyond the scope of this book. But in any event – without intending to reject any of the suggestions for introducing elements of Continental procedure into Anglo-American fact finding – it should be noted that 'legal transplants' need to be approached with caution.[145] Thus both legal and cultural differences between the 'donor' and 'recipient' systems can undermine effective implementation because of a lack of acceptance and possibly also subversion of the new procedures (transplant rejection) and/or result in the importation of unwanted values into the host system (alien species invasion).[146]

In addition, critical epistemology[147] would suggest going beyond both classical procedural models in order to enhance the accuracy of legal fact finding. The competitive argumentation of Anglo-American fact finding may prevent consideration of additional views necessary to a more complete picture of the facts and to have the best chance of resolving disputes. But even if a wider range of views is sought, as in the Continental model, their impact is limited by their binary outcomes and refracted through the eyes and partial perspectives of official investigators. Particularly in a multi-cultural and otherwise highly segmented social world, it seems preferable to seek as many relevant perspectives as possible and to pursue truth through multi-faceted approaches whereby dilemmas are turned into trilemmas or polylemmas through lateral rather than unilinear thinking.[148]

---

[144] Duff et al., above n. 38, 178–80; Baldwin and McConville, above n. 107, Chapter 6; Bottoms and McClean, above n. 107, 233ff; M. McConville, 'Plea Bargaining', in M. McConville and G. Wilson (eds), *The Handbook of the Criminal Justice Process* (2002).

[145] See, for example, J. C. Reitz, 'Why We Probably Cannot Adopt the German Advantage in Civil Procedure' (1989–90) 75 *Iowa Law Review* 987; M. Damaška, 'The Uncertain Fate of Evidentiary Transplants: Anglo-American and Continental Experiments' (1997) 45 *American Journal of Comparative Law* 839; O. G. Chase, 'American "Exceptionalism" and Comparative Procedure' (2002) 50 *American Journal on Comparative Law* 277, but cf. the greater optimism of J. Jackson, 'Transnational Faces of Justice: Two Attempts to Build Common Strategies Beyond National Boundaries', in Jackson, Langer and Tillers, above n. 42.

[146] See L. M. Grande, 'Italian Criminal Procedure: A System Caught Between Two Traditions' and S. C. Thaman, 'The Two Faces of Justice in the Post-Soviet Legal Sphere: Adversarial, Jury Trials, Plea Bargaining and the Inquisitorial Legacy', in Jackson, Langer and Tillers, ibid., but cf. D. Krapac, 'Some Trends in Continental Criminal Procedure in Transition: Countries of South Eastern Europe', in ibid., 134ff. Arguably, however, these problems are lessening with the increasing 'convergence' of the two main legal procedural families: see, for example, R. S. Frase, 'Comparative Criminal Justice as a Guide to American Law Reform: How Do the French Do It, How Can We Find Out and Why Should We Care?' (1990) 78 *California Law Review* 539.

[147] See Chapter 2, section 3 passim, but esp. 3.3.2.

[148] See, for example, Menkel-Meadow, above n. 54; D. Nicolson, 'Gender, Epistemology and Ethics', in Ellison and Childs, above n. 58, 34–5.

Moreover, if all relevant persons affected by disputes have a free and equal opportunity to defend their views and persuade others through dialogue, such as in Jurgen Habermas' 'ideal speech situation', which involves a commitment to the free, tolerant, non-dogmatic and respectful exchange of views,[149] this may ensure more sources of information and hence (hopefully) more accurate fact finding. Of course, meeting such a utopian ideal will be extremely difficult, particularly where parties are diametrically opposed and not interested in co-operation, and where one cannot wait for or afford the resources to conclude open-ended debate between all relevant parties. However, if the aim is to improve the truth-determining function of legal fact finding, reform needs to consider how far it can borrow from the sorts of ideas of critical epistemologists and communication theorists like Habermas which were discussed in Chapter Two. Indeed, the latter seem to have influenced more recent versions of the second approach to Anglo-American fact finding which, as we have seen, looks beyond truth finding to its role in resolving disputes and communicating cherished procedural values. It is to this approach we now turn.

3 Fact Finding and Liberal Values: Civilised Dispute Resolution and Norm Communication

3.1 The Arguments

One variant of this approach points to the many rules designed to protect the liberties of criminal suspects which may obstruct truth finding. Indeed, it is argued that, while Anglo-American procedure might lose out to its Continental comparator as regards truth finding, it is far superior in relation to the protection of an accused's procedural rights.[150] Moreover, according to Laurence Tribe, in upholding such rights, trials act as rituals affirming 'respect for the accused as a human being – affirmations that remind him [sic] and the public about the sort of society we want to become and, indeed, about the sort of society we are'.[151] In other words, the very process of legal fact finding acts to communicate valued social norms. Contemporary proponents of this approach see criminal trials playing an educative role, not just in relation to the substantive, but also

---

[149] See Chapter, 2, section 3.2.2.3.
[150] See Bradley, above n. 124.
[151] 'Trial by Mathematics: Precision and Ritual in the Legal Process' (1971) 84 *Harvard Law Review* 1329, 1392. See also S. J. Clark, '"Who Do You Think You Are?" The Criminal Trial and Community Character', in Duff et al., above n. 143, esp. 83, 85, and for a critique, M. L. Seigel, "A Pragmatic Critique of Modern Evidence Scholarship" (1993) 88 *Northwestern University Law Review* 995.

the procedural, norms applied.[152] They see criminal trials as a public forum in which accused are called to answer charges of, and if proved guilty to answer for, wrongdoing. In order for a verdict to be legitimate, it must emanate from a process in which the accused fully participates and the state upholds its professed commitment to procedural fairness. At the same time, however, many of those who argue that trials should have such a 'principle of integrity'[153] recognise that, if guilty verdicts are to effectively communicate social norms, they need to be based (knowingly, in the view of some)[154] on the truth.

Others, however, seem to regard truth finding as less important than other functions, especially in civil cases. Thus, according to Charles Nesson, while a trial is ostensibly structured to find the truth, 'it is also a drama that the public attends and from which it assimilates behavioral messages . . . the judicial process inculcates and reinforces standards by which each person should judge himself'.[155] A slightly different function for fact finding sees it as primarily providing a civilised forum for resolving conflict which dissuades its citizens from taking the law into their hands and hence helps prevent anarchy.[156] In the words of Henry Hart and John McNaughton:

> The law's handling of its task of fact-finding . . . is a last ditch process in which something more is at stake than the truth only of the specific matter in contest. There is at stake also that confidence of the public generally in the impartiality and fairness of public settlement of disputes which is essential if the ditch is to be held and the settlements accepted peaceably.[157]

However, even under this view, truth finding is not irrelevant. Decisions which are too far removed from the truth will lack legitimacy and hence be less likely to resolve disputes through acceptance of the outcome.

---

[152] See, for example, Duff, above n. 38; R. A. Duff, *Trials and Punishments* (1986), esp. Chapter 4; I. H. Dennis, 'Reconstructing the Law of Criminal Evidence' (1989) *Current Legal Problems* 21; P. Roberts and A. Zuckerman, *Criminal Evidence* (2nd edn, 2010), 22, 188–91.

[153] Duff et al., ibid., Chapter 8.

[154] Ibid., esp. 89, 252–3. See also H. L. Ho, *A Philosophy of Evidence Law: Justice in the Search for Truth* (2008), Chapter 2.

[155] 'The Evidence or the Event? On Judicial Proof and the Acceptability of Verdicts' (1985) 98 *Harvard Law Review* 1357, 1360.

[156] See Frank, above n. 55, 7; E. M. Morgan, 'Suggested Remedy for Obstructions to Expert Testimony by Rules of Evidence' (1942) 10 *University of Chicago Law Review* 285; M. S. Ball, 'The Play's the Thing: An Unscientific Reflection on Courts Under the Rubric of Theatre' (1975) 28 *Stanford Law Review* 81, 107–9. For evidence of this function, even by those not convinced of the justice of decisions made in their cases, see Merry, above n. 9, esp. 170–1, 176.

[157] 'Evidence and Inference in Law', in D. Lerner (ed.), *Evidence and Inference* (1958), 52–3.

In any event, whatever the exact extent to which truth is necessary for the acceptability, legitimacy and communicative value of fact-finding decisions, these views clearly fit within the liberal tradition, which, as we saw in Chapter Two,[158] favours maximising individual freedom and sees law as protecting such freedom through both substantive and procedural rights, and as ensuring equality before the law. The view that law provides a civilised forum for dispute resolution fits within liberalism, in that it sees the functions of litigation other than that of truth finding in a benign light; as valuable and benefiting all in society. The view that trial verdicts communicate and educate people about substantive and procedural norms assumes that the norms of the liberal legal order are worthy of communication.

3.2 Critique

3.2.1 Civilised Values and Procedural Fairness

If accurate, there might be much of value in this view of legal fact finding. But how accurate is it? One version of the argument is to the effect that the Anglo-American procedural system, and particularly its adversarial nature, provides an effective – indeed, compared to Continental systems, a more effective – means of ending disputes and ensuring acceptable decisions because it best accords with people's sense of fairness. Here, however, we are back to a battle of hypotheses. The main, and only empirically supported,[159] argument is to the effect that Anglo-American fact finding is perceived as fairer than state-controlled Continental proceedings because it provides individuals with maximum involvement in and control over proceedings affecting their lives and this makes them more likely to accept the outcome and put aside their quarrels.[160]

However, all empirical support derives from laboratory experiments rather than actual legal proceedings.[161] Indeed, lay respect for the legal system is often found to be reduced in those who appear in court, especially

---

[158] Section 2.2.

[159] For additional, untested, arguments, see Fuller and Randall, above n. 45, 1161–2; M. R. Damaška, *The Faces of Justice and State Authority: A Comparative Approach to the Legal Process* (1986), 120.

[160] Freedman, above n. 49, 39–41; Thibaut and Walker, above n. 49. See also Damaška, ibid., 120–1.

[161] See Thibaut and Walker, ibid.; the references cited in W. O'Barr and J. M. Conley, 'Lay Expectations of the Civil Justice System' (1988) 22 *Law & Society Review* 137, 138. For a critique of the methodology used, see J. McEwan, 'Ritual, Fairness and Truth: The Adversarial and Inquisitorial Models of Criminal Trial', in A. Duff et al. (eds), *The Trial on Trial: Volume One – Truth and Due Process* (2004), 56.

as litigants and even if victorious.[162] This is perhaps not surprising given that, as we have seen or will see:[163]

- lawyers 'steal' their clients' disputes[164] by controlling interviews, pressurising them into settlements and plea bargains, and even expressly overruling their instructions and betraying them in court;
- cross-examining lawyers strive to 'make witnesses appear so inconsistent, forgetful, muddled, spiteful or greedy that their word cannot safely be believed';[165]
- unrepresented accused and other lay participants are often too bewildered and/or intimidated to make use of their day in court and may be treated 'as being either out of place, out of time, out of mind or out of order';[166]
- trial processes are calculated to control lay participants, whether witnesses or litigants.

But even if individual effort and party control were widespread in Anglo-American proceedings, research suggests that various other factors like consistency of decisions, the absence of bias, and opportunities for appeal have a greater impact on perceptions of fairness, and here Continental systems may have the edge.[167] More importantly, the fact that Anglo-American proceedings are *perceived* as fairer than others does not *in fact* mean that they are fairer. Indeed, the impact of inequalities between the parties in terms of abilities, commitment and resources may in fact make Anglo-American civil proceedings less fair. If so, it surely cannot be thought that *perceptions* of fairness[168] should take precedence over *actual* fairness?

Admittedly, the argument that Continental systems are in fact fairer than Anglo-American systems has not been tested, let alone established – even if it were possible to find some way of objectively testing actual

---

[162] Genn and Paterson, above n. 99, 202, 222 (who also note much higher rates of perceptions of fairness on the part of those who resolved their disputes by agreement); A. Sarat, 'Studying American Legal Culture: An Assessment of Survey Evidence' (1971) 11 *Law & Society Review* 427, 438–41.

[163] Sections 2.3–2.4 and 3.2 respectively.

[164] N. Christie, 'Conflicts as Property' (1977) 17 *British Journal of Criminology* 1.

[165] Rock, above n. 75, 267.

[166] Carlen, above n. 107, 129.

[167] McEwan, above n. 161, 59ff; T. R. Tyler, 'What is Procedural Justice? Criteria Used by Citizens to Assess the Fairness of Legal Procedures' (1988) 22 *Law & Society Review* 103, 104–5.

[168] For evidence of such perceptions about English and Welsh proceedings, see, for example, H. Genn, *Paths to Justice: What People Do and Think about Going to Law* (1999), 221–5, 228–33; Davis, above n. 9, 197–8; J. Baldwin, 'Raising the Small Claims Limit', in Zuckerman and Cranston, above n. 69, 189.

fairness. Consequently we are limited to evaluating the extent to which Scottish and other Anglo-American processes of proof uphold their own standards of fairness. Here the situation differs markedly between different types of cases, both in terms of formal standards and the empirical reality.

Thus, as we saw in Chapter Three,[169] the high standards of procedural justice in formal proceedings are watered down for administrative decision-making, especially the further one moves from quasi-judicial proceedings which resemble those of the courts. Unfortunately there is a dearth of sociological research into whether even these watered-down principles are upheld, but the (to put it mildly) cavalier approach to truth and governing substantive law revealed by the studies already discussed[170] does not inspire confidence that administrative decision-makers with power over citizens are particularly concerned by their procedural rights.[171] Certainly, many immigration and social security officials do not always approach applications with open minds or provide applicants with the opportunity to dissuade them from converting their initial assumption into final decision.

A similar lack of research prevents certain conclusions on the extent to which procedural rights are respected in civil proceedings. We do, however, know that the vast majority of disputes are resolved by private negotiation and hence that, without an impartial adjudicator and public and media scrutiny of proceedings, notions of equality and fairness are subject to being overridden by prevailing power relations between the parties.[172] Indeed, feminists and others argue that the increasing resort to negotiation and various forms of ADR may work to the disadvantage of those in positions of subordination in personal relations.[173]

By comparison to administrative and civil fact finding, there is a wealth of research on the criminal justice system. Although far less numerous, it is criminal cases which liberals largely have in mind when referring to law's role in upholding civilised values and communicating social norms. Clearly,

---

[169] Section 4.3.

[170] See section 2.1.

[171] Though cf. Baldwin, Wikely and Young, above n. 13, Chapter 4, on the high levels of procedural fairness in social security appeals (as opposed to initial decision-making).

[172] But cf. T. Tyler, 'Procedure or Result: What do Disputants Want From Legal Authorities', in K. J. Mackie (ed.), *A Handbook of Dispute Resolution: ADR in Action* (1991), 24, referring to (unidentified) studies reporting that participants in ADR and even plea bargaining perceive such proceedings as fair when given an opportunity to participate.

[173] See Chapter 3, section 4.3.1.

as we have seen,[174] the law takes into account the imbalances between state and defendant and the much more serious consequences of wrongful convictions as opposed to acquittals by various measures going well beyond the general right to a friar trial and fair treatment: the higher standard of proof, the presumption of innocence, the privilege against self-incrimination, the right to silence, exclusionary rules of evidence, etc. Moreover, it provides specific protection of their civil liberties when in contact with the police and other state agencies. Officially then, the law adheres to Packer's due process model.[175]

Sociological research reveals, however, that this model is far more prevalent in the superior courts, though even here formal protection is frequently watered down by qualifications, exceptions and contrary legal doctrines. By contrast, the competing criminal control model is far more evident in the lower courts and pre-trial proceedings, and hence governs the vast majority of criminal cases. Thus research[176] reveals that procedural rules are frequently ignored in the courts of summary jurisdiction. More importantly, many have never been extended to the lower courts in the first place or have been abolished. Instead, an 'ideology of triviality' reigns.[177] Because cases are seen as trivial, they are thought not to require the full panoply of procedural rights. Moreover, what procedural rights remain are more easily ignored as the lack of public interest in lower court proceedings removes the protection afforded by the full glare of publicity,[178] and low levels of legal representation mean that many accused lack knowledge or the skills necessary to assert their rights. In any event, as we saw in the previous section, representation will not necessarily make much difference, especially if the lawyers also view cases as trivial. For these reasons, compared to the visible face of the contested jury trial, most trials are brief and may amount to little more than bureaucratic processing.

However, it should now be obvious that the greatest threat to civil liberties flows from the fact that most criminal cases are concluded by guilty pleas without judicial oversight. Reviewing the literature on plea bargaining, Mike McConville asserts that '[e]xperience in many jurisdictions has shown that where plea bargaining is rife, probity, rectitude, and fair dealing are at a disadvantage'.[179] In fact, he argues that plea bargaining in and of itself

---

[174] Chapter 3, section 3.
[175] See at n. 5 above.
[176] McBarnet, above n. 3, Chapter 7; Bankowski, Hutton and McManus, above n. 3, esp. Chapter 3.
[177] McBarnet, ibid., but cf. Bankowski, Hutton and McManus, ibid., 176–9, noting that, despite classifying cases as trivial, JPs do not see their work as unimportant nor as requiring less care.
[178] Cf. Chapter 3, section 4.3.1.
[179] Above n. 133, 376.

'offends against the right to a fair trial set out in Article 6 because it acts to discourage all defendants from going to trial by the threat of more severe punishment if they do and are convicted'.[180] More fundamentally, the fact that a worrying proportion of those convicted following guilty pleas might have been acquitted on procedural grounds suggests that procedural rights are being ignored.[181]

It is just about possible to argue that such accused only have themselves or, where relevant, their legal advisors to blame for rendering the high standard of proof irrelevant or for waiving their procedural rights, and that the police are only doing their job of efficiently pursuing offenders. However, as we saw earlier,[182] many police officers are prepared to stretch or even ignore the law in order to obtain the convictions of those they see as (or sometimes merely those who can be made to seem) guilty. Many officers view civil liberty protections as making them work with one hand tied behind their backs and as only legitimately applying to decent people rather than most suspects.[183] Not only do they ignore the evidential tests for stop, search and seizure and for arrest and detention, but many are also unconcerned to ensure that suspects understand rights like those to a solicitor, and sometimes do their best to ensure that these rights are not taken up. Furthermore, they constantly push the boundaries of what are regarded as fair procedures for conducting interrogations, identity parades, searches of property and the person, and various others forms of obtaining evidence. And when one considers that such breaches do not automatically lead to the quashing of convictions,[184] once again we see that the breaches of procedural rights pre-trial may render irrelevant the full panoply of procedural rights available at trial.

3.2.2 Peaceful Means of Resolving Legal Disputes[185]
But if the law does not always meet its commitments to civilised values and procedural fairness, what about its role as a peaceful means of resolving legal disputes? An obvious preliminary point is that courts and other adjudicative bodies do not actually *resolve* disputes. In a winner-takes-all

---

[180] Ibid., 372.
[181] See section 2.4.2.
[182] Section 2.4.2.
[183] See, for example, the police officer quoted in Sanders, Young and Burton, above n. 5, 69.
[184] See F. Raitt, *Evidence – Principles, Policy and Practice* (2nd edn, with E. Keane, 2013), Chapters 9 and 10, regarding the tests applied in relation to confession and illegal searches.
[185] This section draws extensively on R. Cotterrell, *The Sociology of Law: An Introduction* (2nd edn, 1992), 210–16.

system, where solutions are 'dictated by an outsider, won by the victor, and imposed upon the loser',[186] one party is always likely to come away feeling aggrieved. In almost all cases there will be a residuum of attitudes and sensitivities that will colour any ongoing relationships between the parties and even lead to new grievances, especially where, as with child maintenance cases, court awards are often ignored.[187] Rather than resolve disputes, most legal decisions merely declare that they are no longer significant for legal purposes, while simultaneously affirming the norms that will govern future disputes.

A second point is that adversarial proceedings tend to simplify disputes and hence cannot cope with multi-faceted issues involving a network of different relationships and issues.[188] In addition, because judicial remedies are usually limited to findings of guilt or innocence or the award of damages and at best interdicts ordering the cessation of wrongful behaviour, the courts tend to look to the past in reaching decisions, whereas the resolution of disputes may require forward planning and an awareness of their underlying causes, especially where personal relationships are involved.

The conclusion that courts and other adjudicative bodies are not in fact primarily concerned with dispute *resolution* is reinforced by empirical research in the UK and US. Thus, given that most criminal cases are based upon guilty pleas, much of the courts' time is taken up with other aspects of 'conveyor belt justice' involving the formalities of charging accused or bail hearings and sentencing of those marked out for prosecution and condemnation.

Similar findings have been made in relation to civil courts. For example, one study of the work of two Californian courts over eighty years concluded that their main function was not to resolve disputes but to administratively process routine cases.[189] Similarly, in Maureen Cain's study of the English county courts, only 25 per cent of non-familial family work involved any form of dispute.[190] One of the reasons is that the most common form of court

---

[186] C. Menkel-Meadow, 'Portia in a Different Voice: Speculations on a Women's Lawyering Process' (1985) 1 *Berkeley Women's Law Journal* 39, 55.

[187] See, for example, W. L. F. Felstiner, R. L. Abel and A. Sarat, 'The Emergence and Transformation of Disputes: Naming, Blaming, Claiming . . .' (1980–1) 15 *Law & Society Review* 631, 639; M. Bayles, 'Principles for Legal Procedure' (1986) 5 *Law and Philosophy* 33, 39.

[188] Menkel-Meadow, above n. 54.

[189] L. M. Friedman, and R. V. Percival, 'A Tale of Two Courts: Litigation in Alameda and San Benito Counties' (1975) 10 *Law & Society Review* 267.

[190] M. Cain, 'Where are the Disputes? A Study of a First Instance Civil Court in the UK', in M. Cain and K. Kulcsar, *Disputes and the Law* (1983). See also Rock, above n. 105.

proceedings involves debt collecting or other forms of enforcement proceeding by large institutions (business companies, public bodies, etc.) against private individuals. For instance, private citizens constituted 84 per cent of defendants but only 10 per cent of plaintiffs in Cain's study, whereas in Scotland around 90 per cent of all small claims involve debt proceedings.[191] Such debt-enforcement proceedings hardly resemble a dispute, especially as defendants are rarely in court to mount a defence[192] (and, if they are, they are usually unrepresented).[193] Coupled with the mounting cost of judicial proceedings and the possibility of delays, this tends to increase the move towards efficient bureaucratic processing rather than genuine dispute resolution.

An interesting finding of these studies is that judgments are not enforced against debtors in a high percentage of cases (one-third in Cain's study), yet companies continue to use the courts for enforcement proceedings. Cain concludes that their main aim in doing so is to deter debtors from defaulting, and the courts' main aim is to reaffirm the legal norms relevant to the particular dispute,[194] thus constantly reminding the public of the rules of the system: how they should behave and the consequences of not doing so.

Indeed, the importance of norm reinforcement can also be seen in the fact that repeat players will settle cases to avoid rules being generated which are contrary to their long-term interests[195] or go to proof because of the possibility of favourable rule generation, even where there is little chance of their claim succeeding. In fact, the existing values contained within the law are more likely to be reinforced if courts are deprived of opportunities for law reform,[196] thus adding to the various other pressures channelling disputants into negotiated settlements.

Accordingly it can be argued that, rather than solving the parties' problems and ending disputes, courts are often more concerned with communicating how they will view the rights and wrongs of such relationships in the future. Settlements and other forms of ADR more effectively resolve

---

[191] Consumer Focus Scotland, *Ensuring Effective Access to Appropriate and Affordable Dispute Resolution: The Final Report of the Civil Justice Advisory Group* (2011), 4. See also Jacob, above n. 143, 37; C. Whelan, *Small Claims Courts: A Comparative Study* (1990), esp. 232–3.

[192] In Rock's study, above n. 105, only 17 per cent attended. Indeed, attendance by most defenders would bring the system to a halt.

[193] Consumer Focus Scotland, above n. 191; C. Hennessy, *Civil Procedure and Practice* (4th edn, 2014), 29.

[194] See also Cotterrell, above n. 185, 214.

[195] Galanter, above n. 100, 101.

[196] Ibid., 121–2.

disputes,[197] albeit, as already noted,[198] at the expense of a concern for procedural rights and factual truth. This suggests that the goals of dispute resolution cannot be so easily reconciled with the aims and values of fact finding as liberals seem to assume. However, for those who reject the prevailing legal order, the fact that ADR always takes place within currently accepted legal norms – and hence will tend to reaffirm the status quo – is much more problematic. In fact, for those critical of the status quo, all forms of fact finding can be seen as problematic. This takes us to the third view of legal fact finding.

4 Legal Fact Finding as Politics and Power

4.1 The Arguments

This view has been expressed in various ways. For example, Kenneth Graham calls trials 'political theatre'.[199] Douglas Hay vividly describes how the rituals and majesty of eighteenth-century criminal trials acted as both theatre and education,[200] enabling law to replace religion as the main source of inculcating morality in the masses. Judges would deliver homilies on the evils of crime, the status of which was bolstered by the awe and majesty of proceedings. In this way, trials acted as ideological instruments of the ruling class, who made the law, judged its infractions and controlled its execution. Of more contemporary relevance, Harold Garfinkel labels criminal trials' status 'degradation ceremonies', in which carefully managed dramas involving the presentation and examination of evidence, formal procedures and role playing allow for the successful denunciation of accused as transgressors of social norms.[201] Through the process of accusation, proof and sentencing, and the close examination of their past and present actions, and demeanour, accused are effectively created as new persons who can be presented to the outside world for the purposes of denunciation and the reaffirmation of social values. While this argument echoes the views of trials as a means of

---

[197] Genn, above n. 168, 165–6; Genn and Paterson, above n. 99, 196. See also Tyler, loc. cit., n. 172 on participant satisfaction with procedural fairness of ADR proceedings, but cf. M. S. Melli, H. S. Erlanger and E. Chambliss, 'The Process of Negotiation: An Exploratory Investigation in the Context of No-Fault Divorce' (1987) 40 *Rutgers Law Review* 1133, 1159–60, noting the high percentage of consensual divorce settlements which do not satisfy both parties.

[198] See section 3.2.1 above.

[199] 'The Instrumental Ideology of Evidence' (1987) 85 *Michigan Law Review* 1204, 1232. See also Z. Bankowski and G. Mungham, *Images of Law* (1976), Chapter 5.

[200] 'Property, Authority and the Criminal Law', in D. Hay, P. Linebaugh and E. P. Thompson (eds), *Albion's Fatal Tree* (1975).

[201] 'Conditions of Successful Degradation Ceremonies' (1956) 61 *American Journal of Sociology* 420; see also Bankowski and Mungham, above n. 199, 42, 87–93.

communicating social values, it is the community at large[202] rather than just the accused (or person held responsible in civil cases) which is the focus of persuasion. Consequently, instead of this process being seen in positive terms as reinforcing shared values, critical scholars see it as one of affirming the values of the powerful and a repressive socio-legal order.

4.2 Empirical Studies[203]

These views of trials as exercises in political power are based more on polemic than detailed study (Graham), on eighteenth-century trials (Hay) or on criminal cases alone (Garfinkel). However, when we look at contemporary sociological studies of litigation and trials, as well as the few on tribunals,[204] we find support for these views and a challenge to many vaunted features of Anglo-American fact finding. Given that we have already explored the implications of these studies in relation to truth finding and civilised dispute resolution, we will confine discussion to exploring other aspects of Anglo-American fact finding which are directly challenged by these studies. Most relevant of these are the autonomy of parties to pursue their legal claims, which is said to reflect Anglo-American support for the value of individual effort,[205] and the value of lay participation by witnesses, jurors and other lay adjudicators, which is said to reflect a desire to ensure community involvement in legal proceedings and to mitigate strict formal justice.[206]

4.2.1 Party Autonomy and Lay Participation

It should already be abundantly clear that sociological studies undermine the ideas that parties to disputes pursue their interests with total freedom and witnesses provide evidence in unfettered fashion. As regards the former, we have seen that represented litigants may have their disputes 'stolen' by lawyers by taking important decisions out of their hands.[207]

---

[202] Cotterrell, above n. 185, 224; L. Harmon, 'Etchings on Glass: Reflections on the Science of Proof' (1999) 40 *South Texas Law Review* 483, 505–6, but cf. Merry, above n. 9, esp. at 11, on the fact that working-class participants are not always persuaded of the vision of society presented to them in court.

[203] See generally, McBarnet, above n. 3, esp. Chapter 7; Carlen, above n. 107; Rock, above nn. 63 and 75; Goodrich, above n. 73, Chapter 6; Bankowski and Mungham, above n. 199, Chapters 4 and 5; J. Jackson, 'Law's Truth, Lay Truth and Lawyer's Truth: The Representation of Evidence in Adversary Trials'(1992) III *Law and Critique* 29; J. M. Conley and W. M. O'Barr, *Rules versus Relationships: The Ethnography of Legal Discourse* (1990), Chapter 9.

[204] See at n. 237 below.

[205] Above n. 142.

[206] See Chapter 3, section 3.2.4.

[207] Section 2.4.2 above.

This is most invidious in relation to decisions about whether to co-operate
with the state in criminal cases, not least because suspects are already subject to an overwhelming degree of control by state officials. Given that so
many cases are not subject to formal proof and, even if they are, that much
of the damage occurs outwith court, pre-trial behaviour has far more of
an impact on the truth finding and procedural fairness aims of fact finding than the conduct of trials. However, as this aspect of fact finding has
already been extensively canvassed, the rest of the discussion will focus on
the experiences of parties and witnesses at trial.

Echoing Graham, Garfinkel and Hay, legal sociologists portray trials as tightly controlled theatrical spectacles,[208] in which participants are
manipulated to play their part in producing verdicts acceptable to the law
and which reveal its power and majesty. This, it is argued, helps 'to generate a belief not only in the authority of law, but in authority in general'.[209]

Whether intentionally or not,[210] certain features of trials are likely to
inspire fear, awe and anxiety in lay participants, thus making them much
more pliable and willing to play their allotted role in producing orderly
trials, especially – as is often the case[211] – if they are not prepared by
their lawyers for trial. Even before they arrive in court, participants are
made aware that they are in an unfamiliar world known and controlled by
professionals. The summonses, pleadings and charges are all in a formal,
legalistic language, with threats of sanctions for breach. Court buildings
are designed to display law's power and majesty,[212] though lower courts
tend to be less grandiose. The demarcation of space between court insiders and outsiders signals who is in control, whereas the difficulty of finding
one's way around often badly signposted court buildings enhances lay participants' sense of unease.[213]

Before they get to court, parties and witnesses may have waited for
hours, simultaneously bored and anxious, whereas the location might be
switched at the last minute, leaving the parties on their own with family

---

[208] But cf. Ball, above n. 156, esp. at 100ff, arguing that theatricality has the benefits of inducing
a sense of urgency and greater creativity in judgment, humanising justice, and presenting an
image of a legitimate political community.

[209] P. Gabel and P. Harris, 'Building Power and Breaking Images: Critical Legal Theory and the
Practice of the Law' (1982) *Review of Law and Social Change* 369, 372.

[210] Carlen suggests that not all of these features are unintentional and quotes a magistrate who
recommended scaring lay participants as it 'makes them tell the truth' (above n. 107, 30).

[211] See section 2.4.2 regarding the fact that counsel are reluctant to speak to clients and witnesses.

[212] Even to put the 'fear of god into the ungodly' in the view of a court architect quoted by Rock,
above n. 63, 202.

[213] In addition to the references in n. 203, see Bottoms and McClean, above n. 107, 156–60;
P. Robson and J. Rodger, *The Spaces of Justice: The Architecture of the Scottish Court* (2017).

and friends waiting bemused in another court. In all these ways, lay participants may be softened up even before entering the court room. Then, when in court, they are subject to the control of court officials, police officers, lawyers and judicial personnel. For criminal accused this process starts with having to plead to charges in terms of categories which might seem irrelevant or even incomprehensible, thus forcing submission to law's authority.[214] Similarly they are constantly told to stand up, sit down, keep quiet, speak when spoken to, answer the question, 'just say yes or no', etc. According to one criminal accused: 'I thought it was a bloody farce. I never had the chance to speak my piece. I was just sitting there like a dummy.'[215] This perceptively echoes not just the theatrical image used by many sociologists, but Pat Carlen's argument that the whole process involves a game played by court regulars who treat the accused like a dummy player in bridge.[216] This control is enhanced by the fact that most lay participants are unfamiliar with court proceedings and hence expect to be told what to do or at least feel unable to challenge those doing so.

The intimidating nature of legal proceedings is further enhanced by their formality and majestic rituals, which are both solemn and often theatrical – a fact not lost on some participants:

> The fellow who's prosecuting and the fellow who's defending are not really interested in me. One is looking over the notes of the other as he's going along, to make sure he doesn't make any mistakes. After all they are near enough mates in the same play. They're the cast of the play, you're just the casual one-day actor. It's just another day's work to them.[217]

Like theatre, trials involve an idealised form of speech, dressing up, choreography, a planned physical layout, role-playing, and all the tension of a whodunnit.

For the witness, proceedings will start with the quasi-religious ceremony of oath-swearing. While the 'frequently formulaic, automatic way of taking the oath'[218] undermines its solemnity, the promise to 'tell

---

[214] Goodrich, above n. 73, 195.

[215] Baldwin and McConville, above n. 107, 87; see also ibid., citing another accused: 'They were all talking to each other and I just seemed to be watching and listening . . . It was like watching a press conference on the television.'

[216] Above n. 107, 81–2.

[217] Baldwin and McConville, above n. 107, 85. See also Carlen, above n. 107, esp. at 38, and cf. Davis, Cretney and Collins, above n. 60, describing settlement proceedings in chambers as 'like a Greek drama' and the parties' roles as 'spectators rather than actors'.

[218] D. Kurzon, 'Telling the Truth: The Oath as a Test of Witness Competency' (1989) II *International Journal for the Semiotics of Law* 49, 49. But see Carlen, ibid., 30, who observed magistrates making witnesses retake the oath if taken carelessly or derisorily.

the whole truth and nothing but the truth' is likely to bring to mind the drama of trials portrayed in television and films. Subsequently, the highly stylised nature of court-room language, so different from everyday discourse, augments control by professionals and further intimidates and bemuses lay participants.[219] The archaic and technical terms, meanings and concepts are not merely unfamiliar but also often incomprehensible and tend to silence lay participants, and enhance the power and authority of legal insiders. Particularly, because of frequently poor court acoustics, those giving evidence must speak louder than normal, often about intimate details and sensitive issues. Sometimes they respond to repeated attempts to make themselves heard by retreating into silence. Nor do they have the normal freedom to negotiate the right to speak, qualify their words, demand respect, and withdraw, if necessary, to save face.[220] And when speaking, they must also address their answers not to the person questioning them, but to the bench. Nor can they speak in the usual turn-taking or narrative manner, with listeners providing sympathetic prompts, acknowledgment and questions. Instead, as we have seen,[221] witness testimony is closely controlled so that it is likely to emerge in a totally alien form. Furthermore, witnesses and victims may unexpectedly find that when testifying about someone else's wrongdoing it is their probity which is on trial and their characters that are subjected to the sort of re-casting that Garfinkel describes.[222] Indeed, echoing his view of trials as degradation ceremonies, Brenda Danet and Byrna Bogoch argue that prosecutorial questioning of accused may involve a form of symbolic punishment.[223]

Power relations are also reflected in court-room architecture.[224] In some courts, the poor acoustics and the placement of the accused furthest away from the bench and jury mean that they may be oblivious to much of what is being said. In all courts, the distance between the

---

[219] See further M. Atkinson and P. Drew, *Order in Court: The Organisation of Verbal Interaction in Judicial Settings* (1979); J. McEwan, *The Verdict of the Court: Passing Judgment in Law and Psychology* (2003), 98–9; W. M. O'Barr, *Linguistic Evidence: Language, Power and Strategy in the Courtroom* (1982); R. Penman, 'Regulation of Discourse in the Adversary Trial' (1987) 7 *Windsor Yearbook of Access to Justice* 3.

[220] Penman, ibid., 16.

[221] Section 2.3 above.

[222] Rock, above n. 75, 267.

[223] 'Fixed Fight or Free-for-All? An Empirical Study of Combativeness in the Adversary System of Justice' (1980) 7 *British Journal of Law and Society* 36, 59–60.

[224] See references in n. 213 and A. Duff et al., above n. 38, 273–4, on how court rooms were expressly modified to enhance law's authority.

adjudicator, lawyers questioning witnesses and the witnesses themselves exceed that which is normal for the disclosure of what might be intimate and embarrassing information. In other words, mounting an observable spectacle takes precedence over witnesses' 'interactional comfort'.[225]

In criminal cases, the siting and nature of the dock area carry important psychological messages. The accused's isolation from the rest of the court suggests their alienation from the rest of the community and a second-class status. Surrounding the dock with bars suggests that the accused is already guilty, and elevating it enhances public scrutiny.[226] The judicial bench is also elevated, but higher than the accused, and often set against the backdrop of the emblems of the state. This layout arguably reflects religious ideas in symbolising the judge's greater proximity to heaven, whereas the steps from the dock to the jail below represent the accused's descent to hell. Similarly, there is a protected space around the adjudicators to which entry is closely controlled. All of this reinforces the impression of the adjudicator's power.

Also inspiring awe, while arguably dusting their wearers 'with the divinity that befits the augur',[227] are the judge's robes and wigs[228] and the slightly less impressive garb of advocates. These enhance their status and contrast markedly with the appearance of the lay participants, particularly criminal accused who emerge in handcuffs.[229] The court's power and authority is further augmented by its various rituals: having to rise and wait in silence until the judge arrives from a door to the rear of the bench; the various terms of respect for the court; the deference paid by lawyers to the court; and the affected politeness between lawyers, which contrasts with the way the accused might be addressed or spoken of simply by surname, as 'the panel' or even 'this man/woman'. All of this, and perhaps most importantly the tension which builds as the court waits for the verdict, contributes to the decision's appearance as something which emerges inexorably from the austere machinery of justice, run – but not programmed – by lawyers, adjudicators and court officials.

---

[225] Atkinson and Drew, above n. 219, 222–32.

[226] But cf. *T* v. *UK* and *V* v. *UK* [2000] *Criminal Law Review* 187, in which the European Court of Human Rights held that this and the general incomprehensibility caused by the ritualistic and formalistic nature of proceedings in the notorious trial of the eleven-year-olds Robert Thompson and Jon Venables breached Article 6 of the ECHR.

[227] Frank, above n. 55, 255.

[228] But cf. P. Roberts, 'Faces of Justice Adrift? Damáska's Comparative Method and the Future of Common Law Evidence', in Jackson, Langer and Tillers, above n. 42, 297, arguing that they are '(mostly) harmless quaint anachronisms'.

[229] See Jackson, above n. 203, 48, for evidence of the impact.

Admittedly, these descriptions of formal fact-finding proceedings are based largely[230] on criminal proceedings. Although lacking equivalent studies of civil proceedings, it is apparent to any observer that they also involve ritualistic formality and control of lay participants, albeit in less dramatic form.[231] The elements of dramatic ritual are also far less prevalent in the lower courts, where the conveyor belt nature of justice and the crucial importance of what happens outwith court renders trials 'dull, commonplace, ordinary and after a while downright tedious'.[232] Here, the ritual and solemnity of proceedings remains important, but rather than adding to the drama of proceedings, they mask the fact that courts are merely involved in rubber-stamping outcomes already largely predetermined.[233] A show might still be put on but its audience is not the rarely present public or press, but the lawyer's client. Implicitly acknowledging both the play-acting and confidence game involved in trials, one English solicitor explained that:

> Provided that the solicitor gives them [that is, defendants] a run in the courts, they feel that everything has been done for them. After all, most defendants are guilty of offences. They just form the centre of attraction for the day – when they become the 'prisoner' or the 'accused'. It is important to make them feel they've been looked after. They expect a bit of a show to be put on, even when they know they're 'done for' so to speak.[234]

But even without the rituals and attempts to impress clients, legal fora seem likely to intimidate lay participants. For example, studies of social security appeal tribunals show that appellants do not feel in control, but on trial themselves, and have to adopt humiliating postures in order to obtain favourable decisions,[235] whereas those subjected to Children's

---

[230] But cf. Davis, above n. 9, 188–91; Davis, Cretney and Collins, above n. 60, Chapters 9 and 10, and their conclusion at 254, which echoes the quotation by Goodrich at n. 237 below.

[231] Cf. Davis, Cretney and Collins, ibid., 228ff, regarding the less formidable court architecture in family courts, but also arguing that even judges' chambers are imposing and designed to put the judge in a central position.

[232] Bottoms and McLean, above n. 107, 226; and for a description of this conveyor belt in the Scottish Magistrates' Courts, see Bankowski, Hutton and McManus, above n. 3, 50–3.

[233] Cf. Bankowski, Hutton and McManus, above n. 3, 52, referring to the ever-present 'tension between the symbolic functions of court ritual and the lowly ordinariness of daily practices'.

[234] Bankowski and Mungham, above n. 199, 100, and see also at 97, analogising this show to the mock fights of professional wrestlers; McConville et al., above n. 63, 205–6, on how the lawyers present 'boiler-plate' speeches 'without any expectation of them having an effect'.

[235] Baldwin, Wikely and Young, n. 13, 97, Chapter 6, referring to their own findings and other studies. See also Genn and Genn, above n. 15, Chapter 7; T. G. Ison, 'Administrative Law – The Operational Realities' (2009) 22 *Canadian Journal of Administrative Law and Practice* 315, 326.

Hearings report being lectured and shamed in ways similar to Garfinkel's degradation ceremony.[236]

What these studies reveal, among other things, is that party control and the vaunted day in court, which are meant to help ensure the civilised resolution of disputes, are more myth than reality. In Peter Goodrich's succinct summary, '[t]he day in court is likely to be experienced in terms of confusion, ambiguity, incomprehension, panic and frustration . . .'[237] To a large extent, litigants, accused and witnesses are so overawed that they can do little more than play the roles allotted to them. Even if not a full-blown degradation ceremony, trials in the higher courts certainly resemble theatre performances. The argument that such theatre is political tracks that made in relation to the bureaucratic processing of summary cases. In other words, what is more important than truth finding or dispute resolution is the routine reaffirmation of the social values embedded in substantive law. The aim is not so much to test the facts against the law, but to impose the law's way of looking at things on the facts. Every case which is successfully able to achieve this contributes to law's legitimacy and the social order it supports. By carefully managing what is said and done at trials by investing this process with ritual and majesty – or merely solemnity in the case of the lower courts – verdicts and the law on which they are based are legitimised by seeming to emerge from some natural and neutral process.

The plausibility of this view of trials as about constructing an official version of reality based upon legal ideology gains support from trials in which lay participants refuse the 'dummy player' role of sitting quietly and letting lawyers and officials define the issues, and decide whose input is important and whose values should govern the issues. A good example is the trial of the 'Chicago 7' for alleged crimes flowing from demonstrations against the US military during the Vietnam War.[238] Early in the trial, the accused dismissed all but one of their lawyers because they had allowed the state to define the agenda and were speaking in the language

---

[236] S. Asquith, *Children and Justice: Decision-Making in Children's Hearings and Juvenile Courts* (1983), esp. 202–4.

[237] Above n. 73, 188.

[238] See, for example, Bankowski and Mungham, above n. 199, 130–9; Gabel and Harris, above n. 209, 379ff, for this and other examples of political trials; T. Palmer, *The Trial of Oz* (1971). See also M Combe, 'The Indycamp: Demonstrating Access to Land and Access to Justice' (2017) 21 *Edinburgh Law Review* 228, describing litigants who unsuccessfully invoked Jesus Christ in his second coming, the United Nations Declaration on the Rights of Indigenous People, and the legitimacy of the Anglo-Scottish Union, the court and its judges in an attempt to prevent the removal of a camp set up on land near the Scottish Parliament which was intended to remain until the achievement of Scottish independence.

of the law, both of which made it very difficult for the trial to involve issues of politics and morality rather than merely the application of what the accused saw as repressive law. Consequently they sought to expand the notion of legal relevance by bringing in issues like the validity of the war and to challenge the idea of judicial impartiality by so annoying the judge that he began to work hand-in-hand with the prosecution and even to express racist sentiments. Thus, by refusing to follow the official trial script, the accused were able to delve behind the myth of legal neutrality to expose the trial as a performance designed to persuade the public of the legitimacy of the verdict and to reaffirm the idea that the only way to oppose the Vietnam War was through the electoral process. In fact, they were so successful that their initial convictions were set aside on appeal due to judicial bias and procedural irregularities.

Such successes are, however, rare. Usually attempts to challenge the neutrality of proceedings and law's legitimacy are likely to be suppressed as being as 'out of place . . . or out of order'.[239] Unrepresented litigants are particularly susceptible to having their political challenges defused in this way, but conversely, apart from exceptional cases like the Chicago 7 case where in fact one of the lawyers became politicised by his involvement, legal representation tends to lead to any political challenges being muted by the lawyer's insistence on presenting the arguments within the narrow and often already biased terms of the law. In other words, this picture of trials lends support to the theoretical critique of orthodox theories of evidence and proof as attempting to create closure around law's values.

4.2.2 Lay Adjudication, Democracy and Substantive Justice

At the same time, this picture undermines fact positivism's model of fact adjudication as involving depoliticised rational reasoning. There is, however, one exception to this model, namely the institution of lay adjudication. As we have seen,[240] lay adjudicators are authorised to go beyond expletive justice to leaven formal justice with substantive justice.

In reality, however, the role of juries and JPs in injecting 'lay acid'[241] into fact finding is far more limited than paeans to lay adjudication suggest. Not only, as we have seen,[242] does substantive law and the concept of relevance

---

[239] Carlen, loc. cit., n. 166.
[240] Chapter 3, section 3.2.4.
[241] Bankowski, Hutton and McManus, above n. 3, 181; Z. Bankowski, 'The Jury and Reality', in M. Findlay and P. Duff, *The Jury Under Attack* (1988), 20.
[242] Chapter 1, section 1.2; Chapter 2, section 4.2.

limit what they can consider, but their decisions are also made in an unfamiliar context tightly controlled by lawyers in which they report feeling like bystanders rather than active participants in the adjudicative process.[243] Thus research suggests that JPs are significantly influenced by their legally qualified 'silent partners', the clerks, and tribunal 'wing members' by legally qualified chairs.[244] Similarly judicial views about how to decide cases are conveyed to juries through the charge to the jury[245] as well as by demeanour, body language and tone of voice throughout the trial.[246] Indeed, according to Zenon Bankowski and Geoff Mungham,[247] the whole trial experience teaches jurors that it is the judge and not them who is most important and to whom everyone defers. Accordingly studies suggest that, notwithstanding their higher acquittal rates,[248] juries rarely reach decisions with which the presiding judge or other participating legal actors disagree,[249] and even more rarely can it be said that acquittals represent the triumph of lay and substantive over formal justice.[250] Similarly, while JPs and other lay adjudicators occasionally exercise benevolence, they tend to act within the confines of both substantive and adjectival law.[251] In this light, it becomes clear that the well-publicised acquittals of Clive Ponting for breaking the Official Secrets Act by leaking information about the Falklands War,[252] of

---

[243] Young, Cameron and Tinsley, above n. 89, 13, 29.

[244] Baldwin, Wikely and Young, above n. 13, Chapter 5 passim; Bankowski, Hutton and McManus, above n. 3, Chapter 7, 170.

[245] For a detailed analysis of two cases, see J. Winter, 'The Truth Will Out? The Role of Judicial Advocacy and Gender in Verdict Construction' (2002) 11 *Social & Legal Studies* 343.

[246] Bankowski, above n. 241; G. Mungham and Z. Bankowski, 'The Jury in the Legal System', in P. Carlen (ed.), *The Sociology of Law* (1976), 207, 211–12; D. Wolchover, 'Should Judges Sum up on the Facts?' (1989) *Criminal Law Review* 781, 787–8; but cf. McEwan, above n. 60, 92, citing research which shows that obvious attempts to influence juries may backfire.

[247] Bankowski and Mungham, above n. 199, 127; Mungham and Bankowski, ibid., 206–7.

[248] Darbyshire, above n. 90, 869–71, noting factors like the greater difficulties of proof for more serious offences, which make juries more likely to acquit than the lower courts – a tendency which may be enhanced by the Scottish not proven verdict.

[249] Young, Cameron and Tinsley, above n. 89, 68–9; H. Kalven and H. Zeisel, *The American Jury* (1966); S. McCabe and R. Purves, *The Shadow Jury at Work* (1974); London School of Economics Jury Project, 'Juries and the Rules of Evidence' (1973) *Criminal Law Review* 208; M. Zander, 'Are Too Many Professional Criminals Avoiding Conviction?' (1974) 37 *Modern Law Review* 28; N. Vidmar, 'The Performance of the American Civil Jury: An Empirical Perspective' (1998) 40 *Arizona Law Review* 849, 853ff; T. Eisenberg et al., 'Judge-Jury Agreement in Criminal Cases: A Partial Replication of Kalven and Zeisel's The American Jury' (1995) 2 *Journal of Empirical Legal Studies* 171, but cf. the greater variance found by J. Baldwin and M. McConville, *Jury Trials* (1979).

[250] See Baldwin and McConville, ibid., Chapter 4.

[251] Bankowski, Hutton and McManus, above n. 3, esp. Chapter 9.

[252] *R* v. *Ponting* [1985] *Criminal Law Review* 318 – see further C. Ponting, *The Right to Know* (1983).

anti-war protestors for damaging property[253] and of doctors who engage in euthanasia[254] are famous partly because they are exceptional.[255]

Yet, notwithstanding vociferous attacks by fact positivists as well as establishment figures on the jury's lack of scientific rationality and ability to discern factual truth,[256] lay adjudication arguably supports more than undermines fact positivism. While juries rarely challenge the legal values protected by fact positivism, lay adjudication, and in particular high-profile jury trials, act as an iconic symbol of the democratic and egalitarian nature of legal proceedings, thus helping to legitimise the substantive law applied and other political aspects of the criminal justice system. In fact, by seeming to infuse equity and community values into the process of adjudication after they have been so carefully excluded from the processes of fact handling leading up to judgment, lay adjudication can also be said to act like the safety valve of a pressure cooker,[257] allowing a lid to be kept on the politics of the justice system by occasional releases of pressure when feelings of injustice boil over. In fact, given that juries and other lay adjudicators rarely allow the equities to override expletive justice and lay common sense to override unpopular and unjust law, it is the existence of lay adjudication itself and the jury's pre-eminence in public perceptions of the courts, rather than their actual decisions, which can be said to constitute the safety valve.

5 Conclusion: Truth, Fairness and Justice

Overall, our discussion of the operation of fact finding provides little evidence to support the view of fact positivists and other liberals that legal fact finding in Scottish and other Anglo-American legal proceedings is a particularly effective means of obtaining factual truth or providing a civilised forum for dispute resolution. One reason for this mismatch between assumptions and reality is that orthodox evidence scholars rarely

---

[253] McEwan, above n. 219, 136.

[254] Ibid., 136–7. For more examples, see Baldwin and McConville, above n. 107, Chapter 4.

[255] According to Mungham and Bankowski, above n. 246, 208, juries are more likely to depart from expletive justice in longer, more overtly politically and emotionally charged trials where they both develop confidence in their own powers and where law's legitimacy is weakest.

[256] See, for example, Frank, above n. 55, and *Law and the Modern Mind* (1930), Chapter 16; G. Williams, *Proof of Guilt: Study of the English Criminal Trial* (2nd edn, 1963) Chapter 10; P. Darbyshire, 'The Lamp That Shows That Freedom Lives – Is It Worth The Candle?' (1991) *Criminal Law Review* 740.

[257] Williams, ibid. 260. Cf. also Bankowski, Hutton and McManus, above n. 3, Chapter 9; Mungham and Bankowski, above n. 246, 216–17, arguing that juries provide a 'whipping-boy' for those losing cases.

look at how fact finding actually operates in practice. More importantly, however, when thinking about evidence and proof they have in mind the very public fora of contested trials in the higher courts, where there seems to be a genuine attempt at truth finding and where standards of procedural fairness are relatively high – though not nearly as high as legal rhetoric claims.

The famous metaphor based on Monet's many paintings of different sides of Rouen Cathedral illustrates the fact that things look very differently depending on what is in view. Accordingly, it can be said that fact positivists and liberals are looking at the front of the Anglo-American fact-finding cathedral and hence, as with many Italian Renaissance cathedrals, they see the glorious façade but do not venture around the back or sides to see the crumbling brickwork. In other words, behind the public face of contested trials with their day in court, publicity, party control, etc., is the routine processing of summary trials, in which the parties are largely silent if not silenced and allowed merely to play their allotted role in spectacles designed to reaffirm legal values. Even further out of sight are administrative decisions by hard-pressed and often unsympathetic officials, the resolution of most civil disputes through negotiation, and the conveyor belt of guilty pleas to criminal charges. Here particularly, though not exclusively, socio-legal research reveals that institutional practices and the attitudes they engender undermine both fact positivist and liberal assumptions about the truth finding and civilised dispute resolution qualities of Anglo-American legal proceedings. Instead, they provide substantial support for the critical view that fact-finding processes are more about control, power, and the maintenance and legitimation of the legal status quo.

This chapter has already raised serious questions about the current procedural system's ability to find truth, and indeed provides a compelling case for the argument of fact sceptics, namely that the facts found in legal settings are not so much discovered, but constructed by relevant actors in various institutional settings. We have seen that through a process of interaction in court, tribunal, judicial inquiry, administrative office, etc. an official version of the facts emerges, with labels such as guilty/innocent; negligence, intention, misrepresentation 'attached to situations, actions and individuals in such a way that the labels are accepted as correct representations of reality'.[258] Indeed, this process of turning 'facts' into '*the* facts' begins long before the trial or other climactic fact-finding process. Fact construction starts when

---

[258] Cotterrell, above n. 185, 222.

individuals or state officials perceive facts as having legal relevance, and continues when decisions are made to take matters further by seeking legal advice, arresting suspects, etc.[259] But even here there is no guarantee that facts will be considered as having legal relevance or that proceedings will be commenced.[260] However, where they are, the process of fact construction is significantly accelerated once clients are interviewed by lawyers, the police or other relevant state officials aware of the relevant legal rules and tactical manoeuvres which require one rather than another version of ambiguous reality. Then, *if* cases progress to litigoation, the process of case construction becomes increasingly sharper as the context becomes increasingly adversarial (though likely to stop or temporarily cease during co-operative forms of ADR). At the same time, it should also be clear that fact construction cannot be looked at in isolation, as it occurs at trial or indeed any stage at which facts are handled. Fact handling at one stage will have crucial consequences for later stages, with the die often cast at an early stage of proceedings.

By establishing the highly constructed nature of legal facts, sociological studies do not necessarily establish epistemological scepticism in its cognitive form, which denies that it is ever possible to establish true facts; it is always possible that the facts constructed in legal proceedings correspond with true facts. However, by revealing the numerous barriers to ascertaining truth which emerge from the institutional context of fact finding, these studies certainly lend much support to anti-dogmatic scepticism which accepts that finding the truth is never easy.

Obviously various problematic aspects of this institutional context can be reformed to make it more amenable to upholding civilised legal values and to improving the experience of lay participants in legal proceedings. As regards the former, an obvious starting point would be simply to take seriously the procedural rights and civil liberties already provided by law by ensuring that they are actually upheld. But this is likely to come up against state resistance based on penal populism, cost and other crime control considerations.[261] Were it not for costs, greater use of ADR to ensure that disputes are not just ended but resolved would also be uncontroversial. However, while a managerialist drive for efficiency has indeed ensured greater emphasis on ADR, the drive to reduce costs means that this has to be at the parties' own expense and hence take-up is unlikely to

---

[259] See Chapter 1, section 2.3, and further, J. M. Conley and W. M. O'Barr, *Just Words: Law, Language and Power* (2nd edn, 2005), Chapter 5.

[260] See section 2.4.2 regarding guilty pleas and Genn and Paterson, above n. 99, Chapter 5, regarding attrition rates in civil cases.

[261] See Chapter 3, section 4.2.

be affected.[262] In any event, as we have seen, ADR is far from a pana-cea for the problems of formal fact finding. Similar contradictions beset possible means of improving the experience of lay participants in trials by making legal proceedings more user-friendly to participants through changes to court-room design, dress, the form of witness questioning, and court language and rituals. However, the more effective they are likely to be, the less they are likely to be introduced because of cost, a conserva-tive desire to uphold tradition or simple inertia. Conversely, 'low hanging fruit', such as instructing juries on law before cases begin and/or in writ-ing, and allowing jurors to take notes, directly ask questions of witnesses, lawyers and judges, read transcripts and even call witnesses,[263] are not likely to make much difference.

We thus see that, while it is possible to reform institutional practices to move the processes of evidence and proof closer to orthodox assumptions about their goals, many changes are controversial and hence cannot be relied upon to come about. But even if the institutional context of evidence and proof could be constructed to be as favourable as possible, orthodox evidence theory places great faith in the ability of legal actors to use reason and other human cognitive abilities to find truth and thereby to achieve justice. We thus turn to exploring this ability in the final three chapters.

---

[262] Cf. M. Stevenson, 'Vulnerable Children in Separation: Does Mediation Make Economic Sense?' (2014) *Family Law Journal* 102.

[263] See, for example, R. Lempert, 'Civil Juries and Complex Cases: Taking Stock After Twelve Years', in R. E. Litan (ed.), *Verdict: Assessing the Civil Jury System* (1993), 220ff; S. A. Saltzburg, 'Improving the Quality of Jury Decisionmaking', in Litan, ibid.

CHAPTER FIVE

The Scientific Context: Truth, Reason and Expertise

1 Introduction: Documents, Real Evidence and Expert Testimony

We saw in Chapter One that legal actors utilise three main forms of evidence: testimony, documents and real evidence. In Chapter Six, the first of two chapters on the psychological context of evidence and proof, we will look at the most common form, namely the testimony of *observational* (or fact, ordinary, lay or percipient)[1] witnesses who testify as to their direct observation of relevant events, situations, people, documents and objects encountered in the course of their daily lives. By contrast, this chapter examines *expert* witnesses, whose testimony and pre-trial reports help legal fact finders understand and utilise documents, real evidence and the testimony of observational witnesses, as well as facts directly in issue such as the causes of accidents, the mental states of accused, the dangerousness of countries from which asylum is being sought, etc.

This book does not therefore look directly at documents or real evidence, despite their frequent appearance in fact handling.[2] While a book about a narrow area of practice such as motor vehicle law might – just – be able to discuss all relevant documents and forms of real evidence (forged licences, skid marks, etc.), a general book about evidence and proof cannot possibly cover all potentially relevant documents and real evidence.

---

[1] Law Commission, *Expert Evidence in Criminal Proceedings in England and Wales* (Law Comm. No. 325) (2011), para. 6.7; S. Lubet, *Modern Trial Advocacy: Analysis and Practice* (4th edn, 2009), 193.

[2] See, for example, W. Young, N. Cameron and Y. Tinsley, *Juries in Criminal Trials, Part Two: A Summary of Research Findings* (1999), 21–2, reporting that such evidence appeared in two-thirds of the forty-eight New Zealand criminal trials they studied and that generally it proved useful. See also section 2 on the use of forensic evidence more specifically.

In any event, documents and real evidence[3] often 'speak for themselves' in that fact finders can observe them directly, such as when they read a will or observe the murder weapon. Here, all that might be needed is for someone to 'speak to' the document or object in order to confirm its origin and authenticity. But very often issues relevant to documents (for example, whether the will was forged) or real evidence (for instance, the source of blood on the murder weapon) might be too complex or opaque to be capable of evaluation by legal fact finders without expert assistance.

Such assistance can come in three forms.[4] First, as an exception to the normal prohibition on witnesses expressing opinions on (rather than just reporting their observation of) facts,[5] experts may provide an opinion on the relevance, meaning and value of facts – for example, that a will was not a forgery or that traces of DNA (the common abbreviation for deoxyribonucleic acid) on the knife match that of the suspect – and even predict future facts such as a deceased person's expected life earnings. This can be called the expert's *inferential* function, in that fact finders are guided by the expert's opinion as to what inferences to draw from evidence provided by others.

Secondly, experts may perform an *investigative* function themselves by producing what can be called *subsidiary evidence*, which helps illuminate the facts in issue, such as when ballistic experts perform tests to ascertain whether alleged murder weapons could have caused the fatal wound, or doctors examine car accident victims to see if injuries are consistent with those claimed in the pleadings.

Thirdly, experts may provide fact finders with general background information of which they are unaware. As we will explore in more detail in Chapter Seven,[6] to make inferences from facts (for example, about the potential bias of a witness), fact finders must draw upon some background information about the world (that witnesses married to litigants are likely to be biased). But not all such background information is a matter of 'common-sense'. Some information – like the braking distances of cars and changes in the body after death – is beyond the knowledge and experience

---

[3] See C. E. Renoe, 'Seeing is Believing?: Expert Testimony and the Construction of Interpretive Authority in an American Trial' (1996) 9 *International Journal for the Semiotics of Law* 115 on how apparently unambiguous interpretations of CCTV images can be manipulated; P. Haldar, 'Law and the Evidential Image' (2008) 4 *Law Culture and the Humanities* 139 more generally on visual images.

[4] For a similar analysis, see R. Lempert, 'Experts, Stories and Information' (1993) 87 *Northwestern University Law Review* 1169, 1175–8.

[5] See F. Raitt, *Evidence: Principles, Policy and Practice* (2nd edn, with E. Keane, 2013), Chapter 4.

[6] Section 3.3.

of legal fact finders, Thus, instead of experts informing fact finders about what inference they should make – and impinging on their allotted role of determining the facts – experts can play an *informational* function in providing them with the necessary information to draw their own inferences.

In performing these three functions, experts can employ the theoretical knowledge gained from their education or training and/or their experience in performing specialised tasks such as diagnosing physical and mental illnesses, the causes of death, etc. In fact, if witnesses have relevant experience, they need not have been formally educated, let alone admitted to a professional body, to qualify as an expert for the purposes of being permitted to give opinion evidence.[7] However, because the types of such 'pure experience expertise' are virtually unlimited, on the one hand, and the vast majority of experts will have some training in a recognised field of knowledge, on the other hand, this chapter is limited to more formal areas of scientific knowledge. Etymologically and historically, 'science' can be interpreted even more broadly as any organised critical examination of knowledge (*scienta* in Latin) and may therefore include formal disciplines like art theory, history and philosophy.[8] But adopting such a broad definition here would involve too many forms of expert knowledge to cover in just one chapter. It will therefore focus only on experts commonly conceived of as scientific in the broad sense of making knowledge claims which can be empirically tested,[9] not least because this allows a critical evaluation of fact positivism's borrowing of this scientific model as the means to reliable and objective truth.

2 Experts and the Law

Even if we confine scientific disciplines to those that make empirically testable claims, law makes use of a vast array of such disciplines. These range from what is variously called the *pure, theoretical* or *research* sciences such as physics or biology, which pursue knowledge largely for its own sake, at one extreme, to the *applied* sciences such as engineering or medicine, which use existing theoretical knowledge for practical applications, at the other

---

[7]   Raitt, above n. 5, 49.

[8]   The word 'scientist' only became associated with paradigmatic scientific methods from the eighteenth century: D. M. Risinger, M. P. Denbeaux and M. J. Saks, 'Exorcism of Ignorance as a Proxy for Rational Knowledge: The Lessons of Handwriting Identification Expertise' (1989) 137 *University of Pennsylvania Law Review* 731, 766; D. Faigman, *Legal Alchemy: The Use and Misuse of Science in the Law* (1999), 7.

[9]   Cf. B. Black, F. J. Ayala and C. Saffran-Brinks, 'Science and the Law in the Wake of *Daubert*: A New Search for Scientific Knowledge' (1994) 72 *Texas Law Review* 715, 756.

extreme. Cutting across these categories is the more controversial[10] distinction between the so-called *hard* (or *mature*) and *soft* sciences. The former are usually regarded as constituted by the natural sciences (themselves divided into life sciences like biology and physical sciences like physics, chemistry and astronomy), and the latter by the social, human or behavioural sciences (henceforth social sciences only) like sociology, psychology and economics.

The use of science to resolve legal questions is said to go as far back as Archimedes' Eureka moment,[11] and from at least the early Middle Ages, common law courts have drawn upon experts to help resolve legal disputes.[12] However, with the Enlightenment's scientific discoveries, the explosive development of new technology during the Industrial Revolution and the scientific development of medicine and later psychiatry, scientific experts became increasingly familiar figures in court. In addition, certain disciplines were developed specifically – and in some cases (like fingerprint analysis or forensic toxicology) exclusively – to serve legal needs and hence are described by the adjective *forensic* (from the Latin for forum). Forensic medicine developed from the sixteenth century in Europe, and some forensic science disciplines like fingerprint matching also have a long history. But it was from the nineteenth century that there increasingly developed 'armies of experts in medicine, dentistry, pathology, psychiatry, psychology, fingerprinting, toxicology, biological sciences (blood, hair, and bodily fluids[13] analysis) genetics, ballistics, narcotics, trace mark examination (paint, glass, fibre, toolmarks, and footprint inspection), and document and handwriting analysis, to mention only some of the most common expertises . . .'[14]

According to an English and Welsh study in the early 1990s, around one-third of all contested trials on indictment involved scientific evidence.[15]

---

[10] See section 5 below.
[11] Which was prompted by discovering the method for proving that a coin was not made of gold as claimed in a legal dispute.
[12] See L. Hand, 'Historical and Practical Considerations Regarding Expert Testimony' (1901) 15 *Harvard Law Review* 40; C. M. Bowers, 'The History of Experts in English Common Law, with Practice Advice for Beginning Experts', in C. M. Bowers (ed.), *Forensic Testimony: Science, Law and Expert Evidence* (2014); C. Jones, *Expert Witnesses: Science, Medicine and the Practice of Law* (1994), Chapters 2–6 passim.
[13] Sometimes called serology.
[14] P. Roberts and A. Zuckerman, *Criminal Evidence* (2nd edn, 2010), 470; and see also the first edition at 301, which refers dismissively to 'a multitude of "small ologies" on the periphery including forensic entomology, forensic archaeology, forensic odontology, facial mapping, psychological profiling, and countless other exotica'. Notable omissions from these lists include computer and canine forensics (dog-tracking and identification), forensic phonetics and anthropology, and fire investigation.
[15] M. Zander and P. Henderson, *Crown Court Study* (Royal Commission on Criminal Justice Research Study No. 19, 1993), 84–5.

But, as Paul Roberts argues, this underplays the actual use of scientific expertise in criminal proceedings, given that 'most experts make their most regular and significant contributions prior to the trial'.[16] This is most marked in relation to the constantly improving and ever-expanding range of forensic disciplines,[17] particularly in relation to investigating the causes and perpetrators of crimes and other legally relevant acts. While in the past forensic evidence was usually sought as a last resort, largely as corroborative evidence,[18] and usually only in relation to serious crimes, recent decades have seen an increasing 'scientification'[19] of British policing as forensic science has become a routine and central aspect of factual investigation. For example, the increasing use of CCTV (closed-circuit television) in public and private places makes detecting and convicting perpetrators significantly easier, and thus a routine and core investigative tool.[20] Similarly the establishment of national DNA databases and digitised fingerprinting records increasingly allows suspects to be identified solely from forensic traces (so-called 'cold hits'). As a result, and particularly because of DNA profiling,[21] detection rates have increased dramatically, especially for crimes which have remained unsolved for some time ('cold cases').[22] For example, one study reported that from the mid-1990s to early 2000s the rate at which forensic evidence played a direct role in crime detection in England and Wales rose from 6 per cent to 24 per cent[23] – an increase which is likely to have continued with subsequent technological improvements and greater awareness of the ability of forensic technologies to analyse physical evidence such as DNA,

---

[16] P. Roberts, 'Science, Experts, and Criminal Justice', in M. McConville and G. Wilson (eds), *The Handbook of the Criminal Justice Process* (2002), 259. See further section 6.4 below.

[17] See, for example, J. Fraser and R. Williams, 'The Contemporary Landscape of Forensic Science' and P. Gill and T. Clayton, 'The Current Status of DNA Profiling in the UK', in J. Fraser and R. Williams (eds), *Handbook of Forensic Science* (2009), 4–5 , as well as the essays in Part 2.

[18] Jones. above n. 12, 211; P. Roberts, 'Science in the Criminal Process' (1994) 14 *Oxford Journal of Legal Studies* 469, 474, 477.

[19] R. V. Ericson and C. Shearing, 'The Scientification of Police Work', in G. Böhme and N. Stehr (eds), *The Knowledge Society: The Growing Impact of Scientific Knowledge on Social Relations* (1986).

[20] M. P. J. Ashby, 'The Value of CCTV Surveillance Cameras as an Investigative Tool: An Empirical Analysis' (2017) 3 *European Journal on Criminal Policy and Research* 1.

[21] See B. Bramley, 'DNA Databases', in Fraser and Williams, above n. 17, 316.

[22] J. Fraser and R. Williams, 'Introduction', in Fraser and Williams, ibid., 282.

[23] Cited by T. Wilson, 'Forensic Science and the Internationalisation of Policing', in Fraser and Williams, ibid., 502–3. See also A. Cooper and L. Mason, 'Forensic Resources and Criminal Investigations', in Fraser and Williams, ibid., 287–8 citing a study which showed that forensic evidence was the first link to a suspect in 45 per cent of cases and another that DNA evidence provided the initial identification of a suspect in 70 per cent of 'volume' crimes (that is, those that occur frequently and affect many people).

fingerprints and tyre marks (collectively called 'trace' evidence) which is also almost inevitably left at crime scenes.[24]

While there are no estimates of the use of experts in Scottish civil proceedings, expert evidence has been shown to play a significant role in civil cases elsewhere,[25] most notably in personal injury litigation, but also frequently in disputes over paternity, patents, trading practices and fire damage.[26] Indeed, one of the factors motivating the managerialist reforms of civil procedure discussed in Chapter Three[27] was the time and expense taken up by expert evidence.[28]

This 'creeping scientisation'[29] of legal fact finding and rise of 'experts in everything'[30] is perhaps not surprising given that scientific and other forms of specialist knowledge and technology are now so embedded in modern life that legal actors have no option but to rely on experts to make sense of our brave new world. However, the law is also gradually opening its door to the relatively new disciplines which focus on understanding human behaviour rather than just physiology and mental illness. But here the law has been far more cautious, not least because it has always maintained – albeit not consistently – that fact finders do not need 'psychiatrists to tell them how ordinary folk who are not suffering from any mental illness are likely to react to the stresses and strains of life'.[31] However, law's ambivalence stretches beyond these social sciences.[32]

Like society itself, which realises that science and technology can just as easily cause widespread harm and destruction as make our lives safer,

[24] M. Redmayne, *Expert Evidence and Criminal Justice* (2001), 17, citing a US study reporting that physical evidence is present at 88 per cent of crime scenes.

[25] An early 1990s US study found that experts testified in 86 per cent of civil cases tried in a particular court with an average of 3.3 experts per trial, and a 1998 study reported an average of 4.1 per case: S. K. Ivkovic and V. P. Hans, 'Jurors' Evaluations of Expert Testimony: Judging the Messenger and the Message' (2003) 28 *Law & Social Inquiry* 441, 443–4.

[26] Jones, above n. 12, 129.

[27] Section 4.2.

[28] C. Jackson, 'The Uses and Abuses of Experts and Their Evidence' (2000) *Journal of Personal Injury Litigation* 19, 19; G. Edmond, 'Merton and the Hot Tub: Scientific Conventions and Expert Evidence in Australian Civil Procedure' (2009) 72 *Law and Contemporary Problems* 159, 161.

[29] M. R. Damaška, *Evidence Law Adrift* (1997), 143–4. See also his 'Free Proof and its Detractors' (1995) 43 *American Journal of Comparative Law* 343, 352ff; Jones, above n. 12, 96, 270; M. King and F. Kaganas, 'The Risks and Dangers of Experts in Court', in H. Reece (ed.), *Law and Science: Current Legal Issues Volume 1* (1998), esp. 223–9.

[30] Roberts, above n. 16, esp. 255.

[31] *R* v. *Turner* [1975] QB 834, 841, adopted, for example, in *HMA* v. *Grimmond* 2002 SLT 508.

[32] See, for example, Roberts, above n. 16, passim, and 'Paradigms of Forensic Science and Legal Process: A Critical Diagnosis' (2015) 370 *Philosophical Transactions of the Royal Society B* 201240256, available at http://rstb.royalsocietypublishing.org/content/370/1674/20140256; P. Alldridge, 'Forensic Science and Expert Evidence' (1994) 21 *Journal of Law and Society* 136, 137–9.

healthier, more comfortable and more enjoyable, so has law an ambiv-alent approach to scientific expertise. As an incredibly useful means of ascertaining and proving facts, and uncovering miscarriages of justice,[33] science can be hailed as the 'hero of the day'.[34] On the other hand, it may also be labelled 'the villain of the piece'[35] when it leads to wrongful convic-tions.[36] Indeed, some US studies claim that, after mistaken identification, erroneous or misleading scientific evidence is the second most common cause of miscarriages of justice.[37]

Science's double-edged nature is mirrored in law's deeply contradictory views towards it and expertise more generally. Thus, on the one hand, experts have a special legal status. Not only are experts exempt from the opinion evidence rule, but, contrary to the hearsay rule, they are also allowed to rely on the reports of others encountered in studying and prac-tising their discipline[38] and, unlike other witnesses, may charge for their testimony and sit in court before testifying. Furthermore, the Scottish (and other UK) courts have generally[39] taken a very liberal approach to decid-ing who qualifies as an expert and only very recently asserted the power to exclude insufficiently reliable expert evidence.[40] Even so, some[41] think that law makes insufficient use of science and bemoan the fact that adjudi-cators tend to pay more heed to the more dramatic, comprehensible and memorable evidence of observational witnesses.[42]

On the other hand, there is also a long-standing fear among judges and others that purported experts 'might lack proper credentials, exhibit bias, or even be outright imposters or charlatans' selling opinions to the highest

---

[33]   Especially via DNA evidence in the US: see the Innocence Project's running total of cases, avail-able at http://www.innocenceproject.org/exonerate (354 at last access on 18 March 2018).
[34]   Roberts, above n. 18, 469.
[35]   Ibid.
[36]   For examples, see at nn. 236 and 259, and more generally, R. Smith, 'The Trials of Forensic Science' (1988) *Science as Culture* 71 and 'Forensic Pathology, Scientific Expertise and the Criminal Law', in R. Smith and B. Wynne (eds), *Expert Evidence: Interpreting Science in the Law* (1989), 77–80; M. Redmayne, 'Expert Evidence and Disagreement' (1997) *UC Davis Law Review* 1027, 1039–46; C. Walker and R. Stockdale, 'Forensic Evidence', in C. Walker and K. Starmer (eds), *Miscarriages of Justice: A Review of Justice in Error* (1999).
[37]   M. J. Saks and J. J. Koehler, 'The Coming Paradigm Shift in Forensic Identification Science' (2005) 309 *Science* 892, 893; B. L. Garret and P. Neufeld, 'Invalid Forensic Science Testimony and Wrongful Convictions' (2009) 95 *Virginia Law Review* 1.
[38]   Raitt, above n. 5, 50.
[39]   But see section 5 below regarding the 'soft' sciences.
[40]   In *Young* v. *HM Advocate* 2014 SLT 21; 2014 SCL 98; *Kennedy* v. *Cordia (Services) LLP*, [2016] UKSC 6; 2016 SLT 209, para. 44.
[41]   See, for example, Roberts and Zuckerman, above n. 14, 471; E. J. Imwinkelried, 'A Minimalist Approach to the Presentation of Expert Testimony' (2001) 31 *Stetson Law Review* 105, 105–6.
[42]   See Chapter 6, section 1.

bidder.[43] Even if these views[44] are in fact based on little more than 'war stories and some isolated instances of documented bad practice',[45] there is a more legitimate fear that, faced with difficult and unfamiliar concepts and arcane knowledge, legal fact finders may be incapable of identifying scientific errors and faulty techniques, and adjudicating hotly contested scientific controversies. When this combines with science's 'aura of special reliability and trustworthiness'[46] and 'mystic infallibility',[47] commentators worry that fact finders will be so dazzled by scientific evidence that they succumb to the so-called 'white coat syndrome'[48] and automatically defer, or at least give undue prominence, to expert testimony – especially if bathed in the 'aura of precision'[49] associated with statistical information.

These contradictory views do not just represent competing opinions, but also reflect a fundamental paradox at the heart of law's relationship with expertise.[50] Officially the expert's function is to educate fact finders on matters beyond their knowledge so that they can 'form their own independent judgment'.[51] However, the very fact that legal actors need to turn to experts raises the possibility that they might be unable to make sense of the assistance provided, especially when it involves complex areas of knowledge like the theory of relativity or neuroscience, or even basic statistics.[52] Consequently fact finders may simply unquestionably accept what

---

[43]   Roberts and Zuckerman, above n. 14, 478–9, but cf. G. Edmond, 'Judicial Representations of Scientific Evidence' (2000) 63 *Modern Law Review* 216, 234, noting that this attitude is less prevalent in the UK compared to the US.

[44]   But see A. E. Moenssens, 'Foreword: Novel Scientific Evidence in Criminal Cases: Some Words of Caution' (1993) 84 *Journal of Criminal Law and Criminology* 1, 9–10.

[45]   Roberts and Zuckerman, above n. 14, 479. See also Smith, 'Forensic Pathology', above n. 36, 72–3. Although referring to England and Wales, there is no evidence of greater problems in Scotland. See also R. A. Posner, 'An Economic Approach to the Law of Evidence' (1999) 51 *Stanford Law Review* 1477, 1536–7, noting that paid experts have a professional and commercial interest in maintaining a reputation for honesty.

[46]   *United States* v. *Fosher*, 590 F 2d 381 (1st Cir 1979), 383.

[47]   J. Schklar and S. S. Diamond, 'Juror reactions to DNA Evidence: Errors and Expectancies' (1999) 23 *Law and Human Behavior* 159, 159.

[48]   M. Findlay, 'Juror Comprehension and the Hard Case – Making Forensic Evidence Simpler' (2008) 36 *International Journal of Law, Crime and Justice* 1, 23.

[49]   Schklar and Diamond, above, n. 47, 160.

[50]   See R. J. Allen and J. S. Miller, 'Common Law Theory of Experts: Deference or Education' (1992) 87 *New York University Law Review* 1131; R. J. Allen, 'Expertise and the *Daubert* Decision' (1993) 84 *Journal of Criminal Law and Criminology* 1157. See also Roberts and Zuckerman, above n. 14, 471–5; and the other articles in (1993) 87 *New York University Law Review* 1148–87.

[51]   *Davie* v. *Edinburgh Magistrates* 1953 SC 53, 54.

[52]   See section 7.3 below, but cf. Allen's confidence (above n. 50, 1158) in adequately educated fact finders.

they are told, especially when already suffering from cognitive overload.[53] However, such deference clashes with the cherished values of adjudication by representatives of the community rather than by elite experts[54] and the formal rule[55] prohibiting experts from giving an opinion on the ultimate issue requiring decision. Such deference also limits fact finders to only two options – either accept expert evidence in its totality or reject it altogether. Where this occurs, such choices may be based on 'irrelevant considerations, like the eloquence or charisma of a particular expert witness, as well as prejudicial grounds for accepting or rejecting testimony, such as a juror's personal conceits or lack of comprehension'.[56] Even more problematically, fact finders may be faced with two competing expert views and have little ability to rationally decide between them.

3 Law and Science: Sparring Partners or Marriage Made in Heaven?[57]

The tension between education and deference is not, however, the only conflict generated by the expert's legal role. More fundamentally, the relationship between law and science is often described as involving a clash of cultures[58] or civilisations,[59] but most commonly in marital terms. While this marriage might be 'stormy'[60] or 'troubled',[61] it is nevertheless

---

[53]   Cf. also Risinger, Denbeaux and Saks, above n. 8, 732, referring to the 'wish to be spared the burdens of living in a world of unacceptably imperfect knowledge'.

[54]   See, for example, Damaška, 'Free Proof and its Detractors', above n. 29, 352–5.

[55]   See, for example, Raitt, above n. 5, 58–9.

[56]   Roberts and Zuckerman, above n. 14, esp. 474; Allen, above n. 50, esp. 1175.

[57]   In addition to the more specific references cited below, see Faigman, above n. 8, passim; Jones, above n. 12, Chapter 1; Smith, above n. 36 (both references); B. Wynne, 'Establishing the Rules of Law: Constructing Expert Authority', in Smith and Wynne, above n. 36; S. Jasanoff, *Science at the Bar, Law Science and Technology in America* (1995) esp Chapters 1–3, 10, and 'Law's Knowledge: Science for Justice in Legal Settings' (2005) 95 *American Journal of Public Health* S49; P. H. Schuck, 'Multi-Culturalism Redux: Science, Law, and Politics' (1993) 11 *Yale Law & Policy Review* 1; D. Nelken, 'Can Law Learn from Social Science?' (2001) 35 *Israel Law Review* 205; S. Haack, 'Truth and Justice, Inquiry and Advocacy, Science and Law' (2004) 17 *Ratio Juris* 15 and 'Irreconcilable Differences? The Troubled Marriage of Science and Law' (2009) 72 *Law and Contemporary Problems* 1; P. Roberts, 'Renegotiating Forensic Cultures: Between Law, Science and Criminal Justice' (2013) 44 *Studies in History and Philosophy of Biological and Biomedical Sciences* 47.

[58]   For example, Jasanoff, *Science at the Bar*, ibid., 7 and 'Law's Knowledge', ibid., s.5; 1; L. Roberts, 'Science in Court: A Culture Clash' (1992) 257 *Science* 732.

[59]   S. Brown and S. Willis, 'Complexity in Forensic Science' (2009) 1 *Forensic Science Policy and Management* 192, 196.

[60]   T. Ward, 'Law, Common Sense and the Authority of Science: Expert Witnesses and Criminal Insanity in England, CA. 1840–1940' (1997) 6 *Social & Legal Studies* 343, 346.

[61]   Haack, 'Irreconcilable Differences?', above n. 57; cf. also Roberts, above n. 18, 469 who speaks of a love-hate relationship.

misleading to describe it as a 'marriage of opposites'.[62] Law and science both emphasise logical thinking[63] and share a common language of 'investigation', 'proof', 'law', 'fact' and 'evidence'. More fundamentally, as we saw in Chapter Two,[64] law and science share epistemological assumptions about the possibility of true knowledge corresponding to reality and, following science's lead, in the superiority of gaining knowledge via logical inferences from personal observations. Both disciplines are concerned with preventing mistakes and thus, respectively, have burdens and standards of proof, and conventions about the confidence levels required before accepting hypotheses as proved. Finally, both law and science claim to be authoritative social institutions deserving of trust as neutral and apolitical purveyors of truth generated for the good of society through standardised testing procedures (the trial and experiments, respectively).

However, digging deeper reveals some important differences relating to the goals, values and methods of law and science, albeit far less so as regards the forensic sciences given that they were specifically developed to serve the law. Thus, notwithstanding that both enterprises are concerned with factual truth, science – particularly in its pure form – treats this goal as primary and as an end in itself, whereas – as we saw in Chapter Four – law is also concerned to resolve disputes justly, communicate normative values, regulate society and maintain order. Science's goals are descriptive or explanatory; law's are prescriptive or normative. Science is interested in all facts relevant to the future as well as the past, and builds knowledge cumulatively as new findings and theories build on previous ones. In its adjudicative, as opposed to legislative, mode[65] law is largely only interested in retrospectively ascertaining historical facts relevant to one-off occurrences. Although science, albeit more in its purer rather than its forensic forms, can accommodate uncertainty and admit doubt while investigation and experiments are ongoing, law prioritises the finality of decisions, not least because justice delayed can be tantamount to justice denied.[66]

---

[62] Cf. A. K. Y. Wonder, 'Science and Law, A Marriage of Opposites' (1989) 29 *Journal of the Forensic Science Society* 75.

[63] D. L. Burk, 'When Scientists Act Like Lawyers: The Problem of Adversary Science' (1993) 33 *Jurimetrics* 363, 365.

[64] Section 2.2. See also T. D. Barton, 'Law and Science in the Enlightenment and Beyond' (1999) 13 *Social Epistemology* 99.

[65] See Chapter 1, section 1.

[66] See E. E. Deason, 'Incompatible Versions of Authority in Law and Science' (1999) 13 *Social Epistemology* 147, 156ff.

Far more problematic for legal fact finding is the possibility that law and science may involve 'incompatible discourses'[67] stemming from their differing values and concerns. This view draws theoretical support from autopoietic theory, which sees society comprising of different self-regulating sub-systems with their own language, methods, and modes of operation, which are autonomous of each other.[68] Each sub-system may respond to inputs from outside its system (in other words, it is cognitively open) but does so by converting these inputs into its own language and methods (because it is normatively closed). Thus law deals in rights and wrongs; science in factual truth. Admittedly law is concerned with factual truth, but translating scientific truths into legal discourse may result in 'hybrid artefacts'[69] that are true neither to science nor law.

A good example involves questions of whether death or ill-health was caused by exposure to radiation or toxic products where the alleged effects might only manifest years later or following a cluster of similar cases found in the general population.[70] Here scientists focus on 'general causation' – whether as a matter of probabilities the product is likely to cause harm to those exposed to it – whereas law is interested in 'specific' causation – whether it is likely that the particular pursuer suffered the harm because of exposure. Moreover, scientists assess causation by formulating hypotheses based on probabilities and then testing and refining them in the light of other probabilistic evidence, and will only declare a causal link when this can be demonstrated unequivocally. Law, however, looks to see whether there is a causal chain between the alleged harm and the product. It then compares this possible cause with others to decide which is the most 'proximate', based not just on statistical likelihood but on considerations of policy and equity, such as whether defenders recklessly sold their products before testing them and whether the law needs to deter such behaviour.

---

67   Nelken, above n. 57, 217.
68   See, for example, R. Cotterrell, *The Sociology of Law: An Introduction* (2nd edn, 1992), 65–70; M. King, 'The "Truth" About Autopoiesis' (1993) 20 *Journal of Law and Society* 218; A. Beck and G. Teubner, 'Is Law an Autopoietic System?' (1994) 14 *Oxford Journal of Legal Studies* 401.
69   D. Nelken, 'A Just Measure of Science', in M. Freeman and H. Reece (eds), *Science in Court* (1998), 16.
70   What are called toxic tort cases in the US: see, for example, Jasanoff, *Science at the Bar*, above n. 57, Chapter 6; G. Edmond and D. Mercer, 'Litigation Life: Law-Science Knowledge Construction in (Bendectin) Mass Toxic Tort Litigation' (2000) 30 *Social Studies of Science* 265. See also Redmayne, above n. 36, 1062–70; S. M. Solomon and E. J. Hackett, 'Setting Boundaries between Science and Law: Lessons from *Daubert v. Merrell Dow Pharmaceuticals, Inc.*' (1996) 21 *Science, Technology & Human Values* 131; E. Beecher-Monas, *Evaluating Scientific Evidence: An Interdisciplinary Framework for Intellectual Due Process* (2007), Chapter 4.

This and similar examples[71] suggest a marriage between partners from different countries whose different culture and languages create the potential for communication breakdowns. Such breakdowns may also derive from procedural differences. Thus, unlike the scientific search for truth which is only marginally constrained by normative considerations such as research ethics, legal truth finding is (as we saw in Chapters Two and Three) often overridden by a concern with procedural fairness, national security and expediency, the value of lay justice and the concomitant perceived need to protect lay adjudicators from faulty reasoning through exclusionary evidential rules. Given the arguably laudable nature of these values, one can argue that as science has voluntarily emigrated to join law, it can be expected to adapt to the local culture.[72] Moreover, the only procedural difference that poses assimilation problems is the adversarial nature of legal fact finding. Whereas, as we shall see,[73] science is said to be based on mutual respect, collegiality and consensus-building, the legal process 'enshrines scepticism and mistrust'.[74] Implicit here is a view of science as the less powerful partner pressurised into undermining its essential purity[75] and requiring relationship counselling to unleash its full potential.

A final variation on the marital metaphor also sees the relationship as rocky. But, while ultimately law owns and controls the marital home, power is not one-sided because both partners come from powerful rival families. This view draws on Michel Foucault's argument outlined in Chapter Two[76] that we live in a society in which we are controlled (that is, disciplined) by various disciplines like science, medicine, psychiatry, etc. through their use of expert knowledge. By purporting to provide neutral, objective and apolitical knowledge, these disciplines control people and even persuade them to control their own behaviour. Sharing these same regulatory goals, the older power regime of law has an interest in harnessing this new disciplinary power to its methods of control and, by drawing on science's allegedly direct and objectively true access to the world, to

---

[71]   See, for example, the differing legal and psychiatric approaches to insanity discussed by Faigman, above n. 8, 27–32; Ward, above n. 60, 'Psychiatric Evidence and Judicial Fact-Finding' (1990) 3 *International Journal of Evidence and Proof* 180, and 'Law's Truth, Lay Truth and Medical Science: Three Case Studies', in Reece, above n. 29; R. Smith, 'Expertise and Causal Attribution in Deciding between Crime and Mental Disorder' (1985) 15 *Social Studies of Science* 67.

[72]   See Roberts, above n. 57, 54–7.

[73]   Section 4.4, below.

[74]   Wynne, above n. 57, 37.

[75]   For examples of this 'trial pathology approach', see Haack, 'Irreconcilable Differences', above n. 57, 16–18; Nelken, above n. 57, esp. at 215–16; Burk, above n. 63.

[76]   Section 3.2.2.2.

gain legitimacy.[77] However, this need stands in tension with law's desire to retain control in its own domain. Consequently law has always acted to undermine the probity and competence of the experts who assist it.[78] Its self-contradictory attitude seems to be that 'while "science" is reliable, there has never been a scientist who is'.[79]

But, like all disciplines, science also strives for privileged authority to speak the truth.[80] Accordingly, law and science 'co-exist or collaborate under conditions of unstable compromise',[81] constantly negotiating over truth-claims and who has the authority to speak the truth – what sociologists describe as 'boundary work'.[82] Moreover, law and especially the courts provide a forum for penetrating 'deconstructions'[83] of scientific certainty and rationality. While this may place science's epistemic status in the spotlight, science nevertheless benefits from its fractious relationship with law. Emerging scientific disciplines like the forensic sciences gain in status from their association with law.[84] More pragmatically, legal controversies expose unreliable science and stimulate scientific research which – as with DNA sampling – has led to improved knowledge and techniques,[85] whereas those scientists whose views prevail in controversies aired in court can enrol law's authority to support claims to scientific closure.[86]

We thus see rather different views of the health of the law–science relationship depending on whether law is seen as the patriarchal and uncomprehending despoiler of scientific purity or involved in a marriage of convenience with a partner who speaks a different language. If the former

---

[77] See King and Kaganas, above n. 29; Smith, 'The Trials of Forensic Science', above n. 36, esp. at 78; R. Wheate, 'The Importance of DNA Evidence to Juries in Criminal Trials' (2010) 14 *International Journal of Evidence & Proof* 129, 143.

[78] See especially Jones, above n. 12, Chapter 4.

[79] Wynne, above n. 57, 54. See also Roberts, above n. 18, 505.

[80] Cf. C. Smart, *Feminism and the Power of Law* (1989), Chapter 1.

[81] Nelken, above n. 57, 216.

[82] See T. F. Gieryn, 'Boundary-work and the Demarcation of Science from Non-science: Strains and Interests in Professional Ideologies of Scientists' (1983) 48 *American Sociological Review* 781 and *Cultural Boundaries Of Science: Credibility on the Line* (1999). See also, for example, Solomon and Hackett, above n. 70, 143–4; S. S. Jasanoff, 'Contested Boundaries in Policy-Relevant Science' (1987) 17 *Social Studies of Science* 195.

[83] Albeit not in the technical sense used in literary theory and postmodernism more generally: M. Lynch and R. McNally, 'Science, Common Sense and Common Law: Courtroom Inquiries and the Public Understanding Of Science' (1999) 13 *Social Epistemology* 183, 186–8.

[84] Jones, above n. 12, Chapter 4.

[85] See, for example, Redmayne, above n. 36, 1073, but see S. A. Cole, 'More than Zero: Accounting for Error in Latent Fingerprint Identification' (2004) 95 *Journal of Criminal Law and Criminology* 985, 990 on how tighter admissibility rules lead to fingerprint examiners making even more exaggerated claims about their abilities.

[86] Edmond and Mercer, above n. 70, esp. 284, 299 and 303.

view is correct, legal reform may ensure that law benefits fully from scientific rationality and certainty. But if the latter view is also correct, it seems naïve to assume one can simply transfer unmediated scientific knowledge into law to obtain truth and ensure justice.

4 Truth, Reason and the Scientific Way

4.1 Introduction

An important question then arises as to the accuracy of the picture of science as rational producer of infallible truths about the world – a picture primarily associated with the research, as opposed to applied and social, sciences. While research scientists play far less of a role in legal fact finding than forensic and social scientists, they do sometimes appear as experts, especially in civil cases. Yet it is the assumption that they can reveal truths about the natural world which has led to science gaining its authoritative epistemic status in society and which has sprinkled its stardust on forensic and other applied hard sciences, while simultaneously making the social sciences seem far less valuable. This status rests on the related claims that:

- science is uniquely (or at least optimally)[87] able to deliver truth because its 'firm conclusions . . . are determined by the physical, and not the social, world'[88] or, more poetically, because it has 'discovered the language which nature itself uses';[89]
- in terms of an ideology of scientism,[90] scientific method provides objective and rational methods of inquiry that are uniquely capable of delivering truth in a neutral and value-free manner;[91]
- scientists are subject to norms and practices which ensure that they stick to the path of truth and reason, and maximise their contribution to knowledge.

[87] Cf., for example, Roberts, above n. 16, 263; L. Wolpert, 'What Lawyers Need to Know about Science', in Reece, above n. 29. See also at n. 124, below.
[88] M. Mulkay, 'Knowledge and Utility: Implications for the Sociology of Knowledge' (1979) 9 *Social Studies of Science* 63, 64.
[89] R. Rorty, *Consequences of Pragmatism* (1982) 191.
[90] Jones, above n. 12, 5; R. Smith and B. Wynne, 'Introduction', in Smith and Wynne, above n. 36, 2.
[91] For a succinct summary, see National Research Council of the National Academies, *Strengthening Forensic Science in the United States: A Path Forward* (2009) 112–13.

By contrast, an alternative perspective to this 'standard view of science'[92] draws on historians, philosophers and sociologists[93] to argue that 'the procedures and conclusions of science are, like all other cultural products, the contingent outcome of interpretive social acts'; its empirical findings 'are intrinsically inconclusive and the factual as well as the theoretical assertions of science depend on speculative and socially derived assumptions'.[94]

4.2 Scientific Truth[95]

In terms of this alternative perspective, scientific claims to mirror reality are undermined by the fact that the world does not speak for itself, but needs to be represented in language which – even if expressed in technical terms emphasising precision and mathematical gradations – is, as argued in Chapter Two,[96] socially constructed. However, the social construction of scientific facts is argued to go deeper.

This argument draws on the observation that research findings only count as 'facts' if they successfully navigate a complex process of accreditation by the scientific community.[97] First, they need to be converted into the conventional language of scientific papers, which involves making modest claims for findings, preferably in statistical form,[98] and which conceals possible political, moral and sometimes financial[99] choices as to which phenomena to investigate and how to interpret ambiguous findings. Then, to gain publication in a scientific journal, findings may have to be modified following reviewer comments. Yet most published scientific findings are ignored. Only if noticed and subject to positive replication by others using the same methods – which again may subtly alter the facts asserted – do they attain the status of accepted fact. This process of fact construction is highly dependent on the informal judgments of other

[92] M. Mulkay, *Science and the Sociology of Knowledge* (1985), passim, taking the term from I. Scheffler, *The Anatomy of Inquiry* (2nd edn, 2014).
[93] Who often go under the name of Science and Technology Studies, Science, Technology and Society or the Sociology of Scientific Knowledge.
[94] Mulkay, above n. 88, 65.
[95] See generally, Jasanoff, above n. 57 (both references); Wynne, above n. 57; Beecher-Monas, above n. 70; Mulkay, above n. 92; K. P. Addelson, 'The Man of Professional Wisdom', in S. Harding and M. B. Hintikka (eds), *Discovering Reality: Feminist Perspectives on Epistemology, Metaphysics, Methodology and the Philosophy of Science* (1983).
[96] Section 3.3.1.
[97] See, for example, J. R. Ravetz, 'Conventions in Science and in the Courts: Images and Realities' (2009) 72 *Law and Contemporary Problems* 25, 34–5.
[98] S. A. Cole, 'Forensic Culture as Epistemic Culture: The Sociology of Forensic Science' (2013) 44 *Studies in History and Philosophy of Biology & Biomedical Science* 36, 42.
[99] Funding sources are now usually acknowledged in published papers.

scientists, based, for instance, on the researcher's institutional affiliation and reputation, on the journal's prestige and on the type of science being done (theoretical versus experimental, etc).[100]

Equally important is the crucial relationship between scientific facts and theories. To be valuable, and to avoid drowning in a sea of trivial facts, science must go beyond producing isolated facts about the world and organise them into coherent theories which account for patterns in the way the world works. But extracting theories from facts is obviously a matter of judgment, which history shows is affected by the specific social, cultural and political contexts in which scientists work and the outcome of extensive social negotiations between them.[101] Moreover, the shared assumptions contained within these theories further construct new knowledge in influencing what new issues to investigate, which aspects of reality are noticed during investigation and how they are interpreted. In other words, 'all empirical statements are "theory-laden"'.[102]

It is thus difficult to argue that scientific conclusions are determined 'by the physical, and not the social, world'.[103] Instead, they can only be measured by consistency with other knowledge claims, and with conventional and often tacit standards of adequacy such as simplicity, accuracy, scope, fruitfulness and elegance. However, the consistency and adequacy criteria potentially clash. Adequate knowledge might be inconsistent with other knowledge, whereas consistent knowledge might be inadequate. Moreover, individual adequacy criteria also potentially conflict with each other, most obviously in the case of simplicity and accuracy. Such criteria also tend to vary with geography, particular scientific fields and over time. Nor can scientific conclusions be regarded as conclusive. New facts and insights may always modify existing theories and even occasionally result in 'scientific revolutions' (in Thomas Kuhn's famous phrase)[104] which occur when one existing knowledge paradigm is replaced by a totally incompatible paradigm. In other words, '"knowledge" is a temporary and fluid state, representing agreement among scientists to accept certain things as true

---

[100] See M. Mulkay, 'The Mediating Role of the Scientific Elite' (1976) 6 *Social Studies of Science* 445. Reputation also affects what research gets funded and hence may block challenges to orthodox views: Addelson, above n. 95, 178–80.

[101] See, for example, Mulkay's account of how Darwin's theory of evolution was infused with prevailing philosophical and theological presuppositions and Malthus' views on the dangers with population growth were politically motivated: above n. 92, 100–10.

[102] Ibid., 34; see also at 37 and 50.

[103] Mulkay, loc. cit., n. 88.

[104] *The Structure of Scientific Revolutions* (3rd edn, 1996).

for the time being, while acknowledging that the boundary of agreement will be disputed by some'.[105]

Admittedly, many scientists do not see themselves (or at least their colleagues)[106] as providing infallible and immutable knowledge. Indeed, careers are made precisely through successfully challenging existing knowledge claims. Nevertheless, some argue that science's value can be measured in other ways, such as its practical usefulness.[107] But this only applies to a fraction of scientific research, the vast majority of which is ignored by other scientists and those responsible for developing useful technology.[108] Moreover, while scientific research can undoubtedly lead to useful technologies such as DNA profiling, it has also unleashed existential challenges to life on earth.

4.3 Scientific Method(s)[109]

Given that science's claims to infallible truth and unambiguous utility are less than wholly convincing, a less ambitious claim for science's epistemic authority points to the superiority of scientific methods in delivering objective, value-free knowledge through rational means. It is argued that, not only has science developed sophisticated instruments which expand our ability to observe the world, such as microscopes, CAT scanners and hadron colliders,[110] but that it has also developed strict technical criteria to evaluate truth-claims through rigorous empirical testing aimed at eradicating the impact of subjective values, preferences and prejudices on knowledge. The traditional picture[111] of how science works is one of intuitive flashes of imagination leading to a hypothesis (the 'discovery' stage), which is then subject to rigorous and repeated testing – most notably through controlled experiments – to see if it is confirmed (the 'justification' stage). This picture was altered by Karl Popper, who responded to Hume's argument that hypotheses about the world based on experience can be invalidated by just one disconfirming instance.[112] Instead, he argued that what is important is not repeated confirmations but repeated attempts at

---

[105] Smith, 'The Trials of Forensic Science', above n. 36, 80.

[106] B. L. Campbell, 'Uncertainty as Symbolic Action in Disputes among Experts' (1985) 15 *Social Studies of Science* 429.

[107] For a critique, see Mulkay, above n. 88.

[108] See also Wolpert, above n. 87, 294.

[109] See generally, Wynne, above n. 57, 25–7; Beecher-Monas, above n. 70, esp. Chapter 3; Mulkay, above n. 92, 50–9, 76ff; G. Edmond and D. Mercer, 'Trashing "Junk Science"' (1998) 3 *Stanford Technology Law Review* 3.

[110] J. Sanders, 'Jury Deliberation in a Complex Case: *Havner v Merrell Dow Pharmaceuticals*' (1993) 16 *Justice System Journal* 45; A. I. Goldman, *Knowledge in a Social World* (1999), 251.

[111] See, for example, Black, Ayala and Saffran-Brinks, above n. 9, 753ff.

[112] See, for example, *The Logic of Scientific Discovery* (1959).

falsification. Consequently Popper asserts that only knowledge claims that can be stated precisely enough to be capable of being falsified deserve the status of science, even though their claim to truth must be downgraded from timeless certainty to provisional probability.

Recent years have seen attacks on all aspects of this standard view. Most notably, falsification – science's alleged hallmark – has been argued to involve an infinite regress, in that empirical observations which allegedly falsify some theory are themselves subject to falsification by another empirical observation, which is subject to falsification, and so on.[113] More importantly, science rarely displays a culture of 'organised scepticism', as the sociologist Robert Merton alleges.[114] When promising novel theories conflict with the perceived facts, such as Copernicus' reversal of the then-prevailing idea that the sun rotates around the earth, receptive scientists will temporarily suspend falsification of the new theory until theory can catch up to explain away the conflicts or provide a better alternative. More generally, there is simply insufficient time, resources or prestige to be gained from attempting to falsify all scientific findings. At some stage (sometimes almost immediately) the scientific community will accept there has been sufficiently adequate testing to treat theories as established (at least provisionally until new evidence emerges). Deciding when this point has been reached involves tacit understanding and negotiation within the relevant scientific community as to what constitute effective testing methods and criteria, and whether tests confirm or falsify relevant hypotheses. The decision may also be influenced by intrinsic factors like the theory's explanatory power, simplicity or elegance, and extrinsic factors like the reputation of the theory's proponents, funders' interests and the theory's political or moral acceptability. Indeed, studies of how scientists actually behave show that falsification operates more as a rhetorical tool used when negotiating scientific disagreements than a categorical rule of validity.[115]

But even if science is permeated with 'organised scepticism', the processes of replication and falsification are limited. For various reasons, many well-accepted theories are incapable of being falsified. Thus there may be no independent criteria by which to measure the theory's confirmation. For example, Charles Darwin's survival of the fittest theory was

---

[113] See, for example, Allen, above n. 50, 1169–71; G. Edmond and D. Mercer, 'Keeping "Junk" History, Philosophy and Sociology of Science Out of the Courtroom: Problems with the Reception of *Daubert v Merrell Dow Pharmaceuticals Inc*' (1997) 20 *University of New South Wales Law Journal* 48, 82–97.

[114] See, for example, *The Sociology of Science: Theoretical and Empirical Investigations* (1973), Chapter 13.

[115] See, for example, M. Mulkay, 'Applied Philosophy and Philosophers' Practice' (1981) 6 *Science Technology & Human Values* 7, 13–14.

accepted despite there being no means of testing it other than noting that some biological species have survived and others have not. Other theories are impossible to test, such as those about the origins of the universe or a pathologist's view of the cause of a violent death. Here, researchers in a wide variety of fields like those of climate science and epidemiology have to abandon the paradigmatic scientific method of experimentation in favour of 'statistical analyses of populations, reviews of long-term trend data, clinical studies of illness in individuals, observations of organizational behaviour, computer simulations, and even historical, literary, or cultural records'.[116] In other words, there is no scientific method – merely different scientific *methods*.[117] Admittedly experiments in controlled environments like the laboratory allow variables affecting outcomes to be carefully managed so that cause and effect can be reported with precision. But to downgrade all other research methods as unscientific would expel from the club many disciplines traditionally regarded as scientific. Consequently the justification for science's claim to authoritative epistemic status switches from its methods to the alleged existence of norms governing scientific behaviour, reinforced by various forms of control such as the requirements of strenuous training and publication in peer-reviewed journals.

4.4 Scientific Norms[118]

Most famously, Merton stressed the norms of *communism* (the idea that scientists should work together in transparent ways), *universalism* (participation in science should not depend on personal characteristics), *disinterestedness* (scientific knowledge should be pursued for its own sake rather than personal gain) and the already noted *organised skepticism*.[119] Others have added subsidiary norms such as emotional neutrality, impartiality, humility and an attitude of agnosticism towards the truth of one's own findings.

However, sociologists and historians of science question the prevalence of these norms and the effectiveness of these controls. As regards the latter, peer review has been shown to be affected by informal factors like institutional affiliation and established reputations.[120] On the other hand,

---

[116] Jasanoff, 'Laws Knowledge', above n. 57, S54.

[117] See Edmunds and Mercer, above n. 115, 72ff.

[118] See generally, Edmond and Mercer, ibid., 70–2; Mulkay above n. 92, 21–5, Chapter 3; M. J. Mulkay, 'Norms and Ideology in Science' (1976) 15 *Social Science Information* 637.

[119] At n. 166, above.

[120] See, for example, Cole, above n. 98, 40; D. Crane, 'The Gatekeepers of Science: Some Factors Affecting the Selection of Articles for Scientific Journals' (1967) 2 *The American Sociologist* 195; F. E. Raitt and M. S. Zeedyk, *The Implicit Relation of Psychology and Law: Women and Syndrome Evidence* (2000), 30–2.

while publication in a peer-reviewed journal cannot itself guarantee valid findings, rejection by reviewers or, worse still, the failure to even submit to a peer-reviewed publication provide useful clues as to validity.[121]

As regards universalism and organised scepticism, the operation of peer review and the patchy approach to testing research should already make it clear that these norms are often respected in the breach. Indeed, if organised scepticism were as thorough as is portrayed, scientists would have little time to develop new ideas and the communism norm would be undermined. Indeed, not only do the Mertonian norms sometimes conflict with each other, but studies[122] reveal that many orthodox norms stand in tension with opposing counter-norms which may equally further the scientific enterprise. For example, keeping research activities and findings secret conflicts with the transparency norm, but prevents later disputes over the origins of discoveries, protects commercial interests, and allows scientists to thoroughly check preliminary findings instead of being demotivated by criticism over insufficiently supported claims. The importance of personal motivation to ensure perseverance with lengthy and laborious research and withstand disappointing results also suggests that disinterestedness and emotional neutrality may be counter-productive.

Scientists therefore seem to face competing sets of norms and counter-norms, neither of which represent 'the operating rules of science'.[123] Instead, sociologists argue that none of these norms constrain behaviour. Instead they act more as rhetorical tools used to persuade outsiders of the rationality, objectivity and accuracy of scientific truth, and rival insiders of the superiority of competing theories. Like claims to truth and rational scientific method, perceived adherence to controlling scientific norms thus depends on considerable negotiation within the scientific community.

4.5 Conclusion

Nevertheless, notwithstanding that the standard view of science is less than convincing, few seem to doubt that the sciences 'constitute the richest and most extensive body of human knowledge'[124] and hence deserve '*respect* rather than *deference*'.[125] At the same time, some of the marital metaphors for the law–science relationship seem rather overblown.

---

[121] Black, Ayala and Saffran-Brinks, above n. 9, 777–8.

[122] Most notably by I. I. Mitroff, *The Subjective Side of Science: A Philosophical Inquiry into the Psychology of the Apollo Moon Scientists* (1976).

[123] Mulkay, above n. 118, 641.

[124] P. Kitcher, 'Scientific Knowledge', in P. K. Moser (ed.), *The Oxford Handbook of Epistemology* (2002), 385. See also Goldman, above n. 110, Chapter 8.

[125] S. Haack, *Manifesto of a Passionate Moderate* (1998), 94 (emphasis in original; see also at 95, 105).

If science is secretive, competitive and subject to conflict, then the image of a patriarchal legal husband disrupting the purity of science's collaborative and disinterested pursuit of truth has less purchase. Similarly, if its truth-claims and particularly its methods are subject to internal negotiation, then the impression of science as providing law with infallible and objective facts to bolster its epistemic authority suggests that law might gain less from its marriage of convenience than it expects, but science more so, given that its legal role may enhance its claims to epistemic authority in society.

5 'Hard' versus 'Soft' Science[126]

5.1 Introduction

The recognition that there is no such thing as a paradigmatic scientific method guaranteeing inexorable progress to comprehensive and infallible truth about the world has implications for the legal status of the so-called 'soft' sciences. As we have seen,[127] law's approach to the social sciences has been erratic, but over time it has increasingly found it difficult to resist the attractions of a younger lover,[128] especially in its psychological guises.[129] The 'affair' started in the nineteenth century with the turn to psychiatry in dealing with issues of insanity and later diminished responsibility, though this was facilitated by psychiatrists' socially elevated status as medical professionals. However, it was only in the latter years of the twentieth century that UK law[130] began to draw on insights into human behaviour (largely of a psychological nature) provided by the explosion in social science research which started in the 1970s. Indeed, according to Roberts, '[a]long with the advent of DNA evidence, the growing prevalence and

---

[126] In addition to the specific references below, this section draws heavily on D. L. Faigman, 'To Have and Have Not: Assessing the Value of Social Science to the Law as Science and Policy' (1989) 38 *Emory Law Review* 1005, as well as Raitt and Zeedyk, above n. 120; J. McEwan, *The Verdict of the Court: Passing Judgment in Law and Psychology* (2003); F. E. Raitt, 'A New Criterion for the Admissibility of Scientific Evidence? A Metamorphosis of Helpfulness', in Reece, above n. 29.

[127] Section 2.

[128] See Faigman, above n. 126, 1008 who describes social science as a 'suitor . . . alternately embraced and rejected by the law'; Raitt and Zeedyck, above n. 120, 27.

[129] For brief histories, see Raitt and Zeedyk, ibid., Chapter 1; D. Howitt, *Introduction to Forensic and Criminal Psychology* (2015), 7–14.

[130] US courts have been more amenable to use of social science research as exemplified in *Brown* v. *Board of Education* 347 US 483 (1954), where the Supreme Court cited research on the psychological impact of racial segregation.

influence of "psy-experts" must qualify as the late twentieth century's most significant development in forensic science'.[131]

Much of its impact has occurred outside the court room, such as in guidance on interviewing witnesses and clients[132] or detection strategies based on crime scene, offender and psychological profiling.[133] Other techniques like polygraphs or other lie-detector tests are also confined to use outwith formal fact finding, not least because of their lack of acceptance among many psychologists.[134] However, even if inapplicable or inadmissible in court,[135] such techniques may be useful if they lead to other cogent and admissible evidence being found.

But as regards formal fact finding, there are some notable differences in the way that the law treats the physical and social sciences. Thus the courts are reportedly less likely to allow social science experts to breach the hearsay rule[136] and more likely to require evidence of their credentials, the tests they have conducted and the criteria used to derive their opinions.[137] Most crucially, they seem to apply different rules of admissibility, at least where psychological evidence is thought to invade the court's fact-finding jurisdiction.[138]

The justification given for this hierarchical distinction[139] between the physical and social sciences draws heavily on the former's alleged objectivity, certainty, exactitude, and hence usefulness.[140] But while the various claims have varying degrees of plausibility, we have already seen that they are far from fully realised. Conversely, as we shall now see, they are in some cases equally or even more fully realised in the social sciences.

---

[131] Above n. 16, 261.

[132] See Chapter 6, section 2.4.3.

[133] See, for example, Howitt, above n. 129, Chapters 14 and 15; McEwan, above n. 126, 150–72; A. Kapardis *Psychology and Law: A Critical Introduction* (4th edn revised by I. Freckleton, 2014), 364–78.

[134] Howitt, ibid., Chapter 19.

[135] As in the case of offender profiling: *Young* v. *HM Advocate*, above n. 140.

[136] Jones, above n. 12, 109.

[137] Edmond, above n. 43, 238; A. Good, 'Expert Evidence in Asylum and Human Rights Appeals: An Expert's View' (2004) 16 *International Journal of Refugee Law* 358, 369.

[138] See D. Nicolson and D. Auchie, 'Assessing Witness Credibility and Reliability: Engaging Experts and Disengaging *Gage*?', in P. Duff and P. Ferguson (eds), *Current Developments in Scottish Criminal Evidence Law* (2017).

[139] Or, more accurately, a sliding scale with physics at the top, biology lower down, psychology close to the bottom, and sociology, anthropology and political science at the bottom: see Raitt and Zeedyk, above n. 120, 25–6; S. Cole, 'The Hierarchy of the Sciences?' (1983) 89 *American Journal of Sociology* 111.

[140] See, for example, S. M. Fahr, 'Why Lawyers are Dissatisfied with the Social Sciences' (1960) 1 *Washburn Law Journal* 161.

5.2 How Reliable are the Social Sciences?

A core reason for the alleged inferiority of the social sciences is their subjectivity. This in turn allegedly derives from their 'non-scientific' methods, the inherently socially constructed nature of their concepts,[141] and the fact that humans studying other humans are likely to allow ideological baggage to affect the interpretation of behaviour,[142] and may even use the label of objective science 'as a smokescreen to cloak their personal values'.[143]

Admittedly a fair amount of social science research does not involve testing falsifiable propositions by controlled experiments. Not only do the complex psychological causes and social influences on human behaviour make it difficult to isolate hypothesised causal variables for studies, but in relation to many of the issues which concern the law, like the impact of child abuse, rape or domestic violence, it would be unthinkable to cause such trauma for research purposes. Consequently social scientists rely on various other methods like correlation studies, which, because they cannot control variables, can only show that two variables coincide rather than are causally linked, and case studies in which, for instance, clinicians look at the commonalities between those who have been subjected to certain life events based on interviews, observation, case records, etc.

Being furthest from paradigmatic scientific methods, the case study method relied on by clinicians comes in for most criticism. In many cases, the samples relied on are too small and unrepresentative to justify certain conclusions, and the hypothesised phenomenon so widely and vaguely defined, that just about any behaviour can be regarded as confirmatory. Moreover, clinicians and subject may have a pre-existing relationship causing the former to succumb to what is known as the 'confirmation bias',[144] whereby their hypotheses shape the questions asked, and/or the 'belief bias'[145] or 'expectancy effect',[146] which shapes the interpretation of the answers so that '[d]isconfirmatory information is ignored, dismissed or discarded and spurious salience and significance given to detail which

---

[141] Cf. Redmayne, above n. 24, 8–9; M. King, *Psychology in and out of Court: A Critical Examination of Legal Psychology* (1986), Chapter 3.

[142] Cf. Faigman, above n. 126, 1026.

[143] M. Rustad and T. Koenig, 'The Supreme Court and Junk Social Science: Selective Distortion in Amicus Briefs' (1993) 72 *North Carolina Law Review* 91, 115 (but not endorsing this view).

[144] See, for example, J. St B. T. Evans and D. E. Over, *Rationality and Reasoning* (1996), 103–9.

[145] Ibid., 109–12.

[146] G. Edmond et al., 'Contextual Bias and Cross-Contamination in the Forensic Sciences: The Corrosive Implications for Investigations, Plea Bargains, Trials and Appeals' (2015) 14 *Law, Probability and Risk* 1, 7.

apparently confirms the hypothesis'.[147] In addition, a 'feedback effect' may cause subjects to shape their answers to please their clinicians or respond to subconscious cues from them.

On the other hand, it is possible to mitigate the effects of the personal nature of the research relationship, whereas the limitations of small and unrepresentative samples, and vague and general descriptions of phenomena, will recede as findings accumulate. In the meantime, social scientists can and should limit themselves to making modest research claims. In any event, as we have seen,[148] the physical and especially the medical sciences are also forced to rely on experience and judgment rather than experimental testing,[149] and hence cannot escape the influence of subjective factors. By contrast, the very fact that social scientists study human behaviour may alert them to the need to mitigate associated problems. Moreover, much social science research, such as that on the psychology of witnessing,[150] the reliability of confession evidence[151] and the impact of sexual stereotyping,[152] closely replicates paradigmatic scientific methods. Thus they can be designed to ensure experimental falsification and 'internal validity', which involves controlling study variables to ensure that cause and effect can be established, such as through the exclusion of rival hypotheses which provide plausible alternative explanations for the results, and randomly selecting subjects so that results cannot be said to be coincidental or unrepresentative of a wider class of subjects.

However, internal validity is often bought at the expense of 'external validity', which requires that results obtained are generalisable to other situations and people. Most crucially, research should reflect real-life conditions – what is known as ecological validity – which is undermined by the fact that, outwith the artificial environment of highly controlled experiments, human behaviour is subjected to numerous internal and

---

[147] E. Shepherd and R. Milne, 'Full and Faithful: Ensuring Quality Practice and Integrity of Outcome in Witness Interviews', in Heaton-Armstrong et al., *Analysing Witness Testimony* (1999), 126, also noting the related processes of 'ironing out' inconvenient information and 'selectively synthesising' details from different accounts into a coherent account supporting the initial hypothesis.

[148] Section 4.2.

[149] See, for example, Edmond and Mercer, above n. 109, para. 29; E. I. Imwinkelried, 'The Meaning of "Appropriate Validation" in *Daubert v. Merrell Dow Pharmaceuticals, Inc.* Interpreted in Light of the Broader Rationalist Tradition, Not the Narrow Scientific Tradition' (2002) 30 *Florida State University Law Review* 735, 742–3.

[150] See Chapter 6, section 4.1.3.

[151] See Chapter 6, sections 2.4.3 and 2.5.2.

[152] See, for example, S. T. Fiske et al., 'Social Science Research on Trial: Use of Sex Stereotyping Research in *Price Waterhouse v. Hopkins*' (1991) 46 *American Psychologist* 1049.

external factors going beyond the variables isolated for study. Because it is impossible to control all such factors, social science research is criticised for being unable to develop general explanatory theories capable of predicting future behaviour with the exactitude and certainty of the 'laws' of physics, chemistry and biology. Instead it can only predict the impact of a few isolated variables and does so with decreasingly less certainty as these variables increase. However, the physical sciences are hardly free from similar problems of external validity, imprecision and uncertainty. For instance,[153] the paradigmatic 'hard' science of physics can accurately predict the speed and trajectory of a falling leaf in a vacuum, but not in a stiff wind. Even in laboratory conditions, certainty may be impossible. For example, scientists trying to predict whether a given photon from a light source projected onto a glass block will end up in one of two light receptors can say no more than that 4 per cent of photons will end up at the front receptor. In other words, as David Faigman notes, '[n]ature permits us to calculate only probabilities. Yet science has not collapsed.'[154]

At the same time, however, it is undeniable that the physical sciences have achieved much greater precision and consensus in answering many more questions than the social sciences. Rather than describe the physical sciences as 'hard', with all the implicit associations with privileged masculinity, objectivity and fact,[155] they are better described as 'mature'[156] or 'established'.[157] Even more controversially, they could even be labelled as 'easy', given that, compared, for instance, to the chemical ingredients of matter, it is far harder for the social sciences to define (or 'operationalise') their objects of study for the purposes of measurement.[158] Moreover, there is arguably no reason why, despite the more ideologically contested nature of some questions, the social sciences cannot in time achieve a similar status for many of their knowledge claims. Indeed, in some areas social science knowledge is far more settled and less 'speculative'[159] than that in certain intractable areas of the physical sciences like the origins of the universe and even minute variations in planetary orbits. Furthermore, law is far more frequently concerned with understanding human behaviour rather than the physical world, which is often better understood by the judgment and 'art' of experienced clinicians based on holistic assessment

---

[153] This and following example are taken from Faigman, above n. 126, 1046 and 1048.
[154] Ibid., 1048–9.
[155] E. F. Keller, 'Gender and Science', in Harding and Hintikka, above n. 95, 188.
[156] Haack, 'Irreconcilable Differences?', above n. 57, 10; Faigman, above n. 126, 101.
[157] Campbell, above n. 106, 449.
[158] J. Diamond, 'Soft Sciences are Often Harder than Hard Sciences' (1987) 8 *Discover* 34.
[159] Cf. Haack, 'Irreconcilable Differences?', above n. 57, 10; Roberts, above n. 16, 263.

of those they treat rather than the study of subjects in laboratories performing artificial tasks far removed from the social and historical background which gives meaning to 'real-life' behaviour and motivations.[160]

5.3 How Useful are the Social Sciences?

We thus see that there is no clear divide between the natural and social sciences as regards the reliability and precision of their knowledge claims. This suggests that other factors might play a role in the latter's inferior legal status. One might be the fact that the social sciences compete with law for authority to interpret and assess human behaviour and the law jealously guards its fact-finding authority.[161]

However, this has not led to the total expulsion of the social sciences from the legal domain. For instance, diagnoses of mental illness[162] and opinions of offender dangerousness[163] have been accepted even though they suffer from the unavoidable shortcomings of non-experimental methods, and individual psychiatrists and psychologists frequently differ in their diagnoses of the same people (though evidently not much more so than medical doctors).[164] Yet scientifically rigorous psychological research on witnessing which has produced findings which are not known or fully appreciated by jurors or even professional adjudicators has been excluded on grounds that they are matters of common sense.[165] Here, what seems to be more important than reliability or protection of legal authority is the extent to which expertise is useful to law. Thus, as unreliable as diagnoses of mental illness are, it seems inconceivable that they would be made by legal fact finders rather than psychiatrists, who after all are clothed with the authority and class status of medical professions. Equally important, forensic psychiatrists have reached an accommodation with the law in which they merge medical with legal ways of understanding human behaviour.[166] If so, the courts' assertion of the ability of juror common sense and experience to cope with assessing witness testimony may not just

---

[160] See Raitt and Zeedyk, above n. 120, 53ff; A. E. Taslitz, 'Myself Alone – Individualizing Justice Through Psychological Character Evidence' (1993) 52 *Maryland Law Review* 1, 98ff.

[161] See, for example, Jones, above n. 12, 96; Raitt, above n. 126, esp. at 165–6.

[162] See, for example, M. Zimmerman, 'A Review of 20 Years of Research on Overdiagnosis and Underdiagnosis in the Rhode Island Methods to Improve Diagnostic Assessment and Services (MIDAS) Project' (2016) 61 *The Canadian Journal of Psychiatry* 71. On the contested nature of standard diagnostic descriptors, see, for example, Raitt and Zeedyk, above n. 120, 13–14.

[163] See Beecher-Monas, above n. 70, Chapters 6–8; Howitt, above n. 129, Chapter 27.

[164] G. J. Meyer et al., 'Psychological Testing and Psychological Assessment: A Review of Evidence and Issue' (2001) 56 *American Psychologist* 128.

[165] See Chapter 6, section 4.

[166] See Smith, 'Expertise', above n. 71.

reflect its ignorance of research findings that show the exact opposite,[167] but also a desire to protect lay justice and indeed the judge's own epistemic and adjudicative authority, as well as a faith (largely misguided, as we shall see)[168] in law's ability to cope with any obvious problems through its own epistemic procedures of cross-examination and jury instructions. In other words, while the law might trade on the ideology of scientism in handling expert evidence, it seems to be as much interested in its own epistemic and legal authority and the usefulness of expert evidence than its reliability.

6 Forensic Science[169]

6.1 Introduction

The focus on usefulness rather than reliability is even more prominent in law's attitudes to forensic science and forensic medicine – the progeny of its marriage to hard science. Here, the law seems happy to trade on the authority conferred by these 'hard', albeit applied, sciences without looking closely, if at all, at their scientific credentials.[170] Admittedly the various different forensic science and medicine disciplines (henceforth just forensic sciences) vary considerably, not only in terms of the validity of their scientific bases but also the techniques they use (instrument-based or naked observation), by whom (trained scientists, laboratory technicians or experienced specialists; state employees or private practitioners) and where (in laboratories, morgues, offices), and the level of subjective interpretation involved in the production of results.

6.2 Taking the Science out of Forensic Science[171]

Nevertheless, despite these variations, the applied nature of the forensic sciences and the way they operate give rise to various problems which compromise the accuracy of the results produced. One set of problems involves the inherent accuracy of forensic techniques and the way they are used. Inherent inaccuracy in turn can stem from problems of *validity* – the

---

[167] Above n. 165.

[168] Section 7.4, below; Chapter 6, section 4.2.

[169] See generally, Fraser and Williams, above n. 17; Redmayne, above n. 24, Chapter 2; Roberts, above n. 18.

[170] Thus in *Young* v. *HM Advocate*, above n. 40, at para. 55, it was simply assumed that DNA and fingerprint expertise is unproblematic.

[171] In addition to specific references below, the following draws on Roberts, above n. 16, 264–71 passim, and above n. 18, 472–88; the chapters in Smith and Wynne, above n. 36; Cole, above n. 98; Moenssens, above n. 44; W. C. Thompson, 'A Sociological Perspective on the Science of Forensic Testing' (1997) 30 *University of California Davis Law Review* 1113.

extent to which the science underlying the technique accurately represents the phenomenon described – and *reliability* – the extent to which the technique consistently produces the same results irrespective of who uses them. In addition, as regards the application of techniques, questions of *proficiency* relate to the extent to which individual practitioners or investigative organisations (most notably, laboratories) apply these techniques without error. While we have seen that scientific methods backed up by Mertonian norms do not ensure the infallibility of even the pure sciences, for a number of reasons the forensic sciences are generally far worse in this regard.

One reason relates to the inherent nature of the phenomena being investigated. Thus, compared to pure science's tightly controlled experiments, forensic investigators may work with unsatisfactory materials, such as samples which are degraded, contaminated or mixed with other samples, or those whose size makes testing difficult. Ideally forensic scientists should attend localities to oversee the collection of forensic evidence, as forensic pathologists do.[172] But in criminal cases this only occurs in relation to serious offences. Consequently the lack of necessary knowledge and experience on the part of those collecting samples – who are at best specially trained prosecutors or police officers, but at worst ordinary officers – may result in important evidence being overlooked.[173] Equally, bodily fluids may have been washed away or personal injuries healed by the time victims are examined. Finally, the adversarial nature of case construction may mean that material which challenges case theories is subconsciously or even deliberately withheld from forensic investigators.

A second inherent problem relates to the fact that most forensic investigation relies extensively on subjective decision-making.[174] Instruments may enable observation of phenomena invisible to the naked eye, but conclusions are usually based on subjective judgment, creating potential for human error. Moreover, practitioners cannot learn from experience by testing the results of their analyses against 'reality' in the way that research science is said to gain '"feedback", so to speak, from nature'.[175] Thus there is only rarely conclusive evidence that, for instance, a fingerprint or bite mark identification was wrong (or right), such as when convictions are overturned by contradictory (or confirmed by supporting) DNA evidence.

---

[172] Jones, above n. 12, 197.
[173] See, for example, D. Barclay, 'Using Forensic Science in Major Crime Inquiries', in Fraser and Williams, above n. 17, 342–3.
[174] See I. E. Dror, 'Cognitive Neuroscience in Forensic Science: Understanding and Utilizing the Human Element' (2015) 370 *Philosophical Transactions of the Royal Society B*. 1 on the resultant consequences.
[175] Cole, above n. 98, 43.

But then even DNA profiling is not infallible.[176] Moreover, testing the reliability of techniques or the proficiency of practitioners is often impossible because of the difficulty of repeating the same tests on the same forensic materials given their tendency to degrade or be destroyed by testing.

Other challenges to scientific ideals flow from the applied nature of forensic science and medicine. Thus much routine forensic work is performed by technicians who learn on the job without understanding the scientific foundations (or lack thereof) of the techniques they apply or the safeguards provided by scientific methods and norms. Consequently they may be more prone to making mistakes and claiming more for these techniques than is justified.

More importantly, especially in the case of private as opposed to state providers, techniques are not developed or used in a disinterested quest for the truth but as 'products' which can be 'sold' to meet the instrumental needs of the 'legal masters' to which the providers are 'inextricably tethered', if not mere 'handmaidens'.[177] Thus reward structures in forensic science undermine any motivation to gain independent testing of the validity and reliability of their techniques or the proficiency levels of forensic practitioners, or indeed be honest about problems which emerge. Where forensic scientists do engage in research, it is usually to find new ways to serve their customers. Testing the validity and reliability of these new methods, if it occurs at all, usually follows rather than precedes its use by legal actors. For example, DNA profiling was only put on a solid scientific basis years after regular use in determining paternity and identifying criminals.

The close relationship between forensic practitioners and those they serve affects all stages of the process whereby raw forensic materials (fingerprints, DNA, fire debris, etc.) are transformed into proof of particular facts (the perpetrator's identity, the child's paternity, the fire's cause), namely: (1) the collection of the forensic materials; (2) their analysis; (3) the interpretation of the results; and (4) the reporting of the results. Thus, contrary to Mertonian norms of emotional neutrality, impartiality and agnosticism towards the accuracy of one's own findings, forensic scientists are exposed

---

[176] Especially when DNA samples might have come from more than one source: for example, W. C. Thompson, 'Accepting Lower Standards: The National Research Council's Second Report on Forensic DNA Evidence' (1997) *Jurimetrics* 405, 414 n. 25; J. M. Taupin, *Introduction to Forensic Evidence for Criminal Justice Professionals* (2013), Chapters 5 and 8; and see more generally on the fallibility of DNA sampling: W. C. Thompson, 'Subjective Interpretation, Laboratory Error and the Value of DNA Evidence: Three Case Studies' (1995) 96 *Genetica* 153; W. C. Thompson, 'Tarnish on the "Gold Standard": Understanding Recent Problems in Forensic DNA Testing' (2006) 30 *The Champion* 10.

[177] National Research Council, above n. 91, 52.

to a variety of contextual factors[178] which are likely to cause 'cognitive contamination (where interpretations and judgments are swayed, often without awareness or conscious control, by contextual cues, irrelevant details of the case, prior experiences, expectations and institutional pressures)'.[179] This in turn leads to various types of biases which cause errors in analysis.

'Hot biases' may flow from forensic investigators learning of the heinousness of the crime being investigated or other factors likely to arouse their emotions. More common are 'cold' biases, which stem from examiners learning, for instance, that the alleged sources of forensic material have a criminal record, have confessed or been positively identified by other examiners. The impact of such biases has been demonstrated by numerous studies which build on Daniel Tversky and Amos Kahneman's pioneering work on heuristic reasoning.[180] Heuristics are a form of 'bounded rationality',[181] which involves people reasoning less than optimally in order to make quick and efficient ('fast and frugal') decisions when they are distracted or suffering from cognitive overload caused by information which is too voluminous, ambiguous, incomplete, probabilistic or complicated. They allow shortcuts to lengthy deliberation processes through applying rules of thumb or educated guesses, which usually work effectively as they are based on past experience. However, they may also lead to 'severe and systematic'[182] errors or biases, of which the most pertinent are:[183]

- the already noted[184] confirmation bias and expectation effect – the tendency, respectively, to search for information that confirms our prior beliefs and interpret ambiguous information in ways which support what one expects;[185]

---

[178] See generally, Redmayne, above n. 24, 13–16; Edmond et al., above n. 146; I. E. Dror and S. A. Cole, 'The Vision in "Blind" Justice: Expert Perception, Judgment and Visual Cognition in Forensic Pattern Recognition' (2010) 17 *Psychonomic Bulletin & Review* 161.

[179] Edmond et al., ibid., 2.

[180] For example, D. Kahneman, P. Slovic and A. Tversky (eds), *Judgment under Uncertainty: Heuristics and Biases* (1982). For useful overviews, see M. Saks and R. Kidd, 'Human Information Processing and Adjudication: Trial by Heuristics' (1980) 15 *Law & Society Review* 123; E. Greene and L. Ellis, 'Decision Making in Criminal Justice', in D. Carson et al. (eds), *Applying Psychology to Criminal Justice* (2007); L. van Boven et al., 'Judgment and Decision Making', in E. Carlston, *The Oxford Handbook of Social Cognition* (2013).

[181] See H. Simon, *Models of Bounded Rationality* (1982).

[182] A. Tversky and D. Kahneman, 'Judgment under Uncertainty: Heuristics and Biases', in Kahneman, Slovic and Tversky, above n. 180, 3.

[183] For an overview, see Edmond et al., above n. 146.

[184] Section 5.2 above; and for a good example, see W. C. Thompson, 'Beyond Bad Apples: Analyzing the Role of Forensic Science in Wrongful Convictions' (2008) 37 *Southwestern University Law Review* 1027, 1033ff.

[185] See further Cole, above n. 85, 1060–1.

- the hindsight bias (or 'knew-it-all-along' effect) – the tendency to see events as predictable once we know the outcome;[186] and
- the anchoring and adjustment bias – the reluctance to depart from the first item of information encountered and sufficiently adjust first impressions when new information emerges.[187]

Cumulatively these biases lead to people attending to, exaggerating and emphasising what they expect ('sharpening') and ignoring or down-playing what they do not ('levelling'). In the forensic context the influence of such cognitive biases has been revealed by numerous studies in which contextual information has caused examiners to change their analysis of a previously examined sample.[188]

In fact, cognitive biases may affect even the more precise forms of forensic analysis, such as that of DNA and the refractive index of glass fragments. Here, sophisticated methods of analysis rely on relatively pre-cise evaluations of the statistical likelihood of a conclusion, for instance that blood found on the suspect came from the victim. However, tradi-tional statistical methods suffer from a 'fall off a cliff' effect, in terms of which, if a specified probabilities threshold is not met even by a fraction, analysts conclude that there is no match, yet declare a match if it is mar-ginally exceeded.[189] Consequently forensic scientists prefer approaches based on Bayes' Theorem. This allows one to estimate the probability of a hypothesised event based on first allocating a numerical probability to its likely occurrence prior to any new evidence (the prior odds) and then combining this with the probability calculation attached to some new evi-dence to give a new, posterior, estimate of its probability (posterior odds) by dividing the former by the latter to generate a likelihood ratio.[190] More specifically, Bayes' Theorem allows one to compare the likelihood that the sample and trace match with a paired opposite (match or non-match) to produce a likelihood ratio, and allows for a constant updating of the prob-ability of each proposition as new information is received. However, while this method is said to have numerous advantages,[191] it – and arguably all

---

[186] See, for example, K. D. Markan and E. A. Dyczewski, 'Mental Simulation: Looking Back in Order to Look Ahead', in Carlston, above n. 180.

[187] See, for example, R. Hastie and R. M. Dawes, *Rational Choice in an Uncertain World: The Psychology of Judgment and Decision Making* (2010), Chapter 4.

[188] See Edmond et al., above n. 146; Dror and Cole, above n. 178.

[189] For a detailed discussion, see Redmayne, above n. 24, Chapter 3.

[190] For a good introduction, see I. Hacking, *An Introduction to Probability and Inductive Logic* (2001), Chapters 7 and 15.

[191] But also disadvantages; see, for example, Redmayne, above n. 24, 41ff.

forensic analysis[192] – requires evaluators to be informed of all information relevant to the question of whether there is a match or not, thereby exposing them to both cognitive and emotional biases.[193] It may also extend the legitimate role of experts beyond reporting on the question of whether samples match (what are called source-level propositions) to encroach upon the court's decision as to who might have left them (activity-level propositions).[194]

We thus encounter a paradox: forensic scientists need contextual information to do their job properly, but such information may prompt confirmation and expectancy biases – especially the latter, which is likely to pervade all forensic science work that involves being asked to determine whether two items of forensic evidence are similar rather than dissimilar. Similarly the more expertise a scientist gains the more they become 'susceptible to contextual influences and bias because [they] take more "shortcuts", rely on past experience, attend to information more selectively, and a whole range of cognitive mechanisms that make up expertise'.[195]

Bias can also be caused by social biases rather than specific information. When forensic practitioners enter into an ongoing relationship with one particular 'customer', as occurs with the provision of most forensic services to the Scottish police,[196] it seems inevitable that practitioners will identify with their 'customer's' interests and values, and shape their investigations and analyses accordingly.[197] More generally, the fact that forensic practitioners are 'inextricably tethered'[198] to the legal system means that they become accustomed to subordinating their own values and practices to those of the legal system. For instance, the immersion in an adversarial system of justice in which every small error, hint of uncertainty or nuance is exaggerated and used against forensic practitioners is likely to make them reluctant to disclose anything that can be used against them or those

[192] Barclay, above n. 173, 345; J. Allard, 'Bodily Fluids in Sexual Offences', in Fraser and Williams, above n. 17, 143.
[193] See Roberts, above n. 18, 478–80, noting also that forensic scientists who attend the scene of crimes or other legal incidents will inevitably pick up contextual information.
[194] See R. Cook et al., 'A Hierarchy of Propositions: Deciding which Level to Address in Casework' (1998) 38 *Science & Justice* 331.
[195] I. Dror, 'The Ambition to be Scientific: Human Expert Performance and Objectivity' (2013) 53 *Science & Justice* 81, 82.
[196] All forensic science laboratories are contained within the four major police forces, although forensic pathology and toxicology services are provided by independent laboratories.
[197] See R. Stockdale, 'Running with the Hounds' (1991) 141 *New Law Journal* 772 who, as a forensic scientist working actively for the prosecution, admits that to point out all weakness in the case to the defence 'is rather like expecting the hound who has just caught the hare to set with a will to give it the kiss of life'.
[198] Loc. cit., n. 91.

they serve, such as disagreements between examiners, disciplinary action, or failed proficiency tests, laboratory accreditations and audit reports.

As regards the final stage of the forensic process, forensic reports often repeat and consolidate preceding contraventions of the Mertonian norm of transparency and disinterestedness. Reports tend[199] – increasingly so as economic imperatives dominate – to be brief, written in highly stylised language and standardised form, and with conclusions often stated in definite and categorical terms (for example, that the forensic material could only have come from the suspect), instead of being expressed in more justified probabilistic terms. Whereas the assumed scientific illiteracy of their intended audience provides some justification for simplicity, this and the formulaic nature of reports also conveniently allows them to conceal negative or ambiguous results as well as any factors detracting from the accuracy of results.

More recently, the increasing drive to reduce costs has exacerbated these problems in relation to forensic services provided to the police. While Scotland has resisted the wholesale privatisation of state forensic services which occurred in England and Wales in 2011, this does not necessarily[200] mean that the state provision of forensic services via the Scottish Police Authority has avoided the cold winds of 'austerity' which currently penetrate every crevice of neo-liberal society,[201] and have resulted in budgetary cuts to all state services. Moreover, all civil litigants and criminal accused are required to turn to commercial forensic service providers.

The resultant focus on economic considerations means that, instead of assiduously checking for accuracy, forensic scientists – especially those private providers on block contracts – are likely to be pressurised and/or incentivised to produce as many reports as possible, and as quickly and cheaply as possible. This has led to an increased role for managers lacking scientific experience, routinisation of techniques and procedures and a consequent de-skilling of practitioners. While this standardisation of forensic work may make it less responsive to the particular nuances of individual cases, it does, however, also make it easier to impose good practice

---

[199] But cf. Roberts, above n. 18, 484, on the more comprehensive reports of tool mark, glass fragment and medical examiners.

[200] One cannot say more than this given the intense secrecy surrounding the Scottish Police Authority.

[201] Neo-liberalism refers to an extreme form of laissez-faire economic theory which champions economic liberalisation, privatisation, free trade and deregulated markets, and seeks to minimise government spending, inter alia, through imposing market forces on state services. For the impact on English forensic science services, see C. Lawless, 'Policing Markets; the Contested Shaping of Neo-Liberal Forensic Science' (2011) 5 British Journal of Criminology 671.

on practitioners.[202] Thus commercial pressures have led to the growing adoption by both commercial and state providers of the Case Assessment and Interpretation method,[203] which was designed to integrate commercial imperatives into the investigative process, as well as to ensure greater control by investigative authorities over the laboratory. Based on Bayesian methodology, it is also more likely to increase the possible impact of biasing contextual information. At the same time, not only does it allow forensic scientists to respond to the particular nuances of each case, but the requirement to formulate hypotheses as alternative propositions for prosecution and defence simultaneously reduces the impact of the expectation bias, and the extent to which investigation and analysis will be prosecution-driven.

But whatever the reason for problems with handling forensic evidence, miscarriages of justice, investigative journalism and even far from rigorous proficiency tests reveal that individuals and organisations make numerous errors due to both mistaken analysis, and the contamination and mislabelling of forensic evidence, even in the case of the scientifically more rigorous technique of DNA profiling.[204] When uncovered, these errors are usually blamed on humans rather than the systems or the techniques used,[205] and this in turn creates an incentive for individuals to seek to conceal errors to protect themselves.[206]

6.3 The Scientific Deficit Illustrated: Forensic Identification Methods[207]

Cumulatively the above factors ensure that the methods and norms said to characterise 'proper' science are far less evident in the forensic, as opposed

---

[202] Fraser and Williams, above n. 22, 282.
[203] See R. Cook et al., 'A Model for Case Assessment and Interpretation' (1998) 38 *Science & Justice* 151; I. W. Evett, 'The Impact of the Principles of Evidence Interpretation on the Structure and Content of Statements' (2000) 40 *Science & Justice* 233, and for more critical analyses, Lawless, above n. 201, 677–9; C. J. Lawless and R. Williams, 'Helping with Inquiries or Helping with Profits? The Trials and Tribulations of a Technology of Forensic Reasoning' (2010) 40 *Social Studies of Science* 731.
[204] See, for example, National Research Council, above n. 91, 100.
[205] Thompson, above n. 184.
[206] Thompson, 'Tarnish on the Gold Standard', above n. 76, 12.
[207] In addition to specific references below, the following draws on Beecher-Monas, above n. 70, Chapter 5; the National Research Council, above n. 91, Chapter 5 passim; Dror and Cole, above n. 178; Saks and Koehler, above n. 37 and 'The Individualization Fallacy in Forensic Science Evidence' (2008) 61 *Vanderbilt Law Review* 199; S. A. Cole, 'Where the Rubber Meets the Road: Thinking about Expert Evidence as Expert Testimony' (2007) 52 *Villanova Law Review* 803 and 'Forensics Without Uniqueness, Conclusions Without Individualization: The New Epistemology of Forensic Identification' (2009) 8 *Law, Probability and Risk* 233; G. Edmond et al., 'Admissibility Compared: The Reception of Incriminating Expert Evidence (i.e., Forensic Science) in Four Adversarial Jurisdictions' (2013) 3 *University of Denver Criminal Law Review* 31.

to the pure and even many social, sciences. For the most part, forensic scientists use methods which are intrinsically less trustworthy than those of pure science, and do so in ways which produce less accurate and precise results. In fact, to describe many forensic methods as involving a scientific technique is to give them a spurious legitimacy. As Jonathan Koehler notes, 'where a method depends as heavily on subjective human judgment as does fingerprint examination, the method literally *is* the people who employ it'.[208]

Given the 'bewildering variety'[209] of forensic sciences, it is impossible to give more than an overview of validity and reliability problems. Consequently we will focus on the most common use of forensic science, which is to identify people or objects suspected of involvement in legal incidents. This occurs in the criminal context and usually through investigating whether some trace or mark (for example, a print from a shoe, finger, palm or ear; a mark from a bite, tool or tyre; or a bloodstain, hair or fibre) left by some relevant legal actor or (the 'reference' or 'exemplar') derived from the suspected source. The validity and reliability of such 'source attribution'[210] techniques range from the new 'gold standard' of DNA profiling[211] to the highly speculative theories and unproven techniques of firearm, tool mark, hair fibre and teeth mark analysis,[212] with the previous 'gold standard' of fingerprint identification[213] and the long-accepted technique of handwriting analysis[214] falling between these extremes.

To be probative of identity, forensic scientists must accurately match samples (the question of 'consistency') and this in turn requires confirmation that the technique used is reliable in general and was applied

---

[208] 'Fingerprint Error Rates and Proficiency Tests: What They Are and Why They Matter' (2008) 59 *Hastings Law Journal* 1077, 1090. See also Cole, above n. 85, 1039.

[209] See Fraser and Williams, above n. 17, 2.

[210] For a discussion of the validity and reliability of other examples of forensic identification, see, for example, A. E. Taslitz, 'Does the Cold Nose Know? The Unscientific truth of the Dog Scent Lineup' (1990) 42 *Hastings Law Journal* 15; G. Edmond et al., 'Law's Looking Glass: Expert Identification Evidence Derived From Photographic And Video Images' (2009) 20 *Current Issues in Criminal Justice* 337; G. Edmond, K. Martire and M. San Roque, 'Unsound Law: Issues with ("Expert") Voice Comparison Evidence' (2011) 35 *Melbourne University Law Review* 52; G. Edmond, 'Just truth? Carefully Applying History, Philosophy and Sociology of Science to the Forensic Use of CCTV images' (2013) 44 *Studies in History and Philosophy of Science Part C: Studies in History and Philosophy of Biological and Biomedical Sciences* 80.

[211] See, for example, Gill and Clayton, above n. 17.

[212] See National Research Council, above n. 91, 150–61, 173–6.

[213] See, for example, Redmayne, above n. 24, 48–51; National Research Council, ibid., 136–45; Koehler, above n. 208; G. Edmond, M. B. Thompson and J. B. Tangen, 'A Guide to Interpreting Forensic Testimony: Scientific Approaches to Fingerprint Evidence' (2014) 13 *Law, Probability and Risk* 1; C. Champod and P. Chamberlain, 'Fingerprints', in Fraser and Williams, above n. 17.

[214] Risinger, Denbeaux and Saks, above n. 8; National Research Council, above n. 91, 164–7.

accurately in the particular case. On its own, though, consistency between samples does not prove identity. It must also be established that the trace or mark could only have come from the relevant person or object (the question of 'rarity' or 'uniqueness').

However, while it has long been assumed that no two people have, for example, the same fingerprints or handwriting, such uniqueness has never been established. Nor could it. Even if one could collect all existing prints or handwriting samples, there may be past or future examples of identical prints or handwriting which disprove uniqueness. The best that can be done is to combine relevant scientific theories about the likely uniqueness of the characteristic in question with databases of as many samples as possible from which to develop probabilistic claims about the possibility of coincidental matches. In the case of DNA profiling, genetic theory and impressive statistical databases allow analysts to provide a relatively, but not entirely, discretion-free[215] evaluation of the statistical chance of two identical DNA profiles coming from the same source and to represent this evaluation by a numerical statement (for example, one in a million, billion or even trillion). By contrast, not only are other identification techniques unsupported by scientific theories regarding their uniqueness assumptions, but attempts to provide statistical databases have only recently begun. Accordingly, while examiners should be confined to making very rough estimates of the relatively high chances of random matches (for instance, one in twenty, ten or even less), the courts[216] blithely accept assertions by those analysing fingerprints, earprints, handwriting, etc. that they have identified the source of the suspect or trace. Moreover, while the claim that human and animal marks and traces have a unique source has some plausibility, it is far less plausible in relation to those left by manufactured objects like tools, weapons, shoes and tyres. At best, one could provide some indication as to the likelihood of a random match, but current research supports only very vague guesses.

A similar lack of published and peer-reviewed research undermines the assertions by many forensic identification examiners – frequently accepted by the UK courts[217] – that they can infallibly match suspect with trace, notwithstanding that in many cases the same source can produce

---

[215] At least as regards DNA from a single source: see, for example, J. M. Taupin, *Introduction to Forensic DNA Evidence for Criminal Justice Professionals* (2013), Chapters 5 and 8.

[216] See, for example, W. E. O'Brian, 'Court Scrutiny of Expert Evidence: Recent Decisions Highlight the Tensions' (2003) 7 *International Journal of Evidence and Proof* 172 in relation to England and Wales.

[217] See, for example, C. Chambod and P. Chamberlain, 'Fingerprints', in Fraser and Williams, above n. 17, 78–9.

non-identical prints or marks. For instance, differences in factors like the skin's elasticity and the pressure imparted mean that no two print impressions are ever identical, even if derived from the same finger, palm, sole, ear or set of teeth. Similarly, one study revealed that two people sometimes have the same signature.[218] Moreover, questions of similarity and difference are always matters of social construction rather than essence. Relying on Ludwig Wittgenstein, Simon Cole notes that 'the terms "the same" and "different" are meaningless until we articulate rules for what we mean by them'; otherwise all things can be argued to differ from or be the same as each other in some way.[219] Many forms of identification, such as fingerprint analysis, require a certain number of agreed similarities in a sample before declaring a match, but the number is entirely arbitrary and unsupported by evidence that the threshold delivers infallible matches. Even the interpretation of DNA test results is a matter of subjective opinion.[220]

Despite the mythical nature of uniqueness, it may be that expert experience can deliver accurate matches because samples are so different as to prevent one being mistaken for another. Indeed, recent research has shown that expert fingerprinting examiners make significantly fewer identification errors than lay people.[221] However, they still declare matches for non-identical samples and more frequently non-matches for identical samples. And when one moves from fingerprinting to other identification 'sciences', error rates rise substantially.[222] Moreover, proficiency tests are often run in optimum conditions and with samples which are easiest to identify because they are not partial, smudged, degraded, contaminated or mixed with other sources. Nor are the examiners subject to the myriad contextual factors and operational constraints which affect 'real-life' forensic practice. More worryingly, despite these optimum conditions and the fact that examiners are sometimes aware that they are being tested, proficiency tests, at least in the US, 'reveal disturbingly high error rates'.[223]

---

[218] J. J. Harris, 'How Much Do People Write Alike – A Study of Signatures' (1957) 48 *Journal of Criminal Law, Criminology and Police Science* 647.

[219] 'Forensics without Uniqueness', above, n. 207, 242.

[220] See, for example, Thompson, above n. 171, 1123ff.

[221] See Edmond, Thompson and Tangen, above n. 213, 7–8, but see the study cited by the National Research Council, above n. 91, 143 revealing considerable differences between different examiners applying the standard method.

[222] Saks and Koehler, above n. 37, 895 cite rates of 64 per cent for false positive for bite marks and an average of 40 per cent and 63 per cent overall errors rate (false positives and negatives combined) respectively for handwriting experts and spectrographic voice identification.

[223] Saks and Koehler, above n. 207, 202. See further Koehler, above n. 208. Given the secrecy about proficiency in Scotland, it is impossible to say whether the position is better or indeed worse, though there is no reason to suspect substantial differences.

While some forensic practitioners like fibre and paint coating analysts limit identification to the class from which the suspect samples derive (for example, the type of, rather than the actual, carpet), others still continue to make – and courts continue to accept – categorical claims that two marks or prints are identical or (trespassing on the fact finders' jurisdiction) even that the mark or print in question must have come from the suspect. Indeed, such 'over-claiming' is said to emanate most commonly from the 'weakest areas of forensic science'.[224] Moreover, unless base rates for rarity and error rates in the application of particular techniques in general or by particular examiners or their organisations are provided, testimony as to a certain match again trespasses on the fact finders' territory, given that they have no information by which to assess the claimed match and hence must either treat it as conclusive or ignore it altogether.

A final problem with forensic identification is the language used to report conclusions. In addition to unjustified assertions that two samples categorically come from the same source, there are myriad terms that can be used to convey conclusions about disputed and known sources of forensic material, such as that they 'match', 'are (entirely) consistent', 'there is an association between', or the former is 'not inconsistent' with the latter). Similarly, in going beyond the basic 'source' level to the higher 'activity' level of identifying the suspect, examiners might conclude, for instance, that they 'cannot exclude' the suspect as the source of the disputed evidence or that it 'was very likely to come from' the suspect.[225] Each of these statements may be understood differently by different examiners and fact finders.[226] For instance, does the claim of a 'match' merely mean that the sample is consistent with the trace, but that traces from other sources might also be, or does it mean that no traces from other sources are consistent with the sample?

6.4 Conclusion

In the light of the above discussion, it is hardly surprising that a major US report on forensic science concluded that 'among existing forensic methods, only nuclear DNA analysis has been shown to have the capacity to consistently and with a high degree of certainty, demonstrate a connection between an evidentiary sample and a specific individual or source'.[227]

---

[224] Cole, above n. 207, 822.

[225] Examples taken from G. Jackson, 'Understanding Forensic Science Opinions', in Fraser and Williams, above n. 17.

[226] See, for example, D. McQuiston-Surrett and M. Saks, 'Communicating Opinion Evidence in the Forensic Identification Sciences: Accuracy and Impact' (2008) 59 *Hastings Law Journal* 1159.

[227] National Research Council, above n. 91, 100.

As regards forensic science more generally, it stated that while 'some of the techniques used by the forensic science disciplines – such as DNA analysis, serology [the analysis of bodily fluids], forensic pathology, toxicology, chemical analysis, and digital and multimedia forensics – are built on solid bases of theory and research', many others lack 'an underlying scientific theory, experiments designed to test the uncertainties and reliability of the method, or sufficient data that are collected and analyzed scientifically'.[228] In other words, they are not 'informed by scientific knowledge, or are not developed within the culture of science'.[229] Even more starkly, William Thompson argues that 'it is a mistake . . . to view forensic science as a science'.[230]

It is also unsurprising that, as we have already seen,[231] DNA profiling is increasingly uncovering miscarriages of justice caused by the use and abuse of older forensic techniques. As with all miscarriages of justice, it is well-nigh impossible to gain an idea of the true incidence of those stemming from forensic science[232] and no attempts have been made to look at equivalent problems in civil cases.[233] However, the obstacles in the way of reversing convictions[234] suggest that the clear-cut cases of miscarriages recorded in the US and the few causes-célèbres revealed elsewhere, such as the case of Shirley McKie, a Scottish police officer falsely accused of perjury due to the mistaken identification of her fingerprints at a crime scene,[235] are merely the tip of the proverbial iceberg.[236] This is particularly so given the important indirect effect unreliable forensic evidence might have in encouraging the police to use all possible means to construct cases against those apparently condemned by such evidence and non-expert witnesses to assume guilt,[237] and in discouraging suspects from putting the state to proof.[238]

Admittedly the success of DNA profiling has, as we have seen,[239] belatedly prompted other forensic disciplines to seek a sounder scientific

[228] Ibid., 128.
[229] Ibid., 39.
[230] Above n. 171, 1131.
[231] See at n. 33.
[232] But see C. M. Bowers, 'Preface', in Bowers, above n. 12, xiv, providing a figure of 'nearly 50% of wrongful convictions'.
[233] Though see the debate over 'junk' science most notably in toxic tort cases: section 3 above.
[234] See Chapter 3, section 3.2.2.
[235] See, for example, Raitt, above n. 5, 64–7; Cole, above n. 85, 1009–11.
[236] Cole, ibid., 1017ff in relation to the twenty-two cases of fingerprint misidentification he discusses..
[237] Edmond et al., above n. 146, 3.
[238] Roberts, above n. 18, 484, 493.
[239] Section 6.2, above.

footing by attempting to establish the accuracy of their methods and develop databases from which accurate probabilistic conclusions can be derived regarding the likelihood of random matches. But not all disciplines have striven to emulate the new 'gold standard' and those that have done so still have far to go. Similarly few disciplines have followed the recommendations of the 2011 report of the *Fingerprint Inquiry*[240] (established in response to the McKie case) and prohibited examiners from asserting absolute confidence in declaring matches and using an arbitrary number of similarities to justify such conclusions.

Recent years have also seen improvements in the training of forensic scientists and investigators who handle forensic evidence,[241] and an expanding array of regulatory practices such as inspection, validation, quality control, sampling and batch-testing, monitoring, auditing, certification, and the publication of regulatory protocols and codes of conduct by numerous organisations.[242] The more prominent and overarching of these is the United Kingdom Accreditation Agency, which must accredit all forensic laboratories in terms of adherence to international standards regarding their technical competence, integrity and quality management system standards. In addition, a Forensic Science Regulator seeks to ensure that forensic service providers comply with accreditation and quality assurance requirements, and publishes forms of guidance and a code of conduct, though she holds no legislative powers, and exercises a light touch. Moreover, her powers do not extend to Scotland, though the Scottish Police Services Authority does comply on a voluntarily basis, and scientists who are members of professional bodies are bound by these bodies' regulatory requirements.

Apart from these forms of regulation, the trial process and, in particular, opposing parties challenging forensic evidence before and during trials and instructing their own experts, are meant to safeguard against the sort of problems highlighted here. Consequently we need to look at how effective these safeguards are in redressing the problems with forensic and other forms of scientific evidence.

---

[240] Part 8, Chapter 42, available at http://www.aridgetoofar.com/documents/TheFingerprintInquiry Report_Low_res.pdf (last accessed 22 March 2018).

[241] C. Roux and J. Robertson, 'The Development and Enhancement of Forensic Expertise: Higher Education and In-Service Training', in Fraser and Williams, above n. 17.

[242] See A. Kershaw, 'Professional Standards, Public Protection and the Administration of Justice', in Fraser and Williams, ibid.

7 Science in the Legal Process

7.1 Introduction

Inquiring as to the effectiveness of trial safeguards forms part of the wider question of how scientific evidence is dealt with in the legal process in general. Important here are two features of the procedural context of evidence and proof. The first is the adversarial nature of legal proceedings, which ensures that the selection and preparation of experts, and the presentation and testing of their evidence, is controlled by partisan litigants intent on victory not truth. This prompts the criticism, noted in Section Three, that the legal process distorts science's essential nature and undermines its potential to deliver truth. The second feature is that scientific evidence is evaluated by those who usually lack scientific training, which leads to the worry, noted in Section Two, that they will overvalue or, conversely, ignore scientific evidence.

7.2 The Adversarial Expert[243]

As regards worries about the adversarial distortion of science, it should now be clear that scientific truth is as much a matter of negotiation as a direct reflection of 'reality', and that adherence to scientific methods and norms is patchy, not just in relation to the social and forensic sciences, but also the physical sciences. Nevertheless, it is a very rare scientist who acts like an adversarial partisan. So, while the adversarial system cannot sully some mythical scientific purity, it may nevertheless undermine the potential value science has in contributing to the fact-positivist goal of the rational determination of truth. In fact, as we shall see, while the legal handling of experts and scientific evidence largely mirrors that of other witnesses and forms of evidence, in some respects problems for truth finding are even greater. Such problems arise in all stages of the handling of expert evidence: expert selection, preparation and forensic examination.

7.2.1 Expert Selection

Whereas the selection of observational witnesses is largely limited by who can give relevant evidence, experts can be selected according to whether their views on contested issues align with litigants' interests. Although legitimate, shopping around for experts may expose fact finders to mavericks keen to float their pet theories in court. Yet, in the hands of skilful lawyers and in the context of one party matching the other expert for expert, their views

---

[243] This section draws on Jones, above n. 12, Chapters 7–10; Roberts, above nn 16, 274–7 passim and 18 passim. See also R. S. Thompson, 'Decision, Disciplined Inferences and the Adversary Process' (1991) 13 *Cardozo Law Review* 725.

can be successfully portrayed as equally plausible alternatives to received scientific wisdom.[244] The quality of experts exposed to fact finders may also be affected by experts, being selected not for their knowledge but for being expert at being experts in the sense of being trusted not to leak sensitive information and being skilled at communicating to a lay audience.[245]

Power and resource differentials between the wealthy and the less well-off, repeat players and one-shotters, and the state and accused, which have an effect on adversarial proceedings generally,[246] are particularly prominent in relation to access to expertise. For one thing, few experts are willing to work for those with limited resources. Along with problems of the concentration of experts in big cities, this is particularly problematic for criminal accused who, in addition, like civil litigants without deep pockets, may only be able to pay experts to comment on their opponent's scientific evidence rather than conduct their own investigations.

7.2.2 Case Preparation

In the case of sensitive forensic material, there are additional obstacles for those seeking to challenge it. Materials may be destroyed during their first examination or become degraded with time, especially as opposition lawyers may not appreciate the need for urgency or be held up waiting for legal aid or by other formalities. Even if available, the party holding the forensic materials may prevent access to them or control tests conducted by opposition scientists on their turf. In criminal cases this means defence scientists 'literally "looking through the prosecution microscope", as well as doing so in the figurative sense of being presented with the refined product of the prosecution's investigation rather than having access to raw evidential materials for a fresh scientific enquiry'.[247] On the other hand, sometimes the 'communist' scientific norm takes precedence over adversariality and opposing scientists might co-operate with each other.[248]

As regards the construction of scientific evidence more generally, like forensic scientists, many experts may instinctively act more like advocates than neutral investigators because of ongoing relationships with

---

[244] See Sanders, above n. 110, 61, 64.

[245] See a US survey cited by S. Brewer, 'Scientific Expert Testimony and Intellectual Due Process' (1998) 107 *Yale Law Journal* 1535, 1623, in which over 75 per cent of lawyers admit choosing doctors as witnesses for factors other than their medical expertise. See also Smith, 'Forensic Pathology', above n. 36, 69–70; D. J. Gee, 'The Expert Witness in the Criminal Trial' (1987) *Criminal Law Review* 307, 307–8.

[246] See Chapter 4, section 2.4.2.

[247] Roberts, above n. 18, 491.

[248] Burk, above n. 63, 371.

repeat players or in order to ensure future work. In any event, they may be subtly (or not so subtly) encouraged to ensure that reports and testimony favour those commissioning them.[249] Those instructing experts will formulate questions and control information so as to ensure favourable answers, and can rebuff complaints by experts by hiding behind alleged legal requirements. Experts may even be pressurised into altering their reports or at least expressing results in categorical terms rather than as opinions about probabilities. As with forensic science, the picture of the facts simply speaking for themselves is enhanced by the formal and neutral language of expert reports, and by the omission of references to theoretical underpinnings, investigative assumptions and methods, investigative limitations, doubts and negative findings. Even more fundamentally, in Scotland only the prosecution – but not the accused or civil parties[250] – is required to disclose expert reports and only in specified circumstances.[251] This close control over the report and its contents are crucial to case outcome. Particularly where opponents cannot afford to commission their own reports, they may throw in the towel by pleading guilty or settling when faced with apparently confident and categorical negative findings (though reports may also lead those commissioning them to abandon proceedings).

7.2.3 Experts at (and on) Trial[252]

Unlike in England and Wales, where most expert evidence is presented as a written report, all expert evidence in Scotland is given orally at trial. Unfortunately research suggests that few lawyers thoroughly prepare their experts for the ordeal of court testimony.[253] While forensic scientists and

---

[249] See, for example, Jones, above n. 12, Chapter 10, discussing police and prosecution tactics like withholding relevant information from forensic scientists or pressuring them into adjusting their reports.

[250] Unless judges use case management powers (see Chapter 3, section 4.2) to require civil parties to obtain and share expert reports.

[251] Raitt, above n. 5, 60.

[252] In addition to the references below, this section draws on Edmond and Mercer, above n. 113; S. Yearley, 'Bog Standards: Science and Conservation at a Public Inquiry' (1989) 19 *Social Studies of Science* 421; A. Howe, 'Imagining Evidence, Fictioning Truth – Revisiting (Courtesy of O. J. Simpson) Expert Evidence in the Chamberlain Case' (1997) 3 *Law Text Culture* 82; G. Edmond, '*Down by Science*: Context and Commitment in the Lay Response to Incriminating Scientific Evidence during a Murder Trial' (1998) 7 *Public Understanding of Science* 83 and 'Azaria's Accessories: The Social (Legal-Scientific) Construction of the Chamberlains' Guilt and Innocence' (1998) 22 *Melbourne University Law Review* 396.

[253] At least in England and Wales (Roberts, above n. 18, 496–8) and Australia (K. Cashman and T. Henning, 'Lawyers and DNA: Issues in Understanding and Challenging the Evidence' (2012) 69 *Current Issues in Criminal Justice* 69, 73, 78–9).

other repeat players will know what is coming and many individual scientists, doctors and academics are sufficiently confident to maintain their professional commitment to truth, experts unaccustomed to giving testimony are as susceptible as lay witnesses to being 'softened up' by an alien and intimidating environment, and hence to control by lawyers and other trial actors.[254] Compared to the past when scientific experts were accorded authoritative and sometimes star status,[255] today they face a climate of 'institutionalized pure mistrust'[256] and a barrage of adversarial – often 'unsavoury'[257] – tactics designed to undermine their evidence by attacking their competence, motives, methods and/or conclusions.[258] Conversely, those calling experts can seek to strengthen expert testimony, leaving fact finders the difficult task of separating tactics from truth; rhetoric from reality. Given that such negative and positive tactics largely mirror each other, and that negative tactics prompt most concern, we will look primarily at them.

A preliminary tactic involves challenging the expert's formal qualifications, on-job training, level of experience (either as too callow or alternatively as out of touch with recent developments), and whether they or their employing organisations have a history of errors. Alternatively cross-examiners may question experts' competence in relation to the issues at stake and attempt to lure them into overreaching such expertise. On the other hand, as recent miscarriages of justice demonstrate,[259] such overreaching may also be prompted by the expert's own lawyer yet go unchallenged by oblivious opponents.[260] Rhetorical play is also made of hierarchical distinctions between most obviously the physical and social sciences, but also between 'esoteric' pure disciplines and 'useful' applied disciplines. Even more obviously, lawyers may hint at or directly accuse scientists of bias due to working closely with the instructing party, being bankrolled by those with commercial or ideological interests in particular findings, or pursuing their own agenda or dogmatic position on scientific controversies.

---

[254] Cf. Roberts, ibid., 503–4.
[255] Jones, above n. 12, 80ff.
[256] Wynne, above n. 57, 33.
[257] Roberts, above n. 18, 501.
[258] See J. S. Oteri, M. G. Weinberg and M. S. Pinales, 'Cross-Examination of Chemists in Narcotic and Marijuana Cases' (1973) 2 *Contemporary Drug Problems* 225; also the examples in J. M. Shellow, 'The Limits of Cross-Examination' (2003) 34 *Seton Hall Law Review* 317.
[259] See, for example, R. Hill, 'Reflections on the Cot Death Cases' (2007) 47 *Medical Science and the Law* 2, regarding the misuse of probabilities by a doctor untrained in statistics which led to two miscarriages of justice.
[260] See Roberts and Zuckerman, above n. 14, 480–1.

As regards the content of expert testimony itself, the integrity of procedures used in collecting and storing physical evidence may be challenged, especially if there have been breaches of accepted protocols. Experts can be asked whether all known tests were conducted, and were conducted blind and with relevant controls, equipment was tested or known to be in good working order, and whether all relevant steps involved were recorded. More fundamentally, the methods used can be challenged as lacking empirical and peer-review testing, theoretical underpinning and support from the relevant scientific community, as chosen for reasons of cost and speed rather than accuracy, and/or excessively based on subjective discretion.

We thus see that those challenging expert evidence seek to hoist science by its own idealistic petard. Particular play is made of the chimeric nature of scientific certainty. Mertonian norms require experts to admit this in court and display modesty about their conclusions. Those who do not can be criticised as complacent, if not misguided. But, equally, advocates can exploit any admission of uncertainty, the negotiated nature of scientific truth and the role of tacit judgment to undermine expert testimony. Not all experts are so easily manipulated. Nevertheless, according to Roberts, '[t]he most brilliant scientists in the land could be made to look foolish by a lawyer's tricky questions, whilst a fool with bravado and a pleasing court manner might appear to the layman to be a scientific genius'.[261] And then the waters can be further muddied by matching experts testifying to scientific orthodoxy with an equal or greater number of those supporting maverick ideas. This latter tactic is obviously only open to litigants with deep pockets and thus provides a further reason – along with inequalities relating to expert selection, and access to material evidence and other resources – why adversarial trials may not be best suited to allowing scientific truth to emerge at trial. To make matters worse for criminal accused, defence lawyers frequently fail to cross-examine prosecution experts; and if they do, they fail to challenge scientific evidence effectively.[262]

7.2.4 Conclusion

In general, adversarial proceedings are an uncomfortable place for scientists because they test to the limit their adherence to Mertonian norms, especially those of impartiality, communism, transparency and modesty. While the adversarial system does not distort some mythically pure state where science

---

[261] Above n. 16, 266.

[262] For a good overview of the disadvantages faced by criminal accused, see Roberts, above nn. 16, 274–76 and 18, 489–95.

delivers objective and certain truths, it does exploit and exacerbate pressures within science to depart from its ideals, thereby exposing the negotiated nature of scientific truth and the haphazard adherence to scientific methods and norms. Adversarialism can seriously disrupt the delicate balance in the scientific world between conflict and consensus, and between scepticism and respect. Moreover, it subjects scientific truth-claims to a scepticism which extends well beyond science's own 'organised scepticism'.

7.3 Evaluating Expert Evidence

7.3.1 Introduction

Thorough-going scepticism is problematic for law as well, given that law potentially benefits from science's aura of certainty and objectivity. In addition, while unchallenged experts may be able to play their allotted role of educating fact finders as to relevant areas of knowledge, this might be difficult when fact finders are subject to a bewildering barrage of claims and counterclaims, which may lead them to ignore rather than attempt to grapple with the conflicts. However, even uncontested scientific testimony might be difficult to comprehend, leading, as we have also seen,[263] conversely and paradoxically to the worry that fact finders may automatically defer to it or at least give it undue prominence.

Such worries draw strength from psychological theories on the persuasiveness of communicative messages, such as those delivered by experts, other witnesses and indeed all legal actors. These theories distinguish between, on the one hand, 'systematic'[264] or 'central route'[265] processing, and, on the other, 'heuristic' or 'peripheral route' processing. The former involves consideration of the testimony's content, its coherence and consistency with other evidence, and relevant factors affecting the communicator's reliability. It is more likely when fact finders find the case intrinsically interesting or compelling, take their responsibilities seriously and can cope cognitively, such as when there are uncontested expert explanations and a small or simple body of evidence. By contrast, heuristic or peripheral route processing relies on non-content-based cues, such as witnesses' status or attractiveness, whether they look questioners in the eye, and how long they speak. Such processing is more likely to occur when fact finders suffer from cognitive overload because of contradictory or multiple witnesses,

---

[263] See at nn 46–8, above.

[264] See, for example, S. Chaiken, 'Heuristic versus Systematic Information Processing and the Use of Source Versus Message Cues in Persuasion' (1980) 39 *Journal of Personality and Social Psychology* 752.

[265] See, for example, R. E. Petty and J. T. Cacioppo, 'The Elaboration Likelihood Model of Persuasion', in L. Berkowitz (ed.), *Advances in Experimental Social Psychology* (1986).

evidence which is voluminous, complex and/or technically detailed, and/or when lengthy fact-finding processes or other distractions make it difficult for fact finders to concentrate.

7.3.2 Non-statistical Evidence[266]

However, roughly forty years of research suggest that worries about the ability and motivation of fact finders to understand expert evidence are somewhat exaggerated, at least when such evidence does not involve statistics or probabilities. Admittedly there are serious limitations to the research, albeit no longer an exclusive focus on jurors rather than other legal fact finders. Indeed, studies of judges and lawyers show that their scientific knowledge or ability to evaluate scientific experts is no greater than that of jurors.[267] More problematic is the research methodology. One method involves mock trials in which subjects assess the persuasiveness of expert witnesses. However, even when these involve subjects eligible for jury service rather than just students and video-taped trials rather than subjects reading witness testimonies or transcripts, such trials are heavily edited and devoid of the tensions and/or tedium of real trials, the sense of urgency which comes from deciding another's fate and the impact of the personalities and demeanour of legal actors, and other factors prompting peripheral rather than central route-processing.[268] Such trials may also lack judicial instructions, cross-examination and collective juror decision-making; all of which may affect individual views. Even less insightful, albeit more reliable, is the use of questionnaires to test scientific knowledge and mathematical skills. Such problems of artificiality are avoided by studies involving post-trial interviews with actual jurors.[269] On the other hand, these studies have involved small and unrepresentative samples, a small subset of cases and types of experts,[270] and relied on the

---

[266] The following draws on the overviews in Ivkovic and Hans, above n. 25; R. Lempert, 'Civil Juries and Complex Cases: Taking Stock After Twelve Years', in R. E. Litan (ed.), *Verdict: Assessing the Civil Jury System* (1993); N. Vidmar, 'The Performance of the American Civil Jury: An Empirical Perspective' (1998) 40 *Arizona Law Review* 849; N. Vidmar and S. S. Diamond, 'Juries and Expert Evidence' (2001) 66 *Brooklyn Law Review* 1121; B. D. McAuliff et al., 'Juror Decision-making in the Twenty-First Century: Confronting Science and Technology in Court', in D. Carson and R. Bull (eds), *Handbook of Psychology in Legal Contexts* (2003).

[267] Vidmar and Diamond, ibid., 1177; G. Edmond and K. Roach, 'A Contextual Approach To the Admissibility of The State's Forensic Science and Medical Evidence' (2011) 61 *University of Toronto Law Journal* 343, 366.

[268] See, for example, W. Weiten and S. S. Diamond, 'A Critical Review of the Jury Simulation Paradigm: The Case of Defendant Characteristics' (1979) 3 *Law and Human Behavior* 71.

[269] However, contempt of court rules prevent this in Scotland and the rest of the UK.

[270] Studies of actual jurors concentrate on complex cases and medical malpractice trials, and mock trials on medical and psychological experts.

subjects' honesty and memory in recounting how they and other jurors coped with expert evidence. Finally, all studies suffer from a lack of objective standards for evaluating fact finders' performance.

Nevertheless, despite these limitations, the various studies consistently show fact finders motivated to critically assess expert evidence in terms of its comprehensiveness, internal consistency, consistency with other evidence and consistency with their own knowledge and 'common sense' experience. Fact finders also make appropriate use of expert evidence, especially where witnesses explicitly relate their expertise to the case rather than just giving background knowledge.[271] There is thus no evidence that fact finders automatically defer to experts or give scientific evidence disproportionate weight. In fact, they tend to prefer the more vivid testimony of observational witnesses.[272] One exception is DNA evidence, which many jurors now expect to see in criminal trials. [273] But even this so-called 'CSI effect'[274] does not cause them to ignore other evidence.

On the other hand, as theory predicts, when expert evidence is unduly complex and/or involves contradictory or confusing expert opinion, especially if emanating from different disciplines, fact finders often switch to peripheral route processing and focus on factors like:

- the expert's credentials – educational level and institution, and publication record;
- assumed motives – for instance, as highly paid 'hired guns' frequently appearing in court or sympathetic towards one of the parties;
- body language and demeanour; and
- possibly[275] their personal characteristics[276] – pleasant personality and possibly even physical attractiveness.

---

[271] See Kapardis, above n. 133, 238–40; M. B. Kovera et al., 'Does Expert Testimony Inform or Influence Juror Decision-Making? A Social Cognitive Analysis' (1997) 82 *Journal of Applied Psychology* 178; M. Kovera, B. McAuliff and K. Hebert, 'Reasoning About Scientific Evidence: Effects of Juror Gender and Evidence Quality on Juror Decisions in a Hostile Work Environment Case' (1999) 84 *Journal of Applied Psychology* 362, 363. See further on eyewitness testimony, Chapter 6, section 4.1.3.

[272] In addition to the references at n. 266 above, see E. J. Imwinkelried, 'The Next Step in Conceptualizing the Presentation of Expert Evidence as Education: The Case for Didactic Trial Procedures' (1996) 1 *International Journal of Evidence and Proof* 128, 134.

[273] Named after the popular US TV programme. See National Research Council, above n. 9, 48–9; Wheate, above n. 77; but cf. Young, Cameron and Tinsley, above n. 2, 28, for earlier evidence of this phenomenon.

[274] National Research Council and Wheate, ibid.; see also, for example, D. R. Baskin and I. B. Sommer, 'Crime-Show Viewing Habits and Public Attitudes Toward Forensic Evidence: The "CSI Effect Revisited"' (2010) 31 *Justice System Journal* 97.

[275] See the study discussed by Vidmar and Diamond, above n. 266, 1147–8.

[276] But not race, nationality, age and gender.

While some of these factors clearly involve peripheral route processing, those like motives and credentials[277] are relevant to an expert's credibility and hence augment rather than clash with central route processing. Moreover, complex and conflicting expert testimony does not always cause jurors to entirely ignore scientific evidence or even automatically abandon central route processing. Indeed, the feared 'battle of experts' sometimes causes heightened scrutiny,[278] though not necessarily enhanced comprehension.[279]

As regards fact finders' general ability to comprehend scientific and other expert evidence, no clear picture emerges. Much depends on a complex combination of factors, which, in addition to those already mentioned, include:

- who is evaluating fact finder competence – experts in the field tend to be more critical than those conducting the research;
- how the testimony is delivered – whether it is clear, concise, lively, direct, jargon-free, well-paced, not overly long, and supported by diagrams, models and various multi-media aids;[280]
- how the testimony is evaluated – group deliberation improves comprehension when one or more jurors with relevant knowledge can educate other jurors;
- what type of case is involved – fact finders perform relatively well in certain types of medical cases,[281] but less so with unfamiliar areas of knowledge;
- what the issue is – fact finders are relatively competent in understanding the implications of research results presented by experts but, unless educated about research methodology, poor at assessing the scientific validity of underlying research.[282]

---

[277] But see Brewer, above n. 245, 1624ff.

[278] N. Brekke and E. Borgida, 'Expert Psychological Testimony in Rape Trials: A Social-Cognitive Analysis' (1988) 55 *Journal of Personality and Social Psychology* 372.

[279] In addition to studies cited in references in n. 266 above, see Findlay, above n. 48, esp. 51–2.

[280] See, for example, Young, Cameron and Tinsley, above n. 2, 22; L. Hewson and J. Goodman-Delahunty, 'Using Multimedia to Support Jury Understanding of DNA Profiling Evidence' (2008) 40 *Australian Journal of Forensic Sciences* 55.

[281] See Vidmar and Diamond, above n. 266, 1177.

[282] Kovera, McAuliff and Hebert, above n. 271, 364–6; McAuliff et al., above n. 266, 311–13. See also S. I. Gatowski et al., 'Asking the Gatekeepers: A National Survey of Judges on Judging Expert Evidence in a Post-Daubert World' (2001) 25 *Law and Human Behavior* 433.

7.3.3 Statistical Evidence[283]

One issue which has been extensively researched because of its growing centrality to expert evidence, especially forensic identification, is the ability of fact finders and other legal actors to handle statistical evidence. A common finding is that, contrary to the worries of some commentators and courts,[284] such evidence is generally undervalued rather than overvalued and hence does not 'dwarf'[285] non-statistical evidence. As we have seen,[286] in terms of Bayesian principles, when people learn of new statistical evidence, they are meant to multiply the resulting statistic with the prior odds, represented by the likelihood of the event in question calculated in terms of all prior knowledge about the case, and from this derive an estimate as to posterior odds. However, when this occurs, fact finders usually[287] fail to increase the posterior odds to the extent required by the Bayesian formula, even if given instructions on how to apply it.[288]

A major reason why people (not just potential jurors, but also judges[289] and lawyers, even those with a post-school mathematical education)[290] are 'poor intuitive statisticians'[291] is that they succumb to heuristic reasoning,[292] most commonly the 'representativeness' heuristic.[293] When people evaluate the likelihood of an event or object belonging to a certain category (for example, that a particular mentally ill patient is dangerous) they

283 This section draws on Schklar and Diamond, above n. 47; Vidmar and Diamond, above n. 266, 1149–58, 1163–4, 1170–1; B. Smith et al., 'Jurors' Use of Probabilistic Evidence' (1996) 20 *Law & Human Behavior* 49; K. Martire et al., 'The Expression and Interpretation of Uncertain Forensic Science Evidence: Verbal Equivalence, Evidence Strength, and the Weak Evidence Effect' (2013) 37 *Law and Human Behavior* 197; K. Martire, R. Kemp and B. Newell, 'The Psychology of Interpreting Expert Evaluative Opinions' (2013) 45 *Australian Journal of Forensic Sciences* 305; B. Roberston and G. A. Vignaux, *Interpreting Evidence: Evaluating Forensic Science in the Courtroom* (2nd edn, 2016), esp. Chapter 9.

284 See Smith et al., ibid., 49–51. But see Imwinkelried, above nn 41 and 272, who seems to be more concerned with undervaluing rather than deferring to scientists.

285 Cf. Smith et al., ibid., 75.

286 Section 6.2.

287 However, when the non-statistical evidence on which the prior odds are calculated is very weak, they tend to overvalue the statistical evidence.

288 See, for example, Hastie and Dawes, above n. 187, 97–103.

289 Greene and Ellis, above n. 180, 184–5; C. Guthrie, J. J. Rachlinski and A. J. Wistrich, 'Inside the Judicial Mind' (2000) 86 *Cornell Law Review* 777, noting, however, at 816–18 that in some respects judges performed better than other subjects; cf. also Mcquiston-Surrett and Saks, above n. 226, 1169, reporting a general but marginal judicial superiority.

290 P. Hawkins and A. Hawkins, 'Lawyers' Probability Misconceptions and the Implications for Legal Education' (1998) 18 *Legal Studies* 316.

291 Redmayne, above n. 24, 60.

292 See further Greene and Ellis, above n. 180; Saks and Kidd, above n. 180.

293 See, for example, Kahneman, Slovic and Tversky, above n. 180, Part III; Tversky and Kahneman, above n. 182, 4–11.

tend to focus more on how similar that event or object is to others in the relevant category (in other words, whether the relevant patient is representative of the stereotype of a dangerous patient) than on how commonly the event or object falls within the relevant category (which for dangerousness is very rare in the case of mentally ill patients).[294]

This heuristic explains why many people ignore[295] the impact of base-rate statistics (the so-called base-rate fallacy). For example, in Tversky and Kahneman's famous taxi-cab problem, they regularly hold that a pursuer is entitled to damages against one of only two taxi companies in the city (Blue Cabs), because an eyewitness with a proven accuracy rate of 80 per cent identified a Blue Cab taxi as responsible for her injuries, even though they are also told that 85 per cent of the buses in the relevant vicinity are operated by Green Cab (the base-rate). In fact, the resultant chance of a Blue Cab taxi being responsible is only 41.27 per cent and hence lower than the nominal 51 per cent required by the civil balance of probabilities standard. This also illustrates that fact finders tend to be influenced by 'more salient and vivid' testimonial evidence than 'pallid base-rate statistics'.[296] Translated into more common evidence and proof issues, the representativeness heuristic means that people show little sensitivity to variations in statistical frequencies as regards the extent to which forensic material identified as that of the suspect might be shared by others (the random match probability).

However, in estimating probabilities they are also insensitive to the impact of laboratory error rates (that is, how often mistakes are made in declaring matches). For instance, when provided with a random match probability regarding a DNA sample, especially one of a very low magnitude such as one in a billion, and a much higher rate for errors in the testing laboratory, such as one in a hundred, fact finders will tend to combine the two probabilities and still conclude that there is an infinitely low chance of the DNA not coming from the suspect. This reflects what is known as the 'conjunction fallacy', which encourages people to incorrectly think that the probability of a state of affairs (for example, that a particular woman is a feminist bank-teller) is more than the independent probability of two unconnected states of an affairs (that she is a feminist *and* a bank teller).[297]

---

[294] Howitt, above n. 129, Chapter 27.

[295] However, they are less likely to do so when given a causal explanation for these base rates, such as in the example below, that drivers for the bus company with more accidents are poorly selected and trained: Hastie and Dawes, above n. 187, 114.

[296] Guthrie, Rachlinski and Wistrich, above n. 289, 806.

[297] Hastie and Dawes, above n. 187, 174–7.

In addition to these general problems with dealing with probabilistic evidence, people are often misled by the form in which it is presented and in particular the fallacy variously known as the 'transposition of the conditional' or the 'confusion of the inverse'. For instance, instead of asking 'how likely is it that the animal is a cow given that it has four legs?', it is asked 'how likely is it that the animal has four legs given that it is a cow?'[298] The effect of transposing the conditional in this example is easy to notice, given that the latter likelihood is much higher than the former.

However, it is more difficult in cases where, for example, a prosecutor offers evidence of a DNA random match probability of 1 in 200 million. This figure refers to the probability that a suspect would match the criminal's DNA given that they are innocent, but, as experiments have found, many might assume that it refers to the chance of the accused's innocence given the DNA match, and thus not consider alternative explanations for the match, such as being at the crime scene for an unconnected reason or because the police planted forensic material. This error involves what William Thompson and Edward Schuman have called the prosecutor's fallacy.[299] They also identified 'the defence attorney's fallacy', which involves adjudicators interpreting evidence of a 2 per cent chance of a random match in a city of 1,000,000 as meaning that there could be 20,000 possible other perpetrators and hence acquitting the accused even though other evidence (motive, opportunity, physical capability, etc.) significantly narrows the number of possible perpetrators. While fact finders in mock trials regularly, but by no means universally, make these errors, there is evidence to suggest that erroneous reasoning may be prevented or mitigated by warnings from lawyers or judges, group deliberation by adjudicators and/or the way that experts present statistical evidence (such as in Bayesian form requiring consideration of non-statistical incriminating or exculpatory evidence).[300]

At the same time, however, the way that statistical evidence is presented is usually part of the problem rather than the solution, in that different formulations can ensure very different conclusions. For example, the statement that 'the probability that the suspect would match

---

[298] Lynch and McNally, above n. 83, 183.

[299] 'Interpretation of Statistical Evidence in Criminal Trials: The Prosecutor's Fallacy and the Defense Attorney's Fallacy' (1987) 11 *Law and Human Behavior* 167. For a good explanation, see P. Donnelly and D. J. Balding, 'The Prosecutor's Fallacy and DNA Evidence' (1994) *Criminal Law Review* 711.

[300] Though there is evidence that fact finders might struggle to understand Bayesian formula, and thus English Law prohibits experts from introducing it to jurors: see, for example, Roberts and Zuckerman, above n. 14, 159–63.

the blood specimen if he were not the source is 0.1%' has been shown to be more persuasive than the mathematically comparable statement that 'the frequency with which the suspect would match the blood specimen if he were not the source is one in 1000'.[301] One explanation[302] for such differences lies in a particular instance of another important heuristic, namely the 'availability heuristic'.[303] This involves the tendency for people to judge the frequency or likelihood of an event according to how easy it is to think of examples of it. More specifically, 'exemplar cuing' involves fact finders judging the probative value of a match by the ease with which exemplars of other people who might also match come to mind. Thus when people struggle to think of such examples they will tend to assume that the matching suspect is the source of the relevant forensic evidence.

Instead of using numerical expression of probabilities or frequencies, experts can translate these into verbal expressions. For example, a trace with a random match probability of between 10 and 100 people offers 'moderate' support, one between 100 and 1,000 offers 'moderately strong support' and so on, ending in a random match probability of one person in a million offering 'extremely strong' support. However, while research establishes that people prefer such verbal expressions,[304] they prompt widely varying interpretations. Furthermore, these interpretations are often very different to their intended meaning, with too much weight attached to probabilistic evidence at the lower end of the scale and too little at the top.[305] More problematically, if forensic identifiers like fingerprint examiners are allowed to report a 'match' between a known and suspected source, fact finders are more likely to conclude that the suspect left the print than if the examiner was to provide a more justifiable subjective estimate of the likelihood of a match.

[301] Taken from J. J. Koehler, 'The Psychology of Numbers in the Courtroom: How To Make DNA-Match Statistics Seem Impressive or Insufficient' (2001) 74 *Southern California Law Review* 1275, 1278.

[302] Ibid., esp. 1280–2.

[303] See, for example, Kahneman, Slovic and Tversky, above n. 180, Part IV; Kahneman and Tversky, above n. 182, 11–14.

[304] See, for example, L. M. Moxey and A. J. Sanford, 'Communicating Quantities: A Review of Psycholinguistic Evidence of How Expressions Determine Perspectives' (2000) 14 *Applied Cognitive Psychology* 237, also noting that verbal expressions are more subject to rhetorical manipulation.

[305] In addition to references cited in n. 283 above, see Redmayne, above n. 24, Chapter 4; J. J. Koehler, 'On Conveying the Probative Value of DNA Evidence: Frequencies, Likelihood Ratios, and Error Rates' (1996) 67 *University of Colorado Law Review* 859; J. J. C. Mullen et al., 'Perception Problems of the Verbal Scale' (2014) 54 *Science & Justice* 154.

7.4 Conclusion

We thus see that worries about law's ability to get the most out of scientific evidence are not without foundation. Even accepting that the picture of science's ability to obtain certain truth by objective methods is exaggerated in relation to pure science and downright misleading in relation to some social and virtually all forensic sciences, legal processes vastly increase any problems inherent in these domains. While fact finders appear to take seriously their role in evaluating expert evidence and do not simply defer to experts, on occasion they quite understandably struggle to assess expert evidence competently, especially when credible experts differ and even more so when statistical probabilities are involved. Nor are the assumed safeguards against adversarial excesses and potentially misleading expertise always present. Even if willing to help courts to evaluate the evidence more objectively and accurately through cross-examining experts, adversarial opponents often lack access to their own suitable experts or to the relevant scientific evidence necessary to challenge experts on their own terms. Scientific illiteracy also undermines the effectiveness of judicial instructions – the other main assumed procedural means of ensuring that expertise facilitates the rational ascertainment of truth.

Many have urged that all lawyers should receive relevant training in scientific methods, the main scientific disciplines and statistical analysis.[306] Nevertheless, experimental research and actual miscarriages of justice involving scientific evidence suggest that cross-examination and judicial instructions will always fall short in redressing the various problems with expert evidence in general and those that flow from its adversarial treatment in particular.[307] Indeed, adversarial cross-examination is not necessarily aimed at helping fact finders to evaluate evidence accurately, but at undermining unfavourable, and strengthening favourable, evidence. Moreover, its impact may well owe more to cross-examination ability than exposure of genuine scientific problems.[308] As regards judicial instructions on scientific evidence, they come too late in the proceedings to counter already formed conclusions or to help fact finders struggling to cope with

---

[306] For example, Hawkins and Hawkins, above n. 290, 333–5; Faigman, above n. 8, passim.

[307] Shellow, above n. 258; Kovera, McAuliff and Hebert, above n. 271; D. McQuiston-Surrett and M. J. Saks, 'The Testimony of Forensic Identification Science: What Expert Witnesses Say and What Factfinders Hear' (2009) 33 *Law and Human Behavior* 436, 439; G. Edmond and A. Roberts, 'Procedural Fairness, the Criminal Trial and Forensic Science and Medicine' (2011) 33 *Sydney Law Review* 359, 367–8.

[308] Chapter 4, section 2.3; Chapter 6, section 3.2.2.

information overload, and, like judicial instructions in general,[309] may not be sufficiently comprehensible to be effective.[310]

An additional problem with relying on judges to ensure justice is that they seem to be unduly eager to accept scientific evidence from experts called by the state and civil defenders, but far more sceptical in relation to experts used by criminal accused and civil pursuers.[311] Nevertheless, when fact finders do take sides in scientific controversies, after experts have been subjected to the full arsenal of adversarial deconstructive weaponry the courts often go to great lengths to reconstruct for public consumption the science it relies on as objective and rational truth. Accordingly uncertainties are blamed on individual 'bad apples', organisational malpractice or undue adversariality rather than the fallibility of scientific knowledge.[312] This attitude both reinforces the ideology of scientism and enhances the legitimacy of legal decisions, thus providing support for those who see the law–science relationship in terms of a mutually beneficial, albeit stormy, marriage of convenience. On the other hand, the way scientific evidence is handled also provides some support for the view of law as the dominant marriage partner forcing science to abandon some of its dearest, albeit partially realised, ideals. This leads to the question of whether law can improve its use of science in particular and experts in general.

8 Science, Experts and Reform[313]

The preceding discussion of scientific expertise and the law suggests some obvious ways in which lawyers can enhance their use of scientific evidence, such as by having adequate pre-trial meetings with their experts and encouraging them to provide tuition to adjudicators on how to approach statistical and other technical evidence, and to present evidence in a comprehensible manner, using multi-media aids. Also rather obvious are a number of reforms which are relatively uncontroversial, though not necessarily easy or cheap to implement. For instance, in addition to training

---

[309] See, for example, V. G. Rose et al., 'Evaluating the Comprehensibility of Jury Instructions: A Method and an Example' (2001) 25 *Law and Human Behavior* 409.

[310] See references cited in Edmonds and Roach, above n. 267, 366 n. 84.

[311] For example, Edmond, above n. 43, 226; Edmunds and Roach, ibid., esp. 358, 396, 398.

[312] See, for example, Jones, above n. 12, esp. 13–14, 97–101; Smith, above n. 36, 83–4; Cole, above n. 85, 1034ff; Smith and Wynne, above n. 90, esp. 1 and 16; Wynne, above n. 57, esp. 77ff; Thompson, above n. 184.

[313] For useful overviews of the types of reform, see Jasanoff, *Science at the Bar*, above, n. 57, 218–23; J. Sanders 'From Science to Evidence: The Testimony on Causation in the Bendectin Cases' (1993) 46 *Stanford Law Review* 1, 61ff.

adjudicators in fundamental scientific methods and statistical principles, a uniform set of written materials on relevant areas of scientific knowledge could be produced,[314] and supplemented by the parties if they regard them as partial. Other reforms could include:

(1) (perhaps most urgently) investigating the validity and reliability of *all* forensic techniques in order to test their core assumptions, developing databases to provide statistical base-rate information on likely random matches for identification techniques, and requiring rigorous proficiency testing of all forensic science providers;[315]

(2) establishing a Scottish body with statutory powers to promulgate and enforce quality assurance measures such as accreditation, proficiency testing, the promulgation of protocols to guide forensic procedures and other means of ensuring quality control, such as requiring documentation of all steps taken in the collection, analysis and reporting of forensic evidence, including exposure to biasing contextual information;[316]

(3) ensuring that those faced with forensic and other scientific evidence, especially criminal accused, have the right to access (where possible) the relevant evidence and their own experts[317] and to observe any tests being carried out by the other side;[318]

(4) standardising the terms used to report forensic identification and confining such reports to conclusions that can be supported by evidence;[319]

(5) strengthening the disclosure obligations of prosecuting authorities[320] and indeed any party who 'controls' relevant scientific evidence, including an obligation to disclose negative findings from tests, and any known error rates of the scientists and their organisations who conduct relevant work;

---

[314] Black, Ayala and Saffran-Brinks, above n. 9, 798, 800; P. A. Rao, 'Keeping the Science Court out of the Jurybox: Helping the Jury Manage Scientific Evidence' (1999) 13 *Social Epistemology* 129, 142.

[315] For example, Saks and Koehler, above n. 37, 895; National Research Council, above n. 91, passim, but esp. Chapter 6; I. Evett, 'The Logical Foundations of Forensic Science: Towards Reliable Knowledge' (2015) 370 *Philosophical Transactions of the Royal Society B* 1, 9 regarding Australian fingerprint examiners who must provide courts with the results of blind tests of their accuracy.

[316] Edmond, Thompson and Tangen, above n. 213, 20.

[317] Roberts, above n. 18, 506; Stockdale, above n. 197.

[318] *Report of the Royal Commission on Criminal Justice* (1993 Cm. 2263), para. 9.52.

[319] For example, National Research Council, above n. 91, 185–6; Cole, 'Forensics without Uniqueness', above n. 207, 250.

[320] Law Commission, above n. 318, para. 6.15; P. Roberts, 'Forensic Science Evidence After Runciman' (1994) *Criminal Law Review* 780, 783.

(6)   extending and strengthening the mechanisms in Scotland[321] to require experts to meet in order to agree as far as possible evidence before trial along the lines provided in England and Wales,[322] and elsewhere;[323]

(7)   grouping expert testimony around issues rather than according to who calls the witness[324] and freeing it from the constraints of the fragmented[325] style of testimony,[326] such as by using concurrent evidence (or 'hot tub') sessions involving all experts from similar or closely related fields initially testifying together without lawyers and cross-examination;[327]

(8)   providing juries with judicial instructions throughout long and complex trials[328] and brief[329] training on how to evaluate scientific and probabilistic evidence.

Not at all of these suggestions are equally uncontroversial. The sixth, for instance, might be seen as undermining the right of accused persons to keep their cards close to their chest, and the seventh to challenge the fundamental nature of the adversarial trial. Other suggestions are even more controversial. For instance, there are rather esoteric debates over the best form for presenting statistical evidence, such as whether random match probabilities should be replaced by likelihood ratios, whether verbal scales should replace or complement numerical scales, and whether fact finders should be given separate figures for random match probabilities and error rates or whether these should be aggregated.[330]

---

[321] See M. Ross and J. Chalmers, *Walker and Walker: The Law of Evidence* (4th edn, 2015), 304.

[322] See, for example, Jackson, above n. 28, and more critically, Edmond, above n. 43, esp. 242ff; cf. also Roberts, above, n. 320, 785–91 in relation to criminal cases.

[323] See, for example, in relation to Australia, Edmond, above n. 28, 165.

[324] Damaška, *Evidence Law Adrift*, above n. 29, 145; Vidmar and Diamond, above n. 266, 1179.

[325] See Chapter 3, section 3.1.4.

[326] Cf. Roberts, above n. 266, 16, 269.

[327] See Edmonds, above n. 28.

[328] See, for example, Smith et al., esp. 52, 78, but cf. Schklar and Diamond, above n. 48, 179 citing studies where instructions failed to help correct statistical errors.

[329] Vidmar and Diamond, above n. 266, 1136–7 arguing that even brief training can improve reasoning.

[330] See, for example, Redmayne, above n. 24, Chapter 4; A. Ligertwood and G. Edmond, 'Expressing Evaluative Forensic Science Opinions in a Court of Law' (2012) 11 *Law, Probability and Risk* 289; W. C. Thompson and E. J. Newman, 'Lay Understanding of Forensic Statistics: Evaluation of Random Match Probabilities, Likelihood Ratios, and Verbal Equivalents' (2015) 39 *Law and Human Behavior* 332.

Moreover, there are still other suggestions which are so controversial that they have come to nothing.[331] One is the idea of replacing jurors with judges where cases involve complex science issues, or even establishing 'science courts' staffed by scientifically trained judges, which can be mandatory in all cases or only in relation to certain issues (such as causation in delict cases), or alternatively only used if requested by the parties. In support, it can be noted that it is easier to make judges as opposed to jurors scientifically and statistically literate, and they may gain relevant knowledge over time, use research assistants or teach themselves.[332] On the other hand, studies reveal that knowledgeable jurors may tutor their fellow jurors and that general group deliberation improves the quality of jurors' evaluation of scientific evidence.[333] Also problematic is the dilution of the idea of being judged by community representatives who can 'import a social sense of justice'.[334] Although this problem applies less to 'blue ribbon' juries comprised exclusively of scientifically qualified jurors,[335] the latter's relative scarcity in a small jurisdiction like Scotland would mean their almost continuous jury service.

Instead of using scientists as adjudicators, many suggest that they should act as advisors to judges or provide neutral, non-adversarial, testimony in court and even, as on the Continent, investigate cases from the outset.[336] Such neutral investigators would alleviate problems regarding inequalities between parties in investigating and preparing cases, while all neutral

---

[331] For overviews, see, for example, Burk, above n. 63, 371–5; E. Di Lello, 'Fighting Fire with Firefighters: A Proposal for Expert Judges at the Trial Level' (1993) 93 *Columbia Law Review* 473; 'Developments in the Law – Confronting the New Challenges of Scientific Evidence' (1995) 108 *Harvard Law Review* 1481, 1590–1604.

[332] On the relative merits of judges and jurors in this regard, see, for example, Brewer, above n. 245, 1678, 1680; Black, Ayala and Saffran-Brinks, above n. 9, 787–8; Lempert, above n. 266, 216–17 and 'The Jury and Scientific Evidence' (1999) 9 *The Kansas Journal of Law and Public Policy* 22, 24ff.

[333] See, for example, McQuiston-Surret and Saks, above n. 226, 1180; Vidmar and Diamond, above n. 266, esp. 1173–6; but see Beecher-Monas, above, n. 70, 27–32, noting that this might not apply to complex decision-making and that groups may amplify systematic biases and that individuals might put less effort into group decision-making.

[334] G. Edmond, 'The Next Step or Moonwalking? Expert Evidence, The Public Understanding of Science and The Case against Imwinkelried's Didactic Trial Procedures' (1998) 2 *International Journal of Evidence and Proof* 13, 22.

[335] But cf. Damaška, *Evidence Law Adrift*, above n. 29, 144.

[336] In addition to the references at n. 331, the merits and de-merits of this proposal are canvassed by Jones, above n. 12, 37ff; Roberts and Zuckerman, above n. 14, 505–9; Roberts, above n. 16, 277–80; Alldridge, above n. 32, 142–4; M. Howard, 'The Neutral Expert: A Plausible Threat to Justice' (1991) *Criminal Law Review* 98; J. Spencer, 'The Neutral Expert: An Implausible Bogey' (1991) *Criminal Law Review* 106; D. L. Faigman, 'Expert Evidence: The Rules and the Rationality the Law Applies (or Should Apply) to Psychological Expertise', in Carson and Bull, above n. 266, 394–8.

experts would eradicate problems associated with the adversarial selection, preparation and questioning of experts. Neutrality is also said to be particularly appropriate in the case of psychiatric or psychological assessments, given that it is more likely to increase the degree of confidence and trust in the expert necessary for a good working relationship, while also halving the number of examinations of those who are assessed.[337]

However, neutral experts are far from problem-free. Given that they might still have partisan views on scientific controversies, they should still be subject to adversarial testing, even if only acting as court advisors. Indeed, many accept that parties should retain the right to lead their own experts, which would then increase rather than reduce the time and cost of legal proceedings and the confusion caused by multiple experts. A court-appointed expert might also exacerbate problems of fact finder deference to expertise in that jurors might be influenced by the expert's official status (though this has not been confirmed by mock jury studies).[338] There is also the thorny issue of expert selection. Judges are not themselves qualified to choose the most suitable experts, but delegation to scientists creates the potential for personal and professional rivalries to distort selection and for an existing elite to block those in the vanguard of new developments. In addition, there may be insufficient experts in some disciplines to both accredit and be accredited.

Problems such as these (or indeed simple inertia) has meant that there have been no significant changes to the standard Scottish procedures for dealing with experts. However, the courts have, as already noted,[339] now assumed a new gatekeeping role in relation to the reliability of scientific evidence. In principle, such a role is likely to garner the support of many commentators.[340] Indeed, some argue that the onus of establishing reliability should be on those who lead scientific evidence,[341] or that evidence led by the prosecution should be tested more rigorously than that of the defence or civil parties.[342] Others argue that admissibility should relate not just to the reliability of the techniques used, but should extend also to the manner in which they were used, taking into account, for instance, error rates and breaches of appropriate protocols regarding the collection, stor-

---

[337] B. Irvine, 'Independent Expert Advice' (1991) 2 *Journal of Forensic Psychiatry* 242, 244–5.

[338] Burk, above n. 63, 374.

[339] At n. 40 above.

[340] For example, Raitt, above n. 5, 70; Roberts, above n. 16; Edmond and Roberts, above n. 307; G. Edmond, 'Advice for The Courts? Sufficiently Reliable Assistance with Forensic Science and Medicine (Part 2)' (2012) 16 *The International Journal of Evidence & Proof* 263.

[341] For example, P. C. Giannelli, 'The Admissibility of Novel Scientific Evidence: *Frye v. United States*, a Half-Century Later' (1980) 80 *Columbia Law Review* 1197.

[342] Edmonds and Roach, above n. 267.

age and proper use of relevant techniques.[343] On the other hand, it is also argued that leaving the reliability of scientific evidence to judicial assessment would mean that unreliable evidence will continue to influence legal fact finding until challenged in court, and that judges do not have the necessary knowledge[344] or political will[345] to challenge experts led by the state or powerful civil litigants. Consequently some recommend that questions of the reliability of scientific disciplines or their techniques are referred for assessment to some sort of independent standing body before or even during trial.[346]

However, whatever the exact solution to the problems with the relationship between law and science, and between legal fact finding and expertise, it is clear that very often law cannot operate in modern society without relying on scientific experts. Nor would it in general benefit from trying to do so. Nevertheless, this close encounter with science should undermine the assumptions by orthodox evidence theory that reasoning about evidence is capable of delivering objective and certain factual truths if it models scientific methods. Leaving aside the argument that all truth-claims are socially constructed, even the knowledge claims of pure science cannot escape the impact of subjective biases and the social context. And if this applies to pure science, it applies even more to social and forensic sciences, which play a much greater legal role. In other words, if legal fact finding is a form of 'scientific rationality', it is not as rational as the honorarium 'scientific' would suggest. Nor is science guaranteed to deliver objective and certain truth.

In addition, we have also seen that, even to the extent that science offers an imperfect means of helping to find truth, law's methods and its form of adjudication further water down its potential to do so. Moreover, apart from ensuring that all regular fact finders are provided with more training in scientific knowledge and testing the reliability of scientific evidence far more rigorously, there are few simple means of enhancing this potential without simultaneously harming those features of the Scottish procedural model which are regarded as highly beneficial, most notably its focus on adversariality, lay adjudication and the procedural rights of criminal accused. In other words, while beneficial to both sides, the marriage between law and science seems destined to remain troubled.

---

[343] E. J. Imwinkelried, 'The Debate in the DNA Cases Over the Foundation for the Admission of Scientific Evidence: The Importance of Human Error as a Cause of Forensic Misanalysis' (1991) 69 *Washington University Law Quarterly* 19.

[344] See at n. 267 above.

[345] At least in other jurisdictions (see above at n. 311).

[346] Edmond, above n. 340; Edmonds and Roberts, above n. 307, 389–92; P. Alldridge, 'Recognising Novel Scientific Techniques: DNA as a Test Case' (1992) *Criminal Law Review* 687, 694–5.

CHAPTER SIX

The Psychological Context I: Witnesses and Truth

1 Introduction

Having looked indirectly at documents and real evidence while exploring the scientific context of evidence and proof, we now turn to the other main form of evidence, namely the testimony of observational witnesses. As the first of two chapters devoted to the psychological context of evidence and proof, this chapter describes the two broad psychological processes relevant to witnessing, namely those involved in observing, remembering and recalling relevant facts, and those involved in evaluating the accuracy and honesty of these witnesses. Chapter Seven then explores the psychological processes involved in investigating, analysing, presenting and evaluating the facts relevant to a case as a whole, as opposed to individual items of evidence in the form of testimony, documents and real evidence. The fact that two chapters are devoted to psychology shows that it is central to the processes of evidence and proof[1] – almost by definition, as suggested by Bentham's already quoted[2] definition of evidence as 'any matter of fact, the effect, the tendency or design of which, when presented to the *mind*, is to produce a persuasion either affirmative or disaffirmative concerning the existence of some other matter of fact'.[3] Simply put, investigating and evaluating facts are impossible without psychological processes and hence these are central to our understanding of evidence and proof.

In addition to the general importance of psychology, understanding the psychological processes of witnessing and witness evaluation is

---

[1] It is also central to evidence law given that many rules, especially those of an 'intrinsic exclusionary nature' (see Chapter 3, section 3.2.4) are premised on 'fireside inductions' (P. E. Meehl, 'Law and the Fireside Inductions: Some Reflections of a Clinical Psychologist' (1971) 27 *Journal of Social Issues* 65) of varying degrees of plausibility about human psychology, which have been subjected to interrogation: see, for example, B. R. Clifford and R. Bull, *The Psychology of Person Identification* (1978), 3–4.

[2] Chapter 1 at n. 35.

[3] *Rationale of Judicial Evidence* (1827), quoted in W. Twining, *Theories of Evidence: Bentham and Wigmore* (1985), 29 (emphasis added).

particularly important for a number of reasons. First, eyewitness (and, occasionally, earwitness)[4] accounts are central in launching the processes of naming, claiming and blaming which may flower into legal proceedings.[5] Certainly witness reports are the most common reason for launching police investigations[6] and, along with confessions,[7] the principal determinant of whether crimes are solved.[8] Indeed, where suspects are guilty they can be described as witnesses to their own offences,[9] and hence, where relevant, the psychology of confessions will be discussed in this chapter.

Secondly, whereas historically the law has been highly suspicious of testimony because of its unreliability and likely bias, and hence disqualified a wide range of witnesses,[10] today testimony usually forms the bulk of trial evidence. For example, in one study, 78 per cent of cases in the English Magistrates' Courts were based on observational witnesses, though this ranged from 99 per cent of wounding and assault charges to 52 per cent of property offence charges,[11] and overall rates are likely to have fallen due to the increasing role played by forensic and CCTV evidence.[12]

Thirdly, research suggests that, perhaps with the exception of confession evidence,[13] fact finders give witness testimony far more weight than other

---

[4]   Generally (but see section 2.5.1) we will not distinguish ear- from eye-witnesses.

[5]   W. L. F. Felstiner, R. L. Abel and A. Sarat, 'The Emergence and Transformation of Disputes: Naming, Blaming, Claiming . . .' (1980–1) 15 *Law & Society Review* 631 and the discussion in Chapter 1, section 2.3.

[6]   See, for example, P. A. Tollestrup, J. W. Turtle and J. C. Yuille, 'Actual Victims and Witnesses to Robbery and Fraud: An archival Analysis', in D. F. Ross, J. D. Read and M. P. Toglia (eds), *Adult Eyewitness Testimony: Current Trends and Developments* (1994), 152.

[7]   Based on studies, G. Gudjonsson, *The Psychology of Interrogations and Confessions: A Handbook* (2003), 131–40 estimates that confessions are crucial to the UK police in 24 per cent of cases and that suspects confess in 55–59 per cent of cases.

[8]   P. G. Greenwood and J. Petersilia, *The Criminal Investigation Process Volume III: Observations and Analysis* (1975), ix, Chapter 6; M. McConville, A. Sanders and R. Leng, *The Case for the Prosecution: Police Suspects and the Construction of Criminality* (1993), 57.

[9]   G. H. Gudjonsson, 'Testimony from Persons with Mental Disorder', in A. Heaton-Armstrong, E. Shepherd and D. Wolchover (eds), *Analysing Witness Testimony: A Guide for Legal Practitioners and Other Professionals* (1999), 63–4.

[10] F. P. Davidson, *Evidence* (2007), 303–4.

[11] J. Vennard, *Contested Trials in Magistrates' Courts: The Case for the Prosecution* (Royal Commission on Criminal Procedure, Research Study No. 6, 1980), 6. For similar figures, see B. L. Cutler and S. Penrod, *Mistaken Identification: The Eyewitness, Psychology and the Law* (1995), 6; W. A. Wagenaar, P. J. van Koppen and H. F. M. Crombag, *Anchored Narratives: The Psychology of Criminal Evidence* (1993), 139; W. Young, N. Cameron and Y. Tinsley, *Juries in Criminal Trials, Part Two: A Summary of Research Findings* (1999), 27.

[12] See Chapter 5, section 2.

[13] A. D. Yarmey, 'Eyewitnesses', in D. Carson and R. Bull (eds), *Handbook of Psychology in Legal Contexts* (2003), 533; S.M. Kassin and K. Neuman, 'On the Power of Confession Evidence: An Experimental Test of the Fundamental Difference Hypothesis" (1997) 21 *Law and Human Behavior* 469.

forms of evidence.[14] Witness testimony plays an important role in all legal systems. However, where – as in Scotland – there is a climactic day in court at which all evidence is delivered orally, oral reports by those who observed the relevant facts are likely to be more dramatic and more memorable than witness statements or even transcripts in written dossiers. They also allow for the observation of witness demeanour, which, as we have seen, is thought to be a significant clue as to credibility.[15] Moreover, to the extent allowed by examining lawyers,[16] witnesses will tend to relate facts in narrative form and this, as we shall see,[17] enhances its impact on fact adjudicators.

Finally, the importance of witness testimony is shown by the consistent finding that mistaken witness identifications of accused are the most common cause of miscarriages of justice[18] – and may consequently be assumed to play a role in wrongful acquittals and dubious verdicts in civil cases. Similarly, while it is impossible to accurately gauge the prevalence of false confessions, it is clear that they cause many miscarriages of justice,[19] though fewer than mistaken identifications.

We therefore need to critically interrogate the legal system's apparent faith in humans to deliver truth through personally observing facts and accurately evaluating such witnesses. Since the late nineteenth century, countless psychological studies, including staged incidents during law

---

[14] Cutler and Penrod, above n. 11, Chapter 12; E. F. Loftus, *Eyewitness Testimony* (1996), Chapter 2; M. R. Leippe, 'The Case for Expert Testimony about Eyewitness Memory' (1995) 1 *Psychology, Public Policy and Law* 909, 930–2; M. Boyce, J. Beaudry and R. C. L. Lindsay, 'Belief of Eyewitness Identification Evidence', in R. C. L. Lindsay et al. (eds), *The Handbook of Eyewitness Psychology: Volume II: Memory for People* (2012); M. R. Leippe and D. Eisenstadt, 'The Influence of Eyewitness Expert Testimony on Jurors' Beliefs and Judgments', in B. L. Cutler (ed.), *Expert Testimony on the Psychology of Eyewitness Identification* (2009), 170–1.

[15] See Chapter 3, section 3.2.3.

[16] See Chapter 3, section 3.1.4.

[17] Section 3.2.2; see also Chapter 7.

[18] Estimates range from around 74–90 per cent of US cases involving post-conviction exoneration through DNA evidence: see K. A. Findley, 'Learning from Our Mistakes: A Criminal Justice Commission to Study Wrongful Convictions' (2002) 38 *California Western Law Review* 333, 339–40; G. L. Wells et al., 'Eyewitness Identification Procedures: Recommendations for Line-ups and Photospreads' (1998) 23 *Law and Human Behavior* 603, 615. Although Scottish pre-trial identification procedures (see section 2.4.2) are somewhat better than those in the US, the problems they cause are swamped by the impact of inherent limits to witnessing ability: cf. C. Walker, 'Miscarriages of Justice in Scotland', in C. Walker and K. Starmer (eds), *Miscarriages of Justice: A Review of Justice in Error* (1999), 324–5.

[19] Estimates range from 18–24 per cent in the US studies cited by Findley, ibid.; 20 per cent by the US Innocence Project: D. Howitt, *Introduction to Forensic and Criminal Psychology* (2015), 341. Given differences in police tactics and governing law, the UK rate *may* be lower (though detailed estimates have not been made), but the role of false confessions in so many notorious wrongful convictions suggests a serious problem here as well: see, for example, McConville, Sanders and Leng, above n. 8, esp. Chapters 3 and 4; Gudjonsson, above n. 7, esp. Chapter 7; Walker, ibid., 346–7.

lectures designed to illustrate witness fallibility,[20] have examined these questions. The methods used have largely involved those of behavioural science, in which researchers manipulate certain factors or stimuli in order to ascertain whether and to what extent they influence behaviour.

However, after an initial spurt of activity, studies fell away from around the 1930s, possibly because of unmet expectations regarding their value. But then, from around the 1970s, research resumed and laboratory studies began to be augmented by field experiments involving the observation of actual behaviour in real-life localities such as police stations or court rooms, or situations designed to mirror such conditions, and by archival studies involving the analysis of reports of actual cases.[21] Whether this new wave of research has gained the necessary rigour to overcome early scepticism will be explored after examining the vast body of knowledge it has generated. Most of it is concerned with honest witnesses who provide inaccurate or incomplete evidence or both,[22] which poses most challenges for truth finding in law. We will start with these studies before moving on to those evaluating the extent to which fact finders can accurately assess witness reliability and honesty.

2 The Psychology of Witnessing[23]

2.1 An Overview[24]

Before looking at the ability of witnesses to provide accurate accounts of facts they observe, it is useful to have an understanding of some basic psychological concepts. One sees memory in terms of three types of stores.

---

[20] See, for example, D. S. Greer, 'Anything But the Truth? The Reliability of Testimony in Criminal Trials' (1971) 11 *British Journal of Criminology* 131, 132–42; S. Lloyd-Bostock, 'The Benefits of Legal Psychology: Possibilities, Practice and Dilemmas' (1988) 79 *British Journal of Psychology* 417, 417–19.

[21] For a useful overview of methods, see A. Kapardis, *Psychology and Law: A Critical Introduction* (4th edn revised by I. Freckleton, 2014), 34–8.

[22] Note, however, that accuracy can be gained at the expense of completeness (for example, witnesses only notice and/or remember central details of incidents), extensive detail might stem from inaccuracies (for example, witnesses fill in factual details based on false assumptions or suggestions or reports from others) and insufficient detail might lead to inaccuracies (for example, partial accounts may mislead).

[23] For useful introductions, see, for example, B. S. Jackson, *Making Sense in Law* (1995), Chapter 10; R. N. Haber and L. Haber, 'Experiencing, Remembering and Reporting Events' (2000) 6 *Psychology, Public Policy and Law* 1057; E. F. Loftus, D. Wolchover and D. Page, 'General Review of the Psychology of Witness Testimony', in A. Heaton-Armstrong et al. (eds), *Witness Testimony: Psychological, Investigative and Evidential Perspectives* (2006).

[24] See, for example, Clifford and Bull, above n. 1, Chapter 2; P. B. Ainsworth, *Psychology, Law and Eyewitness Testimony* (1998), 27–33; G. Cohen, 'Human Memory in the Real World', in A. Heaton-Armstrong, E. Shepherd and D. Wolchover (eds), *Analysing Witness Testimony: A Guide for Legal Practitioners and Other Professionals* (1999), 5–14.

The *sensory store* holds un-interpreted information perceived by the sense organs for between one to four seconds, with each sense having its own repository. From here, information passes into *short-term memory* (STM) for between six to twelve seconds. STM can only hold about seven items of information simultaneously. Consequently newly acquired information easily pushes out existing information, which may then be lost forever. However, if attempts are made to retain information or if the information is sufficiently noteworthy, it passes into *long-term memory* (LTM), where it can last indefinitely.

LTM stores both personally observed individual facts – known as 'auto-biographical' or 'episodic' memory – and general knowledge of the world. Some of this latter 'theoretical' or 'semantic' memory is based upon direct observation (for example, that day follows night) but most is gained from formal education or informally from the reports of others (for example, that John Logie Baird invented television and that Glasgow is the largest Scottish city).

While the information on which witnesses report always involves autobiographical memories, these differ from and interact with theoretical memory in crucial ways. Unlike autobiographical memory, which is stored in order of arrival and constantly updated, theoretical memory is more constant and organised in terms of myriad categories. These are grounded in both autobiographical and theoretical knowledge, and organised according to content (as in a library) and level of generality (as in the biological divisions of genus and species), and linked in a 'rich network of associations'.[25]

Together, theoretical knowledge and its commonalities form what are called schemas or schemata. These are knowledge or cognitive structures which represent 'abridged, generalised, corrigible, organised stereotypical knowledge derived from first or second-hand experience concerning situations, persons, roles, events, problems, and context-relevant thought and action'.[26] Particularly important to legal fact handling are schemas relating to events which manifest as story schemata or 'scripts'.[27] Research establishes that people have relatively common scripts both for previously experienced events, such as eating in restaurants and attending lectures, and for

[25] G. Cohen, ibid., 8.

[26] E. Shepherd and R. Milne, 'Full and Faithful: Ensuring Quality Practice and Integrity of Outcome in Witness Interviews', in Heaton-Armstrong, Milne and Wolchover, above n. 24, 125. See also, for example, A. J. Moore, 'Trial by Schema: Cognitive Filters in the Courtroom' (1989) 37 *UCLA Law Review* 273.

[27] R. K. Sherwin, 'Law Frames: Historical Truth and Narrative Necessity in a Criminal Case' (1994) 47 *Stanford Law Review* 39, 50–1.

events such as robberies, muggings and shoplifting that they may only have learned from television, films and books, and so on.[28] These scripts contain compulsory slots which are filled with variable details. For instance, a restaurant script involves food eaten at tables, but the particular food served, the décor, size of tables, etc. will obviously differ. Moreover, slightly different details involved in repeated experiences, such as beach trips, may merge into a single script of a stereotypical beach trip unless there is some significant memorable event such as one's dog going missing.[29]

Schemas play at least five different roles in witnessing. The first is *selection*. Contrary to the view of naïve empirical foundationalists,[30] the mind does not operate like a video camera faithfully recording all images or sounds to which it is exposed. Given our highly limited attention span, we can only attend to a fraction of the plethora of sense data we encounter every second and hence much will never make it into memory. While, as we shall see in the next section, many factors affect the quality of knowledge acquisition, schemas play a crucial role in drawing attention to and guiding the selection of what is stored in memory. However, information which we notice is not just mechanically recorded, but stored in schemas. Before such *storage* can be done, it needs to be sifted and interpreted for categorisation purposes. This process of 'encoding' is highly 'active, creative and subjective',[31] and can cause information to be transformed in two ways. First, the process of *generalisation* transforms information from the specific form in which it is perceived to a more general form, with specific details dropping out and aspects common to other experiences incorporated into general schemas and retained. The second way information is transformed is through *normalisation*, in terms of which memories are altered to fit with prior expectations and made more consistent with likely examples of their kind. Finally, schemas may provide the basis for *making inferences* about aspects of incidents which were not directly observed (for example, that an assaulted victim felt pain).

---

[28] See, for example, V. F. Holst and K. Pezdek, 'Scripts for Typical Crimes and Their Effects on Memory for Eyewitness Testimony' (1992) 6 *Applied Cognitive Psychology* 573; M. S. Greenberg, D. R. Westcott and S. E. Bailey, 'When Believing Is Seeing: The Effect of Scripts on Eyewitness Memory' (1998) 22 *Law and Human Behavior* 685.

[29] Example taken from J. Cohen, 'Questions of Credibility: Omissions, Discrepancies and Errors of Recall in the Testimony of Asylum Seekers' (2002) 13 *International Journal of Refugee Law* 293, 295.

[30] See Chapter 2, section 3.2.1.

[31] Ainsworth, above n. 24, 10.

Allied to this final role of schemas is the operation of heuristics. As we saw in the last chapter,[32] these enable people to make 'fast and frugal' decisions when they are distracted or suffering from cognitive overload. However, whereas schemas cause witnesses to fill in gaps in their knowledge using generic knowledge, heuristics cause them to make inferences from existing information. For instance, the causality heuristic will encourage people to infer that if one thing (for example, screaming) happens after another (an assault), the first caused the second.

To sum up, we can see that, rather than resembling a video camera faithfully recording the growth of a plant for a nature programme, the mind works more like a film-maker or author who needs to decide on which elements of 'reality' to focus and how to interpret events and organise them for the final edit. In addition, there are other sources of witnessing failures flowing from the fact the mind does not retain information in pristine form. As we shall see, like a video recording, it can become degraded or contaminated by outside information, or problems may arise during playback.

Consequently it is common to discuss witnessing in terms of three separate and consecutive stages: *perception* – the acquisition and encoding of information; *memory* – its storage; and *recall* – the retrieval and communication of information. This approach will be followed here, although it is sometimes difficult to ascertain exactly why someone cannot recall information (or do so accurately) – were the problems caused by failures of perception, memory or recall (or even the closely related process of 'enunciation' whereby witnesses struggle to represent their memories accurately in words)?

2.2 Perception – The Acquisition Stage[33]
What information is noticed and how it is encoded can be affected by factors relating to the conditions of observation, the type of facts being observed and those that stem from witnesses themselves.

2.2.1 Conditions of Observation
Factors relating to the conditions of observation are probably rather obvious. They include:

• the distance from the facts observed;
• weather conditions;

---

[32] Sections 6.2 and 7.3.2.
[33] See generally Loftus, above n. 14, Chapter 3; Jackson, above n. 23, 362–6; Kapardis, above n. 21, 40–8; Ainsworth, above n. 24, Chapter 1 and 36–48; M. Stone, *Proof of Fact in Criminal Trials* (1984), Chapters 2–3.

- the state of lighting (particularly in the case of elderly witnesses),[34] as affected, for instance, by the time of day;
- conditions obstructing the view of witnesses (such as moving vehicles) or occluding their hearing (such as loud music);
- the amount of time for observation;
- the ability to observe all aspects of an event (for example, that an apparently unprovoked assault was preceded by an unseen attack);
- distractions affecting witnesses' concentration on the facts (such as a child calling for attention).

However, the effect of some of these factors might be more nuanced than first appears. For example, certain kinds of street or internal lighting can have distinct effects on the perceptions of particular colours; moving suddenly from dark to light or vice versa results in a temporary loss of accuracy in vision; the size of some objects may appear bigger or smaller depending on what they are being contrasted with; and moving objects may seem faster or slower than they actually are. And while it is clear that longer exposure to events enhances accurate perception, research has not and probably cannot establish exactly how long is needed for optimal accuracy.[35] For example, some facts, such as those familiar to witnesses, may be grasped far quicker than others. Exposure time is also complex in its impact on identification evidence in that longer periods increase not only 'correct hits' – witnesses correctly identifying the relevant person – but also 'false alarms' – witnesses identifying the wrong person.[36] The presence of noise and other distractions make the accurate perception of spoken words particularly problematic.

2.3.2 The Nature of the Facts Observed
Words are also far more ambiguous and subject to nuanced meaning than actions and thus require observation of factors like the facial expressions or body language of the speaker and person addressed, and an understanding of the mental and emotional context of the verbal engagement.[37]

---

[34] K. Mueller-Johnson and S. J. Ceci, 'The Elderly Eyewitness: A Review and Prospects', in M. P. Toglia et al. (eds), *The Handbook of Eyewitness Psychology: Volume 1: Memory for Events* (2007), 580, noting also the greater difficulty elderly witnesses have in perceiving colours, distinguishing foreground from background and dealing with glare.

[35] E. B. Ebbesen and V. J. Konečni, 'Eyewitness Memory Research: Probative v. Prejudicial Value' (1996) 5 *Expert Evidence* 2, 7.

[36] Ibid., 7.

[37] D. Davis and R. D. Friedman, 'Memory for Conversation: The Orphan Child of Witness Memory Researchers', in Toglia et al., above n. 34.

Interpreting these factors is particularly difficult for those without relevant experiences, such as young children and those from different cultures.

Given its importance to fact finding and to miscarriages of justice, we will discuss face recognition separately, but particular problems arise – especially for children – in relation to facts requiring measurement, such as distance, speed and time.[38] People, especially if stressed, also tend to overestimate the duration of events – ranging from around twice to six times the actual time.[39] Estimating people's age, height and weight is similarly taxing. Interestingly witnesses tend to overestimate the height and weight, respectively of short and light persons, and underestimate that of tall and heavy persons, especially in the latter case if they themselves are short or light.[40] Finally, and perhaps surprisingly, non-violent events tend to be perceived more accurately than violent events. Less surprisingly, incidents with fewer participants and which are more static are more accurately perceived.[41]

As regards the details of events, those features regarded as most salient by witnesses more readily capture their attention and interest, and accordingly are more accurately perceived than details regarded as commonplace or unimportant. Some facts, such as an assault or the words used in an argument, are of obvious salience. Otherwise, it is '[t]he extraordinary, colorful, novel, unusual and interesting scenes [that] attract our attention and hold our interest'.[42]

2.2.3 Witness-related Factors

Turning to witness-related factors, a number of obvious *physical factors* or *mental disorders* reduce perceptive ability, such as vision or hearing impairments, to which the elderly are again particularly prone.[43] Older witnesses may also notice fewer details.[44] Alcohol and drug intoxication,[45] mental[46]

---

[38] See J. R. Spencer and R. H. Flin, *The Evidence of Children: The Law and the Psychology* (2nd edn, 1993), 290.

[39] See studies cited by Loftus, above n. 14, 29–30.

[40] See, for example, C. A. Meissner, L. S. Sporer and J. W. Schooler, 'Person Descriptors as Eyewitness Evidence', in Lindsay et al., above n. 14, 7–8.

[41] B. R. Clifford and C. R. Hollin, 'Effects of the Type of Incident and the Number of Perpetrators on Eyewitness Memory' (1981) 66 *Journal of Applied Psychology* 364.

[42] D. S. Gardner, 'The Perception and Memory of Witnesses' (1933) 18 *Cornell Law Quarterly* 391, 394.

[43] See Mueller-Johnson and Ceci, above n. 34, 580–1.

[44] Mueller-Johnson and Ceci, ibid., 582.

[45] See M. Lader, 'The Influence of Drugs on Testimony', in Heaton-Armstrong, Shepherd and Wolchover, above n. 24; S. A. Soraci et al., 'Psychological Impairment, Eyewitness Testimony, and False Memories: Individual Differences', in Toglia et al., above n. 34, 286–8.

[46] Gudjonsson, above n. 9.

and physical illness,[47] fatigue or injury may reduce perceptive ability, depending on their degree, the witness' tolerance levels and the complexity and nature of the event being observed. For example, even very drunk witnesses may be able to accurately observe simple facts.

More subtle *psychological and emotional conditions* affect perception. Thus anxiety and even neuroticism have been shown to reduce accuracy.[48] Experiments also reveal a 'mood congruity effect'.[49] For example, experimental subjects made to experience anger before encountering a stranger asking for help tended to interpret his actions as merely interference, but when made fearful perceived him as a potential mugger.[50]

An obvious and frequently relevant psychological condition affecting perception is the stress caused by witnessing events such as those involving violence, especially as actual or potential victims. However, the effect of stress is far from straightforward – not least because individual responses differ dramatically.[51] In general, however, many but not all[52] researchers report that stress tends to have a contradictory effect: up to a certain point it improves perception but beyond that has a negative effect, and at extreme levels can cause total confusion or hysteria. One much-discussed phenomenon is the apparent 'weapon focus effect'.[53] Thus numerous laboratory experiments – but not all archival studies of actual cases – reveal that when weapons are involved in incidents, witnesses tend to see only the weapon, particularly if directed at them, and not the perpetrator's face or other facts. Leaving aside the complex impact of stress, emotional arousal in general may enhance the detail and accuracy of perception, especially as regards central rather than peripheral aspects of events.[54]

---

[47] G. A. Norfolk, 'Physical Illnesses and their Potential Influence', in Heaton-Armstrong, Shepherd and Wolchover, above n. 24.

[48] See studies cited by Loftus, above n. 14, 153–6.

[49] G. H. Bower, 'Mood and Memory' (1981) 36 *American Psychologist* 129, though largely using the term in connection with recall not perception.

[50] C. Z. Malatesta and A. Wilson, 'Emotion Cognition Interaction in Personality Development: A Discrete Emotions, Functionalist Analysis' (1988) 27 *British Journal of Social Psychology* 91, 98.

[51] See, for example, D. Reisberg and F. Heuer, 'The Influence of Emotion on Memory in Forensic Settings', in Toglia et al., above n. 34.

[52] See Ebbesen and Konečni, above n. 35, 8–12; R. Elliott, 'Expert Testimony About Eyewitness Identification: A Critique' (1993) 17 *Law and Human Behavior* 423, 426–7.

[53] See, for example, Ainsworth, above n. 24, 40–1; Reisberg and Heuer, above n. 51, 87–92; K. Pickel, 'Remembering and Identifying Menacing Perpetrators: Exposure to Violence and the Weapon Focus Effect', in Lindsay et al., n. 14, 347ff, but again see the scepticism of Ebbesen and Konečni, ibid., 12; Elliott, ibid., 427–8.

[54] See E. A. Phelps, 'Emotion's Impact on Memory', in L. Nadel and W. P. Sinnot-Armstrong (eds), *Memory and Law* (2012).

The final set of witness-related factors affecting perception are those caused by *prior expectations*, which are particularly influential when the observed facts are complex and events are brief.[55] It is here that schemas play their most influential role in shaping perception. Elizabeth Loftus[56] divides these expectations into four types:

(1) *Cultural expectations*

The influence of beliefs 'held by large numbers of people within a given culture'[57] has been shown most famously by experiments by Gordon Allport and Loe Portman involving people seeing a Red Cross ambulance as carrying medicines when it actually carried explosives, and North Americans as seeing distance signposts in kilometres as being in miles.[58] Their studies also confirmed the impact of stereotypes, which can be described as beliefs about common attributes or traits of a group of people or common situations.[59] For instance, over half of subjects in one of their experiments who viewed a picture of an underground railway carriage containing a black man in a suit and a white man with a razor blade transposed the razor blade into the hands of the former, and some even described him as using it to threaten the latter. Similarly, experimental witnesses tended to see male perpetrators and victims of staged incidents as more active than their female counterparts.[60]

(2) *Personal prejudices*

These are closely related to stereotypes, but are less widely held and may even be confined to a single witness. Loftus includes here an inclination towards one or other side in a dispute and cites a study involving two opposing sets of fans[61] that was replicated in a study involving a heated Scotland–England football match which was interpreted very differently according to whether the spectators were Scottish or English.[62]

[55] See E. Balcetis and S. Cole, 'On Misers, Managers and Monsters: The Social Cognition of Visual Perception', in D. E. Carlston, *The Oxford Handbook of Social Cognition* (2013).
[56] Loftus, above n. 14, Chapter 3.
[57] Loftus, ibid., 37.
[58] *The Psychology of Rumor* (1965), cited in Loftus, ibid., 37–9.
[59] See, for example, M. J. Monteith, A. Woodstock and J. E. Gulker, 'Automaticity and Control in Stereotyping and Prejudice: The Revolutionary Role of Social Cognition Across Three Decades', in Carlston, above n. 55.
[60] T. Lindholm and S.-A. Christianson, 'Gender Effects in Eyewitness Accounts of a Violent Crime' (1998) 4 *Psychology, Crime & Law* 323.
[61] Loftus, above n. 14, 40–2.
[62] J. Boon and G. Davies, 'Extra-Stimulus Influences on Eyewitness Perception and Recall: Hastorf and Cantril Revisited' (1996) 1 *Legal and Criminological Psychology* 155.

(3)   *Past experience*

Because of the way things have been in the past, we expect them to be the same in the present. Thus in experiments most subjects who looked at a Roman numeral watch identified the symbol for four o'clock as 'IV' whereas it was (and usually is) 'IIII'.[63] Similarly, many subjects did not notice that a few cards in a pack of playing cards had their traditional colours reversed.[64] In other words, people both change and ignore unexpected information. Conversely, based on past experience, or indeed any of the other three types of expectations, witnesses might also report non-existent facts which are usually part of the relevant scenario. A particular instance involves 'confabulation' whereby gaps in information are filled based on our expectation of commonly occurring temporal sequences of events. Thus, for example, if we are told that someone had a birthday party, games were played, she received presents, and blew out candles, our party script is likely to include a birthday girl and a cake, whereas in fact her family might have been unable to afford a cake or she was an adult playing drinking games.

(4)   *Temporary expectations or biases*

A much-cited real-life example of the impact of temporary expectations involves two Canadian hunters who shot a companion who they thought had gone for help in getting their car unstuck.[65] Both accused were convinced that they had seen and heard a deer because they were expecting one. Yet, conversely and unsurprisingly, a police officer involved in an immediate reconstruction saw a man and not a deer. This phenomenon has been replicated in experiments. For instance, subjects were briefly exposed to the written quasi-words 'dack' and 'sael', after half had been told that the words they were being shown involved animals or birds and the other half that they involved transport. When asked what words they had seen, most of the former group 'saw' 'duck' and 'seal', whereas most of the latter 'saw' 'deck' and 'sail'.[66]

More generally, the impact of prior perceptions or schemas about how the world works in leading to information being omitted, modified or even invented shows that there is no such thing as pure perception. Even in

---

[63] C. C. French and A. Richards, 'Clock This! An Everyday Example of a Schema-Driven Error in Memory' (1993) 84 *British Journal of Psychology* 249.

[64] J. S. Bruner and L. Postman, 'On the Perception of Incongruity: A Paradigm' (1949) 18 *Journal of Personality* 206, 214–15.

[65] Reported by R. Sommer, 'The New Look on the Witness Stand' (1959) 8 *Canadian Psychologist* 94.

[66] E. M. Siipola, 'A Group Study of Some Effects of Preparatory Set' (1935) 46 *Psychological Monographs* 27.

optimal witnessing conditions, as George Santayana declared, 'every perception . . . involves an act of judgment, nay is an act of judgment . . .'[67]

2.3 Memory – The Storage Stage[68]
2.3.1 Introduction
Before looking separately at memory storage and recall, it needs to be noted that these processes are often difficult to distinguish in practice, since an inability to recall information may be because it has been lost from memory or, alternatively, while stored, cannot be brought to mind. Nevertheless, as the expression 'it's on the tip of my tongue' shows, there are clearly differences between failures of memory and recall. Information lodged in memory may be later recalled given the right conditions, but not if lost from memory. Consequently we shall first look separately at memory and recall where they are clearly distinguishable, and then at a number of general factors affecting both processes where they are not.

As regards memory, far from witnesses passively storing acquired information and then recalling it in pristine form, it can be altered, deleted and created in three ways. First, it decays over time. However, delay between perception and recall is also important in creating the opportunity for memory to be altered after encoding, especially shortly after events before memory becomes more fixed.[69] This can occur through the operation of the witness' own cognitive processes or contamination of memory by external influences. Each of these three processes will be explored in turn.

2.3.2 Memory and Time[70]
Repeated experiments confirm what everyone knows: memory fades over time. Thus delays between perception and recall affect the accuracy and detail of memory. Less well known is the fact that, according to most psychologists,[71] memory is rapidly lost immediately after perception, but then the rate of forgetting slows over time. Unfortunately it is not possible to specify the exact trajectory of this 'forgetting curve'. Not only do experiments differ between themselves as to the impact of delay, but differences

[67] Quoted by J. B. Weinstein, 'Some Difficulties in Devising Rules for Determining Truth in Judicial Trials' (1966) 66 *Columbia Law Review* 223, 231.
[68] See generally Loftus, above n. 14, Chapter 4; Jackson, above n. 23, 367–75 passim; Ainsworth, above n. 24, Chapters 2–4; Stone, above n. 33, Chapter 4.
[69] J. Cohen, above n. 29, 298.
[70] In addition to the references in n. 68, see J. D. Read and D. A. Connolly, 'The Effects of Delay on Long-Term Memory for Witnessed Events', in Toglia et al., above n. 34.
[71] But see Ebbesen and Konečni, above n. 35, 7–8.

can also be caused by variables such as the type of stimulus observed, the witness' age and type of recall used.

We will return to such factors later,[72] but first we can note the impact of schemas. Thus memory loss increases when information is inconsistent, rather than consistent, with existing schemas and is greatest when it is irrelevant to them. For instance, we are more likely to remember (as opposed to initially notice) expected rather than highly unusual and hence unexpected aspects of a robbery (the wearing of a balaclava rather than an Indian headdress), or those aspects of a robbery which are neither expected nor particularly out of the ordinary (that the balaclava was green). Here again we see the importance of stories; the clearer an event's narrative structure, the more accurately it will be recalled.[73]

Also highly influential is the way in which a memory is cognitively processed, both at the time of initial encoding and subsequently.[74] Thus the more such processing, the stronger the memory 'trace', as psychologists term it, and the more resistant such traces are to decay (as well as to subsequent alteration and problems of recall). Strong memory traces are created by 'deep processing' through, for instance, concentrating on making inferences about character from faces rather than simply classifying them in terms of shape, and by 'elaborative encoding', which involves relating the perceived stimulus to similar experiences and puzzling over its meaning. Greater cognitive processing also occurs in relation to facts which are novel, distinctive from similar facts, or which have personal relevance, salience or emotional meaning and which witnesses are motivated to remember.

Subsequent to encoding, memory can be strengthened by further cognitive processing, such as by repeated rehearsals of information, replaying and mulling over significant events in our minds and 'overlearning', as when we repeat telephone numbers. Moreover, being asked repeatedly to reproduce a memory may protect against memory loss, increase the amount of information recalled and strengthen memory – though it also increases the potential for memory contamination during recall, especially as regards peripheral details.[75]

---

[72] Sections 2.5 and 2.4 respectively.

[73] J. M. Mandler and N. S. Johnson, 'Remembrance of Things Parsed: Story Structure and Recall' (1977) 9 *Cognitive Psychology* 111, 132.

[74] See, for example, G. Cohen, above n. 24, 8–9; N. Brewer, N. Weber and C. Semmler, 'A Role for Theory in Eyewitness Identification Research', in Lindsay et al., above n. 14, 204ff.

[75] G. Cohen, ibid., n. 24, 15.

2.3.3 Self-induced Memory Changes

But even without outside influences, a witness' own cognitive processes may result in memories being altered. An obvious cause is a witness' interests or motivations. For example, those who originally acknowledged blame for an accident may gradually over time reduce their acceptance of fault, even to vanishing point. It has also been shown that witnesses who lie about, or pretend not to remember, facts may over time come to remember them less accurately. Conversely, witnesses who guess about facts of which they are uncertain may become increasingly certain about their answers over time. Closely related to this is the common 'freezing'[76] or 'commitment' effect.[77] This stems from a reluctance to retract publicly expressed views, especially if witnesses are worried about wasting others' or court time. It causes witness reports to remain stable over different retellings, even though the original memory was precarious or mistaken on some details, and sometimes even if the witness re-encounters the original stimulus. Labelling information may also have a similar effect. Thus, if ambiguous information is given one label rather than another, it may later be confidently recalled under that label. For example, subjects shown a bluish-green colour tended to remember it clearly as either blue or green depending on how they labelled it shortly afterwards.[78]

Schemas again play a central role. Thus, in all cases where memory starts to fade, features of the observed facts may be altered by, or replaced with, details taken from existing schemas. This is more likely to occur with weak memory traces, when schema information was acquired directly from personal observation rather than from others and when recall occurs long after the witnessed events. Moreover, memory alteration or replacement is more likely where central details of schemas and peripheral details of events are involved.[79]

2.3.4 Memory Contamination[80]

Post-perception information which potentially contaminates memory can arrive in many ways. One is through exposure to media reports or

---

[76] See, for example, Loftus, above n. 14, 84–6.

[77] See, for example, H. A. McAllister, 'Mug Books: More Than Just Large Photospreads', in Lindsay et al., above n. 14, 41–7.

[78] See, for example, D. R. Thomas and A. Decapito, 'Role of Stimulus Labeling in Stimulus Generalization' (1966) 71 *Journal of Experimental Psychology* 913.

[79] See, for example, Greenberg, Westcott and Bailey, above n. 28.

[80] In addition to the references in n. 68, see G. Davies, 'Contamination of Witness Memory', in Heaton-Armstrong, Shepherd and Wolchover, above n. 24; D. Davis and E. F. Loftus, 'Internal and External Sources of Misinformation in Adult Witness Memory', in Toglia et al., above n. 34.

conversations with other witnesses, as both research and real-life cases show, leading to witnesses being unable to distinguish between originally and subsequently acquired information. A striking illustration of this 'source monitoring error' is a study in which 44 per cent of subjects asked about the death of Princess Diana reported seeing a non-existent film of the car crash they had heard or read about.[81]

Another source of memory contamination is leading or otherwise suggestive questions asked of witnesses. The insinuation of such information can be relatively crude, such as asking a witness who has not recalled the colour of a car, 'How fast was the blue car travelling?' But it can be far more subtle, as shown by an experiment in which witnesses were twice as likely (16 per cent as opposed to 7 per cent) to report seeing non-existent broken glass when the verb 'smashed' rather than 'hit' was used in asking them about the speed of cars involved in an accident.[82] Witnesses who read a police officer's summary of their own statement may also have their memory affected if it is not verbatim but in the officer's own language and contains subconsciously or surreptitiously inserted nuances or even new information.[83] Finally, witnesses may be shown props, photographs, diagrams or drawings to prompt their memory, but which may also contaminate existing memory. A common example is where witnesses recognise innocent persons from prior exposure to a photograph or Photofit or Identikit of them.

Loftus, who has done much of the research on the impact of post-event information, reports three possible effects.[84] First, it may reinforce accurate memories. Secondly, and more worryingly, it can cause witnesses to remember non-existent facts.[85] Thus 17 per cent of people shown a picture of a car later reported seeing a non-existent barn after being asked, 'How fast was the white sports car going when it passed the barn while travelling along the country road?'[86] Even more worryingly, given the frequent use of photographs and constructed images to identify criminal suspects, 40 per cent of 'witnesses' to a staged shoplifting were misled by being shown a photofit of the 'suspect' a week earlier, which had been altered to change

---

[81] J. Ost et al., 'Crashing Memories and Reality Monitoring: Distinguishing Between Perceptions, Imaginations and "False Memories"' (2002) 16 *Applied Cognitive Psychology* 125.

[82] E. F. Loftus and J. Palmer, 'Reconstruction of Automobile Destruction: An Example of the Interaction Between Language and Memory' (1974) 13 *Journal of Verbal Learning and Verbal Behavior* 585, 587.

[83] Wagenaar, van Koppen and Crombag, above n. 11, 149; though this is counselled against in the Crown Office and Procurator Fiscal Service, *Code of Practice: Disclosure of Evidence in Criminal Proceedings* (2011), section 22.

[84] Above n. 14, 54–63.

[85] See also J. S. Neuschatz et al., 'False Memory Research: History, Theory, and Applied Implications', in Toglia et al., above n. 34.

[86] E. F. Loftus, 'Leading Questions and the Eyewitness Report' (1975) 7 *Cognitive Psychology* 560.

the latter's hair from straight to curly or by giving him a moustache.[87] Relevant to this 'misinformation effect' is research on the so-called 'recovered memory syndrome' (dubbed the 'false memory syndrome' by sceptics), in terms of which it is claimed that adults can recover vivid and detailed memories of traumatic incidents, often involving sexual abuse, which previously had only been experienced as a vague feeling that something had happened to them.[88] Thus one experiment reported that 25.5 per cent of participants recovered 'memories' of non-existent events when subjected to three sessions devoted to intensive reminiscence,[89] though it should be noted that by no means are all 'recovered memories' fictitious.[90]

Finally, new conflicting information might not totally replace old information, but lead witnesses to remember some sort of compromise between the two. For instance, in an experiment in which subjects witnessed a simulated incident involving eight demonstrators,[91] those who were asked a week later whether the leader of the *four* demonstrators was male, reported seeing an average of 6.4 demonstrators, whereas those who were asked whether the leader of the *twelve* demonstrators was male, reported an average of 8.9 demonstrators – a clear illustration of the 'anchoring and adjustment heuristic' encountered in Chapter Five.[92]

Studies have also highlighted various features of the process of memory contamination. One is that central and salient details are not just perceived and remembered more accurately than those seen as peripheral, but also that the chances of being able to change them is considerably reduced. Other important findings are that witnesses tend to be more resistant to misleading information when memories are fresh, rather than much later after the observed incident.[93] They are also resistant if the misleading information is implausible, contradicts clearly perceived information, is

---

[87]   F. Jenkins and G. Davies, 'Contamination of Facial Memory Through Exposure to Misleading Composite Pictures' (1985) 70 *Journal of Applied Psychology* 164.

[88]   See, for example, Kapardis, above n. 21, 80–7; A. Memon, A. Vrij and R. Bull, *Psychology and the Law: Truthfulness, Accuracy and Credibility* (2nd edn, 2004), Chapter 7; C. R. Brewin, 'Recovered Memory and False Memory', in Heaton-Armstrong et al., above n. 23; S. M. Smith and D. H. Gleaves, 'Recovered Memories', in Toglia et al., above n. 34.

[89]   I. E. Hyman, T. H. Husband and F. J. Billings, 'False memories of Childhood Experience' (1995) 9 *Applied Cognitive Psychology* 181, 192.

[90]   For example, in the study by B. Andrews et al., 'Characteristics, Context and Consequences of Memory Recovery Among Adults in Therapy' (1999) 175 *The British Journal of Psychiatry* 141, 41 per cent of recovered memories were corroborated in some way.

[91]   E. F. Loftus, 'Reconstructive Memory Processes in Eyewitness Testimony', in B. D. Sales (ed.), *The Trial Process* (1981).

[92]   Section 6.2.

[93]   E. F. Loftus, D. G. Miller and H. J. Burns, 'Semantic Integration of Verbal Information into a Visual Memory' (1978) 4 *Journal of Experimental Psychology: Human Learning and Memory* 19.

embedded in simple rather than complex sentences, and is inconsistent with or even irrelevant to existing schemas. Conversely, memory changes are more likely if witnesses are:[94]

- uncertain and reluctant to admit this, but feel pressurised to provide an answer;[95]
- involved in frequent attempts at recall;
- repeatedly exposed to the contaminating information; and
- not alerted to any discrepancy between their initial and later recall.

Memory changes are also more likely if the new information:

- comes from a source that seems authoritative, credible or, in the case of people, attractive;
- is received some time after the event;
- relates to peripheral rather than central details of the facts, and
- involves typical rather than atypical elements of schemas.[96]

Moreover, whatever the reason for memory contamination, once this occurs it is difficult to reverse.

2.4 Recall – The Retrieval Stage[97]
2.4.1 The Psychology of Recall[98]
Unless memory is permanently lost or altered, it is always capable of accurate recall. This might result spontaneously from what is variously called 'involuntary remembering', or 'serendipitous' or 'pop-up recall'.[99] But given that involuntary remembering is by definition beyond human control, we will concentrate on more controllable conditions that may help or hinder recall.

First, it can be noted that recall can take three forms:

(1) *Recognition*, which can vary from total certainty to merely a vague feeling of familiarity, involves witnesses re-encountering the original stimulus and regarding it as familiar, such as when they see or hear the person they are trying to remember;

---

[94] In addition to the specific references cited, see Haber and Haber, above n. 23, 1069–70.

[95] J. McEwan, *The Verdict of the Court: Passing Judgment in Law and Psychology* (2003), 97.

[96] E. García-Bajos and M. Migueles, 'False Memories for Script Actions in a Mugging Account' (2003) 15 *European Journal of Cognitive Psychology* 195. See further, Davis and Loftus, above n. 14, 214.

[97] See Loftus, above n. 14, Chapter 5; Jackson, above n. 23, 367–75 passim; Ainsworth, above n. 24, Chapter 7.

[98] See G. Cohen, above n. 24, 13–14.

[99] L. J. Jackson, R. Sijbing and M. G. Theicke, 'The Role of Human Memory Processes in Witness Reporting' (1997) 5 *Expert Evidence* 98, 100.

(2)   *Cued recall* occurs when a memory is recalled because of something with which it is linked. It may be spontaneous, such as when a smell or sound suddenly evokes a memory, or it may flow from a specific question such as, 'Do you remember that boring lecture on evidence?' The effectiveness of cued recall is dependent on whether the cues are part of the fact's original encoding. Hence, if the lecture was not originally encoded as boring, the cue might fail;

(3)   *Free recall* involves witnesses responding to open-ended questions like, 'Tell me everything you saw that day.'

In general, recall through recognition is easiest: one needs merely to accept or reject the stimulus in question. This is particularly so for stimuli which are difficult to put into words, such as music, faces and complex pictures, as opposed to incidents, which can be labelled with descriptors such as 'fight' or 'conversation' which evoke story schemas. Because of the questioner's assistance, cued recall is second in terms of ease of recollection. Without such help, free recall is most difficult. Consequently, in looking at the factors which help or hinder recall, we can start with how the information is sought, noting, however, that ease of recall or the amount of information generated does not necessarily denote accuracy.

2.4.2 Recall by Recognition: Identifying People[100]
While recall by recognition may involve an object or document, usually it will involve a person whose identity is crucial to fact finding. Notwithstanding that recognition is the easiest method of recall, as already noted,[101] mistaken identifications constitute the most common cause of miscarriages of justice, and presumably also lead to mistakes in non-criminal cases. In non-criminal cases, however, problems are confined to the already discussed inherent difficulties in accurately perceiving and remembering observed facts. Following Gary Wells,[102] factors affecting witnessing accuracy which relate

---

[100] The following draws generally on Ainsworth, above n. 24, Chapter 6; Cutler and Penrod, above n. 11, Chapter 8; Wagenaar, van Koppen and Crombag, above n. 11, Chapter 7; Wells et al., above n. 18; Kapardis, above n. 21, Chapter 9; Memon, Vrij and Bull, above n. 88, 120–5; R. P. Fisher and M. C. Reardon, 'Eyewitness Identification', in *D. Carson*, et al. (eds), *Applying Psychology to Criminal Justice* (2007); S. D. Gronlund, C. A. Goodsell and S. M. Andersen, 'Lineup Procedures in Eyewitness Identification', in Nadel and Sinnott-Armstrong, above n. 54. More specific references are given below. For an analysis of the Scottish position, see P. R. Ferguson, 'Identification Evidence and Its Problems: Recommendations for Change', in P. Duff and P. Ferguson (eds), *Current Developments in Scottish Criminal Evidence Law* (2017).

[101] Section 1.

[102] 'Applied Eyewitness-Testimony Research: System Variables and Estimator Variables' (1978) 36 *Journal of Personality and Social Psychology* 1546.

to the witness, the type of facts and conditions of observation are called 'estimator factors' because, while they may be manipulable in research, they cannot be controlled in real life by fact investigators, and hence their impact can only be estimated post hoc.[103] However, the process of identifying people in criminal proceedings carries with it additional problems arising from 'system variables' which *can* be controlled by fact investigators attempting to identify relevant persons.

While the Scottish courts still accept dock identifications,[104] notwithstanding obvious problems with the persuasiveness of witnesses pointing out an accused as the perpetrator, police officers attempt to provide more cogent evidence of out-of-court identifications by holding line-ups including the suspect and (hopefully) similar-looking 'foils' (also called 'stand-ins', 'fillers' or 'distractors'). If a foil is identified or no identification made, further investigation is required, but if the suspect is identified, this suggests that the witness is reliable and charges should be brought. Evidence of such identifications seems very powerful, but can be highly misleading, both because of the impact of estimator variables and because a desire to be helpful, see justice done and/or gain revenge may make witnesses – especially victims – overly ready to choose a line-up member. Little can be done to prevent such human motivations. The same does not apply to various 'system biases' relating to the conduct of line-ups and other recognition tests, such as showing witnesses photographs ('mugshots') or photo- or identikits of them or confronting them with suspects (called 'show-ups' in the US).

In fact, since 2007 the *Lord Advocate's Guidelines to Chief Constables on the Conduct of Visual Identification Procedures*[105] (henceforth, the *Guidelines*) have redressed most of these biases, not least because it has led to Video Identification Electronic Recordings (VIPERs) becoming the standard means of formal identification.[106] VIPERs involve witnesses being presented sequentially with video images of the head and shoulders of suspects and foils rotated 180 degrees. This accords with psychological research which shows that the optimum stance for identification is not full frontal, as in traditional live line-ups or photographs, but a three-quarter view.[107] On the other hand, it does not allow witnesses to draw on their recall of

---

[103] For an overview of estimator variables relating to identification evidence, see, for example, Cutler and Penrod, above n. 11, Chapters 6 and 7; Memon, Vrij and Bull, above n. 88, 109–20.

[104] Ferguson, above n. 100, 143.

[105] Available at http://www.copfs.gov.uk/images/Documents/Prosecution_Policy_Guidance/Lord_Advocates_Guidelines/Lord%20Advocates%20Guidelines%20-%20Conduct%20of%20Visual%20Identification%20Parades%20-%20February%202007.PDF (last accessed 25 March 2018).

[106] Ferguson, above n. 100, 141.

[107] Ainsworth, above n. 24, 67.

the suspect's whole physical appearance, which improves accuracy considerably.[108] Being easy to organise, VIPERs also reduce the impact of delay on memory, while their virtual nature prevents witnesses being intimidated by the suspect's presence and foils indicating the suspect's identity through body language and their lack of anxiety. Unsurprisingly, research shows the benefits of VIPERs over traditional live line-ups, reducing false alarms at least, though not in inducing more correct hits.[109]

The *Guidelines* also redress most system biases.[110] *Instruction biases* increase false identifications by encouraging witnesses to make identifications even when uncertain rather than, for instance, warning witnesses that suspects might not be present. It is therefore unfortunate that the *Guidelines* confine their recommended unbiased instructions to VIPERs and live line-ups, and then only as an example of 'appropriate' instructions.

More effectively dealt with are *investigator biases*, which involve officers conducting identity tests subconsciously – if not consciously – communicating the suspect's identity through body language, tone of voice, placement of the suspect, etc. Even if officers only confirm a witness' choice, this is likely to increase their confidence in that choice and this in turn, as we shall see,[111] artificially boosts their credibility. Thus, albeit again only in relation to VIPERs and live line-ups, the *Guidelines* prohibit officers involved with the investigation from administering the identification processes.

Even more obvious are *clothing biases* and closely related *foil biases* which, respectively, encourage witnesses to pick out suspects because they are dressed distinctively or otherwise dissimilar to stand-ins. Foil bias also flows from having insufficient numbers of similar foils,[112] because this increases reliance on vague recollections of the suspect's general features. Finding the right balance between reducing the consequent chances of false identifications and making correct identifications very difficult through too many similar foils has proved to be an intractable problem. By contrast, researchers have shown that using witnesses' initial description of suspects rather than their actual appearance to construct similarity with foils increases the rate of correct hits without increasing false alarms. While the *Guidelines* ignore this advice, they do require concealment of distinguishing features of suspects, whereas the requirements of a

---

[108] Cf. M. D. Macleod, J. N. Frowley and J. W. Shepherd, 'Whole Body Information: Its Relevance to Eyewitnesses', in Ross, Read and Toglia, above n. 6.

[109] T. Valentine, 'Forensic Facial Identification', in Heaton-Armstrong et al., above n. 23, 293–5.

[110] The following categorisation derives from Cutler and Penrod, above n. 11, Chapter 8. For other useful discussions of identification procedures, see Lindsay et al., above n. 14, Chapters 6–10.

[111] Section 3.2.2.

[112] See, for example, R. S. Malpass, C. G. Tredoux and D. McQuiston-Surrett, 'Lineup Construction and Lineup Fairness', in Lindsay et al., above n. 14.

minimum of eleven foils for photograph arrays and five for VIPERs and live identification parades exceed the minimum number suggested by researchers.

The final and most subtle bias identified by psychological research is *presentation-style bias*. Experiments repeatedly show that people who observe all suspects simultaneously are more likely to make a relative judgment of which line-up members most resemble their memory of the perpetrator rather than an absolute judgment of whether the person in front of them is the perpetrator. This in turn makes them more likely to make an identification rather than admit uncertainty, thus increasing both correct – but crucially, also false – identifications.[113] VIPERs and sequentially conducted photograph parades are thus an improvement on traditional simultaneous live line-ups. However, the encouragement of absolute rather than relative judgment is undermined by the *Guidelines*' requirement that witnesses consider all faces twice,[114] whereas not allowing witnesses to immediately identify the person they think is the perpetrator prevents fact finders relying on the fact that the spontaneity and swiftness of identifications are relatively reliable indicators of accuracy.[115]

It should be clear that VIPERs are far superior to traditional live parades in eliminating system biases. Moreover, live parades are, in turn, preferable to photospreads, unless the latter are presented sequentially and subjected to the same guidelines relating to eliminating investigator and instruction bias which expressly apply to VIPERS and live line-ups. Accordingly the *Guidelines* can be criticised for giving officers too broad a discretion to hold traditional live line-ups – if they think witnesses need to adopt a particular posture or moves – or photograph line-ups – where circumstances do not allow for physical identification.

Also prima facie problematic is the condonation of 'show-ups' where witnesses are presented with single suspects and asked whether they were the person they observed. This might occur where witnesses identify some-one near the place and shortly after the relevant incident (called 'informal identifications' by the *Guidelines*) or the accused is in custody and no other method is possible ('confrontation identification'). Although the absence of foils is unfair, show-ups have been shown to decrease the overall rate

---

[113] See especially P. R. Dupuis and R. C. L. Lindsay, 'Radical Alternatives to Traditional Lineups', in Lindsay et al., above n. 14.

[114] Cf. J. D. Pozzulo and R. C. L. Lindsay, 'Elimination Line-Ups: An Improved Identification Procedure for Child Witnesses' (1999) 84 *Journal of Applied Psychology* 167.

[115] D. D. Caputo and D. Dunning, 'Distinguishing Accurate Identifications from Erroneous Ones: Post-Dictive Indicators of Eyewitness Accuracy', in Lindsay et al., above n. 14, 439. See also L. B. Stern and D. Dunning, 'Distinguishing Accurate from Inaccurate Eyewitness Identifications: A Reality Monitoring Approach', in Ross, Read and Toglia, above n. 6; S. Charman and G. L. Wells, 'Applied Lineup Theory', in Lindsay et al., above n. 14.

of identification, thus ensuring more correct (but also incorrect) rejections of innocent suspects.[116] The accuracy of informal identifications is also enhanced by being conducted shortly after the relevant incident rather than days or weeks later afterwards.

However, the *Guidelines'* biggest flaw is that they do not regulate informal show-ups, the occasional use of voice identifications[117] or the more common form of informal identification aimed at finding rather than confirming a suspect by showing witnesses a series of 'mugshots' of previously arrested suspects. Moreover, limiting the requirement to record proceedings to serious cases allows unregulated investigator and instruction biases to go unnoticed in non-serious cases. Arguably resultant false identifications can be subsequently rectified by formal identification tests, but even leaving aside the anxiety, inconvenience and possible loss of liberty flowing from becoming a suspect, the 'commitment effect' discussed above[118] makes witnesses more likely to repeat in formal tests their previous informal identification of innocent persons. Equally we shall see that in terms of what is called 'unconscious transference',[119] even those who do not identify a suspect from mugshots may later subconsciously 'remember' them as the perpetrator.

2.4.3 Recall through Questioning[120]

While recognition tests are the most effective means to recall, far more common is questioning either in or outwith courts or other fact-finding fora by relevant legal actors like lawyers, administrative officials and police officers. Here, the accuracy of recall in response to questioning is a reflection of both a number of general factors as well as the techniques used.

One of these general factors is the *questioning style* used. Here, research[121] consistently establishes that more accurate, but less detailed, answers result from open questions which do not provide guidance on how they are to be answered or simply give a choice between options. Particularly effective are 'free narrative' directions such as 'Tell me everything that happened', rather than 'controlled narrative' questions such as 'What happened next?' By contrast, more complete, but less accurate, responses flow from the sort of closed questions asked in direct examination by lawyers, which provide

---

[116] Ebbesen and Konečni, above n. 35, 16; J. E. Dysart and R. C. L. Lindsay, 'Show-up Identifications: Suggestive Technique or Reliable Method?', in Lindsay et al., above n. 14.

[117] Cf. A. D. Yarmey, 'The Psychology of Speaker Identification and Earwitness Memory', in Lindsay et al., ibid., 126–8 on possible guidelines.

[118] Section 2.3.3.

[119] Section 2.5.1.

[120] See generally, Kapardis, above n. 21, 73–9 and 87–94 passim.

[121] See Clifford and Bull, above n. 1, 154–60; Loftus, above n. 14, 90–4; Greer, above n. 20, 148–50.

limited options from which to choose, such as 'Was the car red or blue?' Accordingly, interviewers are recommended to 'funnel'[122] questioning by starting with open-ended questions resulting in free narrative before moving to more closed questions probing for detail and clarification. If they start with closed questions, interviewees might assume that detailed answers are not required and make less effort to recall. Research also makes clear that, while cross-examination might be effective in challenging inaccurate or dishonest testimony (and unfairly disrupting accurate or honest testimony), highly controlled and leading questions cause less complete and accurate answers.

A second important factor affecting recall is *question wording*. Even slight differences in wording can lead to crucially different answers. For example, asking 'how tall' rather than 'how short' was the suspect increases height estimates. One insightful experiment showed that asking subjects who had viewed a simulated accident, 'Did you see *the*', as opposed to '*a* broken headlight?' led to subjects being three times more likely to falsely recalling a broken headlight.[123] Also influential are subtle changes in the meaning of synonyms. For example, in a study involving observation of a car accident, asking how fast were the cars going when they 'smashed' into each other led to estimates of 40.8 mph, dropping to, respectively, 34 mph and 20.8 mph when the words 'hit' and 'contact' were used.[124]

A third set of factors affecting recall involves its *timing, frequency* and the *number of participants*. As regards timing, holding interviews as soon as possible after events unsurprisingly improves the accuracy and completeness of recall, though it also makes more likely inconsistencies between accounts at interview and later testimony. Repeated questioning may increase the overall amount of information recalled (what is called hypermnesia), but also the chances of post-event memory alteration.[125] Consequently interviewers are recommended to hold a few interviews 'within a fairly short period of time'.[126] The impact of collaborative recall by witnesses is also two-edged, leading to both enhanced completeness, but also to cross-contamination of memory with false details.[127]

[122] R. P. Fisher and N. Schreiber, 'Interview Protocols for Improving Eyewitness Memory', in Toglia et al., above n. 34, 58. See more generally, Shepherd and Milne, above n. 26.

[123] E. F. Loftus and G. Zanni, 'Eyewitness Testimony: The Influence of the Wording of a Question' (1975) 5 *Bulletin of the Psychonomic Society* 86.

[124] Loftus and Palmer, above n. 82.

[125] See, for example, J. Cohen, above n. 29, 297–8.

[126] Read and Connolly, above n. 70, 145. See also Meissner, Sporer and Schooler, above n. 40, 18.

[127] Clifford and Bull, above n. 1, 160–2; Kapardis, above n. 21, 66–8; Meissner, Sporer and Schooler, ibid., 17.

Another relevant, but not particularly influential, factor is the *interviewer's identity*. Research reveals that those in authority such as police officers or of high status such as lawyers are likely to obtain longer, but no more accurate, reports and that the ability to influence interviewees increases as perceived credibility increases. It would also seem that questioners' attitudes are important, though supportive and friendly interviewers do not necessarily enhance recall accuracy.[128]

A final and far more determinative factor is that of *retrieval environment*. Studies establish that recall of information is more accurate when conducted in the same place as it was acquired. This was most strikingly shown by a study in which divers who had learnt information underwater had a substantial decrease in accuracy when recalling on land rather than underwater.[129] The atmosphere in which retrieval takes place is similarly important. Thus, in terms of what is called 'state dependent memory', more accurate recall results when witnesses' mood or state of mind when recalling mirrors that when witnessing.[130]

This last factor has obvious implications for *questioning techniques*[131] and has become an important element of the best known of various interview 'protocols' – Ronald Fisher and Ralph Geiselman's 'cognitive interview'. This encourages interviewees to focus their minds on the environment of the original perception, such as the location of objects, its physical conditions (temperature, humidity, etc.) and their feelings at the time, and to report every detail, however peripheral or irrelevant it may seem, including all sensory perceptions. Later they added a focus on ensuring social dynamics conducive to greater disclosure and more effective communication. Like similar but less well-known interview protocols, this 'enhanced cognitive interview' recommends that interviewers:

- establish a good rapport with interviewees;
- encourage interviewees' active participation by explicitly stressing their central role and eschewing closed questions;

---

[128] K. H. Marquis, J. Marshall and S. Oskamp, 'Testimony Validity as a Function of Question Form, Atmosphere, and Item Difficulty' (1972) 2 *Journal of Applied Social Psychology* 167.

[129] D. R. Godden and A. D. Baddeley, 'Context-Dependent Memory in Two Natural Environments: On Land and Under Water' (1975) 66 *British Journal of Psychology* 325.

[130] See Bower, above n. 49, but cf. L. M. Isbell and E C. Lair, 'Moods, Emotions, and Evaluations as Information', in Carlston, above n. 55, 445–7, noting that this impact is fragile and only emerges under very specific conditions.

[131] See, for example, Ainsworth, above n. 24, 99–112; Fisher and Schreiber, above n. 122; Jackson, Sijbing and Theicke, above n. 99, 101ff; B. R. Clifford and A. Memon, 'Obtaining Detailed Testimony: The Cognitive Interview', in Heaton-Armstrong, Shepherd and Wolchover, above n. 24.

- display empathy, understanding and patience in allowing interviewees to answer in their own time;
- anticipate feelings of guilt, shame, embarrassment, suffering, etc., and allow interviewees to regain composure between questions;
- reassure interviewees about their performance during the interview;
- ensure that the interview structure and questions align with the way interviewees think, and their general perceptual and cognitive skills;
- where relevant, encourage interviewees to convey information by drawing or using props (for example, dolls or replica weapons).

In addition, interviewers are advised not to:

- interrupt interviewees as this disrupts concentration, discourages retrieval effort, leads to shorter, less detailed answers, and signals a lack of respect for and interest in them and their answers;
- jump back and forth between topics, as this disrupts retrieval and discourages further effort at remembering detail on abandoned topics;
- immediately and aggressively challenge interviewees about inconsistencies;
- ask closed and in particular leading questions, as they may lead to short and frequently acquiescent affirmative answers as well as memory contamination;
- encourage or pressurise witnesses into making guesses.

Laboratory and field experiments show that the enhanced cognitive interview produces between 25 per cent and 45 per cent more accurate information than typical police interviews which eschew many of its techniques, while also inoculating interviewees against subsequent misleading information. On the other hand, it has had little success in enhancing suspect identification or constructing facial composites, and only mixed success with children. Furthermore, logistical and motivational factors mean that its techniques are not always fully or appropriately utilised by those trained to use them.[132]

Like the cognitive interview, hypnosis involves encouraging interviewees to relax, and concentrate on and take themselves back to the relevant events. However, hypnosis cannot miraculously enhance recall

---

[132] See, for example, R. Milne and R. Bull, 'Interviewing by the Police' and M. B. Powell and T. Bartholomew, 'Interviewing and Assessing Clients from Different Cultural Backgrounds: Guidelines for All Forensic Professionals', both in Carson and Bull, above n. 13. Lawyer training manuals have long drawn on psychological research on effective interviewing (see, for example, A. Sherr, *Client Interviewing for Lawyers: An Analysis and Guide* (1986)), though their impact has not been studied.

performance.[133] Indeed, research shows that it can be used to implant false information and that people lie under hypnosis, and hence that evidence obtained under hypnosis is justifiably treated by the courts with suspicion.[134]

But, whatever the merits of different interviewing techniques, it is clear that the questioning style used in formal proceedings – leading questions, aggressive cross-examination, breaches of conversational rules, arcane terminology, complex syntax, etc. – seems almost deliberately designed to undermine effective recall.

Interview techniques affect in similar ways the effectiveness of the police in obtaining confessions from suspects – and importantly also their accuracy.[135] At one stage, UK police tended to use the sort of 'accusatorial' techniques that are still used in the US, Asia and other parts of the world. These involve trying to pressurise suspects into confessing by controlling interviewing conditions in the way seen in Chapter Four and through coercion (such as by bullying, aggressive questioning and threatening to pursue family and friends), persuasion (emphasising possible leniency or suggesting that resistance is futile), the use of leading questions and other methods of suggestion. Moreover, manipulation and deception may be aimed at either 'maximisation' – suggesting that the case against the suspect is more serious than it is, such as by referring to non-existent evidence – or 'minimisation' – trying to lull the suspect into a false sense of security by showing sympathy, suggesting excuses, blaming the victim, etc.

Following legal reforms prompted by miscarriages of justice, UK police officers (or at least those in England and Wales) have come to adopt more 'information-gathering' strategies based, like the cognitive interview, on establishing rapport, being fair and truthful, displaying civilised social skills and using open-ended questions. As with the cognitive interview itself, these methods are more likely to induce confessions than accusatorial methods (though, even so, the police might be ineffective for other reasons like poor preparation, insufficient knowledge of the law, and so on). However, studies also show that when evidence is strong, officers are confident of guilt, and when offences are more serious they fall back on accusatorial methods which, while less effective in inducing confessions, increase the chances of them being false (and being excluded by the courts).

---

[133] Ainsworth, above n. 24, Chapter 8; Loftus, above n. 14, 104–8; G. F. Wagstaff, 'Hypnotically Induced Testimony', in Heaton-Armstrong, Shepherd and Wolchover, above n. 24.

[134] See the contrasting decisions on admissibility in *R v. Mayes* [1995] CLY 930 and *R v. Clark* [2006] EWCA Crim 23.

[135] See Gudjonsson, above n. 7, esp. Chapters 1–4; Howitt, above n. 19, Chapter 17; Kapardis, above n. 21, 347ff; R. Bull (ed.), *Investigative Interviewing* (2014), esp. Chapters 2–4, 9.

2.5 Variables Affecting Memory and Recall

Having looked at the generic factors which affect memory and recall, we turn now to how both processes are affected by the types of information and witnesses involved, concentrating for reasons of space on the main findings.

2.5.1 Types of Information and the Special Case of Face Identification

As regards types of information witnessed, we have hitherto largely concentrated on the witnessing of events, since they are the most common focus of attention in legal proceedings. However, probably because of its important role in miscarriages of justice, researchers have devoted far more effort to studying the identification of criminal suspects.

Here, numerous studies have established that our ability to accurately recognise unfamiliar faces is relatively poor, with rates estimated at between 40 and 65 per cent.[136] But when it comes to false identifications, meta-analyses (in other words, statistical analyses combining the results of multiple studies) reveal an average rate of between 29.8 per cent and 38.7 per cent of foils in parades where perpetrators were absent and 17 per cent to 21 per cent where they were present.[137] One reason for such inaccuracy is the tendency for (at least Caucasian) witnesses to focus more on 'external' face features such as hairstyle, which are not as useful identification clues as 'internal' features such as eyes, noses or face shape. These former are also more capable of being subsequently changed or covered, which is very effective in avoiding identification. In other respects, the ability to accurately recognise faces is affected by the same factors that influence perception, memory and recall generally. For instance, distinctive faces (for instance, those rated as highly attractive or unattractive) are better recognised than non-distinctive faces; longer exposure to unfamiliar faces improves recognition; whereas delay before identification line-ups increases false alarms, though does not reduce correct hits.[138]

If witnesses struggle to recognise unfamiliar faces, they are even worse at describing them, with accuracy estimates ranging from 25 per cent to 35 per cent.[139] This is perhaps one reason why various forms of translating descriptions into a visual representation of suspects to spur recognition are 'very imprecise tool[s] for conveying facial likeness'.[140] Indeed, artist

---

[136] Studies cited in McEwan, above n. 95, 203 n. 4. On face identification in general, see Cutler and Penrod, above n. 11, esp. Chapters 7–8; Loftus, above n. 14, Chapter 7; Ainsworth, above n. 24, Chapter 5; Memon, Vrij and Bull, above n. 90, 109–20.

[137] Reported by D. Davis and E. F. Loftus, 'Inconsistencies Between Law and the Limits of Human Cognition: The Case of Identification Evidence', in Nadel and Sinnot-Armstrong, above n. 54, 33.

[138] But see Ebbesen and Konečni, above n. 35, 7–8 for exceptions.

[139] McEwan above n. 95, 202 n. 3. See also Meissner, Sporer and Schooler, above n. 40.

[140] See, for example, G. Davies and T. Valentine, 'Facial Composites: Forensic Utility and Psychological Research', in Lindsay et al., above n. 14, 64.

impressions based on descriptions are no less effective than technically sophisticated mechanical systems, such as the Identikit and Photofit, or computer-generated images, which build up faces from component features (eyes, noses, mouths, etc.) selected by witnesses and hence allow for them to reject generated images. The role of description in identifying suspects and other relevant actors is even more problematic because of a frequently, but not invariably, observed 'verbal overshadowing effect', in terms of which describing suspects reduces witnesses' ability to later identify them, especially if they were forced to give detailed descriptions.

One very consistent finding is that witnesses are much better at identifying those in the same, as compared to a different, race group.[141] This 'cross-race effect' (mirrored in regard to voice recognition)[142] is mitigated by longer exposure to faces (and voices) and shorter delays between observation and identification, but not necessarily by training or frequent contact with those in the target's race group. Witnesses are also more likely to correctly identify people of the same age rather than those older or younger than themselves,[143] but a 'cross-sex effect' appears to be stronger with women rather than men.[144]

One particular problem with identification evidence – albeit not consistently experimentally supported[145] – involves so-called 'unconscious transference'. This involves witnesses identifying innocent persons as perpetrators because they remember them from some prior but innocent contact.[146] We have already noted this phenomenon in the context of mugshots,[147] but it may arise from any contact with an innocent person prior to the relevant incident, such as in a much-cited miscarriage of justice caused by a ticket attendant picking out an innocent sailor at a line-up because he had previously sold him rail tickets.

---

[141] See, for example, C. A. Meissner and J. C. Brigham, 'Thirty Years of Investigating the Own-Race Bias in Memory for Faces: A Meta-Analytic Review' (2001) 7 *Psychology, Public Policy, and Law* 3, 15; J. C. Brigham et al., 'The Influence of Race on Eyewitness Memory', in Lindsay et al., above n. 14.

[142] A. D. Yarmey, 'Earwitness Speaker Identification' (1995) 1 *Psychology, Public Policy, and Law* 792, 797–9.

[143] See, for example, Boyce, Beaudry and Lindsay, above n. 14, 512; Memon, Vrij and Bull, above n. 88, 115–16.

[144] M. A. Palmer, N. Brewer and R. Horry, 'Understanding Gender Bias in Face Recognition: Effects of Divided Attention at Encoding' (2013) 142 *Acta Psychologica* 362.

[145] See, for example, Elliott, above n. 52, 428–30; Fisher and Reardon, above n. 100, 34.

[146] See J. D. Read, 'Understanding Bystander Misidentifications: The Role of Familiarity and Contextual Knowledge' and D. F. Ross et al., 'Unconscious Transference and Lineup Identification: Toward a Memory Blending Approach', both in Ross, Read and Toglia, above n. 6.

[147] Section 2.4.2.

In general, then, it is fair to say that 'when a person is asked to identify someone he or she is being asked to do something that the normal human was not created to do'.[148] This applies even more to voice recognition, which at least in relation to unfamiliar voices is far less reliable than face identification for various reasons:[149] earwitnesses are far more susceptible to misleading post-event information than eyewitnesses; it is far easier to disguise voices than faces; changes in mood and emotion, as well as delay between exposure and identification, negatively affects voice far more than face recognition; and context reinstatement techniques do not aid voice recognition. Other factors affect voice recognition in ways similar to face identification, such as 'unconscious transference', the result of prior expectations, voice distinctiveness and longer exposure periods.

If face and voice recognition are problematic, witnesses struggle even more in relation to other types of information. Something read or heard sticks in the memory less than a visual scene or a facial image.[150] Consequently people find it more difficult to remember verbal and numerical information, such as dates, car registration and phone numbers and others' names. They also find it difficult to recall exactly what others say, especially if they only observe rather than participate in conversations and are not particularly interested in or motivated to puzzle over their meaning. On the other hand, memory is improved by violations of conversational rules or expectations, such as when low-status speakers make impolite requests. In other respects, however, memory for conversation is affected in much the same way as memory for events.[151]

2.5.2 Types of Witnesses[152]

Psychologists have extensively investigated whether some types of witnesses have better memories and more accurate recall than others. Surprisingly, they have found that work in occupations like the police

---

[148] Clifford and Bull, above n. 1, 16.

[149] See, for example, Ainsworth, above n. 24, Chapter 10; Yarmey, above n. 142; and 'Earwitness Evidence: Memory for a Perpetrator's Voice', in Ross, Read and Toglia, above n. 6; R. Bull and B. Clifford, 'Earwitness Testimony', in Heaton-Armstrong, Shepherd and Wolchover, above n. 24; A. D. Yarmey, A. L. Yarmey and M. J. Yarmey, 'Face and Voice Identification in Showups and Lineups' (1994) 8 *Applied Cognitive Psychology* 453.

[150] Cf. A. D. Yarmey and E. Matthys, 'Voice Identification of an Abductor' (1992) 6 *Applied Cognitive Psychology* 367.

[151] See Davis and Friedman, above n. 37.

[152] In addition to the specific references below, this section draws on Ainsworth, above n. 24, 41–8, Chapter 9; Kapardis, above n. 21, 53–69, Chapter 4 passim; Loftus, above n. 14, Chapter 8; Clifford and Bull, above n. 1, Chapter 7; Stone, above n. 33, Chapter 5; Cutler and Penrod, above n. 11, Chapter 6.

force or intelligence services which involve noticing facts does not improve memory.[153] Even more surprisingly, training in face recognition has only a marginal effect, except in relation to voice identification.[154]

Studies reveal no race and few gender differences in witnessing ability. Thus, in laboratory experiments, but not real-life situations involving stress, women are better at recognising faces, especially of other women, and have better memory for conversations.[155] More generally, each gender recalls some things better than others. For instance, in relation to a staged incident, women were more accurate in relation to female clothing and actions, and men in relation to the suspect's appearance and background information.[156]

Far more influential and probably the most significant individual variable affecting memory and recall is age.[157] Thus extensive recent research[158] shows that from around the age of two the witnessing abilities of children develop rapidly to the point where they may be as accurate as adults, at least for core details, and, contrary to common stereotypes, they are not notably more prone to fantasise. Nevertheless, children display various differences to adults in storing and recalling information. For instance, they tend to forget faster than adults and provide less information on recall, especially in response to open-ended questions and on peripheral details. This latter factor suggests greater use of closed questions and cued recall, but this in turn creates more opportunities for memory contamination. To make matters worse, until around four years old, children tend to be more susceptible than adults to the influence of interviewers.[159] For instance, they are more likely to interpret repeated questioning on the same topic as indicating that their first answer was wrong, be intimidated by those in authority, confabulate based on inferences about people or

---

[153] But cf. the two contrary findings cited by Pickel, above n. 53, 344.

[154] Yarmey, in Lindsay et al., above n. 14, 113.

[155] Friedman and Davis, above n. 37.

[156] P. A. Powers, J. L. Andriks and E. F. Loftus, 'Eyewitness Accounts of Females and Males' (1979) 64 *Journal of Applied Psychology* 339.

[157] For detailed discussions, see the chapters in Part III of Toglia et al., above n. 34.

[158] See, for example, Spencer and Flin, above n. 38, Chapters 11–12; A. Mortimer and E. Shepherd, 'The Frailty of Children's Testimony', in Heaton-Armstrong, Shepherd and Wolchover, above n. 24; M. E. Lamb et al., 'Enhancing Performance: Factors Affecting the Informativeness of Young Witnesses', in Toglia et al., above n. 34; M.-E. Pipe, K. L. Thierry and M. E. Lamb, 'The Development of Event Memory: Implications for Child Witness Testimony', in Toglia et al., ibid. Note that we will only look at children's memory and recall outwith court; as regards the specific problems of child and other vulnerable witnesses, see, for example, L. Ellison, *The Adversarial Process and the Vulnerable Witness* (2001).

[159] See L. Melnyk, A. M. Crossman and M. H. Scullion, 'The Suggestibility of Children's Memory', in Toglia et al., above n. 34.

their behaviour provided by the interviewer, and respond to accusations of lying by changing their story. Furthermore, not only are children more likely to incorporate information provided by others, but they are also subsequently less likely to be able to distinguish information they obtained themselves from that obtained from other sources. Children's greater weakness at such 'source-monitoring' also means that they are more likely than adults to incorrectly incorporate knowledge from general schemas into reports of specific events and to conflate the details of separate but similar experiences. Moreover, unlike adults, they tend to remember unusual events better than those congruent with existing scripts. On the other hand, because stereotypes and heuristics develop over time they are less prone to their influence.

A final difference between adults and children flows from the latter's inferior communication skills. This hinders recall in various ways. First, children are less able to understand interviewers, especially if they use complex syntax and questioning styles, such as double negatives and multi-part questions. Secondly, children may not fully understand words used or conversation rules and this may lead interviewers – who tend in general to overestimate children's linguistic abilities – to misinterpret long pauses as involving incomprehension, lack of inattention or disengagement. Thirdly, children may lack the vocabulary to convey their memories or the necessary episodic and theoretical knowledge to enrich and clarify their descriptions. Finally, children find it difficult to place events in chronological order, appreciate temporal concepts like yesterday or a week ago, and to understand numerical concepts.

Accordingly it is recognised that interview techniques need to be adapted for children,[160] not least because interview quality has arguably the greatest effect on the accuracy and completeness of children's reports. Particularly effective in this regard and in reducing suggestibility is time spent on establishing rapport and assessing the particular child's cognitive understanding and linguistic skills, being supportive and exhaustively using open-ended questions and probes to prompt cued recall before moving to more focused questions. In addition, specific instructions can counter children's desire to please adults by providing answers even when they do not know the answers or understand the questions. Asking children to demonstrate events using dolls or other props or through drawings

---

[160] See the Scottish Government's *Guidance on Interviewing Child Witnesses in Scotland – Supporting Child Witnesses Guidance Pack* (2003), available at http://www.scotland.gov.uk/Publications/2003/09/18265/27045 (last accessed 22 December 2014).

is also helpful in increasing the number of accurate details, but unfortunately it also increases inaccurate details.

At the other end of the age spectrum, the memory and recall (though not
necessarily perception) of elderly witnesses may equal that of younger adults.[161]
Nevertheless, ageing causes brain cell decay and this has disparate effects on
different individuals, making the witnessing performance of the elderly much
more heterogeneous than that of younger adults and children. Moreover,
ageing has some general effects which lead to problems surprisingly similar
to those experienced by children. Thus, compared to younger adults, elderly
witnesses tend to forget information faster and make more source-monitoring
errors, and hence are more susceptible to misinformation effects from post-
event information. Moreover, they struggle to recall the temporal order of
events, the layout of relevant locations, to recognise voices and to remember
more specific as opposed to general details of events. Given such problems, it
is not surprising that in a series of tests, compared to younger adults, elderly
witnesses were 20 per cent less accurate in free recall, 13 per cent in cued recall
and 15 per cent less complete in describing the perpetrator.[162]

Equally unsurprising is the impact on memory and recall of various
physical and mental illnesses, disabilities or impairments.[163] Most problematic are dementia and Parkinson's disease, which start by distorting memory and end with witnesses unable to provide any meaningful testimony.
Those suffering from Alzheimer's Disease, schizophrenia and severe forms
of epilepsy and depression have impaired memory and recall performance,
and make more source-monitoring errors, though they do not generate
significantly high rates of false memories. Head injuries can cause loss of
memory of events before and after the event (retrograde and post-traumatic amnesia respectively) but not necessarily permanently. We have
already seen that stress affects perception.[164] When serious enough to cause
post-traumatic stress disorder, stress can also lead to a failure to remember
some or even all aspects of traumatic events.[165] Depending on the level of
severity, those with learning difficulties may struggle with recall given their

---

[161] See, for example, Mueller-Johnson and Ceci, above n. 34; D. J. LaVoie, H. K. Mertz and
T. L. Richmond, 'False Memory Susceptibility in Older Adults: Implications for the Elderly
Eyewitness', in Toglia et al., above n. 34; and C. J. A. Moulin et al., 'Eyewitness Memory in
Older Adults', ibid.
[162] Mueller-Johnson and Ceci, ibid., 587.
[163] See Gudjonsson, above n. 9; Norfolk, above n. 47.
[164] Section 2.2.3.
[165] Though there are many cases of people who report clear and detailed (though not necessarily accurate) memories of traumatic events: see, for example, J. Thompson, T. Morton and
L. Fraser, 'Memories for the Marchioness' (1997) 5 *Memory* 615.

reduced ability to understand questions and communicate information, but also their weakened memory capacity. They are also more prone to distorting or fabricating evidence, and more suggestible (prone to accepting the version of events being expressly suggested or implied), compliant (eager to please interviewers and thus go along with what is being suggested though not consciously accepting that it is correct) and acquiescent (answering questions affirmatively irrespective of content).[166] By contrast, autistic witnesses may perform as well as or even better than non-autistic witnesses on tasks such as memorising words, but worse on those more common to legal fact finding, such as remembering faces and events.

While the impact of sustained alcohol and drug abuse has not been extensively researched, studies reveal that temporary drug use may not necessarily impair, and in fact may enhance, memory and recall (as opposed to perception). On the other hand, even moderate intoxication may reduce memory, particularly for peripheral details, and make subjects more susceptible to falsely identifying suspects[167] and to memory contamination.[168] The fact that information acquired while intoxicated may be better recalled when intoxicated raises interesting ethical questions for fact investigators!

In addition to the more obvious individual factors affecting witnessing just discussed, psychologists have begun to look at the possible impact of personality differences and cognitive styles of perceiving, remembering and thinking about information.[169] Studies have shown that greater witnessing accuracy is achieved by those who are introverted rather than extroverted, who conceive of items of information as part of (rather than separable from) the context in which they are embedded ('field-dependence' rather than 'field-independence') and who assimilate new information to previously perceived and stored information, rather than keeping new and existing information separate ('levelling' as opposed to 'sharpening'). However, such research is in its infancy and focuses on face recognition, and in any event it is unlikely that many legal actors will have the time and resources to ascertain relevant information about witnesses' personality and cognitive style.

By contrast, given the implications for detecting crime and protecting civil liberties, the legal system has a much greater incentive and justification for

[166] See in more detail, G. H. Murphy and I. C. H. Clare, 'The Effect of Learning Disabilities on Witness Testimony', in Heaton-Armstrong et al., above n. 23.
[167] Memon, Vrij and Bull, above n. 90, 111.
[168] See Soraci et al., loc. cit., n. 45; Lader, in Heaton-Armstrong, Shepherd and Wolchover, above n. 24; H. V. Curran, 'Effects of Drugs on Witness Memory', in Heaton-Armstrong et al., above n. 23.
[169] See Clifford and Bull, above n. 1, 176–85; H. Hosch, 'Individual Differences in Personality and Eyewitness Identification', in Ross, Read and Toglia, above n. 6.

using the much more well-established findings[170] on the propensity of certain types of criminal suspects to confess and crucially to do so even when they are not guilty. More generally, empirical studies establish that suspects' propensity to confess – and crucially to make false confessions – varies according to certain personal characteristics.[171] Thus there is evidence that older suspects are less likely to confess, but that this is not simply a feature of age but related to life experience and that the very old are as prone to confess as the very young. Surprisingly, one life experience which has been shown – albeit not consistently – to increase the chances of a false confession is previous convictions and incarceration. Less surprisingly, being under the influence of alcohol and drugs may increase the chances of false confessions, but even more so does the effect of drug withdrawal. However, perhaps the greatest personal predictor of whether suspects are likely to confess is whether they are subject to various psychological vulnerabilities such as mental disorders, abnormal mental states (such as extreme anxiety and relevant phobias),[172] and learning disabilities. All of these – and possibly also race[173] – make people more prone to suggestibility and compliance[174] – a tendency which the psychologist Gisli Gudjonsson and his colleagues claim can be measured on what are called the Gudjonsson Suggestibilty and Compliance scales.[175]

However, most confessions do not stem solely from individual psychology. Usually also relevant are two other factors. One is the perception by suspects of the strength of the evidence against them, which may make them realise that denial is pointless and confession beneficial. The other is the pressures emanating from the form of the questioning and the tactics employed by the police discussed earlier,[176] as well as the inherent stress and anxiety caused by being in intimidating and unfamiliar environments, isolated from supportive others,[177] in which suspects are under the control of authority figures. Faced with such stress, some suspects confess to end their discomfort and this is why the presence of legal advisors

---

[170] The following discussion draws on Gudjonsson, above n. 7, Chapters 3–8, 13–14; Kapardis, above n. 21, Howitt, above n. 19; K. A. Houston, C. A. Meissner and J. R. Evans, 'Psychological Processes Underlying True and False Confessions', in Bull, above n. 135.

[171] But evidently not gender.

[172] On the other hand, mood variables like anger and suspicion may reduce suspect suggestibility: Gudjonssen, above n. 7, Chapter 14.

[173] Gudjonssen, ibid., noting one study's finding of greater suggestibility on the part of Afro-Caribbeans.

[174] On the other hand, temporary moods like anger may reduce these tendencies.

[175] See Gudjonsson, above n. 7, Chapter 14.

[176] Section 2.4.3.

[177] Gudjonsson, above n. 7, 148–50, at least if they act zealously and effectively (see Chapter 4, section 2.4.2).

for all suspects and appropriate adults for children and other vulnerable suspects[178], plus short periods of interrogation, are important in reducing the likelihood of false confessions.

As a result of these insights, researchers classify confessions into various categories, depending on, firstly, whether the confession is purely voluntary (because of a desire to please or to assuage feelings of guilt, protect others to avoid another more serious crime being investigated) or in some way coerced (for instance, by the situation and/or police tactics), and, secondly, whether the suspect merely goes along with the interviewers or actually comes to believe in their guilt (compliant versus internalised confessions). At the same time, just as Gudjonsson's suggestibility and compliance tests cannot identify when a confession is false, so it has proved impossible in general to identify which confessions are true or false. Nevertheless, it has been found that true confessions are more likely to result from internal pressures, such as a need to confess, but also perceptions of the strength of the evidence, whereas false confessions are more likely to result from external pressures such as police questioning or the stress of being incarcerated.[179] Moreover, according to Gudjonsson, it is easier to identify an internalised, as opposed to a compliant, false confession because of the tentative nature of the language used, the nature of the preceding interviewing and prominent psychological vulnerabilities.[180]

2.6 Conclusion

In general, the preceding discussion should not make us very hopeful of witnesses – including suspects – providing accurate evidence in legal proceedings. As a pithy summary of research findings, the words of Sally Lloyd-Bostock are particularly apposite:

> Our memories may serve us extremely well for the most part, but human memory was not designed for the benefit of the legal system. When a person is asked to describe events or identify someone after seeing them only briefly and possibly not having paid a lot of attention to them, he or she is being asked to do something that the memory is not adapted to do well.[181]

But what of the other side of the witnessing coin – the witnessing of witnesses?

---

[178] See Scottish Government, *Guidance on Appropriate Adult Services in Scotland* (2007), available at http://www.gov.scot/resource/doc/1099/0053903.pdf (last accessed 7 March 2018).

[179] See esp. Houston, Meissner and Evans, above n. 170.

[180] Above n. 7, 626.

[181] S. Lloyd-Bostock, *Law in Practice: Applications of Psychology to Legal Decision Making and Legal Skills* (1988), 4.

3 Witnessing the Witnesses: The Accuracy of Witness Evaluation[182]

3.1 Introduction

Broadly speaking, there are two ways[183] to evaluate the accuracy and honesty[184] of witnesses, including suspects[185] who either deny or confess to committing crimes.[186] *Intrinsic evaluation* involves fact finders evaluating the testimony itself and the testifying witness. More specifically, *testimony-focused intrinsic evaluation* focuses on:

- what is said (for example, its internal consistency, consistency with external information, how much detail is provided and the extent to which it reports not just what happened but also why);
- how it is said (with what degree of confidence, tone of voice, accompanying body language, etc.); and
- by whom (their perceived authoritativeness, status, reliability, honesty, etc.).

This process is sometimes called post-diction evaluation because it involves predicting past events based on current conditions. The other form of intrinsic evaluation – what can be called *witnessing-focused intrinsic evaluation* – involves consideration of the various estimator and system variables which influence the accuracy of witness reports.

Extrinsic evaluation involves assessment of the extent to which one can trust a witness' report given information not derived from the report itself, but which is provided by other witnesses or sources of evidence relevant to the facts in dispute – what can be called *case-specific extrinsic evaluation* – or which is based on general knowledge about how the world works – *generic extrinsic evaluation*.

---

[182] See in general Leippe, above n. 14, 924–32 and 'The Appraisal of Eyewitness Testimony', in Ross, Read and Toglia, above n 6.

[183] Cf. Leippe, 'The Appraisal of Eyewitness Testimony', ibid., 386–8, for a slightly different analysis.

[184] Usually described as reliability and credibility respectively, but cf. D. Nicolson and D. Auchie, 'Assessing Witness Credibility and Reliability: Engaging Experts and Disengaging Gage?', in Duff and Ferguson, above n. 100, for a slightly different definition.

[185] In what follows, witnesses can be taken where relevant to include suspects, but see the discussion of the evaluation of confessions in section 4.1 below.

[186] For a detailed list of relevant factors, see D. A. Binder and P. Bergman, *Fact Investigation: From Hypothesis to Proof* (1984), Chapter 8.

In reality, all fact finders engage in both intrinsic and extrinsic evaluation when assessing witness reports.[187] Even where there is no other direct evidence, fact finders will assess witness plausibility in terms of background information, such as when immigration officials evaluate asylum applicants' stories in terms of consistency with their knowledge of conditions in the originating country. Moreover, intrinsic and extrinsic evaluations often interrelate in important ways. Thus they may confirm each other, such as when intrinsic judgments of the likely inaccuracy of testimony are confirmed by its perceived inherent implausibility or contradictory evidence, or where testimony regarded as intrinsically reliable is supported by other evidence and by theoretical knowledge. Conversely, positive intrinsic evaluations of testimony may be undermined by overwhelming contrary evidence and/or its perceived implausibility, whereas testimony judged to be intrinsically unreliable may in fact be supported by specific evidence or theoretical knowledge.

Given that the factors which affect the extrinsic evaluation of witnesses are not specific to testimony, but apply to all forms of evidence, involve various cognitive processes such as logic, heuristics and narrative, and are affected by presentational rhetoric, we will explore this dimension of witness evaluation as part of the psychology of proof in Chapter Seven. Here we will concentrate on the ability of fact finders to make accurate intrinsic evaluations of witness reports, looking more specifically at their ability to rely on relevant and reliable factors, and to ignore irrelevant and unreliable factors.

However, before doing so, it is worth recalling the distinction discussed in the previous chapter[188] between 'systematic' or 'central route' processing involving consideration of the testimony's content, its coherence and consistency with other evidence and relevant factors affecting witness reliability, on the one hand, and 'heuristic' or 'peripheral route' processing based on non-content-based cues such as witnesses' status or attractiveness, whether they look questioners in the eye, and the length of their message, on the other hand. Intrinsic evaluation may therefore involve both systematic/central route processing where witnessing-focused conditions affecting the reliability of testimony are considered, and heuristic/peripheral route processing when factors involving the witness' status and how they deliver their testimony which have no relation to their likely reliability are considered. We therefore need to focus on the ability and willingness of fact finders to focus on, and only on, relevant witnessing- and testimony-focused factors.

---

[187] For empirical evidence of this, see W. Young, N. Cameron and Y. Tinsley, *Juries In Criminal Trials, Part Two: A Summary of Research Findings* (1999), 27.

[188] Section 7.3.1.

3.2 Assessing Witness Accuracy

3.2.1 Witnessing-focused Evaluation[189]

For over thirty years, numerous studies have investigated the ability of potential and actual fact finders to accurately assess the reliability of witnesses, albeit predominantly in the sphere of eyewitness identification. Most commonly, their knowledge of the various factors affecting witnessing has been directly sought by comparing their knowledge of witnessing with that of experts through multiple choice or simple agree/disagree formats. While early surveys revealed an average agreement rate between subjects and experts as low as 24 per cent, it has steadily increased over the years, rising to as high as 80 per cent in a recent survey.[190] This increase may of course be due to increased public knowledge, but it is equally like to stem from the use of more comprehensible questionnaires and those with agree/disagree formats which increase the possibility of lucky guesses. Gaining an overall picture of accuracy is, however, impossible because the surveys do not always focus on the same factors or use the same question wording. However, a meta-analysis of twenty-three studies involving 4,669 respondents revealed an average agreement rate of 68 per cent on sixteen factors most commonly included in studies on which more than 80 per cent of experts agreed.[191] However, while there was an average agreement rate of 68 per cent, agreement differed substantially between different factors. Thus at one extreme there was an agreement rate of over 80 per cent on the impact of intoxication, pre-existing attitudes and expectations, question wording, and the malleability of witness confidence, but at the other extreme less than 60 per cent on weapon focus, the cross-race effect, hypnotic suggestibility and the link between witness confidence and accuracy. Admittedly these surveys beg the question as to the accuracy of the experts' own views – even an 80 per cent agreement rate between experts suggests serious room for doubt, whereas today's psychological 'truth' can always become tomorrow's 'fallacy'.

Nevertheless, many of the lay misconceptions revealed by the surveys are replicated by studies which indirectly test lay knowledge by ascertaining

---

[189] This section draws on Cutler and Penrod, above n. 11, Part V; T. R. Benton et al., 'Has Eyewitness Testimony Research Penetrated the American Legal System? A Synthesis of Case History, Juror Knowledge, and Expert Testimony', in Lindsay et al., above n. 14; Chapters 1, 3, 6, 7, 8 and 10 in Cutler, above n. 14.

[190] See S. L. Desmarais and J. D. Read, 'After 30 Years, What do we Know about What Jurors Know? A Meta-Analytical Review of Lay Knowledge Regarding Eyewitness Factors' (2011) 35 *Law and Human Behavior* 200.

[191] Ibid.

how it is used in making decisions. One method involves presenting subjects with actual studies on the impact of various factors affecting witnessing accuracy and asking them to predict the outcome.[192] Others involve asking subjects to either identify factors which determine witness reliability in particular situations or to assess witness accuracy either directly or through delivering a verdict in response to situations presented in written descriptions, videotapes or mock trials in which different witnessing factors are manipulated. All paint a far less optimistic picture of fact finders' abilities to accurately assess witness reliability than the surveys where subject performance can be boosted by educated or lucky guesses. Thus, even when prompted, subjects tended to be insensitive to the impact of a wide variety of factors on witness accuracy. These include those that the surveys suggest are relatively well understood, most notably system variables, but extend also, for instance, to the effect of lighting, stress, weapon focus, crime duration on perception, the effect of delay[193] between the incident and recall on memory, and the effect of disguises in preventing identification. Furthermore, when subjects do consider relevant factors they sometimes (as with foil and instruction bias) apply them contrary to their actual effect or (as with the cross-race effect) underestimate their impact.

3.2.2 Testimony-focused Evaluation[194]
Studies also show that participants tend to give undue prominence to estimator variables related to witness characteristics, whereas they have far less of an impact than system and other estimator variables. In any event, their exact contours do not seem to be well-understood by study participants, who are also influenced by characteristics that have no possible link to accuracy such as status, grooming, attractiveness and likeability.[195] No doubt, various stereotypes about different groups of people also affect whether they are believed, but little relevant research has been conducted.[196]

---

[192] Here again, the 'prediction studies' are dependent on the validity of the finding subjects are asked to predict, as well as on how accurately studies are described to subjects.
[193] According to Wells et al., above n. 11, 18, but not R. C. L. Lindsay, 'Expectations of Eyewitness Performance: Jurors' Verdicts do not Follow from their Beliefs', in Ross, Read and Toglia, above n. 6, 367.
[194] This section draws extensively on Leippe, 'The Appraisal of Eyewitness Testimony', above n. 182. Additional references are provided where relevant.
[195] Loftus, above n. 14, 13–14; Lindsay, above n. 193, 368; C. Fife-Schaw, 'The Influence of Witness Appearance and Demeanour on Witness Credibility', in Heaton-Armstrong et al., above n. 23.
[196] Cf., however, S. J. Sherman et al., 'Stereotype Development and Formation', in Carlston, above n. 55, regarding the general impact of stereotypes.

By contrast, extensive research has been conducted on post-dictive factors relating to how witnesses testify.[197] The most influential of these include the consistency of witnesses' accounts,[198] their speech-style and the amount of detail provided. As regards speech-style, witnesses are more likely to be believed if they speak in a narrative rather than fragmented style,[199] and adopt 'powerful' as opposed to 'powerless' speech (with the latter being characterised by the use of hedges, such as 'I think' and 'it seemed', modifiers like 'sort of' and 'kind of', hesitation forms like 'uh' and 'um', rising intonation as if seeking approval, repetition as an indication of insecurity, intensifiers such as '*very* close friends', frequent direct quotations as indicating a deference to the authority of others, polite forms such as the use of 'sir/madam' and 'please', and empty adjectives such as 'divine').[200]

However, probably the most influential of all – not just post-dictive – clues is witness confidence as expressly stated by witnesses themselves or inferred by evaluators. For instance, one study revealed that perceived witness confidence accounted for more than 50 per cent of the variance in participants' assessment of witness accuracy.[201] Moreover, the impact of confidence is difficult to shake even when fact finders are faced with conflicting evidence or when confidence is debunked as an accurate clue by expert evidence.[202]

Recent research suggests that confidence, consistency, detail and speech-style do have some value as indicators of accuracy. Certainly, as we have seen,[203] automatic and spontaneous identifications are good indicators of accuracy. However, identification involves a recognition task, which differs to that of recall, and is usually not observed by fact finders. As regards recall, 'reality monitoring theory' and some studies suggest that the recall of events actually experienced, rather than imagined or

---

[197] See, for example, Loftus, above n. 14, Chapters 2, 12–13.

[198] See Boyce, Beaudry and Lindsay, above n. 14, 510–11; J. Cohen, above n. 29; J. McEwan, 'Reasoning, Relevance and Law Reform: The Influence of Empirical Research on Criminal Adjudication' in P. Roberts and M. Redmayne (eds), *Innovations in Evidence and Proof: Integrating Theory, Research and Teaching* (2007) 196–7; R. Byrne, 'Assessing Testimonial Evidence in Asylum Proceedings: Guiding Standards from the International Criminal Tribunals' (2007) *International Journal of Refugee Law* 609.

[199] See Chapter 3, section 3.1.4.

[200] See, for example, J. M. Conley, W. M. O'Barr and E. A. Lind, 'The Power of Language: Presentational Style in the Courtroom' (1978) 27 *Duke Law Journal* 1375; W. M. O'Barr, *Linguistic Evidence: Language, Power, and Strategy in the Courtroom* (1982).

[201] See, for example, G. L. Wells, R. C. L. Lindsay and T. J. Ferguson, 'Accuracy, Confidence, and Juror Perceptions in Eyewitness Identification' (1979) 64 *Journal of Applied Psychology* 440. See also Cutler and Penrod, above n. 11, 207–9; Lindsay, above n. 193, 373.

[202] See studies cited in Leippe, above n. 14, 926 and 942.

[203] At n. 115.

the result of misleading suggestions, will contain more contextual, spatial and sensory detail (for instance as to time, place, colour and shapes), and be delivered more confidently, with fewer verbal hedges, admissions of uncertainty and reference to cognitive processing such as what witnesses were thinking while observing facts. Unfortunately, however, experiments suggest that people are not particularly good at assessing accuracy from these clues.

In any event, they are less helpful in assessing whether the recall of actually observed rather than imagined or suggested facts is mistaken and incomplete. Thus witnesses with accurate memories of central details of events may remember few or no peripheral details or may make mistakes on them.[204] As we have also seen,[205] peripheral details are also more susceptible to subsequent alteration, especially if witnesses are required to make repeated reports and are questioned closely on these details.[206] Moreover, skilled lawyers can easily induce witnesses into contradicting themselves, such as by asking witnesses to repeat information in order to suggest that their first account was unsatisfactory and entice them to supply different details. Conversely, even important details may be omitted from early accounts because of their traumatic impact,[207] embarrassment or other understandable reasons. Consequently fact finders ought to be cautious about attaching significance to inconsistent or sketchy reports, not least because consistent accounts may reflect an ability to organise information rather than a coherent memory. Similar caution also needs to be exercised in making inferences about witnesses who appear to be unconfident or use powerless speech, as this may be due to personality traits like shyness or due to gender, race or class rather than unreliability, especially as research confirms that people are influenced by the perceived social origins of speakers.[208]

As regards confidence more generally, years of research reveal that, whereas it *may* reliably indicate accuracy in certain circumstances, such as when witnesses are confident about one aspect of the fact but not others,[209] more commonly there is at best only a modest link between con-

---

[204] See, for example, G. L. Wells and M. R. Leippe, 'How Do Triers of Fact Infer the Accuracy of Eyewitness Identifications? Using Memory for Peripheral Detail Can Be Misleading' (1981) 66 *Journal of Applied Psychology* 682.

[205] Section 2.3.4.

[206] McEwan, above n. 198, 196–7.

[207] See J. Cohen, above n. 29.

[208] The classic study is H. Giles and P. F. Powesland, *Speech Style and Social Evaluation* (1975).

[209] But even then there is a 15 per cent error rate: H. L. Roediger, J. H. Wixted and K. A. Desoto, 'The Curious Complexity between Confidence and Accuracy in Reports from Memory', in

fidence and accuracy, sometimes no link at all, and in rare cases even a negative correlation.[210] For example, the modest relation between the confidence and accuracy of person identification exists only for those who pick out, rather than decline to identify, suspects in identification tests,[211] and for the identification of familiar rather than unfamiliar voices.[212] The accuracy–confidence relation also depends on a number of variables,[213] with confidence being more predictive of accuracy of suspect identifications the sooner they are made after observation, the longer the exposure time and the more the attention paid to suspects. But whereas these factors increase confidence *and* accuracy, other factors like the familiarity or vividness of the facts being recalled and the fact that their reports led to legal proceedings, may increase witnesses' confidence without being related to accuracy.

More worryingly, confidence can be inadvertently or even deliberately enhanced by repeatedly going over the same issues, repeatedly asking witnesses to think about their answers, preparing witnesses for trials, and providing positive feedback on witness reports or identification of suspects.[214] Fortunately such line-up abuses are addressed by the ban in the *Lord Advocate's Guidelines*[215] on investigating officers conducting VIPERs and traditional live line-ups (but not other forms of formal identification) and the requirement that officers take steps to prevent witnesses communicating with each other and thereby boosting confidence levels. On the other hand, confidence or at least the appearance of it can be reduced by aggressive cross-examination, as well as the general unfamiliarity of and stress associated with court and other legal proceedings.[216]

Nevertheless, a recent summary of research concludes that confidence is a relatively reliable but imperfect indicator of accuracy, at least in the absence of any possible sources of post-event memory and confidence

---

Nadel and Sinnott-Armstrong, above n. 54, 109.

[210] See, for example, Roediger, Wixted and Desoto, ibid.; J. S. Shaw, K. A. McClure and J. A. Dykstra, 'Eyewitness Confidence from the Witnessed Event Through Trial', in Toglia et al., above n. 34; C. A. E. Luus and G. L. Wells, 'Eyewitness Identification Confidence', in Ross, Read and Toglia, above n. 6. More specific references are given below.

[211] Memon, Vrij and Bull, above n. 88, 112; Caputo and Dunning, above n. 115, 432.

[212] Yarmey, in Lindsay et al., above n. 14, 110–11.

[213] For example, Caputo and Dunning, above n. 115, 431–2; Brewer, Weber and Semmler, above n. 74, 210–12; Kapardis, above n. 21, 62.

[214] See, for example, Fisher and Reardon, above n. 100, 32–3; Brewer, Weber and Semmler, ibid., 213–14.

[215] Above n. 106.

[216] Leippe, 'The Appraisal of Eyewitness Testimony', above n. 182, 396; McEwan, above n. 95, 99.

manipulation, and particularly as regards recognition and recall shortly after the relevant incidents rather than much later in court.[217] But even so, it is generally accepted that it is too risky in criminal cases to rely on the evidence of one highly confident witness – even if this were allowed in Scotland.

3.2.3 Conclusion

While there are numerous problems with methodology and consistency of results, overall the studies are said to 'converge' on the broad findings that lay adjudicators have an incomplete and sometimes incorrect understanding of the factors which affect witness accuracy and that even when they correctly understand such factors, they do not necessarily incorporate them into their decision-making. Moreover, evaluating the clues to witness accuracy is sometimes too taxing for fact finders, who might then respond to the resultant cognitive overload by relying on irrelevant factors like witness attractiveness and status or, at best, giving undue prominence to other testimony-focused factors like confidence and consistency. Indeed, research suggests that many mock jurors are unaware of the factors that affect their decisions about witness reliability and, when asked, provide ex post facto rationalisations for decisions about witnesses which stem from preconceived hypotheses about the facts as a whole.[218]

But whatever the exact reasons for the limits to fact finders' capabilities, it is clear that they have at best only a moderate ability to discern witness accuracy. For instance, in relation to identification evidence, studies repeatedly show that subjects are rarely able to outdo chance in assessing accuracy, with rates never rising above 61 per cent.[219] However, while such poor performance should lead fact finders to wrongly reject accurate accounts as often as they wrongly accept inaccurate witness accounts, in fact study participants tend to overestimate the accuracy of eyewitness evidence.[220] For instance, in one study[221] 83.7 per cent of subjects

[217] Roediger, Wixted and Desoto, above n. 210, esp. 111–12.
[218] Cf. Boyce, Beaudry and Lindsay, above n. 14, 516–18; Lindsay, above n. 193, 381.
[219] Caputo and Dunning, above n. 115, 442–3; Leippe, above n. 14, 925; Boyce, Beaudry and Lindsay, ibid., 506–7.
[220] Cutler and Penrod, above n. 11, 179, 186; R. S. Schmechel et al., 'Beyond the Ken? Testing Jurors' Understanding of Eyewitness Reliability Evidence' (2006) 46 *Jurimetrics* 177 (arguing at 196 that this might flow from their over-confidence in their own abilities).
[221] J. C. Brigham and R. K. Bothwell, 'The Ability of Prospective Jurors to Estimate the Accuracy of Eyewitness Identifications' (1983) 7 *Law and Human Behavior* 19. See also Boyce, Beaudry and Lindsay, above n. 14, 508–9; Leippe and Eisenstadt, above n. 14, 171; Leippe, 'The Appraisal of Eyewitness Testimony', above n. 182, 388.

overestimated the chances of witnesses accurately identifying a suspect in a line-up. Moreover, fact finder faith in eyewitnesses may be very hard to shake, even in experiments when their evidence was discredited by opposing lawyers.[222]

Despite this rather pessimistic picture of the chances of fact finders accurately assessing witness reliability, it has been argued that matters have improved and that adjudicators no longer unquestioningly accept eyewitness testimony,[223] as exemplified by the fact that 89 per cent of respondents in a 2006 survey accepted that even multiple identification witnesses may be wrong.[224] Yet in the same survey, 46 per cent of respondents thought memory operates like a video camera in relation to traumatic events and 87 per cent believed that identification evidence by honest eyewitness was somewhat or very reliable. Nor can a more optimistic view be derived from the fact that most fact finding is conducted by judges, lawyers and trained legal officials rather than potential jurors who constitute the main subjects of study. While the performance of these legal insiders has not been indirectly tested, none of these groups have performed better in survey studies than lay subjects.[225] Indeed, in one survey law students outperformed judges with years of experience.[226]

3.3 Assessing Witness Honesty[227]

When we turn from assessing the accuracy of witnesses to assessing their honesty, we find no greater ability on the part of fact finders. Whereas witness accuracy is an ubiquitous problem, it is impossible to gauge the incidence of lying witnesses, though studies repeatedly reveal

---

[222] See Cutler and Penrod, above n. 11, 191–5; Leippe, above n. 14, 930–2.

[223] P. J. Bailey and S. H. Mecklenburg, 'The Prosecutor's Perspective on Eyewitness Experts in the Courtroom', in Cutler, above n. 14, 233–5.

[224] Schmechel et al., above n. 220, 211.

[225] See Benton et al., above n. 189, 485–7; H. M. Hosch et al., 'Expert Psychology Testimony on Eyewitness Identification: Consensus Among Experts?', in Cutler, above n. 14, 156–8; J. L. Devenport, C. D. Kimbrough and B. L. Cutler, 'Effectiveness of Traditional Safeguards Against Erroneous Conviction Arising From Mistaken Eyewitness Identification', in Cutler, ibid., 53–9.

[226] R. A. Wise and M. A. Safer, 'A Survey of Judges' Knowledge and Beliefs About Eyewitness Testimony' (2003) 40 *Court Review* 6.

[227] The following draws on Kapardis, above n. 21, Chapter 8; McEwan above n. 95, 94–117; M. Stone, 'Instant Lie Detection? Demeanour and Credibility in Criminal Trials' (1991) *Criminal Law Review* 821; O. G. Wellborn, 'Demeanor' (1991) 76 *Cornell Law Review* 1075; A. Vrij, 'The Assessment and Detection of Deceit', in Carson and Bull, above n. 13 and 'Credibility Assessments in a Legal Context', in Carson et al., above n. 100; J. A. Blumenthal, 'A Wipe of the Hands, A Lick of the Lips: The Validity of Demeanor Evidence in Assessing Witness Credibility' (1993) 72 *Nebraska Law Review* 1157. Additional references are given below.

that many miscarriages of justice are caused by perjurious prosecution witnesses, especially accomplices and others testifying in return for favourable treatment.[228]

We saw in Chapter Three[229] that many features of the Anglo-American trial are thought to flush out lying witnesses – the requirement of orality, the oath, the dialectic confrontation between accuser and accused and, perhaps most importantly, the tool of cross-examination. Laboratory research provides some support for the assumption that the possibility of perjury charges and the solemnity of trials – though not swearing to tell the truth – may discourage lying in court.[230] Anecdotal and some empirical research also suggests that an effective cross-examiner can expose lies.[231] But what about the general ability of fact finders to detect lies?

Here again this may be done – arguably most effectively – by extrinsic evaluation of the witness' testimony in the context of all the evidence. But as regards intrinsic evaluation, there are no predictive clues to lying. Fact evaluators must rely on what is said and how, and here studies[232] show that people make assumptions about particular witnesses' propensity to lie based on stereotypes about particular situations and types of people. Somewhat more justifiable is the reliance on the consistency of what is said, though here also there may be understandable reasons why, for instance, asylum applicants and others affected by traumatic experiences may tell different stories at different stages and to different people.[233] In fact, however, there is evidence to suggest that at least in relation to interviewed suspects, as opposed to observational witnesses, liars are more consistent than truthful suspects in terms of the details they report ('within-statement consistency'), the statements they make at different times ('between-statement consistency') and the details reported by different associates ('within-group consistency').[234]

---

[228] See Gudjonsson, above n. 7, Chapter 7; Findley, above n. 18, 339–40; S. Kassin, 'Judging Eyewitnesses, Confessions, Informants and Alibis: What is Wrong with Juries and can they do Better?', in Heaton-Armstrong et al., above n. 23, 357–8.

[229] Section 3.

[230] See Chapter 3 at n. 127.

[231] See, respectively, F. L. Wellman, *The Art of Cross Examination* (1903); G. Davis, S. Cretney and J. Collins, *Simple Quarrels* (1994), 246ff.

[232] T. M. Burke, J. W. Turtle and E. A. Olson, 'Alibis in Criminal Investigations and Trials', in Toglia et al., above n. 34.

[233] See J. Cohen, above n. 29.

[234] A. Vredeveldt, P. J. van Koppen and P. A. Granhag, 'The Inconsistent Suspect: A Systematic Review of Different Types of Consistency in Truth Tellers and Liars', in Bull, above n. 435.

However, when people testify or are interviewed, the clue most frequently relied on is witness demeanour, no doubt due to folk-wisdom
which holds that liars are betrayed by the three 'communication channels' of face, body and voice. Apparently 'from the United States across
Europe, we look for a change in voice pitch, hesitations and speech errors,
pauses, gaze aversion, fidgeting, smiling, and blinking'.[235] Moreover,
while demeanour is primarily important because of its role in witness
evaluation, it may also affect the way witnesses perceive the behaviour of
others. For instance, it is thought that fist clenching indicates aggression,
face touching reveals anxiety and scratching suggests self-blame.

Only some of these clues are reliable. Given that facial clues are easily
controlled, this is the least revealing communication channel. For instance,
there is no evidence that liars are prone to averting their gaze or smiling
less. More reliable signs emanate from the less controllable communication
channels of body and voice. Thus some studies suggest that liars frequently
shift body posture and make fidgety feet and hand movements, though other
studies suggest that they tend to perform fewer body movements, particularly hand gesticulations. More consistently reliable is the tendency of liars to
speak with raised voice pitch, more hesitantly and with greater speech errors.

Unfortunately, however, people pay most attention to faces and after
that the body. And here, not only are some commonly assumed signs of
lying misconceived, but even the more reliable signs may turn out to be
caused by the stress and anxiety of testifying in court or being interviewed
by those in authority. Ironically it may be the suspicion that one is not
being believed that leads to the signs associated with lying. Similarly,
averting one's gaze or other supposed indicia of lying such as evasive or
vague answers to questions may reflect shyness or – as is endemic in immigration cases – different cultural norms.[236]

Moreover, there are problems even with the more reliable clues. One is that
they cannot be easily detected with the naked eye or ear, but require special
training or equipment. Secondly, not everyone displays the same behaviour
when lying. Accordingly, unless we know their usual behaviour, we cannot
assess the significance of witnesses displaying or not displaying behavioural
signs thought to indicate lying. For example, raised voice pitch may reflect
anger or excitement rather than untruthfulness. In one Australian case, a
voice tremor turned out to be caused by a speech impediment rather than

---

[235] McEwan, above n. 95, 107.
[236] See, for example, Byrne, above n. 198; and see more generally, M. B. Powell and T. Bartholomew,
'Interviewing and Assessing Clients from Different Cultural Backgrounds: Guidelines for All
Forensic Professionals', in Carson and Bull, above n. 13, esp. 630–1.

uneasiness at lying.[237] Finally, practised liars can always train themselves to avoid showing signs commonly thought to indicate untruthfulness. Even children learn to lie effectively at an early age (though there is no evidence that they make more legally relevant false allegations).

In short, 'there is nothing like Pinocchio's nose'[238] which betrays liars. Unsurprisingly then, the success rate for detecting lies in laboratory conditions[239] has rarely been above 60 per cent, with most studies reporting levels of between 45 and 60 per cent.[240] One reason for a success rate little better than chance is the fact that people usually lack the information necessary to confirm or disprove their suspicions and hence to develop expertise in detecting lies. But even so, with the exception of secret service operatives, performance is no better for those employed to detect lies, including police officers,[241] irrespective of the level of their experience or confidence in detecting lies.

We thus see that, while it is impossible not to be influenced by witness demeanour, it is a very unreliable indicator of lies or relevant emotional states, and that if confined to bodily and particularly facial clues, as opposed to voice and words used, may be more misleading than helpful in witness evaluation. Thus in one experiment, those who only listened to witness interviews had an average success rate of 58 per cent in distinguishing lies from truth, but even more surprisingly, this rose to 77 per cent for those who only read the interview transcripts.[242] Greater success has been achieved with verbal lie-detection tests, which analyse the content of witness statements in terms of alleged clues to lying, such as a greater tendency to relate stories chronologically and coherently and with fewer details, and even greater success with physiological lie detectors like polygraphs, which measure a person's state of arousal when answering questions on the assumption that such arousal stems from deception.[243] However, given that the presence or absence of assumed signs of lying

---

[237] P. McClellan, 'Who is Telling the Truth? Psychology, Common Sense and the Law', Local Courts Of New South Wales Annual Conference 2006, page 6, available at http://lawlink .nsw.gov.au/lawlink/Supreme_Court/ll_sc.nsf/vwPrint1/SCO_mcclellan020806 (last accessed 24 March 2018).

[238] Vrij, above n. 227, 68.

[239] Admittedly, where there is far less anxiety and guilt associated with lying than in real-life situations.

[240] P. Ekman and M. O'Sullivan, 'Who Can Catch a Liar?' (1991) 46 *American Psychologist* 913.

[241] See, for example, A. Vrij and S. Mann, 'Who killed my Relative? Police Officers' Ability to Detect Real-Life High-Stake Lies' (2001) 7 *Psychology, Crime and Law* 119.

[242] N. R. F. Maier and J. A. Thurber, 'Accuracy of Judgments of Deception When an Interview Is Watched, Heard and Read' (1968) 21 *Personnel Psychology* 23.

[243] See, for example, A Vrij, 'Detecting Deception in Legal Contexts', in Heaton-Armstrong et al., above n. 23.

may be due to factors like reduced intelligence or nervousness on the part of non-liars or conscious attempts at non-detection on the part of liars, the inadmissibility of such lie-detector tests in Scotland is probably justified.[244]

4 Using the Lessons of Psychology

4.1 Should the Lessons of Psychology be Taught to Fact Finders?[245]

4.1.1 Introduction

The clear message from psychological research is that if people are poor at witnessing facts, they are little better at evaluating witnesses. The same applies to both police officers and adjudicators faced with confessions which might have been fabricated due to external or internal pressures or actually come to be believed by the suspect,[246] even when they learn of factors raising doubts about voluntariness.[247] Indeed, in one study, police officers displayed even less ability to detect false confessions than students.[248] This low level of detection is not surprising given people's general difficulty in detecting deceit. Also at play here is what is known as the 'fundamental attribution error',[249] which involves a tendency to assume that behaviour is caused by personal dispositions rather than environmental factors – in other words, that confessions stem from feelings of guilt rather than situational pressures.[250] In addition, false confessions often contain the sort of details of their alleged actions, motivations for such actions and subsequent feelings of guilt, remorse, etc.[251] Consequently studies show that fact adjudicators remain insufficiently sceptical about confessions,

---

[244] See *HM Advocate* v. *Sheridan* [2011] HCJ 1, para. 10.

[245] This section is a shortened version of Nicolson and Auchie, above n. 184, 181–91.

[246] See, for example, S. Kassin, 'On the Psychology of Confessions: Does Innocence Put Innocents at Risk?' (2005) 60 *American Psychologist* 215, 216–17 and 'True or False: "I Would Know a False Confession When I Saw One"', in P. A. Granhag (ed.), *The Detection of Deception in Forensic Contexts* (2009); D. Bradford, and J. Goodman-Delahunty, 'Detecting Deception in Police Investigations: Implications for False Confessions' (2008) 15 *Psychiatry, Psychology and Law* 105.

[247] See Kassin, above n. 228, 351–2; I. Blandon-Gitlin, K. Sperry and R. A. Leo, 'Jurors Believe Interrogation Tactics are Not Likely to Elicit False Confessions: Will Expert Witness Testimony Inform Them Otherwise?' (2011) 17 *Psychology, Crime and Law* 239.

[248] S. M. Kassin, A. Meissner and R. J. Norwick, '"I Would Know a False Confession When I Saw One": A Comparative Study of College Students and Police Investigators' (2005) 29 *Law and Human Behaviour* 211.

[249] See, for example, G. D. Reeder, 'Attribution as a Gateway to Social Cognition', in Carlston, above n. 55.

[250] Kassin et al., 'Police-Induced Confessions: Risk Factors and Recommendations' (2010) 34 *Law and Human Behaviour* 3, 24.

[251] Kassin, 'True or False', above n. 246.

apparently thinking (like police officers)[252] that no one confesses to crimes of which they are innocent,[253] and hence are more likely to convict accused who confess.[254] It is therefore fortunate that UK courts are showing an increasing willingness to accept expert evidence about an accused's propensity to make false confessions,[255] including that based on the use of the Gudjonssen Suggestibility and Compliance scales,[256] and accordingly to show greater scepticism towards the accuracy of confessions.[257]

This raises the question of whether the law should equally allow research relating to the accuracy of witnesses other than suspects to assist fact evaluators. Most psychologists[258] and many legal commentators[259] think they should, but a vociferous minority of the psychological research community[260] and, more pertinently, the High Court[261] disagree, arguing that using psychological research to inform fact finding is unnecessary, unreliable and more harmful than helpful.

---

[252] See C. Chaplin and J. Shaw, 'Confidently Wrong: Police Endorsement of Psycho-Legal Misconceptions' (2016) 31 *Journal of Police and Criminal Psychology* 208.

[253] Cf. Kassin and Neuman, above n. 13 regarding experimental subjects who saw confessions as more powerful than eyewitness testimony; the survey by L. A. Henkel, K. A. J. Coffman and E. M. Dailey, 'A Survey of People's Attitudes and Beliefs About False Confessions' (2008) 26 *Behavioral Sciences and the Law* 555, in which 64 per cent of members of the public agreed or strongly agreed that confessions are powerful indicators of guilt and 51 per cent that those who make confessions are probably guilty. This view seems to extend to the courts: see, for example, *McCutcheon* v. *HM Advocate* 2002 SLT 27 at para. 6; *Hartley* v. *HM Advocate* 1979 SLT 26, 32; F. P. Davidson, *Evidence* (2007), para. 15.6 regarding the rule that very little evidence is required to corroborate an unequivocal confession.

[254] See in relation to actual cases, for example, R. A. Leo and R. J. Ofshe, 'Consequences of False Confessions: Deprivations of Liberty and Miscarriages of Justice in the Age of Psychological Interrogation' (1988) 88 *Journal of Criminal Law and Criminology* 429, and in relation to experimental studies, Kassin and Neuman, above n. 13; S. M. Kassin and K. Sukel, 'Coerced Confessions and the Jury: An Experimental Test of the "Harmless Error" Rule' (1997) 21 *Law and Human Behavior* 27.

[255] Gudjonsson, above n. 7, 309 estimates that they appear in about 20 per cent of cases involving disputed confessions in England and Wales.

[256] *Gilmour* v. *HMA* [2007] HCJAC 48; 2007 SLT 893.

[257] See the convictions overturned by the English Court of Appeal discussed by Gudjonsson, above n. 7, Chapters 18–20.

[258] For example, Leippe, above n. 14; Cutler and Penrod, above n. 11; R. A. Wise, K. A. Dauphinais and M. A. Safer, 'A Tripartite Solution to Eyewitness Error' (2007) 97 *Journal of Criminal Law and Criminology* 807.

[259] For example, C. J. O'Hagan, 'When Seeing is Not Believing: The Case for Eyewitness Expert Testimony' (1993) 81 *Georgetown Law Journal* 741; A. Heaton-Armstrong, B. Shepherd and D. Wolchover, 'Problematic Testimony', in Heaton-Armstrong, Shepherd and Wolchover, above n. 24; J. Copeland, 'Helping Jurors Recognize the Frailties of Eyewitness Identification Evidence' (2002) 46 *Criminal Law Quarterly* 188; D. Ormerod and A. Roberts, 'The Admissibility of Expert Evidence', in Heaton-Armstrong et al., above n. 23, 408; M. D. MacLeod and D. H. Sheldon, 'From Normative to Positive Data: Expert Psychological Evidence Re-examined' (1991) *Criminal Law Review* 811.

[260] See, for example, Ebbesen and Konečni, above n. 35; Elliott, above n. 52.

[261] *Gage* v. *HMA* 2011 SCL 645.

4.1.2 Can Fact Finders Learn from Psychological Research?

As regards necessity – the current test for admissibility[262] – while many studies merely confirm what many people already know, for instance, that memory fades or children are less reliable witnesses than adults, this knowledge is unlikely to extend to the nuances of such phenomena, such as how memory fades or how soon children catch up with adults.[263] Moreover, as we have seen, many phenomena such as the impact of stress or the ineffectiveness of training on perceptual ability are counterintuitive, whereas fact finders make misleading assumptions about the significance of witness confidence and demeanour as clues to reliability. Finally, many of the phenomena discovered by psychologists, while understandable when raised, are unlikely to spontaneously cross the minds of those unacquainted with psychological knowledge. Indeed, if we could trust fact finders' 'experience of life and human affairs', they would not consistently overestimate the accuracy of witness testimony and cause so many wrongful convictions by trusting identification evidence. Consequently courts in other jurisdictions increasingly recognise the undoubted fact 'that our current scientific understanding of eyewitness memory is beyond the ken of lay and customary knowledge'[264] and hence draw on psychological research to inform jury instructions or even allow expert evidence on the psychology of witnessing.[265]

4.1.3 Is Psychological Research Reliable?[266]

A more plausible objection to using psychological research is that it lacks scientific validity.[267] As we saw in Chapter Five, this complaint applies

---

[262] But cf. Nicolson and Auchie, above n. 184, 163ff.

[263] A. Roberts, 'Expert Evidence on the Reliability of Eyewitness Identification – Some Observations on the Justifications of Exclusion: *Gage v HM Advocate*' (2012) 16 *International Journal of Evidence and Proof* 93, 101.

[264] R. S. Malpass et al., 'The Need For Expert Psychological Testimony on Eyewitness Identification', in Cutler, above n. 14, 18.

[265] See, for example, Kapardis, above n. 21, 231–2; Schmechel et al., above n. 220, 185; E. Stein, 'The Admissibility of Expert Testimony about Cognitive Science Research on Eyewitness Identification' (2003) 2 *Law, Probability and Risk*, 295, 297; L. Dufraimont, 'Regulating Unreliable Evidence: Can Evidence Rules Guide Juries and Prevent Wrongful Convictions?' (2007) 33 *Queen's Law Journal* 261.

[266] This section draws on: McEwan, above n. 95, Chapter 7 and above n. 198; R. Bagshaw, 'Behavioural Science Data in Evidence Teaching and Scholarship', in Roberts and Redmayne, above n. 198; Copeland, above n. 259. See also the more partisan discussions from within psychology of Cutler and Penrod, above n. 11, esp. Chapter 4; Leippe, above n. 14; Davis and Loftus, in Nadel and Sinnott-Armstrong, above n. 54, and the critics cited in n. 267 below.

[267] See references in n. 260 above; Stone, above n. 33, Chapter 1; H. D. Flowe, K. M. Finklea and E. B. Ebbesen, 'Limitations of Expert Psychology Testimony on Eyewitness Identification', in Cutler, above n. 14.

far more to its external rather than internal validity – namely, their generalisability from experimental to real-life conditions, rather than the rigour of their research methods. Nevertheless, despite these problems, many of the phenomena highlighted in this chapter are consistently found in laboratory experiments and increasingly in field experiments which approximate the conditions of 'real' life and also in some archival studies of actual cases. Conversely, there is little clear indication that real-life conditions make a difference to the results of laboratory experiments or, even if there is a potential difference, what the direction of effect will be. It is one thing to say that laboratory conditions are unrealistic; quite another to predict that real-life conditions will cause an observed phenomenon to be reversed, negated or diminished rather than enhanced. Of course, if such evidence emerges, theories based on laboratory experiments need to be altered. But until then, it seems better to take account of phenomena established prima facie by consistent laboratory findings than ignore them because they *might* not be replicated in real life. In fact, it is arguable that evidence from actual cases can never trump laboratory experiments because only very rarely can one derive definitive answers from observing actual incidents. This in turn is because one cannot sufficiently control for the impact of independent variables and also because there is rarely verification of the truth of witness accounts which would be necessary to make inferences about the effect of witnessing conditions and witness accuracy.

Moreover, if views about the negotiated nature of scientific – and indeed all – truth-claims are persuasive,[268] the best we can expect is a consensus among the scientific community based on consistent findings. This, however, raises the question of how much consensus and what degree of consistency is required. For example, a 1989 survey of experts revealed an agreement rate no higher than 70 per cent on thirteen of twenty-one alleged witnessing effects. In two later surveys, the agreement on some existing items increased and new items also received substantial levels of agreement, suggesting that consensus is building as research intensifies.[269] Nevertheless, we need to be wary even when findings attract high levels of consensus.[270] Like all humans, psychological researchers may subconsciously alter their perceptions to suit their interests and preconceived beliefs. Moreover, they have an interest both as academics carving out a

---

[268] See Chapter 5, section 4 and Chapter 2, section 3.3 respectively.
[269] For surveys, see Hosch et al., above n. 225, 146–53.
[270] Moreover, while significant numbers of experts responded, response rates were relatively low and it is possible that the simplicity of the answers on offer forced a choice between two only partially accurate answers.

relatively new discipline and as potential hired experts in being able to point to settled findings. Indeed, agreement among experts has sometimes preceded sufficient supporting evidence. Critics also note that later studies, for instance on unconscious transference, weapon focus, the effect of stress generally and the forgetting curve, have not always replicated earlier findings, or have provided more nuanced details. And this is before we consider the possibility of studies revealing unwanted results sitting in desk drawers.

Nevertheless, given that the vast majority of the findings reported in this chapter are supported by 'multiple studies conducted in systematic programmes of research carried out by multiple investigators working independently of each other' and involve 'methodological variability across paradigms and investigators',[271] it would indeed be startling if 'somehow, most experts are wrong about most eyewitness matters'.[272] Moreover, to dismiss their findings for a lack of absolute certainty would be to hold psychological research to much higher standards than apply to legal decisions – notwithstanding the latter's serious consequences – and indeed to much scientific knowledge, particularly of a forensic nature.[273] As we shall see in the next chapter,[274] legal fact finders regularly rely on 'common sense' generalisations whose applicability and existential validity are far from certain. While it could be argued that, compared to reliance on psychological findings, this is unavoidable, it seems bizarre to prefer leaving fact finders to rely on 'fireside inductions'[275] about human psychology which experts consistently find to be misplaced.

4.1.4 Is Knowledge about Psychology More Harmful than Helpful?

This in fact seems to be the conclusion of some psychological insiders who argue that 'a little learning is dangerous and . . . a little more may be more dangerous still'.[276] Even if findings are scientifically valid and consistent, these critics argue that they cannot be used. One reason is that often the impact of variables affecting witnessing is too small or their contours too imprecise. For instance, while studies consistently find a cross-race effect,[277] it is very small, and while longer exposure time clearly enhances memory of events, the exact ratio between exposure time and memory improvement

---

[271] Leippe, above n. 14, 915.

[272] Leippe and Eisenstadt, above n. 14, 174.

[273] See Chapter 5 sections 4 and 6; also Greer, above n. 14, 140; M. King, *Psychology In and Out of Court: A Critical Examination of Legal Psychology* (1986), 8.

[274] Sections 3.3 and 5.1.

[275] Cf. Meehl, above n. 1.

[276] Elliott, above n. 52, 425.

[277] See at n. 141 above.

is unclear.[278] Secondly, even if research reports precise effects of the factors affecting witnessing, it can only report an average affect which for actual witnesses may be magnified, nullified or diminished because of the unknown effect of other factors. For example, stress clearly affects different people differently, whereas some elderly witnesses may have impeccable memories. Even when we know the effect of a factor in isolation from others or how it combines with specific other factors, there are simply too many variables potentially affecting witness accuracy to allow for precise predictions.

In response, Scotland could follow the example of US courts[279] and prohibit such predictions but allow experts to provide what is called 'social framework evidence'[280] about factors affecting witnessing and caution them about overestimating witness accuracy and their ability to detect inaccuracy and dishonesty. Thus, as long as it is made clear that some effects are smaller than others,[281] that particular findings have been challenged or may lack ecological validity in not being generalisable to conditions outside the laboratory, and that there may be many different witnessing conditions which affect accuracy, it is arguable that fact finders should be educated about the findings of research on witnessing.

A final argument against exposing fact finders to research on witnessing is that, even if the information is useful in the abstract, reference to it may cause more harm than good. Thus exposure to a plethora of relevant findings, but without the means to weigh them up against each other and apply them to the case, might lead fact finders to become confused or paralysed by information overload. This in turn may lead them to resort to peripheral route processing. Conversely, however, it is also possible that general warnings about overestimating witness accuracy and relying on common-sense signs of witness accuracy and honesty might encourage fact finders to concentrate on the content of testimony and its logical plausibility, which might constitute a more reliable means of evaluation.

Speculation aside, experiments have been conducted involving fact finders exposed to research findings through expert evidence or jury

---

[278] See at n. 35 above.

[279] *People* v. *McDonald*, 37 Cal 3d 351 208 Cal Rptr 236 (California Supreme Court) 1984, 371.

[280] See L. Walker and J. Monahan, 'Social Frameworks: A New Use of Social Science in Law' (1987) 73 *Virginia Law Review* 559 describing expert evidence on the social and psychological context relevant to the actions and state of mind of legal actors designed to assist fact finders make more informed interpretation of the facts. While usually associated with various means to counter myths about rape, domestic violence, etc., the concept is also regarded as applying to witness testimony: F. E. Raitt and M. S. Zeedyk, *The Implicit Relation of Psychology and Law: Women and Syndrome Evidence* (2000), 177.

[281] Even though this might negate the impact of their evidence, as has occurred in mock jury studies: see Elliott, above n. 52, 433.

instructions. Ideally this should make them more likely to accept accurate, and less likely to accept inaccurate, evidence. Initially such a 'sensitivity effect' only rarely appeared in the relatively large number of experiments involving expert evidence and in only one of the few experiments involving jury instructions.[282] Instead, some showed no effect at all, whereas most resulted in heightened disbelief in witness testimony irrespective of its accuracy. However, more recent studies have shown less of this latter 'scepticism effect' and more of a sensitivity effect, at least when experts tailored their testimony to the case rather than providing an overview of all research findings. In any event, given fact finders' tendency to overestimate witness accuracy, one can ask whether general scepticism is so undesirable. According to Michael Leippe and Donna Eisenstadt,[283] scepticism occurs usually when it should (for example, when witness testimony is both central to the case and weak) and only sometimes when it should not.

However, while undue scepticism in relation to prosecution witnesses may be desirable given the generally accepted need to overprotect accused against unjust convictions,[284] it is less so in relation to defence witnesses and in civil cases. Moreover, most of the studies on the effect of expert evidence have not been in relation to witness accounts known to be accurate or inaccurate. Instead they have been in relation to assessments of accuracy based on whether witnessing conditions were favourable or not. In the former, more reliable experiments, the impact of expert testimony has been less favourable.[285] One compromise would be to use research findings only where the possible impact of common-sense assumptions about witnessing are likely to lead to patent injustice and where those findings have widespread acceptance and are based on reasonably realistic experiments.

4.2 How should the Lessons of Psychology be Taught?

Assuming that fact finders should receive some exposure to psychological research, the question turns to the form it should take. Aside from cost and possible judicial resistance, an obvious suggestion is the training of lawyers and regular fact finders.[286] If psychology were to be a required element of legal education, fact adjudicators could make more informed

[282] See Cutler and Penrod, above n. 11, Chapter 17; Leippe, above n. 14, 934–47 passim; Wise, Dauphinais and Safer, above n. 258, 837–41; Dufraimont, above n. 265, 301–6.
[283] Above n. 14, 188–9; see also Leippe, ibid.; Dufraimont, ibid., 300–1.
[284] See Chapter 3, section 3.4.1.
[285] See K. A. Martire and R. L. Kemp, 'Can Experts Help Jurors to Evaluate Eyewitness Evidence? A Review of Eyewitness Expert Effects' (2011) 16 *Legal and Criminological Psychology* 24.
[286] MacLeod and Sheldon, above n. 259, 820; Heaton-Armstrong, Wolchover and Shepherd, above n. 259, 336–8; W. Young and S. Katkhuda, 'Judicial training', in Heaton-Armstrong et al., above n. 23.

decisions, trial judges could provide more informed warnings to juries and make more informed decisions themselves, and lawyers could use their psychological knowledge to investigate and argue cases more effectively through, for instance:

- considering all relevant variables affecting perception, memory and recall when questioning witnesses in order to find ways to mitigate (or, if cross-examining, exploit) any problems;
- interviewing witnesses as soon as possible and at the relevant locus, or at least using cognitive interviewing techniques to replicate the effect of such contextualisation and certainly to enhance fact investigation generally;
- ensuring identification procedures are fair and, if not, challenging them in court;
- preparing witnesses to speak confidently and to use powerful speech;
- challenging opponents who use tactics based on unverified 'armchair psychology'.[287]

But what about untrained fact finders? Here, jury members could be introduced to potentially relevant information before cases begin.[288] But it is doubtful how much attention they will pay to abstract knowledge, and whether they can remember and effectively apply relevant knowledge without guidance. We have already seen that cross-examination and judicial instructions are not particularly effective safeguards against uninformed decision-making in general.[289] More specifically in relation to witness testimony, research suggests that cross-examination rarely counters its impact[290] and is 'largely useless' for detecting truthful but mistaken witnesses.[291] Judicial warnings as to potentially unreliable evidence and the factors affecting reliability seem to be similarly ineffective,[292] with the few studies that have been undertaken revealing that, when in rare cases they have an impact, they engender juror scepticism rather than sensitivity.[293] Admittedly these studies suffer from problems

---

[287] Cf. D. Luban, *Lawyers and Justice: An Ethical Study* (1988), 69.

[288] Wise, Daupinais and Safer, above n. 258, 868.

[289] Chapter 5, section 7.4.

[290] Ibid., 924.

[291] Wells et al., above n. 18, 609. See also Devenport, Kimbrough and Cutler, above n. 225; Wise, Dauphinais and Safer, above n. 258, 828–30; Roberts, above n. 263, 98–9; B. L. Garrett, *Convicting the Innocent: Where Criminal Prosecutions go Wrong* (2011), Chapter 3, in relation to actual cases involving miscarriages of justice based on misidentification evidence.

[292] Leippe, above n. 14, 949; Roberts, ibid.; O'Hagan, above n. 259, 753–4.

[293] See Cutler and Penrod, above n. 11, Chapter 17; Devenport, Kimbrough and Cutler, above n. 292, 61–4.

of external validity and use US jury instructions which lack sufficient relevant information.

Although better-designed studies and improved jury instructions are starting to reveal a more positive impact,[294] currently there is some justification for thinking that experts represent the best means of educating lay fact finders about the psychology of witnessing. Certainly, as we have seen, they can produce a sensitivity rather than just a scepticism effect, whereas experts may precede and specifically refer to relevant problems of witness testimony, should be able to convey specialist knowledge better than judges and lawyers, and are open to adversarial challenge. Moreover, as we have already seen,[295] general worries about fact finders being dazzled by experts' credentials and science's aura of reliability are exaggerated. On the other hand, we have also seen that the cost of hiring adversarial experts exacerbates other inequality-of-arms problems. The fact the only studies on the impact of court-appointed experts found that, unlike unopposed defence experts, they caused scepticism not greater sensitivity[296] suggest that more research is needed before it is clearer as to how best to use experts, and whether any advantages of using them rather than relying on lawyers and judicial instructions outweigh the expense and time involved. These drawbacks and the small pool of relevant experts in Scotland suggest that their use might be best limited to more serious cases where witness evidence is determinative and uncorroborated.[297]

4.3 Should Psychology Inform the Practice of Fact Finding?

By contrast, it seems far less controversial to rely on valid and consistent research findings to inform reform of fact-finding processes, as has occurred in England and Wales, where major inquires even commission their own research.[298] As regards possible reforms, while there seems little that can be done to improve witness perception, there are various possible ways of enhancing memory and recall. For instance, recording witnesses' first recall of events will provide more accurate evidence than testimony in

---

[294] F. Leverick, 'Jury Instructions on Eyewitness Identification Evidence: A Re-Evaluation' (2016) 49 *Creighton Law Review* 555. See also L. Ellison and V. E. Munro, '"Telling tales": Exploring Narratives of Life and Law Within the (Mock) Jury Room' (2015) 35 *Legal Studies* 201.

[295] Chapter 5, section 7.3.

[296] See Cutler and Penrod, above n. 11, Chapter 16.

[297] Cf. S. I. Friedland, 'On Common Sense and the Evaluation of Witness Credibility' (1990) 40 *Case Western Reserve Law Review* 165; 221–5; M. M. Koosed, 'Reforming Eyewitness Identification Law and Practice to Protect the Innocent' (2008) 42 *Creighton Law Review* 595, 619.

[298] See McEwan, above n. 198, 187; an approach which contrasts starkly with the Carloway report (*The Carloway Review – Report and Recommendations* (2011)), which ignores highly relevant psychological research relevant to the abolition of corroboration.

formal proceedings after possible memory decay and alteration. Indeed, the superiority of such early recall suggests that witnesses should testify as soon as possible after events before appropriate officials and the parties' lawyers who can cross-examine them, and transcripts should form part of the record and even take precedence over court testimony.

However, because it is subject to human control, witness recall is most conducive to reform. Thus while the *Lord Advocate's Guidelines* regulating pre-court identification procedures are relatively enlightened, they could still be improved by, for instance:

- requiring any negative identifications to be reported;
- basing the choice of foils on witness descriptions rather than suspect appearance;
- removing the requirement that witnesses look twice at line-ups;
- as far as possible, extending the rules applicable to VIPERs to all other forms of identification and making their admissibility depend on judicial permission;
- making inadmissible any reference to a successful show-up or mugshot identification;
- requiring, where practicable,[299] the video recording of all proceedings so that irregularities can be detected and (suitably educated) fact finders can observe post-dictive clues like the speed and confidence with which identifications are made,[300] and discount subsequent confidence enhancement.

In addition, all identifications which breach the *Guidelines* should be presumptively inadmissible until reasonable excuses for non-compliance are provided, judicial instructions on the problems with identification and other eyewitness evidence should be made compulsory and standardised,[301] dock identifications should be prohibited at least where not preceded by pre-trial formal identification,[302] and, if the corroboration requirement is to be abolished, an exception made for identification cases.[303]

---

[299] Cf. A. Roberts, 'The Problem of Misidentification: Some Observations on Process' (2004) 8 *Evidence and Proof* 100, 106–7.

[300] Alternatively witnesses can be asked to provide a description of their thought processes in making identifications: Stern and Dunning, above n. 115, 278.

[301] Cf. F. P. Davidson and P. R. Ferguson, 'The Corroboration Requirement in Scottish Criminal Trials: Should it be Retained for Some Forms of Problematic Evidence?' (2014) 18 *International Journal of Evidence and Proof* 1, 11–13.

[302] See Ferguson, above n. 100, 152–3.

[303] Cf. Davidson and Ferguson, above n. 301.

Interviews by state officials could be similarly regulated. Here one could consider prohibiting leading questions and other cross-examination techniques designed to confuse witnesses or contaminate memory. Alternatively, given the difficulties of enforcement, all interviews could be recorded to enable suitably educated fact finders to respond appropriately to such techniques and all state officials be trained in the cognitive interview protocol or similar interviewing techniques. Leading questions could be prohibited in court on the grounds that their potential for contaminating and confusing accurate memory outweighs their value in challenging inaccurate memory. Far more radically, to mitigate the problems of memory loss, witnesses could be formally examined and cross-examined as soon as possible after the incident and a recording made which could be accessed when the final decision is made. Clearly this would move proceedings far towards the Continental model of episodic fact-finding but, as we saw in Chapter Three,[304] there have been moves in this direction for much less elevated reasons.

As regards improving the evaluation of testimony, apart from the educational measures discussed above, one radical suggestion involves shielding witnesses from the view of fact finders so that only the more reliable paralinguistic clues to honesty can be observed,[305] or even more radically, given that few fact finders have the ability to discern such clues, confining evaluation to transcripts of testimony.

5 Conclusion

Whatever the merits of the proposed reforms to the processes and legal regulation of fact finding and the extent to which psychological research has the potential to improve fact finding, the psychology of witnessing has an important bearing on theoretical debates about the role of truth in fact finding. While the exact degree to which witness testimony falls short of factual truth will never be known, the ubiquitous problems witnesses face in accurately perceiving, remembering and recalling facts, and fact finders in accurately assessing witness accuracy and honesty, suggest that the aim of achieving factual truth can only exist as an aspiration rather than a regularly achieved reality. Moreover, if we accept the crucial role of schemas and theoretical knowledge gained from others, psychology provides clear empirical support for the theoretical positions adopted by anti-realist epistemologists. In other words, humans are fallible observers of

---

[304] Section 4.2.
[305] D. Nicolson, 'Truth and Demeanour: Lifting the Veil' (2014) 18 *Edinburgh Law Review* 254.

the world and whatever they regard as true facts is always predetermined by their previous experience, and the information and opinions provided to them by others. It is thus impossible for humans to escape their social context even if they could accurately perceive remember and recall facts. And it is equally impossible for those who evaluate their accounts to escape their own social conditioning in doing so. As Jack Weinstein, argues, 'the testimony of any witness describes the combination of himself and the event'.[306]

---

[306] 'Some Difficulties in Devising Rules for Determining Truth in Judicial Trials' (1966) 66 *Columbia Law Review* 223, 231.

CHAPTER SEVEN

The Psychological Context II:
Reason, Narrative and Proof

1 Introduction: Atomistic versus Holistic Reasoning

Having in the last chapter concluded the discussion of the three main forms of evidence by looking at the psychology of witnessing and the evaluation of observational witness testimony, we turn in this chapter to the general psychological processes involved in handling facts. Such fact handling can be conducted by a wide variety of legal actors ranging from those with the formal power to determine the facts of cases to those who do so informally, such as lawyers persuading clients to plead guilty or investigating the facts in order to draft contracts, wills, etc. Indeed, the basic psychological processes do not differ substantially according to who is undertaking one or more of the four interlinked and chronologically overlapping[1] but successive tasks in fact handling, namely:

- *fact investigation* – the search for evidence;
- *fact analysis* – the evaluation of evidence by those making strategic decisions, such as whether to settle/plead guilty or go to trial and, if so, about how to present the facts persuasively;
- *fact presentation* (or *advocacy*) – the attempt to persuade fact finders to accept a particular version of the facts;
- *fact determination* (or *adjudication*) – the evaluation of evidence in order to determine the legal facts[2] of a particular case (in other words, convert evidence into proof).

However, in order to make discussion manageable, this chapter will echo the relevant literature and concentrate on lawyers litigating and fact finders adjudicating legal disputes rather than covering all legal

---

[1] Thus, as we shall see, fact investigation and fact analysis may overlap in that analysis may lead to further investigation (see section 3.3), whereas fact adjudicators *are likely to* use some of the logical processes involved in fact analysis (see section 5).

[2] See Chapter 1, section 1.4.

actors who might deal with facts in some way. This literature is fairly extensive, although given the dominance of US studies it focuses disproportionately on jury decision-making.[3] Much of this in turn focuses on highly specific functional issues like the impact of a strong fore(wo)man, methods of deliberation (vote- versus verdict-driven discussion), the size of juries, verdict form (majority versus unanimous), or issues relevant to evidential and procedural rules (such as the impact of pre-trial publicity and the comprehensibility of judicial instructions). Consequently it is of limited value given the rarity of jury trials in Scotland. Potentially more useful are those studies of the effect on decision-making of the juror's personality (for example, as authoritarian or egalitarian), attitudes to various social issues like race or gender, demographic factors and social background such as the age, class, gender and race of jurors, and even the parties' attractiveness and clothing. However, many of the findings are inconclusive, and/or are not necessarily generalisable from the specific type of case or issue studied. Consequently we will confine discussion to those which illuminate the more general question of the psychological process used in fact handling in order to evaluate orthodox theoretical assumptions about evidence and proof.

As we saw in Chapter Two, the Rationalist Tradition is premised on – and indeed is named after – the idea that people can – and do – deal with evidence and proof through rational methods. This approach was expressed most explicitly and influentially by Jeremy Bentham[4] and his 'direct linear descendent'[5] John Henry Wigmore.[6] According to William Twining, they adopt almost identical assumptions about the nature of proof[7] based on the ideas of what is variously called 'scientific rationality', the 'classic scientific method of proof', 'British', 'common-sense empiricism' or what in Chapter Two was called empiricist

---

[3]   Moreover, much of it involves questionable research methods: see, for example, B. S. Jackson, *Making Sense in Law* (1995), 439–58; J. Devine et al., 'Jury Decision Making: 45 Years of Empirical Research on Deliberating Groups' (2001) 7 *Psychology, Public Policy and Law* 622; A. Memon, A. Vrij and R. Bull, *Psychology and Law: Truthfulness, Accuracy and Credibility* (2nd edn, 2010), Chapter 8; A. Kapardis, *Psychology and Law: A Critical Introduction* (4th edn, 2014), Chapter 5.

[4]   *Rationale of Judicial Evidence* (1827).

[5]   W. Twining, *Theories of Evidence: Bentham and Wigmore* (1985), 116.

[6]   *Principles of Proof as Given by Logic, Psychology, and General Experience and Illustrated in Judicial Trials* (1913), later renamed *The Science of Judicial Proof* (1937). See also the very similar approach of J. Michael and M. Adler, 'The Trial of an Issue of Fact: I' (1934) 34 *Columbia Law Review* 1224.

[7]   Above n. 5, ix.

foundationalism,[8] which involves 'a straightforward application of ordinary principles of induction'[9] to draw inferences from '*observation, experience* and *experiment*'.[10]

As we also saw in Chapter Two,[11] rationalists like Wigmore define induction in contradistinction to the syllogistic form of deductive reasoning which comprises of a major premise (a generalisation about the world), a minor premise (the facts) and a conclusion. To take Wigmore's example:

> Major Premise – Persons related by blood to case parties are biased in their testimony;
> Minor Premise – This witness is related by blood to a party;
> Conclusion – This witness is biased.

By contrast, according to Wigmore, inductive reasoning starts with the minor premise, but implicitly relies on the major premise to reach the same conclusion (this witness is related by blood to a party and is therefore biased).

It is, however, more common to distinguish between deductive and inductive logic, not in terms of whether or not reasoning is couched in syllogistic form,[12] but in terms of the certainty of the major premise. Thus, in deductive logic, the major premise admits of no doubt (*all* blood relatives give biased testimony) and hence the conclusion follows as a matter of inexorable logic since it is impossible without self-contradiction not to conclude that the witness is biased. In inductive logic, by contrast, the major premise is couched in probabilistic terms – *most* or merely *some* blood relatives will give biased testimony – and thus one can only conclude that biased testimony is probable or merely possible. Admittedly both Bentham and Wigmore recognised that fact finding is confined to probable rather than certain truth. However, to the extent that they address issues of probability, their ideas are very undeveloped.[13] More recently, as we shall see in more detail,[14] New Evidence Scholars have engaged in an intense and

---

8   Sections 2.2 and 3.2.1.
9   Wigmore, above n. 6, 22–3, quoted by Twining, above n. 5, 125.
10   Bentham, above n. 4, 19, quoted by Twining, ibid., 52 (emphasis in original).
11   Section 3.2.2.3.
12   But cf. Aristotle, who limited syllogistic reasoning to deductive logic involving major premises which are certain, as distinct from the rhetorical device of 'enthymyme' involving uncertain premises: B. Jackson, above n. 3, 178–9; J. C. Rideout, 'Storytelling, Narrative Rationality, and Legal Persuasion' (2008) 14 *Legal Writing: Journal of Legal Writing Institute* 53, 61 and see Chapter 2, section 3.2.1.1 regarding the process of inductive generalisation whereby generalisations are acquired in the first place.
13   Twining, above n. 5, 53 (regarding Bentham) and 125, 144, 178, 183 (regarding Wigmore).
14   Section 3.8.2 below.

arcane debate over the relative merits of different theories about how fact finders should approach questions of probability.

But while this debate raged, mirroring the epistemological debate over foundationalism and coherentism as theories of justification,[15] other evidence scholars[16] began to question the assumption by orthodox rationalists that evidence is evaluated in terms of what can be called an argument-based mode of reasoning.[17] This mode is atomistic and relational[18] in focusing on the logical relationships between individual facts, and elemental[19] in analysing whether these logical relationships establish each of the various legal elements of governing law. Moreover, it involves bottom-up[20] reasoning from individual facts to conclusions about the facts as a whole. By contrast, drawing on epistemology, history, the philosophy and sociology of science, and psychology itself, as well as on laboratory and field studies of fact presentation and adjudication, it is argued that evidence is evaluated holistically in terms of competing theories of what happened. Rather than gradually building towards a conclusion from individual facts, waiting until all the evidence is in before deciding, holistic reasoning starts with a hypothesis about what happened and then involves evaluating facts as they emerge to see whether they fit this hypothesis or whether it needs to be modified or even abandoned due to too many discordant facts. In other words, fact evaluators work top-down from their hypotheses as to what happened and use these frames of reference to help organise, interpret and evaluate individual facts.

More specifically, it is argued that these hypotheses are formulated as stories. We have already seen that memories are stored in narrative form as scripts, scenarios and stories.[21] Indeed, one of the first cognitive

[15] See Chapter 2, section 3.2.
[16] See, for example, J. D. Jackson, 'Theories of Truth Finding in Criminal Procedure: An Evolutionary Approach' (1988) 10 *Cardozo Law Review* 475; M. A. Hareira, 'An Early Holistic Conception of Judicial Fact-Finding' (1986) *Juridical Review* 79; B. Jackson, *Law, Fact and Narrative Coherence* (1988), esp. Chapter 3; R. Allen, 'The Nature of Juridical Proof' (1991) 13 *Cardozo Law Review* 373; W. Twining, *Rethinking Evidence: Exploratory Essays* (2nd edn, 2006), Chapters 9 and 10.
[17] F. J. Bex et al., 'A Hybrid Formal Theory of Arguments, Stories and Criminal Evidence' (2010) 18 *Artificial Intelligence and Law* 123.
[18] P. Tillers and D. Schum, 'Charting New Territory in Judicial Proof: Beyond Wigmore' (1987) 9 *Cardozo Law Review* 907; D. Schum, 'Argument Structuring and Evidence Evaluation', in R. Hastie (ed.), *Inside the Juror: The Psychology of Juror Decision Making* (1993), 176–8.
[19] See M. S. Pardo, 'Juridical Proof, Evidence, And Pragmatic Meaning: Toward Evidentiary Holism' (2000) 95 *Northwestern University Law Review* 399, 400, 440.
[20] W. A. Wagenaar, P. J. van Koppen and H. F. M. Crombag, *Anchored Narratives: The Psychology of Criminal Evidence* (1993), 24.
[21] Chapter 6, section 2.1.

capacities children develop is that of narrative comprehension[22] and some argue that as 'the storytelling animal'[23] humans have an inherent narrative capacity comparable to the linguistic capacity of children to learn grammar.[24] But whether or not narrative is 'hardwired into our brains',[25] it is clear that it is culturally embedded in our collective psyche from the days of storytelling around fires[26] through myths, legends and sagas to the modern age of books, films, theatre, television and myriad new forms of social media.[27] Stories provide an important – if not *the* most important – way in which we learn about ourselves and our world – from family stories to those which are part of our local, national and pan-national culture. Obviously the exact stock of common stories within communities varies over time and place, and from person to person, but it is arguable that stories are not only an incredibly 'elegant'[28] and effective,[29] but also the favoured, form for storing, communicating and understanding information.[30]

While these insights have been accepted – albeit sometimes reluctantly[31] – by modified rationalists, some complain that claims about holism have yet to be 'fully argued'[32] or presented as 'rounded'[33] or 'articulated'[34] theories. This chapter seeks to remedy this gap by exploring in detail the psychological processes involved in the various fact-handling tasks order to map the complex interrelationship between atomistic and holistic reasoning, and how it varies between these tasks.

---

[22] J Bruner, 'The Narrative Construction of Reality' (1991) 18 *Critical Inquiry* 1, 9.

[23] J. Gottschall, *The Storytelling Animal: How Stories Make Us Human* (2012).

[24] B. Jackson, above n. 3, 228ff.

[25] A. E. Taslitz, 'Patriarchal Stories I: Cultural Rape Narratives in the Courtroom' (1996) 5 *Southern California Review of Law and Women's Studies* 387, 434.

[26] J. Yorke, *Into the Woods: How Stories Work and Why We Tell Them* (2013), xviii.

[27] See C. H. Rose, *Fundamental Trial Advocacy* (2nd edn, 2011), 66. In addition to the references cited in this paragraph, see also on the cognitive importance of storytelling: A. G. Amsterdam, R. Hertz and R. Walker-Stirling, 'Introduction' to T. Alper et al., 'Stories Told and Untold: Lawyering Theory Analyses of the First Rodney King Assault Trial' (2005) 12 *Clinical Law Review* 1, 5ff.

[28] B. Jackson, above n. 16, 64–5.

[29] If not *the* most effective: G. P. Lopez, 'Lay Lawyering' (1984) 32 *UCLA Law Review* 1, 10.

[30] See, for example, W. L. Bennett, 'Storytelling in Criminal Trials: A Model of Social Judgment' (1978) 64 *Quarterly Journal of Speech* 1; P. Brooks, 'The Law as Narrative and Rhetoric', in P. Brooks and P. Gewirtz (eds), *Law's stories: Narrative and Rhetoric in the Law* (1998).

[31] See below, section 6.

[32] Twining, above n. 5, 183.

[33] Twining, above n. 16, 309.

[34] Pardo, above n. 19, 401.

2 Fact Investigation, Abductive Reasoning and Lateral Thinking[35]

2.1 Abductive Reasoning[36]

In fact, things are even more complex than the debate between reason and narrative suggests, given that – as we shall see – the first task involves a psychological process which is neither argument- nor story-based (though, as we shall also see, far more holistic than atomistic). When fact investigators commence uncovering facts relevant to their cases – whether through interviewing observational witnesses, instructing expert witnesses, and/or looking for relevant documents and real evidence, etc. – the available evidence will often be thin and patchy. Consequently they will have to generate ideas – theories or hypotheses – about what might have happened. As the philosopher Charles Peirce persuasively argued, these cannot be generated by deduction or induction, because in order to be valid all the information has to be contained in the major and minor premises. Instead, new ideas are generated by a third form of reasoning he called 'abduction' (or simply 'hypothesis').[37]

Compared to the rigidity of logical reasoning, abductive reasoning is highly creative, involving imagination and instinctive flashes of insight. As Sherlock Holmes' method of solving mysteries illustrates,[38] it involves a creative search for hypotheses that are not immediately apparent from available information. Investigators examine the evidence they have and attempt to construct hypotheses to explain those facts – contemplating not just how they are most likely to have occurred but all possible explanations. For instance, if one is trying to ascertain who removed a horse from a stable and knows that a guard dog was present at the time, but did not bark, one may hypothesise that the dog had been poisoned or drugged or,

---

[35] In addition to references cited below, this section draws on Tillers and Schum, above n. 18, 943ff and 'A Theory of Preliminary Fact Investigation' (1991) 24 *University of California Davis Law Review* 931; D. A. Binder and P. Bergman, *Fact Investigation: From Hypothesis to Proof* (1984); D. Schum and P. Tillers, 'Marshalling Evidence For Adversary Litigation' (1991) 13 *Cardozo Law Review* 657; D. A. Schum, 'Marshaling Thoughts and Evidence During Fact Investigation' (1999) 40 *South Texas Law Review* 401. For a brief overview, see, for example, T. Anderson, D. Schum and W. Twining, *Analysis of Evidence* (2nd edn, 2005), 56–60, 98–9.

[36] In addition to the references in n. 35, see P. van Andel and D. Bourcier, 'Serendipity and Abduction in Proofs, Presumptions, and Emerging Laws' (2001) 22 *Cardozo Law Review* 1605; J. R. Josephson, 'On the Proof Dynamics of Inference to the Best Explanation' (2001) 22 *Cardozo Law Review* 1621; D. A. Schum, 'Species of Abductive Reasoning in Fact Investigation in Law' (2001) 22 *Cardozo Law Review* 1645.

[37] Of the references in n. 35 above, see especially Tillers and Schum at 987–91 and Schum at 420ff.

[38] See U. Eco and T. A. Sebeok (eds), *The Sign of Three: Dupin, Holmes, Peirce* (1983).

as it turned out in the Sherlock Holmes' mystery *The Adventures of the Silver Blaze*, knew the culprit.

Given plausible hypotheses, competent investigators will seek corroborating or negating information which might confirm existing hypotheses, destroy others or lead to new ones, and continue until they are satisfied that they know what happened or at least have sufficient evidence to achieve their goals (settle a claim, satisfy the burden of proof, etc.). This top-down process of exploring what evidence might be suggested by a hypothesis is clearly holistic and was called 'reduction' by Peirce (though he sometimes used this term synonymously with abduction). It is a reversal of – and a follow-up to – the bottom-up, but nevertheless still holistic, process of developing hypotheses suggested by the evidence. Instead of asking 'If this evidence is true, what might have happened?', as we saw initially in relation to abduction, reduction involves asking 'If this hypothesis is true, what evidence might one expect?' Moreover, it is usefully combined with the process of 'elimination', identified by Francis Bacon as the way scientists subject hypotheses to a variety of evidential tests in order to eliminate those that are inconsistent with the evidence and gauge their strength by the number of evidential tests they satisfy.[39]

Notwithstanding the importance of abductive reasoning, psychologists provide little understanding of what prompts the 'act of insight'[40] – the 'aha'[41] or Eureka[42] moment. Peirce himself argues that abductive reasoning involves 'putting together what we had never before dreamed of putting together which flashes the new suggestion before our contemplation'.[43] For instance, after first organising the facts chronologically, investigators might rearrange them according to the various legal elements that need to be proved. Moreover, by combining evidence and hypotheses, investigators might see something significant such as interesting patterns of interaction or synergies which elude them when considered separately.[44]

[39] See L. J. Cohen, *The Probable and The Provable* (1977), discussed by, for example, D. A. Schum, 'Probability and the Processes of Discovery, Proof, and Choice' (1986) 66 *Boston University Law Review* 825, 854. Cf. also Sherlock Holmes in *The Sign of the Four*: 'Eliminate all other factors, and the one which remains must be the truth', quoted by T. A. Sebeok, '"You Know My Method": A Juxtaposition of Charles S. Peirce and Sherlock Holmes', in Eco and Sebeok, ibid., 20.

[40] C. S. Peirce, *Collected Papers of Charles Sanders Peirce, Vol. 5 Pragmatism and Pragmaticism* (C Hartshorne and P. Weiss (eds) 1934), para. 1581.

[41] Cf. A. J. K. Green and K. Gilhooly, 'Problem Solving', in N. Braisby and A. Gellatly (eds), *Cognitive Psychology* (2nd edn, 2012), 306.

[42] See Chapter 5 at n. 11.

[43] Loc. cit., n. 40.

[44] Schum, above n. 35, 430–1.

As stressed by the school of gestalt psychology[45] – and as a notable advantage of holistic over atomistic reasoning – 'the force of two or more items of evidence considered jointly is quite different from the aggregate force of these same evidence items when considered separately or independently'.[46]

2.2 Lateral Thinking

Other techniques for generating insights and new ideas are suggested by the psychologist Edward de Bono.[47] Like Peirce, he argues that deductive and inductive logic – what he calls 'vertical thinking' – are useful only in selecting and analysing fixed and finite information in terms of rigid, step-by-step, sequential reasoning in which each step's soundness depends on that of the previous one. By contrast, what de Bono calls 'lateral thinking' is provocative and generative of new ideas, involves fluid categorisations, classification and labels, and jumps in reasoning which may not be valid, leaves gaps to be filled later, and may follow less obvious paths. Like abductive reasoners, lateral thinkers generate as many alternative hypotheses for facts as possible, rather than just accepting the best or most obvious explanation and closing off all investigative avenues other than those which confirm the initial hypothesis. Another shared technique is the arranging and rearranging of information[48] – though de Bono also stresses that this should be combined with the atomistic technique of breaking issues up into small units.[49] In addition, de Bono[50] and other lateral thinkers[51] suggest:

- challenging or even totally reversing assumptions about the problems faced;
- using analogous but not identical fact situations to start a train of thought which escapes the more obvious possibilities;
- suspending judgment in order to look for answers even if it means seeing things from the wrong perspective en route to better solutions;
- varying the entry point from which one views issues, such as working backwards rather than forwards;

---

[45] See, for example, Green and Gilhooly, above n. 41, 306ff; J. Frank, *Courts on Trial: Myth and Reality in American Trials* (1949, reprinted 1973), Chapter 12.

[46] Schum, above n. 35, 431.

[47] See, for example, *Lateral Thinking: A Textbook of Creativity* (1977), upon which the following is based.

[48] Ibid., Chapter 7.

[49] Ibid., Chapter 19.

[50] Ibid., Chapters 8–17 passim.

[51] See Green and Gilhooly, above n. 41 on some common techniques of problem-solving.

- obtaining independent views such as those of experts[52] and drawing on numerous perspectives gained individually or through brainstorming sessions where even outrageous, nonsensical or misinterpreted suggestions can unwittingly spark useful insights;[53]
- refusing to be content with one possible solution to a problem;
- evaluating one's perspective and asking what one is trying to achieve.

This last point is particularly important for litigants who need to view the facts, not just from their own perspective but also from that of opponents, and consider what evidence they might use and arguments they might make. Thus litigants need to commence abductive reasoning and lateral thinking as soon as possible to ensure all factual possibilities are explored.

2.3 Fact Investigation and Law

Fact investigation is not, however, only about investigating factual possibilities in the abstract in order to ascertain what happened. The facts also need to be investigated against the background of the governing law.[54] This can be illustrated by adapting a hypothetical case discussed by Terence Anderson and William Twining[55] in which a lawyer is told by a client that her bracelet was stolen while staying at a hotel. She says she left her room one morning to go to breakfast and on returning found that her bracelet was missing. She blames the housekeeper who she saw entering her room while she was on her way to breakfast. She describes the housekeeper as having brown hair and wearing the hotel uniform. But instead of simply believing the client, the lawyer might develop the alternative hypotheses that she is attempting fraud or that someone else stole the bracelet. Investigation might then reveal that the hotel housekeeper is blonde, the client is sufficiently wealthy to make fraud implausible and the bracelet has important sentimental value. Without absolutely rejecting the hypothesis that there was no theft (for instance, the client might want to falsely accuse the hotel), the lawyer needs to investigate the hypothesis that someone else was the thief. Further investigation might reveal that there is only one housekeeper and that hotels are only responsible for theft by non-employees if due to their negligence. This requires thinking about the

---

[52] See Binder and Bergman, above n. 35, 172–4, 197–8.

[53] See also Binder and Bergman, ibid., 205.

[54] See S. Brewer, 'Scientific Expert Testimony and Intellectual Due Process' (1998) 107 *Yale Law Journal* 1535, 1658ff; K. Vandevelde, *Thinking Like a Lawyer: An Introduction to Legal Reasoning* (1996), 57–8.

[55] *Analysis of Evidence* (1991), xxi.

way in which the hotel management might have been negligent, such as by allowing easy access to hotel uniforms. But then inspection of the hotel might reveal a sign over the reception desk excluding liability for theft, whereas legal research reveals that such notices only exclude liability if brought to the customer's attention. This requires re-interviewing the client to see if this was done. In other words, fact investigation may involve constantly going back and forth between facts, hypotheses and law.

2.4 Marshalling Evidence

This hypothetical case also illustrates how challenging fact investigation is due to its dynamic and continuous nature. New information and new insights may constantly emerge, leading to further investigation, new facts and new insights, which in turn may prompt new investigation, etc. It may soon become impossible to think through all the possible combinations of facts and hypotheses which increase exponentially as each new fact arrives and generates new hypotheses.[56] There is thus a danger of too much information clogging the 'investigative arteries'.[57] Yet as David Schum and Peter Tillers point out, investigators require clairvoyance to foresee whether apparently irrelevant or insignificant evidence may later appear crucial and hence whether they can discard it. Consequently they and other information analysts[58] have developed sophisticated computer-based systems[59] to organise (or 'marshall') evidence to resolve this problem, and thereby improve the generation of ideas, selection of investigatory strategies and ultimately the conclusions reached.

For example, Schum and Tillers' model involves fifteen 'marshalling' operations which represent ways of organising investigators' thoughts during fact investigation.[60] They are linked in a network which is designed to act as a 'net' for capturing or identifying – and a 'magnet' for attracting – facts and thoughts about these facts. Each marshalling operation fits into one of six tiers, each containing different

---

[56] See Schum, above n. 35, 431.
[57] Ibid., 407.
[58] See, for example, Schum, ibid., 406; B. Schafer, J. Keppens and Q. Shen, 'Thinking With and Outside the Box: Developing Computer Support for Evidence', in P. Roberts and M. Redmayne (eds), *Innovations in Evidence and Proof: Integrating Theory, Research and Teaching* (2007).
[59] See, for example, J. Keppens and B. Schafer, 'Knowledge Based Crime Scenario Modelling' (2006) 30 *Expert Systems with Applications* 203.
[60] As described by Schum, above n. 35; see also Schum and Tillers, ibid., for an earlier twelve-stack system.

'stacks' that record information in a way that replicates writing on
subject cards. At the lowest tier are stacks for documentary, real and
testimonial evidence, and for information about witness credibility.
The next tier contains stacks for organising the information chronologically and in terms of whether information precedes, accompanies
or follows the crucial events. Apart from one stack recording information learnt from an opponent, the next three tiers relate more to
thoughts about facts, rather than facts themselves, being devoted to
recording emerging possibilities, eliminated hypotheses, possible scenarios or stories, cases theories, chains of inferences, possible problems in inferential reasoning, and beliefs about degrees of probability.
The sixth and final tier is confined to one stack containing relevant
legal rules.

2.5 Atomistic and Holistic Reasoning in Fact Investigation

While evaluation of this evidence-marshalling model falls outside the
scope of this book, it illustrates a number of implications fact investigation has for orthodox evidence theory. One is that facts do not simply appear in a raw state ready for analysis, presentation and evaluation
in the way that a landscaper takes delivery of gravel to make a path.[61]
We have already seen that facts available for analysis, presentation and
determination always arrive constructed by language and the psychology
of observational and expert witnesses.[62] But we now see that they also
depend heavily on the subjective judgment of fact investigators in relation
to a variety of factors.[63] Of most obvious relevance are the governing
law, their interests (or those for whom they work), and whether gaining
the potential evidence justifies the effort and expense. Also influential
are various assumptions and generalisations about how the world works,
such as the 'working rules' of police officers as to who or what patterns of
behaviour are worth investigating.[64]

Given that many of these assumptions take the form of stories,
scripts and scenarios,[65] stories will inevitably and subconsciously shape
hypotheses developed to explain known facts, the search for further

---

[61] Cf. J. D. Jackson, 'Analysing the New Evidence Scholarship: Toward a New Conception of the
Law of Evidence' (1996) 16 *Oxford Journal of Legal Studies* 309, 318.

[62] Chapters 2, 5 and 6 respectively.

[63] See esp. Tillers and Schum, above n. 18, 943–4.

[64] See Chapter 4 at n. 110.

[65] See, for example, Bex et al., above n. 17, esp, 133–4; M. MacCrimmon, 'What is "Common"
about Common Sense?: Cautionary Tales for Travelers Crossing Disciplinary Boundaries'
(2001) 22 *Cardozo Law Review* 1433, 1453ff.

evidence to confirm or eliminate hypotheses and thus ultimately the evidence presented to fact finders. Indeed, as Tillers and Schum's evidence-marshalling system[66] and David Binder and Paul Bergman's classic account of fact investigation[67] show, using narrative may be deliberate and become increasingly more prominent as investigation proceeds and hypotheses about the facts become more specific.[68] For instance, in the case of the missing bracelet, the hypothesis might sharpen from simply that there was a theft, to the theory that the housekeeper was the culprit and finally to the story that it was stolen by someone impersonating the housekeeper after breaking into the cupboard storing hotel uniforms and using a stolen set of keys to access the client's room while she was eating breakfast. But instead of using stories to fill in the gaps (as with the process of confabulation affecting witness perception, fact presentation and adjudication),[69] missing elements of a plausible story may prompt further investigation (in this case, to see if keys have been stolen). And as with holistic reasoning, if the conjecture turns out to be baseless, the story might have to be changed (the door was unlocked). Crucially, however, facts may be too readily selected for analysis and presentation or conversely not investigated at all because, respectively, they do or do not fit common story scripts.

But while fact investigation may ensure that fact finding takes place within certain narrative structures, and while it largely involves top-down holistic reasoning, it also involves atomistic analysis as demonstrated by the inference network, argument construction and Bayes Net[70] marshalling operations in Schum and Tiller's marshalling model. Indeed, according to Schum, logical methods of analysing evidence, like those involved in Wigmore's chart method discussed below, may serve as 'a very powerful "magnet" for attracting interesting and useful insights'.[71] More specifically, doubts about possible inferences from existing facts, the reliability of evidence, and the soundness of premises used in logical reasoning about the facts[72] may prompt investigators to search for potentially superior evidence. Alternatively, or in addition, they can seek to reinforce (or, as an opponent, undermine) existing evidence.

---

[66] See Tillers and Schum, above n. 35, 958–60.
[67] Above n. 35, passim.
[68] See also Anderson, Schum and Twining, above n. 35, 148.
[69] See Chapter 6, section 2.3.2, and this chapter, sections 4 and 5.
[70] Based on Bayes' Theorem: see Chapter 5, section 6.2.
[71] Schum, above n. 35, 449.
[72] Ibid.

3 Fact Analysis and the Logic of Proof[73]

3.1 Introduction

We thus see that fact investigation involves a complex and complementary interweaving of atomistic and holistic methods reasoning, with abductive reasoning, while sui generis being closer to the top-down nature of holistic reasoning. By contrast, while holistic methods play a role in the later stages of factual analysis, it is logic and atomistic reasoning which dominate Wigmore's attempt to map the 'strictly limited'[74] number of mental processes involved in reasoning about evidence and to represent them in a chart depicting the logical relationship between various evidential items in order to assist lawyers cope with a complex mass of facts relevant to litigation. Although treated as 'nothing more than a quaint, even bizarre, period-piece'[75] during his lifetime, Wigmore's scheme has rightly attracted attention from both evidence scholars and others like intelligence analysts.[76] Whether or not it reflects the way that facts are presented and adjudicated upon will be addressed later, but first we need to gain an understanding and an appreciation of Wigmore methodology, as built upon Bentham before him, and subsequently adapted and simplified by Terence Anderson, David Schum and William Twining in their invaluable book, *Analysis of Evidence*.[77]

3.2 Drawing Inferences[78]

Perhaps the most elementary idea underlying the logical analysis of evidence and proof is that facts do not prove themselves. To conclude that a particular fact is proved involves drawing an inference from some other fact. Even if there is an eyewitness, confession or CCTV recording of an alleged criminal act, one still needs to infer that the eyewitness' observations are accurate, that the confession was made voluntarily or that the CCTV images are not misleading. In other words, there is a difference between the evidence offered for a fact (the testimony/confession/recording) and the fact itself (the commission of the relevant crime), or, in Wigmorean language, between the *factum probans* (the probative fact) and the *factum probandum* (the fact to be

---

[73] This section draws heavily on Anderson, Schum and Twining, above n. 35 esp. Chapters 2–6. For less detailed accounts, see Twining, above n. 5, Chapters 3–4 and Appendix; C. Allen, *Practical Guide to Evidence* (4th edn, 2008), 2–6, and for alternative approaches, Binder and Bergman, above n. 35, Chapters 3–7; Michael and Adler, above n. 6.

[74] Wigmore, above n. 6, cited in Twining, above n. 5, 121, 125.

[75] Twining, ibid., 165.

[76] See Twining, above n. 5, 172–4; Tillers and Schum, above n. 35, 914.

[77] Above n. 35.

[78] In addition to Anderson, Schum and Twining, ibid., 60–3, 100ff, see L. R. Patterson, 'Evidence: A Functional Meaning' (1965) 18 *Vanderbilt Law Review* 875.

proved). Moreover, evidence analysts tend not to refer to facts, but to propositions of fact – namely statements of facts which can be declared to be true or false, proven or unproven, likely or unlikely, etc.

What transforms a *factum probans* into a proven fact is an inference made using inductive reasoning in the Wigmorean sense.[79] Thus, instead of starting with a major premise which is applied to facts to reach a conclusion, the fact finder infers one fact from another by relying on an implicit or hidden generalisation. Of course, one can always – and, as we shall see, usefully – translate such inductive reasoning into deductive reasoning, by making explicit the generalisation relied upon and using it as the major premise of the deductive syllogism. But practically speaking it would be incredibly laborious and tedious, not to say awkward, to do so when presenting facts. Nor is it likely to reflect how people evaluate facts during fast-moving fact-finding episodes.

Reasoning about facts is also inductive in the more usual, non-Wigmorean sense[80] in that it involves premises which are – at best – only probably true. Even when major premises which are infallibly true are relevant to reasoning about evidence, they will usually either be so obvious as to be of little practical use or their application will be subject to doubt because of potential additional information (called additional antecedents) which can suppress the deductive inference (through what is known as default or nonmonotonic reasoning).[81] For instance, if an object is thrown off a roof, we can infer that it will hit the ground unless something intervenes. But if we see it hit the ground, we need only make basic inferences about our perceptive capacities. On the other hand, if our view is obscured, we can only predict that the object is very likely to hit the ground and we are back to using a premise couched in probabilities and not certainties.

3.3 The Role of Generalisations[82]

Whether the premise is couched in terms of certain or only probable truth, all inferences are based upon generalisations. These have been described by

---

[79] See section 1 above.

[80] See section 1, above.

[81] As opposed to monotonic inferences where no new evidence can disrupt the logic of the inference: MacCrimmon, above n. 65; 1456–7; R. Walker, 'Theories of Uncertainty: Explaining The Possible Sources of Error In Inferences' (2001) 22 *Cardozo Law Review* 1523, 1524–5; M. Oaksford, 'Reasoning', in Braisby and Gellatly, above n. 41.

[82] The following discussion draws on Anderson, Schum and Twining, above n. 35, 100–3, 262–80. In addition to the references cited in the rest of the paragraph, see Twining, above n. 5, 143–51 passim; Walker, above n. 81, 1560–2; P. Roberts and A. Zuckerman, *Criminal Evidence* (2nd edn, 2010), 146–8.

Schum as the 'glue holding our arguments together'.[83] Without a generalisation it is well-nigh, if not actually,[84] impossible to infer one fact from another. Even where there is direct evidence of the *factum probandum*, one still needs to rely on a generalisation. For example, if a marriage certificate records a marriage, we still need to rely on the generalisation that marriage certificates are usually accurate in order to infer that the couple were married. If a suspect confesses, we must rely on the generalisation that innocent people do not usually confess to crimes they have not committed and hence will infer guilt unless we think that the confession might be false. Matters are even more complicated in relation to eyewitnesses because we need to rely on the multi-part premise that people with the relevant working perceptive senses, operating under good observational conditions, with good memories and lacking a motive to misrepresent, are likely to give accurate and honest testimony.[85]

The generalisations which enable people to make inferences derive from their own personal experiences, hearing about others' experience, and theoretical knowledge gained from parents, teachers, books, the media, television, films, etc. Together these sources provide 'vast storehouses of commonly-held notions about how people and objects generally behave in our society', which are used to formulate 'generalisation about typical behaviour'.[86] In other words, inferences are based upon a mixture of highly personal experience and 'what passes for common sense or knowledge in a given society (or sub-group) at a given time'.[87] In other words, contrary to L. J. Cohen,[88] there is no common stock of knowledge, shared set of common-sense knowledge or 'universal cognitive competence'.[89]

Moreover, as Anderson, Schum and Twining show, generalisations differ along a spectrum of reliability. At one end are undoubted scientific principles, such as the laws of gravity, and widely shared and undoubted beliefs based upon general knowledge experience (such as the sun sets every night and rises the next morning). Relatively – but, as we have seen,[90] less – reliable are the assumptions by forensic examiners about the uniqueness

[83] A phrase popularised by David Schum: for example, 'Alternative Views of Argument Construction from a Mass of Evidence' (2001) 22 *Cardozo Law Review* 1461, 1472.

[84] Cf. Anderson, Schum and Twining, above n. 35, 263 n. 2.

[85] See Cohen, above n. 39, 251.

[86] Binder and Bergman, above n. 35, 85. See also D. E. Van Zandt, 'Commonsense Reasoning, Social Change, and the Law' (1987) 81 *Northwestern University Law Review* 894, 913ff.

[87] W. Twining, 'Narrative and Generalisations in Argumentation about Questions of Fact' (1999) 40 *South Texas Law Review* 351, 357.

[88] Above n. 39, 274–6.

[89] R. J. Allen, 'Common Sense, Rationality, and the Legal Process', *Cardozo Law Review* 22 (2000): 1417, 1423; C. Geertz, *Local Knowledge: Further Essays in Interpretive Anthropology* (3rd edn 2000).

[90] Chapter 5, section 6.

of fingerprints, weapon markings, etc. In the middle of this spectrum are commonly held, but unproven or unprovable, beliefs, for instance that fleeing a crime scene indicates guilt. Finally, at the other end of the spectrum are biases, misleading stereotypes and prejudices. Other differences regarding generalisations relate to their formulation, in terms of their *universality* (whether they apply always, mostly, sometimes, etc.), *precision* (whether formulated in exact ('always' or 'never') or 'fuzzy' ('often', 'quite often' and 'very often') terms) and *level of abstraction* (whether they apply to a wide range of loosely connected cases or narrowly to only very similar cases).

It is here that legal actors can exploit the difference between deductive and inductive reasoning as understood by Wigmore. Converting inductive into deductive reasoning forces an otherwise hidden generalisation into prominence, allowing it to be challenged or steps taken to redress dubious or inappropriately formulated generalisations. For instance, prosecutors could provide evidence to show that not immediately reporting rape does not mean that the allegations are false.[91] Conversely, drawing attention to the exact generalisation relied on when leading evidence that an offender was traced by a tracker dog may prompt fact analysts to establish that the bloodhound was suitably trained and skilled.

3.4 Proving Facts[92]

3.4.1 Catenate Reasoning

Proof, however, usually involves more than a 'simple' inference from one *factum probans* to a *factum probandum*. All legal cases involve what Bentham and Wigmore called the ultimate *factum probandum*[93] (or ultimate *probandum* for short), which is determined by the requirements of the governing law. Establishing it through just one inference is extremely rare. Usually it requires what is called direct evidence, such as a confession or CCTV footage, which directly and unequivocally establishes the ultimate *probandum*, with the only issue being the reliability of such evidence.

In almost all cases, however, the ultimate *probandum* will have to be proved by more than one inference by what is commonly called circumstantial evidence. This might involve a chain of reasoning in which one fact

---

[91] Cf., for example, J. Clay-Warner and C. Burt, 'Rape Reporting after Reforms: Have Times Really Changed?'(2005) 11 *Violence Against Women* 150.

[92] This section draws on Anderson, Schum and Twining, above n. 35, Chapter 3; Twining above n. 5, 128–30, 180–3.

[93] Also called the major or basic *probandum* (Anderson, Schum and Twining, ibid., 60), major or ultimate fact-in-issue (Tillers and Schum, above n. 35, 927) or 'principal', 'ultimate' and 'operative' facts or 'material propositions' (Michael and Adler, above n. 6, 1252–4).

is inferred from an evidential source (testimony, real evidence, a document, etc.) and then another fact inferred from that inferred fact. For example, if X testifies that A had displayed extreme anger when sacked by B, we could (but not necessarily should) infer that A had a motive to harm B, from this inferred fact that A formed the intention to kill B, and finally from this second inferred fact that A did in fact kill B. In other words, one fact can act as both a *factum probandum* in an initial inference from a *factum probans* but then itself act as a *factum probans* for a further inference to another *factum probandum*. Wigmore described this process as involving 'catenate reasoning', given that it involves a chain (*catena* in Latin) of linked inferences, but more recently the terms 'cascaded inferences'[94] or 'inferential streams'[95] have been used.

3.4.2 Combining Inferences

However, Wigmore failed to provide a vocabulary for the other ways in which circumstantial evidence may be used to establish an ultimate *probandum*. Twining remedies this gap by distinguishing four ways that evidentiary propositions can be combined, which, along with catenate inferences, constitute the 'five Cs' of inferential reasoning,[96] and which are illustrated in Figure 1 in section 3.6 below.

(1)   *Conjunction*

Cases will usually involve a number of issues, each of which has to be proved by a separate chain of inferences. For example, the ultimate *probandum* in a murder trial can be subdivided into a number of penultimate or subsidiary *probanda*, namely that: (1) the accused (A) acted voluntarily; (2) A caused the death of the victim (B); (3) A was sane; (4) A intentionally killed B; and (5) A acted without a legal defence. Unless there is direct evidence of these elements, each needs to be proved by separate inferential chains which when combined constitute conjunction.

(2)   *Compound or complex propositions*

Similar to conjunction, in most cases each penultimate *probandum* will contain a number of elements each of which has to be supported by separate items of evidence, themselves designated as interim *probanda*. For example, establishing that A's act caused B's death requires that A committed an act, did so voluntarily and that it caused B's death. This last proposition itself

---

[94]   For example, D. A. Schum and A. W. Martin, 'Formal and Empirical Research on Cascaded Inference in Jurisprudence' (1982) 17 *Law & Society Review* 105.

[95]   K. W. Graham, 'There Will Always Be an England: The Instrumental Ideology of Evidence' (1987) 85 *Michigan Law Review* 1204, 1223.

[96]   Twining, above n. 5, 180.

can be broken up into its constituent interim *probanda*: (1) B died; (2) without A's act, B would not have died; and (3) that A's act was the legal cause of B's death. Once again, this last proposition can be subdivided into two propositions: that A's act was the proximate or direct cause of B's death and that there were no intervening causes. Propositions that are subdivided into subsidiary propositions in this way are called *compound* or *complex* propositions.

(3)   Corroboration

In relation to a penultimate *probandum*, a particular fact can be useful in a number of ways. First, it can be used independently in a stream of catenate inferences leading to the penultimate *probandum*, as we saw in relation to the evidence that A has been sacked by B. Secondly, it can *corroborate* other evidence which also leads to the same proposition. For example, if you want to prove that A killed B at 4.45 p.m. in B's house and witness X says that she saw A enter B's house at 4.30 p.m., this will be corroborated if witness Y testifies to the same effect because it makes the inference that A was in the house at 4.30 p.m. stronger though by no means irresistible (both could be mistaken or lying).

(4)   Convergence

Obviously testimony by two witnesses that they saw A enter B's house at 4.30 p.m. is insufficient to establish that A killed B at 4.45 p.m. But then witness Z might testify that they saw A leave the house at 5.15 p.m., which independently of X and Y's evidence can show that A was in B's house between 4.30 p.m. and 5.15 p.m (barring evidence that A left and returned to the house between 4.45 pm and 5.15 pm). This in turn can be used to establish the opportunity to kill B between these two times. This combination of two independent facts (entering the house and leaving it) to support the inference of a single proposition (the opportunity to kill) constitutes *convergence*. This evidence can then combine with evidence, say of a motive for revenge (based for instance on B having sacked A), and forensic evidence of B's blood on A's clothes, to justify the penultimate *probandum* that A killed B. There are obviously other facts to be proved, one of which is intention. But here A's motive for revenge will again be relevant, showing that one fact can be used as part of different inferential chains.

3.5 Disproving Facts[97]

Thus far we have explored the logic of proof from the standpoint of someone trying to prove a factual proposition (the proponent). But what can the opponent do when evidence is led from which an unfavourable inference

---

[97]   In addition to references in n. 92, see Binder and Bergman, above n. 35, Chapter 7.

can be drawn? According to Wigmore, there are three logical options. The first involves *denial* of the *factum probans*. For example, if in a shoplifting case, in order to establish a guilty mind, the shop detective testifies that the accused paid for only some of the items in his basket, ran to his car once out of shop and ignored an order to stop, the accused could respond that he was not running and did not hear the order. Secondly, *explanation* involves admitting the *factum probans*, but arguing that it supports an alternative inference which weakens or negates the inference relied on by the proponent. For example, the accused could say that he fled because he was running for an unmissable appointment and did not want to be delayed by having to establish his innocence. Thirdly, *rivalling* entails neither denying the *factum probans*, nor trying to explain away inferences based on it, but leading facts upon which a totally new inference or chain of inferences can be based as a rival to the prosecution's inference of guilt. For instance, the accused could attempt to prove that he was mistakenly identified.

Obviously which and whether any of these strategies can be run depends on the available facts. Moreover, each might themselves be countered. For instance, an explanation may be met with further evidence to corroborate the original inference. Equally the rivalling strategy may be countered by showing that the rivalling inference is unsupported by a solid *factum probans*, or the inference can itself be explained away or countered with its own rival.

3.6 Evidence and Proof

From the discussion thus far it can be seen that while proving a particular set of facts can be very difficult in practical terms, in fact only five logical processes are involved:

- the *assertion* of a *probandum* by the proponent of evidence by relying on an inference from a *probans*;
- a *denial* by the opponent of the existence of the *probans* which provides the basis for the proponent's inference;
- an *explanation* by the opponent of the *probans* in order to show that it does not lead to the proponent's proposed inference;
- the establishment of a *rival probans* leading to a *probandum* which contradicts that asserted by the proponent;
- *corroboration* of a *probandum* asserted by the proponent or opponent.

Even more elegantly, albeit using rather off-putting and sometimes inconsistent terminology, Wigmore reduced the myriad types of evidence[98] which can be relied on to just three categories:

---

[98] See Chapter 1, section 1.4.

- *testimonial evidence* – assertions by observational or expert witnesses as to particular propositions of facts;
- *autoptic proferences* – evidence which fact finders can perceive with their own senses; in other words, real and documentary evidence (sometimes referred to together as tangible evidence);
- *circumstantial evidence* – evidence which is inferred from autoptic proferences.

In fact, given that fact finders can also observe testimony, the awkward nature of the neologism 'autoptic proferences' and the apparent confusion between the usual and Wigmorean definition of circumstantial evidence, one can in fact classify all evidence as either:

- testamentary, real or documentary evidence – which can be called an 'evidential datum',[99] 'evidential fact',[100] 'evidential source'[101] or (reflecting orthodox evidence theory's epistemological roots)[102] 'foundational fact'; and
- a fact inferred from a foundational fact or from another inferred fact.[103]

Another useful distinction[104] which cuts across that between foundational and inferred facts distinguishes *directly relevant* evidence, which can be linked by an inference or chain of inferences to the ultimate *probandum*, from *indirectly relevant* evidence, which enhances or detracts from the probative force of foundational facts. Such indirectly relevant evidence may be direct or circumstantial, may support (or undermine) the foundational fact relied upon (such as where an eyewitness is shown to have good (or bad) eyesight and memory, or DNA evidence was (not) based on a uncontaminated sample) and it may support (or undermine) the generalisation used in the inference chain involving directly relevant evidence (for example, that all bloodhounds are accurate scent-trackers).

Building on these concepts, Tillers and Schum[105] analogise a case as a whole to a piece of fabric consisting of vertical strands (warp) represented by inferential chains running parallel with each other from the foundational facts at the bottom to the ultimate *probandum* at the top of the fabric, and

---

[99] For example, Anderson, Schum and Twining, above n. 35, 92.

[100] For example, Roberts and Zuckerman, above n. 82, 132ff.

[101] For example, A. Stein, 'Against "Free Proof"' (1997) 31 *Israel Law Review* 573, 583.

[102] See Chapter 2, section 3.2.1.1.

[103] Cf. Michael and Adler, above n. 6, 1265ff, who distinguish respectively between evidence and evidential facts.

[104] For this, other terms and related discussion, see, for example, Anderson, Schum and Twining, above n. 35, 62–77 passim; Schum, above n. 35, 448; Walker, above n. 81, 1562–3.

[105] Above n. 18, 941.

horizontal strands strengthening the vertical strands (weft). The stronger each strand, as represented by the plausibility of the inference, and the more tightly wound the warp and weft in terms of the number of relevant inferences and the extent to which each directly relevant evidence is supported by ancillary evidence, the stronger the chances of the resultant fabric constituting proof.

3.7 Methods for Analysing Evidence[106]

In addition to conceptualising proof in terms of various logical relations between evidential propositions, Wigmore developed a 'stunning original'[107] system for representing these relations graphically on a chart in order to make decisions about a complex mass of evidence in a litigated case. Development of the chart, illustrated below, proceeds in two steps.

The *analytical* stage involves generating a key-list of all relevant evidential propositions numbered from the ultimate *probandum*, through the penultimate *probanda* and intermediate propositions which support each penultimate *probandum* – the macroscopic level – down to the mass of facts which in turn support (through assertion and corroboration) or negate (through denial, explanation and rivalling) these intermediate propositions – the microscopic level. The *synthetic* stage then involves plotting on a chart all numbered evidential propositions to be proved and evidence used to prove them, represented by symbols for:

- the types of evidence (testimonial affirmatory, testimonial nugatory, circumstantial affirmatory, circumstantial nugatory);
- their relationship to the ultimate *probandum;*
- the relationship between two evidential propositions (tends to support, negate, explain, corroborate, etc.); and
- the strength of support ('strong', 'provisional' or 'doubt about') provided by the evidence.

At the top of a chart – which is partly[108] illustrated in figure 1, below – is the ultimate *probandum*, numbered 1. Just below are the penultimate *probanda*, numbered from 2, and directly below each of these are their intermediate propositions which need to be proved, all linked via lines and directional arrows to denote the direct and catenate inferences from the foundational facts such as testimony (represented by a square) at the

---

[106] For an overview, see Anderson, Schum and Twining, above n. 35, Chapters 4–6.

[107] Tillers and Schum, above n. 18, 912–13.

[108] In terms of only including some of the symbols and only a few illustrations of inferential chains from foundational facts and combinations of inferences, namely those designed to illustrate the 'five Cs' discussed above in section 3.4.2.

bottom of the chart to various items of circumstantial evidence (represented by circles) until they all culminate in the ultimate *probandum*. It is also possible to list and chart the generalisations relied on in the various inferences linking factual propositions, though to avoid cluttering the key-list and obscuring the arguments, Anderson, Schum and Twining advise only articulating significant, non-obvious and unassailable generalisations.[109]

There are other methods for analysing and constructing arguments about evidence that can be used independently or in conjunction with Wigmore's chart. The outline method uses the same '"task decomposition" or "divide and conquer"'[110] approach to breaking down the ultimate and penultimate *probanda* and intermediate propositions into their constituent parts, but omits the key lists and diagrams, thus replicating the value of the chart method in tracking logical relations between evidence, but in much simpler form. By contrast, the narrative method sets out the facts in chronological order and links each to its potential source of evidential support. This enables advocates to develop a narrative account of the evidence for presentation to fact finders and to identify causal connections between events and any evidential gaps or weaknesses that need to be rectified, as well as logical weaknesses in their own story and that of their opponent. Moreover, whereas Wigmore's chart can only provide a fixed snapshot of the evidence at one moment in time, outlines, chronologies and narratives can be easily updated as new information or ideas emerge. Moreover, they are useful both on their own or in combination with the chart method, and may help with fact investigation as well as fact analysis. Thus Anderson, Schum and Twining[111] suggest that the outline method is usually sufficient on its own before pleadings are filed, but that lawyers should begin to use chronologies, narrative and the chart method when moving to trial preparation.

3.8 Critique

3.8.1 General

Wigmore's methodology is certainly the most rigorous and systematic means of comprehensively analysing all evidence arising in a case, even though his claim that the chart method is the 'only true and scientific method'[112] can be dismissed as modernist rhetoric (what competing method is false

---

[109] Above n. 35, 131.

[110] Schum, above n. 18, 1499.

[111] Above n. 35, 149–53.

[112] Above n. 6, 821–2, quoted by Twining, above n. 10, 307.

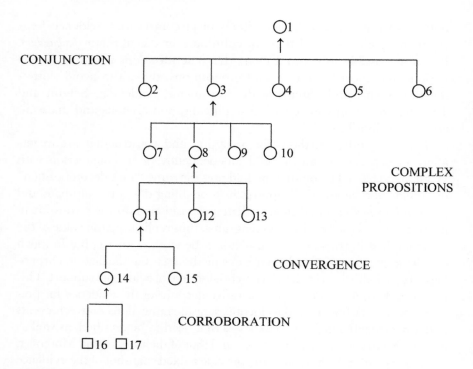

Key list

1. A killed B by stabbing him at A's house on 1/7/17 (the *ultimate probandum*)
2. A acted voluntarily
3. A caused B's death by stabbing
4. A was sane
5. A intentionally killed B
6. A acted without a legal defence
7. B died between 4.30 and 5.15 p.m.
8. A stabbed B between 4.30 and 5.15 p.m. at B's house
9. Without A's stabbing B, B would have not have died
10. A's stabbing B was the legal cause of B's death
11. A was at Bs house between 4.30 and 5.15 p.m
12. B's blood was discovered on A's hands
13. The blood spatters observed on A were consistent with a stabbing
14. A entered B's house at 4.30
15. A left B's house at 5.15 p.m.
16. 'I saw A enter B's house at 4.30' (testimony from X)
17. 'I saw A enter B's house at 4.30' (testimony from Y)

and unscientific?). The chart in particular acts as a useful 'crutch'[113] to cope with the myriad ways evidence can be used and combined and is even – as Wigmore failed to appreciate – a useful aid to fact investigation. Thus, while the evidence to be analysed might be frighteningly complex, the logic behind the chart is simple: all evidence either proves or negates the ultimate *probandum* and it does so through a number of 'strictly limited'[114] logical operations.

However, as Wigmore explicitly acknowledged – and as shall become obvious when we look at fact adjudication – the chart cannot provide an objective representation of the likelihood of the ultimate *probandum* being proved. Instead it provides a diagrammatic and transparent representation of the subjective belief of analysts in the likelihood of proof and the strength of individual evidential items, as well as their choices about which facts support which inferences and how they link to the ultimate *probandum*. The chart is thus 'a map of the mind [rather] than a map of the world'.[115]

But even as a tool of analysis, the chart method has limitations. One is the difficulty of visually depicting a lawyer's reasons for judgments about probative strength based for instance on intuitive impressions of a potential witness' demeanour and the authenticity of their language.[116] Another is that it downplays the importance of analysing the temporal relations among relevant events which may help establish causality.[117] Still further, the chart method 'provides almost no guidance in making *strategic* choices in constructing or criticizing a complex argument'.[118]

But while these limitations can be cured by combining the chart method with alternatives like the narrative method and trial books, other problems with Wigmore's chart method have undermined its potential impact. One is that its symbols are at best 'somewhat quaint'[119] and at worst so obscure and numerous as to seem 'almost calculated to deter the ordinary reader'.[120] Yet even so, there remains a tension between, on the one hand, having insufficient symbols to reflect the facts' true complexity and, on the other hand, having so many that when combined with a key-list of hundreds of items the chart becomes too unwieldy, too time-consuming and laborious to construct and too complex and difficult to interpret – even in

---

[113] Tillers and Schum, above n. 18, 913. See also L. Harmon, 'Etchings on Glass: Reflections on the Science of Proof' (1999) 40 *South Texas Law Review* 483, 500.

[114] Loc. cit., n. 74.

[115] Tillers and Schum, above n. 18, 911.

[116] Harmon, above n. 113, 504–5.

[117] See Schum, above n. 39, 835, 843.

[118] Twining, above n. 16, 310.

[119] Tillers and Schum, above n. 18, 933, referring to 'cosmetic difficulties'.

[120] Twining, above n. 5, 112.

computer form.[121] In response Twining argues, first, that charting becomes easier with practice and that microscopic analysis can be selectively applied where it is most needed and/or only in high-stake cases.[122] Secondly, even if the chart method is 'an over-elaborate and time-consuming way of doing what lawyers do anyway",[123] it – and Wigmorean analysis in general – performs the invaluable pedagogical role of showing students that factual skills are very different to legal skills and that, without training, they tend 'to make logical jumps, to slip in hidden premises, to get away with fallacies, to confuse evidence with inference from evidence, to introduce irrelevant material, or by a switch of standpoint to switch ultimate *probanda*, and so on'.[124] Moreover, these benefits can largely be obtained even if the chart method is substantially simplified or even omitted altogether.

3.8.2 Probabilities Problems

A more serious limitation with the chart method and the logical analysis of proof in general involves the 'transitivity of doubt problem'.[125] As we have seen, virtually all inferences are based on generalisations which are only probably true and thus involve some level of doubt about their certainty. But how does one combine the probabilities involved in one inferential stream with those in subsequent inferences involved in catenate reasoning or when inferences are combined to create convergence or conjunction? Are doubts over the certainty about one inference carried over or ignored when one comes to consider doubts in other inferences? To take a very simple example, the inference that A had a motive to harm B because A had displayed extreme anger at being sacked by B is somewhat doubtful, but it would seem wrong to either treat it as conclusively proved in order to infer A's intention to kill B or to ignore it altogether. However, if we reject these extremes, how do we combine each of the two uncertain inferences and, more acutely, how do we combine both uncertainties with further uncertainties such as the even more uncertain inference of an intention to murder?

---

[121] As developed by Schum and Tillers; see above, n. 35, 679.

[122] Above n. 5, 174 and 'Taking Facts Seriously Again', in Roberts and Redmayne, above n. 58, 80–1.

[123] But cf. Graham, above n. 95, 1218, noting Twining's lack of supporting evidence for this assertion.

[124] Above n. 5, 186.

[125] Raised by Cohen, above n. 39. For a good overview, see Twining, above n. 5, 181–3.

In debating this and other more esoteric problems regarding the proper use of probability theory,[126] all sides agree that one cannot use the sort of frequency-type probabilities used to develop statistical probabilities for matters relevant to law such as we have seen has been done in relation to the likelihood of random matches for DNA and other forensic evidence.[127] This is because one cannot speak of the frequency of one-off events like a murder or car crash happening in the way alleged. Consequently the law cannot use the so-called objective approach to probabilities which is concerned with the actual likelihood of events.[128] Rather, it must draw upon belief-type probability (or epistemic or subjective) theories which are concerned with assessing someone's belief in the likelihood of an event.

Nevertheless, debate between evidence scholars is not between the different proposed approaches to expressing this belief,[129] but over the claim by many that the Bayesian approach to assessing frequency-type probabilities can be used to produce numerical values for the degree of one's belief. As we have seen,[130] Bayes' Rule allows one to estimate the probability of a hypothesised event based on the number given to its likely occurrence prior to any new evidence, combined with the probability calculation attached to the new evidence to give a new, posterior, estimate of its probability by dividing the former by the latter to produce a likelihood ratio. Thus, instead of simply expressing one's belief 'ordinally' in words (for example, 'very likely', 'likely', 'unlikely', 'very unlikely'), it can be expressed 'cardinally' as a number ranging from 0 (denoting impossibility) to 1 (denoting absolute certainty). In response to this mathematical (or Pascalian)[131] approach, Cohen and others argued that probabilities can only be expressed ordinally. Moreover, they espouse an approach based on the Bacanian approach to evaluating the strength of evidence according to the number and completeness of

---

[126] For useful overviews, see, for example, Anderson, Schum and Twining, above n. 35, Chapter 9; Allen, above n. 16, 373–82; J. Jackson, above n. 61, 311–18; Roberts and Zuckerman, above n. 82,148–59; R. C. Park and M. J. Saks, 'Evidence Scholarship Reconsidered: Results of the Interdisciplinary Turn' (2005–6) 47 *British Columbia Law Review* 949, 985–95.

[127] Chapter 5, section 6.2. The following overview of different approaches to probability theory draws on I. Hacking, *An Introduction to Probability and Inductive Logic* (2001), esp. Chapters 11 and 12. For a shorter description using slightly different language, see H. L. Ho, *A Philosophy of Evidence Law: Justice in the Search for Truth* (2008), 110ff.

[128] Or 'aleatory', given much early work on probabilities focused on predicting the outcome of throwing dice (*alea* in Latin).

[129] That is, as to the degree of confidence that one has either that the uncertain fact has or will occur (the personal approach) or that one's belief is supported by available evidence (the interpersonal or evidential approach).

[130] Chapter 5, section 6.2.

[131] Pascal made the first attempt to construct aleatory probability theory.

evidentiary tests it is able to survive (whether witnessing conditions were good, witnesses are competent and unbiased, etc.).

Cohen's intervention was prompted by a number of apparent paradoxes raised by converting probability assessments into numbers. One[132] is the problem of 'naked statistics', exemplified by the promoter of a hypothetical rodeo, attended by 1,000 people, of whom only 499 paid for entry at a turnstile, and who sues randomly chosen spectators as possible gatecrashers because 501 (that is, more than 50 per cent) did not pay. Counter-intuitively, this should succeed because it is slightly more probable than not that each chosen defender was a gatecrasher. Fortunately this paradox does not arise in practice because courts are not prepared to allow proof by naked statistics but require additional evidence, such as witnesses identifying the defender as a gatecrasher.

More problematic are the implications of a numerical approach to the transitivity of doubt issue raised above.[133] To take conjunction as an example, the law requires that each factual element of a case must be proved to the requisite standard of proof. Strictly speaking, this would make proof virtually impossible if one's belief in the existence of each element is expressed in numerical terms because the multiplication rule in probability theory requires that the probability estimate for each independent element is multiplied to provide an overall probability. For instance, if fact finders put the probability of two disputed elements at 0.7 each, then the combined probability of each is only 0.49, which is insufficient for proof even in civil cases. Adding more disputed elements renders results increasingly absurd (adding another element with the same level of doubt leads to a 0.343 overall probability, yet another to 0.2401, etc.). By contrast, Cohen's approach allows pursuers who establish each element on a balance of probabilities to make a judgment on the case as a whole.

According to some commentators,[134] Bayesians have now met Cohen's criticisms (or at least shown that any remaining criticisms apply equally to his own approach), but are still themselves plagued by stubborn problems of their own, such as that:

- the prior probability of facts which is updated by new information to give the posterior probability is based on an arbitrary and highly subjective assessment;
- making prior assessments of criminal guilt before encountering any evidence conflicts with the presumption of innocence;

---

[132] A similar issue is raised by the taxi cab problem discussed in Chapter 5, section 7.3.3.
[133] See at n. 125.
[134] Roberts and Zuckerman, above n. 82, 152. But cf. Pardo, above n. 19, 415ff, who argues that Bayesians have not solved these problems or additional problems raised by others.

- there is no uncontroversial means of translating the numerical probability derived from Bayes' Rule into a decision as to whether this satisfies the non-numerically expressed criminal standard of proof; and
- while one can use Bayes' Rule to assess single items of new information, it is computationally impossible for fact finders to constantly
update prior probabilities and posterior probabilities as each new item
of information emerges.[135]

As we shall see,[136] the last problem has serious implications for orthodox
rationalist assumptions about the ability of fact adjudicators to soundly
assess evidence in terms of inductive logic. More generally, however, the
apparent irresolubility of the debate over the 'one true' normative standard
for making probability assessments[137] means that Wigmorean and other
atomistic methods of assessing evidence in terms of inductive logic have
only limited value in predicting actual decisions – even if one assumes that
facts are presented and evaluated in terms of inductive logic. It is to these
assumptions we now turn, starting with an examination of fact presentation.

4 Fact Presentation and Rhetoric

4.1 Rhetoric: The Art of Persuasion[138]

Because there are few[139] dedicated empirical studies of the way that lawyers and other advocates go about presenting facts, attention will focus

---

[135] But cf. R. Friedman, 'E is for Eclectic: Multiple Perspectives on Evidence' (2001) 87 *Virginia Law Review* 2029, responding to this and some of the more general arguments of 'Bayesioskeptics'.

[136] Section 5.1.

[137] See, for example, Schum, above n. 39, 875, who admits that no probability theory offers the prospect of ensuring sound inferential reasoning by fact adjudicators, but argues (esp. at 874–5) that the
value of each of the different theories varies according to the relevant fact-handling stage; see also
T. J. Anderson, 'Refocusing The New Evidence Scholarship' (1991) 13 *Cardozo Law Review* 783, 785.

[138] See P. Goodrich, *Reading the Law: A Critical Introduction to Legal Method and Techniques* (1986), Chapter 6;
E. A. Scallen, 'Classical Rhetoric, Practical Reasoning and the Law of Evidence' (1995) 44 *American
University Law Review* 1717; J. Hollander, 'Legal Rhetoric' and J. M. Balkin, 'A Night in the Topics: The
Reason of Legal Rhetoric and the Rhetoric of Legal Reason', in Brooks and Gewirtz, above n. 30.

[139] But see the following analyses of single (mostly) US cases, primarily on the use of storytelling:
C. Baldwin, 'Who needs Fact when You've Got Narrative? The Case of P, C & S vs. United Kingdom'
(2005) 18 *International Journal for the Semiotics of Law* 217; A. G. Amsterdam and R. Hertz, 'An Analysis
of Closing Arguments to a Jury' (1992) 55 *New York Law School Law Review* 37; P. N. Meyer, 'Making
the Narrative Move: Observations Based Upon Reading Gerry Spence's Closing Argument in *The
Estate of Karen Silkwood v. Kerr-McGee, Inc.*' (2002) 9 *Clinical Law Review* 229; T, Alper et al., 'Stories Told
and Untold: Lawyering Theory Analyses of The First Rodney King Assault Trial' (2005) 12 *Clinical
Law Review* 1; R. Lempert, 'Narrative Relevance, Imagined Juries, and a Supreme Court Inspired
Agenda for Jury Research' (2002) 21 *Saint Louis University Public Law Review* 15; and the far more exten-
sive observation of over sixty US cases in W. L. Bennett and M. S. Feldman, *Reconstructing Reality in the
Courtroom* (1981), discussed in section 5.2 below.

on advice given to prospective advocates in instruction manuals, which is often illustrated with passages from actual trials, and, as we shall see,[140] confirmed by the behaviour of advocates who continue to ply their art after elevation to the bench when instructing juries and delivering judgments. Much of this advice is too practical and specific for the purposes of this book, being concerned with the technicalities, tactics and ethics of particular aspects of advocacy, such as how to write pleadings, question witnesses, address the court, what to wear, where to stand, and how to control and question witnesses.

Nevertheless, these manuals also contain insights about how advocates go about persuading in general and thus represent the modern incarnation of the ancient art of rhetoric, which until relatively recently was regarded as a serious topic for study. Today the term rhetoric tends to be used pejoratively to denigrate arguments and other forms of discourse as mere hot air or bombast, or as involving illegitimate appeals to emotion, stereotypes and prejudice and dazzling linguistic flourishes designed to pull the wool over people's eyes. By contrast to the implicit dichotomy between rhetoric and reason, emotion and logic, style and substance, Aristotle saw rhetoric as involving *logos* (reason), *pathos* (emotion) and *ethos* (the speaker's credibility as reflected in factors like character, status and authority). Similarly, if we adopt a dictionary[141] or utilitarian definition of rhetoric as simply the art of persuasive communication, we can regard logic and reason as important aspects of rhetoric, rather than implicitly superior to it.[142] After all (he asks rhetorically!), what can be more persuasive than a conclusion that follows as a matter of logical necessity from accepted premises? Equally we can see rhetoric not as illegitimate, but as the unavoidable consequence of communication in which one's words, body language and tone of voice will always convey messages whether one is a witness persuading fact finders to accept one's testimony, an advocate attempting to win a case, a judge instructing the jury or delivering a judgment, or a juror discussing a verdict.

---

[140] See at nn 171–2, 175, 178 and 188, and also Amsterdam, Hertz and Walker-Stirling, above n. 27, 27–30; J. Jackson and S. Doran, *Judge Without Jury: Diplock Trials in the Adversary System* (1995), Chapter 8; J. Winter, 'The Truth Will Out? The Role of Judicial Advocacy and Gender in Verdict Construction' (2002) 11 *Social and Legal Studies* 343.

[141] For example, the *Pocket Oxford Dictionary* (11th edn, 2013) defines rhetoric as 'the art of impressive or persuasive speaking or writing or language used to persuade or impress'.

[142] Cf. J. Michael and M. Adler, 'The Trial of an Issue of Fact: II' (1934) 34 *Columbia Law Review* 1462, 1483–4, distinguishing between the 'proper' art of rhetoric and the 'improper tricks' of sophistry, which are 'not governed by the principles of logic'.

As regards the deliberate use of rhetoric, there are techniques relating to both the content of what is being communicated and the style of delivery, though admittedly they are intimately related since style should support content, whereas content might be chosen partly because of its presentational advantages.

4.2 Content and Structure

Turning first to content, what evidence is presented to adjudicators will obviously depend crucially on the facts available to advocates and their presentational goals. More generically, however, there are ways of structuring facts to be persuasive. Based on a survey of Anglo-American advocacy manuals,[143] Twining lists six such structural devices which guide the choice of what facts to present and how to organise their presentation: theories, themes, stories, thelemas, scenes and situations – though UK manuals, which are generally less theoretically grounded and more restrained in their approach to rhetoric,[144] only refer to the first three[145] and some to none at all.

4.2.1 Theories

In the context of fact presentation (as opposed to investigation, where the term is more of a simile for 'hypothesis'),[146] a theory is a coherent and precise statement of the facts which encapsulates the advocate's argument about the case as a whole. It is selected from the options suggested by the evidence in order to be successfully related in syllogistic form to the relevant governing law and hence to deliver the desired outcome. For prosecutors, and civil pursuers and applicants, choosing a theory is a relatively simple matter of aligning the most provable facts with the governing law and will be found in the indictment, pleadings, etc. Criminal accused and

---

[143] Twining, above n. 16, 288–94 (largely replicated in Anderson, Schum and Twining, above n. 35, 153–8). In addition to the sources he surveys, the following analysis draws on Rose, above n. 27; A. Boon, *Advocacy* (2nd edn, 1993); R. Du Cann, *The Art of the Advocate* (1993); J. Munkman, *The Technique of Advocacy* (1991); K. Evans, *The Golden Rules of Advocacy* (1993); M. O. Miller and T. A. Mauet, 'The Psychology of Jury Persuasion' (1999) 22 *American Journal of Trial Advocacy* 549; D. Napely, *The Technique of Persuasion* (4th edn, 1991); M. Hyam, *Advocacy Skills* (4th edn, 1999); S. Lubet, *Modern Trial Advocacy: Analysis and Practice* (4th edn, 2009); M. Stone, *Cross-Examination in Criminal Trials* (3rd edn, 2009). As regards Scotland, see C. Hennessy, *Practical Advocacy in the Sheriff Court* (2006); R. E. Conway and B. McCann, *The Civil Advocacy Skills Book* (2015).

[144] Probably due to the much greater prevalence of juries in the US: cf. Evans, ibid., 64–5 comparing the two countries.

[145] Which in fact can be said to encompass the other three in that *thelema* is closely connected to theme, and scenes and situations are specific elements of an overall story.

[146] See section 2, above.

civil defenders and respondents have far more leeway to construct a series of alternative competing theories. For instance, in the missing bracelet case, whereas the pursuer's theory might be that 'someone pretending to be a hotel employee stole the pursuer's bracelet due to the hotel's negligence in allowing the imposter to dress in hotel uniform', the hotel could offer the following theories (even if in logical contradiction):[147]

- the pursuer has falsely alleged theft in an attempt at fraud;
- there is insufficient evidence of theft;
- there is insufficient evidence that the thief was wearing a hotel uniform;
- the hotel was not negligent in allowing the thief to gain a hotel uniform;
- the hotel cannot be held liable because a notice excluded liability for theft.

While theory choice will be determined by the available legal options given the available and potentially provable evidence, it will also be significantly influenced by choices regarding the other organisational advocacy devices, especially when more than one theory is possible. And while these organisation devices are likely to prove useless unless they support the theory, theories on their own are unlikely to persuade fact finders.

4.2.2 Themes

Of the other organisational devices, themes are used to strike an emotional, psychological, political, moral or other affective chord with fact finders, and to introduce them as early as possible and to repeat them (at least in jury trials)[148] like a mantra throughout the trial. Whereas advocates use theories to show that law and logic favour them and that fact finders *can* decide in their favour, they use themes to show that morality, justice and/or sympathy is on their side and that fact finders *should* decide in their favour. The aim is to paint their side as the 'good guys' up against the 'bad guys' through such themes as 'a poor investor naively trusting in big business acting at its callous worst' or 'a gold-digging temptress marrying a lonely old man for his money'.[149] In the missing bracelet case, the pursuer could run a theme of 'negligent business too busy making money to bother with security', to which the defender could reply with 'greedy fraudster

---

[147] According to Stone, above n. 143, 11–14, this is far less possible in criminal cases as one cannot simultaneously deny that a crime was committed and that it was not committed by the accused.

[148] Cf. Lubet, above n. 143, 71; Evans, above n. 143, 64 recommending a more toned-down approach for judges.

[149] These can be incorporated into a catchy hook to be constantly repeated for rhetorical emphasis, as in the famous 'if the glove don't fit you must acquit' in the O. J. Simpson trial: see Meyer, above n. 139, 237–40.

using hotel and well-to-do appearance to scam insurance company'. We even see themes in legal judgments such as those discussed in Chapter Two[150] involving women who killed their abusers. Thus Sara Thornton was judicially portrayed as a scheming killer who exploited the very notion of femininity which she transgressed, a woman who 'loved too much' and the author of her own misfortune. Conversely, Kiranjit Ahluwalia benefited from the theme of a tragic and passive victim of fate and an abusive, violent husband.[151] As the implicit referencing in the Thornton case of fictional and historical figures like Lady Macbeth and Lucrezia Borgia, contemporary cod psychology and the genre of Greek tragedy illustrates, there is clearly a link between themes and culturally embedded stories.[152] Also relevant are common idioms like 'hell hath no fury like a woman scorned'.[153] In this way themes may resonate with social beliefs, prejudices and fears (founded or unfounded) about, for instance, rising crime, environmental pollution, and more positively with the espousal of civil virtues or shared values, in order to provide what Steven Lubet calls a story frame or framework.[154]

4.2.3 Thelemas

Closely related to themes is the notion of *thelema* – a Greek term meaning 'to will, wish, want or purpose' and defined by a US judge as 'the universe of things which can combine which create, in a judge or jury, the desire to help'.[155] Clearly *thelema* may be generated by feelings of sympathy or empathy which ought to be triggered at the outset, emphasised throughout[156] and underlined in the closing 'peroration'.[157] Also important here is

---

[150] Sections 1.2 and 4.2 respectively.

[151] See D. Nicolson, 'Telling Tales: Gender Discrimination, Gender Construction and Battered Women Who Kill' (1995) *Feminist Legal Studies* 185. For a similar analysis, see C. Bell and M. Fox, 'Telling Stories of Women Who Kill' (1995) 5 *Social and Legal Studies* 471.

[152] See R. K. Sherwin, 'Law Frames: Historical Truth and Narrative Necessity in a Criminal Case' (1994) 47 *Stanford Law Review* 39, 78 advising that advocates familiarise themselves with 'popular myths, narrative genres, familiar metaphors, schemata and so on'.

[153] See the case discussed at 290, below.

[154] Above n. 143, 8–9.

[155] C. I. Weltner cited in D. L. Rumsey (ed.), *Master Advocates Handbook* (1986), 6 and Twining, above n. 16, 294.

[156] See, for example, Lord Taylor who opens his judgement with 'This is a tragic case' and maintains sympathy for Kiranjit Ahluwalia throughout, inter alia, by quoting extensively from a letter in which she made 'a number of self-denying promises of the most abject kind': *R. v. Ahluwalia* [1992] 4 All E.R. 889, 892.

[157] See, for example, Edward Marshall Hall's closing words to the jury in defending a middle-aged prostitute on a murder charge in the nineteenth century: 'Look at her, gentlemen of the jury. Look at her. God never gave her a chance – won't You?': J. Morton, 'Marshall Hall for the

Aristotle's notion of *ethos* as represented by the advocate's character, credibility, personality, rapport with audience and general demeanour. Thus advocates are advised – perceptively, according to empirical research[158] – to strive to appear to be honest, trustworthy, sincere fair, patient, likeable and respectful of the court, and to encourage fact finders to feel sympathetic not just towards the client, but towards themselves as well.

4.2.4 Stories

Sympathy can be also allied to the 'hard wired human desire for equilibrium and order',[159] which in turn draws on a 'universal story arc'[160] involved in all storytelling. This arc involves a beginning which sets the scene when things were fine (the 'set-up', 'exposition' or '"orientation"'), a situation in which the protagonists encounter conflict or challenges through some inciting incident causing problematic change (the 'complication' or 'crisis'), and finally the 'resolution' of these problems through the restoration of order or the provision of some remedy. This suggests that advocates should aim to engage the 'fact finder as a virtual character in the story – the "hero" who can rectify the disruption and save [their] client from further injustice',[161] thus providing the resolution to the parties' stories which began outside the court room.

In the context of advocacy techniques, a *story* means more than one party's version of what happened ('my story' is that . . .). Twining defines it as 'a narrative of particular events arranged in a time sequence and forming a meaningful totality'.[162] As such, almost all manuals recognise the psychological qualities of stories as a central – if not *the* central – organisational device for presenting facts.[163] These qualities will be explored in

---

Defence' (2001) 151 *New Law Journal* 546, but cf. Stone, above n. 143, 262 who advises that today appeals to the emotions should be minimal and restrained.

[158] W. Young, N. Cameron and Y. Tinsley, *Juries In Criminal Trials, Part Two: A Summary of Research Findings* (1999), 37–8, but see S. M. Wood et al., 'The Influence of Jurors' Perceptions of Attorneys and Their Performance on Verdict' (2011) 23 *Jury Expert* 23, where the sincerity of prosecution and plaintiff lawyers seemed to reduce their chances of success.

[159] Lubet, above n. 143, 427.

[160] Lubet, ibid., 373, 426–7, relying on R. McKee, *Story: Substance, Structure, Style and the Principles of Screenwriting* (1999). See also Yorke, above n. 26, esp. Chapter. 1, but see also Chapter 3, a variant on the classical three-stage model; Amsterdam, Hertz and Walker-Stirling, above n. 27, 20–30; P. N. Meyer, 'Vignettes from a Narrative Primer' (2006) 12 *The Journal of the Legal Writing Institute* 229, 240ff.

[161] Lubet, ibid., 427. For an example of the use of this technique, see Amsterdam and Hertz, above n. 139, esp. at 64ff.

[162] Above n. 33, 290.

[163] In addition to the references in n. 143, see, for example, Rideout, above n. 12; B. J. Foley and R. A. Robbins, 'Fiction 101: A Primer for Lawyers on How to Use Fiction Writing Techniques to Write Persuasive Facts Sections' (2000) 32 *Rutgers Law Journal* 32.

more detail when examining fact adjudication.[164] For now, we can note that it is important that advocates ensure that the form of fact presentation aligns with its likely means of evaluation. In any event, in the context of long trials and in a world where the new forms of communication have reduced human attention spans, stories still have the power to grab and retain the audience's attention. Once a story begins, we all want to know the outcome, especially if we identify with and care about its central characters.[165] Moreover, stories are likely to evoke positive subconscious memories of our early childhood and possibly even the fire-side storytelling of bygone days. Advocacy manuals stress that stories provide a means to integrate disparate facts into a meaningful whole, provide a context to understand them, and create visual images of living events involving real people that are more powerful and memorable than other means of communicating facts. Furthermore, presenting the facts in narrative form encourages fact finders to fill in missing elements of common stories and accept ideas that are better not explicitly expressed.[166]

4.2.5 Scenes

Advocacy manuals also suggest decomposing stories into separate acts and scenes. Thus the story may begin by describing the protagonists' life situation before problems arose, depicting their characters in ways that encourage the audience to identify and sympathise with them, and by providing contextual details suggesting motivations and causal connections. The story may then move to the incidents which led to the event or situation at the core of the legal proceedings – what Binder and Bergman call the 'moment of substantive importance'[167] – and may do so in ways which build tension and imply causality.

Incredibly important in this regard is deciding what facts to include or omit. Thus, depending on the advocate's aims with regard to theory, theme and *thelema*, some scenes may be packed with detail while others may be pared down to their bare essentials or omitted altogether. For instance, those prosecuting women who kill their violent partners are likely to downplay the latter's violence and its impact on her, and any behaviour before, after or during the killing which suggests her mental incapacity, while emphasising evidence suggesting premeditation, an ability to defend

---

[164] Section 5.
[165] Boon, above n. 143, 22.
[166] Lopez, above n. 29, 32–3.
[167] Above n. 35, 191.

herself and more generally her rejection of norms of feminine passivity which seem incompatible with a capacity for murder.[168]

Nor do stories have to be told in chronological order.[169] Using flashbacks or flashforwards may disrupt otherwise seemingly natural inferences or suggest those that are not immediately obvious. For example,[170] instead of referring to Kiranjit Ahuwalia having bought the petrol used to immolate her husband days before killing him in describing the build-up to the killing, Lord Taylor first mentions it when describing Kiranjit suddenly recalling the purchase moments before killing Deepak.[171] By contrast, Lord Beldam in *Thornton* creates a sense of causality and dramatic tension by converting a highly ambiguous threat against the deceased into evidence of premeditation with the words: 'But for subsequent events, Mrs Thomas might well have dismissed this [threat] as no more than an expression of exasperation.'[172]

4.2.6 Situations

The final organisational device referred to by Twining is a *situation*. This refers to 'a state of affairs at a particular moment of time as contrasted with a sequence of events'[173] such as driving without a licence. If the story can be analogised to a film, the situation is a still from the film. Indeed, if one extends it beyond static state of affairs to the events comprising the moment of substantial significance,[174] one can see it as a film's climactic moment shot in slow motion. In films, this is done to emphasise the importance of the scene, but in law an extended focus on the situation allows the theory, themes and story to be brought together in a way that compels the required result. For example, in *Ahluwalia*, Lord Taylor describes the central legal event as follows:

> The appellant went to bed about midnight. She was unable to sleep and brooded upon the deceased's refusal to speak to her and his threat to beat her the next morning. She had bought some caustic soda a few days earlier with a view to using it upon the deceased. She had also bought a can of petrol and put it in the lean-to outside the house. Her mind turned to these substances and some time after 2.30 p.m. she got up, went downstairs,

---

[168] See Nicolson, above n. 151, in relation to Sara Thornton and the almost opposite approach to Kiranjit Ahluwalia.

[169] Lubet, above n. 143, 389–90.

[170] See also Amsterdam, Hertz and Walker-Stirling, above n. 27, 27–30.

[171] Above n. 156, 893.

[172] *R. v. Thornton No. 1* [1992] 1 All E.R. 306, 309.

[173] Anderson, Schum and Twining, above n. 35, 155.

[174] Ibid., n. 10, 155.

poured about two pints of the petrol into a bucket (to make it easier to throw), lit a candle on the gas cooker and carried these things upstairs. She also took an oven glove for self-protection and a stick. She went to the deceased's bedroom, threw in some petrol, lit the stick from the candle and threw it into the room. She then went to dress her son.[175]

Here we see both of the judge's theories, namely that domestic violence led to an excusable boiling over of rather than a murderous cooling down of anger (she 'brooded'), and that she acted while suffering from diminished responsibility (she did not actively remember the petrol but her apparently uncontrolled 'mind turned' to it), as well as the theme of a maternal woman who goes immediately from killing to childcare.

4.3 Form and Delivery[176]
The passage also illustrates the importance of punctuation and word choice in supporting the content of what is being said. This can be done consciously or – as probably in the above example – automatically.[177] Thus, as regards punctuation, the long sentence starting with 'Her mind' was broken up into short clauses, connected by commas and the conjunction 'and', thus suggesting a woman unable to control her actions like a runaway train on a track.[178] Advocacy manuals also recommend a wide range of linguistic tools such as various rhythmic devices (word repetition, alliteration,[179] parallel phrasing,[180] etc.) and choice of linguistic register (conversational involving simple common words rather than technical or legalistic language), verb tense (present rather than past or future), grammatical voice (direct rather than passive voice), speech form (direct, simple and assertive rather than cautious and qualified – that is, 'powerful' rather than 'powerless'[181]).

Even more obvious advice relates to individual word choice, which we have already seen[182] affects the memory, recall and construction of facts,

---

[175] Above n. 156, 893.
[176] See Boon, above n. 143, Chapter 1; Du Cann, above n. 143, esp. Chapters 10 and 11.
[177] See also Amsterdam, Hertz and Walker-Stirling, above n. 27, 117.
[178] Compare the description of the equivalent sequence of events in *Thornton*, above n. 172, 310 f-g, which was twice as long, largely due to its more deliberative pace created by using short sentences with no more than two separate actions, and linking sentences and clauses with conjunctives to suggest a calm, controlled and hence deliberate killing.
[179] Combining words with the same opening consonant (for example, Churchill's 'we shall not flag or fail', quoted by Du Cann, above n. 143, 202).
[180] Phrases which echo others in a sentence (for example, J. F. Kennedy's 'Not merely peace in our time, but peace in all time', quoted by Boon, above n. 143, 11).
[181] See Chapter 6, section 3.2.2.
[182] Chapter 2, section 3.3.1 and Chapter 6, section 2.4.3.

as when different words are used in describing a car crash (collide, hit, smash, etc.). Persuasion can be further enhanced by the use of adverbs (hit carelessly, recklessly, etc.) and adjectives (cruel, vicious or merciless assaults). This power of words to affect fact evaluation is illustrated by recent rape cases in which judges downplayed forced sexual assaults which later culminated in rape as acting in 'an amorous fashion'[183] or attempting 'to cuddle the complainer and become affectionate',[184] and reduced what were likely to be frantic attempts to escape from rapists as mere 'wriggling'.[185] This power may be enhanced by connotations with cultural images and scripts, as when the complainer's reaction to being raped is described as 'hysteria'[186] or attendance at a 'wild teenage party' is used to suggest a willingness to have sex.[187]

This last example in particular illustrates how words may evoke vivid and persuasive images. Another, more well-known, example is Lord Denning's description of the facts in *Miller* v. *Jackson*[188] en route to deciding to discharge an injunction obtained by a property owner against a cricket team:

> In the summer time village cricket is the delight of everyone . . . In the village of Lintz in County Durham they have their own ground, where they have played for these last 70 years. They tend it well. The wicket area is well rolled and mown . . . On other evenings after work they practise while the light lasts. Yet now after these 70 years a judge of the High Court has ordered that they must not play there any more . . . He has done it at the instance of a newcomer who is no lover of cricket. This newcomer has built, or has had built for him, a house on the edge of the cricket ground which four years ago was a field where cattle grazed. The animals did not mind the cricket . . . The newcomer has bought one of the houses on the edge of the cricket ground. No doubt the open space was a selling point. Now he complains that, when a batsman hits a six, the ball has been known to land in his garden or on or near his house. His wife has got so upset about it that they always go out at weekends. . . . So they asked the judge to stop the cricket being played. And the judge, much against his will, has felt that he must order the cricket to be stopped: with the consequences, I suppose, that the Lintz Cricket Club will disappear. The cricket

---

[183] *Cinci* v. *HMA* 2004 SLT. 748, para. 16.

[184] *Spendiff* v. *HMA* 2005 1 JC. 338, para. 11

[185] For example, *GM* v. *HMA* [2011] HCJAC 112, para. 6; *Mutebi* v. *HMA* [2013] HCJAC 142 para. 2; *KH* v. *HMA* 2015 SLT. 380, para. 14.

[186] See, for example, *Lennie* v. *HMA* 2014 SCL. 848, paras 7, 14 and 19.

[187] Taslitz, above n. 25, 437.

[188] [1977] 3 All ER 338, 340–41. Some of the following analysis draws on Twining, above n. 33, 303–4.

ground will be turned to some other use. I expect for more houses or a factory. The young men will turn to other things instead of cricket. The whole village will be much the poorer. And all this because of a newcomer who has just bought a house there next to the cricket ground.

To those familiar with long English summer days resonating to the thwack of willow on leather, one can almost smell the newly mown grass and see the players enjoy the fading light. In fact, Lintz is an ex-mining town which could with similar poetic licence just as easily have been portrayed as an industrial wasteland.

Leaving aside the appropriateness – and possible counter-effectiveness – of such exaggerated rhetoric by a judge, this passage illustrates some common rhetorical tactics: the subtle distancing technique of phrasing an accepted fact as 'the ball *has been known* to land' (emphasis added), the less subtle repetition of 'newcomer' (five times in all) and '70 years' of undisturbed cricket (six times) and the even less subtle speculative commentaries on the facts (the 'newcomer's' lack of love of cricket, the cricket ground being turned into houses or a factory, young men turning to other (impliedly illegal or otherwise insalubrious) activities, and the absurd comment on the cows' views on cricket! Lord Denning also commences with a prominent rhetorical tool, namely a figure of speech (or *trope* in classical rhetorical term), that of exaggeration (*hyperbole* – 'cricket is the delight of everyone'). Other tropes include:

- *simile* – the explicit comparison of one thing with another;
- *metaphor* – referring to one thing by the name of something it resembles;
- *irony* – conveying meaning by referring to its opposite;
- *satire* – ridicule through wit, humour;
- *sarcasm* – using satire to convey scorn or contempt;
- *litotes* – ironic under-statement;
- *pathos* – arousal of pity or sadness;
- *bathos* – change in mood from the dramatic to the absurd or anticlimactic; and
- *rhetorical questions* – asking a question to which the audience knows the answer.

In addition to the actual words used, the way that they are delivered can be extremely persuasive. According to various estimates, only 10 per cent of the message conveyed derives from the words spoken, but 60 per cent from body language and visual appearance, and 30 per cent from tone of voice, etc.[189]

---

[189] See, for example, Evans, above n. 143, 9 (albeit not citing a source).

Thus, in line with the saying that actions speak louder than words, gestures, tone of voice and other paralinguistic forms of communication like the timing of one's delivery and the use of silences can be more effective in subtly allowing fact finders to think that they are making up their own mind rather than being bullied, such as when advocates respond to an invitation to cross-examine a witness with a dismissive wave of the hand rather than expressly stating that there is no need to challenge worthless testimony.

Other ways of enhancing delivery involve using visual aids like maps, diagrams, anatomical models and, particularly in this digital age, 'electronic visuals' (graphs, charts, video re-enactments, etc.).[190] Such tools not only enhance the memorability of the facts portrayed, but can create a sense of drama, such as when murder weapons are put on show. More generally, advocacy manuals often recognise the importance of 'advocacy as theatre'.[191] Still cited are examples of thespian skills from earlier times when advocates pretended to put their reputation and even soul into arguing their cases, expressed indignation at suggestions of client wrongdoing, and even cried on behalf of clients or made closing speeches on their knees. Today such thespianism is declared to be no longer acceptable.[192] Nevertheless, UK advocates are still advised to entertain, modulate their tone of voice, vary their pace, use timing and pauses for dramatic effect, and generally appeal to emotion and the court's sense of morality and justice.[193]

4.4 Conclusion: Rhetoric, Stories and Logic

On the other hand, advocacy manuals make it clear that the art of persuasion is not simply about such appeals. Nor, contrary to Lance Bennett and Martha Feldman,[194] are 'virtually all' rhetorical tactics 'tied to an underlying story frame'. Unless related to a case's governing legal criteria, storytelling is unlikely to succeed on its own.[195] Indeed, Scottish advocacy manuals almost entirely concentrate on relating facts atomistically to the legal elements of liability,[196] though admittedly they are confined

---

[190] See Lubet, above n. 143, Chapter 11 (written by E. R. Stein).

[191] Title chapter of Evans, above n. 143; cf. also Rose, above n. 27, 16.

[192] See, for example, Hyam, above n. 143, 67.

[193] Though empirical research suggests that this can backfire if overdone: Young, Cameron and Tinsley, above n. 158, 38.

[194] Above n. 139, 141.

[195] Lubet, above n. 143, 380ff, 453–4; W. M. O'Barr and J. M. Conley, 'Litigant Satisfaction Versus Legal Adequacy in Small Claims Narratives' (1985) 19 *Law & Society Review* 661, noting how this prejudices unrepresented litigants.

[196] Hennessy, above n. 143, passim, but esp. Chapter 11; Conway and McCann, above n. 143, Part 1 passim.

to civil cases, where juries are rare and issues are often less emotive than criminal cases.[197] But even non-Scottish manuals, and those that focus on jury trials, make it clear that storytelling and an emphasis on emotional and moral themes may have to take a back seat to argument-based reasoning.[198] In addition to the type of case (civil versus criminal) and adjudicator (lay versus professional), the emphasis in advocacy will also depend on variables, such as:

- the stage of fact presentation – for example, it is easier to tell a coherent story in closing submissions or speeches than cross-examination;
- the advocate's standpoint – those representing pursuers and prosecutors are likely to rely more heavily on storytelling than those representing defenders and accused, who merely need to show that the burden of proof has not been met;[199] and
- the available raw materials – for example, it may be easier (though, as we shall see, not necessarily more effective) to disrupt an opponent's superficially persuasive story through exposing its logical inconsistencies and evidential gaps rather than constructing a counter-story; conversely, the weakness of elements of an argument-based approach to presentation may require the use of stories and rhetoric more generally to hide evidential gaps and/or dubious logic.

More generally, logic is likely to play a more negative, destructive role and stories a more positive, constructive role in advocacy. Moreover, as regards logic, what is more important than syllogistic logic (if X, then Y) is the principle of logical consistency (which holds that one cannot accept two contradictory facts – for example, that the accused was at the crime scene and had an alibi). This is not to say that inductive logic (in both its Wigmorean and standard senses) does not play a rhetorical role. But it may only do so due to being embedded in a compelling story which gives it force. For instance, on its own the implicit reliance by Lord Taylor in *Thornton No. 1*[200] on the generalisation that feminine women are unlikely

---

[197] Cf. also in the English context, Du Cann, above n. 143, 196; Munkman, above n. 143, 147; and the fact that lawyers tend to present more complex evidence in non-jury trials: S. S. Diamond, 'What Jurors Think: Expectations and Reactions of Citizens Who Serve as Jurors', in R. E. Litan (ed.), *Verdict: Assessing the Civil Jury System* (2011), 292.

[198] Cf. also the anecdotal evidence of N. Pennington and R. Hastie, 'Evidence Evaluation in Complex Decision Making' (1986) 51 *Journal of Personality and Social Psychology* 242, 244.

[199] Munkman, above nn 143, 144, 158, but see D. W. Maynard, 'Narrative and Narrative Structure in Plea Bargaining' (1988) 22 *Law & Society Review* 449, where the opposite applied in plea bargaining.

[200] Above n. 172.

to murder, which was linked to evidence of Sara's apparent rejection of demure femininity to imply that she murdered, lacks persuasive force. However, when such atomistic logic is converted into what can be called holistic logic it becomes more persuasive by being immersed in a rich narrative about her life history and the build-up to the killing.

5 Fact Adjudication: Logic and Stories

5.1 Rationality and Inductive Logic

Having looked at how lawyers and other legal actors go about investigating, analysing and presenting facts, we now turn to those who make the final determination of the facts. Are they capable of reasoning logically about evidence in the way assumed by orthodox rationalists? And even if they are capable, do they in fact do so, or are they affected by emotion, prejudices, stereotypes and holistic and narrative forms of reasoning?

Before looking at these questions, it can be noted that even if fact finders are capable of using logic in making decisions, this will not by itself make them sound; the generalisations that form the glue for their inferences must also be sound and relevant.[201] Admittedly most humans can function effectively and, in this practical sense,[202] rationally in drawing on common-sense beliefs about how the physical world works (using concepts of time and space, causality, energy, motion, etc.) and about how and why other humans behave (using ideas about motive, intention, desires, goals, etc.).[203] However, when it comes to using these common-sense generalisations to determine the legal fate of others, there are good grounds for concern that fact finders might be unduly influenced by the same sort of stereotypes, biases and prejudices which we have seen influenced knowledge acquisition by witnesses, and more generally by the sort of heuristics and biases[204] we encountered in previous chapters.[205] For instance, empirical research has shown the influence of a wide range of myths about rape[206]

---

[201] Cf. Hacking, above n. 127, Chapter 1; Walker, above n. 81, 1656ff.

[202] Cf. Chapter 2, section 3.1.2 on practical rationality.

[203] In terms of what is variously called, respectively, naive realism or physics and folk psychology: R. Elio, 'Issues in Commonsense Reasoning and Rationality', in R. Elio (ed.), *Common Sense, Reasoning, and Rationality* (2002), esp. 8–9; R. J. Allen, 'Common Sense, Rationality, and the Legal Process' (2001) 22 *Cardozo Law Review* 1417, 1423–5.

[204] For example, the availability heuristic might distract epistemic subjects' attention from all but the most readily available and vivid information and the confirmation bias may prevent new information from being considered.

[205] Chapter 5, sections 6.2 and 7.3.2.

[206] See Chapter 1 at n. 25.

and misconceptions about domestic violence,[207] and a tendency for fact finders to assume that behaviour is caused by personal dispositions rather than environmental factors.[208] In theory, legal actors can challenge fact finders who rely on unsound or irrelevant generalisations, as well as those expressed at the wrong level of universality, precision or abstraction.[209] But given the fast-moving pace of fact finding and the lack of any duty on fact finders to disclose the generalisations upon which they rely, this is unlikely even if legal actors have the necessary knowledge and skills. Whether or not reliance on unsound premises is by itself irrational irrespective of whether they are logically applied is a matter of definition, but it hardly comports with the Rationalist Tradition's conception of rational decision-making.[210]

But what of fact finders' ability to meet their core assumption that decision-makers logically apply premises (whether or not they are sound, relevant and appropriately calibrated) to rationally decide about the likelihood of past events? Surprisingly there has been very little direct study of this question.[211] However, there are some clues from which we can draw logical inferences about the logical inference-making capacities of fact finders.

One derives from relevant studies, which, admittedly, are surprisingly rare.[212] These show that – as one might expect, advocates assume[213] and some judges confess[214] – fact finders may override or bypass logical reason-

---

[207] For example, that abused women can readily leave a shared home and that some women are attracted to and hence condone violent men: see, for example, C. Policastro and B. K. Payne, 'The Blameworthy Victim: Domestic Violence Myths and the Criminalization of Victimhood' (2013) 22 *Journal of Aggression, Maltreatment & Trauma* 329.

[208] Due to what is called the 'correspondence bias' or 'fundamental attribution error': see, for example, Taslitz, above n. 25, 414; G. D. Reeder, 'Attribution as a Gateway to Social Cognition', in D. Carlston (ed.), *The Oxford Handbook of Social Cognition* (2013), 104ff, noting that the bias is not evenly applied across cultures.

[209] Cf. section 3.2.

[210] See M. Damaska, 'Rational and Irrational Proof Revisited' (1997) 5 *Cardozo Journal of International and Comparative Law* 25, 33.

[211] Cf. Elio, above n. 203, 12; Hacking, above n. 127, 248.

[212] See, for example, Young, Cameron and Tinsley, above n. 158, 52–3, though noting that while emotions were brought to the deliberation process in 49 out of 53 cases they studied, they only seemed to affect outcomes in six; H. Kalven and H. Zeisel, *The American Jury* (1971), esp. 165, 218, 494–5, 498, also reporting that juries respond to 'sentiment' in relatively few cases – usually when the closeness of cases 'liberate' them from the dictates of expletive justice (confirmed by subsequent research: Devine at al., above n. 3, 700–1), but cf. A. Farrell and D. Givelber, 'Liberation Reconsidered: Understanding Why Judges and Juries Disagree about Guilt' (2010) 100 *Journal of Criminal Law and Criminology* 1549, questioning this 'liberation thesis'.

[213] See above in relation to themes, section 4.2.2 and at n. 193; see also Schum, above n. 39, 836; Binder and Bergman, above n. 35, 14, 28–9, 105–8, 143, 180–1.

[214] For example, Frank, above n. 45, esp. Chapters 10–12 and 30.

ing because of emotional responses and extra-legal factors like morality, justice, sympathy or antipathy towards one or other party. However, such studies focus on juries, whereas those that include judges suggest that they are more constrained by legal values, training and traditions.[215] In any event, it is misleading to treat decisions affected by emotion and extra-legal values as irrational. As was argued in Chapter Two,[216] relying on extra-legal values to override what would otherwise be the logical application of the law to the facts may be a rational response to the legally legitimated oppressive values of dominant social groups. As regards emotion, psychological studies show that rational decision-making benefits from and indeed may require the exercise of affective faculties.[217] At the very least, emotions such as curiosity, interest, amazement and anger may support rational decision-making by stimulating, defining and sustaining inquiry, concentrating the mind on salient aspects of situations and short-circuiting unnecessary deliberation. They are also useful in interpreting information, heightening memory and allowing us to respond to our beliefs. In fact, research suggests that those who are unable to draw on emotion 'suffer profound deficits in their judgment and decision-making'.[218]

Another clue as to the human capacity for the logical analysis of evidence can be found in the already quoted observation by Twining[219] that untrained law students are prone to making various logical errors. Some support for this observation can be found in numerous studies of deductive reasoning.[220] These show that without training people struggle with the trickier *modum tollens* form of deductive logic (if p, then q; not q, therefore not p) as opposed to the more standard *modum ponens* form (if p, then q; p, therefore q). They also commit standard logical fallacies like confirming the consequent (if p, then q; q, therefore p) or denying the antecedent (if p, then q; not p, therefore not q). However, the research involves highly artificial and abstract reasoning tasks which do not reflect the intuitive, often rule-based, approach people adopt in resolving more realistic and familiar tasks.[221] Moreover,

---

[215] Jackson and Doran, above n. 140, Chapter 8; Kalven and Zeisel, above n. 212, esp. at 498.

[216] Section 4.2.

[217] See, for example, L. M. Isbell and E. C. Lair, 'Moods, Emotions, and Evaluations as Information', in Carlston, above n. 208; P. Greenspan, 'Practical Reasoning and Emotion', in R. Mele and P. Rawling (eds), *The Oxford Handbook of Rationality* (2004).

[218] Isbell and Lair, ibid., 435.

[219] Above, n. 124.

[220] See, for example, Oaksford, above n. 81; R. E. Nisbett (ed.), *Rules for Reasoning* (1993); J. St B. T. Evans and D. E. Over, *Rationality and Reasoning* (1996), Chapters 4 and 6.

[221] In addition to references in n. 220 above, see M. Oaksford and N. Chater, 'Commonsense Reasoning, Logic and Human Rationality', in Elio, above n. 203; G. Gigerenzer, J. Czerlinksi and L. Martignon, 'How Good are Fast and Frugal Heuristics?', in Elio, above n. 203, but see

even in resolving artificial tasks, subjects sometimes use alternative logical processes[222] or reinterpret deductive tasks as involving additional antecedents which suppress the operation of the premise or, as is common to most forms of reasoning outside disciplines like mathematics that are founded on axiomatic truths, premises which are uncertain premises.

This suggests that, while it might be possible for all fact finders to engage in Wigmorean-style fact analysis in the calm of experimental tests, this is less likely if fact finders are untrained. Moreover, it is even less likely if they are immersed in emotionally charged lengthy, and/or complex fact-finding episodes where they are bombarded with a constant stream of new and often contradictory, unclear, ambiguous and rapidly accumulating information.

Indeed, these are the very sorts of factors which contemporary 'dual process' theorists[223] posit as triggering what is variously called common-sense, automatic or sometimes simply System 1 reasoning.[224] Such reasoning is habitual, unconscious, implicit, intuitive and instantaneous, and favours heuristic, narrative and other holistic forms of thinking. It is said to be essential for achieving simple everyday tasks which, like cracking an egg in a bowl or working out which train to catch to attend an appointment,[225] require the simultaneous processing of many items of tacit knowledge (in other words, knowledge one is not aware of or even able to verbalise).[226] By contrast, controlled or System 2 reasoning is deliberative and reflective, involves analytical, atomistic rule-based, decontextualised and depersonalised thinking, operates explicitly and sequentially, and is acquired or at least improved by formal teaching.[227] And whereas most people default most of the time to System 1 reasoning, it may be overridden or corrected by System 2 reasoning when, for instance, stakes are high, common-sense reasoning is recognised as suboptimal, or simply when conditions are conducive to more reflective reasoning.

K. E. Stanovich, *Who is Rational? Studies of Individual Differences in Reasoning* (1999); K. E. Stanovich and R. F. West, 'Individual Differences in Reasoning: Implications for the Rationality Debate' (2000) 23 *Behavioural and Human Sciences* 645, arguing that not all alleged irrationality can be explained away and that some people simply perform better than others.

[222] Such as *reductio ad absurdum*: attempts to refute statements by showing that they inevitably lead to absurd or impractical conclusions or to prove statements by showing that if they were untrue, absurd or impossible consequences would follow.

[223] For an overview of dual process models (which include those relating to persuasive communication discussed in Chapter 5, section 7.3.1 and Chapter 6, section 3.1), see B. Gawronski and L. A. Creighton, 'Dual Process Theories', in Carlston, above n. 208, and for examples, Evans and Over, above n. 220, esp. Chapter 7; Stanovich, above n. 221; Stanovich and West, above n. 221.

[224] Stanovich and West, ibid., 658ff.

[225] Examples taken from Elio, above n. 203, 9–10; Roberts and Zuckerman, above n. 82, 143.

[226] See M. Polyani, *The Tacit Dimension* (1967).

[227] See Nisbett, above n. 220, passim on the impact of training on logical reasoning.

However, as we have already seen,[228] even in less febrile and emo-tionally charged environments like experimental laboratories, untrained fact finders are not natural Bayesian reasoners and, more generally, are prone to commit 'severe and systematic errors'[229] because of heuristic rea-soning.[230] Thus, for example, the likelihood of particular events may be overestimated (or underestimated) because, under the influence of, respec-tively, the representative availability and anchoring and adjustment heu-ristics,[231] events are regarded as a good (or rare) examples of a broader category of similar events, because they can be brought to mind easily (or with difficulty) or because they are given an overly high (or low) first estimate of likely occurrence. We saw in Chapter Five that, in relation to statistical information, such heuristics may lead to fact finders ignor-ing base-rate statistics and insufficiently adjusting expectations when new information arrives, and that such 'errors' in relation to probabilities may also occur when they are evaluated in non-numerical terms.[232] Fact find-ers may also fall prey to the conjunction fallacy,[233] in terms of which they may see the likelihood of a state of affairs combining two elements as more likely than the independent probability of each unconnected element. Equally, such errors may be sustained by various biases. We have already encountered[234] the confirmation bias and expectancy effect in terms of which people interpret facts as confirming their initial expectation of their likelihood. In addition, a hindsight bias may cause people to overestimate the likelihood of an event occurring in a particular way once they know it did occur that way, whereas a simulation bias may encourage people to engage in counterfactual reasoning, leading to them increasing or reduc-ing sympathy for victims depending on how easily their misfortune might have been avoided.[235]

---

[228] Chapter 5, section 7.3.3.

[229] A. Tversky and D. Kahneman, 'Judgment under Uncertainty: Heuristics and Biases', in D. Kahneman, P. Slovic and A. Tversky (eds), *Judgment under Uncertainty: Heuristics and Biases* (1982), 3.

[230] See, for example, Schum, above n. 39, 858; Schum and Martin, above n. 94, 107; for criticisms of the heuristic research which echoes that seen at n. 221, and to which the response by Stanovich and Stanovich and West (both ibid.) also applies.

[231] Discussed, respectively, in Chapter 5, sections 7.3.2 and 6.2.

[232] Cf. Nisbett, above n. 220, 17.

[233] Chapter 5, n. 297.

[234] Chapter 5, sections 5.2 and 6.2.

[235] K. D. Markan and E. A. Dyczewski, 'Mental Simulation: Looking Back in Order to Look Ahead', in Carlston, above n. 208; R. MacCoun, 'Inside the Black Box: What Empirical Research Tells Us About Decisionmaking by Civil Juries', in Litan, above n. 197, 154–5.

Where there is only one simple inference involved in a case, it is *relatively* easy to assign a likelihood of the conclusion being true given the nature of the operative generalisation. Thus if the generalisation is that 'most people who run from the scene of the crime after being accused of committing it are likely to be guilty', one can infer that a fleeing accused is probably guilty. But even with this simple inference, additional uncertainties must be factored in – for instance, how accurate is the generalisation and was the accused in fact fleeing because of guilt rather than some other reason. This causes uncertainty to pile on uncertainty, with no coherent way of assessing the combined effect of two different types of uncertainty,[236] no knowledge of base-rate statistics (here, how many fleeing accused are in fact guilty), and the ever-present possibility of decisions being affected by heuristics.

The problem is, of course, infinitely multiplied when fact finders go beyond deciding about the strength of single inferential streams to decide how such streams combine with other streams to constitute convergence and conjunction, as well as the extent to which ancillary evidence supports various inferences and, finally, what impact to assign to evidence used to deny, explain or rival particular inferences. Here it is conceded by Bayesians that even sophisticated computers – still less trained fact finders – cannot realistically use Bayes' Theorem to constantly update probability assessments as new information emerges,[237] as is assumed by what is sometimes called the meter model of evidential reasoning.[238]

This strongly suggests that fact finders are likely to have to draw on System 1 reasoning in order to cope with the cognitive overload involved in making real-time assessments of a complex mass of evidence when they lack the time and in many cases the training to decompose the evidence into single inferences, evaluate the probabilities involved and combine all of this in some chart or computer system. Equally, disputed cases are likely to be 'richly textured',[239] involving complex issues of human intentions, motivations and other states of mind, sometimes complicated technical issues, and, virtually always, evidential gaps, ambiguous facts and competing views as

---

[236] See Walker, above n. 81, 1565ff, and cf. the transitivity of doubt problem discussed above in section 3.8.2.

[237] R. J. Allen, 'Factual Ambiguity and a Theory of Evidence' (1994) 88 *Northwestern University Law Review* 604, 607.

[238] R. Hastie, 'Introduction' and L. Lopes, 'Two Conceptions of the Jury', in R. Hastie, *Inside the Juror: The Psychology of Juror Decision Making* (1993); see also Jackson and Doran, above n. 140, 214–16; MacCoun, above n. 235, 152–3. Although this meter model is usually linked to atomistic reasoning, it may also describe the way fact finders may constantly adjust their view about the applicability of initial hypotheses about the facts.

[239] Allen, above n. 16, 387.

to what they mean. In fact, when the issue at stake is the meaning of events, rather than whether or not they occurred, atomistic, bottom-up reasoning is of far less value as compared to the imaginative exploration of alternative holistic possibilities which characterises abductive reasoning.[240] To add to the complexity, the governing law may itself be complicated and ambiguous. Similarly the standards of proof, especially for criminal prosecutions, are notoriously difficult to specify with any precision.[241] Consequently they are frequently ignored by jurors, who seem more concerned with deciding between alternative holistic accounts of 'what really happened' than with whether they meet the standards of proof,[242] especially as they struggle to understand what the standards mean.[243]

In fact, the law and legal system encourage holistic reasoning by fact-finders. Generally, except in rare cases where the law reverses the criminal burden of proof,[244] parties must prove or disprove a case as whole rather than individual elements,[245] and evidence is always evaluated against the background of legal requirements, which provides a 'search plan'[246] and check list for fact finding. As we saw in Chapter One, the law determines what facts are relevant and this is likely to encourage fact finders to squeeze the evidence into law's categories. Facts which do not easily fit or which cannot can be squeezed into these categories may be discarded unless they fit an alternative hypothesis relevant to the governing law. Moreover, in an adversarial system, criminal accused and civil defenders and respondents will often – and, as we shall see,[247] are advised – to go beyond merely denying the factual foundations of the hypothesis offered by their opponent and offer a counter-hypothesis. Where they do, fact finders are likely to at least start by seeing which of the two hypotheses best fits emerging information, even if they might ultimately construct their own version of the facts.[248] Indeed, before any evidence is

---

[240] P. Tillers, 'Are There Universal Principles or Forms of Evidential Inference? Of Inference Networks and Onto-Epistemology', in J. Jackson, M. Langer and P. Tillers (eds), *Crime, Procedure and Evidence in a Comparative and International Context* (2008), 183ff.

[241] See, for example, Roberts and Zuckerman, above n. 82, 253ff, and for the technical details of Scots law, F. Raitt, *Evidence: Principles, Policy and Practice* (2nd edn, with E. Keane, 2013), Chapters 4 and 5.

[242] J. A. Holstein, 'Jurors' Interpretation and Jury Decision Making' (1985) 9 *Law and Human Behaviour* 83.

[243] See, for example, L. Ellison and V. E. Munro, 'Getting to (Not) Guilty: Examining Jurors' Deliberative Processes In, and Beyond, the Context of a Mock Rape Trial' (2010) 30 *Legal Studies* 74, 95.

[244] See, for example, Raitt, above n. 241, 82–90.

[245] Allen, above n. 237, 609.

[246] Wagenaar, van Koppen and Crombag, above n. 20, 24.

[247] At n. 299, below.

[248] Cf. Holstein, above n. 242; D. A. Nance, 'Naturalized Epistemology and the Critique of Evidence Theory, Evidence' (2001) 87 *Virginia Law Review* 1491, 1580.

heard, fact finders might already have formed some preconceptions. Judges might have read the pleadings, which research shows have an enduring effect on decisions,[249] whereas the accused's position in the dock (especially if hand-cuffed) may well subconsciously prompt an initial assumption of guilt.[250]

We thus see that fact adjudication may end up being holistic, not just in the sense used up to now whereby the facts are viewed holistically in terms of some overall theory of what happened, but also in the sense of involving an undifferentiated and probably undifferentiable response to law, facts, values and emotions.[251] This is particularly likely if complex fast-moving factual disputes make undue cognitive demands, and artificial and unfamiliar proceedings and sometimes highly emotional issues increase the pressure associated with making a potentially life-changing decision. Moreover, in making such 'gestalt'[252] responses, Richard Posner argues that fact finders draw on a 'grab bag of methods [which] includes anecdote, introspection, imagination, common sense, intuition . . . empathy, imputation of motives, speaker's authority, metaphor, analogy, precedent, custom, the "test of time", memory, "induction" . . . "experience"',[253] as well as tacit knowledge. Interestingly for a judge, Posner omits to mention logic, but equally glaring is the omission of stories.

5.2 Rationality and Narrative[254]

5.2.1 The Importance of Stories

By contrast, a wide range of disciplines – such as semiotics, sociology, anthropology, cultural theory and, most obviously, psychology[255] – suggest that the culturally embedded nature of narrative in people's mental architecture means that stories are the central feature of holistic reasoning.

---

[249] Wagenaar, van Koppen and Crombag, above n. 20, 27.

[250] J. D. Jackson, 'Law's Truth, Lay Truth and Lawyers' Truth: The Representation of Evidence in Adversary Trials' (1992) 3 *Law and Critique* 29, 48; see also Wagenaar, van Koppen and Crombag, above n. 20, 56.

[251] Frank, above n. 45, Chapter 12; Stone, above n. 143, 373; Kalven and Zeisel, above n. 212, Chapter 12; R. P. Burns, 'The Distinctiveness of Trial Narrative', in A. Duff et al. (eds), *The Trial on Trial: Volume 1 – Truth and Due Process* (2004), 169; see also the quotation from Tillers at n. 313 below.

[252] Frank, ibid.

[253] 'The Jurisprudence of Skepticism' (1988) 86 *Michigan Law Review*. 827, 838ff; see also M. L. Seigel, 'A Pragmatic Critique of Modern Evidence Scholarship' (1993) 88 *Northwestern University Law Review* 995, 1025–31.

[254] For brief overviews, see, for example, Allen, above n. 16; Pardo, above n. 19, 402–4; R. P. Burns, 'Some Realism (And Idealism) About The Trial' (1997) 31 *Georgia Law Review* 715, 752–5; J. McEwan, *The Verdict of the Court – Passing Judgement in Law and Psychology* (2003), 118–21.

[255] In addition to the references cited in section 1 above, see Allen, above n. 16, 383ff regarding history.

This is confirmed[256] by various empirical studies of simulated[257] and actual fact adjudication[258] conducted in the Netherlands[259] as well as various Anglo-American jurisdictions, mostly in relation to juries,[260] and solely in criminal cases. They provide compelling evidence that criminal trials at least are organised around storytelling. Just as various 'atomistic' heuristics influence reasoning from one fact to another (as in the reliance on peripheral clues about witness credibility)[261] or when combining a small number of inferential chains (as with the conjunction fallacy),[262] so stories can be said to operate as a super heuristic[263] for assessing disputed facts as a whole.

In discussing advocacy, Twining's 'thin'[264] definition of a story as a 'narrative of particular events arranged in a time sequence and forming a meaningful totality'[265] was quoted. Others[266] have extended its core ideas of *temporality*, *particularity* and *coherence* to include those of *intelligibility*, in that stories give meaning to what might be unconnected facts, and *intentionality* in that, while not necessarily connoting causality,[267] assumptions about human agency mean that stories provide a basis for explaining human action.

---

[256] But cf. Memon, Vrij, and Bull, above n. 3, 160, 166-67 citing J. Macoubrie, *On Stories in Jury Deliberation* (unpublished).

[257] Most notably, by Pennington and Hastie, see, for example, above n. 198, 'A Cognitive Theory of Juror Decision Making: The Story Model' (1991) 13 *Cardozo Law Review* 519, 'Explaining the Evidence: Tests of the Story Model for Juror Decision Making' (1992) 62 *Journal of Personality and Social Psychology* 189 and 'The Story Model for Juror Decision Making', in Hastie, above n. 238; see also Ellison and Munro, above n. 243, 79–80.

[258] Most notably the ground-breaking US study of Bennett and Feldman, above n. 139; see also Jackson and Doran, above n. 140 (Northern Ireland); Young, Cameron and Tinsley, above n. 158 (New Zealand).

[259] Wagenaar, van Koppen and Crombag, above n. 20.

[260] But see Jackson and Doran, above n. 140, which looked at judges.

[261] See Chapter 6, section 3, esp. 3.2.2.

[262] See Chapter 5, section 7.3.3.

[263] Cf. Wagenaar, van Koppen and Crombag, above n. 20, 19, 232; A. J. Moore, 'Trial by Schema: Cognitive Filters in the Courtroom' (1989) 37 *UCLA Law Review* 273, arguing that comparing stories told in court to similar stories known to fact finders involves the representativeness heuristic.

[264] W. Twining, 'Anchored Narratives – A Comment' (1995) 1 *European Journal of Crime, Criminal Law and Criminal Justice* 106, 110.

[265] Above n. 162.

[266] Bennett and Feldman, above n. 139, 7; Bruner, above n. 22, 6–20.

[267] But see Pennington and Hastie, 'A Cognitive Theory of Juror Decision Making', above n. 257, 525, who describe a story as a '"causal chain" of events in which events are connected by causal relationships of necessity and sufficiency'.

As such, empirical research reveals that stories operate on at least[268] two levels in fact evaluation. On the surface there is what can be called the *operative* story or, as in many adversarial proceedings, competing operative stories. Such stories may be spontaneously generated, but are more likely to be drawn from those presented by the parties and first encountered in the charges, indictment and civil pleadings and in opening statements in civil jury trials,[269] or the examination of witnesses.

Secondly, below the surface there is a vast range of *background* (or *stock*)[270] stories that are embedded in the minds of those who are deciding whether or not to accept an operative story either in unadulterated or modified form – though of course the content of these background stories will vary according to the knowledge, experience and hence background of each individual fact finder.[271] While operative stories are case-specific, background stories are formulated at a more generic level, ranging from:

- schema lodged in our memories which are organised in sequential order such as scenarios or scripts for commonly occurring events like eating at a restaurant or encounters with the police; to
- far more general and abstract commonly occurring stories such as the boy-meets-girl narrative in films like *Notting Hill* (boy meets girl; boys loses girl; boy gets girl) or folk mythology (girl meets (old) boy, marries him and inherits when his heart gives out); to
- story genres such as tragedy, farce, romance, noir, Bildungsoman, etc.

But even when background information is stored in non-narrative form, it is frequently subconsciously linked to stories, such as when proverbs like 'look before you leap' call up specific exemplifying stories. Even scientific knowledge may be brought to mind in story form, as when the theory of gravity triggers the story of Newton seeing an apple falling from a tree.[272]

---

[268] Using a broader semiotic approach, Bernard Jackson discussed the stories *within* the trial as told by witnesses (what he calls the 'semantic' level) and the story *of* the trial itself (the 'pragmatic' level): above n. 3, 141ff; n. 16, Chapters 1 and 3; see also at n. 161 regarding adjudicators providing the resolution of the dispute's story.

[269] Though according to Young, Cameron and Tinsley, above n. 158, 16 such statements 'rarely provide a comprehensive picture of the stories that are to be told by the evidence'.

[270] Lopez, above n. 29, esp. 3, 5–6.

[271] For example, in the two story schematas referred to below, wealthy people will have different ideas of eating at restaurants and black working-class men very different perspectives on encounters with the police than white middle- class men (see, for example, A. E. Taslitz, 'African-American Sense of Fact: The O. J. Trial and Black Judges on Justice' (1998) 7 *Buffalo University Public Interest Law Journal* 219.

[272] See http://www.independent.co.uk/news/science/the-core-of-truth-behind-sir-isaac-newtons-apple-1870915.html (last accessed 26 March 2018).

Together, operative and background stories perform four important functions in fact adjudication. First, they enable fact finders to *cope* with the arcane rituals, procedures and technicalities of legal fact finding and a constant stream of constantly changing and conflicting information presented in a disjointed and piecemeal fashion, sometimes over many days. Stories allow fact finders to relate such information back to the plots and subplots contained within possible storylines. By identifying the crucial issues to be decided in terms of the story's central action and by using stories' common temporal, causal and intentional regularities, fact finders are able to form initial hypotheses about what might have happened. Admittedly testimony by witnesses will not fit neatly or easily with operative stories,[273] not least because each will have their own story to tell.[274] They can only speak to those elements of the operative story they observed, and may recount a surfeit of detail or contradict the operative story. In addition, the adversarial nature of formal fact adjudication may mean that some witnesses do not testify in the relevant chronological sequence or in uninterrupted narrative form.[275] But even if the more common fragmented style of witness presentation does allow a clear narrative to emerge, this may immediately be disrupted by cross-examination and other witnesses. Skilled advocates may be able to keep their operative story to the fore, but this is particularly difficult in Scotland because opening statements are only allowed in civil jury trials which are very rare. Consequently it may only be with closing statements that a coherent story is clearly articulated, and even here the focus may be as much on the atomistic analysis of witness credibility and whether the evidence satisfies individual elements of liability. Nevertheless, despite these problems, research still suggests operative stories play an important role in helping fact adjudicators to cope with the demands of fact finding.

Secondly, operative stories combine with background stories to help fact finders *interpret* the evidence as it emerges. Thus it is argued that '[w]thout any context evidence is meaningless' and that it 'derives its meaning from a story context'.[276] Indeed, when as frequently occurs, mental elements are central to a case, 'the "facts" are indistinguishable from the interpretation'.[277] Operative stories allow fact finders to draw inferences about the

---

[273] See, for example, Young, Cameron and Tinsley, above n. 158, 24; P. Gewirtz, 'Narrative and Rhetoric in Law', in Brooks and Gewirtz, above n. 30, 7–8.

[274] For example, police officers may testify in terms of a time-line revolving around the stages of investigation: Jackson and Doran, above n. 140, 216.

[275] See Chapter 3, section 3.1.4.

[276] Wagenaar, van Koppen and Crombag, above n. 20, 33.

[277] Allen, above n. 16, 395.

central action in questions relying on case-specific information acquired during fact finding, knowledge about similar events, about how the world works in general, the meanings associated with particular words, and generic expectations about what makes a complete story.

Bennett and Feldman[278] also note the role played by 'aesthetic responses' to acceptable, familiar, pleasing or satisfying storylines, or conversely those which are strange, awkward, unfamiliar or repulsive. They may result in personal identification with or emotional release at the events and normative understandings of excusable and inexcusable behaviour. Indeed, stories are said to have an inherent normativity, in being a powerful vehicle for making value judgments and hence for encouraging fact finders to accept or reject particular versions of the fact. According to psychologists, humans 'have a chronic disposition to categorise information as either favourable or unfavourable', and these processes 'occur without conscious awareness'.[279] As we saw in the girl-meets-boy stories, many stories contain an implicit value judgment – what Paul Ricouer describes as 'an ethics already realised'.[280] Moreover, certain situations evoke 'canonical scripts'[281] as to how the world works (for example, boy and girl living happily ever after) as well as the ways in which they might be violated or deviated from (gold-digger ends up madly in love with sugardaddy). Even in the absence of more obviously value-laden stories, stock stories contain an implicit judgment about how things ought to be based on the way that they have always been.[282]

Familiar storylines are particularly important in the interpretation of evidence in that, as with witness perception,[283] they may cause fact finders to assume the existence of story elements unsupported by evidence, ignore conflicting evidence or interpret ambiguous or even conflicting evidence so as to ensure it fits with these storylines. While too many evidential gaps or conflicts may cause fact finders to reject an operative story, it is very difficult to shift operative stories once they have been adopted due to the confirmation bias and belief bias (or expectancy effect),[284] which lead fact

[278] Above n. 139, 59–61.
[279] R. S. Wyer, H. Shen and A. J. Ying, 'The Role of Procedural Knowledge in the Generalisability of Social Behaviour', in Carlston, above n. 208, 266.
[280] P. Kemp, 'Ethics and Narrativity', in L. E. Hahn (ed.), *The Philosophy of Paul Ricouer* (1995), 376, quoted by Burns, above n. 251, 172.
[281] Bruner, above n. 22, 11.
[282] Lopez, above n. 29, 9. Cf. van Zandt, above n. 86, 916–17 on the similar normativity of all common-sense reasoning.
[283] See Chapter 6, section 2.2.
[284] See Chapter 5, sections 5.2, 6.2 and 7.2.

finders to filter out and/or reinterpret conflicting information to align with their initial operative stories.[285] So strong is this 'belief perseverance' phenomenon[286] that courts may end up accepting incredible situations such as a witness with severe memory impairment being able to remember the exact dates of twenty-seven arson cases.[287]

A third function of stories in fact adjudication is to provide fact finders with the main means by which they *evaluate* the plausibility of proposed versions of the facts. Here, Nancy Pennington and Reid Hastie found that such judgments are based on three factors. First, the greater the story's *coverage* of the evidence presented to fact finders, the greater is their confidence in the story. Second, *coherence* involves the extent to which the elements of the story are mutually incompatible and do not conflict with other plausible evidence (what they call consistency),[288] the extent to which the operative story is consistent with known background stories about how the world works (plausibility) and the extent to which all the elements of the story are in place (completeness). Thirdly, in terms of what Pennington and Hastie call the quality of *uniqueness*, fact finders will opt for the only coherent story if applicable, but if there is more than one coherent story, have less confidence in their final choice.

The fourth and final role played by stories is to enable fact finders to *choose* which party's version of the facts best fits with relevant legal categories and standards of proof. This task is said to be facilitated by the fact that 'the main attributes of the decision categories . . . – identity, mental state, circumstances, and actions – correspond closely to the central features of human action sequences represented as episodes – initiating events, goals, actions, and states'.[289] While the use of stories to organise, understand and evaluate evidence as it emerges will tend to operate more on an automatic and unconscious level, this final fact-finding stage is far more deliberative and thus likely also to engage more reflective, analytical forms of reasoning.

As the film *Twelve Angry Men* illustrates, this can lead to fact finders questioning the logic or evidential sufficiency of key elements of what

---

[285] Young, Cameron and Tinsley, above n. 158, 24.

[286] Wagenaar, van Koppen and Crombag, above n. 20, 57; see also Moore, above n. 263, 300–3.

[287] Wagenaar, van Koppen and Crombag, ibid., 59, and for other examples, see 58–60.

[288] Which could be classified into internal and external consistency respectively: cf. B. Jackson, above n. 16, 58–9, referring to internal and external coherence; Burns, above n. 251, 172–3, referring to internal coherence and completeness, and 'external factual plausibility'.

[289] Pennington and Hastie, 'A Cognitive Theory of Juror Decision Making', above n. 257, 530–1. See also B. Jackson, above n. 16, 59, who refers to the operative story being compared with the narrative model underlying the relevant law.

is otherwise a coherent and compelling story, especially if prompted by persuasive advocates or fellow fact finders like the juror played by Henry Fonda. A real-life example of the disruption of a coherent narrative by logical analysis involves the murder trial of Jean Harris, the headmistress of a well-known American girls' school who had killed her lover, Herman Tanover, the inventor of the Scarsdale diet.[290] She alleged that she had gone to his house to confront him about his relationship with a younger woman and, if he was not sympathetic, to shoot herself, but that when he had tried to dissuade her from suicide, a struggle had ensued, causing her to accidentally shoot him. This story was backed up through a subplot of his exploitation of her dependency on him while he had affairs with other women. Ultimately, however, it was rejected for the simple reason that he had been shot four times, which common sense (along with a 'hell hath no fury like a woman scorned' theme) suggests is incompatible with a tragic accident.

But the triumph of logic over narrative is by no means guaranteed, especially where logical arguments are made long after fact finders have adopted a clear, coherent and familiar narrative.[291] We have already seen that well-crafted stories can cause fact finders to accept implausible factual scenarios. They might also cause 'inconvenient truths' to be overlooked or reinterpreted. According to Bennett and Feldman, stories are judged according to a 'dual standard of "did it happen that way?" and "could it have happened that way?"'[292] – that is, according to both the available individual facts and the structural properties of their categorisation as a story. However, well-structured but poorly evidenced or complex stories may triumph over poorly structured but simple and well-evidenced stories.[293] Thus, in experiments involving simulated trials, they found no statistical correlation between the actual and perceived truth of stories.

Similarly, Willem Wagenaar, Peter van Koppen and Hans Crombag[294] found that what is more important than an accurate story is a good story – one with a readily identifiable central action and a context that provides an easy and natural explanation for the participants' behaviour. In terms of their theory of 'anchored narratives', each element of the prosecution story (relating to identity, *actus reus* and *mens rea*) ought in principle to be

---

[290] See Twining, above n. 16, 312–14.
[291] See, for example, B. Jackson, above n. 3, 182, and see also research on juries which shows that deliberation among jurors does not usually change already formed views: for example, Devine et al., above n. 3, 690–3; Ellison and Munro, above n. 243, 85–7, but see Kapardis, above n. 3, 169.
[292] Above n. 139, 33.
[293] Ibid. passim, but esp. Chapter 4.
[294] Wagenaar, van Koppen and Crombag, above n. 20, esp. Chapter 3.

anchored to reality via common-sense rules in the form of generalisations or embedded sub-stories which themselves need to be anchored until they reach a point where they rely on universally acceptable generalisations. In actual practice, however, the authors conclude that a 'good story is the better half of proof'.[295] They found that plausible prosecution stories were often accepted without all story elements being anchored, where some or all elements were anchored in unsafe or even absurd common-sense generalisations, and, as we have already seen,[296] even where they involved logical impossibilities. Possibly this undue focus on the plausibility of the prosecution story rather than its evidential support or its comparative plausibility vis-à-vis defence stories owes something to the inquisitorial nature of Dutch criminal procedure, as well as the state's advantages in terms of superior credibility.[297] However, one finding which has wider application is that, of the three strategies Wigmore outlined for challenging an opponent (denial, explanation and rivalling),[298] it is the setting up of a rival story of innocence that was most likely to be successful and, perhaps as a result, usually attempted by defence lawyers.[299]

5.2.2 Conclusion: Not Just Stories!

There seems to be little doubt that narrative plays a central role in fact adjudication. How central is less clear. As we have seen,[300] in some cases arguments attacking the logical flaws contained within stories *may* be determinative, especially when mounted by persuasive advocates or fellow fact finders. While the story model does encompass logical consistency as an important element of a good story, its proponents fail to give due recognition to the impact of forms of advocacy other than storytelling. Furthermore, they also fail to acknowledge that sometimes[301] witnesses' reliability and credibility loom large and are evaluated independently of the content of their story and its fit with operating stories, but in terms

---

[295] Ibid., 44; see also Chapter 3 passim and 225. See also Lempert, above n. 139, 22.

[296] At n. 287.

[297] See at n. 250, above; Chapter 3, section 3.4.1; Chapter 4, sections 2.4, 3.2.1 and 4.2.

[298] Section 3.5.

[299] Above n. 20, Chapter 10. See also Lempert, above n. 139, 21, suggesting that logical attacks on the prosecution story are usually only made when defence stories are weak; J. Sanders, 'From Science to Evidence: The Testimony on Causation in the Bendectin Cases' (1993) 46 *Stanford Law Review* 1, 55–8.

[300] Section 5.2.1.

[301] But not always – see Chapter 6, section 3.2 passim, but esp. at n. 218 regarding research which shows that assessments of witness reliability and credibility often flow from perceptions about the evidence as a whole.

of clues like demeanour, way of speaking, class, etc.[302] More generally, John Jackson and Sean Doran's research on criminal fact finding[303] reveals that stories are likely to be more determinative in relation to issues like witness truthfulness, confessions and causation rather than the reliability of witness identification and forensic evidence. They also suggest that causal models rather than stories may dominate in civil cases, such as when fact finders must ascertain why a vehicle involved in an accident suffered a mechanical failure.[304] Certainly Scottish advice on advocacy in civil cases focuses far more on an argument- rather a narrative-based approach,[305] though this might have more to do with the extreme rarity of civil jury trials. It is also possible that there are differences in the role of stories depending on the issues raised, the potentialities offered by available facts themselves, and a mutually reinforcing synergy between advocates' assumptions about judicial as opposed to jury openness to storytelling, on the one hand, and the impact of the resulting mode of fact presentation on fact adjudication on the other. Thus, by analogy with the apparently greater impact of extra-legal values and emotions on jurors as compared to judges, it may be that stories may also have a similar differential impact. But this issue awaits further research, as does the exact effect of the complex mixture of (often competing) stories, logic, emotion, and its interrelationship with the – currently even less understood[306] – effect of adjudicators' social, political and moral values, personality and social background. In the meantime, however, we can draw some broad conclusions about the admittedly complex and nuanced interrelationship between an atomistic, argument-based mode of reasoning and a holistic, narrative-based mode.

6 Conclusion: Logic, Stories, Proof and Truth

One conclusion is that the role of each mode differs according to the particular fact-handling task being undertaken. At the same time, however, no task is entirely dominated by one or other mode (though atomistic reasoning comes fairly close in relation to fact analysis). Secondly, the influence of each mode waxes and wanes as one moves from one task to

---

[302] See B. Jackson, above n. 16, Chapter 3 passim; J. Jackson, above n. 250, 37–8, 49.

[303] Ibid., esp. 221–2.

[304] Above n. 140, 220, though it can be noted that such issues may equally arise in criminal prosecutions.

[305] Cf. the discussion of civil advocacy in Hennessy and Conway and McCann with that of criminal advocacy in Stone – all in n. 143 above.

[306] See section 1 above.

another. Thus, as legal actors move from uncovering evidence towards analysing it, the holistic, hypothesis-generating form of abductive reasoning gradually gives way to the more atomistic processes of reduction and elimination. Then, when all (or at least most of) the evidence is collected and its probative force evaluated, atomistic and logical reasoning will reach its apex, especially if extending to Wigmorean charting, before the narrative method begins to be used in contemplation of fact presentation. Finally, with fact presentation itself, as with fact adjudication, the exact balance between argument-based and narrative-based reasoning will vary according to factors like the raw factual materials available, the type of case and the type of adjudicator, as well as the personality and attitudes of advocates and adjudicators.

In other words, Wigmore's assertion that narrative methods of analysing evidence are inferior to logical methods[307] is highly questionable even in relation to fact analysis and presentation only. But so is the assumption that fact presentation and adjudication are and can be totally dominated by holistic and narrative methods. As Peter Gay puts it: 'narration without analysis is trivial . . . analysis without narration is incomplete'.[308]

In large part, as modified rationalists argue,[309] the two approaches are complementary, both as regards the way people actually process evidence and, partly as a consequence, the way that evidence is presented. Thus, while evidence only makes sense within a meaningful whole, even the most meaningful holistic versions of the facts are irrelevant or are at least liable to rejection unless linked to the required elements of law. Consequently, even if evidence is presented and evaluated holistically, advocates are strongly advised to spell out and analyse in detail the logical links between, on the one hand, elements of the holistic theory or story relied on and, on the other hand, their relationship to the governing law. Analytical skills are also important in alerting legal actors to potential problems in their own arguments and stories, and hence to the need to rectify these problems with additional ancillary evidence or by a greater focus on the *pathos* and *ethos* dimensions of rhetoric. In other words, whatever the limits of logic and atomistic reasoning during fact finding, it has important functions prior to fact finding. More generally, the methods are complementary in the sense that they are appropriate at different

---

[307] See Tillers and Schum, above n. 18, 942–3.

[308] *Style in History* (1974), 189, quoted by Burns, above n. 254, 768.

[309] See, for example, Anderson, above n. 137, 788; Bex et al., above n. 17; Tillers and Schum, above n. 18, 943, 953, and esp. Twining – for example, above n. 16, 283, 306–11 passim, n. 264, 111 and 'Civilians Don't Try: A Comment on Mirjan Damaška's "Rational and Irrational Proof Revisited"' (1997) 5 *Cardozo Journal of International and Comparative Law* 69, 73.

fact-handling stages.[310] Accordingly, whatever the role of narrative and holistic reasoning at trial and whatever the limits to Wigmorean methodology, the latter is, as Twining has emphasised,[311] at least an excellent means of training students to handle facts rigorously.

But while atomistic and argument-based reasoning complements holistic, abductive and narrative-based reasoning as a method for investigating, analysing, presenting and determining the facts of cases, both can compete with each other as tools for achieving advocacy aims. Similarly, both methods may compete within the thought processes of individual fact finders, such as when they overlook the logical flaws involved in accepting plausible stories or, conversely, fail to grasp the meaning of facts by treating them atomistically and divorced from the context provided by their part of a story. More generally, there are signs of disagreements among modified rationalists as to the relative merits and demerits of atomistic and holistic reasoning. Thus many, like the Scottish jurist James Glassford long ago,[312] have accepted the benefits of a holistic approach to evidence in providing a more contextual and gestalt understanding of the meaning and probative value of evidence than the separate analysis of each isolated fact. In an oft-quoted passage, Tillers goes further to argue that there are distinct benefits of the sort of the implicit and unreflective System 1 reasoning described by dual process theorists.

> [T]he effort to state systematically and comprehensively the premises on which our inferences rest may produce serious distortions in the factfinding process, in part (but only in part) because such systemic statement obscures the complex mental processes that we actually employ and should employ to evaluate evidence. It is not true that we can say all we know, and the effort to say more than we are able to say is likely to diminish our knowledge and our ability to use it. In our daily lives, we confidently rely on innumerable premises and beliefs that we often cannot articulate or explain, but our inability to express these premises and beliefs does not necessarily make them illegitimate or unreliable.[313]

From a more political perspective, as we saw in Chapter Two,[314] many critical theorists celebrate the potential of storytelling to challenge the

---

[310] Anderson, ibid.; Schum, above n. 83, 1500.

[311] See above at n. 124.

[312] *An Essay on the Principles of Evidence and their Application to Subjects of Judicial Enquiry* (1820), 216, quoted with approval by Hareira, above n. 16, 94–5.

[313] J. H. Wigmore, *A Treatise on the System of Evidence in Trials at Common Law* 1 (1983. rev. edn by P. Tillers), 986, quoted by Twining, above n. 5, 184. See also Tillers, above n. 240, 198.

[314] Section 4.3.

status quo.[315] Thus victims of injustice can gain the sympathy of fact finders because of an audience's natural inclination to identify with the story's protagonist and condemn the antagonist. Stories also involve a 'wide-angle opening shot'[316] which includes far more of the background context necessary for a realistic understanding of the causes of events than the more narrow focus of argument-based approaches. More generally, storytelling – or what Richard Delgado calls 'counter-storytelling' – is a powerful means of 'destroying mindset – the bundle of presuppositions, received wisdoms, and shared understandings against a background of which legal and political discourse takes place'.[317] Accordingly they 'can shatter complacency and challenge the status quo'.[318] At the same time, however, critical theorists recognise that such strategies are not necessarily destined to succeed, given the strength of dominant narratives and their incorporation into the law as 'common-sense' and the 'public interest'.[319]

By contrast, while 'sympathetic to the introduction of community values in the administration of justice',[320] Twining exemplifies the ambivalence of many modified rationalists and liberals more generally[321] about storytelling in law. Like the generalisations which provide the glue for logical thinking, stories are portrayed as psychologically 'necessary but dangerous'[322] in allowing in 'social, sexual or other "prejudices"',[323] 'subverting challenging cherished legal principles such as judge the act, not the actors',[324] and as causing familiar, reassuring, easily remembered and well-structured accounts of the facts to push out truthful accounts. It is further argued that, by attempting to impose order and purpose on often random and purposeless events, stories may distort reality. Similarly

---

[315] In addition to references cited in this paragraph, see, for example, Brooks and Gewirtz, above n. 30; L. Sarmas, 'Storytelling and the Law: A Case Study of *Louth v Diprose*' (1993) 19 *Melbourne University Law Review* 701; L. Hayman and N. Levit, 'The Tales of White Folk: Doctrine, Narrative, and the Reconstruction of Racial Reality' (1996) 84 *California Law Review* 377.

[316] K. L. Scheppele, 'Foreword: Telling Stories' (1989) 87 *Michigan Law Review* 2073, 2095.

[317] R. Delgado, 'Storytelling for Oppositionists and Others: A Plea for Narrative' (1989) 87 *Michigan Law Review* 2411, 2413.

[318] Ibid., 2414.

[319] See, for example, Sarmas, above n. 315; D. A. Farber and S. Sherry, 'Telling Stories Out of School: An Essay on Legal Narratives' (1993) 45 *Stanford Law Review* 807.

[320] Above n. 16, 85.

[321] See, for example, Sherwin, above n. 152; Farber and Sherry, above n. 319; D. A. Hyman, 'Lies, Damned Lies and Narrative' (1998) 73 *Indiana Law Journal* 797.

[322] See, for example, W. Twining, 'Necessary But Dangerous: The Role of Stories and Generalizations in Legal Proof', in M. Malsch and J. H. Nijboer (eds), *Complex Cases: Perspectives on Netherlands Criminal Justice System* (1999). See also above n. 309; Anderson, Schum and Twining, above n. 35, Chapter 10.

[323] Above n. 16, 85.

[324] Above n. 10, 283.

because, as Jean-Paul Sartre argues, storytelling starts from a known end, it tends to work backwards, imposing order on messy reality, suggesting causation where perhaps none existed, and involving, as Roland Barthes argues, the *post ad hoc ergo proper hoc*[325] logical error writ large.[326]

However, while as we saw in Chapter Two, some modified rationalists are prepared to reinterpret orthodox concepts of reason to include the narrative-mode of reasoning[327] – at least at the level of communication rather than that of 'rational argument and persuasion'[328] – they decline to see storytelling and holistic reasoning more generally as challenging realist conceptions of truth.[329] While admitting that narrative and holism in evidence entail a coherence theory of truth,[330] they – and indeed some narrative theorists themselves[331] – insist on the existence of 'objective' facts, truth as correspondence with reality and on logical and other 'scientific' methods as a means of verifying story accuracy and ensuring such correspondence. In response, one can argue that, even if one holds on to the possibility of evidence reflecting 'reality', and recognises the dangers of 'good stories pushing out true stories',[332] it does not follow that good stories may not provide a better idea of what happened – and lead to a more just outcome – than drawing logical inferences atomistically from a partial slice of reality deemed relevant by partial law.

If correct, and, at any rate, given that fact finding is probably impossible without narrative reasoning, there are reforms which can make storytelling easier and less susceptible to the worries raised by fact positivists. As regards helping those presenting and evaluating facts to make most effective use of stories, witnesses could be allowed much more leeway to tell their stories in narrative form and more effort made to call them in an order which mirrors the chronology of the events in question.[333] More formally, it has been argued that more holistic approaches to fact finding

---

[325] The idea that because something follows something else it must be caused by it.

[326] Brooks, above n. 30, 19; see also A. M. Dershowitz, 'Life is not a Dramatic Narrative', in Brooks and Gewirtz, above n. 30.

[327] Section 3.2.2.4.

[328] Twining, above n. 16, 287, though somewhat contradictorily he goes on to say that narrative may legitimately contribute to rational arguments; cf. also, ibid., 295.

[329] Twining, ibid., 310.

[330] See, for example, J. Jackson, above n. 16, 517.

[331] Bruner, above n. 22, 4.

[332] Anderson, Schum and Twining, above n. 35, 281; see also Twining, above n. 16, 283; C. S. Vick et al., 'Building Bayesian Networks for Legal Evidence with Narratives: A Case Study Evaluation' (2014) 22 *Artificial Intelligence and Law* 375, 377.

[333] Shown by experiments to increase witness plausibility: N. Pennington and R. Hastie, 'Explanation-based Decision Making: Effects of Memory Structure on Judgment' (1988) 14 *Journal of Experimental Psychology: Learning, Memory, and Cognition* 521.

require the increased eradication of evidential rules excluding evidence from court.[334] Another formal change would involve allowing opening statements to be made in criminal and non-jury civil trials.[335] While this will give the prosecution (and pursuer) the psychological advantage of introducing their story first,[336] some of the studies canvassed in this chapter show how important alternative stories are for an accused's chances of success and, if so, it seems better that this alternative story is introduced as early and as coherently as possible by accused (or civil defenders or respondents), who in any event will have the important last word.[337]

At the same time, as Wagenaar, van Koppen and Crombag persuasively argue,[338] safeguards could be developed to prevent good stories trumping inaccurate stories, such as requiring each of the legally required elements of stories to be independently anchored in admissible evidence and in 'common sense rules [that is, generalisations] that are generally accepted as safe'. However, leaving aside the vague nature of these requirements, it is difficult to see how they can be enforced except indirectly through two of the authors' other recommendations. The first requires fact finders to articulate the narrative and supporting anchors relied on, and the second makes breach of their rules grounds for an appeal. However, in Scotland these innovations are likely to be seen as unacceptable inroads on the idea that the evidence is best evaluated by those who observe it, especially given Tillers' point[339] about the difficulty of consciously expressing every legitimate view of the evidence, and given the law's traditional unwillingness to expose jurors' decision-making to scrutiny lest it curtail their discretion to act as a 'lay parliament'.[340]

Possibly all that effectively can be done is to expose legal actors to the necessary Wigmorean skills so that they can challenge stories, as well as allegedly logical arguments which involve, for instance, dubious logical inferences, are based on suspect generalisations, contain evidential gaps

---

[334] Pardo, above n. 19, 441.

[335] Cf. Young, Cameron and Tinsley, above n. 158, 16, 24, calling for jurors to be provided early on with 'a more coherent factual framework'.

[336] Chapter 3, n. 92.

[337] Though not all psychological studies support such a 'recency effect': see, for example, McEwan, above n. 254, 145–6, noting that it is likely to be lessened in short trials.

[338] Above n. 20, 40–1, 67–73, Chapter 12. Other 'rules' include requirements that the prosecution 'must present at least one well-shaped narrative' and 'a limited set of well-shaped narratives', and that there should be no 'competing story with equally good or better anchoring', 'falsifications of the indictment's narrative and nested sub-narratives' and 'anchoring onto obviously false beliefs'.

[339] See at n. 313, above.

[340] See Chapter 3, section 3.2.4.

or do not address all the elements of legal liability. As we have seen,[341] such training for students is a key justification for the focus on Wigmorean analysis by Twining and others. This chapter, however, suggests that there is a need for an equal focus on storytelling[342] and other rhetorical skills.

Indeed, the book as a whole suggests that it is not only law students who should be exposed to information about and training in the various contexts of evidence and proof, but also all those who determine facts for legal purposes. Apart from issues of time and cost, there seems to be little objection to introducing fact finders to the aims and assumptions of legal fact finding and the extent to which they are upheld in practice, as well as specific background information on how to assess expert and lay witnesses, and the different dangers of heuristic, narrative and atomistic reasoning. However, while this is possible for professional and permanent lay fact finders, it is obviously impractical for jury members. The benefits to accurate fact finding in serious criminal cases from an introduction to the various contexts of fact finding, especially the scientific and psychological contexts, would thus suggest that juries are replaced with more professionalised fact finders. On the other hand, this would entail a loss of the value of multiple perspectives on truth[343] and being able to draw on a variety of skills, knowledge and experience relevant to particular issues.[344] One solution might be for all formal fact finding – or at least in serious cases – to be undertaken by a judge assisted by one or more lay adjudicators[345] who could be educated as to the various contexts of fact finding and associated skills. Such a step is, however, likely to be controversial and will require much greater consideration than is possible in a book which is aimed primarily not at exploring reform of fact handling in the Scottish legal system, but at critically examining the various contexts of evidence and proof.

---

[341] Section 3.8.1, above.

[342] Cf. Sherwin, above n. 152, 81–2.

[343] See Chapter 2, esp. section 5, and for a suggestion for reform based on this insight, J. Jackson, above n. 16, esp. 522–6.

[344] See, for example, D. M. Risinger, 'Unsafe Verdicts: The Need for Reformed Standards for the Trial and Review of Factual Innocence Claims' (20005) 41 *Houston Law Review* 1281, 1308–9.

[345] As in some civilian system: see, for example, Kapardis, above n. 3, 173.

Afterword

Readers who have persevered this far in grappling with the various non-legal factors which shape the processes of evidence and proof in the Scottish legal system will doubtless now be too exhausted to engage in anything more than the peripheral route processing of the book's main findings. Nevertheless, for those readers who are willing to stick it out for a few more pages, it may be worth briefly summarising what this contextual discussion has told us about the accuracy of fact-positivist views on the aims and assumptions of evidence and proof, and what implications this has for the future treatment of fact handling in the legal process.

Probably the most important assumption of traditional evidence scholarship involves the goal of truth finding. While orthodox rationalists regard the empiricist conception of reason as the most effective means of ascertaining true facts, it was argued in Chapter Seven that narrative and other forms of holistic reasoning might ensure more accurate fact finding. Ultimately, however, it matters less how true knowledge is obtained as long as it corresponds with objective reality and that this enables justice to be done. But this book has raised serious questions about whether truth can ever correspond with reality. This is not only because humans are highly fallible as witnesses of facts, and as assessors of the reliability and honesty, or the authenticity and meaning, of witnesses and other forms of evidence, but, more fundamentally, because of the way that the human mind inevitably places filters between reality and knowledge.

As we saw in Chapter Six,[1] all information – both autobiographical and theoretical – is stored in schemas which have been shaped by the individual's upbringing and social milieu, and which in turn filter out, mould or even alter the detail of incoming information. These schemas provide multiple filters between observed reality and determination of the facts in cases. Thus, even when fact finders directly observe evidence, such as documents, objects and CCTV, decisions as to their authenticity

---

[1]   Section 2.1.

and meaning will be affected by these schemas, and this may vary considerably according to who is making them.[2] However, fact finders rarely encounter legally relevant facts directly. Usually they have to rely on witnesses whose own schemas first shape what they perceive, remember and recall before their reports are filtered through the schemas of fact finders evaluating the accuracy, honesty and meaning of their reports.[3]

Moreover, as we saw in Chapter Seven,[4] proof of facts is rarely constituted only by direct evidence of the facts in issue. Instead, proof usually requires a combination of chains of inferences from different evidential sources. Here schemas again play an important role, whether in the form of the fact finders' own schemas or, as we saw in Chapter 5,[5] those of experts who provide legal actors with scientific generalisations to make their own inferences or are delegated the power to make inferences from scientific evidence themselves. Finally, Chapter Seven[6] showed that schemas play a crucial role in helping fact finders deal with the surfeit of often contradictory and ambiguous information they encounter by comparing possible narrative accounts of the facts with the story schemas embedded in their memories. In other words, the role of stories and other socially constructed schemas in the acquisition and assessment of evidence goes all the way down: from the holistic evaluations of the evidence to atomistic evaluation of individual items via generalisations to perception of the facts themselves. When this role is combined with the argument that truth-claims are always socially constructed by being expressed in the social construct of language,[7] it is difficult to see how truth can involve anything more than the most coherent and plausible account of the world.

However, as was argued in Chapter Two,[8] rejection of the correspondence theory of truth does not (as contemporary evidence scholars worry) disqualify one from making claims about the accuracy, rationality or justice of legal processes of evidence and proof. Indeed, it was also argued that it may be more likely than epistemological realism to encourage a critical stance on such issues. Whether this is true or not remains a matter of unprovable prediction, but certainly this book cannot be faulted for eschewing subjecting the processes of fact handling in Scotland to critical

---

[2] See Chapter 5 at n. 3.
[3] See Chapter 6, sections 2 and 3 passim.
[4] Section 3.2.
[5] Sections 3–6 passim.
[6] Section 5.2.
[7] See Chapter 2, section 3.3.1.
[8] Ibid.

evaluation. This evaluation has, moreover, extended well beyond the traditional focus of evidence scholars, not just in Scotland but elsewhere.

Accordingly various chapters have shown orthodox assumptions about most[9] (if not all) of the procedural mechanism for maximising the accuracy of fact finding to be either psychologically naïve or undermined by actual practice. For example, the value of orality is weakened by the misleading nature of witness demeanour as a clue to reliability and honesty,[10] whereas adversarial cross-examination may destroy the credibility of accurate and honest witnesses – both expert and observational – or at least alter their testimony through leading questions, suggestion and innuendo.[11] The ability of witnesses to testify accurately is also hampered by the fragmented style of witness testimony[12] and by the fact that they may testify weeks, if not months, after events and in a locality and environment not calculated to enhance recall.[13] There is also reason to believe that the face-to-face confrontation between parties undermines more than enhances truthfulness and accuracy by causing honest witnesses to struggle with problems and show signs associated with lying, and even to be deterred from testifying.[14] Most notably, Chapter Four[15] showed the assumptions behind the belief in the superiority of adversarial over inquisitorial fact finding (namely that it ensures the discovery of more information and prevents adjudicators jumping to conclusions) to be misguided, largely because of the way that excessive adversariality combines with differences in litigants' power, ability and resources. And, as Chapter Five showed,[16] such problems also diminish the extent to which legal fact finding benefits from the ostensibly more disinterested and accurate testimony of scientific expert witnesses.

In fact, however, it was argued in Chapter Four that much fact finding – formal as well as informal – is not overly concerned with truth finding, as opposed to bureaucratically processing cases[17] and choreographing trials as a form of political theatre designed to legitimise law and the values it

---

[9]   One exception might be the oath – see Chapter 3 at n. 127.
[10] Chapter 6, section 3.3.
[11] Chapter 4, section 2.3, and Chapter 5, section 7.2.3 – see also Chapter 6, section 2.4.3, on problems with leading and other types of questioning used in cross-examination.
[12] See Chapter 3, section 3.1.4.
[13] See Chapter 6, sections 2.3.2 and 2.4.3 respectively, on interviewing witnesses as soon as possible and at the location of the observed events; and Chapter 4, section 4.2.1, on the unrelaxing atmosphere of court proceedings.
[14] See Chapter 4, section 2.2.
[15] Sections 2.3 and 2.4.
[16] Section 7.2.
[17] Sections 2.4.2 and 3.2.2.

espouses.[18] In some instances, such as the desire to allow juries to democratise justice or prioritising the protection of civil liberties, the downplaying of truth and expletive justice is justifiable. However, we also saw in Chapter Four that lay justice was fairly tightly controlled[19] and that civil liberties are frequently ignored in 'trivial cases',[20] and in Chapter Three[21] that, like truth finding itself, they are also increasingly vulnerable to considerations of expediency and national security. Also problematic is the extent to which the individual political and moral views of state officials affect the way they investigate and determine facts relevant to legal issues. While this occurs in all spheres of fact finding, it is particularly problematic in the contexts of interviewing suspects,[22] plea bargaining[23] and administrative decision-making,[24] given the impact on civil liberties and the well-being of some very vulnerable members of society. Perhaps most disturbing for legal educators is the way that some law graduates are co-opted by the system to betray their clients or at least fail to do enough to protect those who cannot pay handsomely.[25]

Hopefully this book will lead to more of the next generation of lawyers developing an awareness of the truth and justice deficit as regards fact handling in law, and the necessary skills to play a more positive role. Thus the book should provide a better understanding not just of how facts are handled in the Scottish legal system, but also how lawyers can more effectively investigate, analyse, present and evaluate evidence.[26] More specifically, it has provided an understanding of the limits to and factors affecting the perception, memory and recall of observational witnesses,[27] various forms of scientific expertise[28] and fact-evaluation processes.[29] Such knowledge can be used both positively, such as improving interviewing techniques and the couching of arguments to fact finders which are more likely to succeed, or negatively, such as highlighting known problems with

---

[18] Section 4.2.1.
[19] Section 4.2.2.
[20] Section 3.2.1.
[21] Section 4.2.
[22] See Chapter 4, section 2.4.2.
[23] See Chapter 4, sections 2.4.2 and 3.2.1.
[24] See Chapter 4, section 2.1.
[25] See Chapter 4, section 2.4.2.
[26] See Chapter 7, sections 2–5, as well as Chapter 5, section 8 and Chapter 6, section 2.4.3, on how to maximise the reports and testimony of expert and lay witnesses respectively.
[27] Chapter 6, section 2.
[28] Chapter 5, sections 4–6.
[29] See Chapter 5, section 7.3, and Chapter 6, section 3, regarding the evaluation of expert and observational witnesses respectively, and Chapter 7 regarding evidence as a whole.

the perception, memory and recall of observational witnesses or the scientific validity of expert testimony.

In addition, at various places in the book, I have made some general and highly tentative suggestions about possible improvements to the processes of evidence and proof in Scotland. These include moving away from the climactic 'day in court' and the principle of orality,[30] greater regulation – if not the abolition of – plea bargaining,[31] providing adjudicators with greater powers to question witnesses,[32] and replacing some lay adjudication with mixed benches of trained professional and lay assessors[33] – albeit also expanding the range of fact finders in order to draw upon a wider variety of views and perspectives.[34] Other suggested and admittedly ambitious institutional reforms include extending the respect shown for civil liberties in serious criminal cases to 'trivial' cases, as well as making legal proceedings more user-friendly for lay participants and less an exercise in bureaucratic processing and political theatre.[35] Less ambitious, but in some cases equally controversial, are various suggestions for improving law's use of scientific experts, such as greater training for adjudicators and adjusting or even abandoning elements of current fact-finding procedures (such as greater disclosure of reports, the separation and/or non-adversarial treatment of scientific issues from the rest of proceedings, and the use of neutral experts).[36] Less controversial are various means of improving forensic evidence itself, such as by requiring greater proof of the validity and reliability of its methods and the proficiency of its practitioners.[37] By contrast, given that scientific understanding of the problems with, and factors affecting, witness testimony and its evaluation are on a much more solid footing, suggestions for reform were focused on how best to use such knowledge.[38] These included more training for adjudicators, greater use of judicial instructions and expert witnesses, and various changes to how and when observational witnesses are used – such as refinements to the regulation of identification parades and requiring less adversarial forms of questioning, conducted much earlier in proceedings.

---

[30] Chapter 4, section 2.4.3, and Chapter 6, section 4.3.
[31] Chapter 4, section 2.5.
[32] Chapter 4, section 2.5.
[33] Chapter 4, section 2.5, and Chapter 7, section 6.
[34] Chapter 2, section 5.
[35] Chapter 4, section 5; see also the discussion of restorative justice in Chapter 3, section 4.2.
[36] See Chapter 5, section 8.
[37] Ibid.
[38] Chapter 6, section 5.

One reason for the undeveloped nature of these reform suggestions is that much of the research on the relevant processes and contexts of evidence and proof is out of date and/or was conducted outwith Scotland. Consequently, before moving too quickly to reform, there is a pressing need to answer a plethora of questions about the current state of fact handling in Scotland. In no particular order of importance, these include:

- To what extent are the problems of administrative fact finding, plea bargaining, the treatment of unrepresented litigants, insufficiently zealous lawyers and, conversely, overzealous lawyers evidenced largely in past decades in other Anglo-American jurisdictions equally applicable in contemporary Scotland?
- How has the reduction in the provision of legal aid (at least in civil cases), changes to lower court procedures, the growth of ADR and the introduction of case management affected civil liberties, and the ability of disputing parties to gain a fair hearing and the courts to rule on the truth of matters?
- What techniques and other tactics do police officers, administrative officials and other legal actors use in interviewing witnesses, suspects, applicants for state benefits and immigration status, etc.? What presumptions, working rules and stereotypes do they bring to this task?
- How do scientists – especially forensic scientists – operate in Scotland and how is their evidence dealt with by the courts and other legal actors?
- What methods, if any, do lawyers use to analyse evidence?
- How do fact advocates go about presenting the facts? Do stories, emotions and other 'irrational' factors play more of a role in presenting and evaluating evidence than as suggested by Scottish advocacy manuals?
- Finally, do proceedings in the Scottish courts operate as political theatre and, if so, does this enhance or diminish the legitimacy of their decisions?

Answering these questions is a vast undertaking which requires, inter alia, a cohort of interested researchers. Unfortunately, as shown by the increasingly outdated nature of most of the empirical studies, especially in relation to civil and administrative fact finding, and not just in Scotland, there is currently far less interest than previously in the sort of research which has informed this book. Admittedly, small jurisdictions like Scotland will always struggle to produce a comprehensive and up-to-date range of relevant empirical studies. However, there is no reason why those interested in evidence and proof need confine themselves to analysing the law of evidence, which has such a marginal impact on the actual practice of fact handling. By demonstrating the importance of a wide range of relevant processes and contextual factors, it is hoped that this book will encourage current and future evidence scholars to explore the sort of theoretical and empirical questions raised here, and more generally encourage those interested in law to 'take facts seriously'.

Index